Catalogue of the
Ethiopic Manuscript Imaging Project

Ethiopic Manuscript Imaging Project

Ethiopic Manuscripts, Texts, and Studies

Series Editor
Steve Delamarter

Forthcoming volumes

Steve Delamarter and Melaku Terefe. *Ethiopian Scribal Practice 1: Plates for the Catalogue of the Ethiopic Manuscript Imaging Project* (Companion to EMIP Catalogue 1).

Veronika Six, Getatchew Haile, Melaku Terefe, Jeremy R. Brown, Erik C. Young, and Steve Delamarter. *Catalogue of the Ethiopic Manuscript Imaging Project: Volume 2, Codices 106–200 and Magic Scrolls 135–284.*

Steve Delamarter and Melaku Terefe. *Ethiopian Scribal Practice 2: Plates for the Catalogue of the Ethiopic Manuscript Imaging Project* (Companion to EMIP Catalogue 2).

Getatchew Haile, Melaku Terefe, Jeremy R. Brown, Erik C. Young and Steve Delamarter. *Catalogue of the Ethiopic Manuscript Imaging Project: Volume 3, Codices 201–300 and Magic Scrolls 286 ff.*

Steve Delamarter and Melaku Terefe. *Ethiopian Scribal Practice 3: Plates for the Catalogue of the Ethiopic Manuscript Imaging Project* (Companion to EMIP Catalogue 3).

Getatchew Haile, Melaku Terefe, Jeremy R. Brown, Erik C. Young and Steve Delamarter. *Catalogue of the Ethiopic Manuscript Imaging Project: Volume 4, Codices 301–400 and Magic Scrolls.*

Steve Delamarter and Melaku Terefe. *Ethiopian Scribal Practice 4: Plates for the Catalogue of the Ethiopic Manuscript Imaging Project* (Companion to EMIP Catalogue 4).

Catalogue of the Ethiopic Manuscript Imaging Project

Volume 1: Codices 1–105, Magic Scrolls 1–134

Getatchew Haile,

Melaku Terefe, Roger M. Rundell,
Daniel Alemu, and Steve Delamarter

☙PICKWICK *Publications* • Eugene, Oregon

CATALOGUE OF THE ETHIOPIC MANUSCRIPT IMAGING PROJECT
Volume 1: Codices 1-105, Magic Scrolls 1-134

Ethiopic Manuscripts, Texts, and Studies 1

Copyright © 2009 Steve Delamarter. All rights reserved. Except for brief quotations in critical publications or reviews, no part of this book may be reproduced in any manner without prior written permission from the publisher. Write: Permissions, Wipf and Stock Publishers, 199 W. 8th Ave., Suite 3, Eugene, OR 97401.

Pickwick Publications
A Division of Wipf and Stock Publishers
199 W. 8th Ave., Suite 3
Eugene, OR 97401

ISBN 13: 978-1-60608-871-5

Cataloging-in-Publication data:

Haile, Getatchew.
    Catalogue of the Ethiopic Manuscript Imaging Project : volume 1, codices 1–105, Magic Scrolls 1–134 / Getatchew Haile, Steve Delamarter, Melaku Terefe, Roger M. Rundell, and Daniel Alemu.

    p. ; cm. —Includes bibliographical references, and indexes.

    Ethiopic Manuscripts, Texts, and Studies 1

    ISBN 13: 978-1-60608-871-5

    1. Manuscripts—Ethiopic—Catalogs. 2. Codicology. 3. Scribes—Ethiopian. 4. Scribes—Africa. I. Delamarter, Steve. II. Terefe, Melaku. III. Rundell, Roger M. IV. Alemu, Daniel. V. Title. VI. Series.

    BS4.5 E75 v.1

Manufactured in the U.S.A.

Cover Art: EMIP 16 (Marwick Codex 12), f. 46v; depicting the Archangel Michael and Balaam; a nineteenth-century copy of the Homiliary in Honor of the Archangel Michael, ድርሳነ፡ ሚካኤል፡.

To the memory of the Late Abune Yisehaq,
former Archbishop of the Western Hemisphere

Contents

Series Foreword / xi
Preface / xiii
Abbreviations / xxi
Introduction to the Collection and Its Codicology / xxiii
Introduction to the Scrolls of Ethiopian Spiritual Healing / xxxiii

Catalogue of the Codices / 1
Catalogue of the Scrolls of Ethiopian Spiritual Healing / 271

List of the Manuscripts by EMIP Number and Owner Number / 399
List of Dated or Datable Manuscripts / 403
List of Undated and Composite Manuscripts / 405
Bibliography / 407
Index of Works in the Codices / 411
Index of Names and Places in the Codices / 419
Index of Miniatures in the Codices / 422
Index of Scribal Practices in the Codices / 427
Index of Works in the Scrolls of Spiritual Healing / 430
Index of Names in the Scrolls of Spiritual Healing / 443

Series Foreword

The series *Ethiopic Manuscripts, Texts, and Studies* offers, in the first place, catalogues of the Ethiopic Manuscript Imaging Project whose purpose it is to digitize and catalogue collections of Ethiopic manuscripts in North America and around the world. Beyond this, though, the series offers a venue for monographs, revised dissertations, and texts that explore the rich historical, literary, and artistic traditions of Ethiopia and the Ethiopian Orthodox Church.

    The series has particular interest in Ethiopic manuscripts and the scribal practices in evidence within them. This includes analytical studies of particular manuscripts or particular scribal practices and illuminations. Moreover, the interest extends to synthetic studies that explore the developments of scribal and artistic practice across time or those that probe the interconnections between common elements in manuscripts, scribal practices, scribal education, and community ideology.

Steve Delamarter, series editor

Preface

This work goes to press after a long season of preparation and with much help and support by a host of friends and colleagues. The Ethiopic Manuscript Imaging Project (EMIP) began its work in the Spring of 2005 and it has taken four years not only to digitize the first 700 manuscripts, but to work out the plan for a catalogue, engage a team of contributors, and finalize details for publication.

The purpose of EMIP is to locate, digitize, and catalogue Ethiopic manuscripts and to make the images and catalogues widely available for research by scholars. The work involves many distinct operations, each requiring a very different skill set, but each one essential to the overall success of the project. These operations include a preliminary physical description, a detailed mapping of the architecture of the codex, digitization of the manuscript (one pass for "down shots" of the content, another pass for details of scribal, codicological, and artistic practice), digital foliation of the images, processing of two different sets of digitial images (one for bundling into PDF files, another for posting on the internet), analysis and documentation of scribal practices, the general layout of a catalogue entry based on a template, the detailed cataloguing of content and determination of the date of the manuscript, and, finally, the editing, indexing and preparation of the catalogue volume for publication and the posting of the images online.

The roles of the contributors to this volume are very different from one another and should be clarified. A host of students helped with various aspects of the physical descriptions, quire mapping and digitization of the manuscripts: Jarod Jacobs, Dylan Morgan, Matt Versdahl, Jenifer Manginelli, Paul Hays, Lisa Barnes, Ivana Barnes, and David Budd. A few have mastered a further set of skills in manuscript photography, digital foliation, image processing, preparation of the initial catalogue entry, and the analysis and recording of details of scribal practice. These have worked with me for months and become true colleagues in the project: Roger Rundell, Jeremy Brown, and Erik Young. With reference to this first catalogue, Mr. Roger Rundell and *Ato* Daniel Alemu worked tirelessly in a month-long workshop in Collegeville to process images and prepare intial catalogue entries and have earned the honor of listing as contributing authors. Mr. Rundell mastered almost every aspect of the project and worked with me in

2005 and 2006. I met *Ato* Daniel in Jerusalem in January of 2004 and took him with me to Ethiopia in April and May of the same year to serve as my translator in a project to locate and interview scribes in various locations in Ethiopia.

The heart of the cataloguing process—and the operation that requires the greatest scholarly expertise—was performed by our senior scholar (listed first among the authors), Professor Getatchew Haile, who finalized, in detail, all of the entries in this catalogue in the Fall of 2006. Getatchew's influence on the entire field of Ethiopian studies is monumental and it would be difficult to overestimate his influence on the Ethiopic Manuscript Imaging Project. In my very first meeting with him in the Spring of 2005 he offered to help with the cataloguing of the manuscripts that we might locate and digitize. Neither of us had any idea that the number would grow from the thirty-nine manuscripts I had at the time to the more than seven hundred we have now digitized in North America. And in spite of my attempts to release him from his offer, he has remained a steadfast supporter of our work. At least six times between 2005 and 2009 I and others have travelled to Collegeville to work on cataloguing the EMIP collection at the HMML. Each time Getatchew has worked tirelessly with us. In the early days it was to help us formulate catalogue entry templates and to understand the issues involved in addressing every aspect of the entry correctly. Since then it has included mentoring me and other scholars (like *Ato* Demeke Berhane and *Kesis* Melaku Terefe) in the fine points of cataloguing Ethiopic manuscripts. He has personally looked at every codex that has passed through the project and helped to produce at the very least a handlist entry for each item. And, he has been the one to establish the date of the codices, particularly when the judgment had to be made on the basis of paleography alone. I have learned so much from Getatchew and his contributions extend even to the correction of my English!

I met *Kesis* Melaku Terefe, a priest in an Ethiopian Orthodox Church in Los Angeles, in March of 2008 when I went to UCLA to inspect their collection of Ethiopic manuscripts. The visit was coordinated with Genie Guerard, head of special collections in the Young Research Library, who not only generously provided everything I needed for the study of the manuscripts, but also introduced me to Dr. Wendy Belcher (now at Princeton) and also to *Kesis* Melaku. Melaku was just completing a catalogue of the collection at UCLA, most of which had been left by Professor Wolf Leslau. Almost immediately Melaku expressed his interest in working with our project to digitize and catalogue manuscripts in North America.

In the summer of 2008, I arranged for a two-week workshop at Collegeville and Melaku joined the work. His knowledge of the language and literature of the Church is very extensive and his knowledge of Western conventions of scholarship has grown considerably. Throughout the time there Professor Getatchew mentored us in the cataloguing process. Melaku now works regularly with me in the cataloguing of newly-acquired materials. Although Melaku's contributions to subsequent volumes is very extensive, his involvement in this volume is limited to the analysis of the Songs of Songs in the psalters to determine whether the editions are the common one or the so-called Hebraic version.

While supervising the whole, my attentions in the project have been given specially to closeup manuscript photography, analysis of scribal practice, finalization of preliminary catalogue entries, working with the head cataloguers, preparing indices, and editing the catalogues for publication.

Mr. Wayne Torborg, director of digital collections and imaging at the Hill Museum and Manuscript Library (HMML) at Saint John's University in Collegeville, Minnesota, consulted with me at various points regarding manuscript photography and is responsible for the construction and management of the collection of manuscript images on HMML's website, *Vivarium*.

I wish to thank the Association of Theological Schools'/Lilly Theological Scholars' Grant Program that has provided me with two grants in support of this work. The first grant facilitated my trip to Ethiopia in the spring of 2004 to study the sociology of religious scribal communities. The second, in the summer of 2006, supported work on this catalogue and the digitization project to that point.

In addition, we are grateful for grants from the Gerald and Barbara Weiner Family Foundation and for matching funds from Morgan Stanley that have enabled us to continue the work of digitization and manuscript description not only for the Weiner collection but also for several other collections.

A recent grant from the Christiansen Fund has supported the ongoing work of EMIP and, in particular, the digitization workshop held in Addis Ababa and described in a bit more detail below.

George Fox University has supported the project in several ways: a sabbatical grant in the 2003/04 academic year, research leaves (load reductions) in 2005-09. In particular, I wish to thank my deans, Drs. Jules Glanzer and (later) Charles Conniry, for their multi-faceted support of the project and to Amy Karjala, Executive Director of Development, for her work in receiving grant funds for the project.

The Hill Museum and Manuscript Library is not only where Professor Getatchew has lived and worked for over three decades; it has become for me a research haven and environment with major support of the EMIP generally and specifically in the preparation of this catalogue. The HMML has paid travel and living expenses for scholars to work there (*Ato* Demeke Berhane and *Kesis* Melaku Terefe), for Mr. Torborg to travel with me to Addis and conduct a workshop on manuscript digitization in June/July of 2008, and for a team of three (myself, Jeremy Brown and Erik Young) to travel to Addis and assist the Institute of Ethiopian Studies in the digitization of 1,120 of her manuscripts in December 2008 and January 2009. Just about every aspect of the work of EMIP has been assisted and informed by the team at HMML. Our special gratitude goes to Father Dr. Columba Stewart, Executive Director and University Vice-President for Programs in Religion and Culture, who has guided and supported our work at every turn.

The Institute of Ethiopian Studies (IES) in Addis Ababa is another institution whose personnel have greatly assisted our research. I met the director, Elsabet Giyorgis, on my first trip to Ethiopia. She has provided extravagant support for our work there ever since. Dr. Yonas Admassu, interim director for a period, was gracious to receive images of our collection at the International Conference of Ethiopian Studies held in Trondheim, Norway in 2007. *Ato* Assefa, director of the Library, has been very supportive and played a key role in facilitating the manuscript digitization workshop at the IES in June/July of 2008. *Ato* Demeke Berhane has become a dear friend and colleague. We have travelled far and wide together, collaborated on a *A Catalogue of Previously Uncatalogued Ethiopic Manuscripts in England: Twenty-three Manuscripts in the Bodleian, Cambridge University and John Rylands University Libraries and in a Private Collection,* Journal of Semitic Studies Supplement 21 (Oxford: Oxford University Press, 2007), and have spent countless hours working together over manuscripts in the IES. I have learned a great deal from him and believe that his leadership on the digitization of the IES collection will benefit the entire field of Ethiopian Studies for years to come.

Besides publishing our catalogue on manuscripts in England, Professor George J. Brooke, one of the editors of the *Journal of Semitic Studies*, has been a constant source of encouragement and counsel in this project. Demeke and I still hope one day to deliver to him and the *JSS* a catalogue of the manuscripts in the Institute of Ethiopian Studies Library.

I have been fortunate to renew acquaintance with Dr. K.C. Hanson, a former classmate at Claremont Graduate School, and who is now editor-in-chief of Wipf & Stock. His support for the idea for establishing the series *Ethiopic Manuscripts, Texts, and Studies* was almost immediate; his expertise and enormous expenditures of time have helped it to become a reality.

I have never met an owner of a manuscript that has not had to face the temptation of thinking that their manuscript should be held for ransom. Indeed, despite all of the talk about world heritage and the cultural legacy of a nation, many manuscript owners are apt to take quite a mercenary attitude toward their possessions. Ironically, this is perhaps nowhere more evident than in a few of the research libraries that hold Ethiopic manuscripts. How extraordinary, then, to come across private individuals, independent dealers, and institutional manuscript curators who have freely and enthusiastically embraced the notion that images of their manuscripts should be made available for everyone to study. For me, it has been the dealers of artifacts that have most defied the stereotypes about them (i.e., that they are only in it for the money). I have been inspired and humbled at their generosity and trust. The first two dealers I met—Eliza Bennett of Colorado and Blake and Claire Marwick of Oregon—have provided around 150 manuscripts between them. Eliza's manuscripts are catalogued here as codex numbers EMIP 2–4, 25–28, 33–54, 60–66, 78–82, and magic scroll numbers EMIP MagSc 3–5. The Marwicks' manuscripts include codex numbers EMIP 5–24, 70, 86, 93 and magic scroll numbers EMIP MagSc 6–37. Further, it was Eliza who provided access to the two manuscripts (EMIP 29 and 30) of the Wisnant galleries (in New Orleans) and gave me introduction to Gerald Weiner, financier and philanthropist and—on the side—rare book dealer in Chicago. His entire collection of nearly 160 Ethiopic manuscripts and hundreds of magic scrolls have been made available to the project as well as grants from the family foundation to support the work of digitizing and cataloguing. His manuscripts in this catalogue are EMIP codex numbers EMIP 75, 76, 83, 87–92, 94–97, 100–105, and magic scroll numbers EMIP MagSc 40–126, and 130–34. Weiner, in turn, introduced me to Mohammad Alwan, owner of Worldwide Antiquarian in Massachusettes, who has provided around 50 manuscripts to the project (catalogued in later volumes). I also contacted Ms. Lee Kirk, a dealer handling one codex for the owner of the Tsunami bookstore in Eugene, Oregon. She not only worked with the owner to gain access to that manuscript (EMIP 58), she also introduced us to another private owner of a manuscript, Hazel Kahan of New York (EMIP 59).

Recently, I have recently found another dealer in my own city of Portland, Oregon, Mr. Jerry Shover, owner of The Gold Door, who has opened his collection to the project (catalogued in a later volume). These dealers have made a profound contribution to EMIP and to the wider field of Ethiopian studies.

To these dealers we add the list of the private individuals who have given us access to their manuscripts for the project. Besides Hazel Kahan, mentioned above, in this catalogue there are Paul Herron (EMIP 1) of Oregon, Sheppard and Sharon Earl of Oregon (EMIP 31), Luigi Focanti of Utah (EMIP numbers 67, 68, and 69), and Theodore Bernhardt Jr. of New Jersey (EMIP 77). Sadly, the Focanti manuscripts were stolen from their residence in 2008 and have not been returned. It is specially gratifying to have digital images of these stolen manuscripts. Two of my own codices are included in this catalogue (EMIP 32 and 84), as well as two magic scrolls (EMIP MagSc 1 and 2). The manuscripts of several other private owners—Daniel Holcomb of Portland, Oregon; Getatchew Haile of Collegeville, Minnesota; Jim Subers of Overland Park, Kansas; Greg Marquart, Rhea DeStefano of Washington, D.C.; Michael Rudulph of Alabama; and Mr. Douglas Walter of Chicago—appear in later volumes.

And beyond dealers and private owners there have been university libraries that have submitted their codices and magic scrolls for digitization. Sylvia Stopforth at Trinity Western University, in Langley, British Columbia, worked with us to digitize the four codices in their collection (EMIP 55–57 and 85). Pam Endzweig, director of collections, and Jon Erlandson, director of the University of Oregon Museum of Natural and Cultural History in Eugene, Oregon, worked with us to digitize their collection of the three codices (EMIP 71–73) and two magic scrolls (EMIP MagSc 38 and 39) in the Bowerman-Hall collection. Carisse Berryhill, special services librarian at Abilene Christian University in Abilene, Texas, worked with us to digitize their collection of two codices (EMIP 98 and 99) and three magic scrolls (EMIP MagSc 127–129). Victoria Ertelt of the Mount Angel Abbey Library in St. Benedict, Oregon, worked with us to digitize their sole Ethiopic codex (EMIP 74).

Surely, it is these manuscript owners who deserve the fullest credit for the success of the EMIP.

One of assumptions of the project is that copies of the images of the manuscripts should be returned to institutions within Ethiopia so that scholars there can have access to their own cultural heritage. In a sort of homegoing, a set of digital images of the first 240 manuscripts was sent back to Ethiopia with *Ato* Demeke in the summer of 2006 for preservation and research at the Institute of Ethiopian Studies in Addis Ababa. A second set of images for the next 300 or so manuscripts was presented to Dr. Yonas Admassu, acting director of the IES, at the Sixteenth International Conference of Ethiopian Studies in Trondheim, Norway, in 2007. A third set of images for the next 170 or so manuscripts was presented to Elsabet Giyorgis, director of the IES, in the summer of 2008. And in January of 2009 a complete set of images (all 710 manuscripts digitized to that point) were presented to his holiness, Abuna Paulos, the head of the Ethiopian Orthodox Church, at his residence in Addis Ababa. These are to be used in the Patriarch's library and museum.

Besides the images online, two further complete sets of the images—in higher resolution than that available on the internet—have been deposited at research libraries. The first is at the HMML; the other is at the Septuagint Institute of Trinity Western University. Our intent is to update these sets of images as more manuscripts are digitized.

Steve Delamarter
Pentecost 2009

Abbreviations

AṢZ	አምስቱ፡ ጸዋትወ፡ ዜማዎች፡፡ እነርሱም፤ ጾማ-ጾም፡ ድጓ፤ ጾማ-ምዕራፍ፤ ጾማ-ዚቅ፤መዝሙር፤ እስመ፡ ለዓለም፤ ዓማ-ዝማሬ፤ ጾማ-መዋሥዕት፡፡ Bərhanənna Sälam Press, Addis Ababa 1965 EC.
Bartos	ጸሎተ፡ እግዝእትነ፡ ማርያም፡ ዘሀገረ፡ ባርቶስ፡ Täsfa Press, Addis Ababa 1963 EC
CSCO	Corpus Scriptorum Christianorum Orientalium
DM	ድርሳነ፡ ሚካኤል፡ ወድርሳነ፡ ሩፋኤል፡፡ መልክአ፡ ሚካኤል፡ ወመልክአ፡ ሩፋኤል፡፡ ዘአንተሞ፡ ተስፋ፡ ገብረ፡ ሥላሴ፡ ዘብሔረ፡ ቡልጋ፡፡ [Dərsanä Mika'el wä-Dərsanä Rufa'el. Mälkə'a Mika'el wä- Mälkə'a Rufa'el. zä-aḫətämo Täsfa Gäbrä Śəllase zä-bəḥerä Bulga] Artistik Press (Addis Ababa), 1940 EC
EC	Ethiopian Calendar, seven to eight years behind AD
EMML	Ethiopian Manuscript Microfilm Library, Addis Ababa, Ethiopian, and Collegeville, Minnesota, USA, described in Getatchew Haile and William F. Macomber, *A Catalogue of Ethiopian Manuscripts Microfilmed for the Ethiopian Manuscript Microfilm Library, Addis Ababa and for the Hill Monastic Manuscript Library, Collegeville*, 1973ff.
JA	*Journal asiatique*
JAOS	*Journal of the American Oriental Society*
JSS	*Journal of Semitic Studies*
MBB 52	መጽሐፈ፡ ስዓታት፡ በገዕዝና፡ በአማርኛ፡፡ ዘሌሊት ÷ ወዘነግህ፡ አሳታሚያቹ፡ አለቃ፡ መኩንን፡ ሰሎሞን፡፡ አቶ፡ ብሥራት፡ ማስረሻ፡፡ አጋፋሪ፡ በየነ፡ አሊ፡፡ Tənśa'e Zä-Guba'e Press Addis Ababa 1952 EC
MD 59	መዝሙር፡ ዘዳዊት፡ [= *Mäzmurä Dawit*], Bərhanənna Sälam Press, Addis Ababa 1959 EC
MD 59	መዝሙረ፡ ዳዊት [= *Mäzmurä Dawit*] Bəhanənna Sälam Press, Addis Ababa 1959 EC
MG 59	ሰባቱ፡ ኪዳናት፡፡ ቅዳሴ፡ ማርያም፡ መልክአ ጉባኤ፡፡ [= *Säbattu Kidanat. Qəddase Maryam Mälkə'a Guba'e.*]Täsfa Press, Addis Ababa 1959 EC
MQ 51	መጽሐፈ፡ ቅዳሴ፡፡ በገዕዝና፡ በአማርኛ፡፡ [= *Mäṣḥäfä Qəddase. Bä-Gə'əzənna bä-Amarəñña.*], Täsfa Press, Addis Ababa 1951 EC.
NEAS	*Northeast African Studies*
Or	*Orientalia*

PO	*Patrologia Orientalis*
ROC	*Revue de l'Orient Chrétien*
RRAL	*Rendiconti della Reale Accademia dei Lincei. Classe di scienze morali, storiche e filologiche*, Rome
SBL	Society of Biblical Literature
TM 61	ተአምረ ማርያም፡፡ በግዕዝ እና በአማርኛ፡፡ [= *Tämmərä Maryam. Bä-Gəʿəzənna bä-Amarəñña.*], Täsfa Press, Addis Ababa 1961 EC
ZDMG	*Zeitschrift der deutschen morgenländischen Gesellschaft*
ZS	*Zeitschrift für Semitistik*
እግ"	እግዚአብሔር

Introduction to the Collection and Its Codicology

Steve Delamarter

The Collection and Its Presentation

This is a catalogue of the digital collection of images produced from the first two hundred and thirty nine Ethiopic manuscripts digitized by the Ethiopic Manuscript Imaging Project (EMIP). These include 105 codices and 134 scrolls of Ethiopian spiritual healing photographed in 2005 and 2006. While many of the manuscripts remain in the hands of the parties who owned them in 2005 and 2006, many others have changed hands since that time. Since the collections themselves cannot be stabilized, the plan of EMIP has been to create a new, digital entity from the manuscripts. This collection of digital images has been stabilized and is now available as an object of study. In fact, all of the images of all of the manuscripts are available online at http://www.hmml.org/vivarium/sgd.htm.

The history of EMIP and the process of digitization used in the first two years of the project have been described elsewhere. We made an initial report about the project in the online venue, *Society of Biblical Literature Forums*, in February of 2007. In that notice we referred to it as "The SGD Digital Collection: Previously Unknown and Uncatalogued Ethiopian Manuscripts in North America." but later changed the name of the collection to the EMIP collection. In November of the same year, and in the same venue, we gave notice of "More Ethiopian Manuscripts in North America." As of this time, the most complete written description of the project is to be found in our contribution to the Proceedings of the Sixteenth International Conference of Ethiopian Studies, for the meeting held in Trondheim,

Norway, in July of 2007. We have given illustrated lectures about the project in various venues.[1]

In November of 2008, we convened a panel of scholars to report on the ten largest collections in North America at the annual Society of Literature Meeting in Boston, November 2008 as part of the Textual Criticism of the Hebrew Bible section of the meeting.[2] Before our report, the most widely-known published report accounted for "slightly over 400 manuscripts" in the United States.[3] Our panel reported on the collections at Princeton University (Dr. Wendy Belcher), Howard University School of Divinity (Dr. Alice Ogden Bellis), the Library of Congress (*Ato* Fentahun Tiruneh), Duke University (Dr. Lucas van Rompay), UCLA (*Kesis* Melaku Terefe), the collection of images at the Hill Museum and Manuscripts Library (Dr. Fr. Columba Stewart), and the four largest private collections in

---

[1] "The Ethiopian Manuscript Imaging Project: History, Goals, Methods, and Issues" (Pacific Northwest Regional SBL meeting in May of 2006); "The Characterization of God in Ethiopian Manuscript Illuminations in the SGD Collection (at the conference called "Descriptions of God in Ancient and Modern Monotheistic Traditions" held at the Septuagint Institute of Trinity Western University in September of 2006); "Ethiopian Codices and Scrolls for the Septuagint Institute: History, Significance, Method, and Contents" (at the same conference at Trinity Western in September of 2006); "Scribal Practice in Ethiopian Psalters" (at the annual SBL meeting in Washington D. C. in November 2006); "A Digital Collection of previously unknown Ethiopian Manuscripts in North America" (at the same annual SBL meeting in November 2006); "In a Foreign Land: Amazing Stories of Ethiopina Manuscripts in Exile" (at the George Fox Evangelical Seminary faculty research forum in January, 2007); "More Ethiopian Manuscripts in North America" (at the annual SBL meeting in San Diego in November of 2007); "Who Guides the Hand of the Scribe? Scribal Practices in Ethiopic Manuscripts" (at the graduate students' seminar, Trinity Western University, Langley, British Columbia, Canada, February 20, 2008); "What Do You Do with 110 Ethiopian Psalters? The Statistical Analysis of Scribal Practices" (at the Library of Congress, African and Middle East Division, May 21, 2008); "On the Digital Edge of the Ethiopic Manuscript Imaging Project," (at the Pacific Northwest Regional SBL Meeting in May of 2008); "The Statistical Analysis of Scribal Practices" (to the staff of the Hill Museum and Manuscript Library, in August 2008); and "The EMIP Manuscript Digitizing Expedition to Addis Ababa in December 2008—January 2009" (at the Library of Congress,African and Middle East Division. on 19 February 2009).

[2] I co-chair the SBL's Textual Criticism of the Hebrew Bible Section with Brent Strawn of Emory University.

[3] Richard Pankhurst, "A Serious Question of Ethiopian Studies: Five Thousand Ethiopian Manuscripts Abroad, and the International Community," *Addis Tribune*, 17 December 1999; available online at http://www.afromet.org/Archives/AddisTribune/17-12-99/Five.htm, accessed 30 November 2008.

North America (myself). By the time we were done, we had accounted for 2,017 manuscripts.

Layout of the Catalogue

For codices, each catalogue entry is laid out in seven sections: 1) number, name and title; 2) physical description and dating; 3) list of contents; 4) list of miniatures; 5) varia; 6) notes; and 7) quire maps.

In the first section is the EMIP number followed by the name of the manuscript (usually involving a form of the owner's name), and the title of the contents of the manuscript (often in English and Gəʿəz). These designations are centered and placed in bold at the head of the entry.

In the first full paragraph under the title comes the physical description followed at the end by the date, and, if applicable, a description of the carrying case for the manuscript. Within the physical description, the following items are detailed: 1) material (usually parchment); 2) the external dimensions of the codex; 3) a description of the binding; 4) a description of the covers; 5) the number of quires (and their balance); 6) the number of folios; 7) the dimensions of the folios and margins; 8) the number of columns of text; 9) the language (usually Gəʿəz, but sometimes Amharic); 10) the number of lines on a typical folio; 11) the date (on which, see below). If the codex has a case, it will be described just following the date of the manuscript.

The date is determined in one of three ways. Occasionally a scribe will provide a colophon where a date is given or reference is made to a known historical figure who appears to be contemporaneous with the production of the codex. Where a colophon is lacking, scribes may nevertheless mention a known historical figure somewhere in the content of the work. This is usual, for instance, in the case of missals, where the leaders of the church are listed within the liturgies to ensure that prayers are made on their behalf. In either of these two cases, the manuscript is said to be "dated or datable." Thirteen of the 105 codices fall into this category. See the "List of Dated or Datable Manuscripts." Dates have been assigned to all manuscript. Where there is neither colophon or other mention of known historical figures, a judgment has been rendered by Professor Getatchew based on the paleography of the script in the codex. See the "List of Undated and Composite Manuscripts."

Occasionally a second paragraph of the physical description will detail the navigation systems in evidence within the codex or give a detailed account of the balance of the quires. The former usually come in the form of strings sewn into the fore edge of the folios to mark either the location of miniatures or to mark the location of contents within the codex.

The third element of each catalogue entry is a detailing, in sequential order, of the content of the major works in the codex. In most every case, Professor Getatchew has provided information about the published edition of the work and/or other important manuscripts containing the same work.

In the fourth element of the entry, the miniatures of the codex are listed by location and theme and any captions are translated. Since many of the illuminations in these codices are secondary and painted over text, we have rendered a judgment about whether the illuminations are apparently original or were added by a later hand.

In the fifth element of the entry, the *varia* are listed. In the first place, these varia are located in the codex in places (e.g., on the end leaves or on folios with some vacant space) and in ways that make it clear that these were not part of the original plan of the codex, but were added later, either by the same scribe or by another. This characteristic differentiates varia from the major works, on the other hand. On the other hand, varia are distinguished from notes in that the content of these additions are known and standard works or excerpts of known and standard works..

The sixth element of the entry is a detailing of notes. These are of two kinds: 1) a description of actual notes (i.e., not works or varia) made by any hand in the codex; or 2) observations by the cataloguers about any feature of the codex (e.g., scribal practices, condition of the parchment, blank folios, etc.).

Finally, the seventh element of each entry is a quire map which details, in graphical form, the architecture of the codex. The system of depiction is fairly self evident, but enables us to specify the location and character of every folio, sheet, and quire, and assigning a folio number to each folio.

The user will notice that more than usual attention has been given to the scribal practices in evidence in the codices. Notes on these appear in both the physical descriptions and in the notes field in each entry. Many of the scribal practices throughout the catalogue have been tagged and a separate index generated: "Index of Scribal Practices in the Codices."

For the scrolls, each catalogue entry contains five elements: 1) number and name; 2) physical description and date; 3) contents; 4) miniatures; and 5) name of the owner.

These fields are essentially the same as the corresponding field in the entries for the codices. To enable the comparison of similar prayers in the scrolls, Professor Getatchew has provided implicits for most of the prayers.

Illuminations

There are 526 illuminations in these first 105 codices. Some of the illuminations, perhaps 15 per cent, are original. A few are, perhaps, important for their old and elaborate illuminations. But most of the illuminations were not part of the original production of the codex. They were painted fairly recently into the codices. This is evident by the fact that they are painted over the top of text (often visible under the paint) and often marked with a string sewn into the fore edge of the folio to draw the attention of a prospective buyer. As such, these manuscripts provide a clear window into the current entrepreneurial practices of dealers in Ethiopia who have keyed into the fact that old books sell, but old book with illuminations sell very well.

From the manuscripts in this first volume we have identified at least two distinctive artistic hands that are well-trained. One we call "the speckled garment artist" who is responsible for fully 177 illuminations across twenty-three manuscripts. We refer to the other as "the beautiful artist" and this artist is responsible for 26 illuminations in four manuscripts in the first volume. Many more manuscripts in the second and third volumes have come through the same shops in Ethiopia. Despite the secondary nature of the illuminations, they are authentic in the sense that they provide us with accurate representations of the traditional themes in Ethiopian artwork and they are executed by authentic Ethiopian craftspeople.

Codicology

The manuscripts described below are distinguished from one another both by the content they contain and also by the physical features they possess. While manuscripts are naturally known for their content, there is actually a great deal to be learned from the study of their physical features. At this time, we will limit ourselves to a few comments about quire construction in the codices and to a few of the general characteristics among the scrolls.

We can note some basic facts regarding quire construction in the codices. Our comments relate to 100 of the codices since four of these are accordion-fold books (EMIP 75, 85, 91, and 92) and two others (EMIP 24 and 27) are so thoroughly rebound that reconstruction of the original architecture of the codex is virtually impossible.

First a word about nomenclature. Quires come in three basic formats: balanced, unbalanced and what we call adjusted balanced. Balanced quires are the natural state of the architecture of a quire: when sheets are folded you end up with a balanced number of folios on either side of the fold. Unbalanced quires and adjusted balanced quires make use of one or more half-sheets. Where one half-sheet is employed the quire ends up unbalanced; where two half sheets are employed, the quire ends up balanced, but we refer to this as adjusted balanced. Theoretically, the half sheets could be placed on the same side of the quire fold and the quire would be doubly out of balance, but this is almost never the case. This is our first indication that the use of half sheets is a normal part of quire construction and that there are certain normal practices in such cases. In the first place, these half sheets are prepared to be about a centimeter wider than a normal folio, thus leaving a folio stub on the other side of the gutter fold and providing a stable space for the half sheet to be sewn into the quire with the rest of the sheets. One can almost always distinguish easily between a prepared half-sheet folio with a folio stub and the remains of a folio t has been cut out of the manuscript. Folio stubs are clearly manufactured edges. Often, there are no scored lines on the stub. And it is not uncommon to find several adjusted balanced quires in the same codex that have the half sheets located in precisely same places in the quires. As we will show, the use of half sheets in the construction of quires is very common. We assume that, in a resource scarce environment, the practice allows for the use of all available material, i.e., pieces of parchment too small to comprise a full sheet.

In all, we analyzed 1,320 quires in these one hundred codices. For the purposes of describing the characteristics of a "normal quire" we subtract from this composite number two categories of abnormal quires: protection quires at the front of a codex and the final quires in codices that are often manufactured to provide just enough space to complete the content of the codex.

Sixty-eight codices have protection quires. Two of these have two protection quires. Thus, we can describe seventy protection quires. Eleven of these are a single folio, i.e., a half-sheet, sewn in some extraordinary way to the codex. Thirty-seven of these are single sheets. Fifteen of these protection quires are comprised of two sheets and five are comprised of a full sheet and a half sheet. In both cases where the codices have two protection quires (EMIP 3 and 9), the second quire is a balanced, single-sheet quire. Besides their abnormal size (i.e., only one or two sheets) two things make it clear that protection quires are not to be considered in the same category as the rest of the quires. First, the content of the first major work of the codex never begins in these quires. Second, and more telling, is that when scribes employed quire numbers, their numbering systems never include the protection quire(s). In such cases, the normal practice is to begin the first major work on the first full quire and begin numbering the quires at the second quire and following.

Forty-nine of the codices have final quires that are abnormal. This is most evident when the number of sheets in the quire is significantly fewer than the rest in the codex. Of these, 16 are single-sheet, balanced quires, 2 are a single folio, 12 are a two-sheet quire, 3 are two-sheet unbalanced quires, 1 is a two-sheet adjusted balanced quire, 11 are three-sheet balanced quires, 3 are three-sheet unbalanced quires and 1 is a four-sheet unbalanced quire. Once again, the primary force behind the design of these quires seems to be a desire to make the quire only big enough to hold the remaining contents of the codex and not to produce a quire that is the same as the ones typically in use in the codex.

When we remove the seventy protection quires and the forty-nine abnormal final quires from the total, we end up with 1,201 quires that we would refer to as "normal." By this we simply mean that the guiding principle behind their construction seems to be to provide one more quire for holding content and that the design and architecture of the quire is determined not by those that guide the design of a protection quire or an abnormal final quire. Instead, we assume that this design would be guided by the scribe's notion of an ideal quire as modified by the dictates of available resources and other economic factors. As we shall see, there is no standard formula for the ideal quire in all Ethiopian manuscripts. Nevertheless, by laying out the details we can see some definite tendencies emerging.

One-Sheet Quires (total: 15 quires or 1.2% of all normal quires)
    Balanced   14
    Unbalanced   1
    Adjusted Balanced   0

Two-Sheet Quires (total: 16 quires or 1.3% of all normal quires)
    Balanced   10
    Unbalanced   3
    Adjusted Balanced   3

Three Sheet Quires (total: 62 quires or 5.1% of all normal quires)
    Balanced   51
    Unbalanced   7
    Adjusted Balanced   4

Four-Sheet Quires (total: 397 quires or 33% of all normal quires)
    Balanced   336
    Unbalanced   28
    Adjusted Balanced   33
Five-Sheet Quires (total: 598 quires or 49.7% of all normal quires)
    Balanced   531
    Unbalanced   34
    Adjusted Balanced   33
Six-Sheet Quires (total: 85 quires or 7% of all normal quires)
    Balanced   67
    Unbalanced   11
    Adjusted Balanced   7
Seven-Sheet Quires (total: 24 quires or 1.9% of all normal quires)
    Balanced   17
    Unbalanced   7
    Adjusted Balanced   0
Eight-Sheet Quires (total: 4 quires or .3% of all normal quires)
    Balanced   3
    Unbalanced   0
    Adjusted Balanced   1

We can make several observations based on this data. Five-sheet quires are the most frequent, but account for only 49.7% of all quires. Four-sheet quires are also very frequent comprising 33% of all the quires. Fully 172, or 14.3%, of the quires employ half-sheets as part of their construction.

When we study the quire maps of the codices other trends emerge. Only twenty seven of the codices employ quires that are entirely or very nearly all of the same size. Codices that use consistent four-sheet quires include: EMIP 18, 25, 26, 78, 83, 102, 105. Codices that use consistent five-sheet quires include: EMIP 14, 29, 30, 35, 38, 44, 48, 49, 60, 61, 62, 64, 70, 71, 79, 88, 94, 96, and, 99. EMIP 97 employs a consistent-six sheet quire. The remaining seventy-two codices in our sample employ quires of varying numbers of sheets.

A fuller study of the codicology of the codices will have to wait until a later time. But already we can see the promise in carrying out such studies. To give just one example related to the data we have presented above, it is already becoming clear that the use of four-sheet or five-sheet quires is not perfectly consistent across time. There appears to be a move from four-sheet quires in the earlier manuscripts to five-sheet quires in later manuscripts.

Professor Getatchew has provided below a thorough introduction to the contents of the scrolls; I will make only a few comments on the collection and the physical attributes of the scrolls.

Dating of the scrolls. The scrolls date from the seventeenth to the twentieth centuries: 65 are from the 20th century; 53 are from the 19th century, 15 are from the 18th century and one is from the 17th century.

Number of strips of parchment in a scroll. In all but two cases (scrolls 1 and 2, which are made up of only one strip), the scrolls are made up of multiple strips of parchment, sewn end to end. The usual number of strips is three; 92 of the scrolls are made up of three strips. But 23 of the scrolls are made up of 2 strips and 17 are made up of four strips. Some of the two-strip scrolls are the result of a strip having become detached and lost. This suggests even more strongly that three is the usual number of strips in the scrolls.

Dimensions of the scrolls. The scrolls vary in length from 78.5 to 265 cm. The average length is 168.9 cm; the average width is 9.44 cm. Since several of the two-strip scrolls have lost one of their strips, the original average length would be slightly larger.

Number of columns of the scrolls. Far and away the majority of the scrolls, 122 of the 134, are laid out in one column, but twelve are laid out in two columns.

Borders of the scrolls. Only fourteen of the scrolls have no border. The rest have some sort of border, but these vary in the following ways. 72 of the scrolls have a single border, i.e., a black line marks a boundary near to the edge of the scroll. But 31 of the scrolls have a double border, i.e., two lines mark a boundary near to the edge of the scroll. In at least 87 cases, the borders have been filled with color, either yellow or a light brown. Sometimes the color is so faded and/or the scroll itself is so aged and worn that it is impossible to tell if the border originally had color. However, the numbers would suggest that the usual practice has been to color the borders. I have designated 30 of the borders as "elaborate." By this we mean that the border itself is something more complex than a simple line or two parallel lines. Elaborate borders can be made in several ways: a series of small horizontal strokes (EMIP scroll 1), wavy lines (scrolls 12, 31, and 34), sawtooth lines (scrolls 23, 65, 90, 92, and 121), "candy cane" patterns of parallel colored slanting lines of red and black (scrolls 18, 19, and 129), interlacing or woven rope patterns (scrolls 44, 58, 59, 61, 63, 113, and 123), and interlinking crescent-shaped lines (scrolls 120 and 126), etc.

Number of prayers per scroll. In all, Professor Getatchew identified 627 separate sections in the scrolls. This works out to an average of 4.67 prayers per scroll, but the numbers vary from one to twelve prayers in one scroll.

Illuminations in the scrolls. We can indicate the most frequently-used illuminations in the scrolls. The most common illumination is the image of an angel standing with sword drawn in one hand and holding the scabbard in the other. Seventy eight of the scrolls employ at least one example of this illumination. Seventy-four scrolls employ the image of the talismanic symbol with a face in the center. Thirty-eight scrolls contain an image of an ornate cross and thirteen contain an image of the four-petal pattern with eyes.

Introduction to the Scrolls of Ethiopian Spiritual Healing

Getatchew Haile

In addition to the catalog of Ethiopian codices, this work contains a catalog of images of 134 scrolls located and digitized by George Fox University Professor Stephen Delamarter. As the identification of each scroll shows, the scrolls themselves belong to individuals (dealers and collectors) and institutions in North America. Copies of the collection have been deposited at The Septuagint Institute of Trinity Western University Langley, British Columbia; the Institute of Ethiopian Studies, Addis Ababa University, Addis Ababa, Ethiopia; and the Hill Museum & Manuscript Library (HMML), Saint John's University, Collegeville, Minnesota, so that they can be available for anyone with a scholarly interest in the scrolls. We thank their owners for making them so available.

The scrolls contain prayers against diseases and the demons that are believed to cause the diseases. All kinds of diseases and natural disasters, such as epidemics and drought, are addressed by the prayers; but most are conditions suffered by women, such as menstruation, miscarriage, and infertility. Of the 134 scrolls in this catalog, 13 do not have the names of their owners, 10 are for men, and 4 for families. The rest carry female names, two of which are the Muslim name Faṭima. The *Ləfafä Ṣədq* ("Bandlet of Righteousness") scrolls are for both genders, as the text is part of the funeral service and for burial.

Demons are believed to attack people directly or indirectly through human and animal media. The power of the special prayers in the scrolls comes from the secret names, *asmat* (plural of *səm* "name" but used as singular), of God, which are abundant in the texts. If this is how these prayers are understood by those who prescribe them and those who use them, calling them magic may not be quite accurate. They are all prayers to God; virtually all of them begin, like any other prayer, with the names of the Trinity in the usual formula: በስመ፡ አብ፡ ወወልድ፡ ወመንፈስ፡ ቅዱስ፡ ፩/አሐዱ፡ አምላክ፡ አሜን፡ ጸሎት፡ በእንተ፡ . . . *Bä-səmä Ab wä-Wäld wä-Mänfäs Qəddus 1/aḥadu Amlak.*

Amen. Ṣälot bä'ətä... or "In the name of the Father, the Son and the Holy Spirit, one God. Amen. Prayer for/against/regarding..."

The Two Spiritual Worlds

The faithful of the Ethiopian Orthodox Church believe that they live in two spiritual worlds, the world of good spirits and the world of evil spirits. These worlds may be called the Kingdom of God and the Kingdom of Satan.

To start from the beginning, one learns from the *Aksimaros* (*Hexemerom* ascribed to Epiphanius, Trumpp, *Hexaëmeron*) and the *Mähafä Ǝla'atqäarfa* (Book of Apocrypha) or "Miracles and Wonders of Jesus" (ascribed to John the Evangelist, Grébaut, *Jésus*), that God first created the world and the elements from which he molded the living creatures. Next, he created ten classes of angels. Eight of these classes were led by archangels while two, the Seraphim and Cherubim, answered directly to God. For his worship, the Lord organized the Archangels and their armies in a descending order from his throne, with the Archangel Sataniel (Satan) or Diyablos (Devil) or Säblyanos and his army being the closest to God's throne.

At their creation, the angels were perplexed by their own sudden appearance. "Who created us?" they asked each other. The archangel closest to the throne (the Devil) and through whom praises of the others were brought to God, felt arrogant when he saw that the rest were all under him. Planning to overthrow his master, he declared, "You should not give glory to any one else but me. For glory, thanks, honor and greatness are meet to me, because I am the creator of all" (Grébaut, *Jésus*, p. 565).

As Sataniel/Säblyanos said this, his fall took place. Gabriel said to the rest, "Let us stay firm where we are until our creator reveals himself to us." When the Almighty God revealed himself, he punished Diyablos by letting him fall from his high position in the seventh heaven to earth. The angels under Diyablos's lordship followed him to earth where he established his kingdom.

For the faithful, Diyablos and his army, *säyṭanat*, "(satans" plural of *säyṭan* "Satan," obviously to mean "demons") on earth, are seen as the enemies of the children of Adam. Some sources say that Sataniel became the enemy of man because God created Adam to take Sataniel's place, just as God was angry with Satan for daring to take His place. Other sources say that it was because Satan's glorious place will be given to the righteous, that is, the loyal servants of God. The overall impression one gets from the literature is that the real fight is between God and Satan/Diyablos for the power to rule man. In any event, in the end the earth is seen as a place where the aggressors (the evil spirits) and defenders (the children of Adam), the two classes of creatures who sinned against their creator and were punished with life on earth, are in constant battle.

One of the homilies in the *Dərsanä Mika'el*, commonly designated as reading for the month of Ṭərr, is an interesting source on the life and organization of these fallen angels and their relation to man. According to this text, there are Angels of Light who guard the children of light, that is, the baptized Christians and the Israelites (!), the Angels of Darkness who guard those who are not baptized and other creatures--the heathen, the wild animals, the beasts, the birds and the fish – "so that they may not die untimely," and Sataniel and his hosts. The Angels of Darkness have an additional responsibility: when God is furious against a group--a community or a nation--he sends the Angel of Darkness to punish the offenders. In such instances, the Angels of Darkness are commanded to act without mercy to any member of the community. The reference to mercilessness is of course to plagues and other natural disasters that affect all members of the community.

The Lord does not use the angels of Sataniel in any way; they exist to mislead people and lure them to disobey God in order to take them to Sataniel's reign. Since they are angels, they will live forever as *säyṭanat*.

Interestingly, there is then another class of man's enemies who are something between human/creature and spiritual. These are called *aganənt* (plural of *ganen*, "demon," Arabic *ǧinn*), who live on land and waters. They have flesh; they live, bear children, and die; and they take and change to all forms--humans, serpents, dogs, hyenas, etc.

The literature is not clear about exactly how the *aganənt* came about. But demons, according to the *Dərsanä Mika'el*, do not involve themselves in misleading people to disobey God; rather, their role is to hurt people:

ወበ፡ አጋንንት፡ እለ፡ ቦሙ፡ ሥጋ፡ እለ፡ ይነብሩ፡ ውስተ፡ የብስ፡ ወውስተ፡ ማያት፡፡ ወእሙንቱሰ፡ ይትዋሰቡ፡ ወይትዋለዱ፡ ከመ፡ ሰብእ፡፡ ወዓዲ፡ ይመውቱ፤ ወአርአያሆሙ፡ ከመ፡ ሰብእ፡ ወበ፡ ከመ፡ አኪይስት፤ ወበ፡ ካልአን፡ ዘዘ፡ ዚአሆሙ፡ ራእዮሙ፡፡፡ ወእሙንቱሰ፡ ኢያስሕቱ፡ መኑሂ፤ አላ፡ ያሐምሙ፡ ወኢያመውቱ፡፡ ወበ፡ እምኔሆሙ፡ ዘይከውን፡ ብድብድ፡፡ ወበ፡ እምኔሆሙ፡ ዘይከውን፡ ፈውስት፤ ወበ፡ እምኔሆሙ፡ ዘይከውን፡ ብዙን፡ ዘዘ፡ ዚአሆሙ፡ ደዌያቲሆሙ፡፡፡ ወአልቦ፡ ደዊ፡ ውስተ፡ ዝ፡ ዓለም፡ ዘእንበሌሆሙ፤ ወባሕቱ፡ ኢይትከሀሎሙ፡ ቀቲል፡ ዘእንበለ፡ ፈቃደ፡ ልዑል፡ ምንተኒ፡፡ ወሰበ፡ ፈቀዱ፡ ይእዜሂ፡ ነፍሰ፡ ወአውዕአ፡ ነፍስት፡ ኢይትከሀሎሙ፡ ዘእንበለ፡ ይደመሩ፡ ዐቃቢያንሃ፡ ለነፍስ፡፡

There are demons who have bodily flesh, which live on land and in the waters. These marry each other, and produce children like people. They also die. Their image is like people; some look like serpents; some are of different images. These do not mislead any one; they only cause/become diseases, but not cause death. Some become epidemics; some become fever; some take many (forms) with their different diseases. There is no disease in this world but by them. However, they cannot kill any one without the consent of the Most High. They can catch a soul whenever they want, but taking life is impossible for them without the involvement of the guardians of the soul (DM, pp. 58–59).

Most likely, the *aganənt* are meant to describe bacteria and viruses. For the list of disease-becoming demons, see no. 91.

Other sources indicate that the *aganənt* are like the other fallen angels, that is, they are part of the misleading angels of Satan. The confusion may be either because the perception of the *Dərsanä Mika'el* about the existence of a third class of demons is wrong or because people wrongly call the *säyṭanat* "*aganənt*." In the scrolls, both the *säyṭanat* and the *aganənt* are usually mentioned paired together as "*säyṭanat wä-aganənt*." It could also be an attempt to characterize people with inhuman demeanor.

The belief that disease-causing demons can appear as people and other creatures makes it difficult to distinguish between real people and animals on one side and the demons that take their images on the other. (For a list drawn up in the prayers, see, as an example, no. 89, 1.) For example, when a dangerous-looking python was found in the abode of *Abba* Ǝsṭifanos, built in the wilderness where there were all kinds of wild animals, his disciples took it for what it was while the *Abba* believed that it was the tempter that came to disrupt his asceticism in seclusion:

> The saint knew that the coming of the serpent was from Satan, to disturb him by fear. Clad with the power of the Lord, the saint entered his abode. The serpent acted like shaking the wall, and moved here and there, and like winding itself on his/its body. But the saint signed it with the cross of Christ, not moving from the firmness of his standpoint. The serpent went out defeated. After that day, the saint saw it dead. The birds ate its flesh.
>
> But Satan called also the dogs, his companions, to perform the temptation of his desire, by which he boasts over those whom he defeated and by which he is also disgraced at

those he was defeated. They were likened to the nature of every frightening beast, such as lions, leopards, hyenas, and snakes. They surrounded him as if to kill, each showing the power of its wishful awfulness. Some roared as one which ravens. Some were as one which scratches with its claws. Some opened their mouths as if to swallow. Some were as which prepares its horns to charge. Some behaved as one which bites. But the saint prayed to the Most High, unmoved, and sought help from him. However, to them, too, he responded saying, "Why do you increase gathering (for) your wretchedness? If you were authorized by the Lord to touch me, one of you would be enough. If not, behold, you only show the weakness in your disgrace." Satan was very angry because of the nullification of all his arrows, by not touching the saint (Getatchew, *Abba Əsṭifanos,* p. 13).

The groundwork for the belief that spirituals can change their images was laid when the Church taught that the crafty serpent that led Eve into error (Gen 3) was Satan; that Abraham's visitors who appeared in the image of men (Gen 18) were not men; and that the dove that appeared when Christ was baptized (Matt 3:16) was the Holy Spirit.

The *aganənt* seem to be identified by the different hours of the day, e. g. *ganenä qätr,* "noontime demon" (mentioned always with Dədq or "one that attacks suddenly") in which they are apparently active. Others are identified by places they are believed to be found. Mothers are often heard restricting the freedom of their children to move at certain times and to certain places.

In general, the *aganənt* and *säytanat* are called *mänafəst rəkusan/rək^wəsan* (plural of *mänfäs rəkus/rək^wəs* "polluted" or "filthy" or defiled" or "unclean spirits." There are others too with names such as *legewon* ("legion," from Matt 8:28; Mark 5:9; and Luke 8:30), Šotälay (fem. Šotälawit), Däsk, Gudale, Mäqawəze, Təgərtya, Däbba, Dobbi (fem, Dobbit). Then there are other demons that use, as their media, individuals (such as the eyes of *ṭäbit* "skilled artisans;" *nähabi,* "carpenter;" *anṭäräñña,* "blacksmith" or "goldsmith") or ethnic groups--Barya, red or black; Šanqəlla; Galla; Fälaša; Amhara; Krəstiyan; Əslam. (For these and the kind of diseases they cause, see Strelcyn, "Wellcome," pp. 43–53.)

Perhaps, the description of the serpent in the Genesis story as "crafty" has had far-reaching consequences regarding the place and class of craftsmen and artisan in Ethiopian society and in the society's technological advancement. The word for "crafty" (ተጠበበ *təṭṭäbbäb*) is from the same root from which wisdom (ጥበብ *ṭəbäb*) and wise (ጠቢብ *ṭäbib*) are derived. People shy away from being carpenters, goldsmiths, weavers, and potters, as such professionals (በጎለ፡ ግብር፡, e.g. no. 50, 1) are believed to belong to people with evil eyes; parents hide their children from such craftspeople when they appear in a village. As transformation from one being to another is assumed to be natural for demons, these class of people roar and howl (people call it "laughter") by night as hyenas.

The evil spirits become or cause diseases. Their weapon is their and their media's (evil) eyes. They devour people by just staring at them. Hence prayers such as ጸሎት፡ በእንተ፡ ሕማመ፡ ዓይነ፡ ባርያ፡ ዘእንበለ፡ መጥባሕት ዘይበልዕ፡ ሥጋ፡ . . . ወዘእንበለ፡ ጽዋዕ፡ ዘይሰቲ፡ ደመ፡ (*Ṣälot bä-əntä ḥəmamä 'aynä Barya zä-ənbälä mäṭbaht zä-yəbällä' śəga . . . wä-zä-ənbälä ṣəwwa' zä-yəsätti dämä:* "Prayer against illnesses caused by the eye of Barya who eats (human) flesh without a knife . . . and drinks (human) blood without a cup," cf. no. 13, 3.).

There seems to be a certain confusion in referring to the evil eye with ዓይን (*'ayn*) and ዓይነት *'aynät*. Although ዓይን (*'ayn*) and ዓይነት *'aynät* were originally different from each other in meaning as well as in form, ዓይነት *'aynät* is now used interchangeably with ዓይን (*'ayn*) to mean "the evil eye." Strictly speaking, ዓይን (*'ayn*) is "(evil) eye" and ዓይነት (*'aynät*) is "a kind of skin disease"--rush or allergic reaction (see Strelcyn, "Wellcome," p. 44). As I have no dependable means of distinguishing the two meanings of ዓይነት (*'aynät*), I have consistently presented both terms as "(evil) eye."

Equally uncertain are the meanings of ዓይነ፡ ጥላ፡ (*'aynä ṭəla*) or ዓይነ፡ ጽላ፡ (*'aynä ṣəla*) and ዓይነ፡ ወርቅ፡ (*'aynä wärq*). Their literal translations would be "eye of shadow" and "eye of gold", respectively. But ዓይነ፡ ጥላ፡ (*'aynä ṭəla*) or ዓይነ፡ ጽላ፡ (*'aynä ṣəla*) must be related to ጥላ፡ ወጊ፡ (*ṭəla wägi*) "piercer of shadow." A person is attacked not only directly but also through attacking his/her shadow. But what is ዓይነ፡ ወርቅ፡ (*'aynä wärq*) or "the eye of gold"? The expression in no. 77, 4, ወምስለ፡ ወለተ፡ ወርቅ፡ ንግስትክሙ፡ ሐተምኩክሙ፡ ወአውገዝኩክሙ፡ (*wä-mälä wälättä wärq nəgəstəkəmu ḥatämkukəmu wä-awgäzkukəmu* or "I seal you and condemn you with the daughter of Wärq your queen") gives the impression that "Wärq" is a name of a female demon.

According to the hagiographical life of Saint Krəstos Śämra, who lived in the 14th century when the bubonic plague or Black Death ravaged the world, including Ethiopia, demons are organized in a manner similar to the Ethiopian feudal system. They have kings and army officers, and invade a region in the form of pestilence, *bədbəd*, when the Lord is angry with the region's inhabitants:

Furthermore, Krəstos Śämra said, "Once upon a time pestilence (*bədbəd*) was sent upon the world, to all ends (of the earth); and many people totally perished. There was crying and lamentation in every house. Three years passed in this situation. And one day, as I was in my cell, a good thought, of asking God for mercy to all mankind came to me. As I was alone in my cell, with the door closed, one from the army of the plague (*bədbəd*) came and sit at the door of my cell. When he sat at my door, (the door) opened for him by itself. At that time, he addressed me saying, 'How are you, Krəstos Śämra, friend of God?' At that time, I answered him, saying, 'Who are you that I may accept your greeting?' He said to me, 'My name is Bädəl Asfärr. I came from a far away country.' I said to him, 'Why did you come here?' He said, 'To have a talk with you.' I said to him, 'Well, let us talk.'

    At that moment, he took a knife and cut beef. He had two dogs lying at my door. He threw to those dogs the beef he cut with the knife. At that moment, one of the dogs picked (it) and started to eat. The other dog did not. I said to their master, 'Why is he not eating while the other is?' At that moment, the dog, which was quietly lying, spoke to me in human language, saying, 'Would I rob my friend as people do? We keep the commandment of our master in this manner; we fear and tremble.' At that time, I marveled and was stunned, saying, 'How does this dog talk in human language?' The master of the dogs replied to me, saying, 'Dogs speak so in human language. We, too, keep the commandment of Our Creator; we do not transgress as you (humans) do. He says to you: do not commit adultery/fornication, but you do; he says to you: do not steal, but you do; he says to you: do not kill, but you do. When you transgress the commandment of God like this, he sends upon you (his) wrath, upon the whole earth.

    Listen, let me tell you, Krəstos Śämra, friend of God: when an order is issued from Our Creator, we are ordered by the words of the Archangel Michael; we (listen in) fear and tremble. He says to us, God says to you thus: Go out of your country to kill all people. We fear and tremble when the Archangel Saint Michael says this to us. At that moment, (our) governors (*mäk^{w}anənt*) and princes (*mäsafənt*) would assemble at (our) king, and counsel with him. The king would say to his governors (*mäk^{w}anənt*): go and counsel with your wives. Do counsel and let us go out quickly so that God may not be angry with us with his wrath.

    At that moment, the governors would go out quickly and counsel with their wives. At that moment, the king and the governors would go out quickly (to attack). None of us would remain behind--neither adults nor children. Listen, let me tell you, Krəstos Śämra: when we arrive at (a region) where God ordered us, (our) king enters the king's palace, and his governors enter the house of the governors. None of us would transgress the order of the Archangel Saint Michael. At that time, we do as we are ordered; we do not transgress as you do: a king kills a king; governors kill governors; adults kill adults; children kill children; women kill women; male servants/slaves kill male servants/slaves; female servants/slaves kill female servants/slaves. We are ordered in this manner. No one kills but his equal. When the Archangel Saint Michael says to us, come out quickly, and go back to your country, we immediately leave, fearing and trembling, and return to our houses in peace. We live thus until the day of death.'" (For the text see, Cerulli, *Krestos Sämrā*, pp. 38–40).

It is widely believed that people are able to use demons in black magic, *śəray*, "charm," to hurt a personal enemy. The literature is short of such prescriptions; there are not many, but the description of the harm that black magic would inflict as found in just one of the prayers for undoing this magic, called መፍትሔ፡ ሠራይ፡ *mäftəhe śəray*, is worth noting:

> Prayer for undoing a charm excerpted from the Eighty-One (Canonical) Books: With this talisman (*tälsäm*) be unbound (diseases caused by) many charmers, liars who do charm with plants and (secret) names (*asmat*), cutting the plant, uprooting a tree, gazing at the sky, piercing the earth, touching a *tabot*, calling a name (of the enemy), spreading aches, tying grass on their heads, burying a whole hen egg, reciting (on) food and drink of Muslims, (using) a donkey, an afterbirth, camel milk, and *fəgen* (?). Bridle and rein the charm of a man and a woman, who has used hair of a woman in child birth bed, owl blood, and that has been recited (by) an Islamic ascetic; undo the charm of the clergy . . . . (For the text, see no. 22, l.)

The list of objects the charmer is said to use is enlarged in no. 99, 5 by adding white incense, *kol* (citrus?), *əfren* (red pepper seed?), parchment (kərtas), parasitic əmb"açço plant, čəfrəgg root, fennel, čəret, əret, copper ring, silver ring, human bone, grave earth, clothes, pillows, bed, carpet, bareqa (probably, barneṭa "hat"), neck thread (ma'əṭäb), mule, saddle, white ash, red silk, qäṭäṭif root, donkey dug, granite pebble, modär, əmb"ay, zägba, massərəčč, bäträ muse, first laid egg, black hen, a dog, a cat, wild hen, adängəzo gall, hyrax hair, monkey heart, genet meat, hyena nose, elephant dung and gall, lion meat, leopard nail, fox meat, black chickpea, black barley, split pea, lentil, nug, honey, butter, 'adbä (?) and milk. And no. 112, adds: sun, moon, darkness, dawn, sea, fountain, day, night, ṭälla, ṭäǧǧ, ənǧära and wäṭ. The list is reminiscent of what is found in ጸሎተ፡ እግዝእትነ፡ ማርያም፡ ዘሰነ፡ ጎልጎታ፡ Ṣälotä Əgzə'ətənä Maryam zä-säne Goləgota or "Prayer of Our Lady Mary (which she prayed) at Golgotha (in the month of) Säne" (Grébaut, "Golgotha.").

The Secretive Nature of the Spiritual Medicine

The defining idea behind these prayers is that the Lord responds or would be obliged to respond if one asks him invoking his secret names. But does the Lord have secret names? The Church's position on this matter is ambivalent. According to the Old Testament, God's chosen people were not allowed to call the Lord by his name; he did not tell it to Moses when he asked for it: "If I come to the Israelites and say to them, 'The God of your ancestors has sent me to you.' And they ask me, 'What is his name?' what shall I say to them?" He just said, "I am who I am." Why did the Lord not reveal his name? It is secret, ḫəbu.'

Why is God's name secret? The religious literature implies that hiding or being secretive had something to do with the fight over mankind. The Lord hides his plans from Satan to prevent Satan from spoiling them. The interpretation of the *Mystagogia* or *Təmhətä Ḫəbu'at* shows that the Incarnation of the Word was a total secret. ፈፈዱስ፡ ይፈውስ፡ ትዝምደ፡ ሰብእ፡ ተገምረ፡ በማሕፀነ፡ ድንግል፡ ተነቢኢ፡ ለኮሉ፡ ኃይል፡ እለ፡ በሰማያት፡ ማኀደር፡ ወለእለ፡ ይትቃወማ፡ ኃይል፡ በኢያእምሮ፡ ሰወርሙ፡፡ "When he willed to heal mankind, he was carried in the womb of a virgin, hidden from all powers who are in heavenly dwelling; and he veiled the opposing power behind ignorance" (Hammerschmidt, *Texte*, p. 48; Lifchitz, *Textes*, p. 42). According to the Amharic commentary, አውቀው ቢሆን የሰውን ሁሉ ጽንስ ያውኩት ነበር, "had they known, they would have disrupted all human conceptions" (Lifchitz, *Textes*, p. 60). Ethiopians' response when hearing good news, ሰይጣን አይስማው "Let not Satan hear it," and their reluctance to count their children must originate in this belief.

The *Mystagogia* itself has been made part of the literature of the spiritual healing. The paragraph in it, ወገጹ፡ ዘፍጹም፡ በጽልመት፡ ፈርሀ፡ ወደንገፀ፡ ዲያብሎስ፡ ርእዮ፡ ብሑተ፡ ልደት፡ በሥጋ፡ አምላከ፡ በሲኦል፡ "The Devil, whose countenance is perfect in darkness, was afraid and startled when he saw in Hades the Only-Begotten, God in flesh," quoted in the scrolls comes from it. A part of the Amharic commentary on this particular sentence may have relevance to the point:

> When there were 25 days remaining before he was born, (the Word) sent the angels to the manger to guard it. At that moment idols started to break to pieces and fall. The demons could not dwell in them. So, they went to their lord, the Devil, and reported to him, saying, "The idols are broken to pieces and have fallen. Therefore, we could not dwell in idols." The Devil said to himself, "When I heard Isaiah say, 'Behold, a virgin will conceive and bear a son,' I had dwelled in Manasseh and caused him cut (a child?) in two pieces with a saw and caused his death. Could it be that he is born?" He has four carriers; he called then and ordered them to carry him and bring him to Bethlehem. When he arrived there, the angels denied him access, shooting arrows of fire at him. At that moment he said to himself, "Woe to me! Now my destroyer is to be born!" (E.g. EMML 1254, folios 292b–293a, *A Catalogue*, vol. IV, p. 247.)

The Testament of Our Lord, of which the *Mystagogia* is a part, states that the Announcer of the Incarnation of the Word (Luke 1:26-38) was the Word himself in the image of the Archangel Gabriel. The following conversation was between Jesus and his Apostles: Our Lord asked the Apostles, "Do you know that the angel Gabriel came and made the annunciation to Mary?" They said to him, "Yes, Lord." He asked them further, "Do you remember what I told you earlier, how for the angels I became like an angel?" They answered, "Yes, Lord." He said, "At that time, I appeared to Mary in the likeness of the Archangel Gabriel and spoke to her. Her heart accepted (what I told her) and believed and smiled, and (I), the Word, entered her and became flesh. I became a messenger for myself in the likeness of the image of an angel." (Guerrier, *Testament*, pp. 196-97).

The miracle-working names (of God) did not remain hidden. Jesus was heard to say "ephphatha" (Mark 7:37), "talitha cumi" (Mark 5:41), "eli, eli, lama sabachthani" (Matt 27: 46). The manufacturers of *asmat* assumed that these words were secret names with the power to perform miracles. But of course these words are just the Evangelists' Greek transliteration of words Jesus uttered in his native language. ("For Christ reciting *asmat* to raise Lazarus from the dead, see, for example, nos. 70, 2; and 84, 3.)

There is also an unstated belief among the clergy that the Disciples were able to work miracles by invoking secret names the Lord equipped them with when he 'called the twelve together and gave them power and authority over all demons and to cure diseases" (Luke 9:1). The book titled አርድእት፡ (*Ardə't*, or "Disciples"— of Jesus Christ)," which is full of *asmat*, reflects this assumption (cf. Littmann, "Arde'et"). The reported understanding of Simon, the Samaritan sorcerer, of their power is not much different. Simon asked Peter and John, in exchange for money, saying: "Give me also this power so that any one on whom I lay my hands may receive the Holy Spirit" (Acts 8:18–19; Harden, *Didascalia*, p. 144).

As reported in the ልፋፌ፡ ጽድቅ፡ (*Ləfafä Ṣədq* or "Bandlet for Righteousness"), secret names were also given to the Blessed Virgin. Worried that her relatives might be thrown into the eternal fire of Hades, Mary asked her Son for a means for salvation:

> On Mäggabit 29, Christ appeared to Our Lady Mary where the righteous live in Paradise and the sinners in damnation. When Our Lady Mary saw this, she was very afraid. The Lord Jesus said to Our Lady Mary, "Fear not, O my Mother, who carried me in your belly and gave birth to me by the Holy Spirit." Our Lady Mary begged him again, saying, "Tell me, O my Son, by what may my relatives be saved from this consuming fire. I fear for myself and for my mother Anne, my father Joachim, my sister Elizabeth (sic), my brother Samuel (sic), and my relative David. Now listen to me, and tell me assuredly by what my relatives may be saved from this consuming fire." The Lord Jesus said to Our Lady Mary, "I shall not tell you; my name is hidden, because what one tells to another will (soon) reach the second and the third. After that it will be scattered to the end of the world; and (people) will commit sins, saying, 'We have by what we will be saved.'"
>
> Our Lady Mary begged him again, saying, "What for had I carried you nine months and five days in my belly?" Our Lady Mary cried a bitter cry. Christ, too, cried with her. The Lord Jesus said to Mary, "Do not cry, O my Mother. I will go and tell my heavenly Father; if he authorizes me, I will tell you (what you want)."
>
> The Son said to his Father, "Behold, my Mother is crying; give me the Book of Life, (the Bandlet of

Righteousness) that you wrote with your hand." His Father said to his Son, "Take (it); I have given you my word. There is nothing that I hide from her; rather I have revealed to her my secrets.

The Lord Jesus copied (it) with golden ink. Bright cloud fell and overshadowed them. [The cloud] made seven curtains of burning fire. None of the angels knew or heard of this incident until he told his Mother Mary. He told her, saying, "Take what my Father has given you. On your part, do not reveal this book to those who are unable to carry it and keep it, but to the wise that believe in me and go according to my commandment."

He who owns this book will not go down into damnation. If he has money let him buy (a copy) with gold and silver and glamorous clothes. If he does not have money, let him be a slave for seven years. For him who carries it round his neck, his sins shall be forgiven. If he recites (it) at communion time, he will be cleansed from his sins. And if he adds in his shroud the three signs of Solomon (?) and is buried with this book, angels will lead him to the presence of God, and let him enter into the Kingdom of Heaven. ...

Having finished telling (Mary) his *asmat* for life and salvation, he said to Our Lady Mary, "Let them shout and say, 'I take refuge with your name Bǝrhana'el, Kiros, and Ṭǝrakos; I take refuge with Mary your Mother. (For the text, see Euringer, "Die Binde," pp. 92–93.)

Mary's prayer titled, ጸሎት፡ ዘእግዝእትነ፡ ቅድስት፡ ድንግል፡ ማርያም፡ ወላዲተ፡ አምላክ፡ ዘጸለየት፡ ባቲ፡ በውስተ፡ ሀገረ፡ ባርቶስ፡ (*Ṣälot zä-Ǝgzə'ətänä Qəddəst Dəngəl Maryam Wäladitä Amlak zä-ṣällä yät batti bä-wəstä hagärä Bartos* or "Prayer of Our Lady Holy Virgin Mary, Mother of God, which she prayed in the city/country of Bartos") is a major source of *asmat*. The prayer begins as follows: "Our Lord, Our God, and Our Savior Jesus Christ, glory be to him, said to his pure Apostles and holy and gracious Disciples, about this prayer, that no one knows, neither the angels nor the Archangels nor the Seraphim, nor the Cherubim nor any one of the celestial hosts, but the Father, the Son, and the Holy Spirit, one God. My name is Alfa and O, the first letters. The name of my Father is Alfa and O, which is the end. And the name of the Holy Spirit is Aradyal . . ." (*Bartos*, p. 7.)

The introduction to *Bartos* is followed by many *asmat*, most of which are found in the scrolls. The prayer ends with these words of her Son: "The Lord answered her, saying, "Salutation, Mary, my Mother. I truly say to

Introduction to the Scrolls of Ethiopian Spiritual Healing · xlv

you, that for every one who asks your intercession on earth, I will fulfill (his/her wish) for your sake in heaven and on earth. (The promise) will be fulfilled upon him who reads this prayer. And for every one who prays in my name and in your name, I shall fulfill for him (his/her wish) on earth, and it will be done for him in heaven; and the wickedness of all demons under the sky and (on) earth will be ineffective; they will flee from him when they hear the words of this prayer."

Another major source of *asmat* is the book on the life of Mary, titled *Nägrä Maryam* or "The Story of Mary." At every hardship, the Holy Family meets, especially during the flight to and sojourn in the wilderness of Lebanon and Egypt, Mary invoked them for immediate and favorable response. The expression ወትቤ ማርያም፡ በነገረ፡ ዕብራይስጥ፡ ፊላላምዮስ፡ ቈራስብያኤል፡ ... (*Wä-təbe Maryam bä-nägärä 'əbrayəst filalamyos qʷərasbəya'el* ... or "Mary said in the Hebrew language, 'filalamyos, qʷərasbəya'el ...,'" no. 62, 6) is the language of the *Nägrä Maryam*.

Dərsanä Mika'el, the homiliary of the most popular Archangel, is another source for a few but widely copied *asmat* in these scrolls and other similar sources: ekos, asle, eppa, eppas, enäkämkam, eboka, kirom, läkaf, fe'e, loke, arnake, gʷa, absola, asbek, abäsaku, ame', awəṣ, eqa, epe, kabə', rew, arhili, ayon, yabsat, ṣ, aka', kəsbə'e, beqa, ṣeqa, seqa, alfa, o, beṭa, yäwṭa, yod, ahya, šarahya el, šaday, ṣäba'ot, adonay, 'amanu'el, əlmäknun are secret names of God found in the *Dərsanä Mika'el*, sanctioned by the Church. (e. g. DM, p. 30.) Actually, *asmat* prayers are composed in the name of every archangel. To see this fact one needs only to consult the ጸሎት፡ በእንተ፡ ዐቃቤ፡ ርእስ፡ (መግረሬ፡ ዐር፡) ወግርማ፡ ሞጎስ፡፡ (*Ṣälot bä'əntä 'aqqabe rə's (mägräre ẓär)wä-gərma mogäs* or "Prayer Regarding Selfguard [A Subduer of the Enemy] and Charismatic Grace,"), Täsfa Press, Addis Ababa 1968 EC.

Combating the Use of Asmat

The use of *asmat* is not limited to Orthodox Ethiopians. Regardless what names such prayers are called, followers of other religions, Christians and non Christians alike, have them. In fact, a good number of Ethiopian *asmat* trace their origin to other traditions (see, for example, Euringer, "Das Netz 6-7;" indices in Strelcyn, *Prières* and Dobberahn, *Zauberrollen*). But at a certain time, it must have reached an intolerable level for concerned Church authorities, especially when producers of the literature established contacts with their Muslim counterparts in the Arabic-speaking world, and expressions such as መሐመድ፡ ሰይዲና፡ (*Mäḥammäd säyyədinä* or "Muhammad is our lord," (cf. no. 66, 4) and new *asmat* started to proliferate.

Proponents of *asmat* went as far as describing every conceivable act the Christian Church ascribed to divine intervention, such as Moses' powers over the Egyptians and David's victory over Goliath, to the power of *asmat*. But the decisive moment for combating the use of *asmat* came when *Aẓe* Zär'a Ya'əqob (1436–1468) claimed that he had foiled a plot by a group of his close relatives and court dignitaries to destroy him by using Satanic power coming from Satanic *asmat*. *Aẓe* Zär'a Ya'əqob took drastic action against the accused plotters and to suppress the use of *asmat* in prayers.

The *Aẓe* believed, in accordance to the prevailing tradition, that both God and demons have *asmat*, and that a person could request demons to hurt his enemy by invoking their *asmat*. The demons obey the person who invokes their name not to help him but to take him from God's lordship and, ultimately, to destroy him. The king wrote a book titled, ጦማረ፡ ትስብእት፡ (*Ṭomarä Täsb't* or "Letter of Humanity") detailing the plot and admonishing the faithful against the practice:

> And now, I disclose to you what I found in the palace: a book of *asmat* which was copied during the time of my brother, King Yəsḥaq. The book was (so) huge and heavy that two men would not be able to carry it on a journey. The clergy of the tabernacle (*kahnatä dätära*) used to read it when a pestilence or other diseases broke out. The *asmat* were not the names of God but names of demons that help the one who invokes them until they destroy him. Behold, I destroyed it by the power of God and did away from the palace all *asmat* not found in the Eighty-One Canonical Scriptures which the apostles gave us, listing them in their *Synodos*. And I have adjured my sons and daughters that they should not carry or read *asmat* not found in the Eighty-One Canonical Scriptures, (a practice) which causes one to depart from the worship of God, because invoking demons in prayer, or in one's other reading, for help is worshipping demons. You, too, O children of the Gospel, do not accept asmat which you have not found in the Eighty-One Canonical Scriptures (Getatchew, *Ṭomar*, p. 91.)

It was, most likely, at about this time, and in connection with the decisive actions taken by *Aẓe* Zär'a Ya'əqob, that the Prayers ሰይፈ፡ መለኮት፡ "Sword of Divinity"; ሰይፈ፡ ሥላሴ፡ "Sword of Divinity"; and ክሕደተ፡ ሰይጣን፡ "Renunciation of Satan" were composed, most likely by the *Aẓe*'s command. These are prayers meant to ward off evil spirits; they were clearly intended to replace *asmat* prayers the king suppressed. They occasionally appear in the scrolls. I suspect that the following standard opening prayer, the first prayer the faithful studies by heart, was also composed at the king's court as prayer against evil spirits:

> በስመ፡ አብ፡ ወወልድ፡ ወመንፈስ፡ ቅዱስ፡ አሐዱ፡ አምላክ፡ በቅድስት፡ ሥላሴ፡ እንዘ፡ አአምን፡ ወእትመሐፀን፡ እክሕደከ፡ ሰይጣን፡ በቅድመ፡ ዛቲ፡ እምየ፡ ቅድስት፡ ቤተ፡ ክርስቲያን፡ እንተ፡ ይእቲ፡ ስምዕየ፡ ማርያም፡ ጽዮን፡ ለዓለመ፡ ዓለም፡፡

In the name of the Father and of the Son and of the Holy Spirit, one God. Believing and taking refuge in the Trinity, I renounce you, Satan, before this church, my mother, as Mary the Sion is my witness for ever (E. g. Wendt, *Milad*, p. 1; MD, 59, p. 456).

The following is from an unpublished hagiographical history of *Abba* Eləyas, presented as nephew of *Aṣe* Zär'a Ya'əqob. *Abba* Eləyas came in a vision to his cousin, *Aṣe* Bä'ədä Maryam (1468-1478), as a messenger of the Blessed Virgin while the king was preparing to renovate his famous church of Atronəsä Maryam:

> ስማዕ፡ እንግርከ፡ ዘለአከተኒ፡ እግዝእትን፡ ማርያም፡ እመ፡ አምላክ፡ ወትቤለከ፡ ሑር፡ ሀገረ፡ እንብሴ፡ ወሐድስ፡ ሕንጻታ፡ ለመርጡልየ፡ ዘአውዓየታ፡ ፀርየ፡ ጉዲት፡ ንግሥተ፡ ሳይንት፡፡ ወለዛቲ፡ ጉዲት፡ አውዓየታ፡ እሳት፡ ንግሥተ፡ መሥርያን፡ ዘሀገረ፡ ሱባ፡ ወእንተዝ፡ ሕንፀ፡ ቀዳሙ፡ መርጡለ፡ ማርያም፡ እስመ፡ ቀዳማዊት፡ እምአትሮንስ፡ ማርያም፡ ዛቲ፡፡ ወድኃራ፡ ተሐንጸ፡ ለዛቲ፡ ደብርየ፡ ዓዲ፡ ዘከመ፡ ሕንን፡ አስተማሲለከ፡ ወአነ፡ እሁብከ፡ መንግሥተ፡ ሰማያት፡ ሀየንተ፡ ዘሃመውከ፡ በእንቲአየ፡ ወየዓሥየከ፡ ወልድየ፡ እጌተ፡ ሥናየ፡ ምስለ፡ ነገሥት፡ ጻድቃን፡፡ ወይዜኒ፡ ዘእንሃ፡ ሰይጣን፡ ውእቱ፡ ዘይትመሰል፡ በአርዌ፡ ምድር፡ በመዋዕለ፡ አቡከ፡ ተመሲሎ፡ ዓቢይ፡ ከይሲ፡ ቦአ፡ ውስተ፡ ደብረ፡ ብርሃን፡ ወለቀፈ፡ ለንብስተ፡ ቁርባን፡ ወእርሁ፡ ካህናተ፡ ይእቲ፡ ቤተ፡ ክርስቲያን፡ ወቦአ፡ አቡከ፡ ነቢሁ፡ ወቀተሎ፡ ብሂሉ፡ ጸሎተ፡ ሰላም፡ ለኪ፡ እንዘ፡ ንሰግድ፡ ንብለኪ፡ ንግሥተ፡ አድኅኖ፡ ማርያም፡ እምነ፡ ናስተቀኍዓኪ፡ እምአርዌ፡ ነዓዊ፡ ተማኅፀነ፡ ብኪ፡፡ በእንተ፡ ሐና፡ እምኪ፡ ወኢያቄም፡ አቡኪ፡ ማነበርነ፡ ዮም፡ ድንግል፡ አድኅኒ፡ ወባርኪ፡፡ አንተኒ፡ ይእዜ፡ በል፡ ዘንተ፡ ጸሎተ፡ ዲበ፡ ዛቲ፡ ቤተ፡ ክርስቲያንየ፡ ወትሬኢ፡ ኃይለ፡ ተአምርየ፡ ዮምኒ፡ ዓዲ፡ በላዕለ፡ ከይሲ፡ እምአዳም፡ አቡየ፡ እስከ፡ ዮም፡፡

(*Abba* Eləyas said to Bä'ədä Maryam:) Listen, let me tell you what Our Lady Mary, Mother of God, has sent me for. She says to you, 'Go to the land of Ǝnnäbse and renovate the building of my shrine which my enemy G^wədit, the queen of Sayənt, has put on fire. And this G^wədit, Fire, the queen of the

sorcerers of the land of Suba, has consumed. Therefore, build
Märṭulä Maryam (in Ǝnnäbse) first because it (it was built)
before this Atronəsä Maryam. You will (re)build this, my
däbr, later, both again in the form they were before. And I
shall grant you the Kingdom of Heaven for your toil for my
sake. And my Son will reward you with a good reward, with
the righteous kings. This time as well, it was Satan, who
resembles a serpent, who demolished it. In the time of your
father, he came into (the church in) Däbrä Bərhan, resembling
a big snake, and embraced the Eucharistic bread. The clergy of
the church were frightened; (but) your father [*Aẓe* Zär'a
Ya'əqob] came to it and killed it, reciting the prayer, "*Peace
to you, we say to you prostrating. O Queen of Salvation, Mary,
we supplicate to you. We take refuge with you from a hunting
serpent. For the sake of your mother Anne and your father
Joachim, save and bless today our community, O Virgin.*"
You, too, recite now this prayer over this my church. And you
will see the power of my miracle today, too, again on the
serpent (as it happened) from my father Adam until today.'"
(EMML 1126, ff. 35b–36a, *A Catalogue*, vol. IV, p. 35.)

This short greeting to the Blessed Virgin, "*Peace to you*," which has
become part of the daily prayer of the faithful (cf. MD 59, pp. 462–63), was
also composed at the court of Zär'a Ya'əqob as an acceptable prayer to
combat evil spirit.

Aẓe Zär'a Ya'əqob's attempt to proscribe and suppress the practice
of *asmat* turned out to be impossible to enforce. Those who knew of his royal
decree sometimes started their scrolls with, ጸሎት፡ በእንተ፡ መፍትሔ፡ ሥራይ፡
ዘተቀድሐ፡ እም፹ወ፩ መጽሐፍት፡ *Ṣälot bä'əntä mäftəḥe śəray zä-täqäḥa əm-80-
wä-1 mäṣaḥət* or "Prayer for undoing charm, copied from the Eighty-One
(Canonical) Scriptures." (See nos. 22, 1; 56, A3; 88, 5; and 110, 6.) Who
among the *däbtäras's* vulnerable and needy clients would ever check whether
or not the *asmat* in the scrolls they purchased were from the Eighty-One
Canonical Scriptures? Furthermore, *Aẓe* Zär'a Ya'əqob did not side with the
monks who brought to his court a case against fellow monks for having
rejected *Bartos* as an authentic prayer of Mary.

The Scrolls

The scrolls described in this catalogue contain prayers to cure diseases
mentioned in the prayers. In theory, there is one prayer that is designed to

combat one specific disease or a group of them. However, the designation is not always observed. As a rule, the introductory prayer lists the ailments with which the prayer that follows deals: ጸሎት፡ በእንተ (*Ṣälot bä'ətä* or "Prayer regarding/for/against"). But despite the introduction, one can find a prayer used against one ailment in one scroll being used against another ailment in another or even the same scroll.

The list of the illnesses and/or demons in the introductory title is in many cases expanded with other illnesses and/or demons in its conclusion. Accordingly, I have been obliged to rely on additional indicators, other than the title, for the identification of the prayers; hence the need for quotation in *extensio* of the *incipit* and of the body and conclusion of some texts.

The variants of a prayer in the different scrolls are some times so extensive that the prayers appear to be entirely different versions. The explanation for this could be simple. First, a copyist might add more ailments than those listed in the scroll from which he copies. Second, the *asmat* are not always common names such as Iyyäsus, Wäld, Adonay, but strange ones, at least for the copyists, especially those who do not know the languages of their possible sources, e.g. Arabic. The producers of this literature generally do not come from the well-educated class and generally have insufficient training in reproducing letters. It is therefore very likely that they simply make mistakes in copying. In quite a few cases, I have difficulty in distinguishing one letter from another, such as ስ from ሰ or ለ, or ዐ, even ር from ኛ, and ጎ from ኅ. Notice how in 11, 1, the copyist has taken ሰያጣናት፡ (*säyṭanot* "satans" or "demons") for ሐጢአት፡ (*ḫaṭl'at* "sin").

It is common practice in copying texts to add the mark "sic" after such incorrect form of a word to indicate that the error is of the *Vorlage*. But my use of this tradition is limited by the fact that I am not knowledgeable of the correct/incorrect forms of many *asmat*, particularly since some of these may well be the inventions of an individual copyist. Furthermore, for the reason given above, the copyists' errors are too many to mark them all with "sic". I have, therefore, limited the use of "sic" to the relatively better texts and when I are certain of the correct word/name.

It is difficult to determine which of the prayers in this collection are unique or even rare as the combinations of diseases and *asmat* are extensive, generating new prayers. However, the seven prayers for the seven days of the week, with an Archangel for its guard, and its star of the Zodiac (nos. 42, 2; 54, 2; 68, 2; 91, 2; and 116, 2), could be at least rare, despite the fact that there are several copies in this collection. Although Strelcyn, *Manchester*, 30, p. 78, also has prayers for the seven days of the week, there are signs in

Strelcyn's descriptions that show that they are different. Another prayer I have not seen elsewhere is Mary's prayer which she prayed when they gave her the bitter water to see whether or not her conception was the result of an illicit relationship (Mum 5:11–31): no. 96, 4.

It is hoped that the scrolls catalogued here contain, by virtue of their number, a representative of every text of this class of literature. There are of course several copies of the same texts, as we did not pre-screen the digitized scrolls prior to the cataloguing. Commonly, each scroll contains several prayers. In cataloguing the scrolls, every effort has been made to identify every one of these prayers. There are cases, however, where it is difficult to determine whether a prayer is a part of the preceding prayer or an independent one. I have addressed this problem in two ways. First, in addition to the *incipits*, a few words from the beginning of a suspected division point are copied, and second, in order to give an idea of the size of a suspected prayer, the lines it occupies are provided.

The Bibliography shows that a great deal of valuable studies have been made by many scholars. I should mention here especially Sebastian Euringer, Sylvain Grébaut, Stefan Strelcyn and Veronika Six, who have made significant contributions by either cataloguing or analyzing many scrolls in several publications. It is hoped that the present catalogue, containing the description of a high number of the scrolls in one volume, will serve as one more source for the study and a tool for describing other similar texts.

Catalogue of the Codices

EMIP 1 — The Herron Codex
Psalter, ዳዊት፡

Parchment, 180 x 165 x 70 mm, four Coptic chain stitches (with later repairs) attached with bridle attachments to the wooden boards, rough-hewn boards covered with tooled leather (except binding) and an inside decorative linen patch (back board only), headband, no tailband, two protection sheets + 22 full quires, quires 2, 4–19 numbered (but the number five is used twice and the number six is left out of the sequence), iii + 177 folios, top margin 20 mm, bottom margin 35 mm, fore edge margin10 mm, gutter margin 15 mm, ff. 1r–158r one column, ff. 158v–175v two columns, Gəʽəz, 20 lines, late 17th cent.

Quire descriptions: protection quire ii and quires 1–21 balanced, protection quire 1 and quire 22 unbalanced. Double-slip case.

Ff. 1r–175v: Psalter, ዳዊት፡ [*Dawit*]. Includes the spiritual meaning of the Hebrew letters of psalm 118 in a line or two. Printed several times in Ethiopia, e. g. MD 59.
1. Ff. 1r–135v: 151 Psalms of David, መዝሙር፡ ዘዳዊት፡፡.
2. Ff. 136r–150r: 15 Biblical Canticles, መሐልየ፡ ነቢያት፡.
    a. Ff. 136r–137r: First Song of Moses, ጸሎተ፡ ለሙሴ፡, Ex 15:1–19.
    b. Ff. 137r–138v: Second Song of Moses, ጸሎተ፡ ሙሴ፡ ዘዳግም፡ ሕግ፡, Deut 32:1–21.
    c. Ff. 139r–140v: Third Song of Moses, ጸሎተ፡ ሙሴ፡ ዘሣልስ፡, Deut 32:22–43.
    d. F. 141rv: Song of Hanna, ጸሎተ፡ ሐና፡ እም፡ ሳሙኤል፡ ነቢይ፡, 1Sam 2:1–10.
    e. F. 142rv: Prayer of Hezekiah, ጸሎተ፡ ሕዝቅያስ፡ ንጉሥ፡ ይሁዳ፡, Isa 38:10–20.
    f. Ff. 142v–143v: Prayer of Manasseh, ጸሎተ፡ ምናሴ፡ ነቢይ፡, Apocryphal, see *The Holy Bible, NRSV*, Oxford University Press 1977, pp. 233–4.

g. Ff. 143v–144r: Song of Jonah, ጸሎተ፡ ዮናስ፡ ነቢይ፡, Jonah 2:2–9.
h. Ff. 144r–145r: First Song of the Three Holy Children, ጸሎተ፡ ዳንኤል፡ ነቢይ፡ ስብሐት፡ ዘእምአዛርያ፡, Dan 3:26–45.
i. F145v: Second Song of the Three Holy Children, ጸሎተ፡ ፫ ደቂቅ፡, Dan 3:52–56.
j. Ff. 145v–146v: Third Song of the Three Holy Children, በ፡ ባረኩ፡ አናንያ፡ ወአዛርያ፡ ወሚሳኤል፡ ለእግዚአብሔር፡, Dan 3:57–88.
k. Ff. 146v–148r: Song of Habakkuk, ጸሎተ፡ ዕንባቆም፡ ነቢይ፡, Hab 3:2–18.
l. Ff. 148r–149r: Song of Isaiah, ጸሎተ፡ ኢሳይያስ፡ ነቢይ፡, Isa 26:9–20.
m. F. 149rv: *Magnificat*, ጸሎተ፡ እግዝእትነ፡ ማርያም፡ ድንግል፡, Luke 1:46–55.
n. Ff. 149v–150r: *Benedictus*, ጸሎተ፡ ዘካርያስ፡ ነቢይ፡, Luke 1:68–79.
o. F. 150r: *Nunc dimittis*, ጸሎተ፡ ስምዖን፡ ነቢይ፡, Luke 2:29–32.

3. Ff. 150r–158r: Song of Songs, ማሕልየ፡ መሐልይ፡ in five parts. ብሉይ፡ ኪዳን፡፡ መጽሐፍ፡ ሣልስ፡፡ Published by the Catholic Mission, Asmara 1917 EC, pp. 283–289; see also H. C. Gleave, *The Ethiopic Version of the Song of Songs*, London 1951. Common version.
   a. Ff. 150r–151v: Part one, Song 1:1–2:7.
   b. Ff. 151r–152v: Part two, Song 2:8–3:5.
   c. Ff. 152v–155r: Part three, Song 3:6–5:8.
   d. Ff. 155r–157r: Part four, Song 5:9–8:4.
   e. Ff. 157r–158r: Part five, Song 8:5–14.

4. Ff. 158v–170r: Praises of Mary, ውዳሴ፡ ማርያም፡ [Wǝddase Maryam]. Arranged for the days of the week (Monday, f. 158v; Tuesday, f. 159v; Wednesday, f. 161v; Thursday, f. 163v; Friday, f. 165v; Saturday, f. 167v; Sunday, 168v). Karl Fries, *Weddâsê Mârjâm. Ein äthiopischer Lobgesang an Maria*, Uppsala 1892; Velat, *Me'erāf* I, pp. 76–91; tr. by Velat, *Me'erāf* II, pp. 284–96; and E. A. Wallis Budge, *Legend of Our Lady Mary the Perpetual Virgin and Her Mother Ḥannâ*, Oxford, 1933, pp. 279–96.

5. Ff. 170r–175v: Gate of Light, አንቀጸ፡ ብርሃን፡ [Anqäṣä Bǝrhan]. Text, Velat, *Me'erāf* I, pp. 69–75; tr. *Me'erāf* II, pp. 279–83; and Christopher Lash, "'Gate of Light': An Ethiopian Hymn to the Blessed Virgin," *Eastern Churches Review*, vol. 4 (1972), pp. 36–46, and vol. 5 (1973), pp.143–56.

Varia:
1. Ff. IIv–IIIr: The Gəʻəz alphabet, with each letter's numerical value.
2. F. IIIr: *Asmat* prayer to protect domestic animals from wild animals.

Notes:
1. Decorative designs: alternating black and red dotted lines on ff. 8r, 25r, 44v, 51r, 61r, 89r, 103v, 128r, 135v, 150r, 158r, and 175v.
2. Prayer for Gäbrä Mikaʼel, in a crude hand, ff. 25r, 44v, 128r, and *passim*; Wälättä Śəllase, ff. 16v, 36r, 118r and *passim*.
3. Note of ownership by the monastery of Däbrä Gännät, in a crude hand, ff. Iv and 175v; Gäbrä Mikaʼel, 135v (the name of his wife and children insufficiently legible), and 175v; and Zäwäldä Maryam, ff 176v and 177r.
4. Columetric layout of text: f. 146rv (tenth biblical canticle)..)
5. The scribe has addressed the problem of lines of text that are too long for the folio mainly in the selection of an aspect ratio that leaves ample room for the lines of text. Occasionally, a line of text is still too long to fit on the folio; in such cases the scribe completes the text above the end of the line (e.g., f. 7r, 10v, 22r, etc
6. Overlooked words of text are written interlinearly (ff. 7r, 19r, 49v, 59r, 71r, 87r, etc.) and overlooked lines of text are written interlinearly (ff. 47v, 77v, 91v, 95r, 121r, 146r).
7. F. Iv: Pen trial, Mäggabit 12, [19]43 E.C. (March 21, 1951 AD.)
8. Ff. Ir, IIr, IIIv, and 176v–177v are blank, save for some scrawls.
9. Copied by Bärtälomewos, f. 175v.

Provenance:
Acquired by Paul Herron in the region of Bahir Dar in 1966.

Quire Map

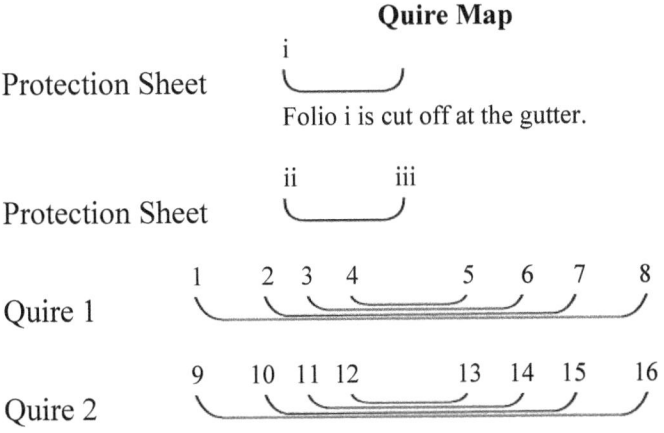

4 · *Catalogue of the Codices*

Quire 3: 17 18 19 20 21 22 23 24 25 26

Quire 4: 27 28 29 30 31 32 33 34

Quire 5: 35 36 37 38 39 40 41 42

Quire 6: 43 44 45 46 47 48 49 50

Quire 7: 51 52 53 54 55 56 57 58

Quire 8: 59 60 61 62 63 64 65 66

Quire 9: 67 68 69 70 71 72 73 74

Quire 10: 75 76 77 78 79 80 81 82

Quire 11: 83 84 85 86 87 88 89 90 91 92

Quire 12: 93 94 95 96 97 98 99 100

Quire 13: 101 102 103 104 105 106 107 108 109 110

Quire 14: 111 112 113 114 115 116 117 118

Quire 15: 119 120 121 122 123 124

Quire 16: 125 126 127 128 129 130 131 132

Quire 17: 133 134 135 136 137 138 139 140

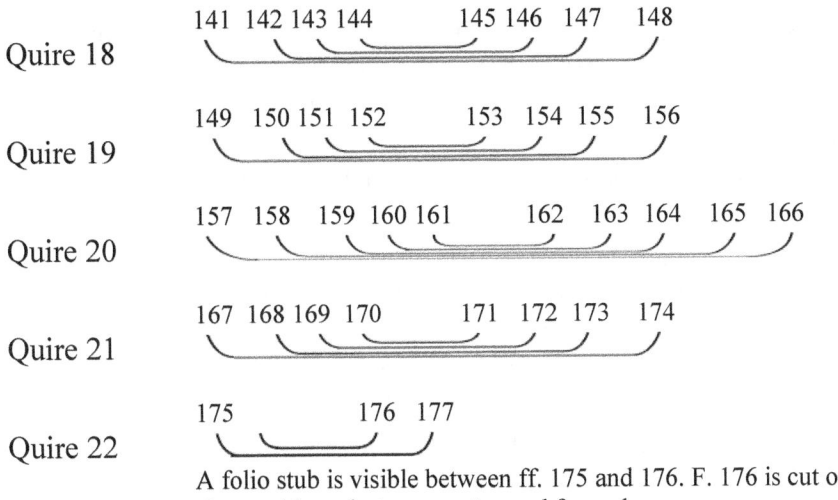

A folio stub is visible between ff. 175 and 176. F. 176 is cut off about midway between gutter and fore edge.

EMIP 2 – Eliza Codex 1
Psalter, ዳዊት፡

Parchment, 150 x 115 x 65mm, four Coptic chain stitches attached with bridle attachments to rough-hewn boards covered with tooled leather, and tailband, protection folio + 14 full quires, no quire numbers, i + 158 folios, top margin 10mm, bottom margin 25mm, fore edge margin15–20mm, gutter margin 5mm, ff. 1r–142r one column, ff. 142v–155r two columns, Gəʻəz, 21–23 lines, 18th cent.

Quire descriptions: quires 1–2, 5–7, 9–13 balanced; quires 3–4 adjusted balanced; quires 8, 14, unbalanced. Navigation system: Brown string sewn into corners of folios to mark the location of content divisions (ff. 14, 22, 40, 80, 93, 107). Single-slip case with heavy linen strap.

Ff. 1r–155v: Psalter [*Dawit*]. Introduced with the first psalm of the Psalter of the Virgin, *Mäzmurä Dəngəl*. cf. Abbadie 244, f. 1r, Conti Rossini, Notice, no. 105. For the contents of the *Dawit* see EMIP 1.

ነዓ፡ ንቤየ፡ ዳዊት፡ ንጉሡ፡ እስራኤል፡፡
በዐለ፡ መዝሙር፡ ሥናይ፡ ወጥዑም፡ ቃል፡፡
ታለብወኒ፡ ነገረ፡ ወፍካሬ፡ ኵሉ፡ አምሳል፡፡
ከመ፡ እወድሳ፡ ለማርያም፡ ድንግል፡፡

1. Ff. 1–120r: Psalms of David.
2. Ff. 120r–133r: Biblical Canticles.
3. Ff. 134r–142r: Song of Songs, common version.
4. Ff. 142v–151r: Praises of Mary [*Wəddase Maryam*]. Arranged for the days of the week (Monday, f. 142r; Tuesday, f. 143r;

Wednesday, f. 144v; Thursday, f. 146r; Friday, f. 148r; Saturday, f. 149r; Sunday, f. 150r).
5. Ff. 151r–155v: Gate of Light [*Anqäṣä Bərhan*].

Miniature:
1. F. 156r: Crude drawing of magical symbol with face in it.

Varia:
1. Ir. Unintelligible note.
2. F. 133r: Price of the manuscript, ten Bərr, detail effaced.
3. F. 157r: Rejected leaf with the words *bäsämay*...
4. F. 158r: The Gəʻəz/Amharic alphabet from *ha* to *so*.

Notes:
1. Decorative designs: ff. 32v, 40r, 46r, 66v, 75r, 80r, 93r, 104v, 107v, 113v, 120r, 134r, 142r (*haräg* using black or late pencil or pen); ff. 1r, 7v, 14v, 22v, (*haräg* using black, red, green, yellow).
2. The aspect ratio for this codex creates consistent challenges for the scribe when it comes to the completion of long lines of text. Almost every folio of the psalms has lines of text that must be completed on another line. In these cases, and where the scribe is free to choose (i.e., when there is not another long line above the line in question), the scribe usually places the final material above the end of the line (e.g., ff. 1v, 2v, etc.).
3. Overlooked words of text are written interlinearly (ff. 64r, 69r, 75v); and overlooked lines of text are written interlinearly (ff. 2v, 3v, 11r, 25r, 69r, 109v, 148r).
4. Columetric layout of text: ff. 119v (Ps. 150), 129rv (tenth biblical canticle).

Quire Map

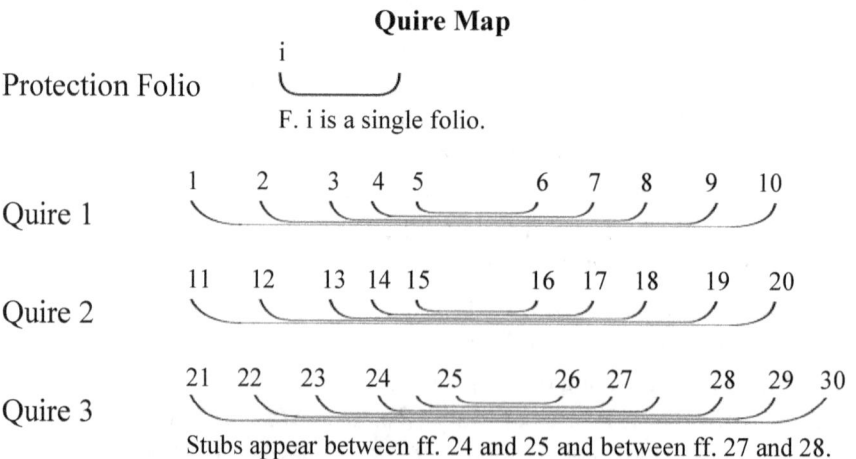

Stubs appear between ff. 24 and 25 and between ff. 27 and 28.

Quire 4: 31 32 33 34 35 36 37 38 39 40

Stubs appear between ff. 33 and 34 and between ff. 38 and 39.

Quire 5: 41 42 43 44 45 46 47 48 49 50

Quire 6: 51 52 53 54 55 56 57 58 59 60 61 62

Quire 7: 63 64 65 66 67 68 69 70 71 72 73 74

Quire 8: 75 76 77 78 79 80 81 82 83 84 85 86 87

A folio stub is visible between ff. 86 and 87.

Quire 9: 88 89 90 91 92 93 94 95 96 97 98 99

Quire 10: 100 101 102 103 104 105 106 107 108 109 110 111

Quire 11: 112 113 114 115 116 117 118 119 120 121 122 123 124 125

Quire 12: 126 127 128 129 130 131 132 133

Quire 13: 134 135 136 137 138 139 140 141 142 143 144 145

Quire 14: 146 147 148 149 150 151 152 153 154 155 156 157 158

A folio stub is visible between ff. 155 and 156. F. 157 is essentially a folio stub, except that there is writing on the verso side.

EMIP 3 – Eliza Codex 2
Gospel of John, ወንጌለ፡ ዮሐንስ

Parchment, 165 x 125 mm, four Coptic chain stitches attached with bridle attachments to rough-hewn boards covered with untooled leather that was, at one time, painted red (flecks of the paint still being visible), protection quire + 15 full quires, quires 2–15 numbered, iv + 128 folios, 165 x 123 mm folio, top margin 25 mm, bottom margin 35 mm, fore edge margin 15–20 mm, gutter margin 8–10 mm, ff. 1–126 two columns, Gǝʻǝz, 14 lines, late 20th cent.

Quire descriptions: quires 1–15 balanced. Double-slip case with leather strap.
1. Ff. 1r–111v: Gospel of John. Text, f. 1r; conclusion, መልእ, f. 111v. Arranged for days of the week (Tuesday, f. 7v; Sunday, f. 8v; Monday, f. 13r; Saturday, f. 21v; Tuesday, f. 27v; Saturday, f. 49r; Wednesday, f. 57r; Saturday, f. 66r; Sunday, f. 67v; Thursday, f. 72; Friday, f. 91v; Sunday, f. 103r; Wednesday, f. 107r)
2. Ff. 112r–121v: Prayer of the Covenant, ጸሎተ፡ ኪዳን፡. As part of the liturgy, the prayer has been copied and printed many times, e.g. MQ 51, pp. 256–62; MD 59, pp. 602–14; see also Dillmann, *Chrestomathia*, pp. 46–50; Velat, *Meʻerāf* I, pp. 1–6; and (tr.) Velat, *Meʻerāf* II, pp.170–74; Sebastian Euringer, "Übersetzung der 'Preces officii matutini' in Dillmanns 'Chrestomathia Aethiopica,'" *Orientalia*, NS, vol. 11 (1942), pp. 333–66; and Daoud–Mersie, *Liturgy*, pp. 314–21.
3. Ff. 121v–126r: Image of Mary's Assumption, መልእክ፡ ፍልሰታ፡. Chaîne, Répertoire, no. 213; MG 59, pp. 668ff; EMIP 17, f. 35v.

Miniatures:
1. F. ivv(erso): Saint George and the Dragon
2. F. 126v: The Crucifixion.

Notes:
1. Decorative designs: f. 1r (*haräg* using black ink); ff. 1r, 111v, 112r, 121v (dotted line using alternating black and red).
2. Ff. ir–ivv, 127rv and 128v blank.
3. F. 128r the name Wälätta Gäbrəʾel.
4. Copied for Wäldä Mikaʾel, ff. 122r and 126r.
5. Overlooked words of text are written interlinearly (ff. 13r, 52r, 53v, 88v, 107v, 124r).

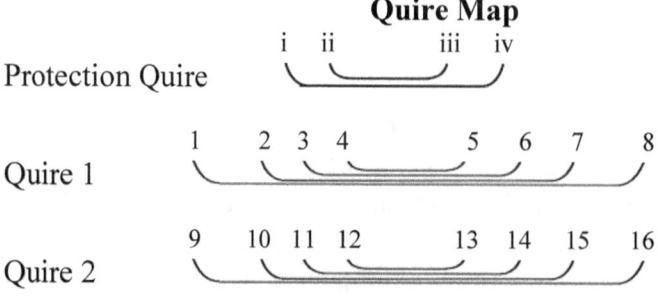

Quire Map

Catalogue of the Ethiopic Manuscript Imaging Project · 9

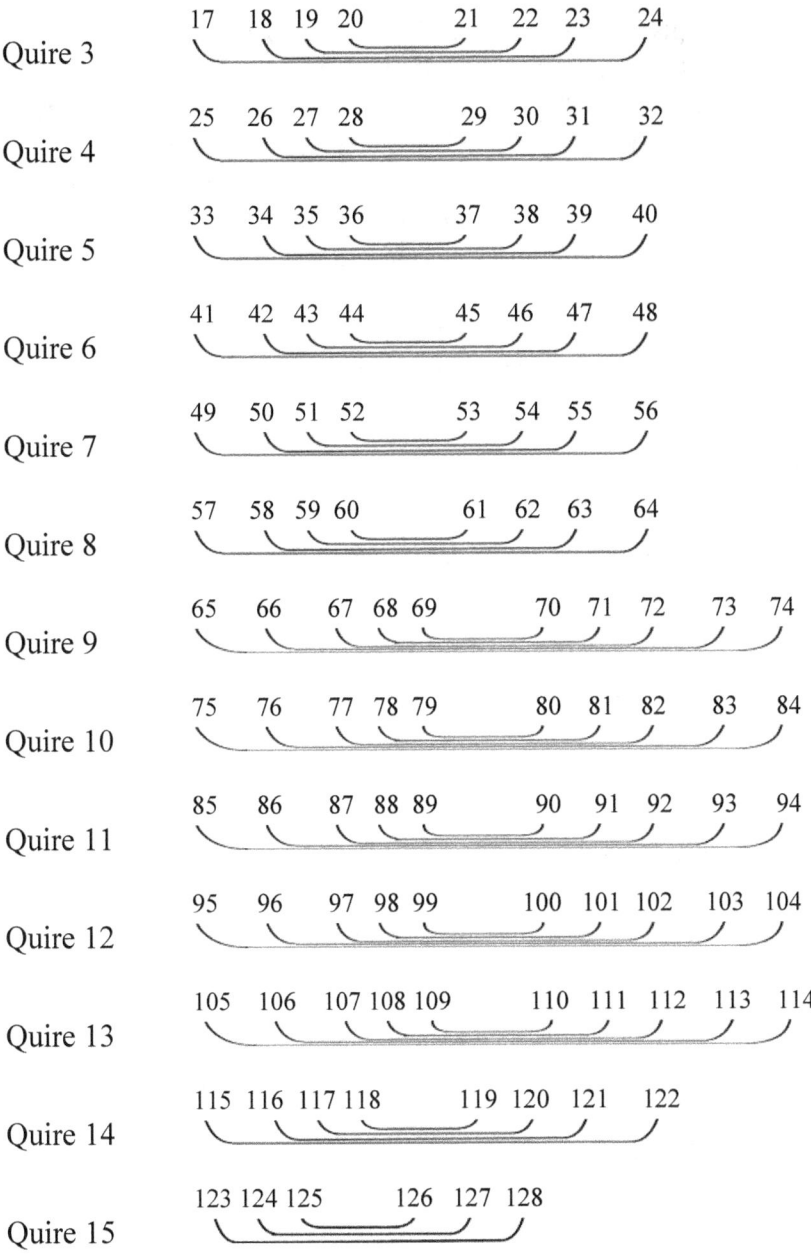

EMIP 4 – Eliza Codex 3
Psalter, ዳዊት፡
Parchment, 120 x 93 x 90 mm, four Coptic chain stitches attached with bridle attachments to rough-hewn boards covered with tooled leather over a

cracked glass plate (front) and "Red Hawk" logo packaging material visible inside the turn-ins on the back cover, headband and tailband, protection quire + 13 full quires, quires 2–12 numbered, iv + 178 folios, 115 x 92 mm, top margin 13 mm, bottom margin 21 mm, fore edge margin 14 mm, gutter margin 7 mm, ff. 1rv, iiv–159v one column, ff. 160r–178v two columns, Gəʿəz, 19 lines, 20th cent.

Quire descriptions: quires 1–13 balanced. Navigation system: 1) various colored string sewn into corners of folios 1, 8, 25, 51, 84, 105, 122, 129, 137 to mark content divisions. Double-slip case.

Ff. 1r–178r: Psalter [*Dawit*]. Introduced with the hymn, *Näʿa Dawit*, cf. EMIP 1 and EMIP 2.
  1. Ff. 1r–136v: Psalms of David.
  2. Ff. 137r–151v: Biblical Canticles.
  3. Ff. 151v–159v: Song of Songs, common version.
  4. Ff. 160r–172v: Praises of Mary [*Wəddase Maryam*]. Arranged for the days of the week (Monday, f. 160r; Tuesday, f. 161r; Wednesday, f. 163r; Thursday, f. 165v; Friday, f. 168r; Saturday, f. 169v; Sunday, f. 171r).
  5. Ff. 172v–178r: Gate of Light [*Anqäṣä Bərhan*].

Varia:
  1. F. 1r: Genealogy of the early Shoan dynasty, in Amharic in a crude hand.
  2. F. 1v: The story of the sorcerer at the Sea of Tiberias.
      በስመ፡ አብ፡ በል፡ አፍጠለሹ፦ም ፫ጊዜ፡ ያሽብክ፡ ጸሎተ፡ ንድራ፡ ዘውእቱ፡ ወእንዘ፡ የሐውር፡ እግዚእን፡ ውስተ፡ ባሕረ፡ ጥብርያዶስ፡ . . .
      Cf. Strelcyn, *Lincei*, no. 32, 7.
  3. F. IIr: List of names in a crude hand.
  4. F. IIv–IVv: Excerpt from the Mystagogia. Hammerschmidt, *Texte*, pp. 48–72; Lifchitz, *Textes*, pp. 40–52; Velat, *Meʿeraf* I, pp. 215–7; MG 59, pp. 9ff.
      ፈትሐ፡ ወዘእምታን፡ (sic) ተንሥአ፡ . . .
  5. F. 178v: Settlement of an unidentifiable dispute.

Notes:
  1. Quire nine (f. 109r) and ten (f. 123r) are both numbered as quire nine making numbers on subsequent quires off by one.
  2. In a later hand, directory for reading: Ps 3 for all occasions, f. 2r; Ps 6 in time of plague, f. 3v; Ps 29 when seeing a dream, f. 22v; Ps 32 for help in falling in love, f. 25v; read Ps 50 with Ps 41, f. 44r; Ps 51 against the enemy, f. 44v; (the directory on ff. 47r and 49r, not clear)

Ps 127 when something bad happens to you, f. 122r; fifth part of the Song of Songs for meal ("daily bread"? *sisit*), f. 159r.
3. The same later hand arranges the codex for the days of the week (Monday, f. 1r; Tuesday, f. 25r; Wednesday, f. 51r; Thursday, f. 74v; Friday, f. 105v; Saturday, f.122v; Sunday, f.137r and f. 151v.)
4. Decorative designs: ff. ii, 1r, 16v, 25r, 44v, 51r, 61v, 74v, 105v, 119r, 122v, 137r, 160r (*haräg* using black and red); ff. 8v, 36r, 84r, 90v, 151v (*haräg* using black); f. 129v (crude *haräg* -like design using pink next to text); ff. 161r, 165v, 169v, 171r (dotted line using alternating black and red); f. 1r (dotted line using black).
5. Note of ownership by Täsfaw Bayyuh, f. 61r and Wäldä Maryam, f. 61v. Other names: Wäldä Ṣadəq Ayyänäw, ff. 177v and 178r, and Gäbrä Iyyäsus Aššäbbər (?), f. 178r.
6. The word for God is rubricated in the first three works; Mary is rubricated in the final two works.
7. The scribe occasionally has to complete a line of text on another line. The challenge is addressed mainly through the selection of an appropriate aspect ratio for the codex combined with an appropriate script size. Where the line of text is still too long, the scribe completes the line of text above the end of the line (e.g., f. 17r, etc.). Occasionally the scribe will try to avoid the problem by writing part of a line in very small print (e.g., f. 35r).
8. Columetric layout of text: ff. 133v (Ps. 145, name of God alternates between red and black from one line to the next), 134v–135r (Ps. 148), 136r (Ps. 150), 147rv (tenth biblical canticle).
9. Overlooked words of text are written interlinearly (ff. 35v, 62r, 174v); and overlooked lines of text are written interlinearly (f. 81r).

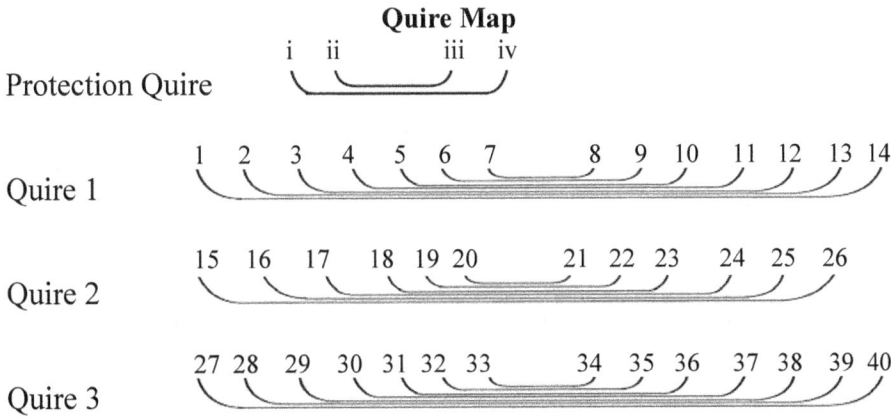

Quire 4	41 42 43 44 45 46 47 48 49 50 51 52 53 54
Quire 5	55 56 57 58 59 60 61 62 63 64 65 66 67 68
Quire 6	69 70 71 72 73 74 75 76 77 78 79 80 81 82
Quire 7	83 84 85 86 87 88 89 90 91 92 93 94
Quire 8	95 96 97 98 99 100 101 102 103 104 105 106 107 108
Quire 9	109 110 111 112 113 114 115 116 117 118 119 120 121 122
Quire 10	123 124 125 126 127 128 129 130 131 132 133 134 135 136
Quire 11	137 138 139 140 141 142 143 144 145 146 147 148 149 150
Quire 12	151 152 153 154 155 156 157 158 159 160 161 162 163 164
Quire 13	165 166 167 168 169 170 171 172 173 174 175 176 177 178

EMIP 5 – Marwick Codex 1
Prayers Against Evil Spirits

Parchment, 125 x 96 x 32 mm, four Coptic chain stitches attached with bridle attachments to rough-hewn boards, both of which are broken and stitched together, protection quire + four full quires, ii + 38 folios, 125 x 97 mm, top margin 3–5 mm, bottom margin 15–19 mm, fore edge margin 5–10 mm, gutter margin 3–7 mm, one column, Gəʿəz, 20–22 lines, 19th/20th cent.

Quire descriptions: quires 1–4 balanced. Navigation system: crimson yarn sewn into corners of ff. 10 and 26 to mark content divisions; Single-slip case with leather strap.

1. Ff. 1r–10r: A collection of prayers against evil spirits. Lifchitz, *Textes,* p. 205–11.
   በስመ፡ አብ፡ ወወልድ፡ ወመንፈስ፡ ቅዱስ፡ ፩ አምላክ፡ . . . በእንተ፡ ሐውረ፡ መስቀል፡ ዘጸሐፈ፡ ኤርምያስ፡ ነቢይ፡ በውስተ፡ ኩኩሕ፡ . . ., f. 1r.
   በስመ፡ አብ፡ . . . ጸሎተ፡ ማኅፀን፡ ተማኅፀንኩ፡ በሰማያዊ፡ ንጉሥ፡ . . ., f. 2v.
   በስመ፡ አብ፡ . . . አውግዘከ፡ ሡይጣን፡ በስሙ፡ ለኢየሱስ፡ ክርስቶስ፡ . . ., f. 2v.
   በስመ፡ አብ፡ . . . ቅድስት፡ ሥላሴ፡ አውግዘከ፡ ወኩሉ፡ አባልከ፡ ወኩሉ፡ ጣያትከ፡ . . ., f. 5r.
   በስመ፡ አብ፡ . . . ተሰደዱ፡ ወርኃቁ፡ በሰርክ፡ ወበነግህ፡ . . ., f. 9r.

2. Ff. 11r–26v: Prayer for protection with the power of the Cross, ሐውረ፡ መስቀል፡. Abbadie 176, Conti Rossini, Notice, no 83; Lifchitz, *Textes,* pp. 92–145.
   በስመ፡ አብ፡ . . . አአትብ፡ ወእትኀሳእ፡ በስመ፡ አብ፡ ወወልድ፡ ወመንፈስ፡ ቅዱስ፡ ነሲእየ፡ ማዕተብ፡ እትመረጉዝ፡ . . . ዲበ፡ መስቀለ፡ ዋህድ፡ አስመኩ፡ እስመ፡ ኃይልየ፡ ወጸወንየ፡ መስቀል፡ . . ., 11r.
   መስቀል፡ መልዕልተ፡ ኩሉ፡ መስቀል፡ ሐውር፡ ወጥቅም፡ . . ., 12r.

3. Ff. 26v–36v: Prayer taking refuge with all powers, ጸሎተ፡ ተማኅፀኖ፡. EMML 1762, f. 165b.
   በስመ፡ አብ፡ . . . ተማኅፀንኩ፡ በእግዚአብሔር፡ አብ፡ ብሁተ፡ ስም፡ ወሥልጣን፡ ተ፡ በኢየሱስ፡ ክርስቶስ፡ ከሣቴ፡ ብርሃን፡ ተበመንፈስ፡ (sic) ቅዱስ፡ ጸራቅሊጦስ፡ ዘዕሩይ፡ ምስለ፡ አብ፡ በመለኮቱ፡ . . .

4. Ff. 36v–37v: Synaxary entry of Roch, ሮቆ, for 23 Miyazya. Used as prayer against pestilence, ሕማም፡ ብድብድ፡:. S. Grébaut, "Prière contre la peste, *Aethiopica. Revue philologique*, New York, vol. 2 (1934), pp.121–23.

Miniatures:
1. F. iiv(erso): Ornate cross with the names of each of the cross' arms (upper, lower, right, left); on the left of the image stands "Mary, Mother of God;" on the right is "John."
2. F. 13v: Cross.
3. F. 20r: Crude painting of two men with arms outstretched.
4. F. 26v: Two small ornate crosses above *haräg* with eyes.

Varia:
1. Ff. iv–iir: Prayer to Jesus Christ for help and protection, in a crude hand. Cf. EMIP 17, f. 1r.

እግዚእየ፡ ኢየሱስ፡ ክርስቶስ፡ ወልደ፡ እግዚአብሔር፡ ወወልደ፡ ማርያም፡ ሥግው፡ በእንተ፡ ማርያም፡ ርድኃኒ፡. . . በእንተ፡ ወላዲትከ፡ ተማሃለኒ፡ ወተዘከረኒ፡ . . .

2. F. 9v: *Asmat* prayer against the enemy, written backward.
3. F. 10r: The first stanza (of five lines) from the hymn "Wise of the Wise," ጠቢበ፡ ጠቢባን፡, as prayer of salvation. Dillmann, *Chrestomathia*, p. 108; MG 59, p. 110.

Notes:
1. Decorative designs: ff. 1r and 26v (*ḥaräg* using black and red, usually with eyes); iv(erso) (*ḥaräg* using black); 29r, 30v, 31v, 33r, and 34v (dotted line using alternating black and red); 36v (red and black lines).
2. The name of the original owner, Wäldä Giyorgis, has been effaced and replaced with Wäldä Maryam, f. 1v, 2r and *passim*.
3. Ff. ir, 10v, 20v, 38rv blank (save for some isolated words).
4. Overlooked words of text are written interlinearly (ff. 5v and 10r).

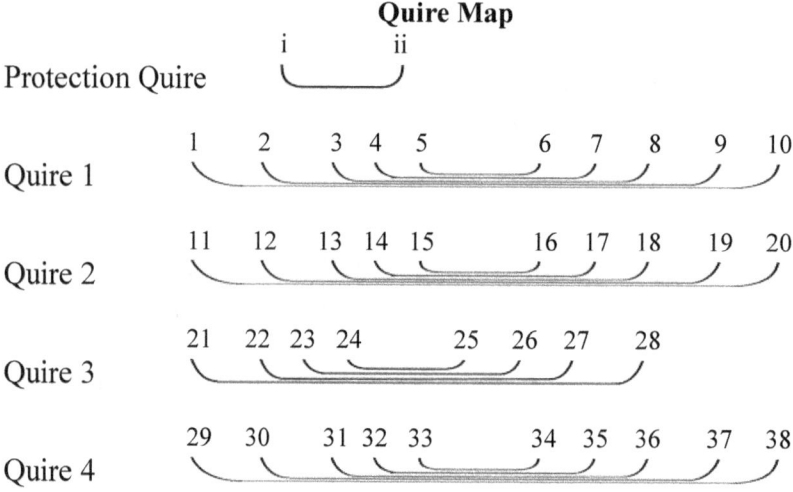

EMIP 6 – Marwick Codex 2
History of the Christological Controversy — Lamentations of the Virgin — Image of Mary of Q^{w}əsq^{w}am, ስቆቃወ፡ ድንግል፡ — መልክዐ፡ ቀሩስቁም፡
Parchment, 125 x 96 x 32 mm, four Coptic chain stitches attached with bridle attachments to rough-hewn boards, the front board is broken ca. 55 mm from the spine and the fore edge piece is missing. The back board is unbroken. One protection sheet + four full quires, ii + 40 folios, 125 x 97 mm folio, top margin 8–10 mm, bottom margin 27–30 mm, fore edge

margin 16–18 mm, gutter margin 6–10 mm, one column, Gəʿəz, 13–16 lines, 18th cent.

Quire descriptions: quires 1–4 balanced. Single-slip case. The case has a set of guiding slots for a leather strap and the staining and wear of the leather shows where a strap has been. However, there is currently no strap.

1. Ff. 1r–3r: On the meaning of አጼ፡ [aẓe] and ጃንሆይ፡ [ǧanhoy].
   በስመ፡ አብ፡ . . . ንዌጥን፡ ታሪከ፡ ነገሥት፡ ብሂለ፡ አጼ፡ ስመ፡ ንጉሥ፡ ተወጥነ፡ በትግሬ፡ . . .
2. Ff. 3r–6r: Palace Etiquette at Susənyos's Court.
   ወአመ፡ ይገብር፡ ፍትሐ፡ ወይትማኅር፡ ምክረ፡ ሱስን(f. 3v)ዮስ፡ (sic) ንጉሥ፡ ይነብር፡ ዲበ፡ መንበሩ፡ . . ., f. 3rv.
   ወአመ፡ የሐውር፡ ንጉሥ፡ በጉዞ፡ . . ., f. 5r.
3. Ff. 6r–20r: On the Christological controversies of the Gonderite era. I. Guidi, "Di due frammenti relativi alla storia di Abissinia," *Rendiconti della Accademia Nazionale dei Lincei. Classe di scienze morali . . .*, vol. 2 (1893), pp. 596–605.
4. F. 20v: List of the first forty abbots of Däbrä Libanos, from *Abunä* Täklä Haymanot to Täsfa Giyorgis of Wəddo.
5. Ff. 21r–34r: Lamentations of the Virgin, ሰቆቃወ፡ ድንግል፡. P. Chrysostome Hayoz, *Portrait de la Vierge. Complainte de la Vierge*, Fribourg (Switzerland), 1956; Chaîne, Répertoire, no. 268.
   በስመ፡ እግ"፡ ሥሉስ፡ ሕፀተ፡ ግጻዌ፡ ዘአልቦ፡፡
   ሰቆቃወ፡ ድንግል፡ እጽሕፍ፡ በቀለም፡ አንብዕ፡ ወአንጠብጥቦ፡፡
6. Ff. 34r–37r: Image of Mary of Q"əsq"am, መልክዐ፡ ቁስቋም፡. Chaîne no. 175; MG 59, pp. 675ff.
   ሰላም፡ ለዝክረ፡ ስምኪ፡ በመጽሐፈ፡ ሕይወት፡ ልኩዕ፡፡
   ወለስእርተ፡ ርእስኪ፡ ጸሊም፡ ከመ፡ ጉብረ፡ ቁዕ፡፡
   ፈለስተ፡ (sic) ቁስቋም፡ ማርያም፡ ተስፋ፡ ፈላስያን፡ ስብእ፡፡

Miniatures:
1. F. 38v: Our Lady Mary praying in the temple.
2. F. 39r: The Archangel Phanuel smiting the sorcerers and driving the demons.
3. F. 39v: *Abunä* Täklä Haymanot standing for prayer.

Varia:
1. F. 37r: *Asmat* prayer against epidemics and dysentery, copied for Wäldä Ḥanna, in a crude hand.
2. F. 37v: Quotation from Matthew 21:23.
3. F. 37v: Directory for funeral ritual, ግንዘት፡, in a crude hand.

4. F. 38r: Greeting to the Archangel Michael, but the content is about the Trinity, in a crude hand.
ሰላም፡ ለሚካኤል፡ ዘእንበለ፡ አምድ፡ ወሰርዌ፡
ዘትሴለሱ፡ በአካላት፡ ወትትዋሐዱ፡ በሀላዌ ፡ . . .
5. Crude drawings in blue ink pen: ff. ir, iir, 40r (the last one being that of *Abunä* Täklä Haymanot).

Notes:
1. Decorative designs: ff. 5r, 6r, 10v, 11v, 12r, 12v, 14r, 14v, 15v, 18r, and 34r (row of multiple full stop symbols in black and red or in red); ff. 21r (*ḫaräg*–like pattern using blue ink).
2. Ff. ir, iv, iir: Pen trial.
3. Note of ownership by *Aläqa* Wäldä Ḥanna, whose father was 'Arkä Śəllus, mother 'Amäta Śəllase Ağori, and whose country was Bašära, f. iiv.
4. F. 40v blank.
5. Overlooked words of text are written interlinearly (ff. 4r, 7v, 23r, 27v, 33v, 36v).

Quire Map

Protection Sheet: i, ii

Quire 1: 1, 2, 3, 4, 5, 6, 7, 8, 9, 10

Quire 2: 11, 12, 13, 14, 15, 16, 17, 18, 19, 20

Quire 3: 21, 22, 23, 24, 25, 26, 27, 28, 29, 30

Quire 4: 31, 32, 33, 34, 35, 36, 37, 38, 39, 40

EMIP 7 – Marwick Codex 3
Sword of the Trinity, ሰይፈ፡ ሥላሴ፡

Parchment, 180 x 115 x 35 mm, four Coptic chain stitches attached with bridle attachments to rough-hewn boards the front one being broken and stitched together. The binding appears to be secondary and very recent. The binding string is still uncut and an unused portion of about 50 cm is hanging free. One protection quire + four full quires, iv + 38 folios, 173 x 110 mm. Either through wear or through trimming, the fore edges of all of the folios are uniformly rounded, extending furthest (115 mm) at the center and 110 mm at top and bottom. Top margin 12–18 mm, bottom margin 28–30 mm, fore edge margin 8–12 mm, gutter margin 5 mm, two columns, Gəʻəz, 17–21 lines, late 18th cent.

Quire descriptions: quires 1–4 balanced. Navigation system: variously-colored string sewn into corners of ff. 5, 7, 17, and 23 to mark content divisions.

1. Ff. 1r–38v: Sword of the Trinity, ሰይፈ፡ ሥላሴ፡. Arranged for days of the week. Abbadie, 244, f. 13r, Conti Rossini, Notice, no. 106; Strelcyn, Lincei, no. 53 and 62; EMML 1170. See ሰይፈ፡ ሥላሴ፡፡ ወመልክአ ሥላሴ፡ ዘደረሰ፡ አባ፡ ስብሐት፡ ለአብ፡፡ Täsfa Press, Addis Ababa 1947 EC.

   a. Ff. 1r–5v: Introduction, intended for Monday (?, not so marked). The prayer to the Trinity, "I take refuge" ተጋንዐንኩ፡, f. 1r.
      በስመ፡ አብ፡ . . . ፩ አምላክ፡ እነቀህ፡ ወእትነሣእ፡ በቅድስት፡ ሥላሴ፡ እንዘ፡ አአምን፡ ወእትመኃፀን፡ . . . አሜን፡ ተጋንዐንኩ፡ . . ., f. 1r.
      ሰላም፡ ለአብ፡ ነቅአ፡ ዘይት፡ (sic) ምህረት፡ (sic) ጥሉል፡ ሰላም፡ ለወልድ፡ ነቅአ፡ ዘይተ፡ ምህረት፡ ጥሉል፡ . . ., f. 2r.
      Miracle(s) of the Trinity, f. 4v.
      ተአምራቲሆሙ፡ ለአብ፡ ወወልድ፡ ወመንፈስ፡ ቅዱስ፡ በረከተ፡ ጸሎቶሙ፡ . . . አሜን፡ ወአሐተ፡ ዕለተ፡ አተዊ፡ ውስተ፡ ገጸ፡ አርያም፡ አብነ፡ ይቤ፡ ወሀለውኒ፡ (sic) ይቤ፡ ጊዜ፡ ይመጽእ፡ ቃልየ፡ ወይትሌአል፡ . . . .

   b. Ff. 5v–7v: Tuesday. Prayer, f. 5v.
      አሐትም፡ ፍጽምየ፡ በመለኮተ፡ ሥሉስ፡ ቅዱስ፡ አሐትም፡ ከዋላየ፡ በመለኮተ፡ ሥሉስ፡ ቅዱስ፡ . . .
      Miracle, f. 6v.
      ተአምራቲሆሙ፡ . . . አሜን፡ ወአሐተ፡ ዕለተ፡ ቦኡ፡ በፈለገ ጻቁዕ. . .

   c. Ff. 7v–11v: Wednesday. Prayer, 7v.
      በስመ፡ አብ፡ ወወልድ፡ ወመንፈስ፡ ቅዱስ፡ ሀቡረ፡ ሀሉ፡ (sic) ሥሉስ፡ ቅዱስ፡ . . .
      Miracle, 11r.
      ተአምራቲሆሙ፡ . . . አሜን፡ ወሀሎ፡ ፩ ብእሲ፡ ወአሐተ፡ ዕለተ፡ ውስተ፡ ሀገረ፡ ፍልስጥኤም፡ . . .

   d. Ff. 11v–17r: Thursday. Prayer, 11v.
      በስመ፡ አብ፡ ወወልድ፡ ወመንፈስ፡ ቅዱስ፡ ፩ በግጻዌ፡ ሥሉስ፡ በሥላሴ፡ ግጽው፡ ዋህድ፡ አምላክ፡ . . .

Miracle, 16v.

ተአምራቲሆሙ፡ . . . አሜን፡ ወሀሎ፡ ፩ መኮንን፡ ውስተ፡ ሀገረ፡
ፍልስጥኤም፡ ወአሐተ፡ ዕለተ፡ አዘዘ፡   ይትጋብኡ፡ ሠራዊቱ፡ . . .

e. Ff. 17r–23v: Friday. Prayer, f. 17r:

አይ፡ ልሳን፡ ወአይ፡ ከናፍር፡ ዘይክል፡ ነቢበ፡ ዕበየ፡ ግብሮሙ፡ . . ., f. 17r.

ስብሐት፡ ለሥላሴ፡ ፈጣሪየ፡ ስብሐት፡ ለሥላሴ፡ ንጉሥየ፡ . . ., f. 19r.
Miracle, f. 23r.

ተአምራቲሆሙ፡ . . . ወ፡ አይ፡ (sic) ከናፍር፡ ወአይ፡ ልቡና፡ . . .
አሜን፡ ወአሐተ፡ ዕለተ፡ ቦኡ፡ አብ፡ ወወልድ፡ ወመንፈስ፡ ቅዱስ፡
ወአግረፉ፡ ላዕለ፡ መንበሮሙ፡ . . .

f. Ff. 23v–27r: Saturday. Greeting to the love of the Trinity. Chaîne, Répertoire, no. 214.

ሰላም፡ ለፍቅረ፡ መለኮት፡ በትስብእቱ፡ ዘጾመ፡ እንበይን፡ ዘ[አ](f. 24r)ርአያሁ፡ ከመ፡ የሀበን፡ ሰላም፡ ለፍቅረ፡ መለኮት፡ ዘይጼአን፡ ላዕለ፡ ሰረገላ፡ ኪሩቤል፡ . . .

g. Ff. 27r–33v: Sunday.

አንሥሥ፡ ጽድቀ፡ ዘእምነቢከ፡ አቀመ(f. 27v)ረ፡ ጽድቅ፡ . . .

2. Ff. 33v–38v: Image of the Trinity, መልክዐ፡ ሥላሴ፡. Chaîne no 20; MG 59, pp. 189ff.

ሰላም፡ ለህላዌክሙ፡ ዘይመውዕ፡ ሀላውያተ፨
ለረኪበ፡ ስሙ፡ ኅቡዕ፡ አመ፡ ወጠንኩ፡ ተምኔተ፨

Varia:

1. F. 12r: Note that (the manuscript) was bound by *Mämmǝre* Gäbrä Iyyäsus Wä[l]dä Śǝllase.

Notes:

1. Crude drawings in pencil: ff. ir, iir–ivv.
2. Names of owners erased, f. 4v, 5v, 6v and *passim*. Names not erased: WäldäYoḥannǝs, f. 6v, and the copyist Gäbrä Wäld, ff. 11r, 16v and 33v.
3. Decorative designs: ff. 1r and 5v (*ḫaräg* using black and red); ff. 11v, 23v, 27r, and 33v (*ḫaräg* using black).
4. F. irv, iiir, ivr blank save for some words that do not make sense.
5. Overlooked words of text are written interlinearly (f. 20v); and overlooked lines of text are written interlinearly (f. 29r).

Quire Map

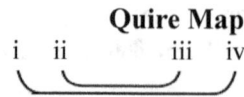

Protection Quire

Quire 1   1 2 3 4   5 6 7 8

Quire 2   9 10 11 12 13   14 15 16 17 18

Quire 3   19 20 21 22 23   24 25 26 27 28

Quire 4   29 30 31 32 33   34 35 36 37 38

EMIP 8 – Marwick Codex 4
Antiphonary for the Fast, ጾም፡ ድጓ፡

Parchment, 163 x 110 x 48 mm, four Coptic chain stitches attached with bridle attachments to rough-hewn boards. The front board is split in two directions and in danger of breaking; it has been sewn together at two places. In the center of the inside cover, a small rectangle (52 x 30 mm) of wood has been carved out of the cover to hold a mirror or some such. The binding appears to have some original elements as well as some secondary. Twelve quires, 95 folios, 156 x 110 mm, top margin 12 mm, bottom margin 33–38 mm, fore edge margin 11–15 mm, gutter margin 5–8 mm, folios are in two columns except for ff. 92rv, Gǝʿǝz, 22–25 lines per page, 19th cent.

Quire descriptions: quires 1–9 and 12, balanced; quire 11, adjusted balanced; quire 10 unbalanced. Navigation system: marginal notations to indicate readings, some of which may include inserted lines of overlooked text.

Ff. 1r–93v: Antiphony for the Fast of Lent, ጾም፡ ድጓ፡. EMML 1135; Bernard Velat, Ṣom Deggua. Antiphonaire du carême. Quatre premières semaines, PO, vol. XXXII, 1–2 (1966) and vol. XXXII, 3–4 (1969); and AṢZ, pp. 1–101.

1. Ff. 1r–10v: First Week, Maḫtǝwä drarä ṣom.
   ዘወረደ፡ እምላዕሉ፡ አይሁድ፡ ሰቀሉ፡ ወሚም፡ ኢያእመሩ፡፡
2. Ff. 11r–20V: Second Week, Qǝddǝst.
   ዛቲ፡ ዕለት፡ ቅድስት፡ ይእቲ፡፡
3. Ff. 20v–31v: Third Week, Mǝkʷrab.
   በዕለተ፡ ሰንበት፡ ቦአ፡ ኢየሱስ፡ ምኩራብ፡ አይሁድ፡፡
4. Ff. 32r–43r: Fourth Week, Mäzagʷǝʿ.
   ውእቱ፡ እግዚአ፡ ለሰንበት፡ ወአቡሃ፡ ለምሕረት፡፡

5. Ff. 43r–57r: Fifth Week, *Däbrä Zäyt*.
   እንዘ፡ ይነብር፡ እግዚእነ፡ ውስተ፡ ደብረ፡ ዘይት፡ ወይቤሎሙ፡ ለአርዳኢሁ፡ ዑቁኬ፡
6. Ff. 57r–65v: Sixth Week, *Gäbr ḫer*.
   ገብር፡ ኄር፡ ወገብር፡ ምእመን፡ ገብር፡ ዘአሥመሮ፡ ለእግዚኡ፡
7. Ff. 65v–75v: Seventh Week, *Niqodimos*.
   ወሀሎ፡ ፩ብእሲ፡ እምፈሪሳውያን፡ ዘስሙ፡ ኒቆዲሞስ፡ ዘሐረ፡ ኀቤሁ፡
8. Ff. 75v–90v: Eighth Week—Passion Week, *Hośa'na*.
   በእምርት፡ እለት፡ በአልነ፡ ንፍሁ፡ ቀርነ፡ በጽዮን፡ ወስብኩ፡ በደብረ፡ መቅደሱ፡፡
9. Ff. 90v–93v: Index of Halleluiatic chants, አንቀጸ፡ ሃሌታ፡. [*Anqäṣä halleta*]. Supplied with musical notation.

Notes:
1. The codex seems to have undergone some water damage, but it is generally legible. A few folios stick together.
2. Decorative designs: ff. 32r (*haräg*) using black and red); ff. 1r, 3v, 11r, (*haräg* using black); ff. 4r, 4v, 5v, 6r, 6v, 7r, 7v, 8r, 8v, 90v, 91r, 91v, (dotted line using alternating black and red).
3. Ff. 94r–95v blank.

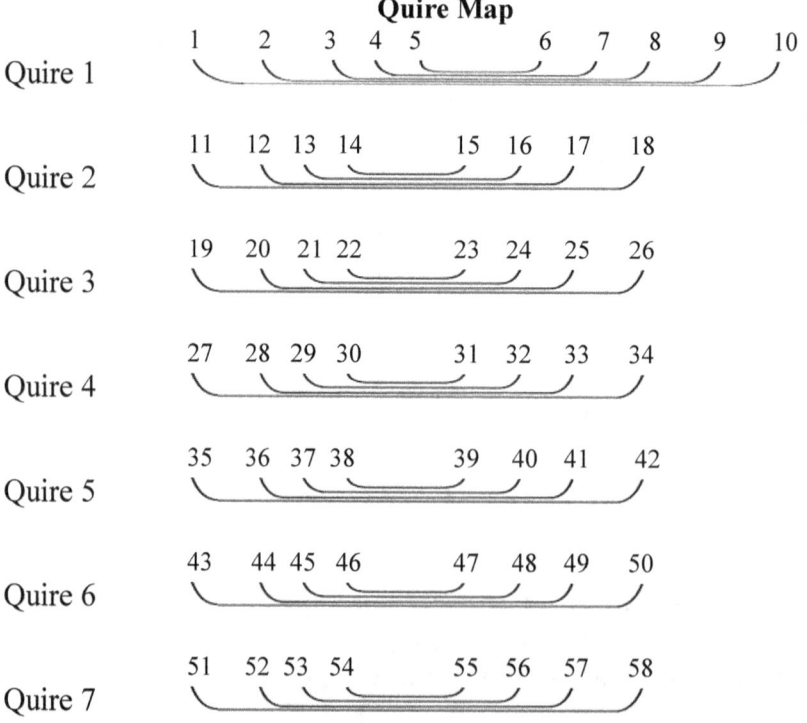

Catalogue of the Ethiopic Manuscript Imaging Project · 21

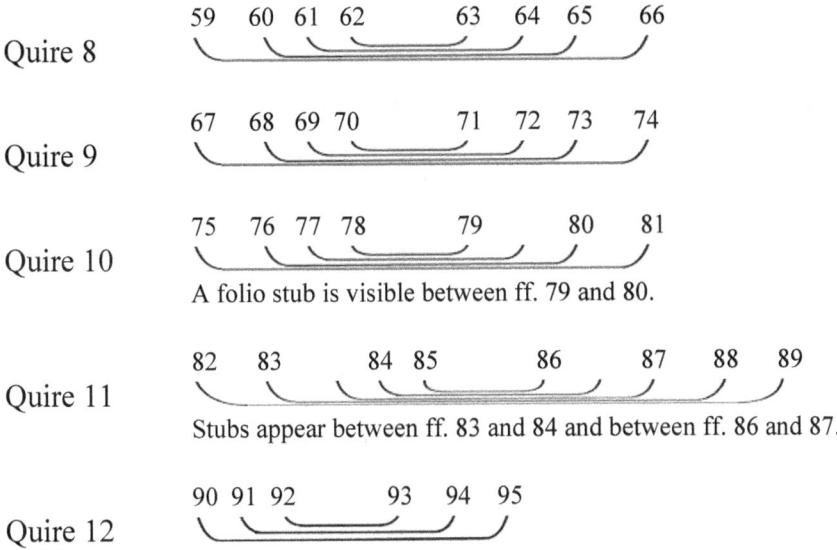

EMIP 9 – Marwick Codex 5
Psalter, ዳዊት፡

Parchment, 175 x 166 x 77 mm, four Coptic chain stitches attached with bridle attachments to the wooden boards, rough-hewn boards covered leather, a sheet of parchment is wrapped around all the quires to cover the spine, protection quire + 22 full quires, reinforcement strips around quires 7 and 14, iii + 170 folios, 109 x 80 mm folio, top margin 12–20 mm, bottom margin 25–27 mm, fore edge margin 12–20 mm, gutter margin 10–15 mm, ff. 1r–155v one column, ff. 156r–168v two columns, Gəʻəz, 20 lines, 18th cent.

Quire descriptions: quires 2–4, 6, 7, 9–11, 13–16, 18, 19, 21 balanced; quires 8, 12 adjusted balanced; quires 1, 5, 17, 20, 22 unbalanced. Navigation systems: 1) brown yarn sewn into corners of folios to mark the location of miniatures; 2) various colored string sewn into corners of folios to mark content divisions; 3) marginal notations to indicate readings.

Ff. 1r–168v: Psalter [*Dawit*]. Cf. EMIP 1.
1. Ff. 1r–136v: Psalms of David.
2. Ff. 137r–149v: Biblical Canticles.
3. Ff. 150r–155v: Song of Songs. Materials from the Hebraic version are inserted here and there by a different hand.
4. Ff. 156r–164r: Praises of Mary [*Wəddase Maryam*]. Arranged for the days of the week (Monday, f. 156r; Tuesday, f. 156v; Wednesday, f.

158r; Thursday, f. 159v; Friday, f. 161v; Saturday, f. 162v; Sunday, f. 163v).
5. Ff. 164v–168v: Gate of Light [*Anqäṣä Bərhan*].

Miniatures (added in the late twentieth-century by "the speckled garment artist"):
1. F. 5r: The Archangel Michael Enthroned, copied erasing the text of Ps 7:10–18.
2. F. 20r: Madonna and Child, copied erasing the text of Ps 23:9–24:7.
3. F. 37r: Saint George and the Dragon, copied erasing the text of Ps 39:11–40:2.
4. F. 58r: The Annunciation, copied erasing the text of Ps 65:18–66:6.
5. F. 76r: The Nativity, copied erasing the text of Ps 79:2–11.
6. F. 95r: The Flight to Egypt, copied erasing the text of Ps 101:22–102:1.
7. F. 117r: Mary Enthroned with the Trinity, copied erasing the text of Ps 118:99–110.
8. F. 136r: Moses "with his tablet and his disciples," copied erasing the text of Ps 150:1–151:4.
9. F. 151r: The Presentation of Jesus in the Temple, copied erasing the text of Song of Songs 2:3–13.
10. F. 169r: Unknown (two white bearded men stand before a multitude), but possibly *Abunä* Täklä Haymanot and his disciples.

Varia:
1. F. IIv: Fragment of a hymn to Mary. Insufficiently legible.
   ዘበሰለ፤ (?) መኑ፡ ተነገሳ፡፡
   በጼሎኪ፡ ዘተወከለ፡ ፍቅርኪ፡ ነየለ፡፡ . . .
2. Ff. IIv and IIIv: Arabic words transliterated in Amharic letters.
3. F. IIIrv: Prayer against the evil eye, *həmamä 'ayn*. Abbadie, 143, f. 49r, Conti Rossini, Notice, no. 109;
   በስም፡ አብ፡ . . . ጸሎት፡ በእንተ፡ እምሕማም፡ (sic) ዓይን፡ እሰሙ፡ መጸእኪ፡ ነቤየ፡ ወእብለኪ፡ አይቴ፡ ተሐውሪ፡ ወትቤ፡ አሐውር፡ ነበ፡ ዕበልዕ፡ ሥጋ፡ ዘእንበለ፡ መጥባሕ፡ (sic) ...
4. F. IIIv: Death record, name and date insufficiently legible.
5. F. 110v: Greeting to the tongue, words and breath of the Archangel Raphael.
   ሰላም፡ ለልሳንከ፡ ዘኢያጸርዕ፡ (sic) ስብሐታተ፡
6. F. 168v: The lucky days of the year, ኢንዕት፡, as opposed to the unlucky days, ጽንጽንት፡; cf. Abbadie 156, f. 19r, Conti Rossini,

Notice, no. 59; and Abbadie 186, f. 14v, Conti Rossini, Notice, no. 233.
7. F. 169v: Medical prescription for an unspecified illness, insufficiently legible.

Notes:
1. F. Ir: Rejected leaf with ሕ፡ and ን in an eighteenth-century hand.
2. F. 96r: words from the text on the same folio copied in a crude hand.
3. F. 170rv: Unintelligible note.
4. Decorative designs: ff. 1r, 94r, 137r (*haräg* using black and red); ff. 8v, 17r, 26r, 38r, 47r, 54r, 64v, 77v, 87v, 93v, 108r, 120r, 123rv, 129v, 136v, 150r, 155v, 156v (dotted line using alternating black and red); 136r, 164rv (black and red lines connecting stops).
5. The scribe rarely has to complete a line of text on another line. The challenge is addressed mainly through the selection of an appropriate aspect ratio for the codex combined with an appropriate script size. Where the line of text is still too long, the scribe completes the line of text above the end of the line (e.g., ff. 7r, 26r, etc.).
6. Overlooked words of text are written interlinearly (ff. 10r, 76v, 85r, 90r, 91r, 95v, 115v, 116v, 118r, etc.); and overlooked lines of text are written interlinearly (ff. 99v and 142r); and in the upper margin with a symbol (+) marking the location where the text is to be inserted (f. 136v, line 6).
7. The reinforcement strip sewn around quire seven is from a rejected leaf of another book and has text on it.
8. Note of ownership by *Abba* Ǝmam, f. IIIv, and *Abba* 'Alämayyähu of Morät, f. 136v.
9. F. IIr: blank.
10. Columetric layout of text: ff. 145v–146v (tenth biblical canticle).

Quire Map

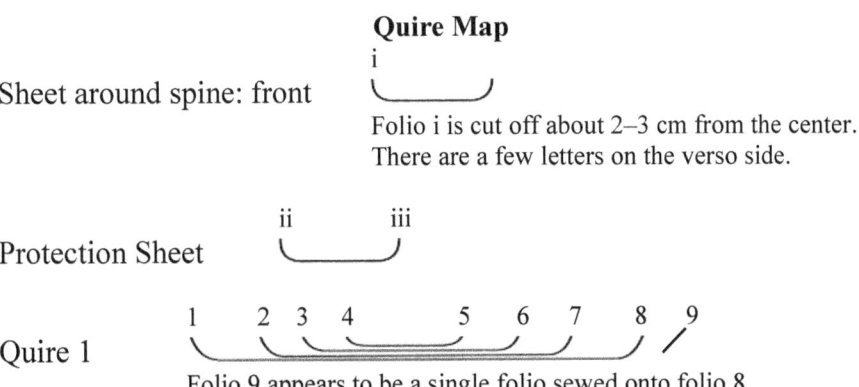

Sheet around spine: front

Folio i is cut off about 2–3 cm from the center. There are a few letters on the verso side.

Protection Sheet

Quire 1

Folio 9 appears to be a single folio sewed onto folio 8.

Catalogue of the Codices

Quire 2 — 10 11 12   13 14 15

Quire 3 — 16 17 18 19 20   21 22 23 24 25

f. 16 appears to be a single folio, sewn to folio 17. Similarly, folio 25 appears to be a single folio, the majority of which is unconnected to the quire.

Quire 4 — 26 27 28   29 30 31

Quire 5 — 32 33 34 35 36   37 38 39 40

f. 32 appears to be a single folio, sewn in, perhaps, to folio 33.

Quire 6 — 41 42 43 44   45 46 47 48

Quire 7 — 49 50 51 52   53 54 55 56

A reinforcement strip has been sewn around the outside of the folio. These are visible between ff. 48 and 49 and between ff. 56 and 57.

Quire 8 — 57 58   59 60   61   62 63 64

Stubs appear between ff. 58 and 59 and between ff. 61 and 62

Quire 9 — 65 66 67 68   69 70 71 72

Quire 10 — 73 74 75 76   77 78 79 80

Quire 11 — 81 82 83 84 85   86 87 88 89

A folio stub is visible between ff. 85 and 86, cut off about 2 cm from the gutter.

Quire 12 — 90 91 92 93   94 95 96 97

Stubs appear between ff. 92 and 93 and between ff. 95 and 96.

Quire 13 — 98 99 100 101   102 103 104 105

Catalogue of the Ethiopic Manuscript Imaging Project · 25

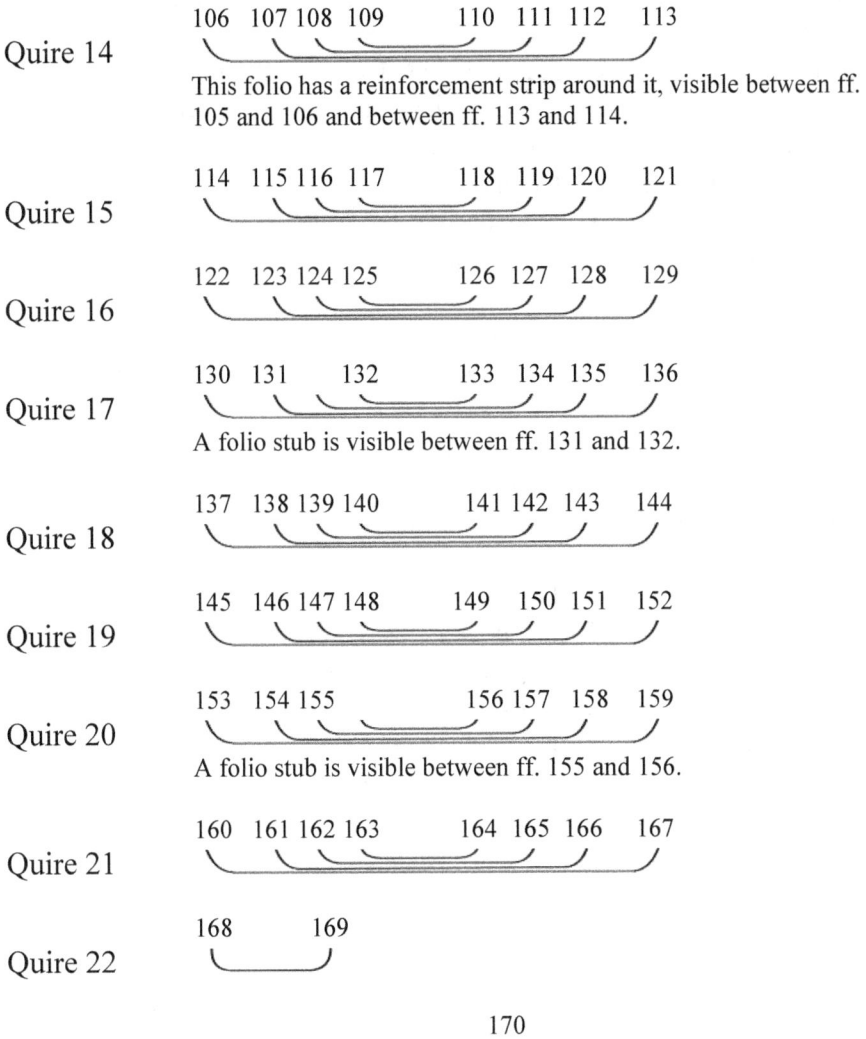

Quire 14 — 106 107 108 109   110 111 112 113
This folio has a reinforcement strip around it, visible between ff. 105 and 106 and between ff. 113 and 114.

Quire 15 — 114 115 116 117   118 119 120 121

Quire 16 — 122 123 124 125   126 127 128 129

Quire 17 — 130 131 132   133 134 135 136
A folio stub is visible between ff. 131 and 132.

Quire 18 — 137 138 139 140   141 142 143 144

Quire 19 — 145 146 147 148   149 150 151 152

Quire 20 — 153 154 155   156 157 158 159
A folio stub is visible between ff. 155 and 156.

Quire 21 — 160 161 162 163   164 165 166 167

Quire 22 — 168 169

Sheet around spine: back — 170

EMIP 10 – Marwick Codex 6
Psalter, ዳዊት:

Parchment, 205 x 153 x 58 mm, four Coptic chain stitches attached with bridle attachments to the wooden boards, rough-hewn boards covered with tooled leather, headband and tailband, protection quire + 16 full quires, ii + 127 folios, 198 x 150 mm folio, top margin 17–21 mm, bottom margin 30–38 mm, fore edge margin 17–19 mm, gutter margin

10–12 mm, ff. 1r–113r one column, ff. 114r–126r two columns, Gəʻəz, 24 lines, 19th, 20th cent.

Quire descriptions: quires 1–3, 5, 7–11, 13–16 balanced; quires 4, 6 adjusted balanced; quire 12 unbalanced. Navigation systems: brown yarn sewn into corners of folios to mark the location of miniatures.

Ff. 1r–126r: Psalter [*Dawit*]. Cf. cf. EMIP 1.
1. Ff. 1r–97r: Psalms of David.
2. Ff. 97r–107v: Biblical Canticles.
3. Ff. 107v–113r: Song of Songs, common version.
4. Ff. 114r–122r: Praises of Mary [*Wəddase Maryam*]. Arranged for the days of the week (Monday, f. 114r; Tuesday, f. 114v; Wednesday, f. 116r; Thursday, f. 117v; Friday, f. 119r; Saturday, f. 120r; Sunday, f. 121r).
5. Ff. 122r–126r: Gate of Light [*Anqäṣä Bərhan*].

Miniatures in a late, twentieth-century hand:
1. F. i v(erso): David beheads Goliath.
2. F. ii v(erso): David Playing the harp.
3. F. 33v: A saint holding a book in his right hand and raising up his left hand, painted erasing the text of Ps 50:6–51:2.
4. F. 46r: A saint receives a book from above, probably the booklet of prayer, cf. EMIP 33, f. 49v, painted erasing the text of Ps 71:16–72:8.
5. F. 70r: Aaron and his rod blooming.
6. F. 94r: Gäbrä Mänfäs Qəddus, painted erasing the text of Ps 142:7–143:5.
7. F. 113v: Angel brandishing a sword, painted erasing the text of Song of Songs 8:10–14.
8. F. 126v: The Crucifixion, painted erasing the text of the rest of the calendar.
9. F. 127r: Resurrected Christ Displays His Wounds.

Varia:
1. F. IIr: Absolution of the Son, ፍትሐት፡ ዘወልድ. As part of the liturgy, this prayer has been copied and printed many times, e.g. MD 59, pp. 640–44; MQ 51, pp. 23–5; Daoud–Marsie, *Liturgy*, pp. 31–3; see also Carl Bezold, "The Ordinary Canon of the Mass according to the Use of the Coptic Church," in Charles Anthony Swainson (ed.), *The Greek Liturgies Chiefly from Oriental Authorities*, New York, 1871, pp. 366–68.

2. Ff. 125v–126r: Calendar of the year, with the text on f. 126v erased to draw the Crucifixion.
3. F. The Ethiopic alphabet from ሀ to ሒ.

Notes:
1. Decorative designs: *harägs* in red and black on ff. 1r, 13r, 19v, 45r (erased), 60r, 64v, 76r, 93r, 97r, 107v, 114v, 122r (one column); *harägs* in black on ff. 28r and 88r. A line of alternating red and black dots marks the division between groups of ten psalms (f. 38v). A row of full-stop symbols marks divisions in the Praises of Mary (ff. 114v, 119r, and 125r).
2. Columetric layout of text: ff. 104v–105r (tenth biblical canticle).
3. F. 67v: An overlooked line of text has been inserted in the upper margin and a symbol (an ornate + sign) markes the place where the text should be read.
4. The scribe regularly has to complete a line of text on another line. Much of the problem is addressed through the selection of an appropriate aspect ratio for the codex combined with an appropriate script size. But, where the line of text is still too long, the scribe completes the line of text above the end of the line (e.g., ff. 5v, 6r, 10v, 11r, 13v, 14r, etc.). This scribe will also reduce the font size at the end of lines to avoid having to go onto the next line (e.g., f. 52r).
5. Overlooked lines of text have been inserted between lines (ff. 13r, 15v, 24rv, 26r, 27r, 86v, 109v).
6. F. 1r: Unintelligible note.

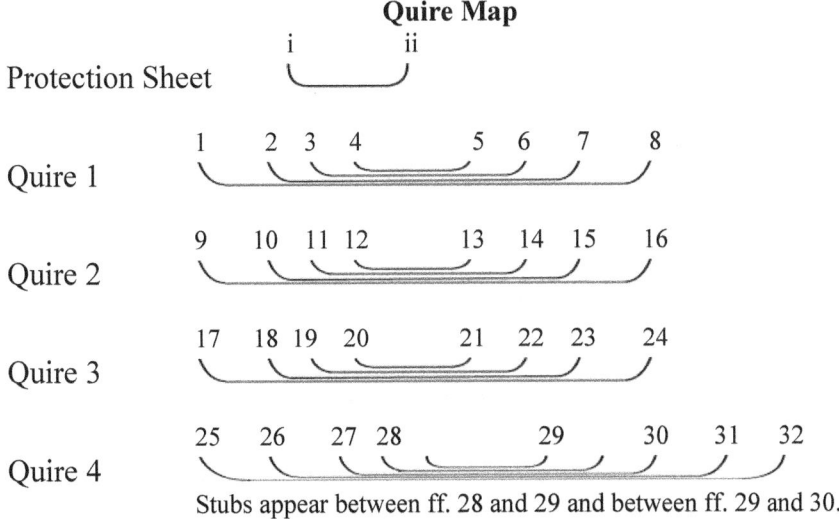

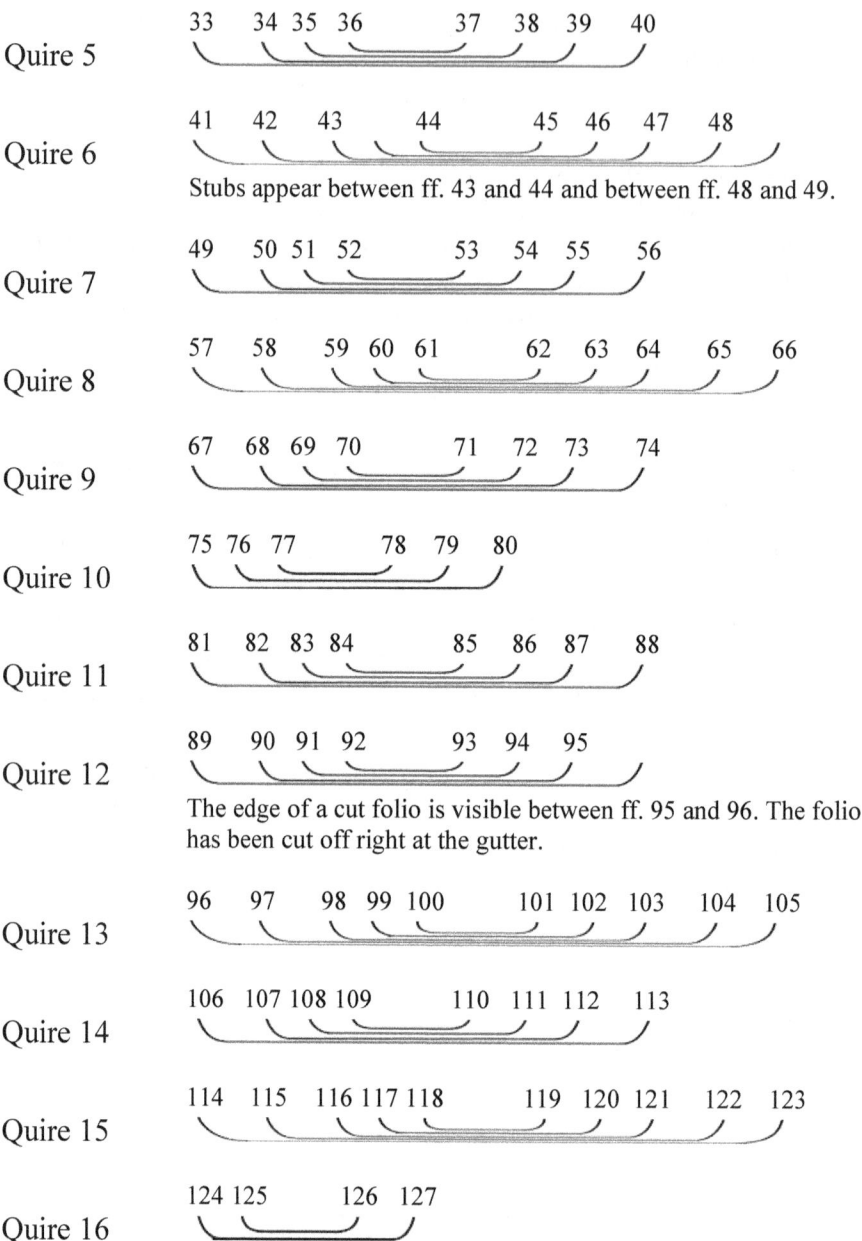

EMIP 11 – Marwick Codex 7
Psalter, ዳዊት:
Parchment, 205 x 156 x60 mm, four Coptic chain stitches attached with bridle attachments to the wooden boards, rough-hewn boards covered

with tooled leather (repaired with blue thread on spine) over decorative linen patches, headband and tailband, protection quire + 13 full quires, quires all numbered, iv + 145 folios, 197 x 150 mm folio, top margin 14–18 mm, bottom margin 40–45 mm, fore edge margin 20–24 mm, gutter margin 10–14 mm, ff. 1r–130r one column, ff. 131r–144r two columns, Gəʿəz, 19–20 lines, Ṭərr 21, 1915 (January 29, 1923), f. 144r. Quire descriptions: quires 1–12 balanced; quire 13 unbalanced. Navigation systems: marginal notations to indicate readings.

Ff. 1r–144r: Psalter [*Dawit*]. Cf. EMIP 1.
1. Ff. 1r–110v: Psalms of David.
2. Ff. 111r–123r: Biblical Canticles.
3. Ff. 123v–130r: Song of Songs, common version.
4. Ff. 131r–140r: Praises of Mary [*Wəddase Maryam*]. Arranged for the days of the week (Monday, f. 131r; Tuesday, f. 132r; Wednesday, f. 133v; Thursday, f. 135r; Friday, f. 137r; Saturday, f. 138r; Sunday, f. 139r).
5. Ff. 140r–144r: Gate of Light [*Anqäṣä Bərhan*].

Varia:
1. Ff. IIr–IVr: Catechism or Christian theology in modern Amharic. For an older version, see Getatchew Haile, "Materials on the theology of Qəbʿat," in (Gideon Goldenberg, ed.), *Ethiopian Studies: Proceedings of the sixth international conference*, Tel-Aviv, 14–17 April 1980, A.A.Balkema, Boston 1986, pp. 210–19; and for a Gəʿəz version, see *idem.*, "*Anqäṣä Haymanot* (or the Gate of Faith)," *NEAS*, vol. 5/1 (1983), pp. 29–37.
   ማን፡ ፈጠረኸ፡ ሥላሴ፡ በማን፡ ታምናለኸ፡ በሥላሴ፡ ሥላሴ፡ ስንት፡ ናቸው፡ . . .
2. F. IIIr: The beginning of Ps 133.

Notes:
1. Decorative designs: *haräg* in black and red f. 96r; *haräg*s in black ff. 1r, 7v, 14v, 22r, 31r, 38r, 43v, 51v, 61v, 69r, 74r, 85r, 99r, 105r, 111r, 123v, 131r; dotted lines in alternating black and red ff. 7v, 14r, 37v, 43r, 51r, 61r, 68v (parallel lines with full-stop symbols between), 73v, 84v, 95v, 98v, 110v, 123r, 144r. Where the scribe places a *haräg* he also places multiple lines of text in red ink to mark the new section.
2. Note of ownership by *Mämhər* Gəday, in Təgrəñña, f. 41r.
3. F. Ir Scrawl in blue ink; f. 145v blank.
4. Columetric layout of text: ff. 110rv (Ps. 150), 119v–120r (tenth biblical canticle).

5. The scribe regularly has to complete a line of text on another line. Much of the problem is addressed through the selection of an appropriate aspect ratio for the codex combined with an appropriate script size. But, where the line of text is still too long, the scribe completes the line of text above the end of the line (throughout). This scribe will also reduce the font size at the end of lines to avoid having to go onto the next line (e.g., f. 52r).
6. Overlooked text is added interlinearly (ff. 45r, 130r).
7. Ff.144v–145r: Record of purchase of the manuscript, Miyazya 5, [19]44 (April 23, 1952).

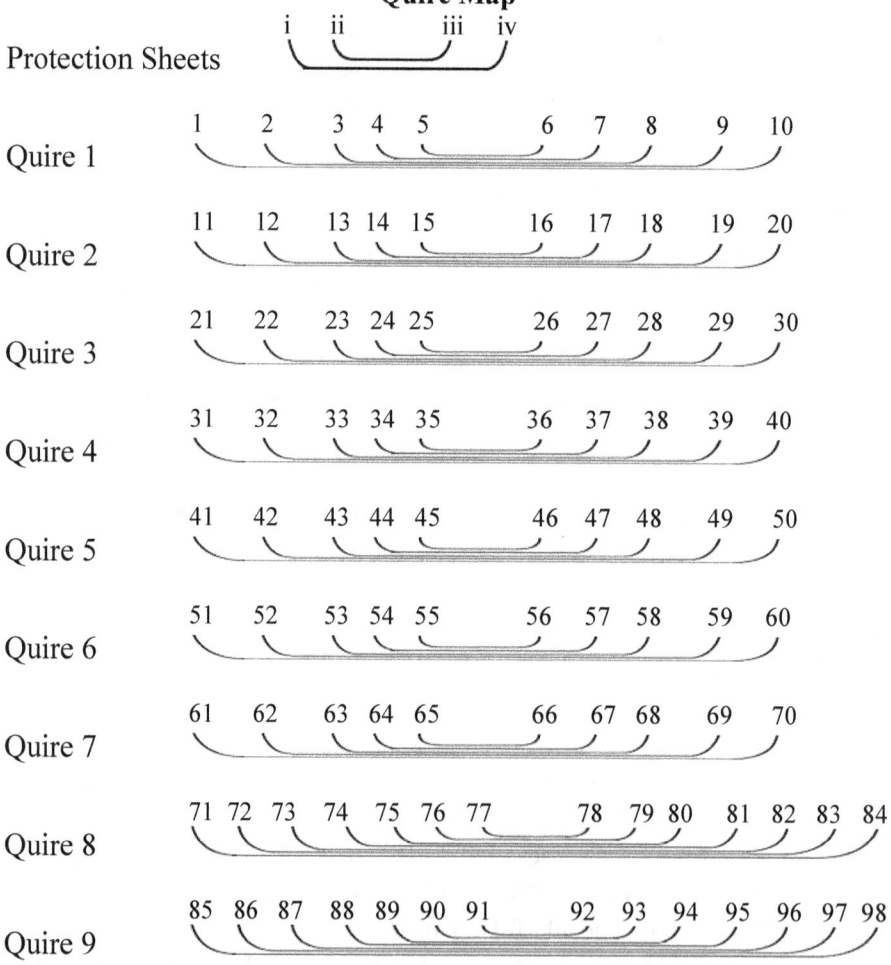

Quire 10   99 100 101 102 103 104   105 106 107 108 109 110

Quire 11   111 112 113 114 115 116   117 118 119 120 121 122

Quire 12   123 124 125 126 127 128   129 130 131 132 133 134

Quire 13   135 136 137 138 139   140 141 142 143 144 145

A folio stub is visible between ff. 134 and 135.

EMIP 12 – Marwick Codex 8
Psalter, ዳዊት፡

Parchment, 108 x 104 x 72 mm, four Coptic chain stitches attached with bridle attachments to the wooden boards, rough-hewn boards covered with leather, spine stitched to quires for repair (head only), protection quire + 18 full quires, iv + 187 folios, 112 x 103 mm folio, top margin 10–12 mm, bottom margin 20–25 mm, fore edge margin 10–12 mm, gutter margin 8 mm, ff. iir–165v one column, ff. 166r–186v two columns, Gəʻəz, 18 lines, late 17th cent.

Quire descriptions: quires 1, 3–11, 13–17 balanced; quires 2, 12, 18 unbalanced. Navigation systems: marginal notations to indicate readings.

Ff. 1r–186v: Psalter [*Dawit*]. Cf. EMIP 1.

1. Ff. 1r–140v: Psalms of David. Arranged for the days of the week (Monday, f. 1r; Tuesday, f. 26v; Wednesday, f. 53r; Thursday, f. 77r; Friday, f. 108r; Saturday, f. 124v; Sunday, f. 141r) and for calendar (*Mäẓagʷəʻ*, f. 3v; *Bərhan*, f. 39v; Paraclete, 46r; Winter [*Krämt*] and John the Baptist, f. 55r; Ascension, f. 57v; Lenten, f. 64r; Epiphany, f. 69v; *Nolawi*, f. 76r; Palm Sunday, f. 76r; *Qəddət*, f.89v; Flower [*Ṣəge*], f. 94v; Easter, f. 102r; Nativity, f. 107r; from *Səbkət* to *Astär'əyo* of Palm Sunday, f. 111r.). The Psalter must have belonged to a church that used it during the liturgical calendar.
2. Ff. 141r–156r: Biblical Canticles.
3. Ff. 156r–165v: Song of Songs, common version.
4. Ff. 166r–178v: Praises of Mary [*Wəddase Maryam*]. Arranged for the days of the week (Monday, f. 166r; Tuesday, f. 167r; Wednesday, f. 169r; Thursday, f. 171v; Friday, f. 174r; Saturday, f. 175v; Sunday, f. 177r).

32 · *Catalogue of the Codices*

   5. Ff. 178v–184r: Gate of Light [*Anqäṣä Bərhan*].
Varia:
   1. F. ir: Note, "David, Prophet of law and order."
   2. F. iv: The opening prayers: the በስመ፡ አብ፡ and the first part of the ነአኩተከ፡ As part of the daily prayers, these prayers have been copied and printed many times, e.g. MD 59, pp. 456–57.
   3. Ff. iir–ivv and ff. 184v–187r: Prayer of the Covenant, ጸሎተ፡ ኪዳን፡. As part of the liturgy, it has been copied and printed many times. See EMIP 3, f. 112r.

Notes:
   1. Decorative designs: *harägs* in black and red ff. 47r, 71r, 93r, 156r, 165v, 166r; late *haräg*-like designs in blue ink ff. 17v, 26v, 38v, 53r; late *haräg*-like design in pencil f. 108r; dotted lines in alternating black and red ff. 124v, 132v, 186r; dotted line in red f. 1r; line in black bars and read dots f. 108r; lines in black (and sometimes red) joined with stops ff. 8v, 73v, 92v, 140v, 178v, 184r.
   2. F. 71r: A red and black *ḥaräg*-like symbol in the margin marks the midpoint of the Psalms.
   3. Isolated names, ff. 5r and 187r.
   4. The name of the original owner erased and substituted by that of Tə'əmrtä Həbu'at, his wife and children, f. 184r.
   5. Pen trial, f. 187v.
   6. Columetric layout of text: ff. 138v (Ps. 148), 139v–140r (Ps. 150), 151r–152r (ninth [sic] biblical canticle).
   7. Small symbols (+) written in pencil in the left margin indicate sections of reading (ff. 48r-53r, 65r-70r, 102r-108r, etc.)
   8. Overlooked lines of text are inserted interlinearly (e.g., ff. 17r, 89v), and in the upper margin with a symbol (⊥) indicating where the overlooked line should be inserted (ff. 106r and 143r).
   9. The scribe regularly has to complete a line of text on another line. Much of the problem is addressed through the selection of an appropriate aspect ratio for the codex combined with an appropriate script size. But, where the line of text is still too long, the scribe completes the line of text above, and sometimes below, the end of the line (throughout).

Quire Map

Protection Quire   i   ii   iii   iv

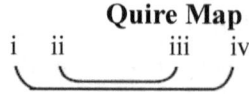

Catalogue of the Ethiopic Manuscript Imaging Project · 33

Quire 1: 1 2 3 4 5 6 7 8 9 10 11 12

Quire 2: 13 14 15 16 17 18 19 20 21 22 23
A folio stub is visible between ff. 14 and 15.

Quire 3: 24 25 26 27 28 29 30 31 32 33

Quire 4: 34 35 36 37 38 39 40 41 42 43

Quire 5: 44 45 46 47 48 49 50 51 52 53

Quire 6: 54 55 56 57 58 59 60 61 62 63

Quire 7: 64 65 66 67 68 69 70 71 72 73

Quire 8: 74 75 76 77 78 79 80 81 82 83

Quire 9: 84 85 86 87 88 89 90 91 92 93

Quire 10: 94 95 96 97 98 99 100 101 102 103

Quire 11: 104 105 106 107 108 109 110 111 112 113

Quire 12: 114 115 116 117 118 119 120 121 122 123 124 125 126
A folio stub is visible between ff. 124 and 125.

Quire 13: 127 128 129 130 131 132 133 134 135 136 137 138 139 140

Quire 14: 141 142 143 144 145 146 147 148 149 150

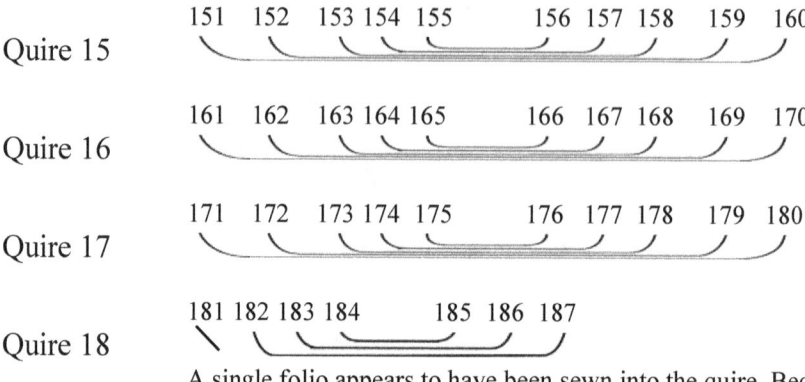

A single folio appears to have been sewn into the quire. Because of the tight binding it is not clear whether it is folio 182 or 183.

EMIP 13 – Marwick Codex 9
General Epistles — Revelation

Parchment, 150 x 128 x 47 mm, four repaired Coptic chain stitches attached with bridle attachments to repaired rough-hewn boards (segment of back board missing), protection quire + 8 full quires, reinforcement strip around protection quire, ii + 70 folios, 145 x 118 mm, top margin 10–13 mm, bottom margin 30–37 mm, fore edge margin 12–14 mm, gutter margin 8–10 mm, ff. iv(erso)–iir, 1r–79v two columns, Gəʻəz, 15 lines, early 18th cent.

Quire descriptions: quires 3–7 balanced; quires 1, 2, 8 unbalanced.

1. Ff. 1r–38v: Epistles
    a. Ff. 1r–10r: 1 Peter.
    b. Ff. 10r–16r: 2 Peter.
    c. Ff. 16r–24v: 1 John.
    d. Ff. 24v–26v: 2 John.
    e. Ff. 26v–27v: 3 John.
    f. Ff. 27r–35v: James.
    g. Ff. 35v–38v: Jude.
2. Ff. 40r–79v: Revelation.

Miniatures:
1. F. ir: Crude drawing of human-like figure.
2. F. iir: Crude drawing of human and flower/cross.
3. F. iiv(erso): Crude drawing of faces peering from behind long slim items.
4. F. 79v: Crude drawing of face peering from behind a small horse-like animal.

5. F. 80v: Crude drawing of face peering from behind a small animal.

Varia:
1. F. Iv–IIr: *Asmat* prayer against thieves and robbers, ሊባ፡ ወቀማኝ፡, insufficiently legible.
2. Ff. 38v–39r: List of the Archangel Michael's twelve feast days of the year, with the reasons for their celebrations.
3. F. 39v: Reward, in quantity of fruits, for praying certain prayers, e.g. The Our Father, and for performing certain good deeds.
4. F. 39v: Greeting letter, in Amharic in a crude hand in pencil.
5. F. 79r: Record of purchase of the manuscript on Mäggabit 2, 1940 EC (March 11, 1948 AD,).

Notes:
1. Decorative designs: f. 79v (dotted line using alternating black and red); ff. 38v, 79v (line of full-stop symbols).
2. Ff. Ir, IIv and 80v: The Gəʿəz version of "In the name of the Father and the Son and the Holy Spirit," in a crude hand.
3. Overlooked lines of text have been added interlinearly (ff. 11v, 24r, 32v, 36v, and 38r), and with text written in the upper margin and a symbol (⊥) to indicate where the text should be inserted (ff. 21r, 25v, 33r, 59v, and 68r).
4. F. 80r: Scrawls and addition of the number of folios of the two parts, 38+42=80, in pencil.

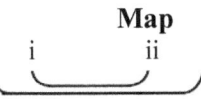

Map
i ii

Protection sheet(s)

There is, perhaps, a reinforcement strip that goes around the spine of the protection sheet. A stub at the gutter is visible before f. i; a folio stub, cut off about 1 cm from the gutter is visible between ff. ii and 1.

Quire 1

1 2 3 4 5 6 7 8 9 10

Ff. 8 and 10 seem to be single sheets sewn into the quire.

Quire 2

11 12 13 14 15 16 17 18 19

Folio 16 is split in half from top to bottom, down one of the creases of the center column. It is sewn together in two places.

Quire 3

20 21 22 23 24 25 26 27 28 29

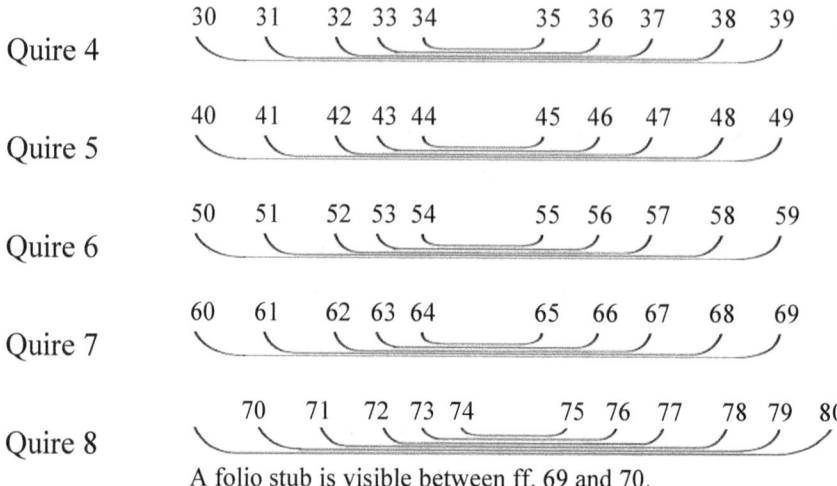

A folio stub is visible between ff. 69 and 70.

EMIP 14 – Marwick Codex 10
Psalter, ዳዊት፡

Parchment, 190 x 150 x 63 mm, four Coptic chain stitches attached with bridle attachments to the wooden boards, rough-hewn boards repaired with string, protection quire + 16 full quires, quires 2–7 numbered, iii + 150 folios, 190 x 133 mm folio, top margin 21 mm, bottom margin 44 mm, fore edge margin 19 mm, gutter margin 5 mm, ff. irv, 1r–131r one column, ff. iir–iiiv(erso), 131r–147v two columns, Gəʽəz, 22 lines, 19th cent.

Quire descriptions: quires 2, 4–16 balanced; quires 1, 3 unbalanced.

Ff. 1r–148r: Psalter [Dawit]. Cf. EMIP 1.
1. Ff. 1r–113v: Psalms of David.
2. Ff. 113v–125r: Biblical Canticles.
3. Ff. 125r–131r: Song of Songs, common version.
4. Ff. 131r–143r: Praises of Mary [Wəddase Maryam]. Arranged for the days of the week (Monday, f. 131r; Tuesday, f. 132r; Wednesday, f. 134r; Thursday, f. 136r; Friday, f. 138v; Saturday, f. 140r; Sunday, f. 141r).
5. Ff. 143r–148r: Gate of Light [Anqäṣä Bərhan].

Varia:
1. Ff. irv: Hymn to Mary, "[Come] with…" The beginning is erased.
2. Ff. iir–iiiv: Image of Mary's Assumption, ማዕጾ፡ ፍልሰታ፡. Chaîne, Répertoire, no. 213; MG 59, pp. 669ff.; and EMIP 17, f. 35v.

Notes:
1. Decorative designs: ff. 1r, 7v, 15r, 23r, 33r, 40v, 46v, 55r, 65v, 73r, 78r, 99v, 102v, 113v, 131r (*haräg* using black and red); ff. 89v, 108r, 125r (*haräg* using black); ff. 131r, 132r, 134r, 136r, 138v, 140r, 141r, 143r (dotted line using alternating black and red).
2. Note of ownership by Wäldä Gäbrə'el (and?) Wäldä Ḥawaryat, f. iiiv.
3. The word for God is written in red ink in the first three works; Mary is written in red ink in the last two works.
4. F. 61r: A line of text in red ink marks the midpoint of the Psalms.
5. Ff. 148v–150rv blank save for senseless scribbles.
6. Columetric layout of text: ff. 121v–122r (tenth biblical canticle).
7. The scribe frequently has to finish the line of text above the end of the line.
8. Overlooked lines of text are added interlinearly (ff. 6r, and 83v).

Quire Map

Protection Quire — i, ii, iii
A folio stub is visible between folio iiiv(erso) and 1r. It is cut off very unevenly near the gutter.

Quire 1 — 1, 2, 3, 4, 5, 6, 7, 8, 9
A folio stub is visible between ff. 3 and 4.

Quire 2 — 10, 11, 12, 13, 14, 15, 16, 17, 18, 19

Quire 3 — 20, 21, 22, 23, 24, 25, 26, 27, 28
A folio stub is visible between ff. 21 and 22.

Quire 4 — 29, 30, 31, 32, 33, 34, 35, 36, 37, 38

Quire 5 — 39, 40, 41, 42, 43, 44, 45, 46, 47, 48

Quire 6 — 49, 50, 51, 52, 53, 54, 55, 56, 57, 58

Quire 7 — 59, 60, 61, 62, 63, 64, 65, 66, 67, 68

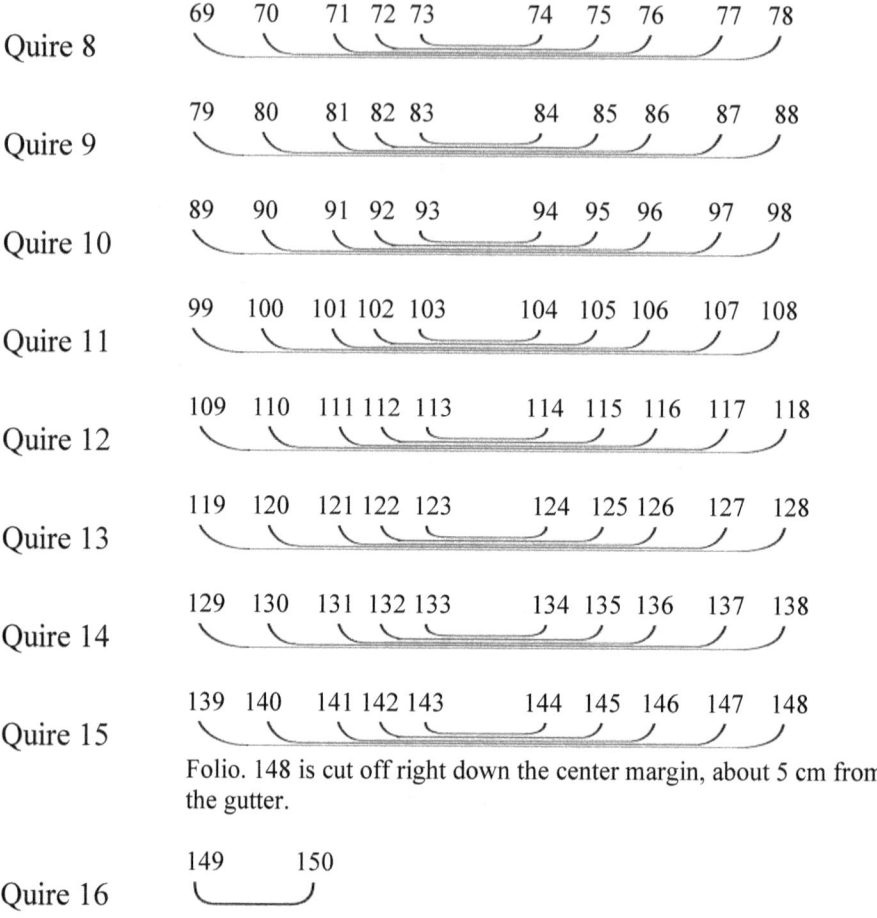

Folio. 148 is cut off right down the center margin, about 5 cm from the gutter.

EMIP 15 – Marwick Codex 11
Psalter, ዳዊት፡

Parchment, 125 x 120 x 90 mm, four Coptic chain stitches attached with bridle attachments to rough-hewn boards repaired with string, protection quire + 24 full quires, quires 2–11, 13 numbered, ii + 219 folios, 122 x 112 mm folio, top margin 10–12 mm, bottom margin 25–27 mm, fore edge margin 15–17 mm, gutter margin 7 mm, ff. 1r–193r one column, ff. 193r–218v two columns, Gəʽəz, 15 lines, late 16th (ff. 47r–50v, 19th) cent.

Quire descriptions: quires 1–11, 13–22 balanced; quires 12, 23, 24 unbalanced. Navigation system: various colored strings have been sewn into the corners of ff. 21, 32, 57, 66, 150, 162, and 186 to mark content divisions.

Ff. 1r–217v: Psalter [*Dawit*]. Cf. EMIP 1.
1. Ff. 1r–172r: Psalms of David. Arranged for the days of the week (Tuesday, f. 32v; Wednesday, f. 66r; Thursday, f. 105v; Friday, f. 150v; Saturday, f. 186r). Some psalms are marked with directory for their reading.
2. Ff. 172r–186r: Biblical Canticles.
3. Ff. 186r–193r: Song of Songs, common version.
4. Ff. 193r–209v: Praises of Mary [*Wəddase Maryam*]. Arranged for the days of the week (Monday, f. 193r; Tuesday, f. 194v; Wednesday, f. 197v; Thursday, f. 200v; Friday, f. 203v; Saturday, f. 206r; Sunday, f. 207v).
5. Ff. 209v–217v: Gate of Light [*Anqäṣä Bərhan*].

Miniatures:
1. F. iir: Crude drawing of a man with a prayer stick and an animal.

Varia:
1. Ff. 47v–48r: Prayer for help in learning, in a crude hand. .
2. F. 87r: Two parallel black and red dotted lines around a line of text and symbols in the margin mark the midpoint of the Psalms
3. F. 113v: What seems to be *asmat* prayer to protect domestic animals from wild animals, in a crude hand.
4. Ff. 217v–219r: Calendar of the year, with the folios obliterated.

Notes:
1. F. 113v: writing in blue ink.
2. Decorative designs: ff. 1r, 113v (*haräg* using black and red); ff. 10v, 32v, 46v, 57v, 66r, 78v, 94r, 105v, 133r, 150v, 154v, 163r, 172r, 186r, 194v, 197v, 200v, 203v, 206r (dotted line using alternating black and red); ff. 10v, 172r, 193r, 209v, 217v (lines in black and/or red connected by stops); ff. 1r, 8v, 21r, 32v, 46v, 57v, 66r, 78v, 86r, 87r, 94r, 105v, 133r, 139r, 140r, 141r, 153v, 154v, 158r, 163rv, 171v, 172r, 186r, 209v, 217v (additional designs in black and/or red).
3. Note of ownership by a certain *Ḥaläqa*, f. iir.
4. F. ir: Pen trial.
5. F. iv, iiv blank.
6. Ff. 47, 48, 49 and 50 have been cut off about 1 cm from the center and new pages attached, sewn into the stubs that are left. Similar repairs have been made to portions of several other folios in the codex.

7. This scribe has avoided the problem of lines of text too long to fit on one line by adopting an aspect ratio that leaves ample room for the width of most lines. On a few occasions, the line would have been too long and the scribe finishes the end of the line with words written smaller so as to avoid leftover text (e.g., f. 22r, line 3, and f. 32r, lines 10 and 12, and f. 116v, bottom two lines). Occasionally a line is still too long and has to be completed above or below the end of the line. In these cases, the scribe places the material above the line (e.g., 9r and 28r), except in the case where he is dealing with the top line (e.g., f. 23r).
8. Overlooked lines of text are written in the upper margin with a mark (⊥) indicating where it should be inserted (ff. 34r, 55r, 135v) and written between lines in the text block (ff. 42r, 44v, 112v, 128r).
9. Many of the psalms have additional superscriptions added later in the margins beside the original superscriptions.
10. Columetric layout of text: ff. 171rv (Ps. 150).

Quire Map

	i	ii
Protection Quire	⌣	

Quire 1: 1 2 | 3 4 5 | 6 7 8 | 9 10

Quire 2: 11 12 | 13 14 15 | 16 17 18 | 19 20

Quire 3: 21 22 | 23 24 25 | 26 27 28 | 29 30

Quire 4: 31 32 | 33 34 35 | 36 37 38 | 39 40

Quire 5: 41 42 | 43 44 45 | 46 47 48 | 49 50

Folios 47, 48, 49 and 50 have been cut off about 1 cm from the center and new pages attached, sewn into the stub that is left.

Quire 6: 51 52 | 53 54 55 | 56 57 58 | 59 60

Quire 7: 61 62 | 63 64 65 | 66 67 68 | 69 70

Catalogue of the Ethiopic Manuscript Imaging Project · 41

Quire 8: 71 72 73 74 75 76 77 78 79 80

Quire 9: 81 82 83 84 85 86 87 88 89 90

Quire 10: 91 92 93 94 95 96 97 98 99 100

Quire 11: 101 102 103 104 105 106 107 108 109 110

Quire 12: 111 112 113

A folio stub is visible between ff. 112 and 113.

Quire 13: 114 115 116 117 118 119 120 121 122 123

Quire 14: 124 125 126 127 128 129 130 131 132 133

Quire 15: 134 135 136 137 138 139 140 141 142 143

Quire 16: 144 145 146 147 148 149 150 151 152 153

Quire 17: 154 155 156 157 158 159 160 161 162 163

Quire 18: 164 165 166 167 168 169 170 171 172 173

Quire 19: 174 175 176 177 178 179 180 181 182 183

Quire 20: 184 185 186 187 188 189

Quire 21: 190 191 192 193 194 195

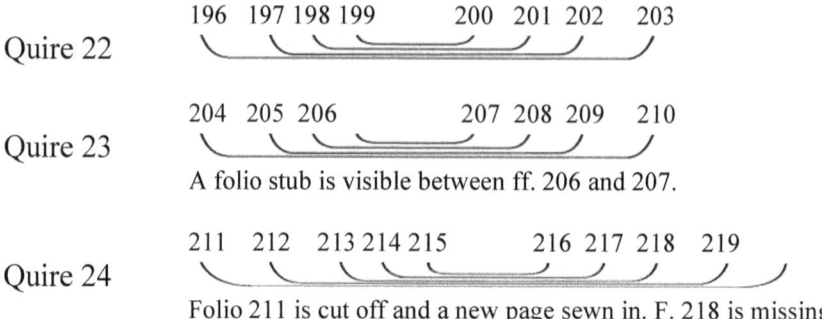

Quire 22 — 196 197 198 199   200 201 202 203

Quire 23 — 204 205 206   207 208 209 210
A folio stub is visible between ff. 206 and 207.

Quire 24 — 211 212 213 214 215   216 217 218 219
Folio 211 is cut off and a new page sewn in. F. 218 is missing the top part of the folio and the bottom part of the folio. F. 219 is mostly missing except for a stub that sticks out from the center. A folio stub about 1 cm wide is visible after f. 219.

EMIP 16 – Marwick Codex 12
Homiliary in Honor of the Archangel Michael, ድርሳነ፡ ሚካኤል፡

Parchment, 215 x 165 x 50 mm, four Coptic chain stitches attached with bridle attachments to rough-hewn boards (both broken), 12 full quires, quires 2–12 numbered, 98 folios, 205 x 162 mm, top margin 17–20 mm, bottom margin 30–35 mm, fore edge margin 22–25 mm, gutter margin 10–12 mm, ff. 1r–97r two columns, Gəʿəz, 15–24 lines, 19th cent.

Quire descriptions: quires 2–4, 6–11 balanced; quire 5 adjusted balanced; quires 1, 12 unbalanced. Navigation system: various colored string sewn into corners of folios 1, 15, 21, 27, 33, 47, 54, 59, 68, 74, 80, 85, 92 to mark content divisions.

1. Ff. 1r–92v: Homiliary for the Monthly Feast of the Archangel Michael, ድርሳነ፡ ሚካኤል፡. The Codex is bound in disorder with folios missing. Published several times in Ethiopia; see for example, ድርሳነ፡ ሚካኤል፡ ወድርሳነ፡ ሩፋኤል፡ መልክአ፡ ሚካኤል፡ ወመልክአ፡ ሩፋኤል፡ Täsfa Printing press, Addis Ababa 1940 EC, pp. 11–205. See also BL Or. 4849, Strelcyn, *British Library*, pp. 94–97; EMML 1133.

   a. Ff. 1r–4r: Introduction on the greatness of the Archangel.
   በስመ፡ አብ፡ . . . ነጽሩ፡ አኃውየ፡ ፍቁራንየ፡ ዕበዮ፡ ወመንክሮ፡ ዘገብረ፡ ሊቀ፡ መላእክት፡ ሚካኤል፡ ለእለ፡ ይስእልዎ፡ በጽሒቅ፡ . . . መፍትው፡ ከመ፡ ንግበር፡ ተዝካሮ፡ . . .

   b. Ff. 4r–14v: Ḫədar:
   (1) Ff. 4r–9r and 10r–13r: Homily. Author not given (other copies have Dämatewos), text wanting in the middle.
   በስመ፡ አብ፡ . . . [ጻጻ]ሳት፡ ዘለእስክንድርያ፡ ዘበዓለ፡ ቅዱስ፡ ሚካኤል፡ ሊቀ፡ መላእክት፡ ያርእየን፡ ኃይለ፡ ወክብረ፡

እግዚአብሔር፡ ... አውሎግሶን፡ ዐቢይ፡ በዓል፡ ፍቁራንየ፡ ኑ፡ ንትጋባዕ፡ ...

(2) F. 9v: Synaxary entry: the Archangel's mission to Joshua son of Nun.
ወበዛቲ፡ ዕለት፡ ተዝካረ፡ በዓሉ፡ ለመልአክ፡ ክቡር፡ ሊቀ፡ መላእክት፡ ሚካኤል፡ ... ዘርእዮ፡ ኢያሱ፡ ወልደ፡ ነዌ፡ በአምሳለ፡ ሐራሁ፡ ለንጉሥ፡ ...

(3) F. 9v: Greeting to the Archangel, *Sälam*, incomplete at the end.
ሰላም፡ ለአስተርእዮትከ፡ ውስተ፡ ደብረ፡ ማሕው፡ ዮም፡

(4) Ff. 13r–14v: Miracle.
Introduction, f. 13r.
በስመ፡ አብ፡ ... ንወጥን፡ (sic) በረድኤተ፡ እግ"፡ ጽሕፈ፡ ተአምሪሁ፡ ... (f. 13v) ይቤ፡ ዐቢይ፡ እግ"፡ ወጥቀ፡ ልዑል፡ ዲበ፡ ኩሉ፡ ፍጥረት፡ ...

Text of the miracle: how the Archangel rescued the people whose boat was troubled by high wind, f. 14r.
ተአምሪሁ፡ ... እክሥት፡ በምሳ[ሌ፡] አፉየ፡ ወእንብብ፡ ኅቡዓተ፡ ዘእምትካት፡ ...

c. Ff. 14v–20v: Taḥśaś.
(1) Ff. 14v–20r: Homily. Author not given; in many other copies this homily is for the month Miyazya; cf. BL Or. 4849, f. 73r, Strelcyn, *British Library*, pp. 95.
በስመ፡ አብ፡ ... ፩ እምጻጻት፡ ዘደረሰ፡ በእንተ፡ ሚካኤል፡ ሊቀ፡ መላእክት፡ ዘይትነብብ፡ (f. 15r) አም፡ ፲ወ፪ለወርኃ፡ ታኅሣሥ፡ በሰላመ፡ እግ"፡ አሜን፨ መፍትው፡ ለነ፡ ፍቁራንየ፡ ንዘክር፡ ዕበዮ፡ ለአብ፡ ኂሩቶ፡ ለወልድ፡ ወጸጋሁ፡ (sic) ለመንፈስ፡ ቅዱስ፡ ...

(2) F. 20rv: Miracle about the farmer who could not make a feast in honor of the Archangel because of drought and famine.
ተአምሪሁ፡ ... ወሀሎ፡ ፩ብእሲ፡ መሃይምን፡ ወይሴፎ፡ ምሕረተ፡ እግ"፡ ወይገብር፡ በዓሉ፡ ለቅዱስ፡ ሚካኤል፡ አም፡ ፲ወ፪ለለኩሉ፡ አውራኅ፡ ወዝንቱ፡ ብእሲ፡ ኮነ፡ ይገብር፡ ግብረ፡ ማኅረስ፡ ...

(3) F. 20v: Greeting to the Archangel, *Sälam*.
ሰላም፡ ለከ፡ ዓቃቤ፡ ቅዱሳን፡ እምተሀውኩ፨

d. Ff. 21r–27r: Taḥśaś (sic), Ṭǝrr added later in pencil.
(1) Ff. 21r–26r: Homily (by John, Bishop of Aksum), on the family of Dorotheos and Theopista.
በስመ፡ አብ፡ ... እም፡ አም፡ ፲ወ፪ ለወርኃ፡ ታኅሣሥ፡ ... አሜን፨ ስምዑ፡ ኩልክሙ፡ አሕዛብ፡ ወአጽምዑ፡ ኩልክሙ፡ እለ፡

ትነብሩ፡ ውስተ፡ ዓለም፡ . . . ወሀሎ፡ ፩ብእሲ፡ ዘርቱዕ፡ ሃይማኖቱ፡ ዘስሙ፡ ዶራታያስ፡ ወስሙ፡ ብእሲቱ፡ ቴያብስታ፡ . . .

(2) F.26rv: Miracle on the farmer who neglected making the feast of the Archangel.

ተአምሪሁ፡ . . . ወሀሎ፡ ፩ብእሲ፡ ክርስቲያናዊ፡ ፈራዬ፡ እግ"፡ ወያፈቅሮ፡ ለቅዱስ፡ ሚካኤል፡ ይነብር፡ በግብረ፡ ማንረስ፡ ወዘርአ፡ ብዙኀ፡ ገራውህ፡ . . .

(3) Ff. 26v–27r: Synaxary entry: Mission to save Jacob from the wrath of Esau.

እስመ፡ በዛቲ፡ ዕለት፡ ፈነዎ፡ እግ"፡ . . . ኀበ፡ ያዕቆብ፡ እስራኤላዊ፡ እመ፡ አፍርሆ፡ ኤሳው፡ እኑሁ፡

(4) F. 27r: *Sälam.*

ሰላም፡ ለከ፡ ሚካኤል፡ አሐዱ፡፡

e. Ff. 27r–32r: Yäkkatit.

(1) Ff. 27r–30v: Homily (anonymous) on the man who prayed to the Archangel for his needs but never worked.

. . . (f. 27v) . . . ወሀሎ፡ ፩ነዳይ፡ ውስተ፡ ውእቱ፡ ብሔር፡ ዐቢይ፡ ሃይማኖቱ፡ ወይስእል፡ መዓልተ፡ ወሌሊተ፡ . . .

(2) Ff. 30v–31: Miracle on the man who gave alms to the poor, who was paralyzed. ተአምሪሁ፡ . . . (f. 31) ወሀሎ፡ ፩ብእሲ፡ ዘይገብር፡ ምሕረተ፡ ለነዳያን፡ ወለምስኪናን፡ ወይገብር፡ ሠናየ፡ ለኩሎ፡ ሰብእ፡ ወሰብ፡ ርእየ፡ ጸላኤ፡ ሠናያት፡ ኂሩቶ፡ . . .

(3) F. 32r: Synaxary entry: Mission to Samson the giant.

. . . ወበዛቲ፡ ዕለት፡ ፈነዎ፡ ኀበ፡ ሶምሶን፡ ረዓታዊ፡ (sic) ወኢሎፍላዊ፡ . . .

(4) F. 32r: *Sälam.*

ሰላም፡ እብል፡ ዘያከ፡ (sic) ናዜ፡፡

f. Ff. 33r–46v: Mäggabit.

(1) Ff. 33r–44v: Homily (by John, Archbishop of Antioch), on (the Christian) Sabbath and Matthew the traveler.

በስመ፡ አብ፡ . . . በዕለተ፡ ሊቀ፡ መላእክት፡ ሚካኤል፡ ወአፍቅርቱ፡ ለሰብእ፡ ወተናገረ፡ በእንተ፡ ስንበት፡ ቅድስት፡ እስመ፡ ኀብረ፡ በ0 (sic) ምስለ፡ ሰንበት፡ በዓሉ፡ . . . ወካዕበ፡ ነገረ፡ በእንተ፡ ደማቴዎስ፡ ነግድ፡ . . .

(2) Ff. 44v–45v: Miracle on the wealthy and generous woman who suffered from skin disease.

. . . ወሀለወት፡ አሐቲ፡ ባዕልት፡ ዘአጎዛ፡ ሕማም፡ ዝልጋሴ፡ ወሀብጠ፡ ኮለንታሃ፡ . . .

(3) F. 45v: Synaxary entry: Mission to Balaam.

... ወበዛቲ: ዕለት: ፈነዎ፡ . . . ኀበ፡ በልዓም፡ መሰግል፡

(4) F. 46r: *Sälam.*

ሰላም፡ እብል፡ ዘይቀውም፡ (sic) ፆታሁ፡፡

g. Ff. 47r–54v: Miyazya (in some manuscripts, Ṭərr).

  (1) Ff. 47r–52r: Homily (anonymous) on the life of the spirituals—angels and demons.

  በስመ፡ አብ፡ . . . ሥሉስ፡ ዘኢይትሌለይ፡ ዕሩይ፡ ዘኢይሰደቅ፡ (sic) ምሉዕ፡ ዘኢይትነገር፡ . . . መፍትው፡ ትስምዕዎ፡ . . .

  (2) Ff. 52r–53v: Miracle on the Christian who denied that he borrowed money from a Jew.

  . . . ወሀሎ፡ ፩ብእሲ፡ ባዕል፡ አይሁዳዊ፡ በንዋየ፡ ዓለም፡ ወርቅ፡ ወብሩር፡ እንዘ፡ የሐውር፡ ፍኖተ፡ በከመ፡ ሕገ፡ አበዊሁ፡ ውስተ፡ ብሔረ፡ ሮሜ፡ ረከበ፡ ብእሲ፡ (sic) ክርስቲያናዊ፡ (sic) . . .

  (3) Ff. 53v–54r: Synaxary entry: Mission to Prophet Jeremiah.

  ... ወበዛቲ፡ ዕለት፡ ፈነዎ፡ . . . ኀበ፡ ኤርምያስ፡ ነቢይ፡ ወአውጽአ፡ እቤተ፡ (sic) ጦቅሕ፡ . . .

(4) F. 27r: *Sälam.*

ሰላም፡ ለከ፡ ዘረሰየከ፡ በክብር፡፡

h. Ff. 54v–58v: Gənbot.

  (1) Ff. 54v–56v: Homily by Yoḥannəs, Bishop of Ethiopia, who came after Bishop Yəsḥaq, on the conflict between the consort of King Arqadewos and John Chysostom.

  በስመ፡ አብ፡ . . . ድርሳን፡ ዘሊቀ፡ መላእክት፡ ሚካኤል፡ ነገር፡ በእንተ፡ ዮሐንስ፡ ጳጳስ፡ ዘኢትዮጵያ፡ ዘመጽአ፡ እምድኀረ፡ አቡነ፡ ይስሐቅ፡ ወነ፡ (sic) በመዐሊሁ፡ ለአርቃዴዎስ፡ ንጉሥ፡ . . .

  (2) Ff. 56v–58r: Miracle on the Roman (Greek) nobleman whose wife was barren.

  . . . ወሀሎ፡ ፩ብእሲ፡ እምሰብአ፡ ሮሜ፡ ክርስቲያናዊ፡ ወብእሲቱ፡ ኮነት፡ መካን፡ . . .

  (3) F. 58rv: Synaxary entry: Mission of the archangel to the Prophet Habakkuk.

  ... ወበዛቲ፡ ዕለት፡ ፈነዎ፡ . . . ኀበ፡ ዕንባቆም፡ ነቢይ፡ . . .

  (4) F. 58v: *Sälam.*

  ሰላም፡ ለሕላዌከ፡ ዘምሥዋዓ፡ [አብ፡] መቅደሰ፡፡

i. Ff. 59r–67r: Säne.

  (1) Ff. 59r–64v: Homily by Bishop of Aksum on the family of Astäraniqos and Euphemia.

  በስመ፡ አብ፡ . . . ድርሳን፡ ዘቅዱስ፡ ሚካኤል፡ ሊቀ፡ መላእክት፡ ዘደረሰ፡ ዮሐንስ፡ ጳጳስ፡ ዘብሔረ፡ አክሱም፡ ቀዳሜ፡ ኩሎን፡

አብያተ፡ ክርስቲያናት፡ . . . ወሀሎ፡ ፩ መኰንን፡ . . . ዘስሙ፡
አስተራኒቆስ፡ ወስም፡ ብእሲቱ፡ አፍምያ፡ . . .
(2) Ff. 65r–66r: Miracle on the Jew who was cleansed from his leprosy.
. . . ወሀሎ፡ ፩ብእሲ፡ ክርስቲያናዊ፡ ዘአስተ፡ ሐመም፡ (sic) ይሕንጽ፡ ቤተ፡ ክርስቲያን፡ ዘደሴተ፡ ቆጵሮስ፡ . . .
(3) Ff. 66r–67r: Synaxary entry: The building of the church of the Archangel in place of a pagan temple in Alexandria.
. . . ወበዛቲ፡ ዕለት፡ ያብዕሉ፡ ለመልአክ፡ ቅዱስ፡ ሚካኤል፡ ወምክንያተ፡ ዘያብዕሉ፡ ሎቱ፡ ሀሎ፡ በእስክንድርያ፡ ምኩራብ፡ ዐቢይ፡ ዘሐነጾ፡ አክላቡጥራ፡ ወለተ፡ በጥሊሞስ፡ . . .
(4) F. 67r: *Sälam.*
ሰላም፡ ለሚካኤል፡ መሐሪ፡ ውእቱ፨

j. Ff. 68r–73v: Ḥamle.
(1) Ff. 68r–72v: Homily by Bishop Yoḥannəs on the wicked wealthy man whose property was inherited by the son of his poor neighbor.
በስመ፡ አብ፡ . . . ድርሳን፡ ዘቅዱስ፡ ወብፁዕ፡ ሊቀ፡ መላእክት፡ ሚካኤል፡ ዘደረሰ፡ ዮሐንስ፡ ጳጳስ፡ . . . ወሀሎ፡ ፩ ብእሲ፡ ባዕል፡ በአሐቲ፡ ሀገር፡ ዘጸዋግ፡ ልቡ፡ ወጽኑዕ፡ ከመ፡ ፈርዖን፡ . . .
(2) Ff. 72v–73r: Miracle on the man from whom the evil spirit was cast out during Mass service.
. . . ወኮነ፡ ካዕበ፡ በአሐቲ፡ ዕለት፡ አም፡ በዐሉ፡ ለሊቀ፡ መላእክት፡ ቅዱስ፡ ሚካኤል፡ እንዘ፡ ሀሎ፡ ኤጲስ፡ ቆጶስ፡ ምስለ፡ ሕዝብ፡ ክርስቲያን፡ ወበገቢረ፡ ቅዳሴ፡ . . .
(3) F. 73rv: Synaxary entry: Mission to the camp of Sennacherib.
. . . ወበዛቲ፡ ዕለት፡ ፈነው፡ (sic) እግ"፡ ለሚካኤል፡ ኀበ፡ ትዕይንተ፡ (sic) ለሡናክሬም፡ . . .
(4) F. 73v: *Sälam.*
ሰላም፡ ለከ፡ ረዳኤ፡ ቅዱሳን፡ ሰግዕ[ት፨].

k. Ff. 74r–79r: Näḥase.
(1) Ff. 74r–77v: Homily (anonymous) on the book of the angels that came from Jerusalem.
በስመ፡ አብ፡ . . . ድርሳን፡ ዘቅዱስ፡ ወብፁዕ፡ ሊቀ፡ መላእክት፡ ሚካኤል፡ . . . ለዛቲ፡ መጽሐፍ፡ ዘወዐት፡ እምኢየሩሳሌም፡ ከመ፡ ትትናገሮሙ፡ ዕበዮሙ፡ . . .
(2) Ff. 77v–78v: Miracle on the blind man.
. . . (f. 78r) . . . ወካዕበ፡ ሀሎ፡ ፩ ብእሲ፡ ክርስቲያን፡ (sic) ዘረከቦ፡ ደዌ፡ ዕውብ፡ ወያፉ፡ ፩ሆሙ፡ አዕይንቲሁ፡ . . .

(3) F.79r: Synaxary entry: Mission to the Emperor Constantine.
... ወበዛቲ: ዕለት: ካዕበ ፈነዎ: (sic) እግ": ... ኀበ: ቄስጠጢኖስ: (sic) ጻድቅ: ላዕለ: ሀገረ: ሮሜ: ...

(4) F. 79r: *Sälam.*
ሰላም: ለከ: መልአከ: መልአከ: (sic) ኪዳኑ: ወምክሩ::

l. Ff. 80r–84v: Mäskäräm.
  (1) Ff. 80r–83v: Homily (anonymous) on not worshipping other gods.
  በስመ: አብ: ... ድርሳን: ... ይቤ: እግ": ኢታምልኩ: ባዕደ: አልቦ: ባዕድ: አምላክ: ዘእንበሌየ: ...

  (2) F. 84rv: Miracle on how the Archangel raised to heaven the relics of Saint George.
  ተአምሪሃ: (sic) ለቅዱስ: ሚካኤል: ዘከመ: ረድአ: ለቅዱስ: ጊዮርጊስ: ወአዕረገ: አዕፅም: (sic) ውስተ: ሰማይ: ...

  (3) F. 84v: Synaxary entry: Mission to Prophet Isaiah.
  ... ወበዛቲ: ዕለት: ፈነዎ: ... ኀበ: ኢሳይያስ: ወልደ: አሞጽ: ...

  (4) F. 84v: *Sälam.*
  ሰላም: ለምቅዋምከ: ዘልዑል: መዓርጋ::

m. Ff. 85r–92v: Ṭəqəmt.
  (1) Ff. 85r–89v: Homily (anonymous) on the need to make the angels sureties by honoring them.
  በስመ: አብ: ... ድርሳን: ... ዘኢኃሠሡት: ነፍስ: በሕይወታ: ዘይትወሐሳ: ወኢይትረከብ: በሰማያት: አመ: ዕለተ: ሞታ: ...

  (2) Ff. 89v–91v: Miracle of the man who prayed to the Archangel for his need but never worked.
  ተብህለ: ከመ: ሀሎ: ፩ ነዳይ: በሐቲ: (sic) ሀገር: ዘገረ: ቤተ: ክርስቲያ(f. 90r)ኑ: ለቅዱስ: ሚካኤል: ሊቀ: መላእክት: ወለለእለተ: ይገይስ: ኀቤሁ: ወይቀውም: ቅድመ: ሥዕሉ: ...

  (3) Ff. 91v–92r: Synaxary entry: Mission to Prophet Samuel.
  ... ወበዛቲ: ዕለት: ፈነዎ: ... ኀበ: ሳሙኤል: ነቢይ: ...

  (4) F. 92rv: *Sälam.*
  ሰላም: ለከ: ዘጎነተ: ጽባሕ: ያፍ:::

2. Ff. 92v–97r: Image of Michael መልክዐ: ሚካኤል:. Chaîne, Répertoire, no. 119; MG 59, pp. 290ff.
ሰላም: ለዝክረ: ስምከ: ምስለ: ስም: ልዑል: ዘተሳተፈ::
ወልደ: ያሬድ: ሄኖክ: በከመ: ጸሐፈ::

Miniatures, depicting the miraculous stories in the *dərsan*:
  1. F. 9r: Diptych, depicting the General Resurrection as told in the homily of the month. Top panel has Christ sitting in diamond shape

48 · *Catalogue of the Codices*

with the Four Living Creatures in the corners and an angel to his right; second panel has church at center and an angel on either side playing Ethiopian musical instruments—the angel blowing the horn.
2. F. 33v: The Archangel Michael helping Samson to kill the Philistines.
3. F. 46v: Balaam, his donkey, and the Archangel Michael.
4. F. 68v: Dedication of the church of the Archangel Michael in Alexandria replacing a pagan temple.
5. F. 79v: The Archangel Michael restores the sight of the blind man; another man stands with eyes shut; a church of the Archangel Michael is in the background.

Varia:
1. F. 97v: Number of years (59) of a certain deed that "His Majesty Haile Sellasie I" performed.
2. F. 98r: List of fourteen contributors of 1 to 2 Bərr.

Notes:
1. Prayer for (the owner of the manuscript) Wäldä Maryam, f. 9v, 52r and *passim*.
2. Decorative designs: ff. 59r, 68r, 74r, 80r, and 85r, (*haräg* using multiple colors); ff. 1r, 47r (*haräg* using black and red); ff. 20v, 32r, 67r, 78v, 83v, and 97r (dotted line using alternating black and red); ff. 46r and 92v (line of black dots connected with a continuous red line).
3. F. 98v: The names of *Mämmərə* Fəśśəḥa and *Abba* Gäbrä Mädḫən
4. Overlooked words of text are written interlinearly (ff. 58r and 59v).

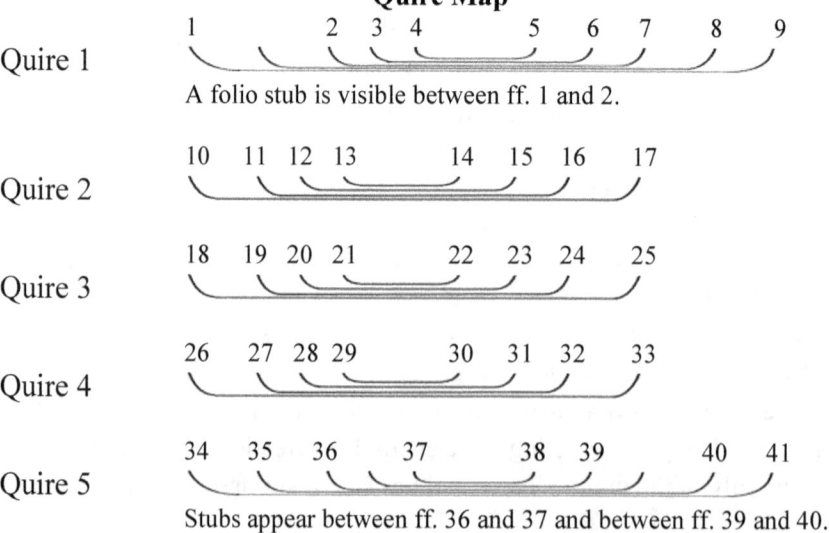

Stubs appear between ff. 36 and 37 and between ff. 39 and 40.

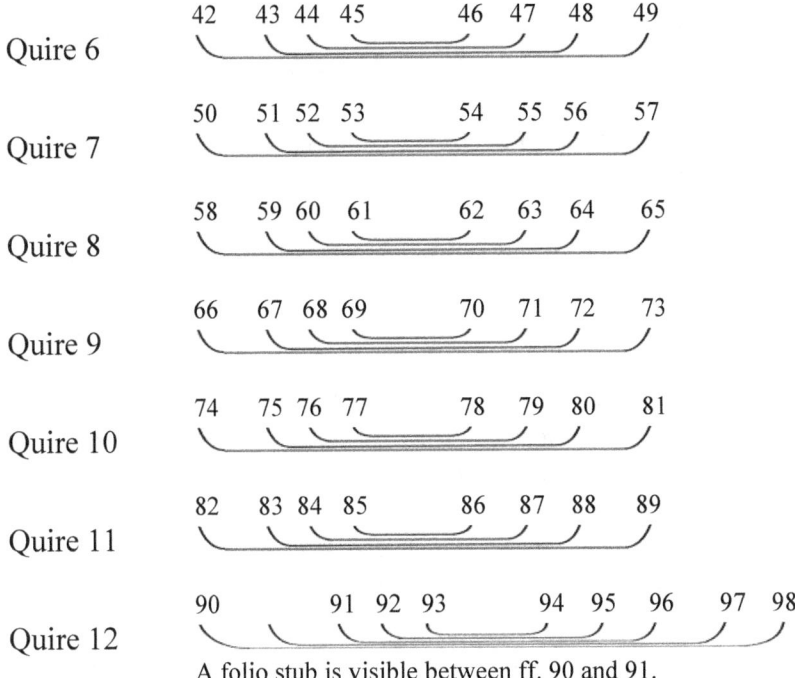

A folio stub is visible between ff. 90 and 91.

EMIP 17 – Marwick Codex 13
A Collection of Prayers: Images and Hymns

Parchment, 207 x 143 x 48 mm, four Coptic repaired chain stitches attached with bridle attachments to rough-hewn boards (front board not square, back repaired), protection quire + 9 full quires, quires 2–8 numbered, iii + 85 folios, 202 x 139 mm, top margin 21 mm, bottom margin 40–42 mm, fore edge margin 25 mm, gutter margin 10 mm, ff. ir–iir, 82v–85r one column, ff. 1r–82r two columns, Gə'əz, 20–35 lines, 20th cent.

Quire descriptions: quires 1–9 balanced.

Ff. 1r–82r: A Collection of Prayers, mostly rhyming hymns.

1. Ff. 1r–17v: Booklet of prayer that came down from heaven for a nobleman in the land of the Afrəgi. Cf. Abbadie 70, Conti Rossini, Notice, no. 111; EMML 1169, f. 143a.

   a. Ff. 1r–9v: Prayer to Jesus Christ, "Guard me," ዕቀበኒ፡.

   በስመ፡ አብ፡ ወወልድ፡ ወመንፈስ፡ ቅዱስ፡ ፩ አምላክ፡፡ ነዓ፡ ኀቤየ፡ አእግዚእየ፡ ኢየሱስ፡ ክርስቶስ፡ ወልደ፡ እግ"፡ ሕያው፡ ወወልደ፡ ማርያም፡ ሥግው፡ ከመ፡ ትዕቀበኒ፡ እምኵሉ፡ እኩይ፡ ለገብርከ፡ "ሀለ፡ ሥላሴ፡ ለዓለመ፡ ዓለም፡ አሜን፡፡ አእግዚእየ፡ ኢየሱስ፡

ክርስቶስ፡ ዕቀበኒ፡ ለገብርከ፡ ሥዕለ፡ ሥላሴ፡ በእንተ፡ ዘኃደርከ፡ በከርሡ፡ ማርያም፡ ድንግል፡ . . . (f. 9v) ...አሜን፤ ድግም፡ አቡነ፡ ዘበሰማያት፡ ወሰላም፡ ገብርኤል፡ ፫ተ፡ ጊዜ።

    b. Ff. 9v–14v: Prayer to Mary, "I take refuge," ተማኀፀንኩ፡. ተማኀፀንኩ፡ እግዝእትየ፡ ማርያም፡ ምልዕተ፡ ጸጋ፡ ንግሥተ፡ ነገሥታት፡ . . .

    c. Ff. 14v–16r: Concluding prayer to Jesus Christ. አእግዚእየ፡ ኢየሱስ፡ ክርስቶስ፡ ዘትሁብ፡ ለኮሉ፡ ዘሰአለከ፡ መፍቅደ፡ ሕሊናሁ፡ . . .

    d. Ff. 16r–17v: History of the book and the benefit of praying with it.
ለዛቲ፡ መጽሐፍ፡ ከመዝ፡ ምጽአታ፡ እስመ፡ ነበረ፡ ፩፡ መኮንን፡ በሀገረ፡ አፍርንጊ፡ ወቦዐ፡ ውስተ፡ ጸሞዕት፡ ከመ፡ ያሥምሮ፡ ለእግ"፡

2. Ff. 17v–23r: Prayer to Mary, "Guard me," ዕቀብኒ፡. Cf. Abbadie 104, f. 85r, Conti Rossini, Notice, no. 104.
በሰመ፡ አብ፡ ወወልድ፡ ወመንፈስ፡ ቅዱስ፡ ፩፡ አምላክ፡ አእግዝእትየ፡ ማርያም፡ እስመ፡ ክብርት፡ አንቲ፡ እምኮሉ፡ ፍጡር፡ በሰማይ፡ ወበምድር፡ አልቦ፡ ዘይከብር፡ እምኔኪ፡ እምታሕተ፡ እግ"። አእግዝእትየ፡ ማርያም፡ ዕቀብኒ፡ ለገብርኪ፡ ሥዕለ፡ ሥላሴ። አእግዝእትየ፡ ማርያም፡ እሙ፡ ለፈጣሪ፡ ኀበ፡ ሐር(f. 18r)ኩ፡ ሑሪ፡ ወኀበ፡ ኃደርኩ፡ ኀድሪ፡ . . .

3. Ff. 23r–26v: Hymn to Mary, commonly called "Image of Edom," መልክዐ፡ ኤዶም፡. Chaîne, Répertoire, no. 221; MG 59, pp. 651ff.
ሰላም፡ ሰላም፡ ለዝክረ፡ ስምኪ፡ በአምኃ።
ሥርከ፡ ወነግሀ።
ማርያም፡ ደብተራ፡ ለኤዶም፡ በከተማሃ።

4. Ff. 26v–32r: The collection of hymns, commonly known by its incipit, "Does not a man?" አኮኑ፡ ብእሲ፡. Composed to conclude each of the original thirty two miracles of Mary. Chaîne, Répertoire, no, 327; Grohmann, *Marienhymnen*, pp. 322–82.
አኮኑ፡ ብእሲ፡ ሶበ፡ ሐነጸ፡ ቤት፡ አፍተም።
ኮሉ፡ ጸጸየ፡ ያቀድም፡ ያስተዳልዎ። (sic).

5. Ff. 32r–35v: Hymn to Mary "Rejoice Mary, the Pasch of Adam," ተፈሥሒ፡ ማርያም፡ ለአዳም፡ ፋሲካሁ፡. Chaîne, Répertoire, no. 302.
ተፈሥሒ፡ ማርያም፡ ለአዳም፡ ፋሲካሁ።
ወማዕዶታ፡ ለሔዋን፡ እንተ፡ ይእቲ፡ አጽም፡ ገቦሁ።

6. Ff. 35v–38v: Image of Mary's Assumption, መልክዐ፡ ፍልሰታ፡. Chaîne, Répertoire, no. 213; MG 59, pp. 668ff.
ሰላም፡ ለፍልሰተ፡ ሥጋኪ፡ ምስለ፡ ነፍስኪ፡ ኢመዋቲ።
በተሰዕዐም፡ አሐቲ፡ ድንግል፡ በ፪ኤ፡ ማርያም፡ ወለተ፡ ማቲ።

7. Ff. 38v–40v: Hymns to Church.
   a. Ff. 38v–40r: "Your power has been known," ኃይልኪ፡ ተዓውቀ፡. Chaîne, Répertoire, no. 397 (probably also 179).
   ኃይልኪ፡ ተዓውቀ፡ ወበርንብ፡ ዓለም፡ ሰፈኑ፡፡
   እንተ፡ ላዕለ፡ ሕይወት፡ ወሞት፡ ሰብ፡ አድምዐ፡ ሥልጣነ፡፡
   ቤተ፡ ክርስቲያን፡ ቅድስት፡ ተራድእኒ፡ ፍጡነ፡፡
   b. F. 40rv: Greeting to Church, ሰላም፡ ለኪ፡ ቤተ፡ ክርስቲያን፡ ሎዛ፡. EMML 1494, f. 1a.
   ሰላም፡ ለኪ፡ ቤተ፡ ክርስቲያን፡ ሎዛ፡፡
   ቤተ፡ ያዕቆብ፡ ወሬዛ፡፡
   እም፡ ሞተ፡ ብኪ፡ ኢየሱስ፡ ቤዛ፡፡
8. Ff. 40v–44r: Hymns to the Christian Sabbath (Sunday).
   a. Ff. 40v–43r: Image of the Christian Sabbath, መልክዐ፡ ሰንበተ፡ ክርስቲያን፡.
   MG 59, pp. 643ff.; EMML 1494, f. 2a.
   ሰላም፡ ሰላም፡ ለዝክረ፡ ስምኪ፡ እምፀሐለ፡ ምሥራቅ፡ ወምዕራብ፡
   ሰሜን፡ ወደቡብ፡፡
   ሰንበተ፡ ክርስቲያን፡ ቅድስት፡ መርዓተ፡ በግዑ፡ ለአብ፡፡
   b. Ff. 43r–44r: Greeting to the Christian Sabbath, ሰላም፡ ለኪ፡ ዕለተ፡ ሰንበት፡.
   ሰላም፡ ለኪ፡ ዕለተ፡ ብርሃን፡ ሰንበት፡፡
   ወሠርቀ፡ ዓለማት፡ ጥንት፡፡
9. Ff. 44r–49r: Halleluiatic hymn to Mary, concluded with a hymn to Christ, "My heart overflows with goodly themes," ጐሥዐ፡ ልብየ፡ ቃለ፡ ሠናየ፡.
   ጐሥዐ፡ ልብየ፡ ቃለ፡ ሠናየ፡ ጐሥዐ፡ ልብየ፡ ቃለ፡ ሠናየ፡ ጐሥዐ፡ ልብየ፡ ቃለ፡ ሠናየ፡
   ሃሌ፡ ሉያ፡ ሃሌ፡ ሉያ፡ ሃሌ፡ ሉያ፡፡
   ሰማይ፡ ወምድር፡ ዘኢያገምሮ፡ መካን፡፡
   በከርሥኪ፡ ተፀውረ፡ በአግን፡፡, f. 44r.
   ሃሌ፡ ሉያ፡ ሃሌ፡ ሉያ፡ ሃሌ፡ ሉያ፡
   ወጤ፡ ትሕትና፡ ክርስቶስ፡ እግረ፡ አርዳኢሁ፡ ሐጸበ፡፡, f. 47v.
10. Ff. 49r–59r: Greeting to the suffering of Jesus Christ, ሰላም፡ ለሕማምከ፡. The second part seems to be image, መልክዕ፡, to Jesus, Emmanuel and Savior of the World, *Mädḫane 'Aläm*. Chaîne, Répertoire, no. 26.
    ሰላም፡ ለሕማምከ፡ ቤተ፡ [አይሁድ፡] ዘአንደደ፡፡
    ወረሰዮሙ፡ ሐመደ፡፡
    ማርያምሃ፡ እለ፡ ወጠኑ፡ ካህደ፡፡, f. 49r.

ሰላም፡ ለስእርተ፡ ርእስከ፡ . . . ሰላም፡ ለላሕየ፡ ገጽከ፡, f. 51r.
መድኃኔ፡ ዓለም፡ ነዓ፡ በዲበ፡ ብድብድ፡ ሀቡነ፡ መዊዐ፡, f. 52r.

11. Ff. 59r–65v: Hymn to Jesus Christ, beginning with "I prostrate before your conception," አስግድ፡ ለፅንስትከ፡. Composed in the style of *mälkə'*.
አስግድ፡ ለፅንስትከ፡ ወለልደትከ፡ መድምም፡፡
እምድንጋሌ፡ ሥጋ፡ ጎቱም፡፡
ኢየሱስ ክርስቶስ መድኃኔ ዓለም፡፡ . . . , f. 59r.
. . . ለዝክረ፡ ስምከ፡ . . . ለሥእርተ፡ ርእስከ፡ . . . ለርእስከ፡ . . . , f. 59v.
ስብሐት፡ ለከ፡ አምላኪየ፡ በጉልቄ፡ ሰብእ፡ ወመላእክት፡ . . . , f. 64v.

12. Ff. 65v–71v: Image of Jesus Christ, መልክዐ፡ ኢየሱስ፡. Chaîne, Répertoire, no. 125.
ሰላም፡ ለዝክረ፡ ስምከ፡ በመጽሐተ፡ መስቀል፡ ዘተለክዐ፡፡
ወለስእርትከ፡ ጸሊም፡ ዘደመ፡ ተኩርየ፡ ተቀብዐ፡፡

13. Ff. 71v–73v: Hymn to Mary, "In heaven and on earth," በሰማይ፡ ወበምድር፡. Abbadie 171, f. 99v, Conti Rossini, Notice, no. 104; Chaîne, Répertoire, no. 248.
በሰማይ፡ ወበምድር፡ አልብየ፡ ባዕደ፡፡
አብ፡ ወእም፡ እኅት፡ ወውሉደ፡፡

14. Ff. 73v–82r: Image of the suffering of George, መልክዐ፡ ሥቃየ፡. Chaîne, Répertoire, no. 6.
በስመ፡ አብ፡ . . . መልክዐ፡ ሥቃይ፡ [ሥ]ዑለ፡፡ (sic).
መጽሐተ፡ ሥጋከ፡ አርአየ፡፡
እምአመ፡ ትቤ፡ ለ[..]ከ፡ እስከ፡ ፈጸምከ፡ ሥቃየ፡፡

Varia:

1. Ff. Ir–IIr: Image of the conception of George, መልክዐ፡ ፅንሰቱ፡. Chaîne, Répertoire, no. 208; MG 59, pp. 505ff.
ሰላም፡ ለፅንስትከ፡ ወለልደትከ፡ ቡሩክ፡፡
በበዓለ፡ ድንግል፡ ቅድስት፡ ወመስቀለ፡ ክርስቶስ፡ አምላክ፡፡

2. Ff. IIv–IIIr: The letters of the Amharic alphabet, each with its numerical value.

3. F. IIIr: Good wishes for the teacher by the student, one of the traditional formulae.
የመምሬን፡ ጠላት፡ አንጠልጥሎ፡ ወደ፡ ጉድፍ፡፡
ጥሩ፡ ጥሩውን፡ ለመምሬ፤ አተላ፡ አተላውን፡ ለገብሬ፡፡

4. Ff. 82v–84r: Absolution of the Son, ፍትሐት፡ ዘወልድ፡. EMIP 10, f. IIr, (varia).

5. F. 84rv: Table blessing, "We beseech you" ሰአላጊከ:, incomplete at the beginning. MD 59, pp. 634ff.
6. Ff. 84v–85r: 1 John 1:1–7.

Notes:
1. Decorative designs: ff. 1r, 17v, 23r, 26v, 32r, 35v, 38v, 40v, 44r, 49r, 59r, 65v, 71v (*haräg* using multiple colors); ff. 17v, 23r, 35v, 40r, 44r (line of stops and/or stops connected by lines).
2. Prayer for Wäldä Mika'el, f. 73v; Wäldä Yoḥannəs, f. 82r and Gäbrä Əgzi'bḥer, f. 84v.
3. Note of ownership by *Mämmǝre* Wäldä Maryam, f. 85r.
4. F. 85v, the beginning of writing a Gə'əz text.
5. Ff. 71v–82r copied in a different hand.
6. Copied beautifully for Śahlä Śəllase, f. 1r and *passim*.
7. F. IIv blank.
8. Overlooked words of text are written interlinearly (f. 76v).

Quire Map

Protection Folio: i ii iii
A folio stub is visible between ff. ii and iii.

Quire 1: 1 2 3 4 5 6 7 8 9 10
Quire 2: 11 12 13 14 15 16 17 18 19 20
Quire 3: 21 22 23 24 25 26 27 28 29 30
Quire 4: 31 32 33 34 35 36 37 38 39 40
Quire 5: 41 42 43 44 45 46 47 48 49 50
Quire 6: 51 52 53 54 55 56 57 58 59 60
Quire 7: 61 62 63 64 65 66 67 68 69 70

Quire 8   71 72   73 74   75 76 77 78 79

Quires 8 and 9 have been sewn together with green string using a stab stitch. A folio stub is visible between ff. 72 and 73.

Quire 9   80 81 82   83 84 85

EMIP 18 – Marwick Codex 14
Psalter, ዳዊት:

Parchment, 164 x 143 x 60 mm, four Coptic chain stitches attached with bridle attachments to a rough-hewn board (rear) covered with tooled leather and one leather cover (front), 22 full quires, 175 folios, 160 x 140 mm folio, top margin 18–20 mm, bottom margin 28–32 mm, fore edge margin 13–18 mm, gutter margin 8–10 mm, ff. 1r–158v one column, ff. 159r–175r two columns, Gəʿəz, 18–19 lines, early 18th cent.

Quire descriptions: quires 1–21 balanced; quire 22 unbalanced. Navigation system: various colored string sewn into corners of folios 17, 36, 84, 123 to mark content divisions.

Ff. 1r–175r: Psalter [*Dawit*]. Cf. EMIP 1.
1. Ff. 1r–137r: Psalms of David. Arranged for the days of the week by a later hand.
2. Ff. 137r–151r: Biblical Canticles.
3. Ff. 151r–158v: Song of Songs, common version. Some verses are paired with other verses by a different hand.
4. Ff. 159r–170r: Praises of Mary [*Wəddase Maryam*]. Arranged for the days of the week (Monday, f. 159r; Tuesday, f. 160r; Wednesday, f. 162r; Thursday, f. 164r; Friday, f. 166v; Saturday, f. 168r; Sunday, f. 169r).
5. Ff. 170v–175r: Gate of Light [*Anqäṣä Bərhan*].

Varia:
1. F. 175r: *Asmat* prayer against the enemy, copied for Wäldä Giyorgis.

Notes:
1. Some psalms are marked with *qəbʿ* that is serially numbered. It must have been used as a prayer on remedial oil. Some versicles are encircled in ink. These were apparently the ones that are used in the liturgy.
2. Decorative designs: ff. 17r, 36v, 43r, 45r, 52r, 62r, 158v, 175r (dotted line using alternating black and red); ff. 75r (dotted line using red); ff.

158v, 175r (full row of stops); f. 175r (section divider using black and red); ff. 1r, 26r, 91r, 123v, 130r, 137r, 151r (late *haräg* using crudely scribbled pencil or pen).
3. F. Ir: The name Abrəha Kasay, possible a one-time owner of the manuscript, and scribbling, in a crude hand.
4. Overlooked lines of text are added interlinearly (ff. 72, 95r, 104v, 141r, 143r, 147v, 148r, and 153r).
5. Note of ownership by *Qes* Hadära Abrəha, f.29v, and *Haläqa* Täsfay, f. 40v, with the name of the original owner on f. 158v erased.
6. Ff. 86r and 158v: The name of *Aläqa* Gäbrä Ṣadəq of Betä Abrəham.
7. Ff. 158v and 175rv words and phrases copied in crude hands.
8. F. Iv blank.
9. This scribe has avoided the problem of lines of text too long to fit on one line by adopting an aspect ratio that leaves ample room for the width of most lines. Occasionally a line is too long and has to be completed above or below the end of the line (e.g., ff. 8r, 12v, 14v, 18v, 19v, etc.).

Quire Map

Front Cover: Parchment

Quire 1: 1, 2, 3, 4, 5, 6, 7, 8

Quire 2: 9, 10, 11, 12, 13, 14, 15, 16

Quire 3: 17, 18, 19, 20, 21, 22, 23, 24

Quire 4: 25, 26, 27, 28, 29, 30, 31, 32

Quire 5: 33, 34, 35, 36, 37, 38, 39, 40

Quire 6: 41, 42, 43, 44, 45, 46, 47, 48

Quire 7: 49, 50, 51, 52, 53, 54, 55, 56

56 · *Catalogue of the Codices*

Quire 8: 57 58 59 60 61 62 63 64

Quire 9: 65 66 67 68 69 70 71 72

Quire 10: 73 74 75 76 77 78

Quire 11: 79 80 81 82 83 84 85 86 87 88 89 90

Quire 12: 91 92 93 94 95 96 97 98

Quire 13: 99 100 101 102 103 104 105 106

Quire 14: 107 108 109 110 111 112 113 114

Quire 15: 115 116 117 118 119 120 121 122

Quire 16: 123 124 125 126 127 128 129 130

Quire 17: 131 132 133 134 135 136 137 138

Quire 18: 139 140 141 142 143 144 145 146

Quire 19: 147 148 149 150 151 152 153 154

Quire 20: 155 156 157 158 159 160 161 162 163 164

Quire 21: 165 166 167 168 169 170 171 172

Quire 22: 173 174 175

Quire 22 has been re-sewed. It appears that a folio is missing between ff. 174 and 175. However, the re-sewing of the quire has made it impossible to inspect the gutter of the quire.

EMIP 19 – Marwick Codex 15
Praises of God, ውዳሴ፡ አምላክ፨

Parchment, 194 x 185 x 65 mm, four repaired Coptic chain stitches attached with bridle attachments to rough-hewn boards, 16 full quires, quires 3–15 numbered, 144 folios, 182 x 175 mm, top margin 22–25 mm, bottom margin 40–42 mm, fore edge margin 27–32 mm, gutter margin 12–15 mm, ff. 1r–142v two columns, Gəʽəz, 18 lines, late 17th cent.

Quire descriptions: quires 1–6, 9–14, 16 balanced; quires 7, 8 adjusted balanced; quire 15 unbalanced.

Ff. 1r–142v: Praises of God, *Wəddase Amlak* (ውዳሴ፡ አምላክ፡). Devotional groups of prayers by Church Fathers, arranged for the days of the week. Incomplete at the beginning, folios missing and rebound in some disorder. Abbadie 198, f. 1r, Conti Rossini, Notice, no. 99; EMML 1432.

1. Ff. 1r–7v, lacuna, 8r–14v, lacuna, and 15r–40v: Tuesday: Prayers taken from a homily by St Ephrem the Syrian.
   ጸሎት፡ ዳግሚት፡ እንተ፡ ዘዐለተ፡ ሠሉስ፡ እምድርሳነ፡ ቅዱስ፡ ኤፍሬም፡ ሶርያዊ፡ አፈ፡ በረከት፡ ወበቁኔት፡ . . . ስብሐት፡ ለከ፡ አመስተዓግሥ፡ . . .

2. Ff. 41r–62r: Wednesday: Prayers taken from a homily by St Ephrem the Syrian.
   ጸሎት፡ ወስእለት፡ ማልሲት፡ እንተ፡ ዘዐለተ፡ ረቡዕ፡ እምድርሳነ፡ ቅዱስ፡ ማሪ፡ ኤፍሬም፡ ካዕበ፨ አእግ"፡ አምላክ፡ መሀሪ፡ ኢየሱስ፡ ክርስቶስ፡ ወልደ፡ እግ"፡ ሶበ፡ ተዘከርኩ፡ ምጽአትከ፡ . . .

3. Ff. 62r–86v: Thursday: Prayers compiled from the words of St. John (Saba), the Spiritual Elder, *Arägawi Mänfäsawi*.
   ጸሎት፡ ዘዐለተ፡ ሐሙስ፡ አስተጋብአዋ፡ እመጽሐፈ፡ አረጋዊ፡ መንፈሳዊ፡ ቅዱስ፡ . . . ቡሩክ፡ ውእቱ፡ አቡሁ፡ ለእግዚእነ፡ ወመድኃኒነ፡ ኢየሱስ፡ ክርስቶስ፡ ዘከሠተ፡ ምሥጢረ፡ አፍቅሮቶ፡ ለነፍሳቲነ፡ . . .

4. Ff. 87r–105v: Friday:
   (1) Ff. 87r–96v: Prayers by John Chrysostom (?, otherwise by *Abba Sinoda the Archmandrite*).
   ጸሎት፡ ወስእለት፡ ሐምስ፡ [እ]ምድርሳነ፡ ቅዱስ፡ ዮሐንስ፡ አፈ፡ ወርቅ፡ (sic) . . . ዘተብህለ፡ ለመዝሙር፡ (sic) እግዚአ፡ በመዓትከ፡ ኢትቅሥፈኒ፡ . . .

   (2) Ff. 96v–105v: Prayer by Abbot Pachomius.

ጸሎት፡ ዘአብ፡ ጳኮሚስ፡ እንበይነ፡ ፍጻሜሃ፡ በዛቲ፡ ዕለት፡ ዘዕለተ፡
ዓርብ፡ . . . ስብሐት፡ ለአብ፡ ስብሐት፡ ለወልድ፡ ስብሐት፡
ለመንፈስ፡ ቅዱስ፡ ሥላሴ፡ በተዋህዶ፡ ወተዋህዶ፡ በሥላሴ፡ . . .

5. Ff. 106r–120v: Saturday: Prayers compiled by Athanasius of Alexandria from Coptic hymns.
ጸሎት፡ ሳድሲት፡ ዘዕለተ፡ ሰንበተ፡ አይሁድ፡ ዘአስተጋብአ፡ እግናሌተ፡
ቅብጢ፡ አቡነ፡ አትናቴዎስ፡   ሊቀ፡ ጳጳሳት፡ ዘሀገረ፡ እለ፡ እስክንድርያ፡
. . . ወትብል፡ ከመዝ፡ ኃሥሥኩከ፡ እግዕምቀ፡ ልብዮ፡ . . .

6. Ff. 121r–135v, 137rv, 136rv, and 138r–140r: Sunday: Prayers compiled from the prayers of St. Cyril of Alexandria.
ጸሎት፡ ወስእለት፡ ሳብዓይ፡ እንተ፡ ዘዕለተ፡ እሁድ፡ አስተጋብእዋ፡
እምቅዱስ፡ ቄርሎስ፡ እምብዙኀ፡ ስእለታት፡ . . . ባርክ፡ እግዚአ፡
ስብሐት፡ ለአብ፡ ወወልድ፡ ወመንፈስ፡ ቅዱስ፡ አአምን፡ ወእትአመን፡

Miniatures:
1. F. 22r: Crude drawing, unknown.
2. F. 40r: Drawing of man mounted on a horse holding a spear.
3. F. 143r: Crude drawing of a man.
4. F. 143v: Crude drawing of an angel.

Varia:
1. Ff. 140r–141v: Image of the Saintly Kings of the Zag^{w}e Dynasty. MG 59, pp. 644ff.
እወጥን፡ (sic) አንስ፡ ማኅሌተ፡ መልክዕክሙ፡ በዘምሮ፨
ወዓዲ፡ ለጣዕሙ፡ እምጣዕሙ፡ መዓር፡ ዘአፈቅሮ፨
ይምርኃን፡ ክርስቶስ፡ ላሊበላ፡ ነአኮቶ፡ ለአብ፡ በአንብሮ፨
2. Ff. 141v–142v: What seems to be on the early life of Däbrä Asbo (Däbrä Libanos), insufficiently legible.

Notes:
1. Decorative designs: f. 62r (dotted line using alternating black and red); f. 140r (full line of stops).
2. Note of ownership by Wäldä Täkle, in a crude hand, f. 143v.
3. New works are indicated by the writing of multiple lines entirely in red ink (ff. 1r, 15v, 18v, 22v, 27v, 41r, 45v, 53r, 56v, 57v, 59v, 62r, 68v, 77r, 82r, 83r, 84v, 85r, 86r, 87v, 96v, 101v, 103v, 106r, 112v, 114r, 121r, 122v, 127v, 130v, 131v, and 138v).
4. F. 144r blank.
5. Copied for Iyyosyas, ff. 1r, 15v, 39v, 40r and *passim*.

Quire Map

Quire 1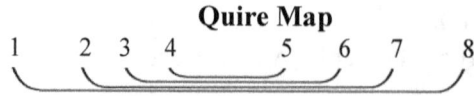

Quire 1 is loose and has been rebound in white string. The sheets seem to have come apart and the folios are loose.

Quire 2: 9 10 11 12 13 14

Quire 3: 15 16 17 18 19 20 21 22 23 24

Quire 4: 25 26 27 28 29 30 31 32 33 34

Quire 5: 35 36 37 38 39 40 41 42 43 44

Quire 6: 45 46 47 48 49 50 51 52 53 54

Quire 7: 55 56 57 58 59 60 61 62 63 64

Stubs appear between ff. 57 and f. 58 and between ff. 60 and f. 61.

Quire 8: 65 66 67 68 69 70 71 72 73 74

Stubs appear between ff. 68 and f. 69 and between ff. 71 and 72.

Quire 9: 75 76 77 78 79 80 81 82 83 84

Quire 10: 85 86 87 88 89 90 91 92 93 94

Quire 11: 95 96 97 98 99 100 101 102 103 104

Quire 12: 105 106 107 108 109 110 111 112 113 114

Quire 13: 115 116 117 118 119 120 121 122 123 124

Quire 14: 125 126 127 128 129 130 131 132 133 134

135 136 137 138 139 140 141 142

Quire 15

This quire has been rebound with white string. Two stubs appear between ff. 141 and 142. Folio 142 is cut off about half way toward the center.

Quire 16   143   144

This folio is made of a different grade of parchment.

EMIP 20 – Marwick Codex 16
Images, መልክዐ፡ ጉባኤ፡

Parchment, 108 x 60 x 65 mm (no covers), four Coptic chain stitches bind the quires together. There are no wooden covers. Twenty-one quires, 143 folios, 108 x 60 mm folio, top margin 8–10 mm, bottom margin 15–22 mm, fore edge margin 7–10 mm, gutter margin 5–6 mm, one column, Gə'əz, 12–21 lines, usually 15–16, reign of Iyyo'as (1747–1761), f. 137r.

Quire descriptions: quires 1–9, 11, 13, and 16–17 balanced; quire 12 adjusted balanced; quires 10, 14, 15, 18–21 unbalanced.

1. Ff. 1r–14v and 95rv: Image of Fasiledes, መልክዐ፡ ፋሲለደስ፡. The beginning (f. 1r) is illegible. Chaîne, Répertoire, no. 287; edited by F. M. Esteves Pereira in *Acta Martyrum I*, CSCO, vol. 37, script aeth. t. 20 reprint (1962), pp. 69–78 (text); vol 38, script aeth. t. 21 reprint (1962), pp. 61–70 (tr.).
2. Ff. 15r–19r: Image of Gäbrä Mänfäs Qəddus, መልክዐ፡ ገብረ፡ መንፈስ፡ ቅዱስ፡. Chaîne, Répertoire, no. 196; MG 59, pp. 553ff.
ሰላም፡ ለዕንስትከ፡ መሡረተ፡ ነገር፡ ወውጣኔ፨
ወለልደትከ፡ ሰላም፡ በብስራተ፡ መልአክ፡ ሠናየ፡ ቅኔ፨
3. Ff. 19r–25v: Image of John the Baptist, መልክዐ፡ ዮሐንስ፡ መጥምቅ፡. Chaîne, Répertoire, no. 279; MG 59, pp. 394ff.
በስመ፡ እግ"፡ እሳት፡ በሐቅለ፡ ሐሊና፡ ነዳዪ፨
ወበስመ፡ ማርያም፡ ድንግል፡ መጥበቢተ፡ ዓለም፡ አባዲ፨
4. Ff. 26r–33r: Image of Jesus Christ, መልክዐ፡ ኢየሱስ፡. Chaîne, Répertoire, no. 125; EMIP 17, f. 65v.
5. Ff. 33v–34r: Greeting, *Sälam*, to Abib.
ሰላም፡ ለከ፡ አቢብ፡ ንሩይ፡ ዘተከለልከ፡ ሞገስ፨
እስመ፡ ምስለ፡ ዐቢይ፡ ንጉሥ፡ ዐረይከ፡ ነጊሠ፨
6. Ff. 35r–38r: Hymn to Mary, commonly called "Image of Edom," መልክዐ፡ ኤዶም፡. Chaîne, Répertoire, no. 221; EMIP 17, f. 23r.
7. Ff. 38r–44r: Image of the Eucharist, መልክዐ፡ ቀርባን፡. Commonly called in the West "Community of the faithful," ማኅበረ፡ ምእመናን፡. Chaîne,

Répertoire, no. 17; MG 59, pp. 261ff; Dillmann, *Chrestomthia*, pp. 131–36; S. Euringer, "Ein orientalisches Kommunionlied," *Theologie und Glaube*, vol. 26 (1934), pp. 200–205.

ማኅበረ፡ ምእመናን፡ ወምእመናት፡ አለ፡ ኪያከ፡ ተአምኑ፡፡
ለነሂአ፡ ሥጋከ፡ ወትረ፡ ኅቡ፡ ተዓፀኑ፡፡

8. Ff. 44r–57v: Image of the Covenant of Mercy, መልክዐ፡ ኪዳነ ምሕረት፡. Chaîne, Répertoire, no. 362; Dillmann, *Chrestomathia*, pp. 136–46; MG 59, pp. 681–700.

እግ"፡ ወሀቤ፡ ብርሃን፡ ዘይሴልስ፡ በአካለ፡፡
እንዘ፡ ተዋህዶ፡ ያጸንዕ፡ በመለኮቱ፡ ወኃይሉ፡፡

9. Ff. 57v–60v: Greetings, *Sälam*, of the *Dərsanä Mika'el*. See EMIP 16, f. 84v, 92rv, 20v, 27v, etc., copied for Aqba Mika'el, f. 60v.

10. Ff. 61v–75v: Image of Michael, መልክዐ፡ ሚካኤል፡. Concluded with a halleluiatic hymn, f. 75rv. Chaîne, Répertoire, no. 119; MG 59, pp. 290ff.; EMIP 16, f. 92v.

11. Ff. 76r–80r: Image of the Trinity, መልክዐ፡ ሥላሴ፡. Chaîne, Répertoire, no. 189.

ሰላም፡ ለዝክረ፡ ስምክሙ፡ ዘእምቅድም፡ ዓለም፡ ሀልው፡፡
ለርእስክሙ፡ ሰላም፡ ወስእርትክሙ፡ ዕእድው፡፡

12. Ff. 80r–91v: Image of Mäzra'tä Krəstos, መልክዐ፡ መዝራዕተ፡ ክርስቶስ፡.

ይትባረክ፡ እግ"፡ ዘአምጽአ፡ ዓለማተ፡፡
ወበአርምሞ፡ ፈጠረ፡ ግሩማነ፡ ራዕይ፡ ኃያላተ፡፡
መዝራዕተ፡ ክርስቶስ፡ ያሬድ፡ እንዘ፡ ትብል፡ ክሡተ፡፡
ኢያዕረፍከ፡ እምተናግሮ፡ ወኢረሰይከ፡ ሀኬተ፡፡

Concluded with a litany for the Nativity:

ምልጣን፤ ተወልደ፡ እምድንግል፡ ሰከበ፡ ውስተ፡ ጎል፡፡, f. 91rv.

13. Ff. 92r–94v: List of the sufferings of Jesus.

ጸዋትው፡ ሐማማት፡ ዘእግዚእነ፡ ወመድኃኒነ፡ ኢየሱስ፡ ክርስቶስ፡ ዘዘበጥም፡ ገጾ፡ . . .

14. Ff. 94v–95r: Greeting, *Sälam*, to Täklä Haymanot. Taken from the *Əgzi'abḥer Nägśä* hymns ascribed to *Aṣe* Zär'a Ya'əqob; cf. EMML 3128, f. 71b.

ሰላም፡ ለተክለ፡ ሃይማኖት፡ ባሕርየ፡ ወንጌል፡ ወወአሪት፡፡ (sic.)
እምአም፡ ተወልደ፡ ስአት፡፡
ለእግ"፡ ባረኮ፡ በሰላስ፡ ዕለት፡፡

15. Ff. 95v–102r: Image of Kiros, መልክዐ፡ ኪሮስ፡. Chaîne, Répertoire, no. 141.

ሰላም፡ ለዝክረ፡ ስምከ፡ ኅቡ፡ ዓምደ፡ ወርቅ፡ ዘተጽሕፈ፡፡
ምስለ፡ አበው፡ ጌራን፡ እንዘ፡ ይከውን፡ ሱቱፈ፡፡

16. Ff. 104r–126v: Image of Täklä Haymanot, መልክዐ፡ ተክለ፡ ሃይማኖት፡. Chaîne, Répertoire, no. 211; MG 59, pp. 566ff.
ሰላም፡ ለጽንስትከ፡ ወለልደትከ፡ እምከርሥ፡፡
አመ፡ ፰ወረቡዑ፡ ለወርኃ፡ ታኅሣሥ፡፡
17. Ff. 127r–129r: Image of the Trinity, መልክዐ፡ ሥላሴ፡. Composed probably by a certain Tabor after Iyyasu (1682–1706) built the Däbrä Bərhan Śəllase church in Gondär, cf. ff. 127r and 129r.
ሰላም፡ ለሕጽንከሙ፡ ምርፋቀ፡ ጻድቃን፡ አግብርቲሁ፡፡
ማያተ፡ ኢያሱ፡ ሥላሴ፡ እለ፡ ትውሕዙ፡ እምሕሊናሁ፡፡
18. F. 129r: Greeting, Sälam, to Abunafər, of Säne 16. EMML 1297, f. 150b.
ሰላም፡ ለአቡናር፡ (sic.) ጊዜ፡ ተዳደቀ፡ መዊት፡፡
እንተ፡ ተወለጠ፡ ገጹ፡ አምሳለ፡ እሳት፡፡
19. Ff. 129v–131r: *Asmat* prayer against rinderpest (*ḫəkor*?). The Greek names of the nails of the cross are copied on f. 130v.
አስማት፡ በእንተ፡ እንሳ፡ ወበእንተ፡ አባግዕ፡ ወበእንተ፡ አጋሌ፡ ወኮሉ፡ ንዋየ፡ ሰብእ፡ ከመ፡ ኢይንድፉ፡ ለዓራዊት፡ ኅኮር፡ ቡነጸ፡ ቀጤን፡ . . .
20. Ff. 132v–132r: Greeting, *Sälam*, to the Archangel Phanuel. Prayer for driving away demons. Chaîne, Répertoire, no 49; William Hoyt Worrell, "Studien zum Abessinischen Zauberwesen," *Zeitschrift für Assyriologie und verwandte Gebiete*, vol. XXIII (1909), p. 177, and vol. XXIX (1914), p. 113.
ሰላም፡ ለከ፡ ሰዳዬ፡ ሰዳዬ፡ (sic.) አጋንንት፡ ፋኑኤል፡ ለእግ"፡ እምጽርሑ፡፡
ከመ፡ ኢይስክዩ፡ ሰብአ፡ እነ፡ ኢነስሑ፡፡
21. Ff. 134v–138r: Prayer, "For the sake of the peaceful holy things," በእንተ፡ ቅድሳት፡ ሰላማዊት፡. Incomplete at the end. MQ 51, pp. 26–29; MG 59, pp. 41ff.; Daoud-Mersie, *Liturgy*, 33–37.
22. Ff. 138v–140r: What seems to be a hymn/song praising what Iyyo'as (1747–1761) has done for the monastery of *Abunä* Täklä Haymanot. Supplied with musical notation, insufficiently legible.

Miniatures
1. Crude drawings on ff. 25v, 141v and 142v
2. Crude geometric patterns drawn on ff. 94r, 102v, and 103r.

Varia:
1. F. 25v: Note that the parchment has been effaced.
2. F. 102v: Note that the design "is *ḥaräg*."
3. Ff 140v–141r: The beginning of 1 John 1:1, in a crude hand.
4. Prayer for Ma'əqbä Krəstos, ff. 60v, 75r, 126v and *passim*.

Notes:
1. The vellum is stained. For all of its wear, the pages seem to be intact.
2. Decorative designs: ff. 25v and 33r (*haräg* using black and red); ff. 13v, 19r, 38r, 91v, and 102r (dotted line[s] using alternating black and red); 44r (line of black dots); 75r, 80r, 94v, 95rv, 130v, and 131r (red line or black line); 75v and 91r (series of full-stop symbols); 126r, 129r (series of black dots or lines interspersed with full-stop symbols).
3. Missing texts are copied in different (later) hands.
4. F. 75v: Unintelligible note.
5. Ff. 136v-137r: an overlooked line is written in the upper margin of f. 136v and a symbol (+, in red ink) shows the place on f. 137r where the text is to be inserted.
6. Ff. 34v, 103v, 133v–134r, 142r and 143rv blank save for some scrawls.

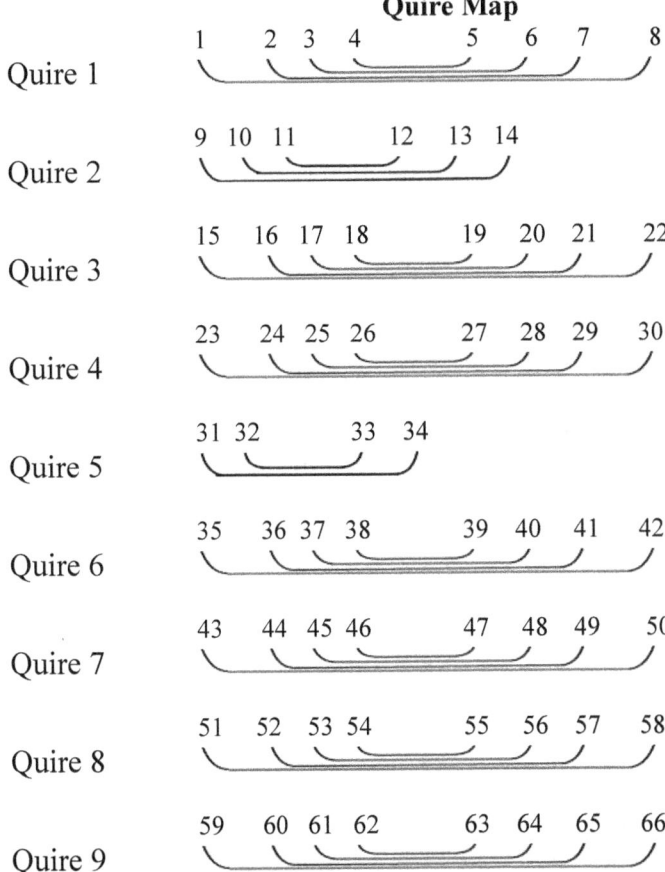

64 · *Catalogue of the Codices*

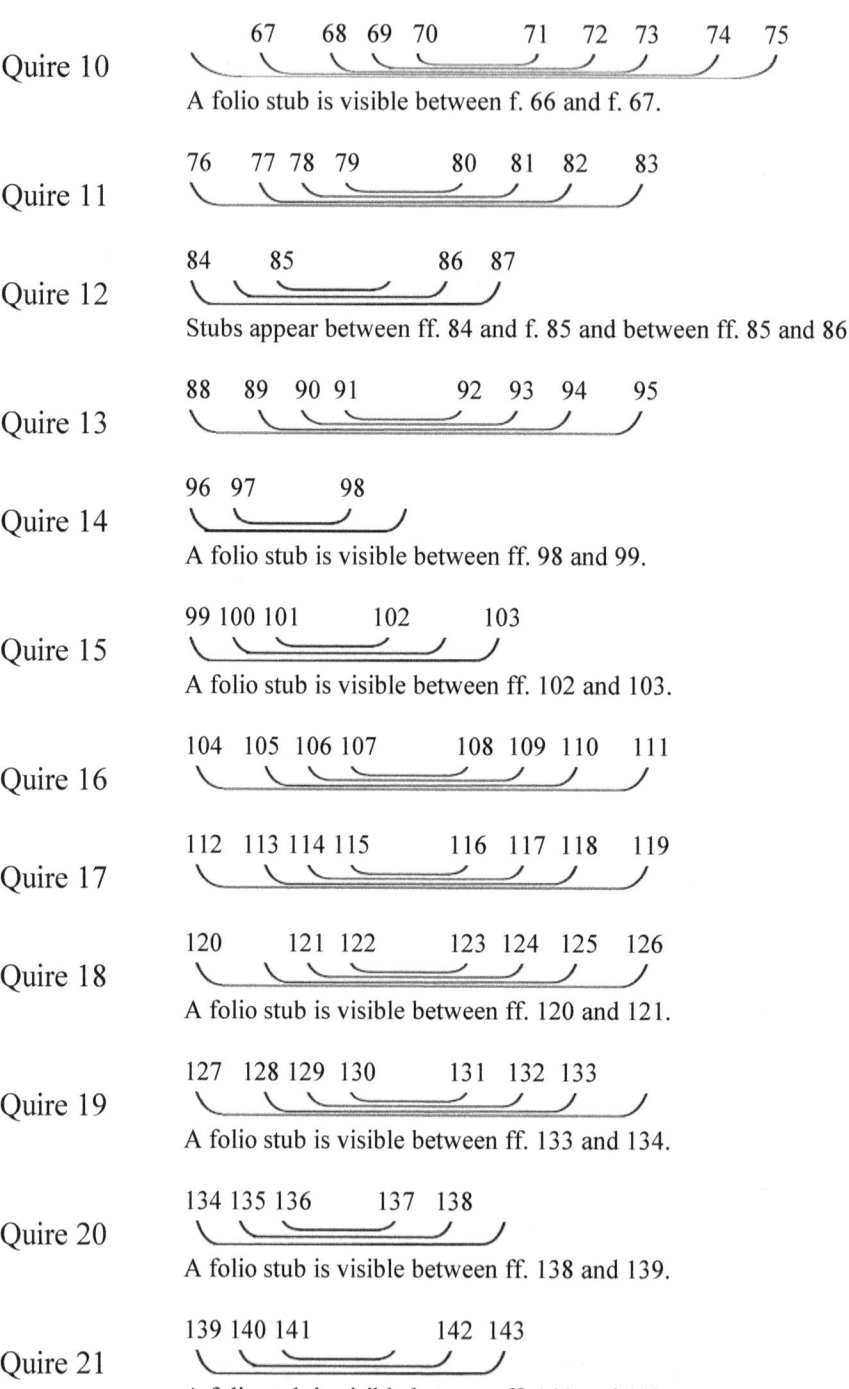

EMIP 21 – Mar wick Codex 17
Praises of Mary, ውዳሴ፡ ማርያም፡ — አንቀጸ፡ ብርሃን፡

Parchment, 140 x 123 x 42 mm, rebound, attached to rough-hewn boards both of which have been broken about 2–3 cm from the spine and the outer portion of the covers have been replaced with rough-hewn boards but with grain going perpendicular to the grain of the original boards, analyzed as three quires (but there is much displacement of folios in the current rebinding), 32 folios, 135 x 118 mm, top margin 12–14 mm, bottom margin 33–35 mm, fore edge margin 15–17 mm, gutter margin 8 mm, two columns, Gəʿəz, 14 lines, early 19th cent.

Quire descriptions: quires 1–3 balanced, but several loose folios have been sewn to folios. Navigation system: at least one example (f. 19) where red string was sewn into the corner of a folios to mark content divisions;

Ff. 1r–20v: Praises of Mary [*Wəddase Maryam*]. Arranged for the days of the week (Monday, with musical notation, f. 1r; Tuesday, f. 2r; Wednesday, f. 6v; Thursday, f. 10r; Friday, f. 14v; Saturday, f. 17v; Sunday, ff. 19v, 30rv, 28rv, 20rv.). EMIP 1, f. 158v.

Ff. 20v–27v, 29rv, 31rv: Gate of Light [*Anqäṣä Bəhan*]. EMIP 1, f. 170r.

Miniatures:
1. Front cover: Crude drawing in pencil.
2. Back cover: Crude drawing of talisman face on back cover (upside down)

Varia:
1. Ff. 3v and 4r: Practice on how to write a letter.
2. Ff. 13v–16r: Isolated sentence from Song 1.
3. F. 32r: Words and sentences copied from the *Wəddase Maryam*, in crude hands.

Notes:
1. Rebound in some disorder. The general condition of the vellum is dirty.
2. F. 32v blank.
3. Decorative designs: ff. 1r and 2v (*haräg* using black and red).
4. Overlooked words of text are written interlinearly (ff. 10r, 16r, 23r).

Quire Map

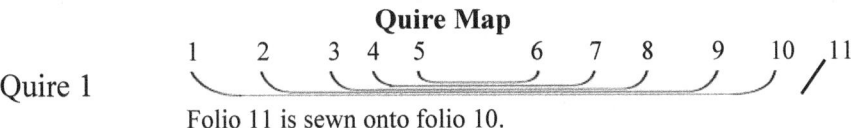

Quire 1

Folio 11 is sewn onto folio 10.

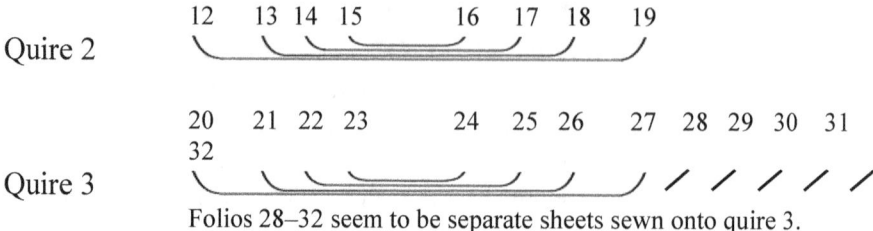

Folios 28–32 seem to be separate sheets sewn onto quire 3.

EMIP 22 – Marwick Codex 18
Psalter, ዳዊት:

Parchment, 175 x 125 x 55 mm, four Coptic chain stitches attached with bridle attachments to rough-hewn boards, protection quire + 14 full quires, quires 1–13 numbered, i + 110 folios, 173 x 122 mm folio, top margin 12–15 mm, bottom margin 35–40 mm, fore edge margin 7–10 mm, gutter margin 7–9 mm, ff. 1r–100v one column, ff. 100v–110r two columns, Gəʿəz, 23–24 lines, 20th cent.

Quire descriptions: quires 1, 2, 7–11, 13, 14 balanced; quire 5 adjusted balanced; quires 3, 4, 6, 12 unbalanced. Navigation system: green string sewn into corners of folios 42, 66, 76, 81, 85, 100, 102 to mark content divisions.

Ff. 1r–110r: Psalter [Dawit]. Cf. EMIP 1.
1. Ff. 1r–86r: Psalms of David.
2. Ff. 86r–95r: Biblical Canticles.
3. Ff. 95r–100v: Song of Songs, common version.
4. Ff. 100v–107r: Praises of Mary [Wəddase Maryam]. Arranged for the days of the week (Monday, f. 100v; Tuesday, f. 101r; Wednesday, f. 102v; Thursday, f. 103v; Friday, f. 105r; Saturday, f. 105v; Sunday, f. 106v).
5. Ff. 107r–110r: Gate of Light [Anqäṣä Bərhan].

Miniatures:
1. F. 110: drawing of Jesus Christ in black and red, with uplifted hands and an unfinished head.

Varia:
1. F. Iv: Hymn to the Archangel Michael, in pencil in a crude hand; insufficiently legible.

Notes:
1. Decorative designs: ff. 1r, 25v, 32r, 36v, 42v, 50v, 56v, 59v, 67r, 77r, 86r, 100v (haräg using black and red); ff. 6r, 11v, 36v, 37r, 47r, 81v, 102v (small haräg using black and/or red drawn next to or over text);

ff. 11v, 17v, 75r, 95r, 107r (dotted line using alternating black and red); f. 75r (additional drawing in black and red).
2. F. 47r: A small red and black symbol in the upper margin marks the midpoint of the Psalms (?).
3. Ff. Ii and 110v blank save for some scrawl.
4. Colometric layout of text: ff. 85v–86r (Ps. 150) and 92r–93r (tenth biblical canticle).
5. Overlooked words of text are written interlinearly (ff. 87r, 103v, 109r).
6. The scribe regularly has to complete a line of text on another line. Much of the problem is addressed through the selection of an appropriate aspect ratio for the codex combined with an appropriate script size. But, where the line of text is still too long, the scribe completes the line of text above the end of the line (throughout). This scribe will also reduce the font size at the end of lines to avoid having to go onto the next line (throughout).

Quire Map

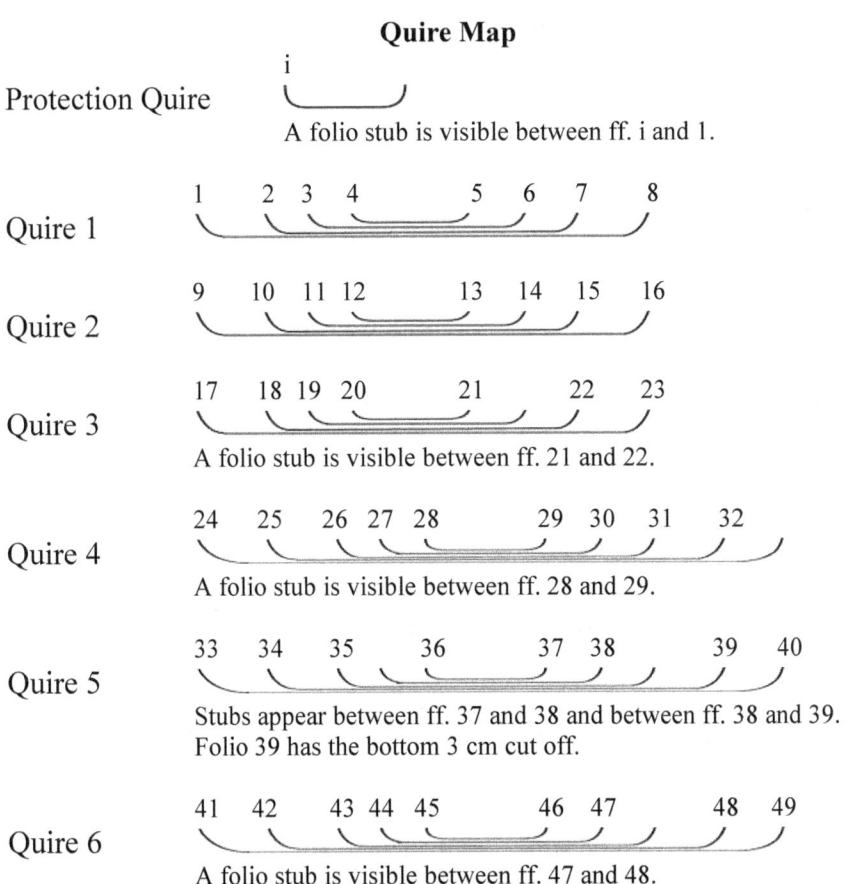

Protection Quire — i
A folio stub is visible between ff. i and 1.

Quire 1 — 1 2 3 4 5 6 7 8

Quire 2 — 9 10 11 12 13 14 15 16

Quire 3 — 17 18 19 20 21 22 23
A folio stub is visible between ff. 21 and 22.

Quire 4 — 24 25 26 27 28 29 30 31 32
A folio stub is visible between ff. 28 and 29.

Quire 5 — 33 34 35 36 37 38 39 40
Stubs appear between ff. 37 and 38 and between ff. 38 and 39. Folio 39 has the bottom 3 cm cut off.

Quire 6 — 41 42 43 44 45 46 47 48 49
A folio stub is visible between ff. 47 and 48.

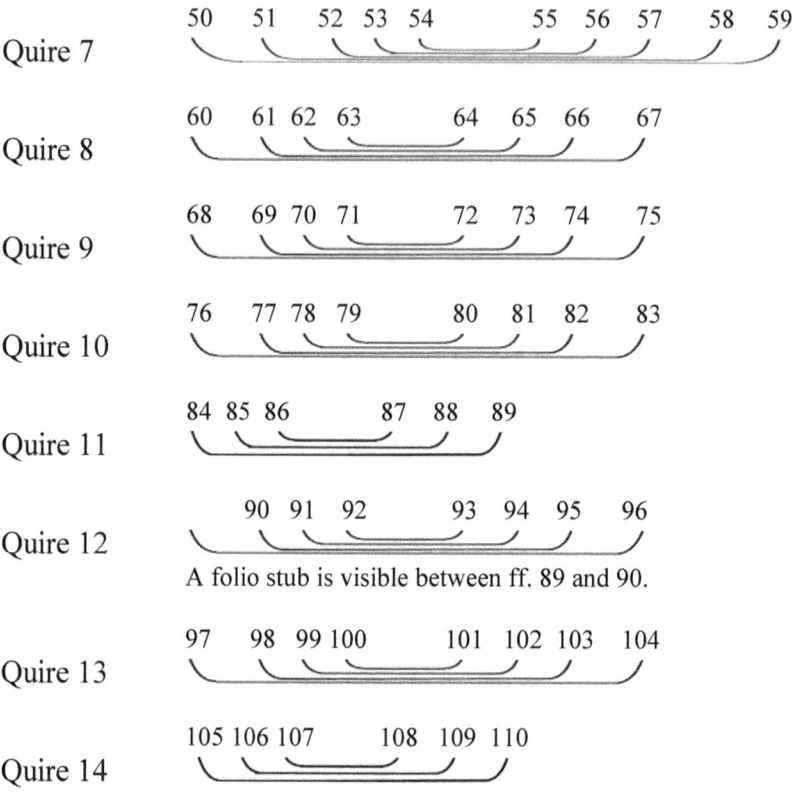

A folio stub is visible between ff. 89 and 90.

EMIP 23 – Marwick Codex 19
Gospel of John, ወንጌለ፡ ዮሐንስ፡

Parchment, 195 x 134 x 57 mm, four Coptic chain stitches attached with bridle attachments to rough-hewn boards. The back board is broken top to bottom in three places. The outer piece is missing; the remaining two are stitched together. The front board is also broken and repaired with three stitches. Tooled leather covers the spine and ca. 60 mm of the boards. Neither headband nor tailband are visible, but the tops and bottoms of the folios are stitched into the spine in such a way as to accomplish the same purpose, eleven quires, 97 folios, 191 x 130 mm, top margin 20–25 mm, bottom margin 40–43 mm, fore edge margin 20–25 mm, gutter margin 5–10 mm, one column, Gəʿəz, 15–16 lines, 19th cent.

Quire descriptions: quires 1–10 balanced; quire 11 unbalanced. Navigation system: various colored string sewn into corners of ff. 15, 33, 43, 59, 70, and 81 to mark content divisions.

Ff. 1r–96v: The Gospel of John.
   Text, f. 1r; conclusion (*mäl'a*), f. 94v; introduction (*mäqdəmä wängelu*), f. 95r; traditional chapters (*ar'əst*), f. 96v. Arranged for the days of the week (Tuesday, f. 15v; Wednesday, f. 33r; Thursday, f. 43r; Friday, f. 59v; Saturday, f. 70r; Sunday, f. 81v).

Varia:
  1. F. 97rv: One miracle of the Archangel Michael about the farmer who could not make a feast in honor of the Archangel because of drought and famine, EMIP 16, f. 20r.

Notes:
  1. The sheets of this codex are particularly thick and uniform. The margins are ample. The letters are large.
  2. Decorative designs: ff. 1r, 15v, 33r, 43r, 59v, 70r, and 81v (*haräg* using black and red).
  3. Copied by Ewosṭatewos for Wäldä Śəllase and his wife Wälättä Maryam 'Omä Gännät, f. 97v.

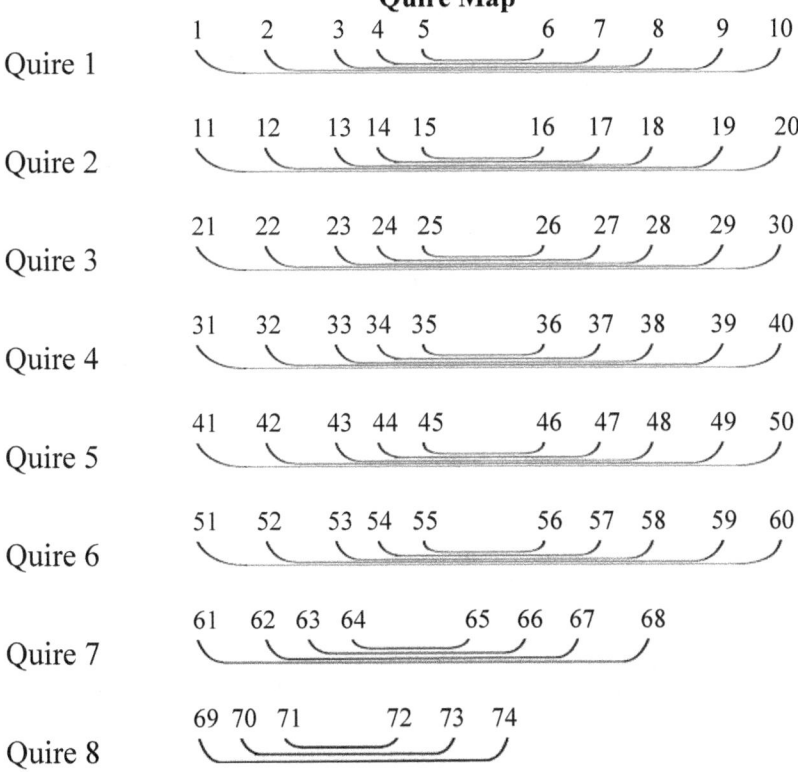

70 · *Catalogue of the Codices*

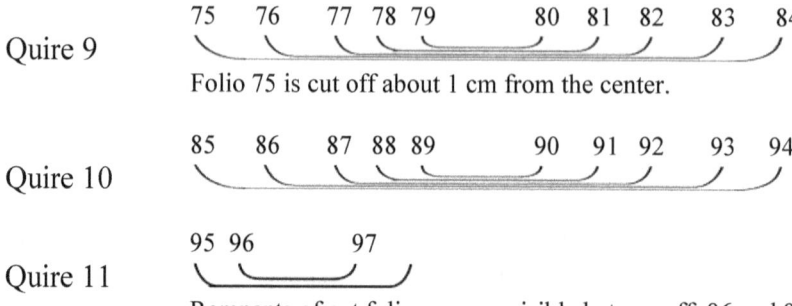

Quire 9

Folio 75 is cut off about 1 cm from the center.

Quire 10

Quire 11

Remnants of cut folios appear visible between ff. 96 and 97 and between 97 and the back cover. These are not folio stubs and the architecture of the final quire is not clear.

EMIP 24 – Marwick Codex 20
Psalter, ዳዊት:

Parchment, 182 x 155 x 95 mm, four repaired Coptic chain stitches attached with bridle attachments to rough–hewn boards, rebound, quire numbers 9, 11–14 visible, i + 153 folios, 180 x 143 mm folio, top margin 10–12 mm, bottom margin 35–38 mm, fore edge margin 10–13 mm, gutter margin 8 mm, ff. 1r–142r one column, ff. 142r–153v two columns, Gəʿəz, 20–30 lines, early 18th cent.

Navigation system: various colored string sewn into corners of folios 8, 23, 52, 59, 61, 67, 70, 78, 84, 94, 97, 109, 117 to mark content divisions.

Ff. 1r–152v: Psalter [*Dawit*]. Cf. EMIP 1.
1. Ff. 1r–123r: Psalms of David.
2. Ff. 123v–135v: Biblical Canticles.
3. Ff. 136r–142r: Song of Songs, common version.
4. Ff. 142r–149v: Praises of Mary [*Wəddase Maryam*]. Arranged for the days of the week (Monday, introduced with the first part of the story of its composition by a Syrian potter, f. 142r; Tuesday, f. 143r; Wednesday, f. 144v; Thursday, f. 146r; Friday, f. 147r; Saturday, f. 148r; Sunday, introduced with the last part of the story, f. 149r. The full story of the Syrian potter is preserved as one of the miracles of Mary, Budge, *Mary*, pp. 129–32).
5. Ff. 149v–152v: Gate of Light [*Anqäṣä Bərhan*].

Miniatures:
1. F. iv: Joab and his brother Abishai (1Sam 26:6), each on horseback.

Varia:

1. Ff. 152v–153v: Symbolic interpretation of parts of a church building and its contents, in Amharic. Marcel Griaule, "Regles de l'Église Éthiopiens (Documents Éthiopiens)," *JA*, vol. 221 (1932), pp. 1–42.
   ሥርዓተ፡ ቤተ፡ ክርስቲያን፡ ታቦቱ፡ ክርስቶስ፡፡ መንበሩ፡ ዐእንስሳ፡፡ ሥዕሉ፡ በከርሡ፡ ማርያም፡ እንደ፡ ኃደረ፡፡ . . .
2. F. 152v: Excerpt from the computus, ባሕረ፡ ሐሳብ፡. For a detailed study of the computus, see Otto Neugebaur, *Ethiopic Astronomy*, Vienna 1970; and ጌታቸው፡ ኃይሌ፡ ÷ ባሕረ ሐሳብ የዘመን ቤጠራ ቅርሳችን ከታሪክ ማስታወሻ ጋራ ÷ Collegeville (Minnesota), 1993 EC.
3. F. 153r: First part of the table blessing, "We beseech you," ሰአልናከ፡. See EMIP 17, f. 84rv.
4. F. 153r: Prayer to de-consecrate blessed baptismal water. Unfinished, cf. EMIP 32, f. 38r.
   ዝንቱ፡ ጸሎት፡ ፍትሐተ፡ ማይ፡ እግ"፡ አምላክነ፡ አኃዜ፡ ኮሉ፡ ፍጥረት፡ እምነበ፡ አልቦ፡ በጥብብከ፡ በአግን፡ አስተጋእኮሙ፡ ለማያት፡ . . .
5. F. 153v: Calendar of the Apostles, Evangelists and few other holy days.

Notes:
1. The codex has been rebound in disorder.
2. Decorative designs: ff. 8r, 13v, 23v, 42r, 48v, 59r, 70r, 78r, 84r, 97r, 109r, 111v, 117r, 123r, 135v, 136r, 142r, 143r, 144v, 146r, 147r, 148r, 149r (dotted line alternating black and red); f. 149v (dotted line using red); f. 152r (division using combined dots and lines in red).
3. F. Ir: two crosses, crudely painted.
4. Overlooked lines are written interlinearly (ff. 20v, 122v, and 143r). On f. 132v there is a case where an overlooked line was written in the upper margin and a mark was made in the text where it was to be inserted, but another scribe has written the overlooked line (beginning with the + symbol) into the text interlinearly a line lower than the location marked in the first case.
5. Some long lines of text have been written in smaller letters to avoid forcing the line of text onto another line: ff. 39v, 44r, 45r, 124r, etc.
6. F. 65r: A small, black and red cross marks the midpoint of the Psalms.
7. Prayer for the soul of Gäbrä Iyyäsus, f. 70r; for Wäldä Giyorgis, f. 84r, 109r and *passim*; and for Täklä Haymanot, f. 148v.
8. F. 1r (top margin) insufficiently legible text of one line.
9. Columetric layout of text: ff. 121v (Ps. 148), 122v–123r (Ps. 150), 132rv (tenth biblical canticle).

Quire Map
This codex has been rebound. There are several clues to the architecture of the original codex and of the rebound version: reinforcement strips surround several quires, original quire numbers are visible on several folios, and the strings are visible at the center of several quires. Nevertheless, it will require a very detailed study to sort out the two systems with any certainty.

EMIP 25 – Eliza Codex 4
Image of Mary — Image of Jesus Christ, መልክዐ: ማርያም: — መልክዐ: ኢየሱስ:

Parchment, four repaired Coptic chain stitches attached with bridle attachments to rough-hewn boards, protection quire + 8 full quires, ii + 60 folios, 118 x 87 mm, ff. 1r–59r one column, Gəʻəz, 13 lines, 20th cent.

Quire descriptions: quires 1 and 4–8 balanced; quires 2 and 3 adjusted balanced. Navigation system: brown yarn sewn into corners of folios ii, 8, 9, 17, 24, 36, 47, 59 to mark the location of miniatures. Single-slip case with a strap of leather.

1. Ff. 1r–24v: Image of Mary, መልክዐ: ማርያም:. Incomplete because of erasure to make room for the miniatures. Chaîne, Répertoire, no. 220; MG 59, pp. 735ff.
   ሰላም፡ ሰላም፡ ለዝክረ፡ ስምኪ፡ ሐዋዝ፨
   እምነ፡ ከልበሊ፡ ወቀኈስጥ፡ ወእምነ፡ ሰንበልት፡ ምዑዝ፨

2. Ff. 25r–46r: Image of Jesus Christ, መልክዐ: ኢየሱስ:. Ff. 24v and 36r erased to make room for the picture. Chaîne, Répertoire, no. 123; EMIP, 26, f. 47r.
   . . . ብቁሉ፤ ወጽፉቅ፡ ጥቀ፡ ለአርዘ፡ ሊባኖስ፡ ቄጽሉ፨
   ኢየሱስ፡ ክርስቶስ፡ ሊቀ፡ ካህናት፡ ዘላዕለ፡ ኮሉ፨

3. Ff. 46r–59v: "Missed text from the Image of Mary," ዘተረስዓ፡ ናይ፡ መልአ፡ (sic) ማርያም፡ The note is in Gəʻəz and Təgrəñña.
   ለዘኢየፈቅርኪ፡ (sic) እግዝእትየ፡ ማርያም፡ ውኩፈ፡ ኢይኩን፡ ጸሎቱ፡

Miniatures, all in twentieth-century hand, on erased folios:
1. F. IIr: painting of a man being fed by a bird.
2. F. IIv: painting of a holy man (Jesus?) looking and pointing up.
3. F. 8v: Saint George and the dragon.
4. F. 9r: Madonna and Child.
5. F. 17r: The Striking of the Head, ኮርንት፡ ርእሱ፡.
6. F. 24v: The Flogging of Jesus.

7. F. 36r: The Crucifixion.
8. F. 47v: Resurrected Christ Displays His Wounds.
9. F. 59v: A man (Christ?) looking ahead and pointing up.

Varia:
1. Verso of the front fore guard board: Words from the Image of Mary's Icon.
2. F. Ir: Prayer to Mary, in a crude hand.
3. F. Ir: Table of contents, in a crude hand.

Notes:
1. Decorative designs: f. 46r (dotted line using alternating black and red).
2. Ff. Iv and 60rv, blank save for some isolated words in a crude hand.
3. Overlooked words of text are written interlinearly (ff. 4v, 11r, 16v, 28v); and in the upper margin with a symbol (+) marking the location where the text is to be inserted (ff. 24r, line 1).

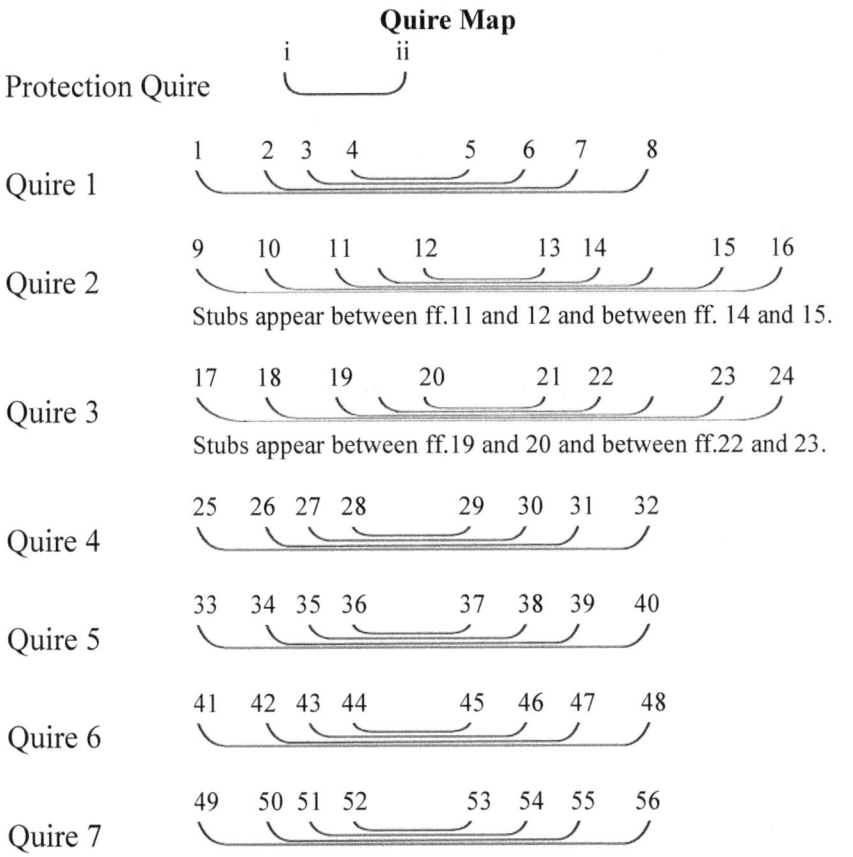

Quire 8   57 58   59 60

EMIP 26 – Eliza Codex 5
Anaphora of Our Lady Mary — Images , ቅዳሴ፡ ማርያም፡ — መልክዐ ጉባኤ ፡

Parchment, three repaired Coptic chain stitches attached with bridle attachments to rough-hewn boards, protection quire + 12 full quires, quires 2–9 numbered, ii + 96 folios, 129 x 98 mm, ff. 1r–77r one column, Gəʻəz, 12 lines, 20th cent.

Quire descriptions: quires 1–9, 12 balanced; quires 10, 11 adjusted balanced. Double-slip case with a strap of leather.

1. Ff. 1r–29v: Anaphora of Our Lady Mary, ቅዳሴ፡ ማርያም፡. Cf. EMIP 27.
2. Ff. 29v–47r: Image of Mary, መልክዐ፡ ማርያም፡. Chaîne, Répertoire, no. 220; MG 59, pp. 735ff.; EMIP 25, f. 1r.
3. Ff. 47r–63r: Image of Jesus Christ, መልክዐ፡ ኢየሱስ፡. Chaîne, Répertoire, no. 123; MG 59, pp. 757ff; EMIP, 25, f. 25r.
   ሰላም፡ ለዝክረ፡ ስምከ፡ ስመ፡ መሐላ፡ ዘኢ.ይሔሱ፡፡
   ዘአንበረ፡ ቅድመ፡ እግ"፡ በአ(f. 47v)ትሮንሱ፡፡
   ኢየሱስ፡ ክርስቶስ፡ ለዳዊት፡ ባሕርየ፡ ክርሁ፡፡
4. Ff. 63r–77r: Image of Michael, መልክዐ፡ ሚካኤል፡. Chaîne, Répertoire, no. 119; MG 59, pp. 290ff.; EMIP 16, f. 92v.

Notes:
1. Decorative designs: ff. 1r (*haräg* using multiple colors); ff. 1r, 29v, 47r, 63r, and 77r (dotted line using alternating black and red); f. 54v (cross using black).
2. F. 96rv isolated names and words.
3. Overlooked words are added interlinearly (ff. 2r, 6v, 8v, 15v, 16r, 61r, 62v, 73v), as is an overlooked line (f. 72r,). On ff. 54v, overlooked lines of text are written in the upper margin and a symbol (+) markes the location where the text is to be inserted.
4. Ff. Ir–IIv and 77v–95v blank.
5. Copied for Wäldä Abib, f. 77r.

Quire Map
Protection Sheet   i   ii

Catalogue of the Ethiopic Manuscript Imaging Project · 75

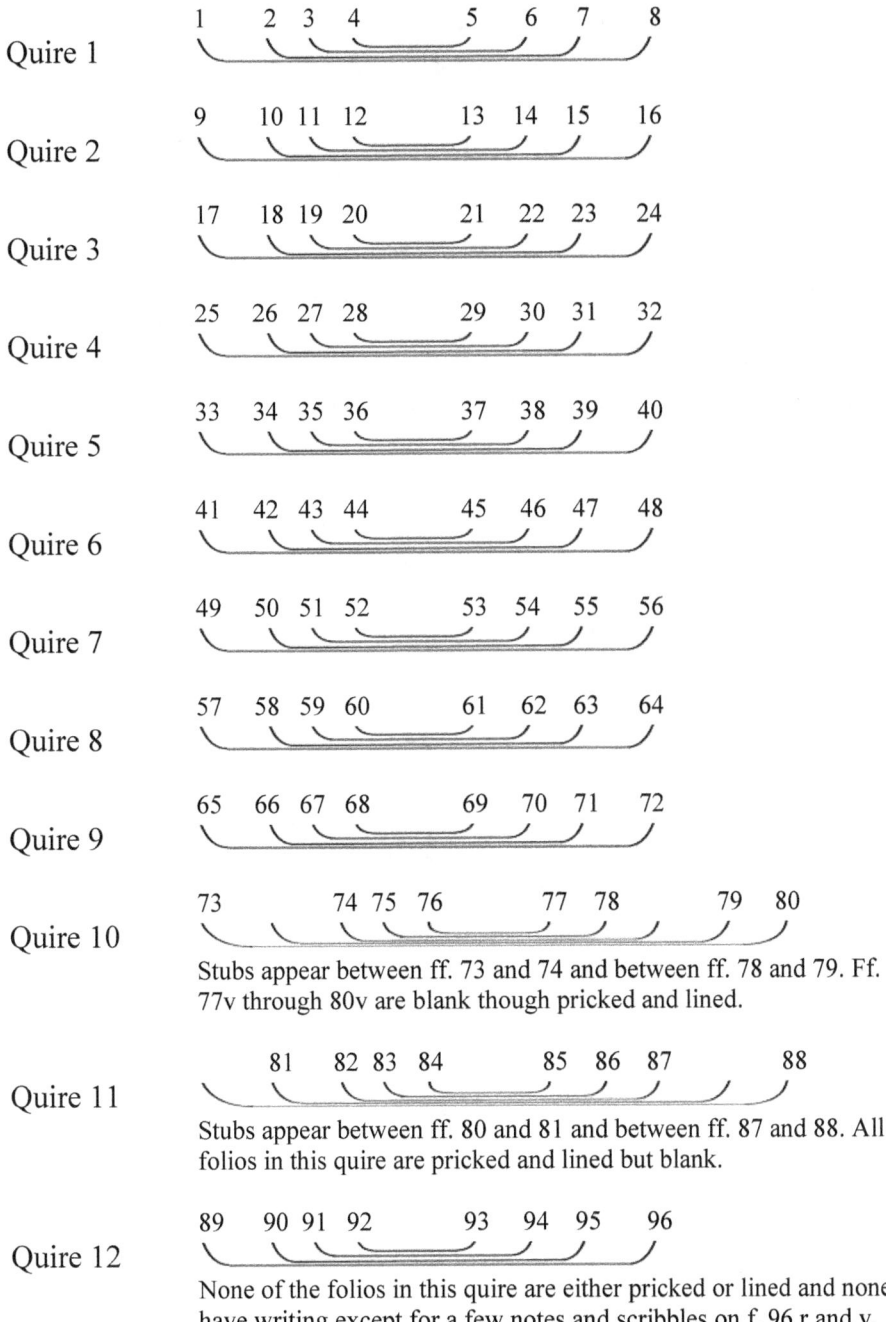

Quire 1: 1 2 3 4 5 6 7 8
Quire 2: 9 10 11 12 13 14 15 16
Quire 3: 17 18 19 20 21 22 23 24
Quire 4: 25 26 27 28 29 30 31 32
Quire 5: 33 34 35 36 37 38 39 40
Quire 6: 41 42 43 44 45 46 47 48
Quire 7: 49 50 51 52 53 54 55 56
Quire 8: 57 58 59 60 61 62 63 64
Quire 9: 65 66 67 68 69 70 71 72
Quire 10: 73 74 75 76 77 78 79 80

Stubs appear between ff. 73 and 74 and between ff. 78 and 79. Ff. 77v through 80v are blank though pricked and lined.

Quire 11: 81 82 83 84 85 86 87 88

Stubs appear between ff. 80 and 81 and between ff. 87 and 88. All folios in this quire are pricked and lined but blank.

Quire 12: 89 90 91 92 93 94 95 96

None of the folios in this quire are either pricked or lined and none have writing except for a few notes and scribbles on f. 96 r and v.

EMIP 27 – Eliza Codex 6
Missal, መጽሐፈ፡ ቅዳሴ፡

Parchment, four Coptic chain stitches attached with bridle attachments to repaired rough-hewn boards, 18 quires rebound, reinforcement strips around most of the quires, i + 129 folios, 141 x 125 mm, ff. 126r–129r one column, ff. iv(erso)–125v two columns, Gəʿəz, 15 lines, reign of Metropolitan Yosab (1770–1803), f. 110v.

Navigation systems: 1) black thread sewn into corners of folios 4, 35, 53, 76, 104, 105, 124, and 125 to mark the location of miniatures; 2) various colored string sewn into corners of folios 15, 20, 23, 25, 28, 41, 45, 52, 66, 87, 100, and 110 to mark content divisions. Single-slip case without strap.

Ff. 1r–129r: Missal, መጽሐፈ፡ ቅዳሴ፡፡. MQ; Daoud-Mersie, *Liturgy*. For the pertinent references and comments, see Ernst Hammerschmidt, *Studies in the Ethiopic Anaphoras*, second revised edition, (Stuttgart 1987).
1. Ff. 1r–28v: Ordinary of the Mass.
2. Ff. 28v–40v: Anaphora of the Apostles.
3. Ff. 40v–45r: Anaphora of Our Lord Jesus Christ.
4. Ff. 45r–52r: Anaphora of John Chrysostom.
5. Ff. 52r–66r: Anaphora of Həryaqos, Bishop of Bəhəna, otherwise dedicated to Our Lady Mary.
6. Ff. 66r–75v: Anaphora of the 318 Orthodox Fathers.
7. Ff. 75v–87r: Anaphora of John Son of Thunder.
8. Ff. 87v–100v: Anaphora of Athanasius the Apostolic.
9. Ff. 100v–103v: Anaphora of Dioscorus.
10. Ff. 103v–110r: Anaphora of Epiphanius.
11. Ff. 110r–121v, and 123v: Anaphora of James of Sarug.

Miniatures, all in twentieth-century hand:
1. F. 4r: God the Father or Jesus, surrounded by Four Living Creatures.
2. F. 35v: The Rod of Aaron Blooms.
3. F. 53r: Man riding a lion.
4. F. 76r: Two men gesturing toward one another, man on right only shows one eye.
5. F. 104v: Mary.
6. F. 105r: Gabriel.
7. F. 124v: Saint George and the Dragon.
8. F. 125r: Madonna and Child.

Varia:
1. F. Iv: Excerpt from the ordinary of the Mass.

2. F.104r, 121v–123r, 125v and 127r: The different prayers of *Śärawitä mäla'əktihu* of the different anaphoras.
3. Ff. 123v–124r: Suggestion of alternative prayers in the anaphoras.
4. F. 126rv: Imposition of the hand of the Anaphora of the 318 Orthodox Fathers.
5. F. 127r: *Asmat* prayers, copied for Iyyob, purpose not clear.
6. Ff. 127v–128v: *Asmat* prayer for help in learning, stained with water. በስመ፡ አብ፡ ወወልድ፡ ወመንፈስ፡ ቅዱስ፡ ዘይበልሕ፡ እምሰይፍ፡ ወእመላጺ፡ ኤልባሕኮን፡ ዘኮነ፡ አጋዜ፡ ኮሉ፡ ወ[.]ተፈታሕ፡ ልቡ፡ በጋለ፡ (sic) ዝንቱ፡ አስማትከ፡ (sic) አብርሁ፡ ፪ አዕይንተ፡ ልብየ፡ ወ፪፡ አዕይንተ፡ መጽሐፍት፡ ለአንብቦ፡ ወለተርጉሞ፡ ወለቃለ፡ ድርሰት፡ . . .
7. F. 129r: Imposition of the hand of the Anaphora of Our Lord.

Notes:
1. The codex has been rebound in some disorder; some missing texts have been copied in different hands.
2. Decorative designs: ff. 5v, 45r, 52r, 66r, 75v, and 103v (stops connected by lines); f. 122v (short strokes framed in box using black).
3. F. 129v: Isolated names.
4. F. Ir blank
5. Splice of page: f. 7.
6. Overlooked lines of text are written interlinearly (ff. 13r, 15v, 23r, 26r, etc.); and in the upper margin with a symbol (⊥) marking the location where the text is to be inserted (ff. 32r, 50v, 71r, 75r, 85v, 86v, 93r, 98r, and 101r), and in another case where the symbol + is used (f. 73r).

Quire Map

Protection Sheet   i
This folio is from a different source than the others.

Quire 1   1 2
The quire has a reinforcement strip, making the analysis of its architecture impossible.

Quire 2   3 4 5
The quire has a reinforcement strip, making the analysis of its architecture impossible.

Quire 3   6 7 8 9 10
The quire has a reinforcement strip, making the analysis of its architecture impossible.

Quire 4	11 12 13 14 The quire has a reinforcement strip, making the analysis of its architecture impossible.
Quire 5	15 16 17 18 The quire has a reinforcement strip, making the analysis of its architecture impossible.
Quire 6	19 20 21 22 23 24 The quire has a reinforcement strip, making the analysis of its architecture impossible.
Quire 7	25 26 27 28 29 30 The quire has a reinforcement strip, making the analysis of its architecture impossible.
Quire 8	31 32 33 34 The quire has a reinforcement strip, making the analysis of its architecture impossible.
Quire 9	35 36 37 38 The quire has a reinforcement strip, making the analysis of its architecture impossible.
Quire 10	39 40 41 42 43 44 45 46 47 48 49 50 51 The quire has a reinforcement strip, making the analysis of its architecture impossible.
Quire 11	52 53 54 55 56 57 The quire has a reinforcement strip, making the analysis of its architecture impossible.
Quire 12	58 59 60 61 62 63 64 65 66 67 68 69 70 71 The quire has a reinforcement strip, making the analysis of its architecture impossible.
Quire 13	72 73 74 75 76 77 78 79 80 The quire has a reinforcement strip, making the analysis of its architecture impossible.
Quire 14	81 82 83 84 85 86 87 88 89 90 91 92 93 94 The quire has a reinforcement strip, making the analysis of its architecture impossible.
	95 96 97 98 99 100 101 102 103

Quire 15   The quire has a reinforcement strip, making the analysis of its architecture impossible.

Quire 16   The quire has a reinforcement strip, making the analysis of its architecture impossible.

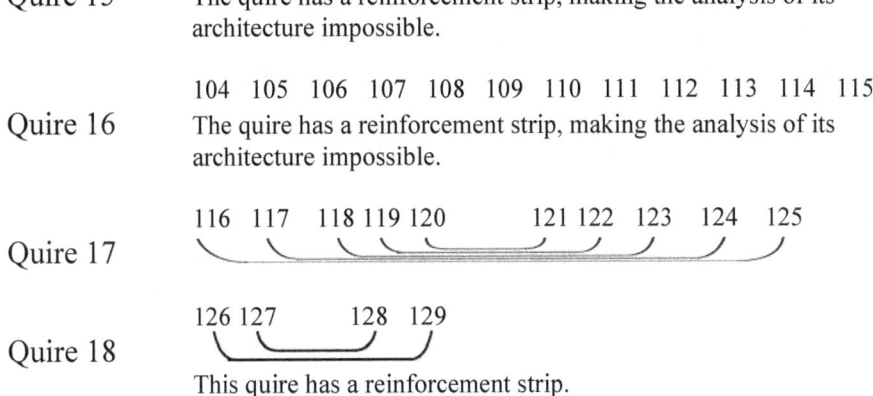

Quire 17

Quire 18

This quire has a reinforcement strip.

EMIP 28 – Eliza Codex 7
Psalter, ዳዊት፡

Parchment, 140 x 83 x 50 mm, four Coptic chain stitches attached with bridle attachments to rough-hewn boards covered with tooled leather, headband and tailband, protection quire + 21 full quires, quires 2–21 numbered, iv + 158 folios, 141 x 83 mm folio, top margin 10 mm, bottom margin 32 mm, fore edge margin 10 mm, gutter margin 6 mm, ff. 1r–127v one column, ff. 128r–157v two columns, Gəʿəz, 26 lines, late 19th cent.

Quire descriptions: quires 1–21 balanced. Navigation system: various colored string sewn into corners of folios 26, 36, 50, 59, 62, 83, 97, 102 to mark content divisions. Single-slip case with a strap of woven rope.

1. Ff. 1r–142v: Psalter [*Dawit*]. Cf. EMIP 1.
   a. Ff. 1r–108r: Psalms of David.
   b. Ff. 108v–119v: Biblical Canticles.
   c. Ff. 120r–127v: Song of Songs, Hebraic version.
   d. Ff. 128r–137r: Praises of Mary [Wəddase Maryam]. Arranged for the days of the week (Monday, f. 128r; Tuesday, f. 128v; Wednesday, f. 130r; Thursday, f. 132r; Friday, f. 134r; Saturday, f. 135r; Sunday, f. 136r).
   e. Ff. 137r–142v: Gate of Light [Anqäṣä Bərhan].
2. Ff. 143r–148v: Image of Mary, መልክዐ፡ ማርያም፡. EMIP 25, f.1r.
3. Ff. 148v–150r: Liturgical hymn to Jesus Christ, አኀወረድከ፡. Hammerschmidt, *Texte*, pp. 20–27; EMML 1203, f. 161b.
   አክርስቶስ፡ አኀወረድከ፡ እምሰማያት፡ በእንቲአነ፡ ስምዓነ፡ አምላክነ፡ ወመድኃኒነ፡፡
   አክርስቶስ፡ አዘተሰባእከ፡ በእንቲአነ፡ ስምዓነ፡ አምላክነ፡ ወመድኃኒነ፡፡

4. Ff 150v–151r: Halleluiatic hymn to Jesus Christ.
መሐረን፡ አብ፡ ሃሌ፡ ሉያ፡ ተማሃለን፡ ወልድ፡ ሃሌ፡ ሉያ፡ መንፈስ፡ ቅዱስ፡ መሐሪ፡ ተዘከረን፡ በሀለክ፡ ለከ፡ ንጌኑ፡ ስብሐት፡ ወለከ፡ ነዓርግ፡ አኮቴተ፡
. . .

5. Ff. 151v–157v: Image of Jesus Christ, መልክ0፡ ኢየሱስ፡. EMIP, 26, f. 47r.

Varia:
1. F. Ir: Prayer of Ǝssetä Mika'el to Mary that she may give her the faculty of eloquence to praise her.
2. F. Iv: Record of purchase of the manuscript in [18]99 EC (1906/7 AD).
3. F. IIr: Prayer to Mary asking her to intercede with her Son "so that he may protect us from a wicked day."
4. F. IIv: Prayer to Täklä Haymanot asking him to intercede with Jesus "so that he may preserve our life."
5. F. IIIr–IVv: One miracle of the Trinity. EMIP 7, f. 6v.
6. Ff. 157v–158r: Prayer to God for forgiveness.
7. F. 158v: *Qəne* poem that some one claimed to have heard in his dream on Miyazya 5, 1894 (4/13/1902).

Notes:
1. Decorative designs: Open space, possibly left for a *haräg*: ff. 1r, 7r, 13v, 20v, 29v, 36v, 41v, 49v, 59v, 67r, 72v, 83v, 94v, 97r, 102v, 108v, 120r, 128r, 143r.
2. The name Wärqu Täsfayä, f. 158v.
3. Columetric layout of text: ff. 105v (Ps. 145), 106v (Ps. 148), 107v (Ps. 150), 112v (fourth biblical canticle), 116rv (tenth biblical canticle).
4. Overlooked words of text are written interlinearly (ff. 21r, 31v, 35r, 101v, 103v, 104r, 121r, 126r, 129v, 130r, 132v, 134r, 135v and 137r); and overlooked lines of text are written interlinearly (ff. 24r, 99r, 101 and 112v).
5. The scribe's chosen aspect ratio for the codex combined with the script size forces the scribe to reduce the font size at the end of lines to avoid having to go onto the next line throughout the codex (see ff. 1rv and 2rv for examples) But, where the line of text is still too long, the scribe completes the line of text above the end of the line (ff. 5v, 6r, 8v, 15v, 36v, 38v, 45v, 48r, 57r, 68r, 71v, 95r and 115r).

Quire Map

Protection Quire

Catalogue of the Ethiopic Manuscript Imaging Project · 81

Quire 1: 1 2 3 4 5 6 7 8

Quire 2: 9 10 11 12 13 14 15 16 17 18

Quire 3: 19 20 21 22 23 24 25 26

Quire 4: 27 28 29 30 31 32 33 34 35 36

Quire 5: 37 38 39 40 41 42 43 44 45 46

Quire 6: 47 48 49 50 51 52 53 54 55 56

Quire 7: 57 58 59 60 61 62 63 64 65 66

Quire 8: 67 68 69 70 71 72 73 74

Quire 9: 75 76 77 78 79 80

Quire 10: 81 82 83 84 85 86 87 88 89 90

Quire 11: 91 92 93 94 95 96 97 98 99 100

Quire 12: 101 102 103 104 105 106

Quire 13: 107 108 109 110 111 112

Quire 14: 113 114 115 116 117 118

Quire 15: 119 120 121 122 123 124

82 · *Catalogue of the Codices*

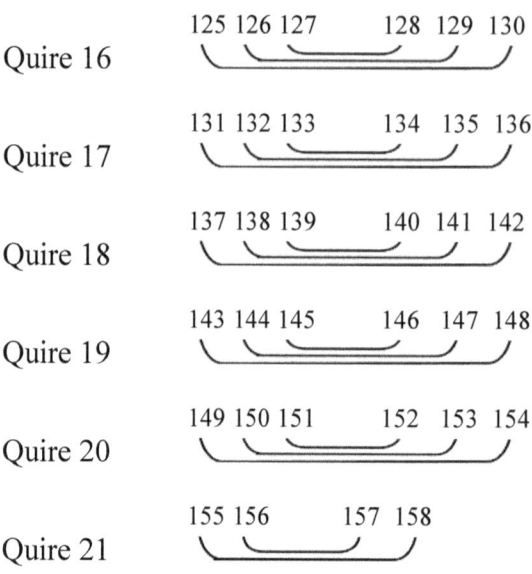

EMIP 29 – Whisnant Codex 1
Psalter, ዳዊት:

Parchment, 185 x 160 x 72 mm, four repaired Coptic chain stitches attached with bridle attachments to rough-hewn boards, 16 full quires, quires 2–14 numbered, 153 folios, 184 x 160 mm folio, top margin 15 mm, bottom margin 40 mm, fore edge margin 7–9 mm, gutter margin 12–13 mm, ff. 1r–134r one column, ff. 134v–153v two columns, Gəʿəz, 20 lines, 18th cent.

Quire descriptions: quires 1–8, 10–15 balanced; quire 9 adjusted balanced; quire 16 unbalanced. Navigation system: marginal notations to indicate readings in psalms.

Ff. 1r–152v: Psalter [*Dawit*]. Cf. EMIP 1.
1. Ff. 1r–115v: Psalms of David.
2. Ff. 116r–127v: Biblical Canticles.
3. Ff. 127v–134r: Song of Songs, common version.
4. Ff. 134v–147v: Praises of Mary [*Wəddase Maryam*]. Arranged for the days of the week (Monday, f. 134v; Tuesday, f. 136r; Wednesday, f. 138v; Thursday, f. 140v; Friday, f. 143r; Saturday, f. 144v; Sunday, f. 146r).
5. Ff. 147v–152v: Gate of Light [*Anqäṣä Bərhan*].

Varia:
1. F. 152v: What seems to be a note on land ownership, unfinished.
2. F. 153rv: Calendar of some feast days of the year.

Notes:
1. Decorative designs: ff. 1r, 40r, 115v (*haräg* using black and red); ff. 8r, 15r, 22v, 32r, 45v, 54v, 66r, 74r, 79r, 90v, 101v, 104r, 110r, 127v, 134r (dotted line using alternating black and red); f. 60 (two words boarded by a box using black and red); f. 152v (full-page line of stops).
2. Columetric layout of text: ff. 115rv (Ps. 150, word dividers using black and red), 123v–124v (tenth biblical canticle).
3. F. 60v: A small text in a black and red box marks the midpoint of the Psalms.
4. Note of ownership by Wäldä Ṣadǝq and his wife Wälätta Ǝgzi'bḫer, f. 134r.
5. Overlooked words of text are written interlinearly (ff. 27v, 72r, 78r, 79r, 105v, 128v, 130rv, 142v, 145v); and overlooked lines of text are written interlinearly (ff. 28r, 110r, 117r, 129r); and in the upper margin with a symbol (⊥) marking the location where the text is to be inserted (f. 78v, line 8); and in the upper margin with a symbol (⊥) marking the location where the text is to be inserted (f. 119r, line 15).
6. F. 103r: an incorrect text was written in the base text. A later hand has utilized correction dots and written the first corrected line interlinearly. The second line is written in the upper margin with no insertion symbol.
7. F. 126: correction dots have been employed in line 10. The text was later erased and the correct text was written in the fore edge margin.
8. F. 129v: an incorrect word was written in the base text. The word has been circled and the correct word is written above.
9. This scribe has largely avoided the problem of lines of text too long to fit on one line by adopting an aspect ratio that leaves ample room for the width of most lines. When the line would have been too long the scribe finishes the end of the line with words written smaller so as to avoid leftover text (e.g., ff. 6v, 10r, 12v, 16r, 22r, etc.). When a line is still too long and has to be completed above or below the end of the line. In these cases, the scribe places the material above the line (e.g., ff. 36r, 52r) or below the line (e.g., f. 37v).

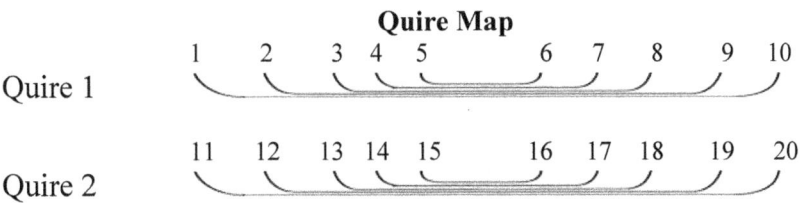

Quire Map

Catalogue of the Codices

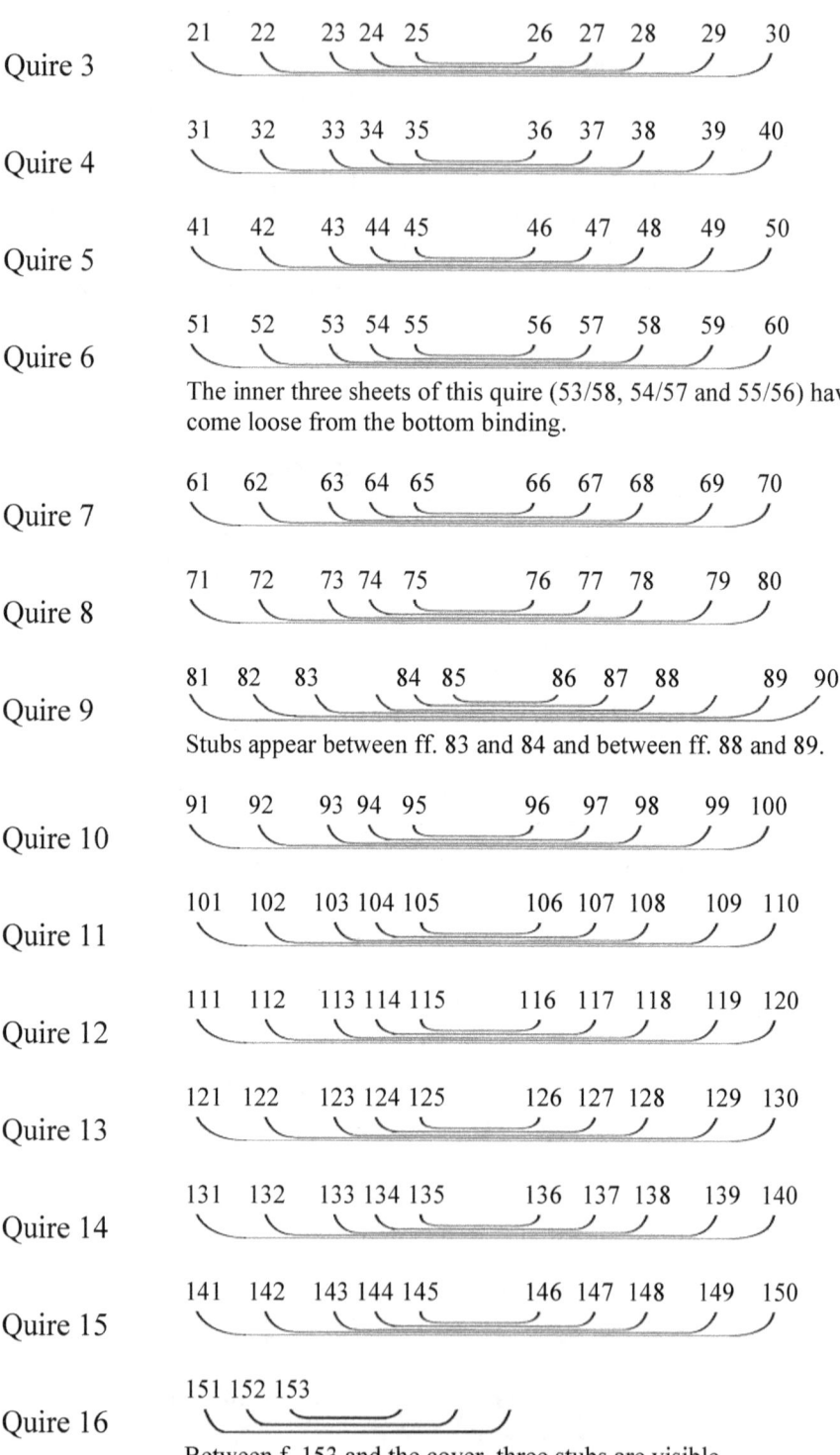

Quire 3: 21 22 23 24 25 26 27 28 29 30

Quire 4: 31 32 33 34 35 36 37 38 39 40

Quire 5: 41 42 43 44 45 46 47 48 49 50

Quire 6: 51 52 53 54 55 56 57 58 59 60

The inner three sheets of this quire (53/58, 54/57 and 55/56) have come loose from the bottom binding.

Quire 7: 61 62 63 64 65 66 67 68 69 70

Quire 8: 71 72 73 74 75 76 77 78 79 80

Quire 9: 81 82 83 84 85 86 87 88 89 90

Stubs appear between ff. 83 and 84 and between ff. 88 and 89.

Quire 10: 91 92 93 94 95 96 97 98 99 100

Quire 11: 101 102 103 104 105 106 107 108 109 110

Quire 12: 111 112 113 114 115 116 117 118 119 120

Quire 13: 121 122 123 124 125 126 127 128 129 130

Quire 14: 131 132 133 134 135 136 137 138 139 140

Quire 15: 141 142 143 144 145 146 147 148 149 150

Quire 16: 151 152 153

Between f. 153 and the cover, three stubs are visible.

EMIP 30 – Whisnant Codex 2
Psalter, ዳዊት፡

Parchment, 196 x 125 x 72 mm, four Coptic chain stitches attached with bridle attachments to rough-hewn boards covered with tooled leather (binding exposed) over decorative linen patches visible inside the turn-ins on front and back cover, 16 full quires, quires 2–10, 12–16 numbered, i + 153 folios, 193 x 125 mm, top margin 15 mm, bottom margin 34 mm, fore edge margin 21 mm, gutter margin 11 mm, ff. 1r–138r one column, ff. 138v–153v two columns, Gəʻəz, 23–24 lines, 18th cent.

Quire descriptions: quires 1–9, 11–15 balanced, though f. i of quire 1 is cut off; quire 10 adjusted balanced; quire 16 unbalanced. Navigation system: various colored string sewn into corners of folios 14, 65, 107, 113, 119 to mark content divisions.

Ff. 1r–178r: Psalter [*Dawit*]. Cf. EMIP 1.
1. Ff. 1r–119r: Psalms of David. Arranged for the days of the week (Monday, f. 1r; Tuesday, f. 22v; Wednesday, f. 45v; Thursday, f. 65v; Friday, f. 92r; Saturday, f. 107v).
2. Ff. 119v–131v: Biblical Canticles, designated for a day of the week (Sunday, f. 119v).
3. Ff. 131v–138r: Song of Songs, common version.
4. Ff. 138v–148v: Praises of Mary [*Wəddase Maryam*]. Arranged for the days of the week (Monday, f. 138v; Tuesday, f. 139v; Wednesday, f. 141r; Thursday, f. 143r; Friday, f. 145r; Saturday, f. 146v; Sunday, f. 147v).
5. Ff. 149r–153v: Gate of Light [*Anqäṣä Bərhan*].

Miniatures:
1. F. 22v: angel drawn in pencil.

Varia:
1. F. 153v: Prayer to Mary by the author whose name has been erased.

Notes:
1. Quires 14 and 15 are both numbered as 14, but quire 16 received the correct number.
2. Decorative designs: ff. 1r, 131v, 143r, 153v (*haräg* using black and red); ff. 32v, 40r, 74r, 79v, 104v, 119v (*haräg* using black); f. 138v (small *haräg* in top margin using red); ff. 1r, 7v, 14v, 22v, 32r, 39v, 45v, 54v, 65v, 73v, 79r, 92r, 104v, 107r, 113r, 119r, 139r, 141r, 145r, 146v, 148v (dotted line using alternating black and red); ff. 22v, 145r,

147v (dotted line using alternating black and red surrounded by *haräg*-like border); f. 146v (outline of a cross using black).
3. F. I cut out.
4. Back cover has tag with the following written: 1100– AF305
5. Columetric layout of text: ff. 76v (Ps. 95), 118v–119r (Ps. 150), 127v–128v (tenth biblical canticle).
6. Overlooked words of text are written interlinearly (ff. 43r and 146r); and overlooked lines of text are written interlinearly (f. 109v); and in the upper margin with a symbol (⊥) marking the location where the text is to be inserted (f. 23v, line 15).
7. The scribe regularly has to complete a line of text on another line. Much of the problem is addressed through the selection of an appropriate aspect ratio for the codex combined with an appropriate script size. This scribe will reduce the font size at the end of lines to avoid having to go onto the next line (e.g., ff. 1r, 4r, 7r, 15r, 18v, etc.). When a line is still too long it is completed above or below the end of the line. In these cases, the scribe places the material above the line (e.g., ff. 3v, 5r, 8v, 10r, 12rv, 14v, 16r, etc.), or below (e.g., ff. 6r, 10v, 14v, 16r, 18r, etc.).

Quire Map

Quire 1	i, 1, 2, 3, 4, 5, 6, 7, 8, 9 (F. i is cut off 1 cm from gutter.)
Quire 2	10, 11, 12, 13, 14, 15, 16, 17, 18, 19
Quire 3	20, 21, 22, 23, 24, 25, 26, 27, 28, 29
Quire 4	30, 31, 32, 33, 34, 35, 36, 37, 38, 39
Quire 5	40, 41, 42, 43, 44, 45, 46, 47, 48, 49
Quire 6	50, 51, 52, 53, 54, 55, 56, 57, 58, 59
Quire 7	60, 61, 62, 63, 64, 65, 66, 67, 68, 69

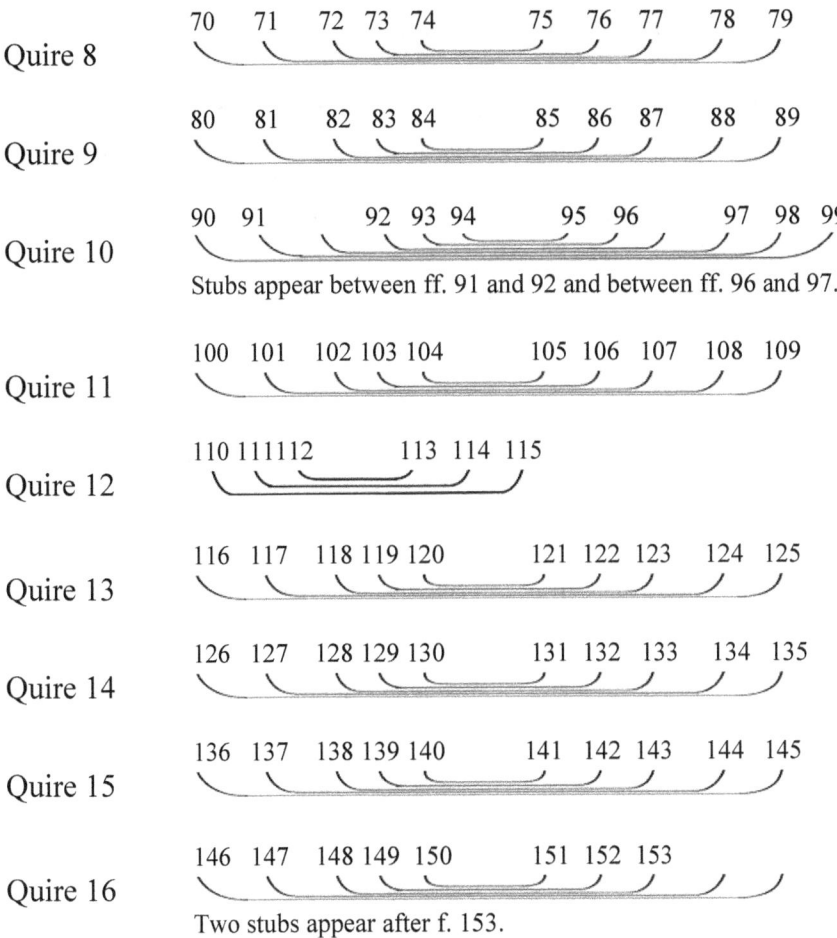

EMIP 31 – The Earl Codex
Miracles of Mary, ተአምረ፡ ማርያም፡

Parchment, 152 x 95 mm, four repaired Coptic chain stitches attached with bridle attachments to rough-hewn boards, 6 full quires, 54 folios, 149 x 95 mm, top margin 22 mm, bottom margin 36 mm, fore edge margin 16 mm, gutter margin 8 mm, ff. 1r–53v one column, Gəʿəz, 13 lines, Ṭəqəmt 27, 1933 EC (11/05/1940 AD), f.44v.

Quire descriptions: quires 1–4 balanced; quires 5, 6 unbalanced.
1. Ff. 1r–44v: Amharic Commentary on the Introductory Rite to the Miracles of Mary. For the Gəʿəz text, see TM 61, pp. 9–20.
2. Ff. 45r–51r: Three miracles of Mary. The standard works on the miracles of Mary are Cerulli, *Maria*, and Budge, *Mary*.

a. King Marəqos (Mark) who abandoned his throne for monastic life, f. 45r. TM 61, pp. 333–37.
b. How Our Lord and the Apostle built the first church dedicated to Mary and how, on the occasion, the Lord ordained Peter head of the Apostles, *arsäy astäfanos*, f. 47r. TM 61, pp. 130–32.
c. What will happen when the Lord comes for the second time, f. 49r. ተአምሪሃ፡ . . . ስምዑ፡ አበውየ፡ ወአኃውየ፡ ዘንተ፡ ምሥጢረ፡ ወመ(f. 49v)ድምመ፡ ዘንገሩኑ፡ አበዊነ፡ ሐዋርያት፡ ቅዱሳን፡ . . . ወይቤሉ፡ አሙ፡ ይመጽእ፡ እግዚእነ፡ በዳግም፡ ምጽአቱ፡ . . .

3. Ff. 51r–53v: Layman's prayer, in Amharic, *Addamən*, or *Noḫən*, expanded.
እግ" ርጎሩኃ፡ ልብ፡ አድጎነኒ፡ አዳምን፡ ከሲአል፡ ኖኅን፡ ከማየ፡ አይህ፡ . . .

Miniatures:
1. F. 54v: Crude drawing of two men, using purple ink.

Notes:
1. Decorative designs: ff. 1r, 45r (*haräg* using pencil).
2. Copied by Täklä Ṣadəq Gäbrä Iyyäsus for Wäldä Ṣadəq, f. 45r, and 53r.
3. Overlooked words of text are written interlinearly (ff. 6r, 12v, 53r).

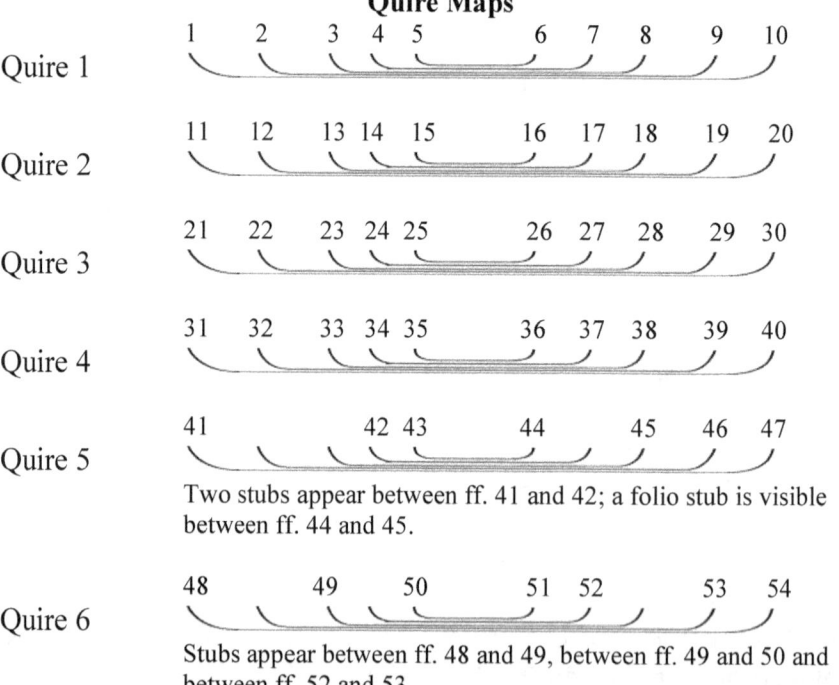

Quire Maps

Quire 1: 1 2 3 4 5 6 7 8 9 10

Quire 2: 11 12 13 14 15 16 17 18 19 20

Quire 3: 21 22 23 24 25 26 27 28 29 30

Quire 4: 31 32 33 34 35 36 37 38 39 40

Quire 5: 41 42 43 44 45 46 47

Two stubs appear between ff. 41 and 42; a folio stub is visible between ff. 44 and 45.

Quire 6: 48 49 50 51 52 53 54

Stubs appear between ff. 48 and 49, between ff. 49 and 50 and between ff. 52 and 53.

EMIP 32 – Delamarter Codex 1
Baptismal Ritual, መጽሐፈ፡ ክርስትና፡ ቅድስት፡

Parchment, three Coptic chain stitches attached with bridle attachments to rough-hewn boards, protection quire + 6 full quires, iv + 46 folios, 135 x 95 mm, ff. 1r–44r one column, ff. iiv(erso)–iiir two columns, Gəʻəz, 11–12 lines, second half of the 20th cent.

Quire descriptions: quires 2–6 balanced; quire 1 adjusted balanced.

Ff. 1r–44r: Baptismal Ritual, መጽሐፈ፡ ክርስትና፡ ቅድስት፡. Sylvain Grébaut, "Ordre du Baptême et de la Confirmation dans l'Église Éthiopienne," *ROC*, vol. 26 (1927–8), pp. 105–89; Ernst Trumpp, "Das Taufebuch der aethiopischen Kircher: Aethiopisch und Deutsch," *Abhandlungen der philosophisch.-philologischen Classe der Königlichen Bayerischen Akademie der Wissenschaften*, vol.14, no. 111 (1878), pp. 147–83; EMML 1106; Or. 11802. Strelcyn, *British Library*, p. 71.

በስመ፡ አብ፡ . . . መጽሐፈ፡ ክርስትና፡ ቅድስት፡ ወይብል፡ መዝሙረ፡ ዘ፻ወጸሎተ፡ አኮቴት፡ ወየሐትት፡ አስማቲሆሙ፡ ለእለ፡ ይጠመቁ፡

Prayer for the de-consecration of the water, f. 38v.

ወፈጺሞ፡ ይበል፡ ዘንተ፡ ፍትሐ፡ ማይ፡ እግዚአ፡ እግ"፡ አምላክነ፡ አምላከ፡ ኩሉ፡ ፍጥረት፡ ወኩሉ፡ እምነበ፡ አልቦ፡ በጥበቡ፡ ፈጠረ፡ ለዘአስተጋባእሙ፡ ለማያት፡ . . .

Prayer of blessing and imposition of the hand, f. 40r.

ጸሎተ፡ ባርኮ፡ ወአንብሮ፡ እድ፡ ለእለ፡ ይጠመቁ፡ ቅድመ፡ ቅብዓ፡ ሜሮን፡ ነአኩተከ፡ እግዚአ፡ ዘረሰይከሙ፡ ድልዋነ፡ ለአግብርቲከ፡ ለሕፅበ(f. 40v)ተ፡ ዳግም፡ ልደት፡

Varia:
1. F. Iv: Rejected leaf from a Synaxary manuscript, 5 Mäggabit: Eudoxia and Gäbrä Mänfäs Qəddus.

Notes;
1. Decorative designs: f. 38v (dotted line using alternating black and red).
2. Ff. Ir–IIr,IIIv–4v and 44v–46v blank
3. Provenance: From Demeke Berhane in Addis Ababa, May 2004.

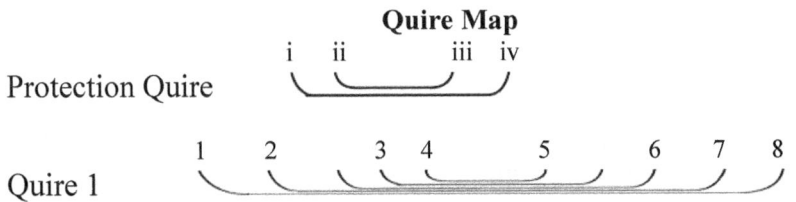

Stubs appear between ff. 2 and 3 and between ff.

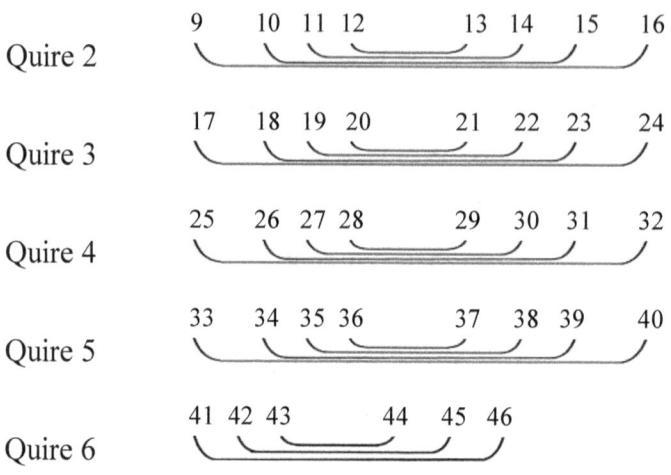

EMIP 33 – Eliza Codex 8
Sword of the Trinity, ሰይፈ፡ ሥላሴ፡

Parchment, four Coptic chain stitches attached with bridle attachments to rough-hewn boards, protection quire + 13 full quires, quires 4–6, 8–12 numbered (as numbers 2–4, 5–9 respectively), i + 118 folios, 159 x 106 mm, top margin 9 mm, bottom margin 30 mm, fore edge margin 23 mm, gutter margin 7 mm, ff. 1r–18v one column, ff. 19r–118v two columns, Gəʻəz, 15–22 lines; 18th (ff. 1r–18v, 19th) cent.

Quire descriptions: quires 1–5, 7–13 balanced; quire 6 unbalanced. Navigation systems: 1) brown yarn sewn into corners of folios 6, 22, 49, 66, 90, 97, 117, 118 to mark the location of miniatures; 2) string sewn into corners of folios 31, 56(?), 107 to mark content divisions. Single-slip case with a strap of leather.

1. Ff. 1r–5: A Story of the Trinity, ዜና፡ ነገሮሙ፡ (ለሥላሴ፡). EMML 1170, f. 7a.
2. Ff. 5r–8r and 10r–15r: Journey to Heaven, መንገደ፡ ሰማይ፡. An extended version; see Getatchew Haile, "Journey to Heaven. The Popular Belief of Reward and Punishment in Ethiopian Christianity," in Verena Böll *et al*, (eds.), *Studia Aethiopica in Honour of Siegbert Uhlig on the Occasion of his 65th Birthday*, Wiesbaden (2004), pp. 41–65.
3. F. 15v: Blessing of *Abunä* Yared.
ቡራኬ፡ ዘቅዱስ፡ ያሬድ፡ ዘይትበሀል፡ ለለዕላቱ፡ ስብሐት፡ ለእግ"፡ ዘፈጠረ፡ ሰማያተ፡ ወምድረ፡ ኪነ፡ ወተግባረ . . .

4. Ff. 16r–18v: History of Priest Yared. Yared was an Aksumite Musician to whom the composition of the *Dəggʷa* is ascribed. This story, which is slightly different from what is in *hid gädl*, is composed in Amharic, but the beginning is in Gəʿəz.
ዝታሪክ፡ ዘቅዱስ፡ ያሬድ፡ ባሕታዊ፡ ወድንግል፡ ዘይነግር፡ ኮነቶ፡ ዕንሰቶ፡ ወልደቶ፡ . . . ያሬድ፡ በተወለደ፡ በ፯፡ ዓመቱ፡ . . .

5. Ff. 19r–49r: Sword of the Trinity, ሰይፈ፡ ሥላሴ፡. Arranged for the days of the week (Monday, f. 19r; Tuesday, f. 22v; Wednesday, f. 27v; Thursday, f. 31v; Friday, f. 36r; Saturday, f. 41v; Sunday, f. 45v). Abbadie, 244, f. 13r, Conti Rossini, Notice, no. 106; EMML 1170; and EMIP 7.

6. Ff. 49r–64r: Wisest of the Wise, ጠቢበ፡ ጠቢባን፡. Arranged for the days of the week (Monday, f. 107r; Tuesday, f. 109v; Wednesday, f. 111r; Thursday, f. 112v; Friday, f. 113v; Saturday, f. 114v; Sunday, f. 116r). Dillmann, *Chrestomathia*, pp, 108–31; MG 59, pp. 118–63.
እግ"፡ ጥበበ፡ (sic) ጠቢባን፡ ከሃሊ፡፥
እስከ፡ ለዓለም፡ እምጥንት፡ እንት፡ (sic) ኢትበሊ፡፥
Concluded with an additional praise to God, ስብሐት፡ ለከ፡
ስብሐት፡ ለከ፡ እግ"፡ በሥርቀ፡ ዕለት፡ ወለያልይ፡ . . .

7. Ff. 64r–76v: Booklet of prayer that came down from heaven for a nobleman in the land of the Afrəgi. EMML 1169, f. 143a; EMIP 17, f. 1r;
በስመ፡ አብ፡ . . . አእግዚእየ፡ ኢየሱስ፡ ክርስቶስ፡ ዕቀ(f. 64v)በኒ፡ ለገብርከ፡ ሎቱ፡ ስብሐት፡ በእንተ፡ ዝኃደርከ፡ በከርሡ፡ ማርያም፡ . . ., f. 64rv.
ዝንቱ፡ (sic) መጽሐፍ፡ ከመዝ፡ ምጽአታ፡ እስመ፡ ነበረ፡ ፩፡ መኰንን፡ በሀገረ፡ አፍርንጊ፡ . . . , f. 73r.

8. Ff. 76v–90r: Prayer of the Twelve Disciples, ጸሎት፡ ዘ፲ወ፪አርድእት፡. Enno Littmann, "Arde'et: The Magic book of the Disciples," *Journal of the American Oriental Society*, vol. 25 (1904), pp. 1–48; for more, see the description of Or. 13265, Strelcyn, *British Library*, p. 15.
በስመ፡ አብ፡ . . . ጸሎት፡ ዘ፲ወ፪አርድእት፡ ዘወሀቦሙ፡ እግዚእነ፡ ኢየሱስ፡ ክርስቶስ፡ አመ፡ የዓርግ፡ ሰማየ፡ በዘይድኅኑ፡ እምኃጢአት፡ ወእምኰሉ፡ ሕማም፡ ሥጋ፡ ወነፍስ፡ ወእምኰሉ፡ ፀራዊ፡ ወሕምዘ፡ አርዌ፡ ምድር፡ ወእምኰሉ፡ ዘቦቱ፡ ሕምዝ፡ ዘይቀትል፡ ወእምኰሉ፡ ሕማም፡ ወድካም፡ . . . (78r) በኢያዜ፡ ስምከ፡ ግሩም፡ በሱራዜ፡ ስምከ፡ ዓቢይ፡ . . .

9. Ff. 90r–93r: Prayer of the Disciples for forgiveness of sin, ጸሎት፡ ስርየተ፡ ኃጢአት፡. Cf. EMML 1289, f. 18b.
ጸሎት፡ (sic) ስርየተ፡ ኃጢአት፡ ዘሰአሉ፡ ሐዋርያት፤ አእግዚአ፡ እግዚእየ፡ ኢየሱስ፡ ክርስቶስ፡ መሐሪ፡ ወመስተሣህል፡ . . . ስሪይ፡ ኃጢአትየ፡ . . .

በሴቃ፡ ወበዬቃ፡ ስምከ፡ እግዚአ፡ ርድአኒ፡ . . . (92r) ዛቲ፡ መጽሐፍ፡ ኢተጽሕፈት፡ በእደ፡ ሰብእ፡ አላ፡ ለሊሁ፡ መድኃኒነ፡ ኢየሱስ፡ ክርስቶስ፡ ዘጸሐፋ፡ በእዴሁ፨

10. Ff. 93r–96v: Sword of Divinity, ሰይፈ፡ መለኮት፡. Abbadie 171, f. 29v, Conti Rossini, Notice, no. 104; Abbadie 186, f. 104, Conti Rossini, Notice, no. 233; Strelcyn, Lincei, 47, f.88v; EMML 1169, f. 120b. በስመ፡ እግዚአብሔር፡ ቀዳማዊ፡ እንበለ፡ ትማልም፡ ወ(f. 93v)መግእክላዊ፡ (sic) ዘእንበለ፡ ዮም፡ ወደኃራዊ፡ ዘእንበለ፡ ጌሠም፡ ብሉየ፡ መዋዕል፡ . . . (f. 94r) ነአ፡ ኀቤየ፡ ኦእግዚእየ፡ ኢየሱስ፡ ክርስቶስ፡ ወልደ፡ እግ"፡ ሕያው፡ ወወልደ፡ ማርያም፡ ሥጋው፡ . . .

11. Ff. 96v–103r: The Mystagogia, ትምህርተ፡ ኅቡአት፡. EMIP 4, f. IIv (varia).

12. Ff. 103r–107r: The prayer, "God of the luminaries," እግዚአብሔር፡ ዘብርሃናት፡. MG 59, pp. 38ff; MQ 51, pp. 199–200; Daoud-Mersie, Liturgy, pp. 244–45; Sebastian Euringer, "Die äthiopische Anaphora des hl. Epiphanius Bischofs der Insel Cypern," Oriens Christianus, third ser., vol. I (1926), pp. 126–28.

13. Ff. 107r–117v: The prayer, "I take refuge," ጸሎተ፡ ተማኅጸንኩ፡. Arranged for the days of the week (Monday, f. 107r; Tuesday, f. 109v; Wednesday, f. 111r; Thursday, f. 112v; Friday, f. 113v; Saturday, f. 114v; Sunday, f. 116r). EMML 1170, f. 1a. በስመ፡ አብ፡ . . . ጸሎተ፡ ተማኅጸንኩ፨ በእግዚአብሔር፡ ብሑት፡ ሥልጣን፨ ተማኅጸንኩ፡ በኢየሱስ፡ ክርስቶስ፡ (f. 107v) ወልዱ፡ ለአብ፡ ከሣቴ፡ ብርሃን፨ . . .

Miniatures, all in twentieth-century hand:

1. F. ir: Crude drawing of the Archangel Michael brandishing his sword.
2. F. 6r: God the Father holding Orb.
3. F. 22r: *Abunä* Gäbrä Mänfäs Qəddus.
4. F. 49v: The Afringi nobleman receiving the Booklet of Prayer, cf. f. 64r.
5. F. 66v: Man looking ahead and pointing up (Jesus praying?).
6. F. 90v: Saint (Peter?) with a Book.
7. F. 97r: The Ascension.
8. F. 117r: The Archangel Michael Enthroned.
9. F. 118r: The Archangel Michael rescuing the Three Holy Children of the book of Daniel.

Varia:
1. F. Iv: Names of the months in the order of one replacing the other (?).
2. F. 8v: *Asmat* prayer against stomachache.
 በስመ፡ አብ፡ . . . ጸሎት፡ በእንተ፡ ሕማመ፡ ቀርፀት፡ ወጉሥምት፡ አከማቺ፡ መሳኪ፡ ወያኑሪ፡ ሐሡረ፡ እጅ፡ ወመግነዘጅ፡ ኪኪን፡ ካውሳን፡ . . .
3. F. 9r: Note that someone's age was 77 years in the Year of Luke.
4. F. 9r: Note that the age of Gäbrä Krəstos was 73 years on the feast day of Abbo in the month of Ṭəqəmt (5 Ṭəqəmt).
5. F. 9r: Will of *Mämhərə* Gäbrä Krəstos.
6. F. 9v: *Asmat* prayer against hemorrhage (and for bladder control).
 በስመ፡ አብ፡ . . . ጸሎት፡ በእንተ፡ ደም፡ ወማይ፡ ሰይፍ፡ ወአዶናይ፡ . . . ሎፍሐም፡ መሐፍሎን፡ ደም፡ ዓቤል፡ ደም፡ ትክቶ፡ ደም፡ ንስር፡ ዜት፡ ትዋራለሽ፡ . . .
7. F. 117v: Prayer of Wäldä Kahən that God may not separate him (by death) from the community.
8. Ff. 118v and Iv: Fragment of the Prayer of the Covenant, MQ 51, p. 260.
 ብ፡ (sic) እምኃጢአት፡ ጸላኢ፡ ንትዓቀብ፡ ስግዕ፡ ዘለዓለም፡ ንገሥ፡ (sic) . . .

Notes:
1. F. 117v: Note of ownership: "This book belongs to Gäbrä Ṣəyon whose teacher is Iyyo'ab; it was given to him by Lottu Səbḥat."
2. Decorative designs: ff. 1r, 107r (*haräg* using black and red); ff. 93r, 96v (dotted line using alternating black and red); ff. 31v, 41v, 49r, 64r, 76v, 103r, 117v (stops connected by lines).
3. Copied by Gäbrä Maryam for Gäbrä Krəstos, f. 15r.
4. Overlooked words of text are written interlinearly (ff. 37v, 38v, 51r, 58v, 60v, etc.); and overlooked lines of text are written interlinearly (ff. 51r, 61v, 73v, 76v, 96v, etc.); and in the lower margin with a line showing where the text is to be placed (f. 133v, line 14).

Quire Map

Protection Folio — i
A single folio is sewn into the front as a protection folio.

Quire 1

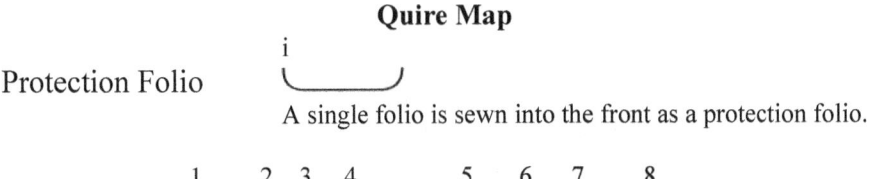

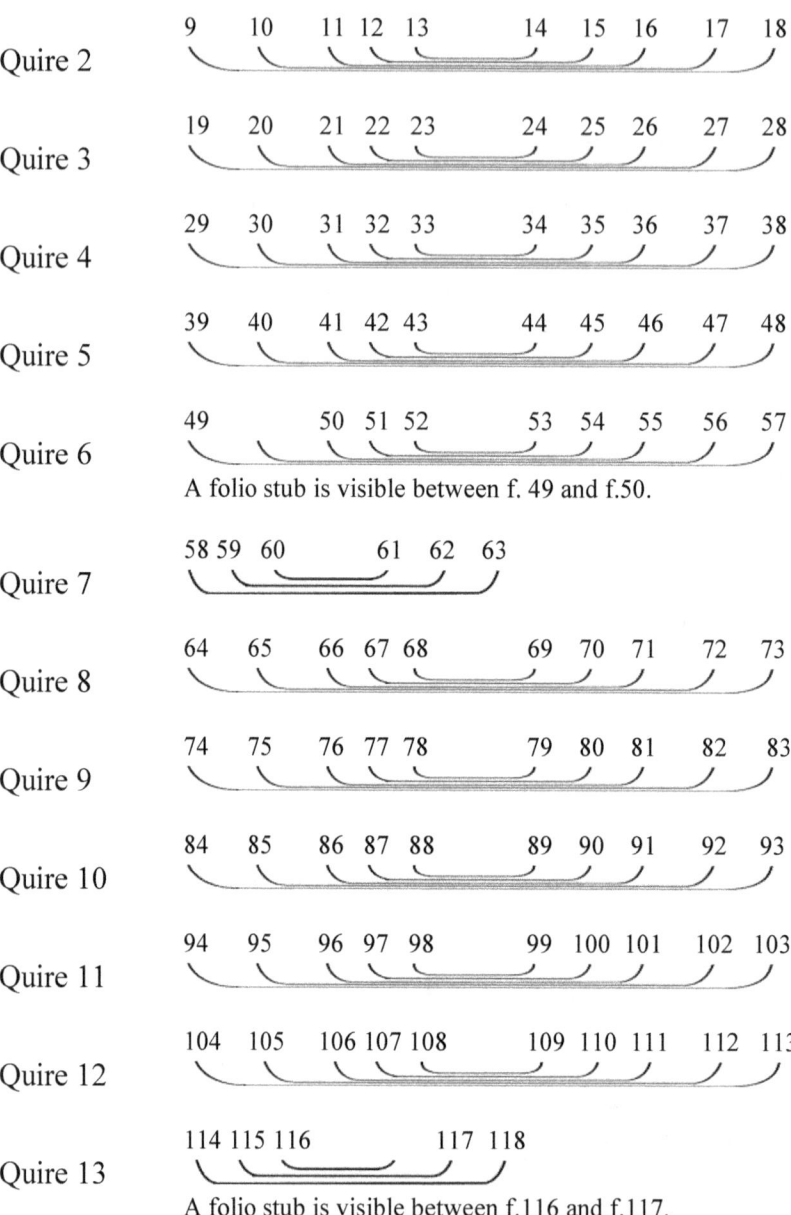

Quire 2: 9 10 11 12 13 14 15 16 17 18

Quire 3: 19 20 21 22 23 24 25 26 27 28

Quire 4: 29 30 31 32 33 34 35 36 37 38

Quire 5: 39 40 41 42 43 44 45 46 47 48

Quire 6: 49 50 51 52 53 54 55 56 57

A folio stub is visible between f. 49 and f.50.

Quire 7: 58 59 60 61 62 63

Quire 8: 64 65 66 67 68 69 70 71 72 73

Quire 9: 74 75 76 77 78 79 80 81 82 83

Quire 10: 84 85 86 87 88 89 90 91 92 93

Quire 11: 94 95 96 97 98 99 100 101 102 103

Quire 12: 104 105 106 107 108 109 110 111 112 113

Quire 13: 114 115 116 117 118

A folio stub is visible between f.116 and f.117.

EMIP 34 – Eliza Codex 9
Psalms of David, መዝሙር፡ ዘዳዊት፡

Parchment, 145 x 130 x 87 mm, four Coptic chain stitches attached with bridle attachments to rough-hewn boards covered with tooled leather, headband and tailband, 16 full quires, 123 folios, 140 x 127 mm, top margin 14 mm, bottom margin 27 mm, fore edge margin 19 mm, gutter margin 10 mm, ff. 1r–123v one column, Gəʿəz, 19–20 lines, 18th cent.

Quire descriptions: quires 1–4, 6, 9–11, 13–15 balanced; quires 5, 16 adjusted balanced; quires 7, 8, 12 unbalanced. Navigation system: crimson yarn sewn into corners of folios 8, 36, 78, 120 to mark the location of miniatures.

Ff. 1r–123v: Psalms of David: 1–139. , Rebound in disorder with few folios missing.

Miniatures, all in twentieth-century hand:
1. F. 8v: Madonna and Child.
2. F. 9r: Moses carrying the tablets.
3. F. 36v: Jesus, holding book, teaching multitude.
4. F. 37r: The Ascension.
5. F. 78v: The Resurrection, raising Adam and Eve.
6. F. 79r: The Striking of the Head.
7. F. 120v: The Visitation.
8. F. 121r: Zechariah and His Disciples.

Notes:
1. F. 51r: contains encircled and blacked-out text.
2. Decorative designs: ff. 43v, 44r, 50r, 73v, 101v (small, crude, *haräg*-like feature using black); ff. 8r, 15v, 34v, 87v (dotted line using alternating black and red); ff. 60v, 82r, 87v (dotted line using black).
3. F. 51r partially effaced.
4. Outer margin of f. 101 is partially cut out.
5. Note of ownership by *Aläqa* Fəssəḥa, f. 1r.
6. Overlooked words of text are written in the upper margin with a symbol (+) marking the location where the text is to be inserted (f. 22r, line 14).
7. The scribe regularly has to complete a line of text on another line. Much of the problem is addressed through the selection of an appropriate aspect ratio for the codex combined with an appropriate script size. But, where the line of text is still too long, the scribe completes the line of text above the end of the line (throughout).

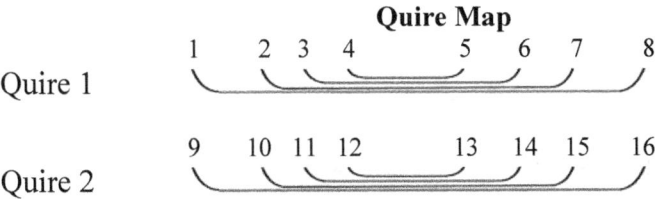

Quire Map

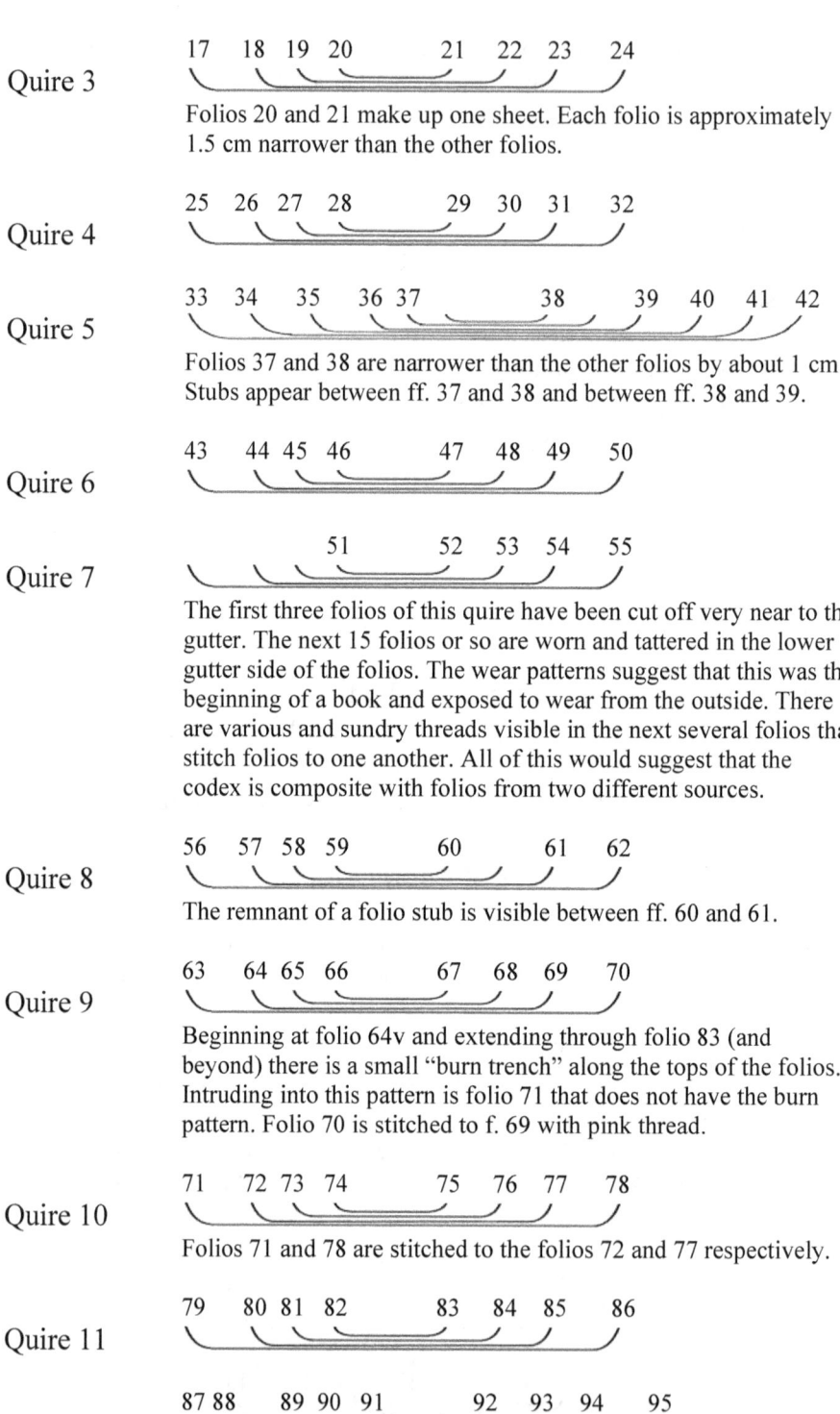

Quire 3

Folios 20 and 21 make up one sheet. Each folio is approximately 1.5 cm narrower than the other folios.

Quire 4

Quire 5

Folios 37 and 38 are narrower than the other folios by about 1 cm. Stubs appear between ff. 37 and 38 and between ff. 38 and 39.

Quire 6

Quire 7

The first three folios of this quire have been cut off very near to the gutter. The next 15 folios or so are worn and tattered in the lower gutter side of the folios. The wear patterns suggest that this was the beginning of a book and exposed to wear from the outside. There are various and sundry threads visible in the next several folios that stitch folios to one another. All of this would suggest that the codex is composite with folios from two different sources.

Quire 8

The remnant of a folio stub is visible between ff. 60 and 61.

Quire 9

Beginning at folio 64v and extending through folio 83 (and beyond) there is a small "burn trench" along the tops of the folios. Intruding into this pattern is folio 71 that does not have the burn pattern. Folio 70 is stitched to f. 69 with pink thread.

Quire 10

Folios 71 and 78 are stitched to the folios 72 and 77 respectively.

Quire 11

Quire 12

Folio 87 appears to be connected as a regular part of the folio, but an object can be run between either side (suggesting the open space between two folios). We judge it to be an individual folio.

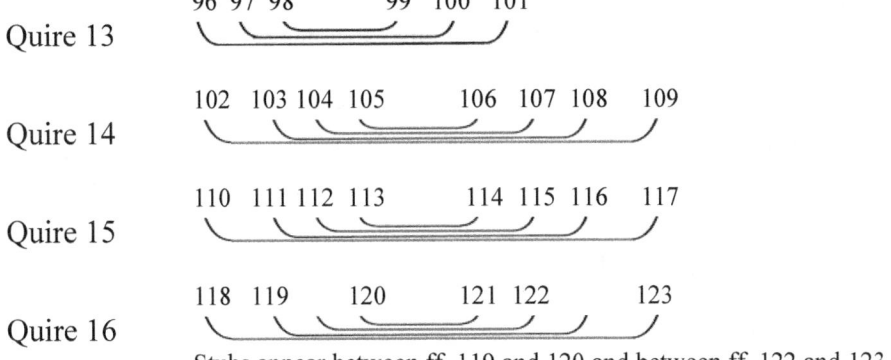

Stubs appear between ff. 119 and 120 and between ff. 122 and 123.

EMIP 35 – Eliza Codex 10
Psalter, ዳዊት:

Parchment, 192 x 122 x 78 mm, four Coptic chain stitches (one repaired) attached with bridle attachments to rough-hewn boards, protection quire + 19 full quires, ii + 177 folios, 187 x 115 mm folio, top margin 20 mm, bottom margin 35 mm, fore edge margin 15 mm, gutter margin 5 mm, ff. 1r–154v one column, ff. 155r–176r two columns, Gəʿəz, 20–24 lines, 19th cent.

Quire descriptions: quires 1, 3–19 balanced; quire 2 unbalanced. Navigation system: various colored string sewn into corners of folios 22, 33, 71, 118 to mark content divisions.

Ff. 1r–176r: Psalter [*Dawit*]. Cf. EMIP 1.
1. Ff. 1r–131v: Psalms of David.
2. Ff. 131v–146r: Biblical Canticles.
3. Ff. 146r–154v: Song of Songs, common version.
4. Ff. 155r–169v: Praises of Mary [*Wəddase Maryam*]. Arranged for the days of the week (Monday, f. 155r; Tuesday, f. 156r; Wednesday, f. 158v; Thursday, f. 161r; Friday, f. 164v; Saturday, f. 166v; Sunday, f. 167v).
5. Ff. 169v–176r: Gate of Light [*Anqäṣä Bərhan*].

Miniatures:
1. F. iiv(erso): crude pencil drawings of two crosses and a man.
2. F. 177v: crude pencil drawings of two crosses.

Varia:
1. Verso of the fore guard board: Prayer of the Archbishop (name not mentioned) and Bishop/Metropolitan Matewos (1881–1926).
2. F. IIv: The beginning of 1 John.
3. F. 154v: Chant for Easter, with musical notation, seven lines.

Notes:
1. Decorative designs: f. 155r (*haräg* using black and red); ff. i, 1r, 7r, 48v, 64v, 106r, 121v, 156r, 158v, 164v, 166v, 169v, 176r (crude *haräg* or *haräg*-like feature using pencil); ff. 7r, 15r, 22v, 33v, 42r, 59r, 71v, 81v, 87r, 101r, 115r, 118r, 124v, 131v, 146r (dotted line using alternating black and red).
2. Note of ownership by *Mämməre* Wäldä Mika'el, f. 109v and Abbäbä, f. 131r.
3. F. Irv: Illegible notes.
4. F. Iv: The name Giyorgis.
5. Ff. IIr, 176v–177v blank, save for some scrawls.
6. F. 67r: A red and black cross in the margin and an interlinear note mark the midpoint of the Psalms.
7. Overlooked words of text are written interlinearly (ff. 29v, 36r, 39v, 43r, 44r, 53v, etc.); and overlooked lines of text are written interlinearly (ff. 14r, 17v, 58v, 60v, 67r, 68v, etc.); and in the upper margin with a symbol (⊥) marking the location where the text is to be inserted (f. line 137v, line 6), and in another case where the symbol + is used (f. 119v, line 14).
8. The scribe regularly has to complete a line of text on another line. Much of the problem is addressed through the selection of an appropriate aspect ratio for the codex combined with an appropriate script size. This scribe will reduce the font size at the end of lines to avoid having to go onto the next line (e.g., ff. 1r, 18v, 19rv, 22v, 23r, 27r, etc.). When a line is still too long it is completed above the end of the line (e.g., ff. 13v, 25v, 27v, 43rv, 68r, 72v, etc.).

Quire Map

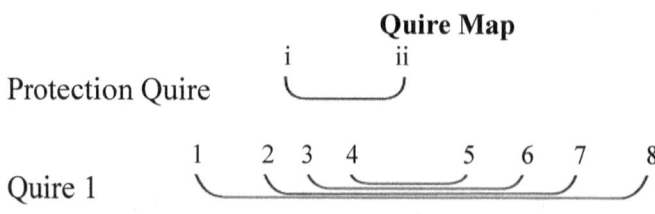

Protection Quire

Quire 1

Quire 2 9 10 11 12 13   14 15 16 17

Quire 2 is not attached to the book anymore and folio 11 is no longer attached to the quire.

Quire 3 18 19 20 21 22   23 24 25 26 27

Quire 4 28 29 30 31 32   33 34 35 36 37

Quire 5 38 39 40 41 42   43 44 45 46 47

Quire 6 48 49 50 51 52   53 54 55 56 57

Quire 7 58 59 60 61 62   63 64 65 66 67

Quire 8 68 69 70 71 72   73 74 75 76 77

Quire 9 78 79 80 81 82   83 84 85 86 87

Quire 10 88 89 90 91 92   93 94 95 96 97

Quire 11 98 99 100 101 102   103 104 105 106 107

Quire 12 108 109 110 111 112   113 114 115 116 117

Quire 13 118 119 120 121 122   123 124 125 126 127

Quire 14 128 129 130 131   132 133 134 135

Quire 15 136 137 138 139   140 141 142 143

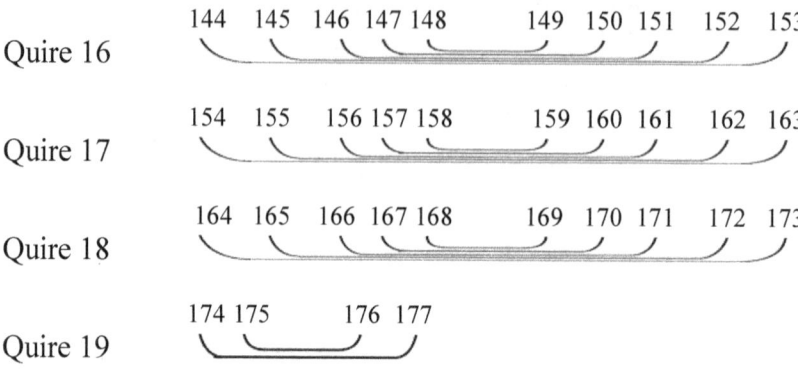

EMIP 36 – Eliza Codex 11
Miracles, ተአምራት፡

Parchment, 235 x 175 x 33 mm, four Coptic chain stitches attached with bridle attachments to rough-hewn boards, protection quire + 5 full quires, reinforcement strips around quires 1, 2 and 3, ii + 36 folios, 232 x 175 mm, top margin 30 mm, bottom margin 37–45 mm, fore edge margin 30–35 mm, gutter margin 7 mm, ff. iir–35r two columns, Gəʿəz, 20 lines, early 19th cent.

Quire descriptions: quires 1–5 balanced.

Ff. 1v–35r: Miracles of Mary, ተአምረ፡ ማርያም፡.

    a. Ff. 1v–7r: Extended version of Introductory Rite from Muʿallaqa, incomplete at the beginning. Cf. Budge, *Mary*, pp. xlvi–liv.
… (f. 6r) አሜን፡፡
አእግዚእትየ፡ ቅድስት፡ ወድንግል፡ በጀማርያም፡ ወላዲተ፡ አምላክ፡ እሙ፡ ለእግዚእነ፡ ኢየሱስ፡ ክርስቶስ፡ ከሃሊ፡፡
ሶበ፡ ይትነብብ፡ መጽሐፈ፡ ተአምርኪ፡ አክናፊኪ፡ ጸልሊ፡፡
ወሕንባቢሁ፡ አልዕሊ፡፡
ወአፀቂሁ፡ አጽድሊ፡፡

    b. Ff. 7r–8v: Introductory exhortation. Cf. Budge, *Mary*, pp. liv–lvii.

    c. Ff. 9r–15r: Four miracles, each concluded with a rhyming hymn.
        (1) Bishop Hildefonsus of Toledo, f. 9r. Budge, *Mary*, 1–2; TM 61, pp. 21–23.
        (2) The farmer to whom Mary spoke, f. 11v. Budge, *Mary*, 6–7.
        (3) The old man from Akhmim whom Mary made young, f. 12v. Budge, *Mary*, 8–9.
        (4) Yoḥannəs Bäkänsi whose sight Mary restored with her milk, f. 13v. Budge, *Mary*, 47–48.

    d. Ff. 15r–16r: Hymn to Mary, "I prostrate before you," እሰግድ፡ ለኪ፡።
Chaîne, Répertoire, no. 336/338.
እሰግድ፡ ለኪ፡ ወእዌድሰኪ፡ አአግዝእትየ፡ ማርያም፡ ለፀሐየ፡ ጽድቅ፡ ሠረገላሁ፡።
እሰግድ፡ ለኪ፡ አአግዝእትየ፡ ማርያም፡ ለመርዓዊ፡ ሰ[ማ]ይ፡ ጽርሐ፡።
    e. F 16r: Fifth miracle: The man who lost his mind when he lost his property.

1. Ff. 17v–21: Image of Mercurius, መልክዐ፡ መርቆሬዎስ፡. Possibly, Chaîne, Répertoire, no. 169. The beginning has been erased to make room for a painting.
ዘተከ፡ (for ዘተከዝከ፡?) ብዙኃ፡።
ሶበ፡ ሰማዕከ፡ እምወንጌል፡ በዓለም፡ ዕበድ፡ ዘረብኃ፡።
እምነ፡ ድልወቴ፡ ወአቅሙ፡ ያጠሪ፡ ስራኃ፡።
ሰላም፡ ለከናፍሪከ፡ ...

2. Ff. 21r–22v: Three Miracles of Mercurius.
    a. How a pagan was able to kill some one by the help of the Martyr, f. 21r.
ተአምሪሁ፡ ... ተብህለ፡ ከመ፡ ሀሎ፡ ፩አረጋዊ፡ ወርእዮሙ፡ ለቅዱሳን፡ ክርስቲያን፡ እንዘ፡ የሐውሩ፡ ውስተ፡ ቤተ፡ ክርስቲያን፡ ...
    b. How the lips of a paramour and a wife of another man remained stuck to each other when they kissed each other as she was preparing drinks for the feast of the Martyr, f. 21v.
ወሀሎ፡ [፩]ብእሲ፡ ዘሠረቀ፡ ብእሲተ፡ ካልዑ፡ ወበዕለተ፡ ተዝካሩ፡ ለብፁዕ፡ ወለቅዱስ፡ መርቆሬዎስ፡ እንዘ፡ ታስተዳሉ፡ [ስ]ቴ፡ ለበዓል፡ ...
    c. How the farmer who worked on the holy day of the Martyr was hit by thunderbolt, f. 22r.
ተአምሪሁ፡ ለብፁዕ፡ ወለቅዱስ፡ መስተጋድል፡ መርቆሬዎስ፡ ጸሎቱ፡ ... ወአመ፡ በዓሉ፡ ለቅዱስ፡ መርቆሬዎስ፡ ዘዐለተ፡ ቅዳሴ፡ ቤቱ፡ ወዕአ፡ ፩ብእሲ፡ ከመ፡ይሕርስ፡ ገራንቶ፡ ...

3. Ff. 22v–24v: Two miracles of *Abunä* Täklä Haymanot.
    a. How *Abunä* Täklä Haymanot called a pagan woman to join the monastic community of Däbrä Libanos, f. 22v.
በስመ፡ አብ፡ ... ወእምዝ፡ ንጽሐፍ፡ እንከ፡ ቅድመ፡ ዘተገብረ፡ በደብረ፡ ሊባኖስ፡ ተአምር፡ ወካዕበ፡ ይቤ፡ ዓዲ፡ በውስተ፡ አሕጉር፡ ስምዑ፡ ፍቁራንየ፡ ... ወሀለወት፡ አሐቲ፡ ብእሲት፡ አረጋዊት፡ ...
    b. How a mule refused to eat the grain belonging to (the monastery of) *Abunä* Täklä Haymanot, f. 24v.
ተአምሪሁ፡ ... ወከመሁ፡ በካልእትኒ፡ ሀገር፡ እምእክለ፡ አቡነ፡ ቅዱስ፡ ተክለ፡ ሃይማኖት፡ ወሀብዎ፡ ለበቅል፡ ...

4. Ff. 25v–35r: Ten miracles of Jesus; the tenth being incomplete at the end.
   a. The stolen calf, f. 25v. Grébaut, Jésus II, pp. 775–79; EMML 2180, f. 49a.
   b. The lions of the land of Asqalon, f. 26r. Grébaut, Jésus III, pp. 821–23; EMML 2180, f. 78a.
   c. The changing of the water to wine at the wedding Cana of Galilee, f. 27r. EMML 2180, f. 90b.
   d. The adulteress, f. 28v. Grébaut, Jésus II, pp. 804–48; EMML 2180, f. 56b.
   e. The Presentation, f. 29v. Grébaut, Jésus I, pp. 605–9; EMML 2180, f. 34a.
   f. Salome praises Christ, f. 31r. Grébaut, Jésus I, 589–92; EMML 2180, f. 28b.
   g. Healing of the Blind and dumb man, f. 32r. Grébaut, Jésus II, pp. 823–26; EMML 2180, f. 61b.
   h. Christ tells how it would be at his second coming, f. 33r.
      ወአሜሃ፡ ይጸርሕ፡ ገብርኤል፡ መልአክ፡ ላዕለ፡ ምስጢራትየ፡ ወሚካኤል፡ መልአክ፡ ይነፍሕ፡ ቀርነ፡ ወትርዕድ፡ ምድር፡ ወኵሉ፡ ዘውስቴታ ፡ ወዓዲ፡ ሰማያትኒ፡ . . .
   i. The betrayal of Judas Iscariot, f. 34r.
      ተአምር፡ ዘገብረ፡ እግዚእን፡ . . . ወእምዝ፡ ይቤሎሙ፡ ለአርዳኢሁ፡ ተንሥኡ፡ ንዑ፡ እምውስተ፡ ጽርሕ፡ ወወዕኡ፡ ኵሎሙ፡ ወበኡ፡ ውስተ፡ ገነት፡ ወሰብ፡ ነበሩ፡ ህየ፡ ወይቤሎሙ፡ እግዚእ፡ ኢየሱስ፡ ናሁ፡ ቀርበ፡ ጊቤየ፡ ዘየገብአኒ፡ . . .
   j. How the high priests conspired to bribe (the witnesses against Christ?), erased, f. 35r.

Miniatures, all in the late twentieth-century hand of the "beautiful artist":
   1. F. IIv: Crude drawing.
   2. F. 1r: Saint George and the Dragon.
   3. F. 16v: Mary Enthroned.
   4. F. 17r: The Resurrection, raising Adam and Eve.
   5. F. 35v: Two men with radiant halos and thin processional crosses, possibly *Abunä* Täklä Haymanot and *Abunä* Ewosṭatewos.
   6. F. 36r: The Annunciation.

Varia:
   1. F. IIr: Miracle of Martyr Märqorewos. The story does not make sense at all.
   2. F. IIrv: Miracle of *Abunä* Täklä Haymanot. The story does not make sense at all.

Notes:
1. Decorative designs: f. 7r (dotted line using alternating black and red).
2. Ff. I (strip of about a quarter of a folio) and 35v blank
3. Copied for Ḥaylä Maryam and (his wife) Wälättä Śəllase, ff. 7r, 9r and *passim*.
4. Overlooked lines of text are written interlinearly (f. 33r).

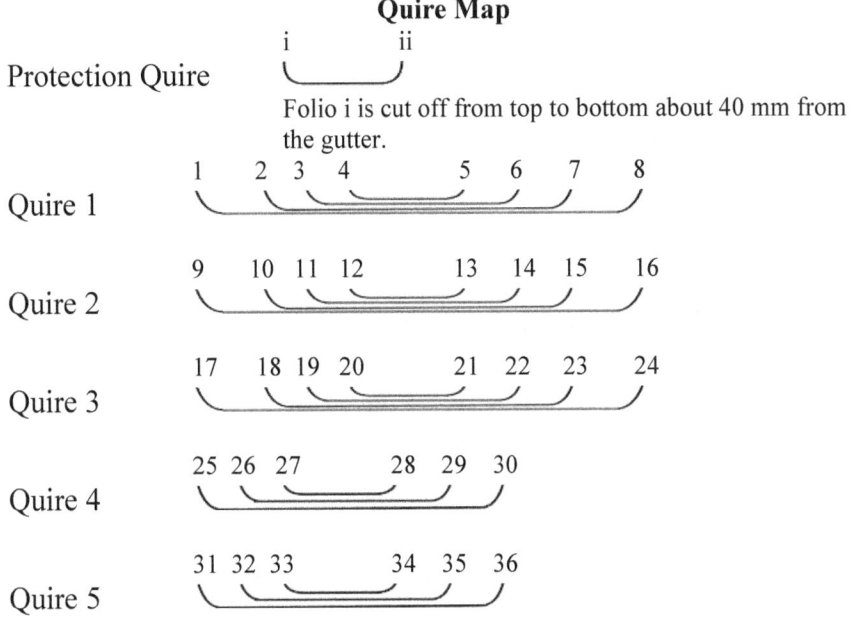

Folio i is cut off from top to bottom about 40 mm from the gutter.

EMIP 37 – Eliza Codex 12
Images — Anaphora of Our Lord, መልክዐ ጉባኤ፡ — ቅዳሴ፡ እግዚእ

Parchment and paper, 140 x 115 x 67 mm, four Coptic chain stitches attached with bridle attachments to rough-hewn boards covered with two linen coverings: 1) a two-pocket sleeve made of linen with a black background and pink flowers and green leaves; 2) an inner two-pocket sleeve made of linen with a red background and white and blue flowers going around both boards and spine. Underneath the second linen cover is a piece of lined paper 30 x 17 cm on which is written a text. One protection quire + 18 full quires, ii + 165 folios, 133 x 105 mm folio, Gəʿəz, 1916 EC (1923/4 AD), f. 78v; but most are late 20th cent.

This codex is comprised of several parts, that is, folios taken from various sources:

Part I: protection quire through quire 2.

Part II: quires 3–8. Note the frequent use of maroon string navigation system in these folios.

Part III: quire 9. This quire has several differences from the prior quires: 1) Its measurements are irregular, apparently to trim it for inclusion in this codex: the height of the sheets are 138 mm; the width varies from 100 mm at the top to 93 mm at the bottom; 2) the quality of the vellum is much finer and drier; 3) the side and bottom margins are mostly trimmed off; 4) there is no use of a full-stop symbol; 5) the hand is different; 6) the cut of the trim is uniform for all the folios of this quire.

Part IV: the outside sheet of quire 10, i.e. ff. 78/93, which may be in the same hand and text layout as that in quires 3–8.

Part V: folio 10 excluding the outside sheet (ff. 78/93) and the inside sheet (ff. 85/86). The folios of this part are made of paper that is lined in blue ink.

Part VI: the inside sheet of quire 10, i.e., ff. 85/86.

Part VII: quires 11–14. These have a new format (single column) but may be a resumption of the hand in quire 8.

Part VIII: quire 15. This quire is different from the others in that the text block is still in one column with 17 lines (as is the previous), however, the bottom has been trimmed and the bottom margin is smaller than normal.

Part IX: quires 16–18 (resumption of hand in quire 8? Note the resumed use of maroon navigation string system.) This quire is different in several respects. 1) The text block is laid out in two columns. 2) The bottom margins are very large (35 mm). 3) There are maroon-colored threads sewn into the upper fore edge of the following folios: 134, 136, 139, 140, 141, and 142. 4) The red ink is very orange in tint. 5) The full stop has only the four black dots.

Description of quires: quires 3–8, 10, 14 balanced; quires 1 and 2 adjusted balanced; quires 9, 11–13 and 15 unbalanced. Navigation system: maroon-colored string sewed into corners of ff. 19, 28, 38, 47, 55, 58, 64, 134, 136, 139, 140, 141, 142, and 144 to mark content divisions; marginal notations to indicate readings.

1. Ff. 1r–16r: Image of Täklä Haymanot, መልክዐ፡ ተክለ፡ ሃይማኖት፡. Chaîne, Répertoire, no. 211; MG 59, pp. 566ff.; EMIP 20, f. 104r.
2. Ff. 19r–66v and 78rv: Prayer of Mary at Bartos, ባርቶስ፡. Arranged for the days of the week (Monday, f. 19r; Tuesday, f. 28r; Wednesday, 37v; Thursday, 46v; Friday, 55r; Saturday, 57v; Sunday, 64r). Strelcyn,

Lincei, no. 54; Abbadie, 153, Conti Rossini, *Notice*, no. 201; C, Conti Rossini, "La redazione etiopica della preghiera della Vergine fra i Parti," *RRAL*, vol. V (1896), pp. 462–79; Basset, *Apocryphes* V, pp. 11–30; ጸሎተ እግዝእትነ ማርያም ዘሀገረ ባርቶስ, Täsfa Press, Addis Ababa 1963 EC.
በስመ አብ . . . ጸሎት፡ ዘእግዝእትን፡ ማርያም፡ ዘጸለየት፡ ባቲ፡ በሀገረ፡ ባርቶስ፡ ወተፈትሐ፡ ኵሉ፡ ሕጻውንት፡ በይእቲ፡ ጊዜ፡ ወአድኃነቶ፡ ለማትያስ፡ ረድእ፡ . . . ይቤ፡ እግዚእነ፡ . . . ለላእካኪሁ፡ ንጽሐን፡ ወለአርዳኢሁ፡ ቅዱሳን፡ ወኔራን፡ በእንተ፡ ጸሎት፡ ከመ፡ አልቦ፡ ዘየአምሪ፡ . . .

3. Ff. 68r–75v: Prayer to Mary, "Guard me," ዕቀብኒ፡. EMIP 17, f. 17v.
4. Ff. 76r–77v: Hymn to St. George (and Mary), "O who is quick for help," አፍጡኖ፡ ረድኤት፡. EMML 1214, f. 38a.
አፍጡኖ፡ ረድኤት፡ ለጽኑእ፡ ወለድኩም፡፡ ወለፍስ፡ ኵሉ፡ ቃውም፡፡ ጊዮርጊስ፡ የዋህ፡ እንበለ፡ መስፈርት፡ ወዓቅም፡፡
5. Ff. 79r–84v and 87r–92r: Image of Gäbrä Mänfäs Qəddus, መልክዐ፡ ገብረ፡ መንፈስ፡ ቅዱስ፡. Copied by Gäbrä Mika'el, f. 92r. MG 59, pp. 534ff.
ገብረ፡ መንፈስ፡ ቅዱስ፡ አቡነ፡ ለጽንስትከ፡ ቅዱስ፡፡ ወለልደትከ፡ ሰላም፡ ለወርኃ፡ (sic) ታኅሣሥ፡፡
6. Ff. 94r–101v: Prayer of the Covenant, ጸሎተ፡ ኪዳን፡. EMIP 3, f. 112r.
7. Ff. 102r–109r: Anaphora of Our Lord, ቅዳሴ፡ እግዚእ፡. See EMIP 27.
8. Ff. 109v–113r: The Prayer, "For the sake of the peaceful, holy things," በእንተ፡ ቅድሳት፡ ሰላማዊት፡. EMIP 20, f. 134v.
9. Ff. 113rv: Prayer after taking Communion.
ቅዱስ፡ ቅዱስ፡ ቅዱስ፡ ሥሉስ፡ ዘኢይትነገር፡ ሀቤኒ፡ ከመ፡ እንግአ፡ ለሕይወት፡ ዘንተ፡ ሥጋ፡ ወደምከ፡ እንበለ፡ ኵነኔ፡ . . .
10. Ff. 113r–117v: The prayer, "God of the luminaries," እግዚአብሔር፡ ዘብርሃናት፡. EMIP 33, f. 103r.
11. Ff. 117v–126r: Supplications titled ዘይነግሥ፡. Velat, *Me'eraf* I, pp. 23–29; MQ 51, pp. 277–84.
12. Ff. 126r–127r: Absolution of the Father.
ዘአብ፡ እግዚእ፡ እግ"፡ አኃዜ፡ ኵሉ፡ ዓለም፡ አንተ፡ ውእቱ፡ ዘትፈውስ፡ ቍስለ፡ ነፍስ፡ ወሥጋ፡ . . .
13. Ff. 131r–133r: Image of the Gate of Light, መልክዐ፡ አንቀጸ፡ ብርሃን፡. Incomplete at the beginning; MG 59, pp. 728ff.
14. Ff. 134r–145r: Image of the Praises of Mary, መልክዐ፡ ውዳሴ፡ ማርያም፡, arranged for the days of the week (Monday, f.134r; Tuesday, f. 135v;

Wednesday, f. 138v; Thursday, f. 140r; Friday, f. 141r; Saturday, f. 142r; Sunday, f. 143v.). Chaîne, Répertoire, 398; MG 59, pp. 701ff; EMIP 43, f. Ir (varia).

በስመ፡ አብ፡ . . . ሰላም፡ ለኪ፡ እንዘ፡ ንሰግድ፡ ንብለኪ፡ . . .
ተዓብዮ፡ ነፍስየ፡ አምጣነ፡ ብየ፡ ክህለ፨
ለእግ"፡ ወልድኪ፡ በከመ፡ አቅደምኩ፡ ብዕለ፡ . . . (134v.) . . .
ፈቀደ፡ እብዚእ፡ ለአዳም፡ ያግእዞ፨
ሡጋኪ፡ ንጹሕ፡ አሙ፡ ረሰየ፡ አራዞ፡

15. Ff. 145v and 154r–155v: Image of Mary, መልክዐ፡ ማርያም፡. EMIP, 25, f. 1r.

Miniatures, most in twentieth-century hand:
 1. F. IIr: Madonna and Child.
 2. F. IIv: Saint George and the Dragon.
 3. F. 11r: The Holy Trinity surrounded by the Four Living Creatures.
 4. F. 18v: Printed picture of the Madonna and Child pasted onto the folio. To the left of her head are the Greek letters MP and to the right are the letters ΘΥ. Under the image in Latin are the words *Sedes Sapientiae, ora pro nobis*! At the bottom of the image is the printer's logo: BLASI, INC.
 5. F. 27r: Two figures (a holy man and a woman) stand looking upward and to their right. A haloed figure is to the left and holds his right hand upward. Thumb is pointing up and the first two fingers are intertwined. The other fingers are folded back toward the palm. The figure to the right looks up.
 6. F. 59r: The Annunciation.
 7. F. 103r: The Resurrection, raising Adam and Eve.
 8. F. 144r: Angel brandishing a Sword.

Varia:
 1. F. 16r: Note on an unidentified legal case, in Amharic.
 2. F. 17rv: Prayer against the evil eye, ጸሎት፡ ንድራ፡. Or.4865, Strelcyn, *British Library*, p. 121; Abbadie 143, f. 49r, Conti Rossini, Notice, no. 109.

    በስመ . . . ጸሎት፡ ንድራ፡ ወእንዘ፡ የሐውር፡ እግዚእነ፡ ኢየሱስ፡ ክርስቶስ፡ ውስተ፡ ባሕረ፡ ጥብርያዶስ፡ . . .

 3. F. 67r: Record of purchase of land, in Amharic.
 4. F. 67v: *Asmat* prayer for the revelation of divine matters, ነገረ፡ መለኮት፡.

    ጸሎት፡ (?) አቀሙርያቅ፡ ወሰዳካኤል፡ እንበለ፡ ጢርስ፡ ቆፋኤል፡ ራኤል፡ በጵጵ፡ ቆጵ፡ የአስፈጫ፡ አርእዩኒ፡ ነገረ፡ መለኮት፡ . . .

5. F. 85r (pasted): Greeting letter from Taffäsä Azzänä to his uncle *Abba* Täklä Iyyäsus, concluded with a *Qəne* poem asking for (material) help from the recipient, written on Mäggabit 22, 1927 EC (3/1/1935 AD).
6. F. 92v: List of the days of the year on which heaven is open to receive prayers.
7. F. 93r: Receipt for money borrowed, Mäggabit 20, 1947 EC (3/29/1955 AD).
8. F. 146r: Record of the purpose of the money *Abba* Tākläyyäs Dačäw sent through his children, Mäggabit 8, 1947 EC (3/17/1955 AD).

Notes:
1. F. 16r: at the bottom of column one are two printed seals; f. 78v also has a seal.
2. Ff. 138v, 140r, and 141r contain a small rectangular box made of 8 smaller boxes (two rows of four).
3. Ff. Irv, 16v, 18r, 86v, 93v, 127v–130v, 133v, 146v–153v and 156r–165v blank.
4. Decorative designs: ff. 19r, 68r, 101v, 109v, and 113v (*haräg* using black and red); ff. 75v, 117v, and 134r (*haräg* using black ink or pencil); ff. 28r, 37v, 46v, and 142r (dotted line using alternating black and red); ff. 16r, 57v, 64r, 78v, and 113r (row or rows of full-stop symbols).
5. Ff. 85v–86r fragment of an Amharic text, insufficiently recognizable, copied by Wäldä Maryam, f. 78v.
6. Prayer for Säyfä Mika'el, ff. 18r, 32v, 34r, 41v and *passim*, and for Wäldä Iyyäsus, f. 78r.
7. Note of ownership by *Qesä Gäbäz Mämməre* Ayyälä, f. 133r.
8. Overlooked words of text are written interlinearly (ff. 10r, 51r, 141v and 142v).

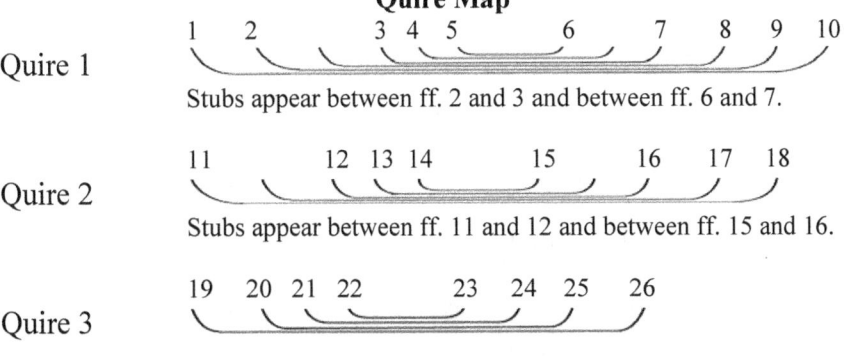

Quire Map

108 · *Catalogue of the Codices*

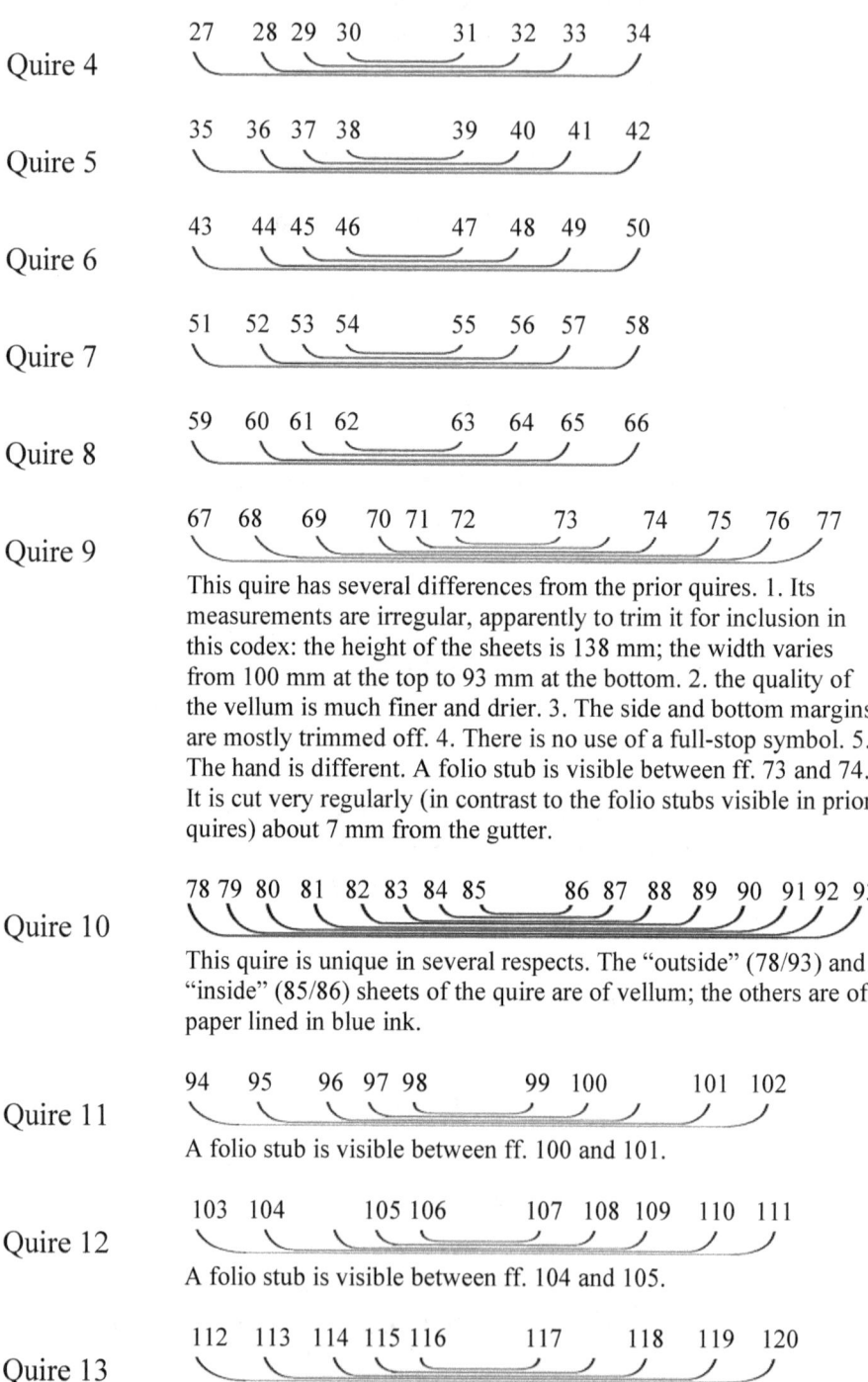

Quire 4: 27 28 29 30 31 32 33 34

Quire 5: 35 36 37 38 39 40 41 42

Quire 6: 43 44 45 46 47 48 49 50

Quire 7: 51 52 53 54 55 56 57 58

Quire 8: 59 60 61 62 63 64 65 66

Quire 9: 67 68 69 70 71 72 73 74 75 76 77

This quire has several differences from the prior quires. 1. Its measurements are irregular, apparently to trim it for inclusion in this codex: the height of the sheets is 138 mm; the width varies from 100 mm at the top to 93 mm at the bottom. 2. the quality of the vellum is much finer and drier. 3. The side and bottom margins are mostly trimmed off. 4. There is no use of a full-stop symbol. 5. The hand is different. A folio stub is visible between ff. 73 and 74. It is cut very regularly (in contrast to the folio stubs visible in prior quires) about 7 mm from the gutter.

Quire 10: 78 79 80 81 82 83 84 85 86 87 88 89 90 91 92 93

This quire is unique in several respects. The "outside" (78/93) and "inside" (85/86) sheets of the quire are of vellum; the others are of paper lined in blue ink.

Quire 11: 94 95 96 97 98 99 100 101 102

A folio stub is visible between ff. 100 and 101.

Quire 12: 103 104 105 106 107 108 109 110 111

A folio stub is visible between ff. 104 and 105.

Quire 13: 112 113 114 115 116 117 118 119 120

A folio stub is visible between ff. 117 and 118.

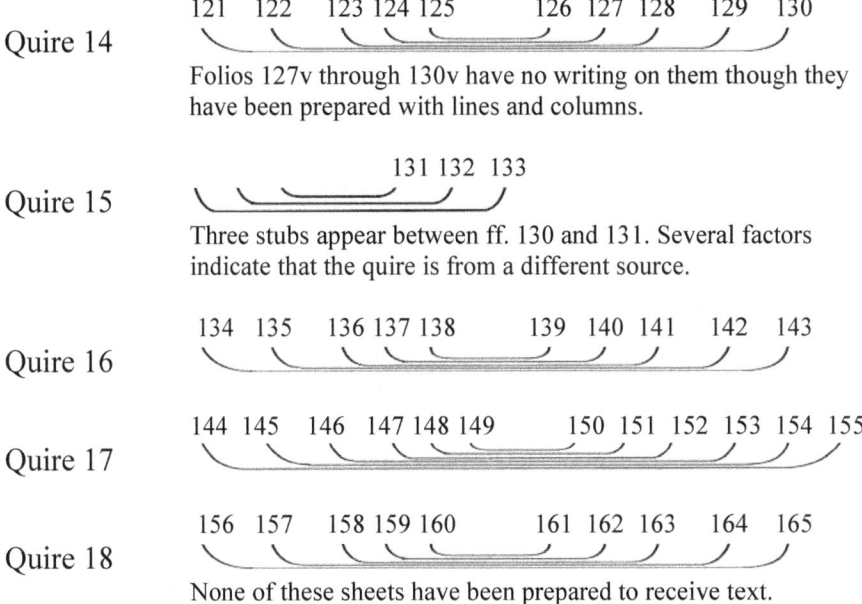

EMIP 38 – Eliza Codex 13
Gospel of John, — Image of Raguel, ወንጌለ፡ ዮሐንስ፡ — መልከዐ፡ ራጉኤል፡
Parchment, 175 x 125 x 35 mm, four Coptic chain stitches attached with bridle attachments to rough-hewn back board covered with a piece of cloth, front board missing, 10 full quires, 100 folios, 170 x 125 mm, top margin 10–15 mm, bottom margin 40–45 mm, fore edge margin 20–25 mm, gutter margin 10–12 mm, two columns, Gəʻəz, 19 lines, Ḫadar 23, 1993EC (12/2/2000), f. 78r.

Quire descriptions: quires 1–10 balanced. Navigation systems: 1) black yarn sewn into corners of folios to mark the location of miniatures; 2) various colored string sewn into corners of folios ff. 7, 14, 17, 31, 37, 42, 59, 67, 70, 74, and 81 to mark content divisions.

1. Ff. 1r–78r: Gospel of John, arranged for the days of the week: Sunday, f. 7r; Monday, f. 8v; Saturday, f. 14r; Tuesday, f. 17v; Saturday, f. 31r; Wednesday, f. 37r; Sunday, f. 42v; Thursday, f. 46r; Friday, f. 59r; Sunday, f. 67v, Wednesday, f. 70v; Sunday, f. 72r.
2. Ff. 78v–100v: Image of Raguel, **መልከዐ፡ ራጉኤል፡**. Chaîne, Répertoire, no. 365; MG 59, pp. 357ff.
3. Ff. 81r–99r: Anaphora of Our Lord Jesus Christ, **ቅዳሴ፡ እግዚእ፡**. See EMIP 27.

Miniatures:
1. F. 2r: Saint John.
2. F. 11r: Madonna and Child.

3. F. 41r: Saint George and the Dragon.
4. F. 61r: The Annunciation.
5. F. 80r: The Nativity.
6. F. 80v: Mary Enthroned.
7. F. 99v: The Baptism of Jesus.
8. F. 100r: Jesus holding orb in front of crowd.

Notes:
1. Decorative designs: ff. 1r, 81r and 99r (*haräg* using black and red); f. 6v (dotted line using alternating black and red).
2. F. 100v blank.
3. Copied for Wäldä Iyyäsus, ff. 1r and 81r.
4. Overlooked words of text are written interlinearly (ff. 90r, 92r and 98r).

Quire Map

Quire 1	1 2 3 4 5 6 7 8 9 10
Quire 2	11 12 13 14 15 16 17 18 19 20
Quire 3	21 22 23 24 25 26 27 28 29 30
Quire 4	31 32 33 34 35 36 37 38 39 40
Quire 5	41 42 43 44 45 46 47 48 49 50
Quire 6	51 52 53 54 55 56 57 58 59 60
Quire 7	61 62 63 64 65 66 67 68 69 70
Quire 8	71 72 73 74 75 76 77 78 79 80
Quire 9	81 82 83 84 85 86 87 88 89 90
Quire 10	91 92 93 94 95 96 97 98 99 100

EMIP 39 – Eliza Codex 14
Miscellaneous Prayers, ትምህርት፡ ኅቡአት፡ — ሰአልናከ፡ . . .

Parchment, 110 x 85 x 35 mm, four Coptic chain stitches attached with bridle attachments to rough-hewn boards, one protection sheet + 8 full quires, 48 folios, 105 x 77 mm, top margin 8–12 mm, bottom margin 10–20 mm, fore edge margin 5–10 mm, gutter margin 6–10 mm, ff. 1v–8v, 14v–45r one column, ff. 9r–14r two columns, Gəʿəz, 9–14 lines, 19th cent.

Quire descriptions: quires 1–8 balanced. Navigation system: black yarn sewn into corners of folios to mark the location of miniatures.

1. Ff. 1v–8v: The Mystagogia, ትምህርት፡ ኅቡአት፡. EMIP 4, f. IIv (varia).
2. Ff. 9r–13v: The different *Śärawitä mäla'əktihu* prayers of the different anaphoras, with musical notations.
3. Ff. 13v–14v: Time table for the use of the different anaphoras.
4. Ff. 14v–16r: Table blessing, ሰአልናከ፡. EMIP 17, f. 84rv.
5. Ff. 17v–19r: Litanical prayer to Jesus Christ, "For the sake of your …," በእንተ፡ . . . Incomplete at the beginning.
   በእን[ተ፡] አስተርዮትከ፡ በእን፡ ጸምከ፡ በእን፡ ሕማምከ፡ በእን፡ ተዕህዞትከ፡ . . .
6. Ff. 19r–21r: Halleluiatic hymn to the Trinity.
   ሃሌ፡ ሉያ፡ ሃሌ፡ ሉያ፡ ሃሌ፡ ለአብ፡ ወወልድ፡ ወመንፈስ፡ ቅዱስ፡ መላእክቲሆሙ፡ ለሥሉስ፡ እሩጾቶሙ፡ ለነፋስ፡ ሃሌ፡ . . .
7. Ff. 21v–22r: Calendar of the feasts of the year. Incomplete at the end, erased to make room for the forged painting.
8. Ff. 23v–26r: Greetings to Mary, በሐኪ፡. Incomplete at the beginning; Chaîne, Répertoire, no. 243.
9. Ff. 26r–32r: Hymn to the Martyr George, "Come, George," ነዓ፡ ጊዮርጊስ፡. EMML 2096, f.172b.
   ነዓ፡ ጊዮርጊስ፡ እንዘ፡ ትጼአን፡ በፈረስ፡፡
   ወነዓ፡ ፍቁርየ፡ ዘልዳ፡ ንጉሥ፡፡
10. Ff. 32r–36v: Rogation of the Archangel Michael, ምህላ፡ ዘሚካኤል፡.
    መልአኩ፡ ለቃል፡ ሚካኤል፡ መልአኩ፡ ለቃል፡ መልአኩ፡ ለቃል፡ ፪፡ ሚካኤል፡ መጋቢ፡ ኮሉ፡ ለነፍስ፡ ኮሉ፡ ፍጥረት፡፡
    አምሕለከ፡ በጸባዖት፡፡
    ምህላነ፡ ስምዓ፡ (sic) በዛቲ፡ ዕለት፡፡

11. Ff. 36v–45v: Hymn to Mary, "In the name of the Father and the Son," በስመ: አብ: ወወልድ:. Incomplete at the end, erased to make room for painting. Composed following the psalms of David. EMML 2481, f. 4a. በስመ: አብ: ወወልድ: ወመንፈስ: ቅዱስ: ሥላሴ:: ብሂለየ: ወጠንኩ: ዘለ(f. 37r)ኪ: ውዳሴ::

Miniatures, all in the late twentieth-century hand of "the speckled garment artist," written over the top of text:
1. F. 3r: Saint Peter holding a text.
2. F. 16v: Angel Surafel (Seraphim) brandishing a sword.
3. F. 17r: Madonna and Child.
4. F. 22v: Saint George and the Dragon.
5. F. 23r: Angel Kirubel (Cherubim) brandishing a sword.
6. F. 35r: Moses with the Ten Commandments and a star falling in background.
7. F. 45v: The Resurrection, raising Adam and Eve
8. F 46r: The Last Supper.

Varia:
1. Verso of the fore guard board and ff. 46v–47r: Isolated letters in a crude hand.
2. F. 1r: Medical prescription for an unidentified illness, in a crude hand.
3. F. 8rv: *Asmat* prayer to protect domestic animals from wild animals.

Notes:
1. Decorative designs: f. 36v (*haräg* using black and red); f. 19r (dotted line using alternating black and red); f. 32r: black line.
2. Copied for Gäbrä Ṣadəq, f. 32r.
3. Overlooked words of text are written interlinearly (ff. 37r, 38v,); and in the upper margin with a symbol (⊥) marking the location where the text is to be inserted (ff. 19v, line 4).

Quire Map

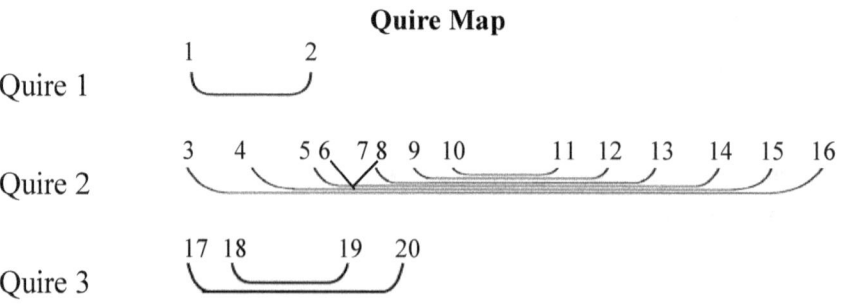

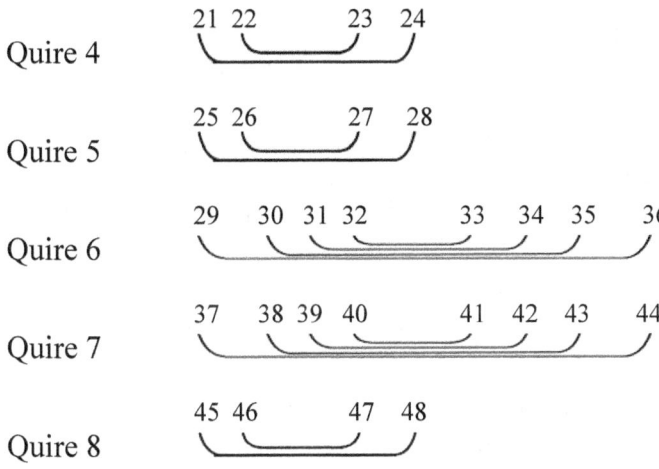

EMIP 40 – Eliza Codex 15
Psalter, ዳዊት:

Parchment, 178 x 120 x 65 mm, four Coptic chain stitches attached with bridle attachments to two rough-hewn boards, 1 protection quire + 16 full quires, quires 2–6, 8–9, 11, 13 numbered (the first folios of quires 7, 10 and 12 are covered with late miniatures), ii + 167 folios, 172 x 120 mm folio, top margin 12–14 mm, bottom margin 30–35 mm, fore edge margin 20–22 mm, gutter margin 10 mm, ff. 1r–150r one column, ff. 150v–167v two columns, Gəʿəz, 21 lines, $19^{th}/20^{th}$ cent.

Quire descriptions: quires 1–8, 12, 14–15 balanced; quires 9–11, 13 adjusted balanced; quire 16 unbalanced. Navigation systems: 1) brown yarn sewn into corners of folios 1, 35, 62, 94, 116, 127, 151, and 167 to mark the location of miniatures; 2) various colored string sewn into corners of folios 71, 80, 86, 101 to mark content divisions.

Ff. 1r–166r: Psalter [*Dawit*]. Introduced with the psalm of the shorter *Mäzmurä Krəstos* "Psalms of Christ. See መዝሙረ: ዳዊት: ምስለ: መዝሙረ: ክርስቶስ: Artistik Press, Addis Ababa 1952 EC, p. 1. For the content of the Psalter, see EMIP 1.

መዝሙረ: ዳዊት: ትመስል: ጎተ::
ታስተጋብእ: አቅማጎ: ወፍሬያተ::

A crude hand has attempted to arrange it for the days of the week.
1. Ff. 1r–130r: Psalms of David.
2. Ff. 130v–143v: Biblical Canticles.

3. Ff. 143v–150r: Song of Songs, common version, except for several lines written in the margin of f. 150r that are from the Hebraic version.
4. Ff. 151r–162r: Praises of Mary [*Wəddase Maryam*]. Arranged for the days of the week (Monday, f. 151r; Tuesday, f. 152r; Wednesday, f. 153v; Thursday, f. 155v; Friday, f. 158r; Saturday, f. 159v; Sunday, f. 160v).
5. Ff. 162r–166r: Gate of Light [*Anqäṣä Bərhan*].

Miniatures, numbers 2–9 are all in the late twentieth-century hand of the "speckled garment artist:"
1. F. Iv: Crude drawing of man brandishing a sword.
2. F. IIv: David Playing the harp.
3. F. 36r: Madonna and Child.
4. F. 63r: Saint George and the Dragon.
5. F. 95r: The Annunciation.
6. F. 117r: The Nativity.
7. F. 126v: The Baptism of Jesus.
8. F. 150v: Jesus Teaching the Multitude (Sending out the Seventy?).
9. F. 166v: The Arrest of Jesus.

Varia:
1. F. Ir: Birth record of Gäbrä Səllase, in an untrained hand.
2. F. Ir: Matt 27:37.
3. F. IIr: Copy from the introduction on f. 1r.
4. F. IIr: What seems to be birth (or death) record of an unidentified person.
5. F. 8r: The year in which some one was ordained priest, 1914 EC (1921/2 AD).
6. F. 167r: *Asmat* prayers whose purpose is not clear, in a crude hand.

Notes:
1. Decorative designs: Decorative designs: ff. 8r, 43v, 50r, 59v, 71v, 80v, 100v, 130r, 143v, (*haräg* using black or late pencil or pen); ff. 1r, 24v, 86v, 117v, 124r, 130v, (*haräg* using black and red); ff. 16r, 35r, 43r, 49v, 59v, 71v, 100r, 114r, 143v, (red and black dotted line).
2. The name Märgeta Gäbrä Maryam, f. Iv.
3. F. 66r: A small black cross above a text circled in black and red ink mark the midpoint of the Psalms.
4. F. 167v: Illegible words, erased.
5. Columetric layout of text: ff. 139v–140r (tenth biblical canticle), and many other places alternating red and black letters on the word "God"

when it appears in a line succeeding another with the word "God" directly above it.

6. Overlooked words of text are written interlinearly (ff. 122r, 151v, 160r); and overlooked lines of text are written interlinearly (ff. 61r, 81v, 92v, 93r, 96r, 98r, 150r).

7. The scribe's chosen aspect ratio for the codex combined with the script size forces the scribe to reduce the font size at the end of lines to avoid having to go onto the next line throughout the codex (e.g., ff. 1r, 3r, 6r, 7v, 10v) But, where the line of text is still too long, the scribe completes the line of text above the end of the line (ff. 2v, 3v, 5v, 6v, 7r, 8r, etc.) or below the end of the line (ff. 15r, 73v, 76v, 107r).

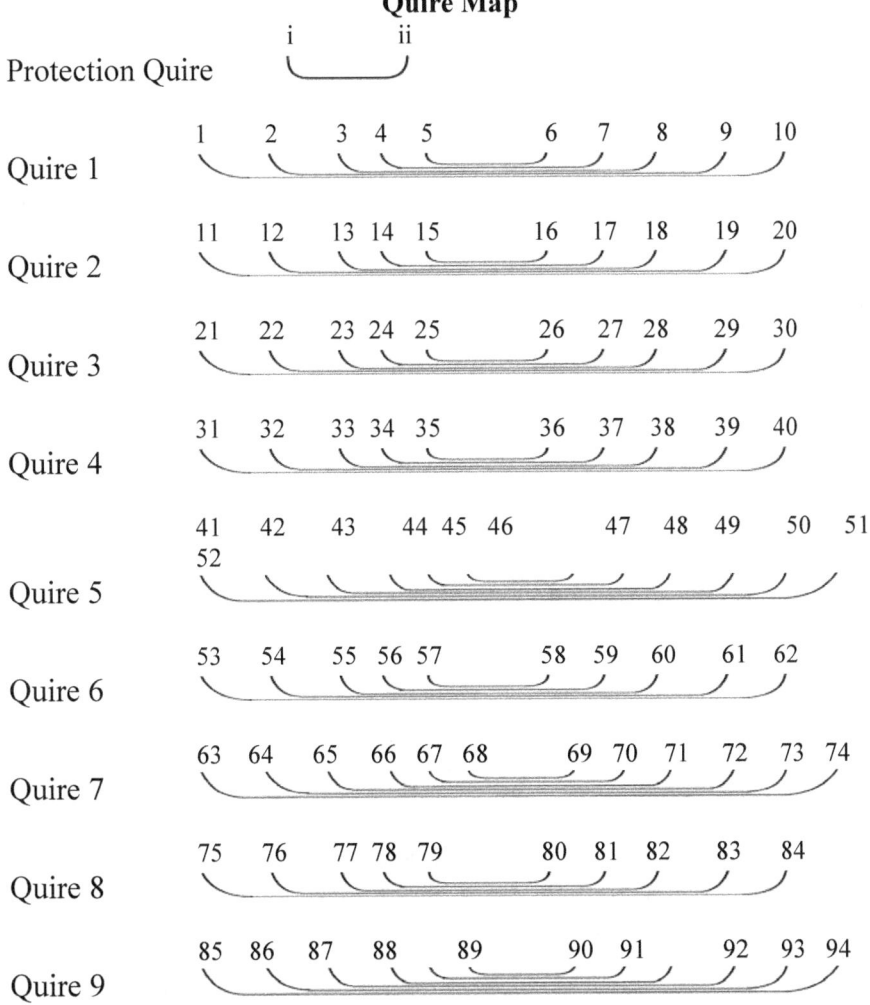

Stubs appear between ff. 88 and 89 and between ff. 91 and 92.

Quire 10: 95 96 97 98 99 100 101 102 103 104

Stubs appear between ff. 98 and 99 and between ff. 101 and 102.

Quire 11: 105 106 107 108 109 110 111 112 113 114 115 116

Stubs appear between ff. 109 and 110 and between ff. 112 and 113.

Quire 12: 117 118 119 120 121 122 123 124 125 126

Quire 13: 127 128 129 130 131 132 133 134 135 136 137 138

Stubs appear between ff. 131 and 132 and between ff. 134 and 135.

Quire 14: 139 140 141 142 143 144 145 146 147 148 149 150

Quire 15: 151 152 153 154 155 156 157 158 159 160

Quire 16: 161 162 163 164 165 166 167

Stubs appear between ff. 161 and 162, between ff. 166 and 167 and after f. 167.

EMIP 41 – Eliza Codex 16
Sword of the Trinity — Image of the Trinity, ሰይፈ፡ ሥላሴ፡ — መልክዐ፡ ሥላሴ፡

Parchment, 164 x 122 x 40 mm, four rebound stitches attached to rough-hewn boards, one protection quire + 8 full quires, 56 folios, ff. 1r–6v: 155 x 110 mm, 7r–56v: 163 x 120, top margin 10 mm, bottom margin 25 mm, fore edge margin 15 mm, gutter margin 10 mm, ff. 7r–56v one column, ff. 1–6v two columns, Gəʽəz, 18–22 lines, 20th cent.

Quire descriptions: quires 1–8 balanced. Navigation system: various colored string sewn into corners of folios 12, 22 and 40 to mark content divisions. Single slipcase with leather strap.

1. Ff. 1r–6v: Excerpts from the Lectionary for Passion Week, ግብረ፡ ሕማማት፡. With musical notation.

ሶበ፡ ሰቀልዎ፡ ሶበ፡ ሰቀልዎ፡ ሶበ፡ ሰቀልዎ፡ ለእግዚእን ፀሐዩ፡ ጸልመ፡ ወወርኅ፡ ደመ፡ ኮነ፡

2. Ff. 7r–8r: Halleluiatic hymn to the Trinity. EMIP 39, f. 19r.
አብ፡ ወወልድ፡ ወመንፈስ፡ ቅዱስ፡ መላእክቲሁ፡ ለስሉስ፡፡ ሩጻሎሙ፡ ከመ፡ ነፋስ፡

3. Ff. 9r–12r: Story of the Trinity, ዜና ነገሮሙ፡. EMIP 33, f. 1r.
4. Ff. 12r–48r: Sword of the Trinity, ሰይፈ፡ ሥላሴ፡. The usual miracles are included. Incomplete; texts are erased to make room for the pictures. Arranged for the days of the week (Monday, f. 12r; Tuesday, f. 17v; Wednesday, f. 22v; Thursday, f. 26v; Friday, f. 33v; Saturday, f. 37r; Sunday, f. 40r). EMIP 7.
5. Ff. 49r–56r: Image of the Trinity, መልክዐ፡ ሥላሴ፡. EMIP 7, f. 33.

Miniatures, all in twentieth-century hand:
1. F. 8v: Madonna and Child with haloed man (the owner of the manuscript) taking refuge.
2. F. 19r: Three Women: the first carrying firewood, the second grinding grain, and the third fetching water.
3. F. 35r: A man writing while inspiring hand of God appears in the clouds.
4. F. 48v: Saint George and the Dragon.

Varia:
1. F. 7r: Excerpt from the Computus, ባሕረ፡ ሐሳብ፡፡
2. F. 56v: Excerpt from the hymn of the Nativity.
ርእይዎ፡ ኖሎት፡ አእኩትዎ፡ መላእክት፡

Notes:
1. Decorative designs: f. 9r (*haräg* using black and red).
2. The name *Qes Mämmǝre* Däggu, recto of the rearguard board.
3. Name of the original owner erased and replaced with Wäldä Maryam of Gämza Safra, f. 56r.
4. Overlooked words of text are written interlinearly (ff. 46r and 53r).

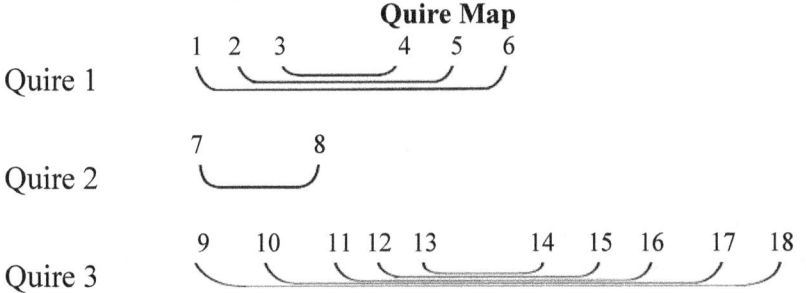

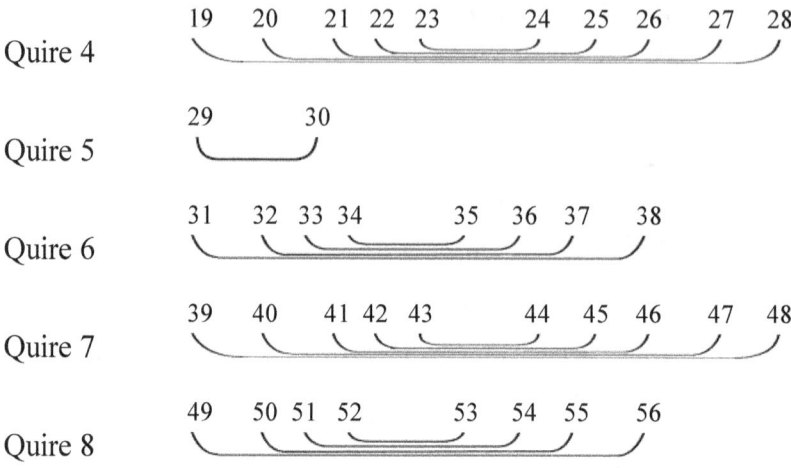

EMIP 42 – Eliza Codex 17
Horologium of *Abba* Giyorgis, ሰዓታት፡ ዘአባ፡ ጊዮርጊስ፡

Parchment, 148 x 140 x 65 mm, rebound with four stitches attached to rough-hewn boards. The front board is broken down the center; six holes have been drilled and the two pieces stitched together with copper wire. Similarly, the back board is broken about 40 mm from the fore edge. Six holes have been drilled and the two pieces stitched together with copper wire. Fourteen quires, reinforcement strips are common between ff. 45 and 98v, 98 folios, 150 x 137 mm, margins vary from quire to quire (cf. discussion below), ff. 1r–2r, 20rv, 27r–29v, and 34rv in one column; ff. 3r–19v, 21r–26v, 31r–32v, 35r–98r in two columns, Gəʻəz, 12–21 lines, 18th (ff. 21r–26v, 16th) cent.

Quire descriptions: quires 1–2, 4, 6–9, 11–12, and 14 balanced; quires 3, 5, 10, 13, unbalanced. Navigation systems: 1) brown yarn sewn into the corners of ff. 3, 29, 34, 58, 69, and 93 to mark the location of miniatures; 2) white string sewn into corners of ff. 63 and 72 to mark content divisions; 3) marginal notations (small crosses in red ink) in ff. 22r and 25r to indicate readings.

This codex is comprised of several parts, that is, folios taken from various sources:

    Part One: Quire 1 (2 folios) comes from one source. Quire 5 (1 folio) comes from the same source. On these quires there are 12 lines of text (Biblical Canticles) per page.

    Part Two: Quires 2 and 3 (15 folios) come from one source and are laid out in 16 lines per page.

Part Three: Quire 4 (2 folios) comes from one source and is laid out in 21, 19, 16 and 14 lines per folio.

Part Four: Quire 6 (6 folios) comes from one source laid out in 12 lines per folio. The hand is different. The page layout is different (2 columns). There are 12 lines per page.

Part Five: Quire 7 is a composite of sheets from various sources laid out in 20, 23 and 24 lines per folio. This quire is from a different source and is, itself, a collection of sheets from various sources. It has been stitched together secondarily with a stitch running about 5mm from the gutter. It has been attached to the codex also secondarily with brown string. The sheet constituted by ff. 27 and 34 has not been pricked and ruled. It bears two hands. The hand on the top of 27r (12 lines) and in 34r (15 lines) is the same and is in black ink; the hand at the bottom of 27r (4 lines) and on 27v (11 lines) and 34v (20 lines) is in a different hand in brown ink. The sheet constituted by ff. 28 and 29 has not been pricked and ruled. A trained hand has written on all four pages in one column. There are 20 lines of text on f. 28r, 24 lines on f. 28v, and 23 lines on f. 29r and v.

Part Six: Quires 8–13 and 14 (first 10 lines on the first folio) constitute a work from one source laid out in 12 lines per folio.

Part Seven: Quire 14, after the first 10 lines in col. 1, constitutes another work from another source laid out in 23 lines per folio.

Ff. 1r–93r: Leaves from the Psalter, Gospel of John and the Horologium bound together in some disorder.

1. Ff. 20v and 1r: *Magnificat*, ጸሎተ፡ እግዝእትነ፡ ማርያም፡ ድንግል፡, Luke 1:46–55.
2. Ff. 1v–2r: *Benedictus*, ጸሎተ፡ ዘካርያስ፡ ነቢይ፡, Luke 1:68–79.
3. F. 2r: One line from the beginning of the prayer *Nunc dimittis*, ጸሎተ፡ ስምዖን፡ ነቢይ፡.
4. Ff. 3r–17v: John 1–6:48. Arranged for days of the week (Saturday, f. 12v; Tuesday, f. 15v).
5. Ff. 18r–19v: Computus, ባሕረ፡ ሐሳብ፡. Based on the Year 7378 AM (1871 AD).
6. Ff. 20rv: The last part of the Song of Isaiah, ጸሎተ፡ ኢሳይያስ፡ ነቢይ፡ (Isa 26:14–20).
7. Ff. 21r–26v: John 20:2–21:17, 16th cent.
8. F. 27r: Excerpt from the first part of the Image of the Icon, መልክዐ፡ ሥዕል፡. Chaîne, Répertoire, no. 368; published as part of the Horologium, e.g. MBB 52, pp. 188–93,

አርነርነተ፡ ሐሊና፡ አፍቅሮተ፡ ሰብእ፡ ልማዳ፡፡
ሰአሊተ፡ ምሕረት፡ ይእቲ፡ ማርያም፡ ሐዉረ፡ መስቀል፡ ዘየዐውዳ፡፡

9. Ff. 28rv: Hymn to Mary, "I prostrate before you," እሰግድ፡ ለኪ፡. Chaîne, Répertoire, no. 336/338; EMIP 36, f. 15r.

10. Ff. 28v–29v: Image of Kiros, መልክዐ፡ ኪሮስ፡. Incomplete at the end.
መልክዕ፡ ዘአብ፡ ኪሮስ፡፡ አንቅሁኒ፡ እምሃኬትየ፡ ወጸግወኒ፡ ልቡና፡፡
ከመ፡ እዜኑ፡ ንስቲተ፡ ለስምከ፡ ውዳሴ፡ ዜና፡፡

11. Ff. 31r–34r: *Asmat* prayer against charm, መፍትሔ፡ ሥራይ፡. Incomplete at the beginning.
ከመ፡ [. . .]ሱ፡ ሚካኤል፡ ወገብርኤል፡ ፍትሑኒ፡ አፍኒን፡ ወራጉኤል፡
ወሳቁኤል፡ ወኮሎሙ፡ መላእክት፡ ሰማያውያን፡ ፍትሑኒ፡ ፱ ወንጌላውያን፡
ማቴዎስ፡ . . .

12. Ff. 35r–54v, lacuna, 55r–58v (59r erased), 59v–69v (70r erased), 70v–74v, lacuna, 75r–93r: Horologium of *Abba* Giyorgis for the night hours, ሰዓታት፡ ዘሌሊት፡ ዘአባ፡ ጊዮርጊስ፡. Incomplete, and rebound in disorder; MBB 52; EMML 1362, f. 1r.
ሰዓታት፡ ዘአባ፡ ጊዮርጊስ፡ ሃሌ፡ ሃሌ፡ ሃሌ፡ ሉያ፡ ሃሌ፡ ሃሌ፡ ሉያ፡ አአትብ፡
ወእትነሣእ፡ በስመ፡ አብ፡ ወወልድ፡ ወመንፈስ፡ ቅዱስ፡ ፩ አስግተ፡ ነዊኤየ፡
እትመረጕዝ፡ እመኒ፡ ወደቁ፡ እትነሣዕ፡ . . .

13. Ff. 93rv (f. 94r erased), 94v–98r: *Asmat* prayers against charm, መፍትሔ፡ ሥራይ፡.
በስመ፡ አብ፡ . . . መፍትሔ፡ ሥራይ፡ ተፈጁን፡ መሐጹን፡ በሀገረ፡ ዳጅን፡
ዘአቅደምኩክ፡ ወዘፈታሕኩክ፡ ሥራየ፡ ብእሲ፡ ወብእሲት፡ ሥራየ፡ ማሪ፡
ወማሪት፡ ሥራየ፡ ካህናት፡ ወዲያቆናት፡ . . .
. . . (f. 93v) . . . በስመ፡ አብ፡ . . . መስቀል፡ መግሬ፡ ፀር፡ ወሰዳዬ፡
አጋንንት፡ አንተ፡ እግ"፡ ኩን፡ ጸዋነ፡ ናዛዜ፡ ለሕዙናን፡ መጽንኤ፡ ለድኩማን፡
. . .

Miniatures, all in the late twentieth-century hand of "the speckled garment artist" and painted over text:
1. F. 2v: Moses with the Law?
2. F. 30r: Madonna and Child.
3. F. 30v: Angel brandishing a Sword.
4. F. 33r: Saint George and the Dragon.
5. F. 33v: Angel brandishing a Sword.
6. F. 59r: The Nativity.
7. F. 70r: Jesus Teaching.
8. F. 94r: The Striking of the Head.

Varia:
1. F. 27v: 1 John 1:1–2.

2. F. 34v: Copy from f. 35v, in a crude hand.

Notes:
1. F. 95r contains rows of identical letters.
2. Decorative designs: f. 31r (*haräg* using black and red); f. 19v (rows of full–stop symbols); f. 19v (ornate cross).
3. Overlooked words of text are written interlinearly (ff. 3r, 4v, 6v, 7r, 10r, 97r); and overlooked lines of text are written interlinearly (ff. 10v, 44r); and in the upper margin with a symbol (+) marking the location where the text is to be inserted (f. 8r, line 7).

Quire Map

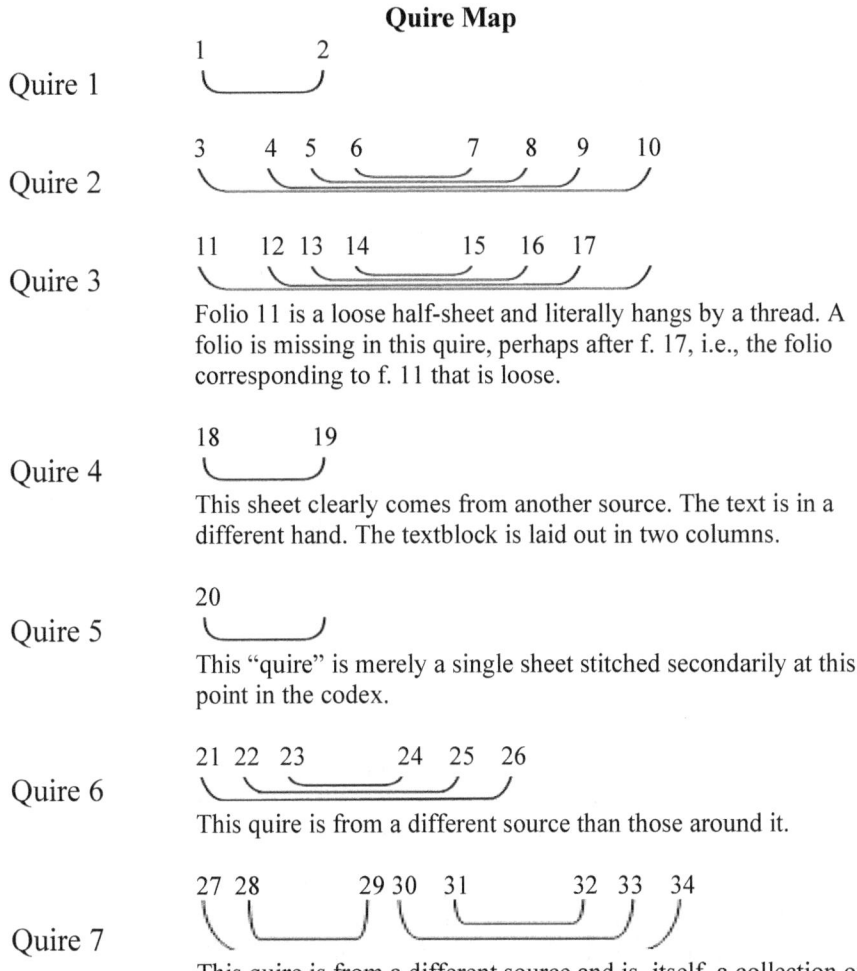

Quire 1

Quire 2

Quire 3

Folio 11 is a loose half-sheet and literally hangs by a thread. A folio is missing in this quire, perhaps after f. 17, i.e., the folio corresponding to f. 11 that is loose.

Quire 4

This sheet clearly comes from another source. The text is in a different hand. The textblock is laid out in two columns.

Quire 5

This "quire" is merely a single sheet stitched secondarily at this point in the codex.

Quire 6

This quire is from a different source than those around it.

Quire 7

This quire is from a different source and is, itself, a collection of sheets from various sources. It has been stitched together secondarily with a stitch running about 5mm from the gutter. It has been attached to the codex also secondarily with brown string.

Quire 8: 35 36 37 38 39 40 41 42 43 44

Quire 9: 45 46 47 48 49 50 51 52 53 54

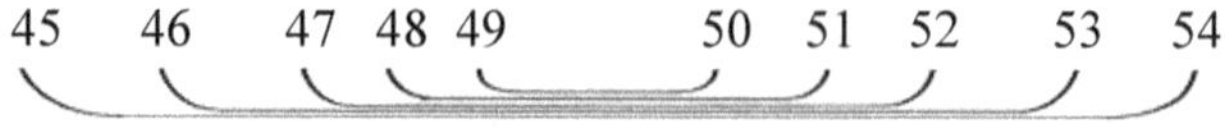

This quire and all subsequent quires have been reinforced with small strips of vellum sewn around the upper and lower outside sheet of the quire. Occasionally, such strips are sewn onto other sheets in the quire besides the outside one.

Quire 10: 55 56 57 58 59 60 61 62 63

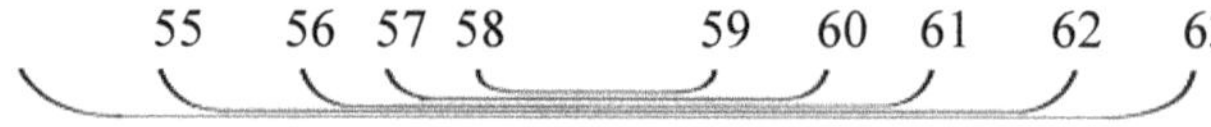

A folio (half-sheet) is apparently missing. It is not clear exactly from where.

Quire 11: 64 65 66 67 68 69 70 71 72 73

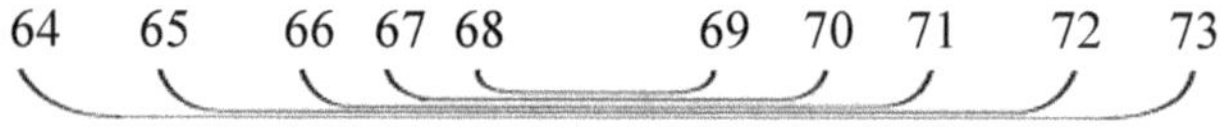

Quire 12: 74 75 76 77 78 79 80 81

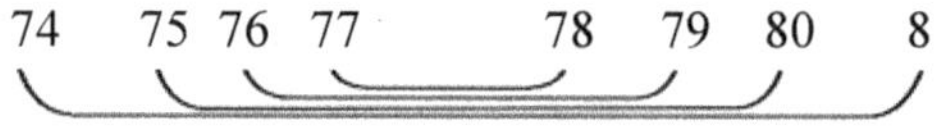

Ff. 75 and 80 are still connected to form a sheet. Folio 81 would be completely detached but for the reinforcement strips.

Quire 13: 82 83 84 85 86 87 88 89 90 91 92

This quire has 11 folios that we have analyzed in the manner depicted above. Folios 83 and 92 are still connected. The textblock in this quire is consistent with two columns per page and 15 lines per page.

Quire 14: 93 94 95 96 97 98

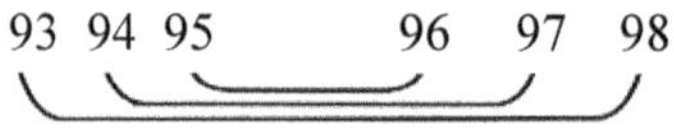

EMIP 43 – Eliza Codex 18
Office Prayers – Praises of Mary, ጸሎተ፡ ኪዳን፡ — ሥርዓተ፡ ቅዳሴ፡ — ውዳሴ፡ ማርያም፡

Parchment, 193 x 110 x 40 mm. The binding is secondary and has come loose at several points. Remains of weavings are visible along all four points in the spine, though none of the weavings is complete. The binding is in a bad state of repair. Attached to rough-hewn boards (the front made of the traditional wood, the back from a different, wide-grained wood), one protection quire + eight full quires, ii + 75 folios, 190 x 113 mm. Top margin quires 1–5, 15 mm; quires 6–8, 25 mm.

Bottom margin: quires 1–5, 35 mm; quires 6–8, 42 mm. Fore edge margin quires 1–5, 8–12 mm; quires 6–8, 22–25 mm. Gutter margin all quires 8–10 mm. Ff. ir and 46r–75v one column, ff. 1r–43r two columns, Gəʿəz, lines per page quires 1–5: 16–22; lines per page quires 6–8: 18, reign of Tewodros (1855–1868), ff 12r, 22v, and *passim.*

Quire descriptions: quires 1–4, 6–7 balanced; quire 8 adjusted balanced; quire 5 unbalanced. Navigation systems: 1) brown yarn sewn into corners of ff. i, ii, 43, 44, 45, and 74 to mark the location of miniatures.

1. Ff. 1r–8v: Prayer of the Covenant, ጸሎተ፡ ኪዳን፡. EMIP 3, f. 112r.
2. Ff. 8v–23v, and 29r–36v: The different supplications, መስተብቍዓት፡. Incomplete; includes the supplication for Mary, containing the expression condemned at the Boru Meda Council of 1878, and the Cross (ff. 34v–36v). Cf. MQ 51, pp. 270ff. On the controversial supplications, see ጌታቸው ኃይሌ፥ ደቂቀ እስጢፋኖስ፥ Collegeville (Minnesota) 1996 EC, pp. 36–41.
3. Ff. 24r–29r: The different litanies, ሊጦን፡. Incomplete; cf. Velat, *Meʿerāf* I, pp. 7–12; MQ 51, pp. 262ff.
4. Ff. 37r–43r: Ordinary of the Mass. Incomplete at the end, erased to make room for the forged picture; cf. MQ 51, pp. 15–19.
5. Ff. 46r–71v: Praises of Mary [*Wəddase Maryam*]. Arranged for days of the week (Wednesday, f. 49r; Thursday, f. 57v; Friday, f. 63r; Saturday, f. 66r; Sunday, f. 68v).
6. Ff. 71r–75v: Gate of Light [*Anqäṣä Bərhan*]. Incomplete in the middle (to make room for forgery) and at the end.

Miniatures, all in a late twentieth-century hand akin to the "speckled garment artist," painted over text:
1. F. Iv: The Annunciation (see miniature on IIr.)
2. F. IIr: the Angel speaking to Mary. The miniatures on Iv and IIr constitute together the Annunciation.
3. F. IVv: *Abunä* Gabra Manfas Qəddus.
4. F. 43v: The Crucifixion.
5. F. 44r: Resurrected Christ Displays His Wounds.
6. F. 44v: Saint George and the Dragon.
7. F. 45r: Madonna and Child.
8. F. 74v: A haloes saint with beard stands holding a book in his left hand and pointing with index finger of his right hand toward the heavens.

Varia:
1. F. 1r: Hymn to Mary, "Peace to you, Mary," ሰላም፡ ለኪ፡ እንዘ፡ ንሰግድ፡ ንብለኪ፡. As one of the daily prayers, this short hymn has been published in Ethiopia many times, e.g., MD 59, p. 462–63.
2. F. 1r, top: Will of *Abba* Wäldä Mädḫən to *Mämmərə* Tägäññ.
3. F. 1r, bottom: Record of payment in grain to Wäldä Giyorgis for prescribing medicine (*leba šay*) to catch a thief, in a crude hand.

Notes:
1. Decorative designs: f.46r (*haräg* using black and red); ff. 1r, (*haräg* using black); f. 53r (row of full-stop symbols).
2. F. 45v blank.
3. Overlooked words of text are written interlinearly (ff. 18r, 31v, 75v); and in the upper margin with a symbol (⊥) marking the location where the text is to be inserted (f. 72r, line 4).

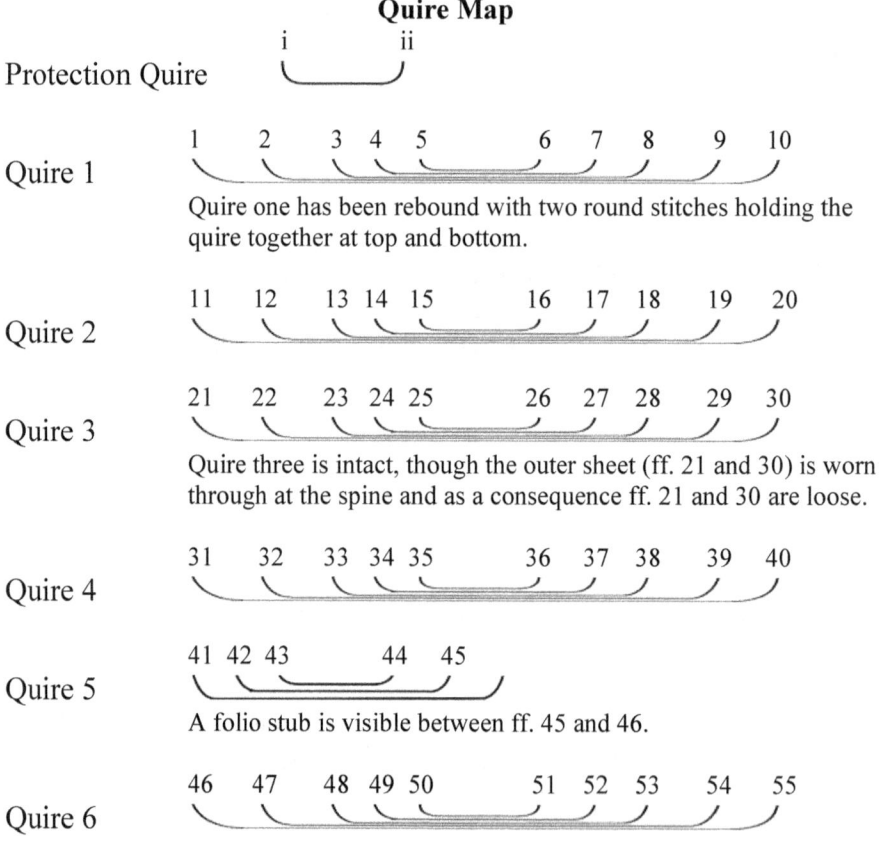

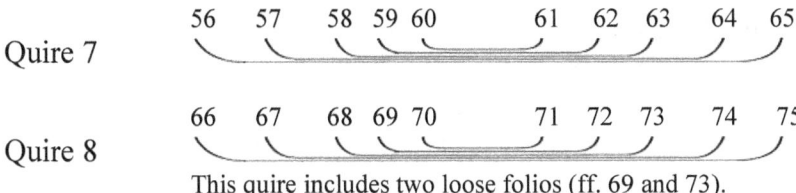

Quire 7: 56 57 58 59 60 61 62 63 64 65

Quire 8: 66 67 68 69 70 71 72 73 74 75
This quire includes two loose folios (ff. 69 and 73).

EMIP 44 – Eliza Codex 19
Psalter, ዳዊት፡

Parchment, 235 x 165 x 54mm, four Coptic chain stitches attached with bridle attachments to the rough-hewn boards covered with tooled leather, headband and tailband, protection quire + 20 full quires, quires 2–20 numbered, iv + 194 folios, 230 x 163 mm folio, top margin 28 mm, bottom margin 45 mm, fore edge margin 25 mm, gutter margin 10 mm, ff. 1r–172v one column, ff. 173r–193v two columns, Gǝ'ǝz, 20 lines, late 20th cent.

Quire descriptions: quires 2–19 are balanced five-sheet quires; quire 20 and the protection quire are both two-sheet, balanced quires. Navigation system: Interwoven red and green yarn or gold yarn sewn into corners of folios 1, 9, 17, 27, 40, 49, 57, 68, 81, 92, 99, 114, 129, 133, 140, 148, to mark the divisions of the Psalms. Double-slip case.

Ff. 1r–193v: Psalter [*Dawit*]. Cf. EMIP 1.
1. Ff. 1r–148r: Psalms of David.
2. Ff. 148v–163v: Biblical Canticles.
3. Ff. 164r–172v: Song of Songs. In the margins are texts that serve as mnemonic aids to the reader, pointing to the *Andǝmta* traditional commentary. In addition, there are several lines from the Hebraic version that have been inserted in smaller interlinear texts.
4. Ff. 173r–187r: Praises of Mary [*Wǝddase Maryam*]. Arranged for the days of the week (Monday, f. 173r; Tuesday, f. 174r; Wednesday, f. 176v; Thursday, f. 179r; Friday, f. 182r; Saturday, f. 184r; Sunday, f. 185v).
5. Ff. 187r–193v: Gate of Light [*Anqäṣä Bǝrhan*].

Miniatures, all in the late 20th century hand of the "speckled garment artist," painted over text:
1. F. Iv: Moses, with the tablet, Aaron and the Holy Spirit.
2. F. IIr: The Holy Trinity surrounded by the Four Living Creatures
3. F. IIv: Saint George and the Dragon
4. F. IIIr: Madonna and Child

5. F. IIIv: Jesus Carrying the Cross and being Flogged.
  6. F. IVr: The Crucifixion
  7. F. IVv: David Playing the Harp
  8. F. 194r: The Resurrection, raising Adam and Eve

Varia:
  1. Ff. 8v and 91v: Glorification of the Trinity (*səbḥat lä-Ab*) and prayer to Mary asking her intercession (*sä'li länä*).

Notes:
  1. Decorative designs: Decorative designs: ff. 1r, 9r, 17v, 27v, 40r, 49v, 57r, 68r, 81v, 92v, 99r, 114r, 129r, 133r, 140v, 148v, 164r, and 173r (*haräg* using black, red, purple, green, yellow and blue); no *haräg* marks the beginning of the Gate of Light.
  2. Columetric layout of text: ff. 147v (Ps. 150), 159r–160r (tenth biblical canticle).
  3. Ff. Ir and 194v blank.
  4. Overlooked words of text are written interlinearly (ff. 98v, 165r, 184v); and overlooked lines of text are written interlinearly (ff. 52v, 55v, 95v, 130r, 151r, 166r, 167rv, 168rv–172v, 175r).
  5. This scribe has avoided the problem of lines of text too long to fit on one line by adopting an aspect ratio that leaves ample room for the width of most lines. When the line would have been too long, the scribe finishes the end of the line with words written smaller so as to avoid leftover text (e.g., ff. 16v, 17r, 29r, 30r, 42r, etc.). Also, the scribe may complete the line above the end of the line (e.g., ff. 2v, 6v, 10r, 19rv, 20v, 27v, etc.).

Quire Map

Quire 5	41	42	43	44	45	46	47	48	49	50
Quire 6	51	52	53	54	55	56	57	58	59	60
Quire 7	61	62	63	64	65	66	67	68	69	70
Quire 8	71	72	73	74	75	76	77	78	79	80
Quire 9	81	82	83	84	85	86	87	88	89	90
Quire 10	91	92	93	94	95	96	97	98	99	100
Quire 11	101	102	103	104	105	106	107	108	109	110
Quire 12	111	112	113	114	115	116	117	118	119	120
Quire 13	121	122	123	124	125	126	127	128	129	130
Quire 14	131	132	133	134	135	136	137	138	139	140
Quire 15	141	142	143	144	145	146	147	148	149	150
Quire 16	151	152	153	154	155	156	157	158	159	160
Quire 17	161	162	163	164	165	166	167	168	169	170
Quire 18	171	172	173	174	175	176	177	178	179	180
Quire 19	181	182	183	184	185	186	187	188	189	190

Quire 20   191 192   193 194

EMIP 45 – Eliza Codex 20
Amharic Commentary on Our Father

Parchment, 103 x 72 x 28 mm, four Coptic chain stitches attached with bridle attachments to rough-hewn boards, 6 full quires, i + 44 folios, 101 x 70 mm, top margin 8 mm, bottom margin 27 mm, fore edge margin 11 mm, gutter margin 8 mm, ff. 1r–42v one column, Gəʻəz, 11 lines, 19th cent.

Quire descriptions: quires 2, 3, 5, 6 balanced; quires 1, 4 unbalanced.
Navigation system: brown yarn sewn into corners of folios 1, 9, 16, 24, 42 to mark the location of miniatures.

1. Ff. 1r–41v: Amharic Commentary on Our Father.
   በስመ፡ አብ፡ ወወልድ፡ ወመንፈስ፡ ቅዱስ፡ ፩ አምላክ፡ ብሎ፡ መጽሐፍ፡ እንዲጀምር፡ ጌታችን፡ እግዚእነ፡ ኢየሱስ፡ ክርስቶስ፡ አንትሙሰ፡ ሶበ፡ ትጸልዩ፡ ከመዝ፡ በሉ፡ አለ፡ . . .

2. Ff. 41v–42v: Notes on orders of the rite of baptism and the Mass, in Amharic.
   እጽሐፍ፡ ሥርዓተ፡ ቤተ፡ ክርስቲያን፡ ቀዳሽ፡ ቢታባ፡ ጥምቀት፡ . . .

Miniatures, all in the late twentieth-century hand of the "speckled garment artist," over the top of text:
   1. F. Iv: Saint Matthew. Caption: "Saint Matthew."
   2. F. 8v: Madonna and Child.
   3. F. 9r: Angel brandishing a sword.
   4. F. 17r: The Striking of the Head.
   5. F. 25r: Removing the Robe of Jesus.
   6. F. 43r: The Holy Trinity.
   7. F. 43v: Jesus Holding Orb.
   8. F. 44r: Angel with Sword.

Varia:
   1. F. Ir: Note that the manuscript is on the interpretation of Our Father.

Notes:
   1. Note of ownership by *Ato* Yazäw Gäbäyyä, f. Ir.
   2. Copied in a beautiful hand, but the text is erased in several places to make room for the forged pictures.
   3. Ff. 18v and 44v blank, save for the expression *bä-səmä* on f. 18v.
   4. In the images, a photographic image seems to be missing in quire one.
   5. Overlooked words of text are written interlinearly (f. 15v).

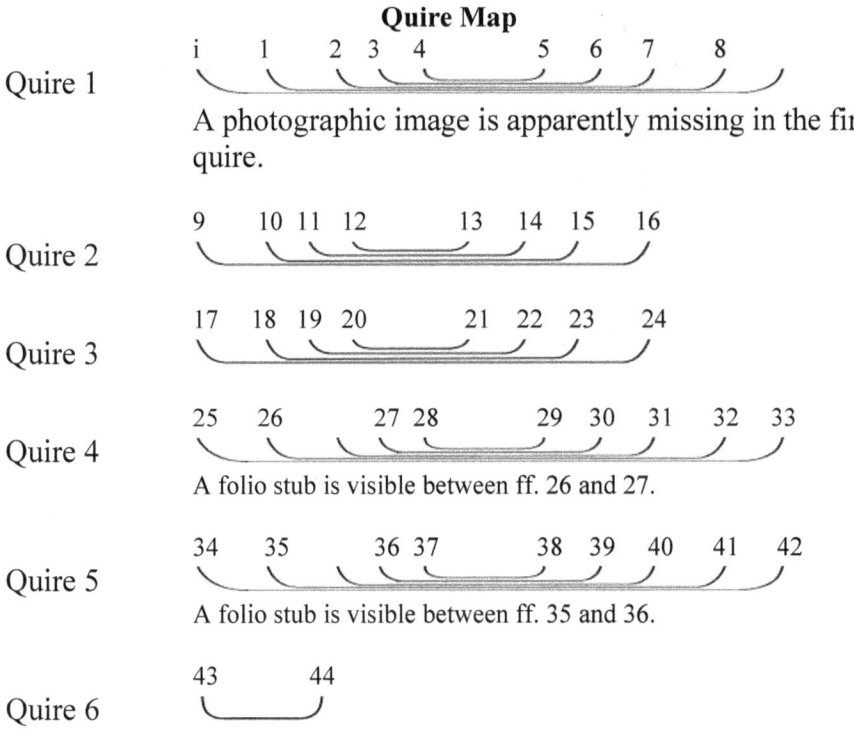

EMIP 46 – Eliza Codex 21
Missal, መጽሐፈ፡ ቅዳሴ፡

Parchment, 143 x 125 x 47 mm, three of four Coptic chain stitches attached with bridle attachments to rough-hewn replacement boards (front repaired), protection quire + 7 full quires, iv + 66 folios, reinforcement strips visible on folio 18 and between 25 and 26, 140 x 125 mm, top margin 23 mm, bottom margin 33 mm, fore edge margin 17 mm, gutter margin 8 mm, ff. iiv(erso)–65v two columns, Gəʽəz, 14 lines, reign of Metropolitan Krestodolu, 1720–1743, f. 8v.

Quire descriptions: quires 1–3, 5–7 balanced; quire 4 unbalanced. Navigation systems: 1) crimson yarn sewn into corners of folios 1, 13, 34, 54, 65 to mark the location of miniatures; 2) various colored string sewn into corners of folios 6, 16, 58 to mark content divisions.

Ff. 1r–17v, lacuna, 18r–65v: Missal, መጽሐፈ፡ ቅዳሴ፡. Supplied with musical notation; incomplete; MQ 51; Daoud-Mersie, *Liturgy*; EMIP 27.
    1. Ff. 1r–17v: Ordinary of the Mass, incomplete at the end.
    2. Ff. 18r–25v: Anaphora of the Apostles, incomplete at the beginning.

3. Ff. 26r–65v: The other anaphoras, rebound in total disorder.

Miniatures, all in twentieth-century hand:
1. F. IVr: Moses, with the tablet, Aaron and the Holy Spirit.
2. F. IVv: The Archangel Michael enthroned.
3. F. 14r: The Baptism of Jesus.
4. F. 34v: Saint George and the Dragon.
5. F. 35r: Madonna and Child.
6. F. 54v: The Flogging of Jesus.
7. F. 55r: Taking off the Robe of Jesus.
8. F. 66r: The Sacrifice of Isaac.

Varia:
1. F. Iv: Unintelligible note.
2. F. Iv: Receipt of loan, written by Bayyä Alämu.
3. F. IIv: Hymn to Mary, "Rejoice you whom we beseech," 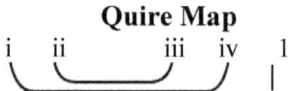 Tənśa'e Zä-Guba'e Press, Addis Ababa, 1951 EC, pp. 26–7; EMML 1867, f. 137v.

4. F. IIIrv: Acts 23:1–11, in a crude hand.
5. F. 66v: Unintelligible note.

Notes:
1. Note of ownership by Məsgan Wəbe, in a crude hand, f. 65v.
2. Ff. ir, iir blank, save for pen trial.

Quire Map

Protection Quire — i ii iii iv 1

The quire construction is secondary. A single folio has been stitched to the back of the quire.

Quire 1 — 2 3 4 5 6 7 8 9

The quire construction is secondary. The quire has been stitched together at three points in a round stitch (one that goes in one side of the quire about a half centimeter from the gutter fold and comes out the other side) at three points, head, middle and foot of the spine edge, thus making it impossible to verify the inner construction of the quire.

Quire 2 — 10 11 12 13 14 15 16 17

The quire construction is secondary. The quire has been stitched together at two points in a round stitch at two points, middle and foot of the spine edge, thus making it impossible to verify the inner construction of the quire. Thus, the image above is imprecise, e.g., ff. 14/15 are one sheet.

Quire 3

18 19 20 21 22 23 24 25 26 27

This quire construction is secondary if not tertiary. There is evidence of not one but two non-original gathering strategies: 1) ff. 18–24 have three small reinforcement strips sewn around them, suggesting a first repair; 2) The current full quire includes the folio constituted by ff. 18–24. The entire folio has been stitched together at three points in a round stitch at three points, head, middle and foot of the spine edge, thus making it impossible to verify the inner construction of the quire. The image above is imprecise.

Quire 4

28 29 30 31 32 33 34

The quire construction is secondary. The quire has been stitched together at three points in a round stitch at three points, head, middle and foot of the spine edge, thus making it impossible to verify the inner construction of the quire. Thus, the image above may be imprecise.

Quire 5

35 36 37 38 39 40

Quire 6

41 42 43 44 45 46 47 48 49 50 51 52 53 54

Quire 7

55 56 57 58 59 60 61 62 63 64 65 66

EMIP 47 – Eliza Codex 22
Psalter, ዳዊት፡

Parchment, 150 x 110 x 60 mm, four Coptic chain stitches attached with bridle attachments to rough-hewn boards covered with tooled leather over decorative linen patches visible inside the turn-ins on front and back cover, headband and tailband, protection quire + 18 full quires, quires 1–17 numbered, iv + 169 folios, 147 x 105 mm folio, top margin 10–12 mm, bottom margin 35–38 mm, fore edge margin 10–13 mm, gutter margin 8 mm, ff. ir–iir, 1r–150v one column, ff. 151r–166v two columns, Gəʿəz, 21–23 lines, 20th cent.

Quire descriptions: quires 1–11, 13–18 balanced; quire 12 unbalanced.
Navigation system: crimson yarn sewed into corners of folios 1, 114, 166 to mark the location of miniatures.

Ff. 1r–166v: Psalter [*Dawit*]. Cf. EMIP 1.
1. Ff. 1r–128v: Psalms of David.
2. Ff. 129r–142v: Biblical Canticles.
3. Ff. 143r–150v: Song of Songs, common version.
4. Ff. 151r–161r: Praises of Mary [*Wəddase Maryam*]. Arranged for the days of the week (Monday, f. 151r; Tuesday, f. 152r; Wednesday, f. 153v; Thursday, f. 155v; Friday, f. 157v; Saturday, f. 159r; Sunday, f. 160r).
5. Ff. 161r–166v: Gate of Light [*Anqäṣä Bərhan*].

Miniatures, all in the late twentieth-century hand of the "speckled garment artist," over the top of text:
1. F. IIIv: Saint George and the Dragon.
2. F. IVr: Madonna and Child.
3. F. IVv: David Playing the Harp.
4. F. 114v: The Triumphal Entry.
5. F. 115r: The Baptism of Jesus.
6. F. 167r: The Sacrifice of Isaac.
7. F. 167v: The Flogging of Jesus.
8. F. 168r: Taking off the Robe of Jesus.

Varia:
1. F. Ir–IIr: *Asmat* prayer of Jeremiah against the evil eye, ጸሎት፡ በእንተ፡ ሕማም፡ ዓይን፡ ወዓይነት፡. Cf. EMIP 9, f. IIIrv (varia). በስመ አብ . . . ጸሎት፡ በእንተ፡ ሕማም፡ ዓይን፡ ወዓይነት፡ ክሽን፡ ረክሽ፡ አባግሂ፡ ጤአን፡ . . . ጸለየ፡ ኤርምያስ፡ ነቢይ፡ የሀቦ፡ እግ"፡ ወይቤ፡ ፈውስ፡ ዮጣ፡ ቤጣ፡ . . . ጸሎት፡ በእንተ፡ ሕማም፡ ናስ፡ (sic, for ርእስ፡) ወዓይን፡ አመ፡ መጸእኪ፡ ሀቤየ፡ ወእቤለኪ፡ አይቴ፡ ተሐውሪ፡ . . .
2. F. 47r: Ps 60:9.

Notes:
1. F. 63v: Marginal symbol and note at 78:14 indicating the point "half" of the way through the Psalms.
2. Decorative designs: f. 1r (*haräg* using multiple colors); ff. 32v, 41r, 47v, 69r, 98r, 129r, 143r (*haräg* using black and red); ff. 7v, 14v, 21v, 22r, 47r, 57r, 78r, 84r, 111v (*haräg* using black); ff. 142v, 150v (dotted line using alternating black and red); ff. 83v (dotted line using black);

ff. 32r, 128v (dotted line using red); ff. 122r, 128v (full row of stops); f. 63v (additional decorative design).
3. F. 63v: An ornate symbol and the word "half" mark the midpoint of the Psalms.
4. Open space left for potential *haräg*: f. 115v.
5. Columetric layout of text: ff. 128r (Ps. 150), 138r–139v (tenth biblical canticle).
6. Copied by Śahlä Ǝgzi', ff. 150v and 166v.
7. Ff. IIv–IIIr, 168v–169v blank.
8. Overlooked words of text are written interlinearly (ff. 9v, 15v, 33v, 70v, 99r, 134v); and overlooked lines of text are written interlinearly (ff. 52r, 80v, 88v, 102r, 117v, 126r, 132v); and in the upper margin with a symbol (⊥) marking the location where the text is to be inserted (f. 18r, line 5), and in another case where the symbol (+) is used (ff. 123v, line 10, 145v, line 6).
9. The scribe regularly has to complete a line of text on another line. Much of the problem is addressed through the selection of an appropriate aspect ratio for the codex combined with an appropriate script size. On some occasions, the line would have been too long and the scribe finishes the end of the line with words written smaller so as to avoid leftover text (e.g., ff. 8v, 9v, 48v, 96r). Other times, a line is too long and has to be completed above (e.g., ff. 2v, 4v, 5v, 6r, 7rv, etc.) or below (e.g., 35r, 45v, 51v, 149v) the end of the line.

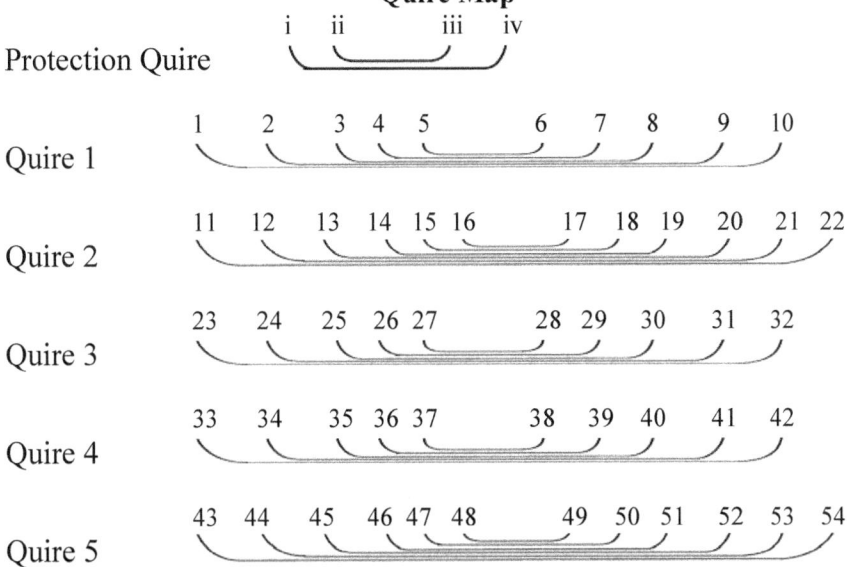

Quire 6	55 56 57 58 59 60 61 62 63 64
Quire 7	65 66 67 68 69 70 71 72 73 74
Quire 8	75 76 77 78 79 80 81 82 83 84
Quire 9	85 86 87 88 89 90 91 92
Quire 10	93 94 95 96 97 98 99 100
Quire 11	101 102 103 104 105 106 107 108 109 110
Quire 12	111 112 113 114 115 116 117 118 119

A folio stub is visible between ff. 114 and 115.

Quire 13	120 121 122 123 124 125 126 127 128 129
Quire 14	130 131 132 133 134 135 136 137
Quire 15	138 139 140 141 142 143 144 145 146 147
Quire 16	148 149 150 151 152 153 154 155 156 157
Quire 17	158 159 160 161 162 163 164 165 166 167
Quire 18	168 169

EMIP 48 – Eliza Codex 23
Psalter, ዳዊት፦

Parchment, 192 x 120 x 59 mm, four Coptic chain stitches attached with bridle attachments to rough-hewn, protection quire + 14 full quires, quires 1–6 numbered, ii + 138 folios, 188 x 123 mm folio, top margin 15–20 mm, bottom margin 27–35 mm, fore edge margin 12–15 mm, gutter margin 8 mm, ff. 1r–118v one column, ff. 119r–135v two columns, Gə'əz, 23 lines, early 20th cent.

Quire descriptions: quires 1–14 balanced. Navigation systems: 1) black thread sewn into corners of folios ii, 31, 50, 81, 109, 134 to mark the location of miniatures; 2) various colored string sewn into corners of folios 6, 13, 19, 29, 35, 47, 56, 63, 68, 88, 89, 91, 96, 102, 112, 119 to mark content divisions; 3) marginal notations to indicate readings (in the Biblical Canticles).

Ff. 1r–135v: Psalter [Dawit]. Cf. EMIP 1.
1. Ff. 1r–102r: Psalms of David.
2. Ff. 102r–112v: Biblical Canticles.
3. Ff. 112v–118v: Song of Songs, common version.
4. Ff. 119r–130r: Praises of Mary [Wəddase Maryam]. Arranged for the days of the week (Monday, f. 119r; Tuesday, f. 120r; Wednesday, f. 121v; Thursday, f. 123v; Friday, f. 126r; Saturday, f. 127v; Sunday, f. 129r).
5. Ff. 130r–135v: Gate of Light [Anqäṣä Bərhan].

Miniatures 2–8 are all in the late 20th century hand of the "speckled garment artist," painted over the top of text:
1. F. Iv: crude pen and pencil drawings of humans or human-like characters.
2. F. IIr: drawings of three men, one with a cross staff, another mounted and slaying a dragon by Ḫaylä Maryam.
3. F. IIv: Madonna and Child.
4. F. 31r: The Crucifixion
5. F. 50v: The Ascension.
6. F. 81r: Jesus Carrying the Cross.
7. F. 109v: Taking off the Robe of Jesus.
8. F. 134r: The Resurrection, raising Adam and Eve.
9. F. 136r: crude pen drawing of a goblin-like figure.
10. Covers (inside): pencil drawings of crosses.

Varia:

1. F. 137r: Record of division of land (to heirs?), Ṭəqəmt, 1913 EC (Oct/Nov1920 AD).
2. F. 137r: Record of marriage, 1915 EC (1922/23 AD).
3. F. 138r: *Asmat* prayer whose purpose is not clear.
   ወደ፡ ዘቄላት፡ ወጅ ናቂራንአ ለገብርከ ጋሌስ (?)

Notes:
1. Decorative designs: ff. 6v, 13r, 19v, 29r, 35v, 40v, 47v, 63r, 68r, 78v, 88v, 91r, 96v, 102r, 112v (dotted line using alternating black and red); ff. 138r, inside covers (geometric pattern using pencil).
2. Columetric layout of text: ff. 101rv (Ps. 150), 109r–110r (tenth biblical canticle).
3. Note of ownership by someone with a crude hand who could not write even his name clearly, f. Ir, Abbäbä, ff. IIr, and 138r, *Ato* Takkälä Abbäbä, ff. 137r and 138r, and by *Mämmərə* Zähay, recto of the rear cover board.
4. F. 1r: The name A/Maryam.
5. Ff. 136v–137r blank save for some scrawl on f. 136v.
6. Sold to Gerald Weiner in 2007; numbered Weiner 158.
7. Overlooked words of text are written interlinearly (ff. 52r, 119v, 121r); and overlooked lines of text are written interlinearly (ff. 2r and 135); and in the upper margin with a symbol (⊥) marking the location where the text is to be inserted (f. 57r, line 10 and f. 70r, line 5).
8. The scribe regularly has to complete a line of text on another line. Throughout the manuscript this scribe will reduce the font size at the end of lines to avoid having to go onto the next line as well as complete the line of text above the end of the line.

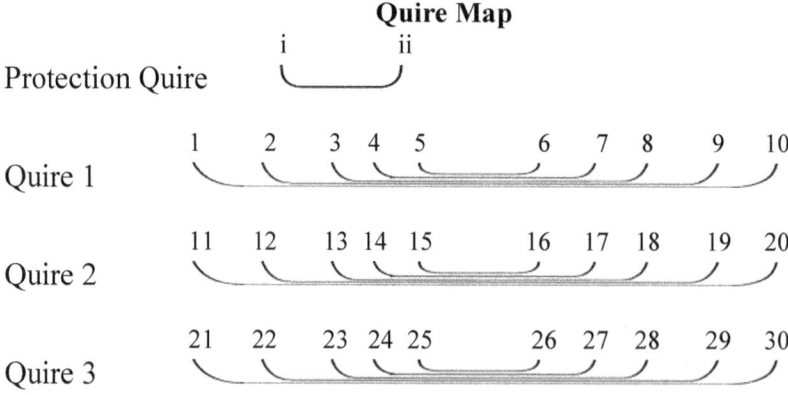

Quire 4: 31 32 33 34 35 36 37 38 39 40

Quire 5: 41 42 43 44 45 46 47 48 49 50

Quire 6: 51 52 53 54 55 56 57 58 59 60

Quire 7: 61 62 63 64 65 66 67 68 69 70

Quire 8: 71 72 73 74 75 76 77 78 79 80

Quire 9: 81 82 83 84 85 86 87 88 89 90

Quire 10: 91 92 93 94 95 96 97 98 99 100

Quire 11: 101 102 103 104 105 106 107 108 109 110

Quire 12: 111 112 113 114 115 116 117 118 119 120

Quire 13: 121 122 123 124 125 126 127 128 129 130

Quire 14: 131 132 133 134 135 136 137 138

EMIP 49 – Eliza Codex 24
Psalter, ዳዊት፦

Parchment, 180 x 120 x 53 mm, four Coptic chain stitches attached with bridle attachments to rough-hewn boards with a few remnants of purple linen, protection quire + 14 full quires, quires 2–14 numbered, iv + 140 folios, 180 x 118 mm, top margin 15 mm, bottom margin 32 mm, fore edge margin 18 mm, gutter margin 7 mm, ff. 1r–123r one column, ff. 123v–138r two columns, Gəʿəz, 26 lines, 20th cent.

Quire descriptions: quires 1–12, 14 balanced; quire 13 adjusted balanced.
Navigation system: brown yarn sewn into corners of folios 1, 51, 91, 99, 138 to mark the location of miniatures.

Ff. 1r–138r: Psalter [*Dawit*]. Introduced with the first psalm of the shorter *Mäzmurä Krəstos*; Cf. EMIP 40. Some psalms are marked with the special occasions for the use, in a crude hand.
1. Ff. 1r–104r: Psalms of David.
2. Ff. 104v–115r: Biblical Canticles.
3. Ff. 115v–123r: Song of Songs, a fine example of the Hebraic version in the base text.
4. Ff. 123v–134r: Praises of Mary [*Wəddase Maryam*]. Arranged for the days of the week (Monday, f. 123v; Tuesday, f. 124v; Wednesday, f. 126r; Thursday, f. 128r; Friday, f. 130r; Saturday, f. 131v; Sunday, f. 132v).
5. Ff. 134r–138r: Gate of Light [*Anqäṣä Bərhan*].

Miniatures, all in the late 20th-century hand of the "speckled garment artist," painted over text::
1. F. IVv: David Playing the Harp.
2. F. 50v: Madonna and Child.
3. F. 90v: Saint George and the Dragon.
4. F. 98v: The Crucifixion.
5. F. 138v: Jesus Carrying the Cross.
6. F. 139r: The Striking of the Head.
7. F. 139v: The Resurrection, raising Adam and Eve.
8. F. 140r: The Ascension.

Varia:
1. F. Iv: Medical prescription against snake, *käysi*, i.e. Satan.
2. F. Iv: Medical prescription "for urine."

Notes:
1. Decorative designs: f. 1r (elaborate, multicolor frame for text); ff. 1r, 6v (*haräg* using multiple colors, sometimes with floral elements reaching into text block); ff. 56r, 123v (*haräg* using pencil); ff. 12v, 27v (unfinished *haräg* using pencil); ff. 124v, 126r, 128r, 130r (dotted line using alternating black and red). Additional space in top margin, potentially meant for a *haräg*: ff. 34r, 39r, 46r, 63r, 67v, 79r, 91r, 93v, 99r, 104v, 115v.
2. Columetric layout of text: ff. 103v–104r (Ps. 150), 111v–112v (tenth biblical canticle).
3. Psalm 118 (ff. 97ff) has the spiritual meanings of the Hebrew letters.

4. Ff. Ir, IIr–IVr and 140v blank.
5. Overlooked lines of text are written interlinearly (f. 45r).
6. The scribe regularly has to complete a line of text on another line. Much of the problem is addressed through the selection of an appropriate aspect ratio for the codex combined with an appropriate script size. But, where the line of text is still too long, the scribe reduces the font size at the end of lines to avoid having to go onto the next line (throughout). This scribe will also regularly complete the line of text above (e.g., ff. 1v, 2rv, 3r, 5v, etc.) or below (e.g., f. 14v, 16v, 25v, 26rv, etc.) the end of the line.

Quire Map

	i	ii	iii	iv

Protection Quire

Quire 1: 1 2 3 4 5 6 7 8 9 10

Quire 2: 11 12 13 14 15 16 17 18 19 20

Quire 3: 21 22 23 24 25 26 27 28 29 30

Quire 4: 31 32 33 34 35 36 37 38 39 40

Quire 5: 41 42 43 44 45 46 47 48 49 50

Quire 6: 51 52 53 54 55 56 57 58 59 60

Quire 7: 61 62 63 64 65 66 67 68 69 70

Quire 8: 71 72 73 74 75 76 77 78 79 80

Quire 9: 81 82 83 84 85 86 87 88 89 90

Quire 10: 91 92 93 94 95 96 97 98 99 100

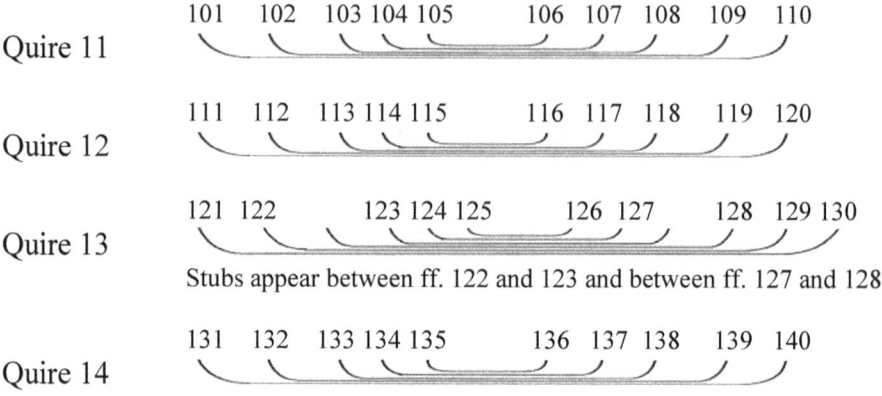

EMIP 50 – Eliza Codex 25
Psalter, ዳዊት:

Parchment, 142 x 109 x 63 mm, four Coptic chain stitches attached with bridle attachments to rough-hewn boards covered with tooled leather over a decorative linen patch visible inside the turn-ins on back cover, headband and tailband, 16 full quires, quires 2–13 numbered, i + 165 folios, 134 x 104 mm, top margin 12–14 mm, bottom margin 27–30 mm, fore edge margin 15–18 mm, gutter margin 5–7 mm, ff. 1r–147v one column, ff. 148r–165v two columns, Gəʿəz, 18–22 lines, 19th cent.

Quire descriptions: quires 2, 5, 6, 10, 14, 15 balanced; quires 1, 3, 4, 7, 9, 11, 13 adjusted balanced; quires 8, 12, 16 unbalanced. Navigation systems: various colored string sewn into corners of folios 34, 48, 55, 125 to mark content divisions.

Ff. 1r–165v: Psalter [*Dawit*]. Some psalms are marked for special occasions. Cf. EMIP 1.

1. Ff. 1r–125v: Psalms of David.
2. Ff. 125v–139v: Biblical Canticles.
3. Ff. 140r–147v: Song of Songs, common version.
4. Ff. 148r–160r: Praises of Mary [*Wəddase Maryam*], arranged for the days of the week (Monday, f. 148r; Tuesday, f. 149r; Wednesday, f. 151r; Thursday, f. 153r; Friday, f. 156r; Saturday, f. 157v; Sunday, f. 159r).
5. Ff. 160v–165v: Gate of Light [*Anqäṣä Bərhan*].

Miniatures, all in the late twentieth-century hand of "the beautiful artist," painted over text:

1. F. Iv: drawing of mounted human over a serpent.

Catalogue of the Ethiopic Manuscript Imaging Project · 141

2. F. 3v: The Annunciation.
3. F. 4r: Saint George.
4. F. 82v: The Resurrection, raising Adam and Eve.
5. F. 83r: Jesus Carrying the Cross.
6. F. 141v: Angel Holding Staff.
7. F. 142r: Jesus Followed by a Line of People.

Notes:
1. Decorative designs: ff. 55r, 77r, 82r (*haräg* using black and red); ff. 1r, 6v, 13v, 96v, 160v (*haräg* using black); f. 148 (crude *haräg* sketched over late text using black); ff. 22r, 33r (*haräg* using red); f. 67r (crude *haräg* using blue); ff. 32v, 125v (*haräg* using pencil); f. 109 (line consisting of alternating blue and red segments); f. 41v (line using stops connected with lines); ff. 61v (cross using black and red).
2. Columetric layout of text: ff. 124v–125r (Ps. 150), 135v–136r (tenth biblical canticle).
3. F. 61v: A small black cross marks the midpoint of the Psalms.
4. F. lr blank.
5. Overlooked words of text are written interlinearly (ff. 6r, 18r, 24v, 26r, 44r, 46r, 50v, etc.); and overlooked lines of text are written interlinearly (ff. 25v, 34v, 35r, 40v, 43v, 45v, 50r, etc.); and in the upper margin with a symbol (+) marking the location where the text is to be inserted (f. 98v, line 7 and f. 165r, line 5).
6. The scribe regularly has to complete a line of text on another line. Much of the problem is addressed through the selection of an appropriate aspect ratio for the codex combined with an appropriate script size. But, where the line of text is still too long, the scribe completes the line of text above the end of the line (throughout).

Quire Map

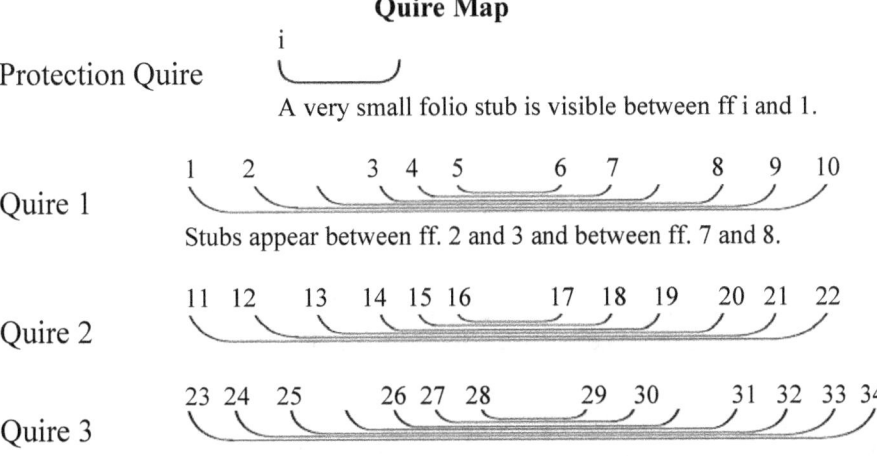

Stubs appear between ff. 25 and 26 and between ff. 30 and 31.

Quire 4: 35 36 37 38 39 40 41 42 43 44

Stubs appear between ff. 38 and 39 and between ff. 41 and 42.

Quire 5: 45 46 47 48 49 50

There are at least two sheets missing between ff. 47 and 48. The text contains a lacuna between the end of f. 47v and the beginning of 48r that represents a break in the Psalms from Psalm 59, next to the last line, until Psalm 65, line 25.

Quire 6: 51 52 53 54 55 56 57 58 59 60

Quire 7: 61 62 63 64 65 66 67 68 69 70

Stubs appear between ff. 63 and 64 and between 66 and 67.

Quire 8: 71 72 73 74 75 76 77 78 79 80 81

Stubs appear between 72 and 73, between ff. 77 and 78 and between ff. 78 and 79.

Quire 9: 82 83 84 85 86 87 88 89 90 91 92 93

Stubs appear between ff. 84 and 85 and between ff. 91 and 92.

Quire 10: 94 95 96 97 98 99 100 101 102 103

Quire 11: 104 105 106 107 108 109 110 111 112 113

Stubs appear between ff. 105 and 106 and between 110 and 111.

Quire 12: 114 115 116 117 118 119 120 121 122

Stubs appear between ff. 122 and 123.

Quire 13: 123 124 125 126 127 128 129 130 131 132 133 134

Stubs appear between ff. 124 and 125 and between ff. 131 and 132.

Quire 14: 135 136 137 138 139 140 141 142 143 144

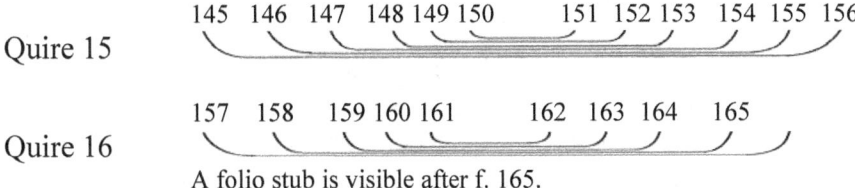

A folio stub is visible after f. 165.

EMIP 51 – Eliza Codex 26
The Five Pillars of Mystery — Admonition — Commentary on Our Father, አምስቱ፡ አዕማደ፡ ምሥጢር፡ — ምዕዳን፡ — ትርጓሜ፡ አቡነ፡ ዘበሰማያት፡, all in Amharic

Parchment, 176 x 128 x 45 mm. The cover appears to have been made off the book and attached not in the usual bridle attachment of the chain stitches to the boards. The boards were prepared to receive attachment; holes for the bridle attachment are visible on the inside. However, the orientation of the holes is backwards from the usual. Likewise, the holes have no strings in them and are oriented backwards: the holes come through the side edge and come out the inside cover. The cover is attached to the quires by sewing string through the gutter of the quires and through the spine of the cover. A line of stitches is visible at both head and tail of the spine and look very much like the stitches that hold head and tail pieces in place. However there are no head and tail pieces. Eleven full quires, quires 1–5 numbered, 101 folios, 175 x 126 mm, ff. 70r–101v one column, ff. 1r–69v two columns, Gəʿəz, $19^{th}/20^{th}$ cent.

The codex appears to be composite with quires from four different sources:

Part one, quires 1-5: all in one hand, quire numbers for each quire, page layout in two columns, top margin 20 mm, bottom margin 36 mm, fore edge margin 20 mm, margin in gutter: 10 mm. There is one additional and secondary hand in quires 1 and 2. This hand writes in light black ink with a very small tip and makes notes between the main lines of text. These are visible in ff. 1r, 2r, 2v, 3v, 4v, 11r, and 11v.

Part two, quires 6-7: a new hand, no quire numbers, page layout in two columns, top margin: 15-25 mm (irregular), bottom margin 35 mm, fore edge margin 10-15 mm, margin in gutter: 5-7 mm.

Part three, quires 8-9: quire dimensions shorter in height than the rest, new hand, page layout in one column of 17 lines of text, top margin 8-10 mm, bottom margin 45 mm, fore edge margin 10 mm, margin in gutter: 12 mm.

Part four, quires 10-11: new hand, page layout in one column of 18 or 19 lines of text, top margin 13-15 mm, bottom margin 32-35 mm, fore edge margin 5-8 mm, margin in gutter 10-13 mm.

Quire descriptions: quires 1, 3-11 balanced; quire 2 unbalanced.

1. Ff. 1r – 45v: The Five Pillars of Mystery, አምስቱ፡ አዕማደ፡ ምሥጢር፡. An Amharic explanation of the teachings of the Church, widely copied, e. g. EMML 1648, f. 16a; EMML 1815; see also ፭ቱ፡ አዕማደ፡ ምሥጢር፡፡ Täsfa Press, Addis Ababa 1952 EC.
    a. Ff. 1r–4r: Introduction.
       በስመ፡ አብ፡ . . . ብለው፡ መጻሕፍት፡ እንዲጆምሩ፡ በአብ፡ ስም፡ ወላዲ፡ . . . ብለን፡ እንጆምራለን፡ አምቅድመ፡ ዓለም፡ ከአብ፡ . . .
    b. Ff 4r–11v: Mystery of the Trinity, ምሥጢረ፡ ሥላሴ፡.
    c. Ff. 11v–26r: Mystery of the Incarnation, ምሥጢረ፡ ሥጋዌ፡.
    d. Ff. 26r–38v: Mystery of the Baptism, ምሥጢረ፡ ጥምቀት፡.
    e. Ff. 38v–45v: Mystery of the Eucharist, ምሥጢረ፡ ቁርባን፡.
    f. Ff. 48r–67r: Mystery of the Resurrection, ምሥጢረ፡ ትንሣኤ፡.
2. Ff. 67v–69v: Hymn to Mary, "All hosts of heaven glorify you," ኩሎሙ፡ ሠራዊተ፡ ሰማያት፡. EMML 1593, f. 92a.
   ኩሎሙ፡ ሠራዊተ፡ ሰማያት፡ ይሴብሑኪ፡፡
   ዘዕምቅድመ፡ አለም፡ ሀለወተኪ፡፡ (sic)
3. Ff. 70r–86v: Admonition, ምዕዳን፡. Three of the nine subjects of the teachings of the Church composed in Amharic, under this title, by "the Seven Monks." EMML 1442.
   በስመ፡ አብ፡ . . . ብለን፡ መጽሐፈ፡ ምዕዳን፡ እንጆምራለን፡ እንዲህ፡ አሉ፡ ሐዋርያት፡ ሕዝቡን፡ በሲኖዶስ፡ ካሁኑ፡ ካላስተማሪ፡ ይሻር፡ አሉ፡፡ እመቦ፡ ካህን፡ ዘኢይምሕር፡ (sic) . . .
    a. Ff. 70r–78v: On the Ten Commandments.
    b. Ff. 78v–82v: On almsgiving.
    c. Ff. 82v–86v: On eating.
4. Ff. 88r–97v: Amharic Commentary on Our Father. Cf. EMIP 45, f. 1r.
5. Ff. 98r–99r: Amharic Commentary on Hail Mary (Gabriel's greetings to Mary).
6. Ff. 99v–100v: Wise saying, in Amharic.
   ተወጥነ፡ ሥራተ፡ ምክር፡ ሰው፡ ደግ፡ ነው፡ ሰው፡ ክፉ፡ ነው፡ ቅንነት፡ ከበዛው፡ ዘንድ፡ ይዋረዳል፡ በእግ"፡ ዘንድ፡ ግን፡ ይከበራል፡ . . .
7. Ff. 100v–101v: Hymn to God, "All spiritual hosts of angels," ኩሎሙ፡ ሠራዊተ፡ መላእክት፡. EMML 1139, f. 28a; EMML 1246, f. 31a.
   ኩሎሙ፡.ሠራዊተ፡ መላእክት፡ መንፈሳውያን፡ እለ፡ ስዑን፡ በነደ፡ እሳት፡

Miniatures, all in the late twentieth-century hand and an artist akin to "the speckled garment artest," painting over text::
1. F. 8v: Madonna and Child.
2. F. 25v: Jesus Carrying the Cross.
3. F. 46r: The Crucifixion.
4. F. 46v: The Resurrection, raising Adam and Eve.
5. F. 47r: Saint George and the Dragon.
6. F. 47v: The Ascension.

Varia:
1. F. 87r: Unfinished letter to *Balambaras* Šawəl.

Notes:
1. Decorative designs: f. 1 (*haräg* using pencil); f. 48v (space in top margin, potentially meant for a *haräg*).
2. F. 68v, 86v pen trial.
3. F. 87v, isolated words and phrases.
4. F. 99r: Prayer for Kidanä Maryam.
5. F. 100v: Note of ownership by *Abba* Asräss;
6. The codex was sold to Gerald Weiner in 2007.
7. Overlooked words of text are written interlinearly (ff. 3v, 4v, 9r, 27v, 28v, 70r, 73v, 82v); and overlooked lines of text are written interlinearly (ff. 1r, 2rv, 11rv); and in the upper margin with a symbol (+) marking the location where the text is to be inserted (f. 59r, line 3).

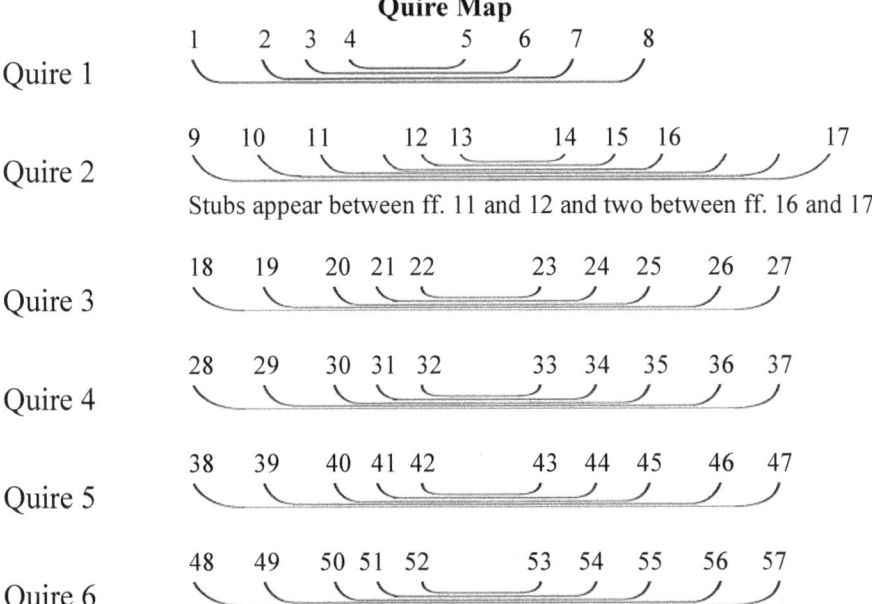

Stubs appear between ff. 11 and 12 and two between ff. 16 and 17.

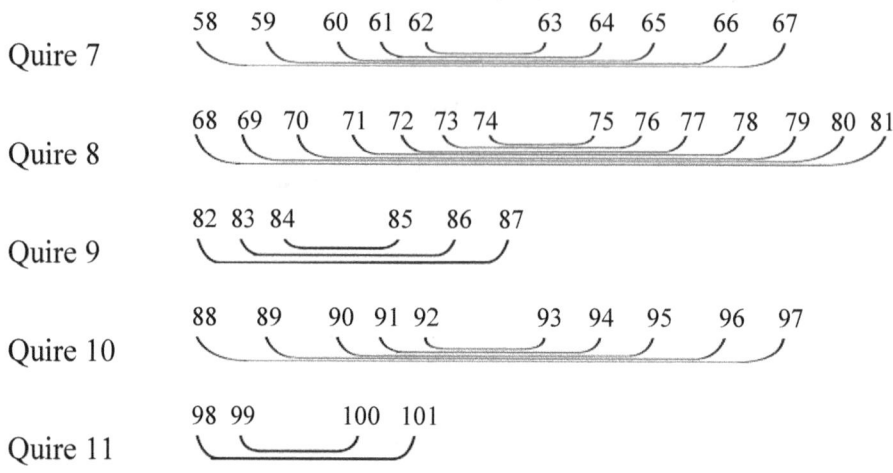

EMIP 52 – Eliza Codex 27
Prayer of Mary at Golgotha, ሰኔ፡ ጎልጎታ፡

Parchment, 122 x 100 x 37 mm, three or four Coptic chain stitches attached with bridle attachments to rough-hewn boards covered with tooled leather, headband and tailband, protection quire + 5 full quires (plus illumination sheets between quires 2 and 3, 3 and 4, and after 5), quires 2–5 numbered (not counting illustration sheets), iv + 42 folios, 113 x 94 mm, top margin 7–10 mm, bottom margin 20–27 mm, fore edge margin 7–12 mm, gutter margin 12 mm, ff. 1r–39v one column, Gəʻəz, 11–16 lines, 19th/20th cent.

Quire descriptions: quires 1, 4, 5 balanced; quire 2 adjusted balanced; quire 3 unbalanced. Double-slip case with a strap of leather.

Ff. 1r–39v: Prayer of Mary at Golgotha, ጸሎተ፡ እግዝእትነ፡ ማርያም፡ ዘሰኔ፡ ጎልጎታ፡. Copied and printed several times in its Gəʻəz and Amharic versions, e.g., ጸሎተ፡ እግዝእትነ፡ ማርያም፡ ዘሰኔ፡ ጎልጎታ፡፡ በመቃብረ፡ እግዚእነ፡ ኢየሱስ፡ ክርስቶስ፡፡ Täsfa Press, Addis Ababa 1949 EC.; ጸሎተ፡ እግዝእትነ፡ ማርያም፡ (ዘሰኔ፡ ጎልጎታ፡) በአማርኛ፡፡ Täsfa Press, Addis Ababa 1963 EC.; see also Sylvain Grébaut, "La prière de Marie au Golgotha," *JA*, vol. 226 (1935), pp. 273–86; and Basset, *Apocryphes*, V, pp. 30–47; Strelcyn, *Lincei*, no. 47, f. 73r; EMML 1213, f. 1a.

በስመ፡ አብ፡ . . . ዛቲ፡ ጸሎት፡ ዘእግዝእትነ፡ ማርያም፡ ወላዲተ፡ አምላክ፡ እንተ፡ ጸሐፉ፡ አብሮኮሮስ፡ ረድአ፡ ዮሐንስ፡ ጸሎታ፡ . . . ጸሎት፡ ዘጸለየ(f. 1v)ት፡ ባቲ፡ አመ፡ ጀወዬ፡ ለወርኃ፡ ሰኔ፡ በደብረ፡ ጎልጎታ፡ ዘውእቱ፡ መቃብረ፡ እግዚእነ፡ ኢየሱስ፡ ክርስቶስ፡ እንዘ፡ ትብል፡ እግዚእየ፡ . . .

Miniatures:
1. F. Iv: Geometric patterns with circular face at center.
2. F. IIr: Angel brandishing a Sword.
3. F. IIv: Geometric patterns with diamond face at center of cross.
4. F. IIIr: Geometric patterns with rectangular face at center of cross.
5. F. IIIv(erso): Madonna and Child.
6. F. IVr: Angel brandishing a Sword.
7. F. 17r: Geometric patterns and four *fleur de Lis*.
8. F. 17v: Angel brandishing a Sword.
9. F. 18r: Angel brandishing a Sword.
10. F. 18v: Nine-box panel with face in center box; others filled with geometric patterns.
11. F. 26v: Ethiopian dignitary with prayer stick.
12. F. 27r: Ethiopian dignitary with prayer stick and sistrum.
13. F. 40v: Saint Nä'akk^{w}əto Lä'ab.
14. F. 41r: Saint Lalibäla.
15. F. 42r: Geometric patterns with rectangular face at center of cross.

Notes:
1. Decorative designs: f. 1r (*ḥaräg* using black and red).
2. F. Ir, 26r, 27v, 40r, 41v–42v blank.
3. Overlooked words of text are written interlinearly (f. 2r).

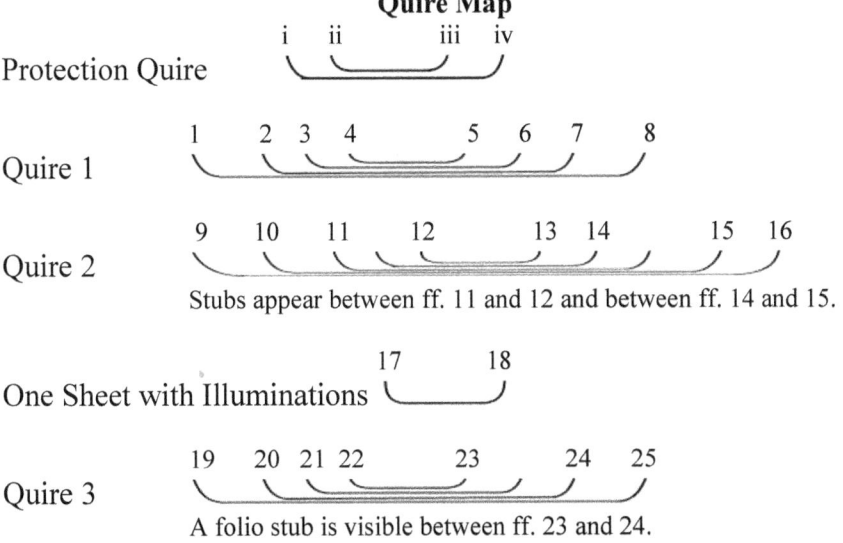

148 · *Catalogue of the Codices*

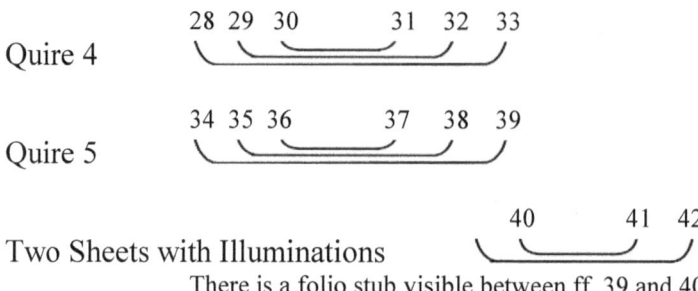

There is a folio stub visible between ff. 39 and 40.

EMIP 53 – Eliza Codex 28
"God Reigns," ascribed to Zär'a Ya'əqob, እግዚአብሔር፡ ነግሠ፡

Parchment, 86 x 78 x 43 mm, four Coptic chain stitches attached with bridle attachments to rough-hewn boards, one protection sheet + eight full quires, ii + 80 folios, 82 x 76 mm, top margin 10–12 mm, bottom margin 18 mm, fore edge margin 12–15 mm, gutter margin 5 mm, one column, Gə'əz, 11 lines, 18th cent.

Quire descriptions: quires 1–8 balanced. Navigation system: brown yarn sewed into corners of ff. 2, 10, 30, 50, and 79 to mark the location of miniatures.

1. Ff. 1r–72v: The hymn "God Reigns" እግዚአብሔር፡ ነግሠ፡, ascribed to Zär'a Ya'əqob. For 12 to 30 Ḥədar (ff. 1r–62r) and 11 Ḥədar (ff. 62r–72v). See Getatchew Haile, *The Different Collection of Nägś Hymns of the Ethiopic Literature* (Oikonomia no. 19), Erlangen (Germany), 1983, pp. 29–52; EMML 3128, ff. 2a–10b, and 92r–94a.
    አም፡ ፲ወ፪ ለወርኃ፡ ኅዳር፡ ሚካኤል፡ ሊቀ፡ መላእክት፡ ሰአል፡ በእንቲአነ፡ ወቅዱስ፡ ገብርኤል፡ አዕርግ፡ ጸሎትነ፡ . . .
    (f. 62r) አም፡ ፲፩ ሰላ፡ ለሐና፡ ሜላተ፡ (f. 62v) ንጽሕ፡ አስከሬነ፡ (sic) ለማርያም፡ አስከሬነ፡፡
    እምአሮን፡ ሌዋዊ፡ ሙላደ፡ መካነ፡

2. Ff. 73r –79r: Three miracles of Mary.
    a. How Mary saved a monk from the temptation of Satan, f. 73r. Budge, *Mary*, p. 299.
    b. The man who was able to learn Hail Mary only, f. 75r. Budge, *Mary*, pp. 138–9.
    c. The virgins Juliana and Barbara, f. 78r. Budge, *Mary*, pp. 39–40.

Miniatures, all in the late twentieth-century hand of "the speckled garment artist," painted over text:
    1. F. Iv: Angel with Sword.

2. F. IIr: Madonna and Child.
3. F. IIv: Saint Mathew.
4. F. 11r: The Sacrifice of Isaac.
5. F. 31r: The Striking of the Head.
6. F. 51r: The Holy Trinity.
7. F. 79v: Saint George and the Dragon.
8. F. 80r: Angel with Sword.

Varia:
1. F. Ir: The beginning of the Image of Michael, Chaîne, Répertoire, no. 119, in a crude hand.

Notes:
1. Decorative designs: f. 72v (row of full-stop symbols).
2. Note of ownership by 'Ǝrgätä Qal, f. 73v and *passim*.
3. F. 80v blank.
4. Overlooked words of text are written interlinearly (f. 10v).

Quire Map

Protection Quire: i — ii

Quire 1: 1 2 3 4 5 6 7 8 9 10
Quire 2: 11 12 13 14 15 16 17 18 19 20
Quire 3: 21 22 23 24 25 26 27 28 29 30
Quire 4: 31 32 33 34 35 36 37 38 39 40
Quire 5: 41 42 43 44 45 46 47 48 49 50
Quire 6: 51 52 53 54 55 56 57 58 59 60
Quire 7: 61 62 63 64 65 66 67 68 69 70
Quire 8: 71 72 73 74 75 76 77 78 79 80

EMIP 54 – Eliza Codex 29
Anaphora of Our Lady by Cyriacus of Bəhənsa — Prayer of Mary at Golgotha, ቅዳሴ፡ ማርያም፡ — ጸሎተ፡ እግዝእትነ፡ ማርያም፡ ዘበሰ፡ ጎልጎታ፡

Parchment, 113 x 80 x 29 mm, three Coptic chain stitches attached with bridle attachments to rough-hewn boards. Inside the back cover, a portion of the wood has been scraped lower than the rest, forming an area 70 x 60 mm. It looks to have held a mirror at some time though now all that appears to remain is the residue of old glue. One protection sheet + eight full quires, ii + 81 folios, 109 x 80 mm, top margin 10–12 mm, bottom margin 25–27 mm, fore edge margin 10 mm, gutter margin 5 mm, one column, Gəʿəz, 12–13 lines, 19th/20th cent.

Quire descriptions: quires 1–4, 5–8 balanced; quire 5 unbalanced. Navigation system: brown yarn sewed into corners of ff. 1, 11, 24, 49, 59, 69 to mark the location of miniatures.

1. Ff. 1r–36v: Anaphora of Our Lady Mary ascribed to Cyriacus of Bəhənsa, *Gʷäsʾa*.
2. Ff. 37r–69r: Prayer of Mary at Golgotha, ጸሎተ፡ እግዝእትነ፡ ማርያም፡ ዘበሰ፡ ጎልጎታ፡. Incomplete at the end; cf. EMIP 52.
3. Ff. 70r–81r: The Mystagogia. EMIP 4, f. IIv (varia).
4. F. 81rv: Calendar of the Apostles and Evangelists.

Miniatures, all in the late twentieth-century hand of the "speckled garment artist," painted over text:
1. F. IIv: Saint Luke.
2. F. 10v: Madonna and Child.
3. F. 11r: Angel brandishing a sword.
4. F. 25r: Saint George and the Dragon.
5. F. 50r: The Last Supper.
6. F. 60r: Moses and the Ten Commandments.
7. F. 69v: The Resurrection, raising Adam and Eve.
8. F. 70r: The Ascension.

Varia:
1. F. Iv–IIr: *Asmat* prayer to protect domestic animals from wild animals.
2. F. IIr: Receipt of the purchase of the manuscript.
3. F. 1r: The title of the Anaphora of Our Lady by Cyriacus of Bəhənsa.

Notes:
1. Decorative designs: f. 37r (*haräg* using black).

2. Copied for Gäbrä Mädḫǝn Abbäbä, f. 81r.
3. F. 1r blank.
4. Overlooked words of text are written interlinearly (ff. 4r, 5v, 6r, 29v, 30r, 31v, 32r, 33rv, 37v, 47r, 61v, 63r, 68v, 75v); and overlooked lines of text are written interlinearly (f. 71v).

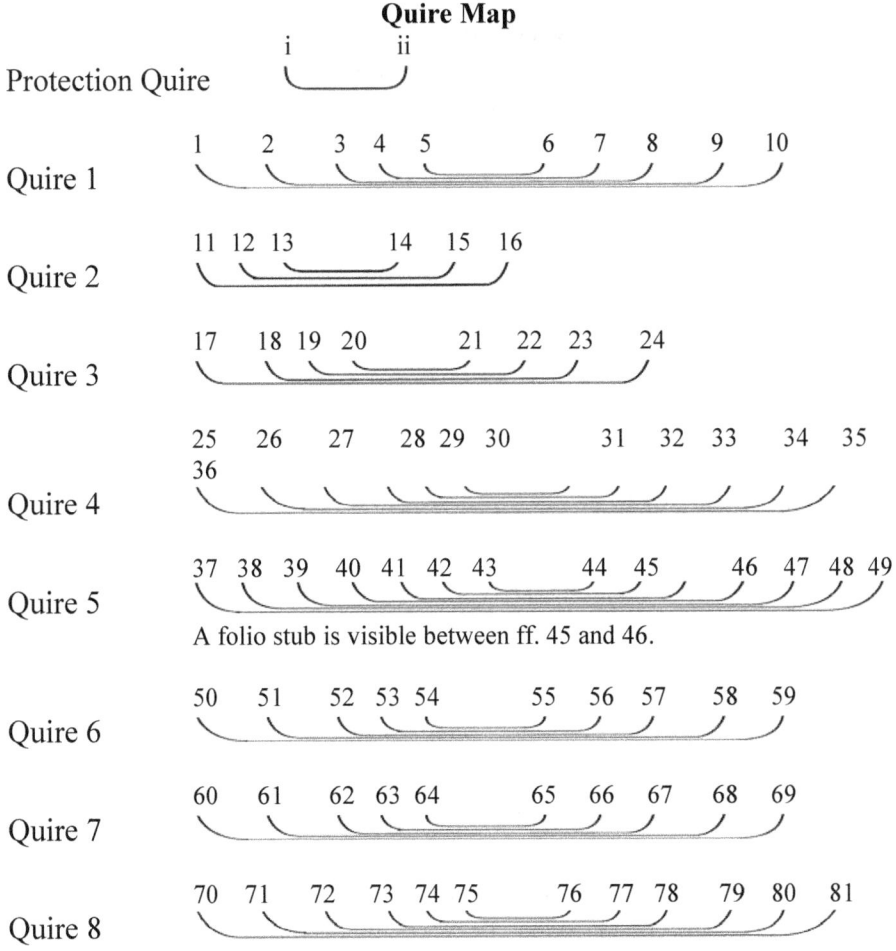

EMIP 55 – Trinity Western University Ethiop MS 1
Psalter, ዳዊት፡

Parchment, 183 x 130 x 65 mm, four Coptic chain stitches attached with bridle attachments to rough-hewn boards covered with tooled leather, headband and tailband, protection folio + 12 full quires, i + 142 folios, 173 x 126 mm folio, top margin 15–18 mm, bottom margin 40–43 mm,

152 · *Catalogue of the Codices*

fore edge margin 15–18 mm, gutter margin 10–12 mm, ff. 1–128r one column, ff. 128r–140v two columns, Gəʿəz, 25 lines, 19th/20th cent.
Quire descriptions: quires 1–3, 5, and 8–10 balanced; quire 7 adjusted balanced; quires 4, 6, 11 unbalanced; 12 adjusted unbalanced.
Ff. 1r–140v: Psalter [*Dawit*]. Cf. EMIP 1.
1. Ff. 1r–108v: Psalms of David.
2. Ff. 109r–121v: Biblical Canticles.
3. Ff. 121v–128r: Song of Songs, common version.
4. Ff. 128r–140v: Praises of Mary [*Wəddase Maryam*]. Arranged for the days of the week (Monday, f. 128r; Tuesday, f. 129r; Wednesday, f. 132r; Thursday, f. 134r; Friday, f. 136v; Saturday, f. 138r; Sunday, f. 139r).
5. F. 140v: Gate of Light [*Anqäṣä Bərhan*]. Incomplete, only one and a half columns from the beginning.

Miniatures:
1. F. iv(erso): Madonna and Child
2. F. 39r: An Ethiopian Dignitary (holding hand cross and book and wearing crown).
3. F. 39v: Savior of the World (Jesus seated holding orb).
4. F. 60r: The Holy Trinity.
5. F. 60v: The Crucifixion.
6. F. 120r: Mary praying (showing only one eye).
7. F. 120v: King David Playing the Harp (reverse direction of normal iconography).
8. F. 130r: Saint Joseph holding Flowers.
9. F. 130v: *Abba* Qerəlos (Archbishop of Ethiopia in the 1920's and 30's) holding a hand cross and a prayer stick.
10. F. 141r: Madonna and Child.

Notes:
1. In every case, the miniatures are on parchment folios that are of a slightly different size than the surrounding folios.
2. Recto of the fore guard leaf (Iv), and ff. 141v–142v blank, save for some scrawls.
3. F. 55r: A note in red ink and circled in red marks the midpoint of the Psalms.
4. Some folios have severe water stains.
5. Decorative designs: line of alternating red and black dots or marks in ff. 1r, 7r, 13r, 20r, 29r, 35v, 41v, 50r, 61r, 68r, 73r, 84r (red dots only),

95r, 97v, 103r, 121v (with black line box around it), 128r (with black line box around it), 129v.
6. Columetric layout of text: ff. 116v–118v (tenth biblical canticle).
7. Overlooked words of text are written interlinearly (ff. 14v, 17r, 123v); and overlooked lines of text are written interlinearly (ff. 73r and 115v).
8. The scribe regularly has to complete a line of text on another line. Much of the problem is addressed through the selection of an appropriate aspect ratio for the codex combined with an appropriate script size. But, where the line of text is still too long, the scribe completes the line of text above the end of the line (throughout) or below the line (ff. 45v, 47r, 48v, 53r, 62v, 119r, 122v, etc.). This scribe will also reduce the font size at the end of lines to avoid having to go onto the next line (e.g., f. 21r, 23v, 32rv, etc.).
9. Provenance, etc. This codex was donated to Trinity Western University in 1993 by Brian L. Fargher, who purchased it in Ethiopia in the 1960's. A placard that is inside the front cover states: "THE PSALMS OF DAVID Hand Written in Ancient Geez Language on Sheepskin Parchment—From Lake Tsana Island Monastery—Ethiopia. Date Unknown—Probably pre 1700."

Quire Map

Protection Quire — i

A folio stub is visible between ff. i and 1.

Quire 1: 1 2 3 4 5 6 7 8 9 10

Quire 2: 11 12 13 14 15 16 17 18 19 20 21 22

Quire 3: 23 24 25 26 27 28 29 30 31 32 33 34

Quire 4: 35 36 37 38 39 40 41 42 43 44 45 46 47

A folio stub is visible between ff. 43 and 44.

Quire 5: 48 49 50 51 52 53 54 55 56 57 58 59

Quire 6: 60 61 62 63 64 65 66 67 68 69 70 71 72

A folio stub is visible between ff. 72 and 73.

Quire 7: 73 74 75 76 77 78 79 80 81 82 83 84

Stubs appear between ff. 76 and 77 and between ff. 79 and 80.

Quire 8: 85 86 87 88 89 90 91 92 93 94 95 96

Quire 9: 97 98 99 100 101 102 103 104 105 106 107 108

Quire 10: 109 110 111 112 113 114 115 116 117 118

Quire 11: 119 120 121 122 123 124 125 126 127 128 129

A folio stub is visible between ff. 128 and 129.

Quire 12: 130 131 132 133 134 135 136 137 138 139 140 141 142

Stubs appear between ff. 129 and 130 and between ff. 130 and 131 and between ff. 132 and 133 and between ff. 137 and 138 and between ff. 141 and 142.

EMIP 56 – Trinity Western University Codex 2
Images, መልክዐ፡ ጉባኤ፡

Parchment, 105 x 77 x 30 mm, three Coptic chain stitches attached with bridle attachments to rough-hewn boards, protection quire + 7 full quires, ii + 72 folios, 101 x 80 mm, top margin 13 mm, bottom margin 28 mm, fore edge margin 12 mm, gutter margin 5 mm, ff. iv(erso)–72r one column, Gəʻəz, 12 lines, 19th (ff.63r–71r, 20th) cent.

Quire descriptions: quires 1–7 balanced.

1. Ff. 1r–19r: Image of Michael, መልክዐ፡ ሚካኤል፡. EMIP 16, f. 92v.
2. Ff. 21r–41r: Image of Jesus Christ, መልክዐ፡ ኢየሱስ፡. EMIP 26, 47r.
3. Ff. 41r–62v: Image of Mary, መልክዐ፡ ማርያም፡. EMIP 25, f. 1r.
4. Ff. 63r–71r: Image of Gabriel, መልክዐ፡ ገብርኤል፡. Chaîne, Répertoire, no. 246; MG 59, pp. 312ff.
   በሰላም፡ ገብርኤል፡ መልአክ፡ በዓለ፡ ማርያም፡ ዘአ (sic) ዘአዕረፈ፡፡
   ከመ፡ እዜኑ፡ ጎዳጠ፡ ወአኮ፡ ትሩፈ፡፡

Varia:
1. F. Iv: Note that the promised vow is one curtain.

2. F. IIv: Note on the vow to kill a cow for Ḥara Mädḫane 'Aläm church if the person who vowed and his/her daughter are healed from the cough.
3. Ff. 19r and 19v: Personal prayer (of Askalä Ṣəyon) to the Lord for salvation.
4. F. Record of an unidentified incident that happened to the writer of the note on Yäkkatit 25, 1935 EC (March 4, 1943 AD).

Notes:
1. Ff. 63r–71v: purple ink used instead of red.
2. Decorative designs: f. 1r (*haräg* using black); ff. 19r, 62v (dotted line using alternating black and red); f. 41 (row of full-stop symbols).
3. Prayer for Askalä Ṣəyon, f. 71r.
4. Ff. Ir, IIr, 20rv 71v and 72v: blank.
5. Overlooked lines of text are written interlinearly (f. 56v).
6. Provenance: This codex was donated to Trinity Western University by Robert N. Thompson, who spent some years immediately following World War II in Ethiopia working with the Ministry of Education. Later, he served with the mission organization, SIM (then "Sudan Interior Mission," now "Serving In Ministry").

Quire Map

Protection Quire — i ii

Quire 1 — 1 2 3 4 5 6 7 8 9 10

Quire 2 — 11 12 13 14 15 16 17 18 19 20

Quire 3 — 21 22 23 24 25 26 27 28 29 30

Quire 4 — 31 32 33 34 35 36 37 38 39 40

Quire 5 — 41 42 43 44 45 46 47 48 49 50

Quire 6 — 51 52 53 54 55 56 57 58 59 60 61 62

Quire 7: 63 64 65 66 67 | 68 69 70 | 71 72

EMIP 57 – Trinity Western University Ethiop MS 3
Fragment of a Psalter, ዳዊት:

Parchment, 170 x 150 mm, unbound stack of quires, loosely connected with strings. Many sheets have been repaired with reinforcement strips. 6 full quires, none of which appear to be numbered (though, the areas where many of the quire numbers would appear are covered with reinforcement strips), 50 folios, 150 x 137 mm, top margin 15–20 mm, bottom margin 35–38 mm, fore edge margin 15–18 mm, gutter margin 10–12 mm, ff. 1–50r one column, ff. 50rv two columns, Ge'ez, 17 lines, 17th cent.

Navigation systems: marginal notations using the symbol for the number 100 to indicate readings.

Ff. 1r–50v: Psalter [Dawit]. Cf. EMIP 1.
1. Ff. 1r–27r: End of Psalms of David, beginning at Psalm 93 (missing Psalms 118–144), and rebound in disorder.
2. Ff. 27r–41r: Biblical Canticles.
3. Ff. 41r–50r: Song of Songs, common version.
4. Ff. 50rv: Beginning of Praises of Mary [Wəddase Maryam].

Notes:
1. Decorative designs: ff. 5v, 27r (crude *haräg*-like design using only black ink); ff. 50r (section divider using a line of alternating red and black marks in conjunction with several full-stop symbols).
2. Overlooked words of text are written interlinearly (ff. 22v, 23r, 28r); and overlooked lines of text are written interlinearly (ff. 17r, 18rv, 20v).
3. This scribe has avoided the problem of lines of text too long to fit on one line by adopting an aspect ratio that leaves ample room for the width of most lines. On a few occasions, the line would have been too long and the scribe finishes the end of the line with words written smaller so as to avoid leftover text (e.g., ff. 7v, 21r). Occasionally a line is still too long and has to be completed above or below the end of the line. In these cases, the scribe places the material above (e.g., ff. 2r, 14r, 25v, 26v, 27r, 29v, 33v, 41v, 43r, etc.) or below (e.g., ff. 21v, 30v, 35r, 39r, 42rv, 43rv, 44r, etc.) the line.
4. Provenance: This codex was donated to Trinity Western University by Robert N. Thompson, who spent some years immediately following World War II in Ethiopia working with the Ministry of Education.

Later, he served with the mission organization, SIM (then "Sudan Interior Mission," now "Serving In Ministry").

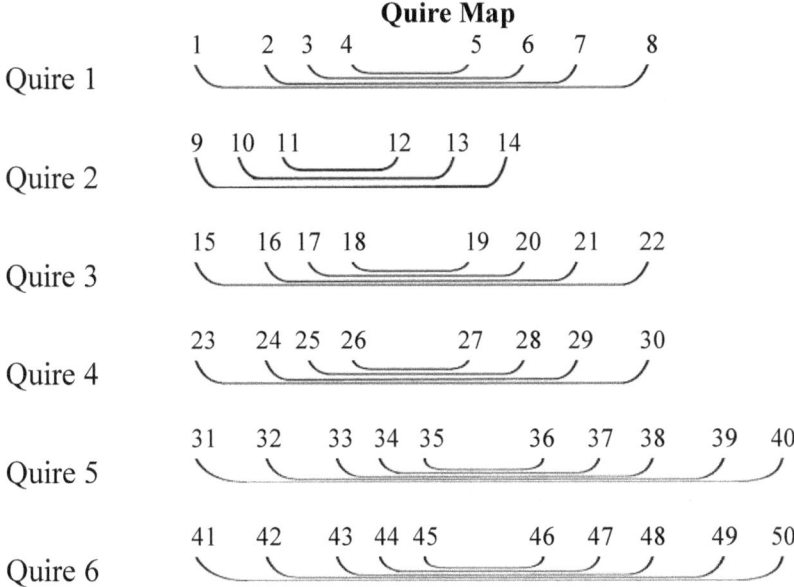

EMIP 58 – Tsunami Codex 1
Anaphora of Our Lady Mary, ቅዳሴ፡ ማርያም፡

Parchment, 120 x 93 x 40 mm, four Coptic chain stitches attached with bridle attachments to rough-hewn boards covered with tooled leather over decorative linen patches (red with yellow floral) visible inside the turn-ins on front and back cover, headband and tailband, protection quire + 9 full quires, iv + 70 folios, 118 x 88 mm, top margin 13–15 mm, bottom margin 27–30 mm, fore edge margin 15 mm, gutter margin 8–10 mm, ff. 1r–69v one column, Gəʿəz, 9 lines, 19th/20th cent.

Quire descriptions: quires 1–4, 6–9 balanced; quire 5 adjusted balanced.

Ff. 1r–69v: Anaphora of Our Lady Mary ascribed to Cyriacus of Bəhənsa, G^was'a. See EMIP 27.

Notes:
1. The general condition of the parchment is quite good, though there is some water staining at the bottom of several pages.
2. Copied beautifully for Gäbrä Ǝgzi'abḥer, ff.1v and 69r.
3. Ff. Ir–IVv and 70rv blank.

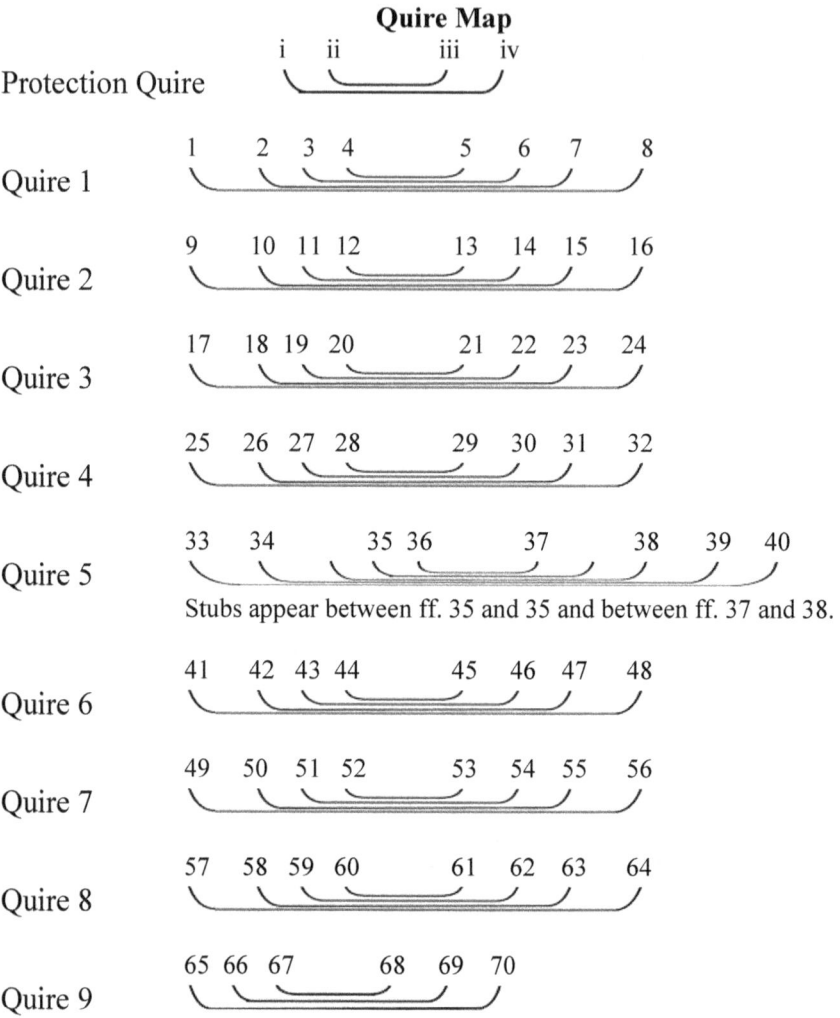

EMIP 59 – The Kahan Codex
Missal, መጽሐፈ፡ ቅዳሴ፡

Parchment, 220 x 160 x 35 mm, two heavy paste boards covered in linen and then covered in tooled, red leather. The quires are stitched together along four points in a chain stitch. However, the stitching does not attach to the board, as is usual in Ethiopic bindings. Instead, the cover appears to be a modified Islamic binding. The cover was made off the book without the envelope flap usual on Islamic bindings before 1700. The spine inside the case is covered in linen. The case was adhered to the book block with hinge linings. It has neither head nor tail bands. The quires are not well trimmed so that the folios are quite uneven at the fore edge and top and bottom. Ten full quires, 94 folios, 190–210 x 150–157 mm, ff. 1v–94v two columns, Gəʻəz, 18–22 lines, reign of Haile Sellassie (1930–1974), f.88r.

Quire descriptions: quires 1–3, 5, 8, 9 balanced; quires 4, 6, 10 adjusted balanced; quire 7 unbalanced.

Ff. 1r–94v: Missal, መጽሐፈ፡ ቅዳሴ፡. Mostly supplied with musical notation. See EMIP 27.

1. Ff. 1r–10v, and 87r–91v: (11r–19v): Office prayers. Prayer of the Covenant, f. 1r; Supplications, f.4r; Litanies, f. 6r; Zä-yənäggəś supplications, ff.9v–19v and 87r–91v.
2. Ff. 91v–94v and 11r–19v: Ordinary of the Mass.
3. Ff. 20r–86v: The Anaphoras. Incomplete at the end. Anaphora of the Apostles, f. 20r; Our Lord Jesus Christ, f. 29v; Our Lady Mary ascribed to Cyriacus of Bəhənsa (*Gwäs'a*), f. 33r; John Son of Thunder, f. 42v; James of Sarug, f. 50v; Dioscorus, f. 56r; John Chrysostom, f. 59r; Cyril of Alexandria, f. 63v; Gregory (I), *Nä'kk^wəto*, f. 70r; Epiphanius, f. 76r.

Miniatures, all in a late twentieth-century hand, over the top of text:
1. F. 31v: Jesus Carrying the Cross.
2. F. 42r: The Flogging of Jesus.
3. F. 70r: Temptation of Jesus by the Devil.

Notes:
1. Decorative designs: ff. 19v, 63r (line of only black stop dots).
2. Overlooked words of text are written interlinearly (ff. 24r and 59r)
3. Provenance: Purchased in January 2005 in a shop in Addis Ababa for about $400.

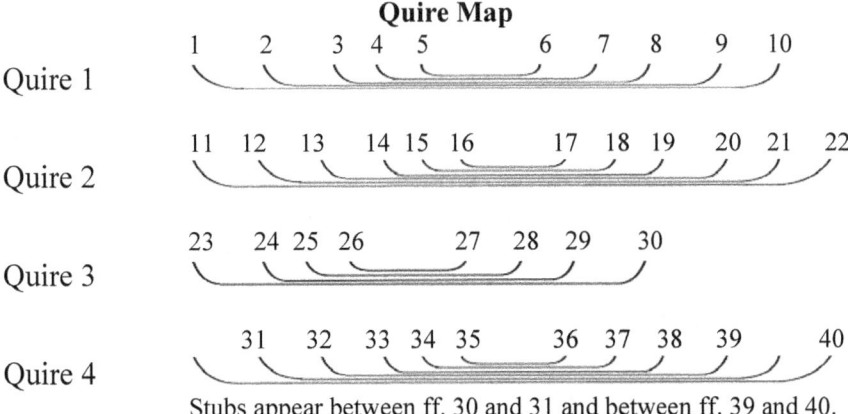

Stubs appear between ff. 30 and 31 and between ff. 39 and 40.

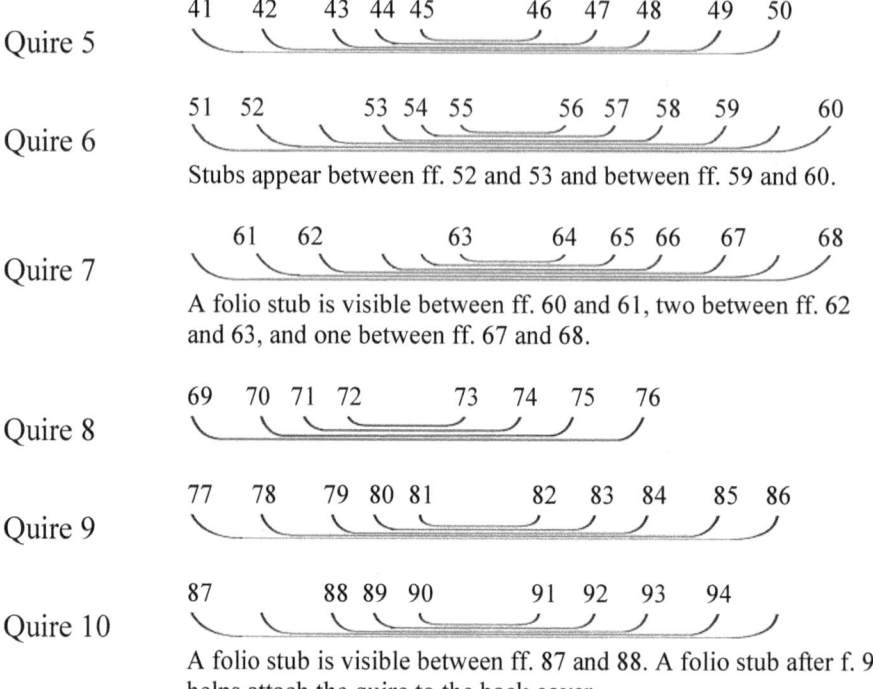

Stubs appear between ff. 52 and 53 and between ff. 59 and 60.

A folio stub is visible between ff. 60 and 61, two between ff. 62 and 63, and one between ff. 67 and 68.

A folio stub is visible between ff. 87 and 88. A folio stub after f. 94 helps attach the quire to the back cover.

EMIP 60 – Eliza Codex 30
Psalter, ዳዊት፡

Parchment, 143 x 147 x 68 mm, four Coptic chain stitches (original with some repairs) attached with bridle attachments to rough-hewn boards, the quires have been punched with holes to affix them to headband and tailband, but none are present, protection quire + 19 full quires, ii + 178 folios, 138 x 138 mm, top margin 13 mm, bottom margin 30–37 mm, fore edge margin 15–18 mm, gutter margin 5–7 mm, ff. i–158r one column, ff. 159r–178v two columns, Gəʽəz, 18 lines, 18th cent.

Quire descriptions: quires 1–19 balanced. Navigation systems: 1) brown yarn sewn into the corners of folios 10, 40, 70, 100, 130, 161, 166, and 177 to mark the location of miniatures; 2) white string sewn into the corners of folios 84, 91, 105, 117, 121, 128, and 135 to mark content divisions.

Ff. 1r–175v: Psalter [*Dawit*]. Cf. EMIP 1.
1. Ff. 1r–135r: Psalms of David.
2. Ff. 135r–150r: Biblical Canticles.
3. Ff. 150r–158r: Song of Songs, common version.

4. Ff. 159r–170r: Praises of Mary [Wəddase Maryam]. Arranged for the days of the week (Monday, f. 159r; Tuesday, f. 160r; Wednesday, f. 162r; Thursday, f. 164r; Friday, f. 165v; Saturday, f. 166v; Sunday, f. 168r).
5. Ff. 170r–175v: Gate of Light [Anqäṣä Bərhan].

Miniatures, all in the late twentieth-century hand of the "speckled garment artist," painted over text:
1. F. 11r: Saint with a book.
2. F. 41r: Breaking the Bread at the Last Supper.
3. F. 71r: The Holy Trinity.
4. F. 101r: Madonna and Child.
5. F. 131r: The Striking of the Head.
6. F. 160v: Taking off the Robe of Jesus.
7. F. 167r: The Flogging of Jesus.
8. F. 176v: The Sacrifice of Isaac.

Varia:
1. Ff. Ir–IIv: Ps 49:14–51:9 from a different manuscript.
2. Ff. 175v–178v: Matt 25:1–14.
3. Ff. 177r: *Asmat* prayer against evil spirits. Insufficiently legible; perhaps Abbadie 143, f. 53r, Conti Rossini, Notice no. 109.
   በስመ፡ አብ፡ . . . ጸሎት፡ [በእን]ተ፡ ባርያ፡ ወተግባረ፡ [ሰ]ብእ፡ ዘይሰልብ፡ ልበ፡ [ሰ]ብእ፡ ወያጻልም፡ አዕይንተ፡ . . .
4. F. 177v: *Asmat* prayer to Jesus Christ against eye disease and headache.
   በስመ፡ አብ፡ በል፡ ክርስቶስ፡ ዘበምራቅከ፡ ከሠትከ፡ አዕይንተ፡ ዕውራን፡ ወበቃልከ፡ ይትፈወሱ፡ ድውያን፡ ለዛቲ፡ ነፍስ፡ ሕምምት፡ ወጥውቅት፡ . . . አድኅን፡ ነፍሶ፡ ወሥጋሆ፡ ወአብርህ፡ አዕይንቲሁ፡ . . . ተገነዐንኩ፡ በስመ፡ እግ"፡ ሕያው፡ ታአስ፡ ሜሎሳዊ፡ . . .
5. F. 177v: *Asmat* prayer for help in learning.
   በስመ፡ አብ፡ . . . በፍንግኃኤል፡ ስሙ፡ ለእግ"፡ በጽምጽማኤል፡ ስሙ፡ ለእ"፡ . . . ረስዮ፡ ለአንበልብሎ፡ መጻሕፍት፡ . . .
6. F. 178r: Matt 26:26–29; Mark 14:22–25; and Luke. 22:19–20.
7. F. 178v: Calendar of the Apostles and Evangelists.

Notes:
1. Decorative designs: Decorative designs: ff. iiv(erso) and 175v (*haräg* using black ink or pencil); ff. 1r, 46v, 91r, and 135r (*haräg* using black and red ink); ff. 8v, 17r, 25v, 37v, 53r, 63r, 75v, 84v, 105r, 117v, 121r, and 128r (line of alternating red and black dots); f. 158r (line of full stop symbols).

2. F. 69r: A two-word note circled in red and black marks the midpoint of the Psalms.
3. The codex arrived with a loose sheet between ff. 16 and 17. The location was clearly wrong since the text of the psalm ran from the bottom of f. 16v to the top of f. 17r. Another loose folio (f. 30) was identified and the gutter join showed itself to match up. F. 30 is the last folio in a quire, suggesting that the loose sheet should be f. 21. The flow of the content made it clear that the correct location of the folio should be after f. 20. The loose sheet was accordingly moved to its correct location.
4. The general condition of the vellum is very worn, stained and dirty.
5. F. 10v has Psalm 15 beginning on line 7 (superscription) and 8. The folio ends with the 11th line of Psalm 15. A full-page illumination is on the next folio, f. 11r. The first line on f. 11v is not the 12th line of Psalm 15, but the 5th line of Psalm 16. There is a lacuna of about 18 lines, precisely the number of lines that would have been on f. 11r, which has apparently been painted over.
6. The back cover is broken in two places along the grain (about 50 mm and 90 mm from the gutter), leaving three pieces that have been stitched together by drilling three small holes (10 mm, 60 mm and 120 mm from the top) and stitching the boards together. The front board is likewise broken and all but 35 mm of it (the part nearest the gutter) is missing. Pieces of heavy cardboard have been sewn together and then attached to the remaining piece of wood to function as a replacement front cover.
7. Overlooked words of text are written interlinearly (ff. ii v(erso), 18v, 46v, 72v, 156v, 167v); and overlooked lines of text are written interlinearly (ff. 105r, 138r).
8. This scribe regularly has avoided the problem of lines of text too long to fit on one line by adopting an aspect ratio that leaves ample room for the width of most lines. When a line is too long, the scribe places the material above the line (e.g., ff. 5v, 9r, 12r, 14r, 19v, 22r, etc.).

Quire Map

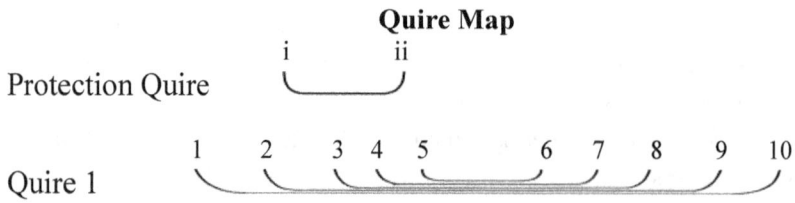

Catalogue of the Ethiopic Manuscript Imaging Project · 163

Quire 2	11 12 13 14 15 16 17 18 19 20
Quire 3	21 22 23 24 25 26 27 28 29 30
Quire 4	31 32 33 34 35 36 37 38 39 40
Quire 5	41 42 43 44 45 46 47 48 49 50
Quire 6	51 52 53 54 55 56 57 58 59 60
Quire 7	61 62 63 64 65 66 67 68 69 70
Quire 8	71 72 73 74 75 76 77 78 79 80
Quire 9	81 82 83 84 85 86 87 88 89 90
Quire 10	91 92 93 94 95 96 97 98 99 100
Quire 11	101 102 103 104 105 106 107 108 109 110
Quire 12	111 112 113 114 115 116 117 118 119 120
Quire 13	121 122 123 124 125 126 127 128 129 130
Quire 14	131 132 133 134 135 136 137 138 139 140
Quire 15	141 142 143 144 145 146 147 148 149 150
Quire 16	151 152 153 154 155 156 157 158 159 160

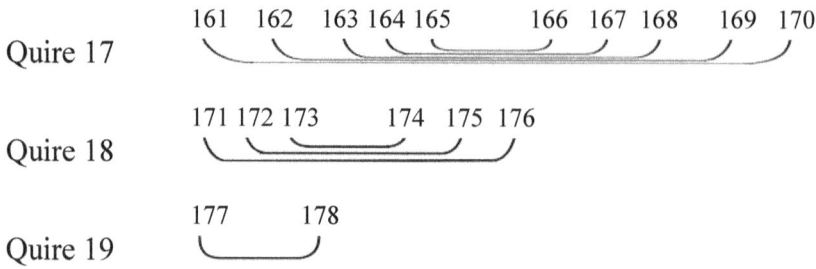

EMIP 61 – Eliza Codex 31
Psalter, ዳዊት፡

Parchment, 185 x 143 x 60 mm, four Coptic chain stitches attached with bridle attachments to rough-hewn boards, one protection folio and additional front quire + 15 full quires, quires 2–15 numbered, though some are faint, i + 151 folios, 180 x 142 mm, top margin 20 mm, bottom margin 30 mm, fore edge margin 18 mm, gutter margin 10 mm, ff. 1r–136v one column, ff. 1r–5r and 137r–149r two columns, Gəʿəz, 21–24 lines, 20th cent.

Quire descriptions: quires 1–5, 9–15 balanced; quires 6–8, adjusted balanced. Navigation systems: 1) brown yarn sewn into corners of folios to mark the location of miniatures; 2) various colored string sewn into corners of ff. 12, 19, 24, 29, 43, 49, 67, 74, 80, 92, 107, 113, 130, 137, 145, and 146 to mark content divisions.

1. Ff. 1r–5v: Image of Michael, መልክዐ፡ ሚካኤል፡. EMIP 16, f. 92v (f. 5v: painting over text).
2. Ff. 1r–151v: Psalter [*Dawit*]. Cf. EMIP 1.
    a. Ff. 6r–119r: Psalms of David.
    b. Ff. 119v–130v: Biblical Canticles.
    c. Ff. 131r–136v: Song of Songs, common version.
    d. Ff. 137r–145r: Praises of Mary [*Wəddase Maryam*]. Arranged for the days of the week (Monday, f. 137r; Tuesday, f. 137v; Wednesday, f. 139r; Thursday, f. 140v; Friday, f. 142v; Saturday, f. 143v; Sunday, f. 144v).
    e. Ff. 145v–149r: Gate of Light [*Anqäṣä Bərhan*], incomplete because illumination painted over last folio of text.

Miniatures (1 and 10 appear to be older; miniatures 2-9 are in the late twentieth-century hand of the "speckled garment artist," painted over text:

Catalogue of the Ethiopic Manuscript Imaging Project · 165

1. F. Ir Madonna and Child.
2. F. Iv: Seated Saint with a Book before Mary.
3. F. 5v: King David Playing the Harp.
4. F. 56v: Madonna and Child.
5. F. 96v: The Crucifixion.
6. F. 149v: Jesus Carrying the Cross.
7. F. 150r: The Last Supper.
8. F. 150v: The Burial of Jesus.
9. F. 151r: The Resurrection, raising Adam and Eve.
10. F. 151v: The Holy Trinity, with the Trisagion as a caption.

Notes:
1. F. 62v: Marginal note at 78:14 indicating the point "half" of the way through the Psalms: "half of it above; half of it below."
2. The general condition of the vellum is unworn and clean.
3. Decorative designs: ff. 1r, 74v, 80r, 92v, and 104v (*haräg* using Green, Red and Brown); f. 6r (*haräg* using red, brown and yellow);. ff. 26v, 49r, 119v, and 137r (*haräg* using black and red); f. 107v (*haräg* using black, yellow and green); ff. 12v, 19r, 26r, 36v, 43v, 104r, 113r, 119r, 130v, 139r, 140v, 142v, 143v, 144v, and 145r (dotted line using alternating black and red); f. 92r (line of pairs of black and red dots); f. 137v (red line).
4. Columetric layout of text: ff. 116v (?)(Ps 145), 117v (Ps. 148), 118v (Ps. 150), 127rv (tenth biblical canticle).
5. F. 62v: Four words in an ornate box in the margin mark the midpoint of the Psalms: "half above; half below."
6. Isolated names are written on many folios in crude hands.
7. Two names are given as the copyists: Wäldä Giyorgis, f. 79v, and Aśrat, f. 119r (possibly for Gäbrä Iyyäsus, ff. 92r, 104r, 119r and *passim*).
8. Overlooked words of text are written interlinearly (f. 148r); and overlooked lines of text are written interlinearly (ff. 57v, 91r).
9. This scribe regularly has avoided the problem of lines of text too long to fit on one line by adopting an aspect ratio that leaves ample room for the width of most lines. When a line is too long, the scribe places the material above (e.g., ff. 6r, 7v, 11r, 14v, 16v, etc.) or below (f. 91r) the line.

Quire Map

Initial (secondary) Quire

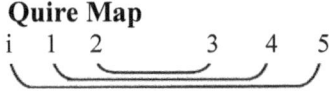

The first quire is of later origin than the rest of the codex. Its binding into the rest of the codex is out of place. The hand and ink are different than the other quires. It is not part of the quire numbering scheme that is on the rest of the quires.

Quire 1: 6 7 8 9 10 11 12 13 14 15

Quire 2: 16 17 18 19 20 21 22 23 24 25

Quire 3: 26 27 28 29 30 31 32 33 34 35

Quire 4: 36 37 38 39 40 41 42 43 44 45

Quire 5: 46 47 48 49 50 51 52 53 54 55

Quire 6: 56 57 58 59 60 61 62 63 64 65

Stubs appear between ff. 59 and 60 and between ff. 60 and 61.

Quire 7: 66 67 68 69 70 71 72 73 74 75

Stubs appear between ff. 69 and 70 and between ff. 70 and 71.

Quire 8: 76 77 78 79 80 81 82 83 84 85

Stubs appear between ff. 80 and 81 and between ff. 81 and 82.

Quire 9: 86 87 88 89 90 91 92 93 94 95

Quire 10: 96 97 98 99 100 101 102 103 104 105

Quire 11: 106 107 108 109 110 111 112 113 114 115

Quire 12: 116 117 118 119 120 121 122 123 124 125

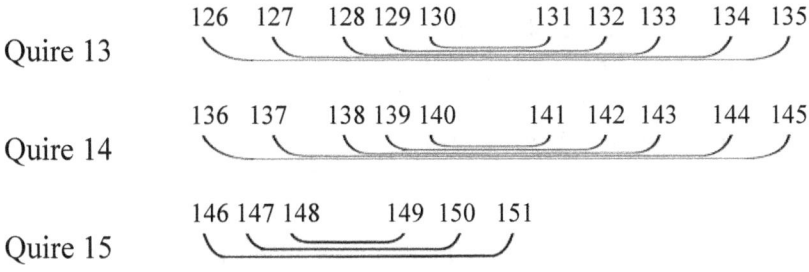

EMIP 62 – Eliza Codex 32
Psalter, ዳዊት፡

Parchment, 160 x 125 x 58 mm, four Coptic chain stitches attached with bridle attachments to rough-hewn boards covered with tooled leather. The back cover has a woven material visible inside the turn-ins, headband and tailband, one protection quire + 17 full quires, ii + 170 folios, 155 x 120 mm, top margin 15 mm, bottom margin 27–30 mm, fore edge margin 20–22 mm, gutter margin 10 mm, ff. 1r–148r one column, ff. 148v–168v two columns, Gəʽəz, 21 lines, 19th/20th cent.

Quire descriptions: quires 1–17 balanced. Navigation system: brown yarn sewn into corners of folios to mark the location of miniatures.

Ff. 1r–168v: Psalter [*Dawit*]. Cf. EMIP 1.

1. Ff. 1r–127r: Psalms of David. Arranged for the days of the week (Monday, f. 1r; Tuesday, f. 23v; Wednesday, f. 48v; Thursday, f. 70r; Friday, f. 98r; Saturday, f. 114r; Sunday, f. 127v).
2. Ff. 127v–140v: Biblical Canticles.
3. Ff. 140v–148r: Song of Songs, common version.
4. Ff. 148v–162r: Praises of Mary [*Wəddase Maryam*]. Arranged for the days of the week (Monday, f. 148v; Tuesday, f. 149v; Wednesday, f. 152r; Thursday, f. 154v; Friday, f. 157v; Saturday, f. 159v; Sunday, f. 160v).
5. Ff. 162v–168v: Gate of Light [*Anqäṣä Bərhan*].

Miniatures (3–10 in late twentieth-century hand of the "speckled garment artist," painted over text):

1. F. Ir: Crude drawing of a person.
2. F. Iv: Crude drawing of a person with crosses on right and left.
3. F. IIr: The twelve Apostles.
4. F. IIv: King David Playing the Harp.
5. F. 24r: The Holy Trinity.
6. F. 51r: The Crucifixion.
7. F. 85r: Jesus Carrying the Cross.

8. F. 141r: The Striking of the Head.
   9. F. 169r: The Last Supper.
   10. F. 169v: Judas Betrays Jesus.
   11. F. 170r: Crude drawing of a man.
   12. F. 170v: Crude drawing of *Qes* Amdu of Bašo Däbr on a horse.

Varia:
   1. F. 148r: The first few words of the Praises of Mary.
   2. F. 168v: Calendar of the holy days of the year, erased at the end to make room for the picture.

Notes:
   1. Decorative designs: ff. 1r, 23v, 48v, 70r, 84v, 98r, 114r, 127v, and 148v (*haräg* using black and red); ff. 8r, 15r, 34r, 42r, 48r, 58r, 69v, 78v, 97v, 110v, 113v, 120r, 127r, 140v, 148rv, 149v, 159r, and 168v (dotted line using alternating black and red), ff. 8r and 159r (full stop symbol); f. 69v (lined black dots).
   2. Columetric layout of text: ff. 126v (Ps. 150), 136r–137r (tenth biblical canticle).
   3. The general condition of the vellum is only slightly worn and dirty.
   4. Overlooked words of text are written interlinearly (f. 4v); and overlooked lines of text are written interlinearly (ff. 37r, 41v, 67r, 71v).
   5. The scribe regularly has to complete a line of text on another line. Much of the problem is addressed through the selection of an appropriate aspect ratio for the codex combined with an appropriate script size. But, where the line of text is still too long, the scribe reduces the font size at the end of lines to avoid having to go onto the next line (throughout). This scribe also will complete the line of text above the end of the line (e.g., ff. 2v, 20r, 23v, 78v).

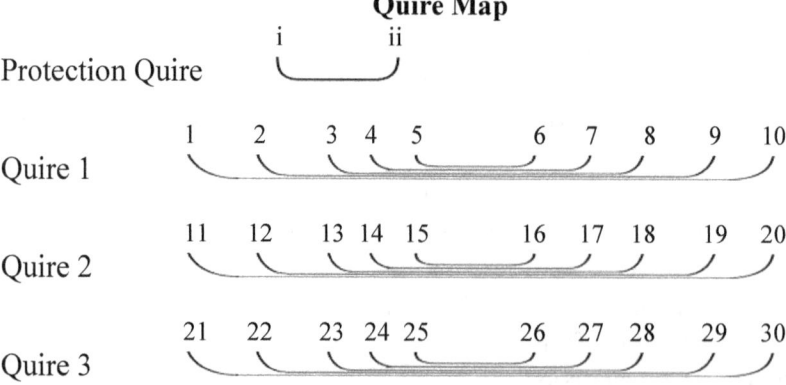

Quire Map

Catalogue of the Ethiopic Manuscript Imaging Project · 169

Quire 4: 31 32 33 34 35 36 37 38 39 40

Quire 5: 41 42 43 44 45 46 47 48 49 50

Quire 6: 51 52 53 54 55 56 57 58 59 60

Quire 7: 61 62 63 64 65 66 67 68 69 70

Quire 8: 71 72 73 74 75 76 77 78 79 80

Folio 76 is a half-sheet that has been sewn onto a stub that extends about .5 cm from the gutter.

Quire 9: 81 82 83 84 85 86 87 88 89 90

Quire 10: 91 92 93 94 95 96 97 98 99 100

Quire 11: 101 102 103 104 105 106 107 108 109 110

Quire 12: 111 112 113 114 115 116 117 118 119 120

Quire 13: 121 122 123 124 125 126 127 128 129 130

Quire 14: 131 132 133 134 135 136 137 138 139 140

Quire 15: 141 142 143 144 145 146 147 148 149 150

Quire 16: 151 152 153 154 155 156 157 158 159 160

Quire 17: 161 162 163 164 165 166 167 168 169 170

EMIP 63 – Eliza Codex 33
Amharic Commentary on Our Father

Parchment, 160 x 118 x 42 mm, three Coptic chain stitches attached with bridle attachments to rough-hewn boards covered with tooled leather over decorative linen patches visible inside the turn-ins on front and back cover, headband and tailband, protection quire + 5 full quires (plus illustration sheets between quires 1 and 2, 2 and 3, 3 and 4, 4 and 5, and after 5), quires 2–4 numbered (ignoring illustration sheets), ii + 42 folios, 153 x 118 mm, top margin 12–20 mm, bottom margin 30–34 mm, fore edge margin 15–18 mm, gutter margin 8 mm, ff. 1r–39r one column, Gə'əz, 14–15 lines per page (though some reduced to 11 or 12 lines, e.g. 10v–12r), 20th cent.

Quire descriptions: quires 1–3, 5 balanced; quire 4 adjusted balanced.

Ff. 1r–39r: Amharic Commentary on Our Father, ትርጓሜ፡ አቡነ፡ ዘበሰማያት፡.

Miniatures:
1. F. Iv: *Abunä* Samu'el riding a lion.
2. F. IIr: Ethiopian Dignitary (St. Yared?) with prayer stick and *sistrum*.
3. F. 7v: The Crucifixion.
4. F. 8r: Ethiopian saint holding small cross, both arms uplifted.
5. F. 15v: Angel with Sword and hand cross; three figures at bottom of image.
6. F. 16r: Madonna and Child.
7. F. 23v: Saint George and the Dragon.
8. F. 24r: *Abunä* Arägawi holding snake.
9. F. 31v: *Abunä* Gäbrä Mänfäs Qəddus.
10. F. 32r: *Abunä* Täklä Haymanot.
11. F. 39v: Geometric drawing, box with cross on top.
12. F. 40r: Nine-box panel with geometric patterns and square face at center.
13. F. 41v: Geometric pattern with rectangular face at center.
14. F. 42r: Geometric pattern with square face at center.

Notes:
1. Decorative designs: f. 1r (*haräg* using multiple colors); ff. 2r (*haräg* using black and red).
2. Ff. Ir, 7r, 8v, 15r, 16v, 23r, 24v, 31r, 32v, 40v–41r and 42v blank.
3. Overlooked words of text are written interlinearly (ff. 12r, 17rv).

Quire Map

Protection Quire   i   ii

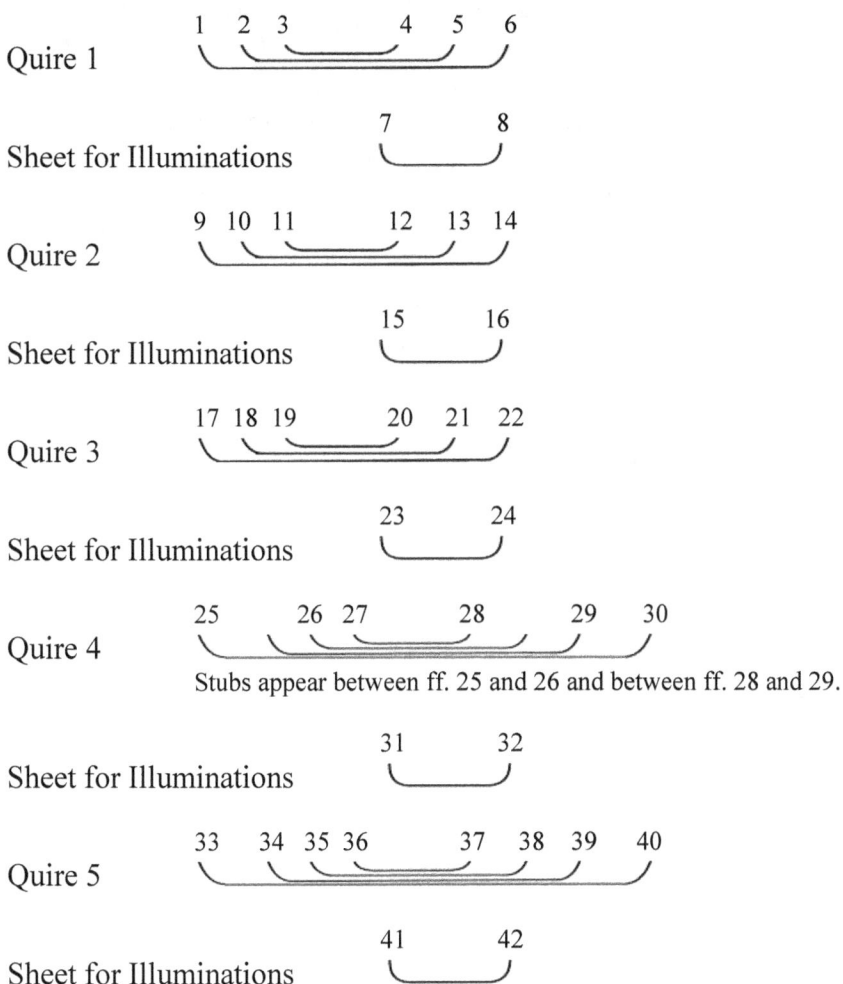

EMIP 64 – Eliza Codex 34
Gospel of John, ወንጌለ፡ ዮሐንስ፡

Parchment, 157 x 123 x 55 mm, four Coptic chain stitches attached with bridle attachments to rough-hewn boards covered with tooled leather, headband and tailband, protection quire + 12 full quires, quire 2 numbered, ii + 120 folios, 150 x 118 mm, top margin 17 mm, bottom margin 35 mm, fore edge margin 18–22 mm, gutter margin 5 mm, ff. ir–120v two columns (except 6 lines on f. 1r and 4 lines on f. 119r), Gəʿəz, 12–15 lines, 18th/19th cent.

172 · *Catalogue of the Codices*

Quire descriptions: quires 1–12 balanced. Navigation systems: 1) crimson yarn sewn into corners of folios 1, 20, 40, 60, 80, 100, 118 to mark the location of miniatures; 2) red colored string sewn into corner of folio 12 to mark content division. Double-slip case with a strap of leather.

1. Ff. ir–iir: Acts of *Abunä* Tärbu, ገድለ፡ አቡነ፡ ተርቡ፡. Incomplete at the beginning and at the end; S. Grébaut, "Abba Tarbou et le chien Koulb," *ROC*, vol. 30 (1835–36), pp. 433–41; EMML 1569, ff. 2ab and 4a.
2. Ff. 1r–118r: Gospel of John. Arranged for the days of the week (Monday, f. 8v; Tuesday, f. 33r; Wednesday, f. 69v; Thursday, f. 82v; Saturday, ff. 26r, 59r; Sunday, ff. 12r, 110v). Text, f. 1r; conclusion, *mäl'a*, f. 118r.

Miniatures, all in the late twentieth-century hand of the "speckled garment artist," painted over text:
1. F. IIv: Saint John.
2. F. 21r: The Striking of the Head.
3. F. 41r: Madonna and Child.
4. F. 61r: Saint George and the Dragon.
5. F. 81r: The Holy Trinity.
6. F. 101r: The Last Supper.
7. F. 119v: The Resurrection, raising Adam and Eve.
8. F. 120r: The Crucifixion.

Varia:
1. F. 118v: *Asmat* prayer whose purpose is not stated.
    ታኬም፡ ኬርአኬም፡ ኬርቴ፡ ሃፉሴ፡ ኃይለ፡ ቀራቶም፡ . . . ፯ ጊዜ፡ ድግ[ም]።
2. F. 118v: *Asmat* prayer and medical prescription for help in learning.
    አላኸየ፡ ኢላኸየ፡ ኤላኽ፡ የበለስ፡ ተቀጽላ፡ ሕፃን፡ አርብ፡ ረቡዕ፡ ይቁረጥ፡ . . .
3. Ff. 118v–119r: *Asmat* prayer whose purpose is not stated.
    እንፈረው፡ አስልጥቤ፡ እንፈሸው፡ እነሩህሉቤ፡ ወአላሃኩም፡ ኢላሁ፡ ዋሂዱ፡ ኢላለ፡ ሀይላለ፡ ወረሂማን፡ ወረሂብ፡ . . .
4. Ff. 119r and 120v: *Asmat* prayer against fever and pestilence. Incomplete in the middle, erased to make room for the pictures. It is not even clear if it is one prayer, but cf. Abbadie 206, f. 19v, Conti Rossini, Notice, no. 136.
    በስም፡ አብ፡ . . . ጸሎት፡ በእንተ፡ ፈሪ፡ ወቸነፈር፡ ሕማም፡ በሸታ፡ ወተስሕቦ፡ ዘያድኅን፡ ወትብል፡ በትሑት፡ ቃል፡ እሎንተ፡ አስማተ፡ ዓቢያተ፡ ኤኮስ፡ ለሚእለኬ፡ . . . በጸሎቱ፡ ለቅዱስ፡ ሚካኤል፡ ሊቀ፡ መላእክት፡ በጸሎታ፡ ወበስእለታ፡ . . .

Notes:
1. Decorative designs: ff. 1r (*haräg* using black and red); ff. 12r, 26r, 32v (dotted line using alternating black and red); ff. 1r (line of full-stop symbols connected by black lines).
2. Note of ownership by Čäkkol Gäbrä Śəllase and his wife Wälättä Mika'el, f. 120v.
3. Copied by Wäldä Gäbrə'el, f. 118r.
4. F. 32v, upper margin: John 5:45–47 is written and a mark at the end of column 2, line 7 indicates where the text belongs.
5. Overlooked words of text are written interlinearly (ff. 26r, 33v, 39r); and overlooked lines of text are written interlinearly (ff. 27r, 40v, 110r); and in the upper margin with a symbol (+) marking the location where the text is to be inserted (ff. 15r, line 4 and 40r, line 4), and in another case where the symbol (⊥) is used (f. 32v, line 7).

Quire Map

Protection Sheet — i, ii

Quire 1: 1 2 3 4 5 6 7 8 9 10
Quire 2: 11 12 13 14 15 16 17 18 19 20
Quire 3: 21 22 23 24 25 26 27 28 29 30
Quire 4: 31 32 33 34 35 36 37 38 39 40
Quire 5: 41 42 43 44 45 46 47 48 49 50
Quire 6: 51 52 53 54 55 56 57 58 59 60
Quire 7: 61 62 63 64 65 66 67 68 69 70
Quire 8: 71 72 73 74 75 76 77 78 79 80

Quire 9: 81 82 83 84 85 86 87 88 89 90

Quire 10: 91 92 93 94 95 96 97 98 99 100

Quire 11: 101 102 103 104 105 106 107 108 109 110

Quire 12: 111 112 113 114 115 116 117 118 119 120

EMIP 65 – Eliza Codex 35
Praises of Mary, ወዳሴ፡ ማርያም፡

Parchment, 120 x 82 x 23 mm, prepared for three rows of stitches and attachments but bound with a loose web of strings to rough-hewn boards made of the atypical wide-grained wood, 3 quires, 22 folios, 117 x 77 mm, top margin 8–12 mm, bottom margin 28–32 mm, fore edge margin 10 mm, gutter margin 5 mm, ff. 1r–22v one column, Gə'əz, 22 lines, early 20th cent.

Quire descriptions: quires 1–3 balanced.

Ff. 1v–21v: Praises of Mary.
1. Ff. 1v–13v: Praises of Mary [Wəddase Maryam]. Arranged for the days of the week (Monday, f. 1v; Tuesday, f. 2v; Wednesday, f. 5r; Thursday, f. 7r; Friday, f. 9v; Saturday, f. 11r; Sunday, f. 12v).
2. Ff. 13v–20r: Gate of Light [Anqäṣä Bərhan]. For the literature on these two praises, see EMIP 1.
3. Ff. 20r–21v: The hymn, "The Angels Praise Mary" [Yəweddəsəwwa Mäla'əkt]. Chaîne, Répertoire, no. 388; MD 59, pp. 519ff.

Varia:
1. F. 1r: The first hymn of the Praises of Mary, Wəddase Maryam.
2. F. 21v: Asmat prayer against the serpent, i.e. the Devil (käysi), in a crude hand.
3. F. 22rv: Record of transaction of a certain good, damaged with water stain.

Notes:
1. Decorative designs: f. 20r (two full rows of stops).
2. Several names, in crude hands, are copied on several pages.
3. Copied by Śahlä Maryam for Täklä Maryam, f. 20r.

4. Overlooked words of text are written in the upper margin with a symbol (⊥) marking the location where the text is to be inserted (f. 10v, line 18).

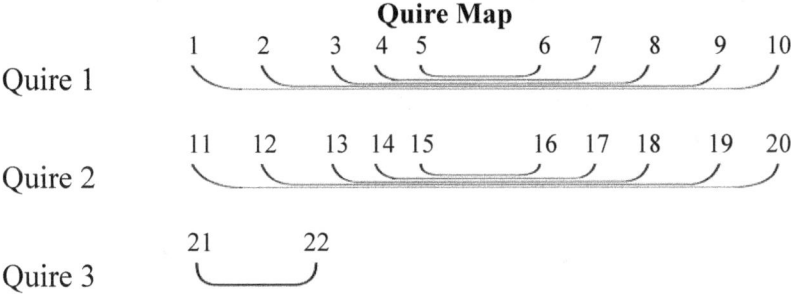

Quire Map

EMIP 66 – Eliza Codex 36
Prayer of Mary at Golgotha — The Mystagogia, ስኔ፡ ጎልጎታ፡ — ትምህርተ፡ ኅቡአት፡

Parchment, 108 x 65 x 40 mm, three Coptic chain stitches attached with bridle attachments to rough-hewn boards covered with floral-patterned (red with blue, white, and yellow), linen double-pouch cover, with a protection strap that runs from head of the spine around the text block fore edge, protection quire + 7 quires, quires 2–5 numbered, ii + 56 folios, 107 x 60 mm, top margin 11 mm, bottom margin 21 mm, fore edge margin 7 mm, gutter margin 7 mm, one column, Gəʻəz, 12–24 lines, 18th cent.

Quire descriptions: quires 1–7 balanced.

Ff. 1r–40r: Prayer of Mary at Golgotha, ጸሎተ፡ እግዝእትነ፡ ማርያም፡ ዘስኔ፡ ጎልጎታ፡. See EMIP 52.
1. Ff. 41r–50v: The Mystagogia. EMIP 4, f. IIv (varia).
2. Ff. 52v–53v, 50v–51r: Sword of Divinity, ሰይፈ፡ መለኮት፡. Incomplete; EMIP 33, f. 93r.
 በስመ፡ እግዚአብሔር፡ ቀዳማዊ፡ እንበለ፡ ትማልም፡.
3. Ff. 53v–55r: The prayer, "God of the luminaries," እግዚአብሔር፡ ዘብርሃናት፡. Incomplete; cf. EMIP 33, f. 113r.

Miniatures, all in twentieth-century hand, over the top of text:
   a. F. ir: Crude drawings of faces in pencil.
   b. F. 4r: Jesus (to the right) holds his hand up to two other people.
   c. F. 28r: Saint George and the Dragon.
   d. F. 56v: Jesus with three others, man in front of Jesus has one eye closed.

Varia:
1. F. Iv–IIv: *Asmat* prayer against evil spirits, damaged.
   . . አጋንንት፡ መግረሬ፡ [ፀ]ር፡ በከመ፡ ተሰዱ፡ [..]ግሙኪር፡ ባሪ [ያ፡] ወመቃውዜ፡ ዛ[ር፡] ወዛሪት፡ ሥራየ፡ [ጉ]ጻሌ፡ ወጠፍንት፡ ኑቢ፡ ወቄደር፡ ባርያ፡ ወነገርጋር፡ . . .
2. F. 40v: Fragment of a prayer to God.
   ሰ፡ (sic) ሕይወት፡ ወሰላም፡ እንዘ፡ ይጸውኑ፡ ብከ፡ ፍ.. ፡ ..ይማኖ..፡ ንጽሐ፡ ወትእግሥተ፡ ፍቅረ፡ ወኂሩተ፡ . . .
3. Ff. 51v–52v: Prayer against evil spirits. Incomplete at the beginning and at the end.
   . . እመሂ፡ በመዓልት፡ ወእመሂ፡ በሌሊት፡ እመሂ፡ በሡርክ፡ ወእመሂ፡ በጽልመት፡ ወበብርሃን፡ እመሂ፡ በቀትር፡ ወበሰአት፡ በኵሉ፡ ጊዜ፡ ወበኵሉ፡ ወርኅ፡ ኢትቅረቡ፡ ኃቤየ፡ . . ., f. 51v.

Notes:
1. Decorative designs: f. 1r (*haräg* using black and red); ff. 50v, 52v (dotted line using black).
2. Copied for Säfonyas, f. 50v.
3. Note of ownership by Wäldä Mäsqäl, ff. 11v, 12v and *passim*.
4. Overlooked words of text are written interlinearly (ff. 13v, 19r, 22v, 27r, 30r, 38v, 43r, 45v); and overlooked lines of text are written interlinearly (f. 37v).

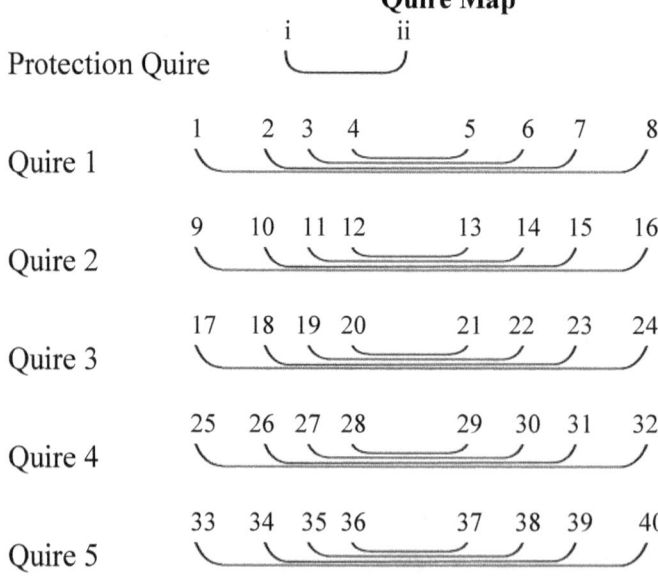

Quire Map

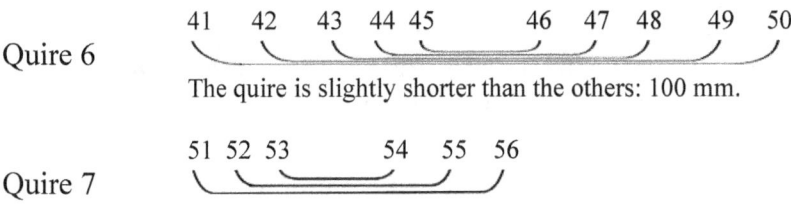

Quire 6

The quire is slightly shorter than the others: 100 mm.

Quire 7

EMIP 67 – Focanti Codex 1
Sword of the Trinity — *Asmat* prayers for the days of the week, ሰይፈ፡ ሥላሴ፡ — አስማት፡

Parchment, 172 x 109 x 50 mm, four altered Coptic chain stitches attached with bridle attachments to rough-hewn boards, protection quire + 11 full quires + 1 loose sheet, quires 1–4, 7 numbered, i + 102 folios, 169 x 105 mm, top margin 10–14 mm, bottom margin 30–38 mm, fore edge margin 15–21 mm, gutter margin 10 mm, ff. 1r–100r, 101r–102v one column, Gəʿəz, 18–20 lines, 19th cent.

Quire descriptions: quires 1–11 balanced. Navigation system: 1) various colored string sewn into corners of folios 11, 37, 52, 72, 77, 88 to mark content divisions.

1. Ff. 1r–40v, 49r–52v, lacuna, 53r–61v: Sword of the Trinity ሰይፈ፡ ሥላሴ፡. Arranged for the days of the week by the original and a later hand, but the manuscript is rebound in disorder. ([red ball-point pen] Monday, f. 4v; Tuesday, ff. 11v; Wednesday, f. 18v; Thursday, f. 23v; Friday, f. 30v; Saturday, f. 37v; Sunday, f. 52r; [black] Thursday, f. 23v; Friday, f. 30v; Sunday, f. 88r; [black framed by black] Friday, f. 77r; Saturday, f. 82r; [red] Wednesday, f. 46r); cf. EMIP 7.

2. Ff. 42v–48v, 62r–100v, and 101r–102v: A collection of *asmat* prayers for the days of the week. Arranged for the days of the week by the original and a later hand, but the manuscript is rebound in disorder. (Wednesday, f. 46r; Sunday, f. 52r; Monday, f. 62r; Thursday, f. 72r; Friday, f. 77r; Saturday, f. 82r; Sunday, f. 88r.
   Preserved in many copies, including Strelcyn, *Lincei*, 47; and EMML 1328, f. 54a.
   a. Ff. 42v–44r: Prayer of mercy that the angels and the clergy prayed. በስመ፡ አብ፡ . . . ጸሎተ፡ ምሕረት፡ ዘጸለዩ፡ መላእክት፡ ወስማዕት፡ ጻጻሳት፡ ወካህናት፡ ወመነኮሳት፡ ዕድ፡ ወአንስት፡ ወኵሎሙ፡ ተጋቢያሙ፡ ጸለዩ፡ ዘንተ፡ ጸሎተ፡ ኀበ፡ እግ"፡ መሐረኒ፡ መዋዒ፡ (sic) ፀር፡

b. Ff. 44rv: Prayer to keep Satan away.
በስመ፡ አብ፡ . . . ዘኢይቀርብከ፡ ሰይጣን፡ ዘንተ፡ ድግም፡ ወበል፡ በአስባኤል፡ (f. 44v) በአቅናኤል፡ በአማኑኤል፡ ...

c. Ff 44v–46r: Prayer to Christ for mercy.
ክርስቶስ፡ መሐረኒ፡ ክርስቶስ፡ ተማሃለኒ፡ ክርስቶስ፡ ርድአኒ፡ . . . እስመ፡ አንተ፡ ውእተ፡ ትመይጥ፡ (sic) ምክሮሙ፡ ለመ(f. 45r)ለእክት፡ (sic) በክስብኤል፡ . . .

d. Ff. 46r–48v: Prayer of salvation that descended to St. Thomas from heaven.
በስመ፡ አብ፡ . . . ጸሎተ፡ መድኃኒት፡ አስጊተ፡ (sic) ኃያላን፡ ዘወረደ፡ እምሰማያት፡ ዘወሀቦ፡ ለቶማስ፡ ሪድዕ፡ . . . ኢያኤል፡ አፍናኤል፡ አስናኤል፡ . . .

e. Ff. 62r–66v: *Asmat* prayer that God gave to Peter
በስመ፡ አብ፡ . . . ጸሎቱ፡ ለጴጥሮስ፡ ዝውእቱ፡ ዘዖጻቢ፡ እምሐዋርያቲሁ፡ ዘኃሪዮ፡ ክርስቶስ፡ . . . ወጸውያሙ፡ ለኩሎሙ፡ ሐዋርያቲሁ፡ . . . ወይቤሎሙ፡ አንትሙ፡ አርዳእየ፡ . . .

f. Ff. 101rv, 41r–42v: Prayer about Melchisedek and the Paraclete.
ጸሎት፡ በእንተ፡ መልከ፡ ጼዴቅ፡ ወበእንተ፡ ጸራቅሊጦስ፡ መንፈስ፡ ጽድቅ፡ ወጸሎት፡ በእንተ፡ እግ"፡ አብ፡ ወወልድ፡ . . . ክርስቶስ፡ አዕትት፡ እምነፍሰየ፡ ሐማም፡ . . .

g. Ff. 67v–72r: Prayer about which the angels asked the Lord. Incomplete at the beginning.
ወቤላሁ፡ (sic) መዋቅሕት፡ (sic) አድማስ፡ ለእግዚእ፡ ኢትመጥን፡ (sic) ለአምሙራ፡ እመ፡ ኢይበክዩ፡ ሕዝብ፡ አንብአ፡ ከመ፡ ክረምት፡ ወካዕበ፡ ይቤላ፡ ለመዋቅሕት፡ (sic) አድማስ፡ ኢታውርደን፡ ምስለ፡ ዲያብሎስ፡ ለእኩይ፡ . . .

h. Ff. 72r–77r: Prayer given to the Apostles and Mary.
በስመ፡ አብ፡ . . . አነ፡ (sic, for ለነ፡) ለሐዋርያት፡ ወሀቦነ፡ ዘንተ፡ አስማተ፡ በደብረ፡ ዘይት፡ ወምስሌን፡ እሙ፡ አሙ፡ ዕለተ፡ ዕርገቱ፡ . . . ወይቤለን፡ ንሥኡ፡ ዘንተ፡ አስማተ፡ ይኩንክሙ፡ ጽንአ፡ ነበ፡ ተሐውሩ፡

i. Ff. 77r–82r: The prayer, "May the names of Christ sanctify us."
በስመ፡ አብ፡ . . . ይቀድሰን፡ አስማቲሁ፡ ለክርስቶስ፡ ሲድላዊ፡ ሊደጋዊ፡ ተድሮፋፊቃዲ፡ . . .

j. Ff. 82r–88r: Prayer of the Apostles and Disciples for the forgiveness of sin.
በስመ፡ አብ፡ . . . ጸሎት፡ (sic) ሥርየት፡ እምነቶሙ፡ ለሐዋርያት፡ ወለኩሎሙ፡ ፫ወ፪ አርድዕት፡ ከማሁ፡ ይቤሎሙ፡ ለአርዳኢሁ፡ አንትሙ፡ ውእቱ፡ አዕርክትየ፡ ወይቤሎ፡ ጴጥሮስ፡ (sic) አንተ፡ ውእቱ፡ ጴጥሮስ፡ . . .

Catalogue of the Ethiopic Manuscript Imaging Project · 179

k. Ff. 88r–91v: Prayer that God gave to Ananiah, Azariah and Michael.
በስመ፡ አብ፡ . . . ብርሃናኤል፡ አጉዴ፡ (sic) ጽድቅ፡ አግላላኤል፡ ዘንተ፡ አስማት፡ ዘወሀበ፡ (sic) እግ"፡ ለአናንያ፡ ወአዛርያ፡ ወሚሳኤል፡ እንዘ፡ ይትናገሮሙ፡ ለሚካኤል፡ (sic) ቀዊሞ፡ ማእከለ፡ እቶነ፡ እሳት፡ . . .

l. Ff. 91v–95v: Prayer that Our Lord told to St. Andrew.
በስመ፡ አብ፡ . . . አስማት፡ ዘነገሮ፡ እግዚእነ፡ ለቅዱስ፡ እንድርያስ፡ ረድእ፡ ሐዋርያ፡ ወሰማዕት፡ ጸሎተ፡ . . . ወይቤሎ፡ ሑር፡ ሀገረ፡ በላዕተ፡ ሰብእ፡ ኅበ፡ ሀሎ፡ እጐከ፡ ማትያስ፡ ከመ፡ ታውጽአ፡ እቤተ፡ (sic) ሞቅሕ፡ . . .

m. Ff. 95v–96: Prayer about the angel of death. EMML 1328, f. 82b; EMML 1486, f. 67; Strelcyn, Lincei, 47, f. 65r.
በስመ፡ አብ፡ . . . ተማኅጸንኩ፡ ከመ፡ ኢይሙት፡ ዘእንበለ፡ ጊዜየ፡ ከመ፡ ሡራቂ፡ (sic) ሌሊት፡ ወከመ፡ ሡራቂ፡ (sic) መዓልት፡ በመንግሥት፡ አብ፡ ወወልድ፡ . . . ዘኢያድለቀልቆ፡ ሞርሞራ፡ . . .

n. Ff. 96v–100r: Prayer that the angels told Enoch. EMML 1328, f. 83b.
በስመ፡ አብ፡ . . . አስማት፡ ዘተናገርዎ፡ መላእክት፡ ለሄኖክ፡ ዘንተ፡ ወመሐርዎ፡ ወይቤልዎ፡ ሶበ፡ መጽአ፡ ድልቅልቅ፡ ወበረድ፡ ወጽዓ፡ ወረኃብ፡ ለብሔር፡ ከመዝ፡ በል፡ እግ"፡ ጉንዴ፡ መዓት፡ ወብዙኃ፡ ምንረት . . .

Varia:
1. On both the inside front and back cover the number "400" is written in modern, black felt-tip pen.
2. F. 61v: The days in the year on which heaven is open to receive prayers, Rəḥwä sämay.

Notes:
1. Decorative designs: ff. 4v, 11v, 30v, 52r (dotted line using black and some faded red).
2. F. 88v: Twenty-box grid (four rows of five columns) with letters in sixteen of the boxes.
3. Copied by Gäbrä Iyyäsus for Wäldä Täklä Haymanot, ff. 61v, and 100r.
4. Overlooked words of text are written interlinearly (ff. 78r and 98r).

Quire Map

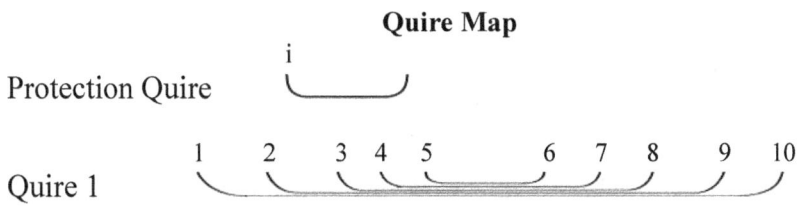

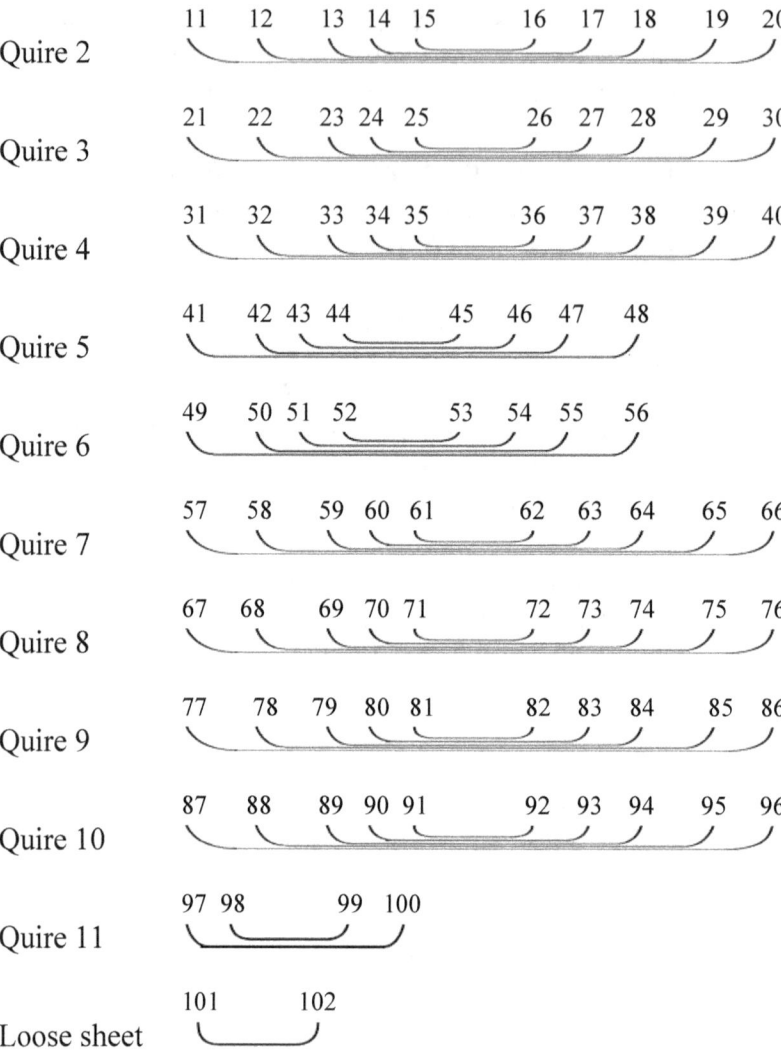

EMIP 68 – Focanti Codex 2

Psalter, with the Psalter of the Virgin, ዳዊት፡ ምስለ፡ መዝሙረ፡ ድንግል፡
Parchment, 233 x 210 x 75 mm, four Coptic chain stitches attached with bridle attachments to rough-hewn boards covered with tooled leather that has been mutilated on one side, 1 protection folio + 18 full quires, i + 168 folios, 230 x 208 mm, top margin 30–32 mm, bottom margin 45–50 mm, fore edge margin 43 mm, gutter margin 15 mm, ff. 1r–145v one column, ff. 146r–168r two columns, Gəʿəz, 22 lines, 18th cent.

Quire descriptions: quires 1–8, 10–18 balanced; quire 9 adjusted balanced.
Ff. 1r–168r: Psalter [*Dawit*], with the Psalms of the Virgin, *Mäzmurä Dəngəl*.
Cf. EMIP 1; and EMIP 2; Abbadie 244, Conti Rossini, Notice, no. 105.
1. Ff. 1r–125v: Psalms of David.
2. Ff. 126r–138v: Biblical Canticles, with the corresponding hymns of the *Mäzmurä Dəngəl*.
3. Ff. 139r–145v: Song of Songs, common version, with the corresponding hymns of the *Mäzmurä Dəngəl*.
4. Ff. 145v: Praises of Mary [*Wəddase Maryam*], with the corresponding Praises of the Virgin [*Wəddase Dəngəl*]. Arranged for the days of the week (Monday, f. 145v; Tuesday, f. 147v; Wednesday, f. 150v; Thursday, f. 152v; Friday, f. 155v; Saturday, f. 157r; Sunday, f. 159r).
5. Ff. 161v–167r: Gate of Light [*Anqäṣä Bərhan*], with the corresponding Praises of the Virgin [*Wəddase Dəngəl*].

Varia:
1. F. Iv: Calendar of the feast days of the year.
2. F. 167rv: Versicles that include the name Zion, *Ṣəyon*.
3. F. 167v: Record of transaction; the good is not mentioned, probably this manuscript.
4. F. 168r:Table blessing, *Sä'alnak*, incomplete at the end.
5. See EMIP 17, f. 84rv.
6. F. 168v: An illegible note.

Notes:
1. The general condition of the vellum is dirty and worn about the edges, but fully intact and good condition inside.
2. Decorative designs: ff. 126r (*haräg* using black and red); ff. 16v, 138r, 161r (line of pairs of black and red dots); ff. 24v, 25r, 35r, 42v, 58r, 83r, 94v, 108r, 112r, 118v (line of black dots); ff. 68v, 76v, 100r (dotted line using alternating black and red); ff. 8v, 16v (lines of full stop symbols).
3. Columetric layout of text: ff. 134v–135r (tenth biblical canticle).
4. F. 64r: A two-word text in a box in the margin marks the midpoint of the Psalms.
5. Note of ownership by Adära Giyorgis, Fəqrä Śəllase Kəflä Maryam, f. 145v.
6. F. Ir. Blank.
7. Overlooked words of text are written interlinearly (ff. 11v, 13v, 14r, 21r, 37r, 38v, etc.); and overlooked lines of text are written interlinearly (ff. 4v, 16r, 30v, 44r, 63r, 72v, etc.); and in the upper margin with a

symbol (⊥) marking the location where the text is to be inserted (f. 96r, line 6).

8. This scribe regularly has avoided the problem of lines of text too long to fit on one line by adopting an aspect ratio that leaves ample room for the width of most lines. When a line is too long, the scribe places the material above (e.g., ff. 7rv, 19r, 24v, 40v, 68r, etc) or below (e.g., ff. 103rv, 104r, 138r, 140r) the line.

Quire Map

Protection Folio — i

Folio i is a loose, single folio that is sewn loosely onto the binding with blue thread.

Quire 1: 1 2 3 4 5 6 7 8 9 10

Quire 2: 11 12 13 14 15 16 17 18 19 20

Quire 3: 21 22 23 24 25 26 27 28 29 30

Quire 4: 31 32 33 34 35 36 37 38 39 40

Quire 5: 41 42 43 44 45 46 47 48 49 50

Quire 6: 51 52 53 54 55 56 57 58 59 60

Quire 7: 61 62 63 64 65 66 67 68 69 70

Quire 8: 71 72 73 74 75 76 77 78 79 80

Quire 9: 81 82 83 84 85 86 87 88 89 90

Stubs appear between ff. 83 and 84 and between ff. 88 and 89.

Catalogue of the Ethiopic Manuscript Imaging Project · 183

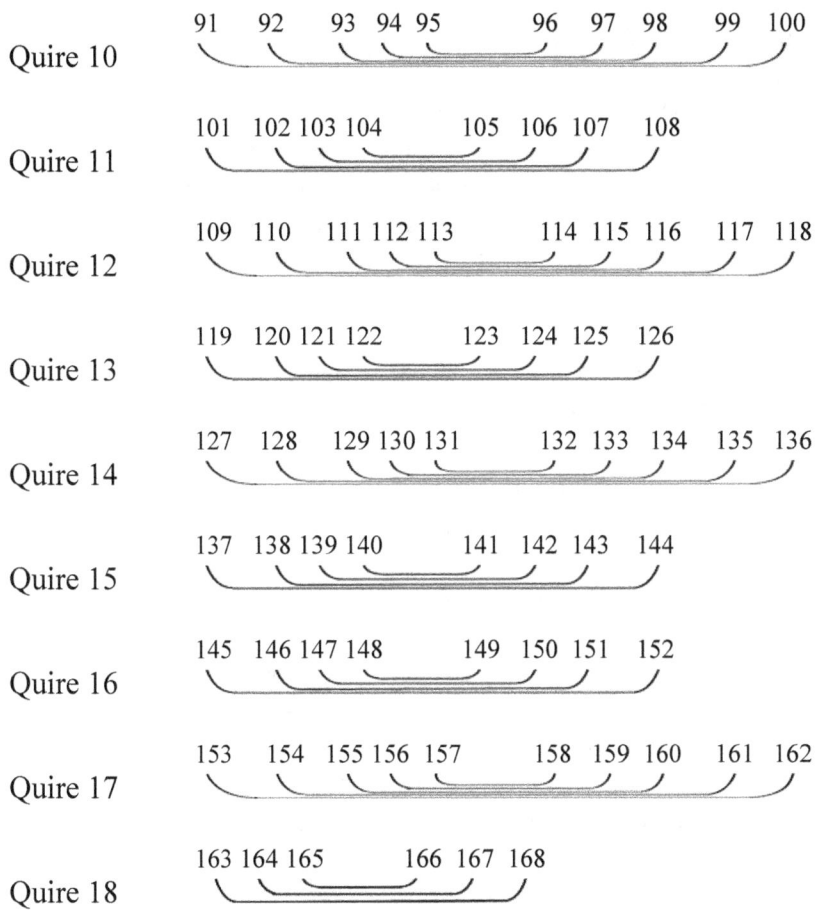

EMIP 69 – Focanti Codex 3
Funeral Ritual, መጽሐፈ፡ ግንዘት፡

Parchment, 288 x 205 x 75 mm, four Coptic chain stitches attached with bridle attachments to rough-hewn wide-grain boards, glue residue and pink dye lines inside front board suggest former cover with decorative patch, nail holes in back board suggest previous use as building material. Seventeen full quires, quires 2, 4, 5, 7–13, 15, 17 numbered, 136 folios, 275 x 183 mm, top margin 25 mm, bottom margin 55–60 mm, fore edge margin 22–25 mm, gutter margin 10 mm, ff. 1r–136v two columns, Gəʻəz, 23 lines, 18th cent.

Quire descriptions: quires 1–4, 6–14 balanced; quires 5, 15–17 adjusted balanced. Navigation systems: 1) black thread sewn into corners of folios 8, 17, 41, 56, 72, 88, 105, 121, 128 to mark the location of miniatures; 2) various colored string sewn into corners of folios 18, 50, 120, 126 to mark content divisions.

Ff. 1r–136v: Funeral Ritual, መጽሐፈ፡ ግንዘት፡.
Copied carefully, but incomplete at the end. Published more than once: መጽሐፈ፡ ግንዘት፡፡ ጸሎት፡ ላዕለ፡ ምውታን፡፡ Tənśaʼe Zä-Gubaʼe Press, Addis Ababa, 1944 EC; መጽሐፈ፡ ግንዘት፡፡ ጸሎት፡ ላዕለ፡ ምውታን፡፡ Täsfa Press, Addis Ababa 1962 EC. For the sources and detailed description, see the description of Hs.or.9645 SBPrK Berlin in Six, *Handschriften*, no. 57, pp. 162–65; see also Friedrich Erich Dobberahn, "Der äthiopische Ritus," in Hansjakob Becker-Herman Ühlein (eds.) *Liturgie im Angesicht des Todes: Judentum und Ostkirchen*, St. Ottilien 1997, Pietas Liturgica nos. 9 and 10, pt. I, pp. 137–316; *idem.*, "Der äthiopische Begräbnisritus," pp. 657–84 and pt. II, 1397–1432. As the quotation from f. 1v shows, this ritual belongs to the Ṣägga sect; see Getatchew Haile, "The *Mäṣḥafä Gənzät* as a Historical Source Regarding the Theology of the Ethiopian Orthodox Church," in *Scrinium. Revue de patrologie, d'hagiographie critique et d'histoire ecclésiastique. Tome 1: Varia Aethiopica in Memory of Sevir B. Chernetsov (1943–2005)*, Byzantinorossica, Saint-Pétersbourg 2005, pp. 58–76.

1. Introduction, summarizing the directory, f. 1r.
   በስመ፡ አብ፡ ... ንጽሐፍ፡ ዘንተ፡ መቅድም፡ ግንዘት፡ ዘአስተጋብኦ፡ እምሲኖዶስ፡ ወእምፍትሐ፡ ነገሥት፡ ወእምዝንተ፡ መጽሐፍ፡ በበሥርዓቱ፡ ወበበመትልዉ፡ ቀዳሜ፡ ኩሉ፡ ጊዜ፡ በጸዓተ፡ ነፍስ፡ ዘቃል፡ አትናቴዎስ፡ ይድግሙ፡ ... (f. 1v) ... ወእምድኅረ፡ ፍጻሜ፡ ፍትሐት፡ ያልክፍዎሙ፡ እምሥጋሁ፡ ቅዱስ፡ ወእምደሙ፡ ክቡር፡ ...
2. On the importance of making memorial feast for the dead, f. 6r.
3. The story of the sinful father of a bishop, f. 7v.
4. The book that came from Jerusalem, f. 22v.
5. Prayer of Our Lady Mary, f. 33r,
6. Prayer for priests and deacons that slept (eternally), f. 35v.
7. *Kəśtät* chant, f. 40v.
8. *Gənzät* for priests, f. 58v.
9. *Gənzät* for deacons, f. 64v.
10. *Gənzät* for monks, f. 67v.
11. *Gənzät* for the elders, f. 73v.
12. *Gənzät* for men and children, f. 76v.
13. Homily of James of Sarug about priests and deacons that died, f. 80v.
14. Homily of Abba Sälama about death, f. 89r.
15. *Gənzät* for nuns, f. 91v.

16. Gənzät for grown women, f. 94r.
17. Gənzät for little girls, f. 96r.
18. Reading for women who die during Passion Week, f. 97v.
19. Absolution at burial, f. 98v.
20. Reading from the second to third day, f. 101r.
21. The Bandlet of Righteousness, ለፋፌ፡ ጽድቅ፡ [Lifafä Ṣədq], f. 123r.
    E. A. Wallis Budge, *The Bandlet of Righteousness. An Ethiopian Book of the Dead. The Ethiopic Text of the Lefâfaf Ṣedek in Facsimile from Two Manuscripts in the B.M.*, edited with an English Translation, London 1949; Sebastian Euringer, "Die Binde der Rechtfertingung (Lefâfa ṣedek)," *Orientalia* NS vol. 9 (1940), pp. 76–96 and 244–59.
    በስመ፡ አብ፡ . . . ጸሎተ፡ ድጎነት፡ ወመጽሐፌ፡ ሕይወት፡ ለፋፌ፡ ጽድቅ፡ ዘተናገረ፡ አብ፡ በቃሉ፡ እምቅድመ፡ ይትወለድ፡ ክርስቶስ፡ በሥጋ፡ እማርያም፡ እንተ፡ ኢታበውዕ፡ ውስተ፡ ፀብ፡ አንቀጸ፡ ወታበጽሕ፡ ውስተ፡ መንግሥተ፡ ሰማያት፡ . . .
22. Prayer for the journey to heaven, f. 126r. This prayer is part of the *Ləfafä Ṣədq*.
    በስመ፡ አብ፡ . . . ጸሎት፡ ዘመን(f. 126v)ገደ፡ ሰማይ፡ ዕቀበኒ፡ ክርስቶስ፡ ከመ፡ ኢያዕቅፍዋ፡ ለነፍስየ፡ መላእክተ፡ ጽልመት፡ ውስተ፡ ፀብ፡ አንቀጸ፡ . . .
23. On the 12th day, f. 130r.
24. On the 40th day, f. 131r.
25. On the 48th, 80th and on the anniversary, f. 133r.
26. Blessing of *Abba* Samu'el, f. 134v.

Miniatures, all in twentieth-century hand:
1. F. 8v: Madonna and Child.
2. F. 17r: Saint George and the Dragon.
3. F. 41r: The Crucifixion.
4. F. 56v: Resurrected Christ Displays His Wounds.
5. F. 72v: A mounted holy man carrying a spear over a slain man holding an ax, most probably St. George helping the Ethiopian army at the 1896 battle of Adwa.
6. F. 88v: Archangel Michael Enthroned.
7. F. 105r: *Abunä* Täklä Haymanot.
8. F. 121r: *Abunä* Gäbrä Mänfäs Qəddus.
9. F. 128v: A man grasps the cloak of Mary so that she may rescue him from the fire of hell.

Note:
1. Decorative designs: f. 42r (dotted line using alternating black and red); f. 122v (stops connected by dotted line using alternating black and red).
2. Overlooked words of text are written interlinearly (ff. 18r, 86r, 108r, 122r and 129v).

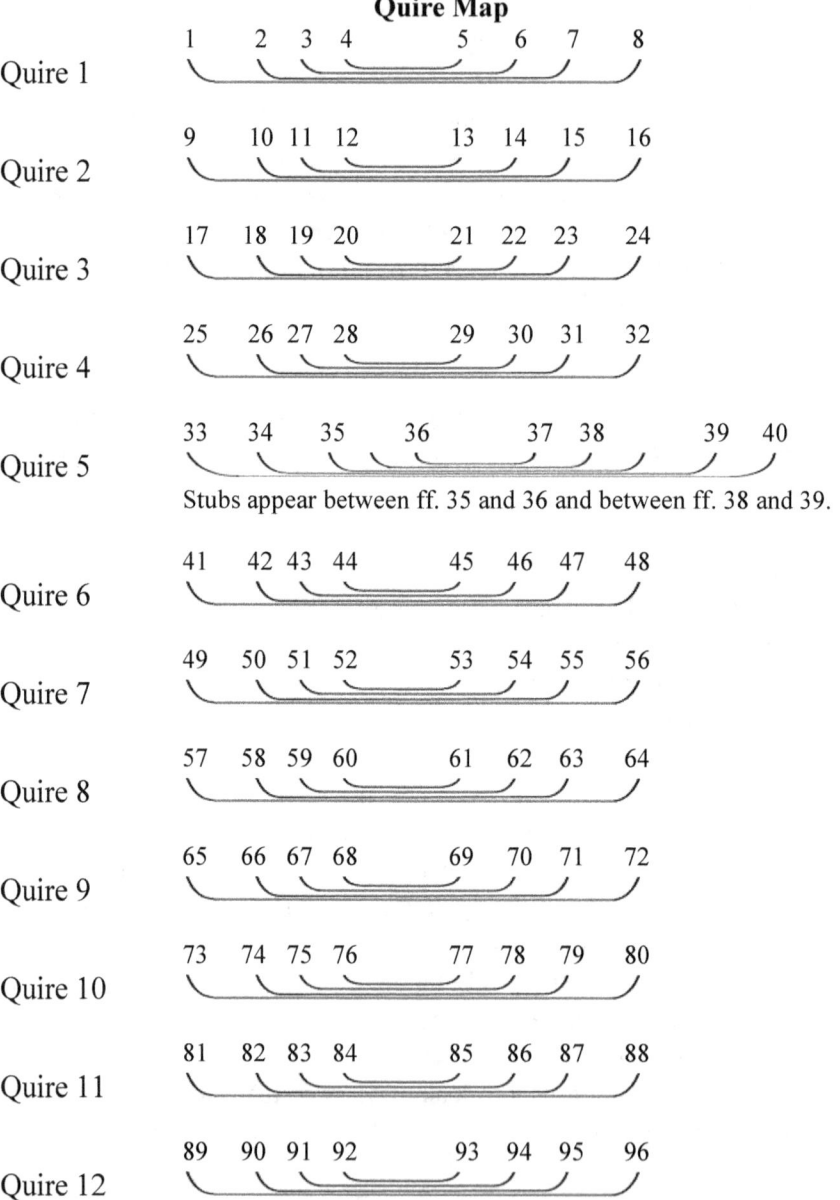

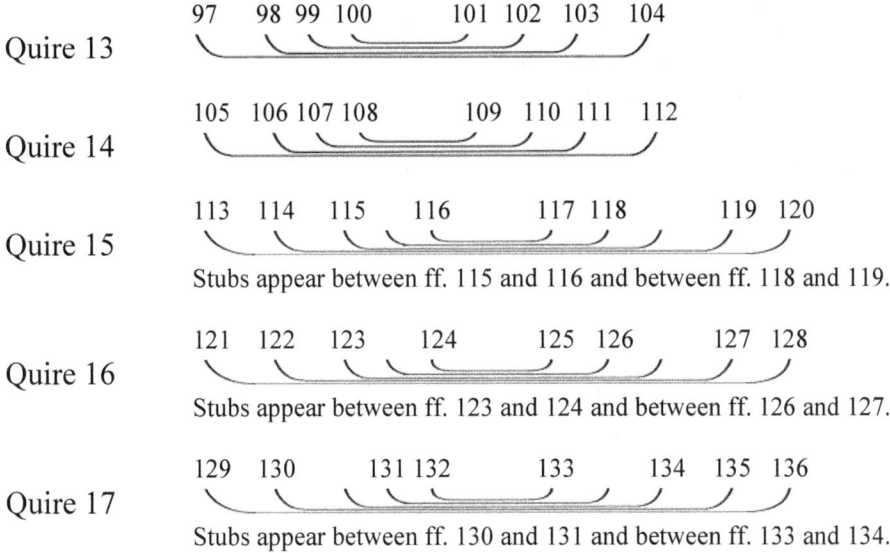

Stubs appear between ff. 115 and 116 and between ff. 118 and 119.

Stubs appear between ff. 123 and 124 and between ff. 126 and 127.

Stubs appear between ff. 130 and 131 and between ff. 133 and 134.

EMIP 70 – Marwick Codex 22
Psalter, ዳዊት፡

Parchment, 167 x 127 x 60 mm, four Coptic chain stitches attached with bridle attachments to rough-hewn boards, protection sheet + 17 full quires, ii + 167 folios, 162 x 122 mm, top margin 13 mm, bottom margin 36–40 mm, fore edge margin 17–20 mm, gutter margin 10–12 mm, ff. 1r–149v one column, ff. 149v–164v two columns, Gəʽəz, 21–22 lines, 20th cent.

Quire descriptions: quires 1–16 balanced; quire 17 unbalanced. Navigation system: brown yarn sewn into corners of folios to mark the location of miniatures.

Ff. 1r–167v: Psalter [*Dawit*]. Introduced with the Psalm 1 of the Psalter of the Virgin, cf. EMIP 1, EMIP 2 and EMIP 68.
1. Ff. 1r–128r: Psalms of David.
2. Ff. 128v–142r: Biblical Canticles.
3. Ff. 142r–149v: Song of Songs, common version.
4. Ff. 149v–160r: Praises of Mary [*Wəddase Maryam*]. Arranged for the days of the week (Monday, f. 149v; Tuesday, f. 150v; Wednesday, f. 152v; Thursday, f. 154r; Friday, f. 156v; Saturday, f. 158r; Sunday, f. 159r).
5. Ff. 160r–164v: Gate of Light [*Anqäṣä Bərhan*].

Miniatures, all in the late twentieth-century hand of the "speckled garment artist, painted over text:

1. F. iiv(erso): David Playing the Harp.
2. F. 21r: Madonna and Child.
3. F. 41r: The Crucifixion.
4. F. 61r: Jesus Carrying the Cross.
5. F. 91r: The Resurrection, raising Adam and Eve.
6. F. 165r: The Ascension.
7. F. 165v: The Burial of Jesus.
8. F. 166r: The Last Supper.

Varia:
1. Ff. Ir–IIr: Ps 118:75–108, possibly from another manuscript.
2. F. 166v: Record that there was a military expedition to Eritrea on Gənbot 16, [19]68 EC (May 24, 1976) that returned on Säne 10, [19]68 (June 17, 1976), copied thrice.
3. F. 167v: Calendar of the Apostles and Evangelists.

Notes:
1. The general condition of the vellum is quite clean and relatively unworn.
2. F. 26 has been cut off about 85 mm from the gutter. A replacement piece of parchment has been sewn onto the fore edge (with a narrow leather strip) to restore the folio.
3. Decorative designs: ff. 8r, 15v, 24r, 34v, 43r, 49r, 59r, 71r, 79v, 85v, 99v, 112r, 115r, and 121v (dotted line using alternating black and red); f. 149v (two lines of alternating red and black dots with five full-stop symbols between).
4. Columetric layout of text: ff. 125r (Ps. 145), 137v–138rv (tenth biblical canticle).
5. F. 167 blank.
6. Overlooked words of text are written interlinearly (ff. 1v, 29v, 47r, 55r, 76r, 77r, 78v, etc.); and overlooked lines of text are written interlinearly (ff. 9v, 14v, 60v, 105r, 132v, etc.); and interlinearly with a symbol (⊥) marking the location where the text is to be inserted (f. 102v, line 18), and in the upper margin where the symbol (⊥) is used (f. 136v, line 4), and in another case where the symbol (+) is used (ff. 10v, line 6, 64v, line 5, 77v, line 21, 78v, line 6 and 164v, line 14).
7. The scribe regularly has to complete a line of text on another line. Much of the problem is addressed through the selection of an appropriate aspect ratio for the codex combined with an appropriate script size. But, where the line of text is still too long, the scribe completes the line of text above or below the end of the line

(throughout). This scribe will also reduce the font size at the end of lines to avoid having to go onto the next line (throughout).

Quire Map

Protection Quire: i, ii

Quire 1: 1, 2, 3, 4, 5, 6, 7, 8, 9, 10

Quire 2: 11, 12, 13, 14, 15, 16, 17, 18, 19, 20

Quire 3: 21, 22, 23, 24, 25, 26, 27, 28, 29, 30

Quire 4: 31, 32, 33, 34, 35, 36, 37, 38, 39, 40

Quire 5: 41, 42, 43, 44, 45, 46, 47, 48, 49, 50

Quire 6: 51, 52, 53, 54, 55, 56, 57, 58, 59, 60

Quire 7: 61, 62, 63, 64, 65, 66, 67, 68, 69, 70

Quire 8: 71, 72, 73, 74, 75, 76, 77, 78, 79, 80

Quire 9: 81, 82, 83, 84, 85, 86, 87, 88, 89, 90

Quire 10: 91, 92, 93, 94, 95, 96, 97, 98, 99, 100, 101, 102

Quire 11: 103, 104, 105, 106, 107, 108, 109, 110, 111, 112

Quire 12: 113, 114, 115, 116, 117, 118, 119, 120, 121, 122

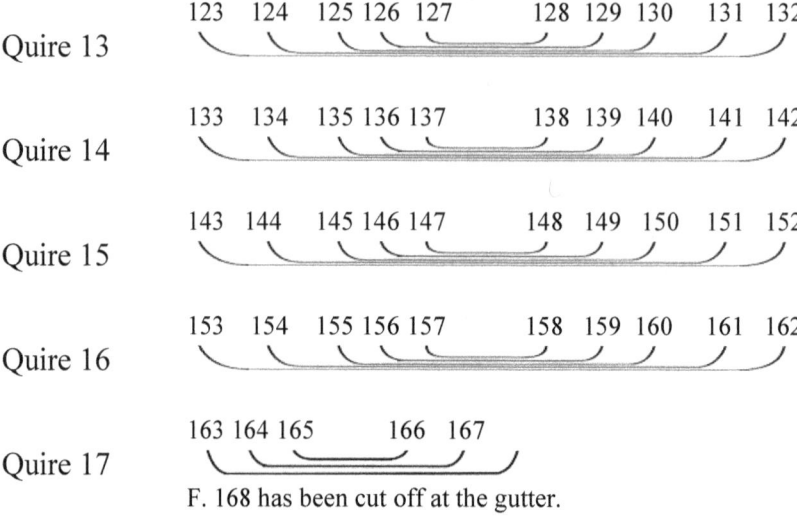

F. 168 has been cut off at the gutter.

EMIP 71 – Bowerman Hall Codex 1
University of Oregon Museum of Natural and Cultural History, Shelf Mark 10–845
Psalter, ዳዊት፡

Parchment, 193 x 140 x 59 mm, four Coptic chain stitches attached with bridle attachments to rough-hewn boards, two protection quires + 17 full quires, quires 2, 4, 6–17 numbered, iv + 173 folios, 185 x 135 mm, top margin 20 mm, bottom margin 47 mm, fore edge margin 25 mm, gutter margin 12 mm, ff. 1r–156v one column, ff. 157r–171v two columns, Gəʿəz, 20–24 lines, 20th cent.

Quire descriptions: quires 1–6, 8–17 balanced; quire 7 unbalanced. Navigation system: various colored string sewn into corners of ff. 8, 16, 74, 83, and 147 to mark content divisions;

Ff. 1r–178r: Psalter [*Dawit*]. Cf. EMIP 1.
1. Ff. 1r–133v: Psalms of David.
2. Ff. 134r–147v: Biblical Canticles.
3. Ff. 147v–156v: Song of Songs, Hebraic version.
4. Ff. 157r–167r: Praises of Mary [*Wəddase Maryam*]. Arranged for the days of the week (Monday, f. 157r; Tuesday, f. 158r; Wednesday, f. 159v; Thursday, f. 161r; Friday, f. 163v; Saturday, f. 164v; Sunday, f. 166r).
5. Ff. 167r–171v: Gate of Light [*Anqäṣä Bərhan*].

Miniature:
1. F. ivv(erso): Crude drawing of King David Playing the Harp, unfinished.

Varia:
1. F. iv: Quotation from Ps 114:3/116:3.

Notes:
1. The general condition of the vellum is almost pristine.
2. Decorative designs: space left for *haräg* unfilled; ff. 8r, 16r, 25r, 36r, 51v, 61r, 73v, 83r, 89r, 103v, 117r, 120r, 126v, 133v, 147v, 156v, 158r, 159v, 161r, 163v, 167r, (dotted line using alternating black and red), f. 35v (3 lines in pencil); f. 171v (dotted line using black ink).
3. Columetric layout of text: ff. 143rv (tenth biblical canticle).
4. F. Irv, IIv–IIIv, 172r–173r blank, save for some scrawls.
5. F. IIr: an attempt to draw a person.
6. F. 173v : an attempt to draw a person.
7. Overlooked words of text are written interlinearly (f. 90r); and overlooked lines of text are written interlinearly (f. 2v).
8. This scribe has avoided the problem of lines of text too long to fit on one line by adopting an aspect ratio that leaves ample room for the width of most lines. On a few occasions, the line would have been too long and the scribe finishes the end of the line with words written smaller so as to avoid leftover text (e.g., ff. 2v, 5r, 105v). Occasionally a line is still too long and has to be completed above or below the end of the line. In these cases, the scribe places the material above the line (e.g., ff. 47v, 50r, 60r, 65r, 87r, 107r, etc.) or below the line (e.g., ff. 50r and 65r).

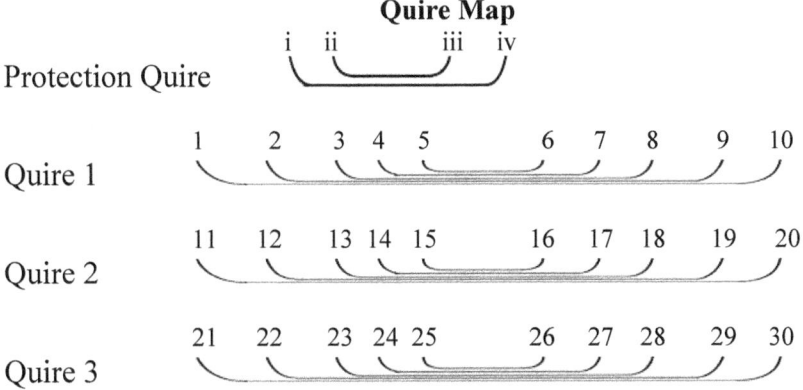

Quire 4: 31 32 33 34 35 36 37 38 39 40

Quire 5: 41 42 43 44 45 46 47 48 49 50

Quire 6: 51 52 53 54 55 56 57 58 59 60

Quire 7: 61 62 63 64 65 66 67 68 69 70 71

A folio stub is visible between ff. 69 and 70.

Quire 8: 72 73 74 75 76 77 78 79 80 81

Quire 9: 82 83 84 85 86 87 88 89 90 91

Quire 10: 92 93 94 95 96 97 98 99 100 101

Quire 11: 102 103 104 105 106 107 108 109 110 111 112 113

Quire 12: 114 115 116 117 118 119 120 121 122 123

Quire 13: 124 125 126 127 128 129 130 131 132 133

Quire 14: 134 135 136 137 138 139 140 141 142 143

Quire 15: 144 145 146 147 148 149 150 151 152 153

Quire 16: 154 155 156 157 158 159 160 161 162 163

Quire 17: 164 165 166 167 168 169 170 171 172 173

EMIP 72 – Bowerman-Hall Codex 2
University of Oregon Museum of Natural and Cultural History, Shelf Mark 10–843
Missal — Miscellanea, መጽሐፈ፡ ቅዳሴ፡

Parchment, 143 x 130 x 69 mm, four altered Coptic chain stitches attached with bridle attachments to rough-hewn boards, 24 full quires, quires 7 and 10 numbered (as 4 and 1 respectively), 177 folios, 140 x 129 mm, top margin 15 mm, bottom margin 35 mm, fore edge margin 20 mm, gutter margin 10 mm, ff. 1r–177v two columns, Gəʿəz, 15 lines, reign of Täklä Haymanot I (1706–08), f. 65v.

Quire descriptions: quires 2–6, 8, 12–23 balanced; quire 24 adjusted balanced; quires 1, 7, 9–11 unbalanced. Navigation system: 1) various colored string sewn into corners of folios 92, 125, 161 to mark content divisions.

1. Ff. 3r–5r: Image of Gabriel, መልክዐ፡ ገብርኤል፡. EMIP 56, f. 63r.
2. Ff. 6r–:13v: Prayer of Incense, ጸሎተ፡ ዕጣን፡. Published in Ethiopia, ጸሎተ፡ ዕጣን፡፡ Tənśaʾe Zä-Gubaʾe Press, Addis Ababa, 1951 EC.
3. Ff. 14r–37v, 44r–170v: Missal, መጽሐፈ፡ ቅዳሴ፡. Rebound in some disorder; cf. EMIP 27. Office prayers, f. 14r; ordinary of the Mass, f. 44r; Anaphoras of the Apostles, f. 71r; Our Lord Jesus Christ, f. 77v; John Son of Thunder, f. 89r; Our Lady Mary By Cyriacus of Bəhənsa (called here *dərsan* "homily," not *akk^{w}ätet*), f. 92r; the 318 Orthodox Fathers, f. 104r; John Chrysostom, f. 114; Epiphanius, f. 120r; Dioscorus, f. 127v; James of Sarug, f. 130r; Cyril of Alexandria, f. 138r; Athanasius the Apostolic, f. 145r; Gregory of Armenia, f. 156v; Basil, f. 161v.
4. Ff. 37v–38v: The litanical hymn to Christ, "For the sake of your Trinity, በእንተ፡ ሥላሴከ፡. Hammerschmidt, *Texte*, pp. 16–19.
5. Ff. 38v–39v: Litanical hymn to Jesus Christ, አዘወረድከ፡. EMIP 28, f. 148v.
6. Ff. 39v–40v: Halleluiatic hymn to the Trinity. EMIP 39, f. 19r.
7. Ff. 40v–42v: Hymn to Saint George.
ቅንት፡ ሰይፈከ፡ ኃያል፡ ውስተ፡ ሐወሕቋከ፡ (sic) . . . ናቀርብ፡ ስብሐተ፡ ወጋዳ፡፡
ለጊዮርጊስ፡ ኮከበ፡ ልዳ፡፡

8. Ff. 42v–43v and 174r–176v: Hymn to Mary, "You are blessed," ብፅዕት፡ አንቲ፡ ወንግሥተ፡ ጽድቅ፡. Chaîne, Répertoire, no. 292 ታዐብዮ፡ ነፍስየ፡ ለእግ"፡ ታዐብዮ፡ ነፍስየ፡ ለእግ"፡ ብፅዕት፡ አንቲ፡ ወንግሥተ፡ ጽድቅ፡ . . .

Most of these hymns (from 4 to 8) are part of the Horologium for night hours, cf. EMIP 105.
9. Ff. 171r–174r Monastic genealogy of the line of *Abunä* Ewosṭatewos. Cf. C. Conti Rossini, "Il Gadla Filpos e Gadla Yohannes di Dabra Bizan," *Atti della R. Accademia dei Lincei. Classe di Scienze Morali, Storiche e Filologiche*, vol. VIII, ser. 5 (1903), pp. 154–6; and Getatchew Haile, "A Fragment on the Monastic Fathers of the Ethiopian Church," *Orbis Aethiopicus: Studia in honorem Stanislaus Chojnacki* (ed. Piotr O. Scholz et al), Albstrat (1992), pp. 231–7.

Miniatures:
1. F. 2v: Crude drawing of two humans.
2. F. 5v: Crude drawing of John, Son of Thunder praying.
3. F. 177v: Crude drawing of Täklä Haymanot.

Varia:
1. F. 1rv: Excerpt from the beginning of the prayer of incense.
2. F. 2r: *Asmat* prayer for help in learning.
በስመ፡ አብ፡ . . . ቤቃ፡ Ïٞ፡ በከመ፡ አርአይኮ፡ ለሄኖክ፡ መጻሕፍት፡ (sic) ዘብሉይ፡ ወዘሐዲስ፡ ከማሁ፡ አርኑ፡ ሊተ፡ . . .
3. F. 2v: What seems to be prayer against the enemy, insufficiently legible.
4. F. 2v: A copy of the few words from the first line of f. 3r, in a crude hand.
5. F. 5v: The title of the Anaphora of John Son of Thunder.
6. F. 177r: Prayer to heal a wound/laceration.
ጸሎተ፡ ቁስል፡ አብድ፡ ቁስል፡ ወአብድ፡ ቁስል፡ ወእመ፡ ይረግዞ፡ ገቦሁ፡ የማኒት፡ (sic) ለእግዚእነ፡ ወእመ፡ ይረግዞ፡ ገቦሁ፡ የማኒት፡ (sic) እንተ፡ ኢየአት፡ . . .
7. F. 177v: *Asmat* prayer against hemorrhage.
ቆርጾግኤል፡ ጸራቁኤል፡ ጥንዋግጥን፡ ፈኪካ፡ ፈኪክሞ፡ በኃይለ፡ ዝንቱ፡ አስማቲከ፡ . . .

Notes:
1. Decorative designs: f. 2r (*haräg*-like feature using black); ff. 13v, 34r, 35r, 36r, 91v, 104r, 120r, 127r, 137v, 144v, 156v, 170v (dotted line using alternating black and red).
2. Copied for Ləssanä Krəstos, ff. 11r, 13v and *passim*.
3. Note of ownership by a certain church dedicated to Gabriel, partly erased, f. 2v.
4. Overlooked words of text are written interlinearly (ff. 39v and 40v); and overlooked lines of text are written interlinearly (ff. 17v and 31r);

and in the upper margin with a symbol (+) marking the location where the text is to be inserted (f. 16r, line 11).

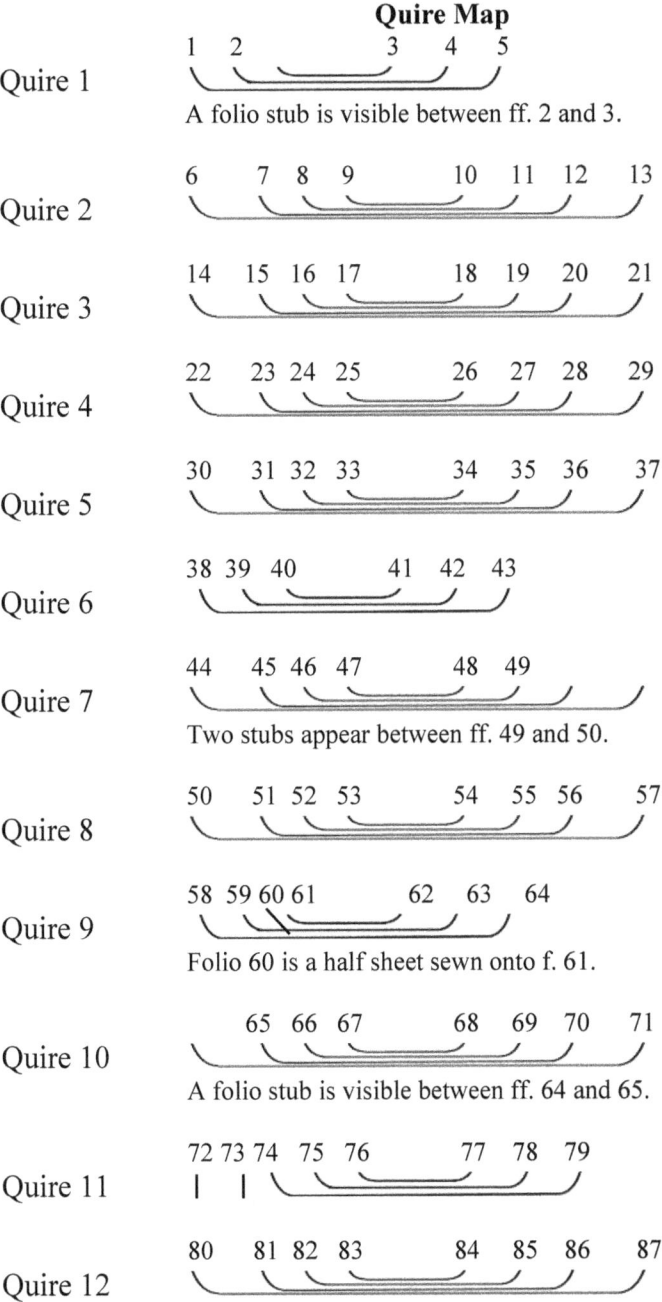

196 · *Catalogue of the Codices*

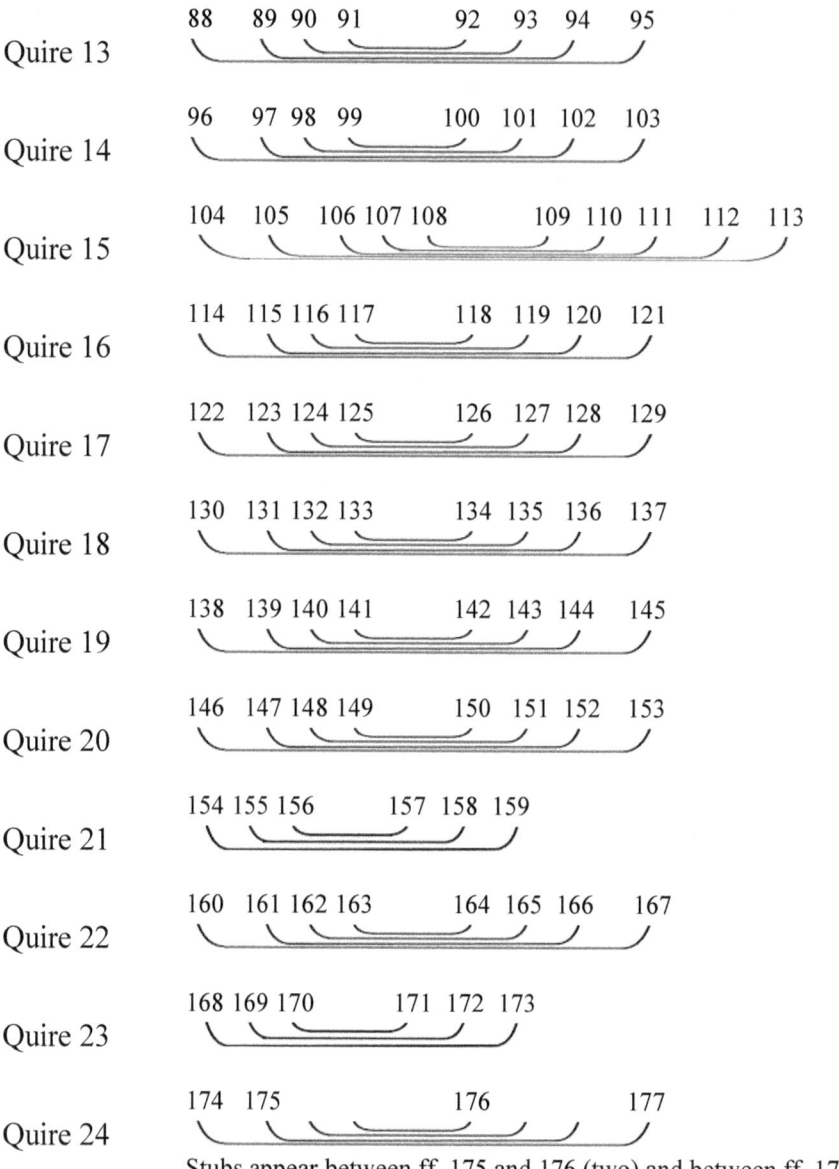

Stubs appear between ff. 175 and 176 (two) and between ff. 176 and 177 (two).

EMIP 73 – Bowerman-Hall Codex 3
University of Oregon Museum of Natural and Cultural History, Shelf Mark 10–844
Psalter, ዳዊት:

Parchment, 140 x 111 x 57 mm, four Coptic chain stitches attached with bridle attachments to rough-hewn boards, protection quire + 12 full quires, ii + 141 folios, 138 x 105 mm, top margin 15 mm, bottom margin 24 mm, fore edge margin 14 mm, gutter margin 8 mm, ff. 1r–139v one column, Gəʿəz, 23–26 lines, 20th cent.

Quire descriptions: quires 1–4, 6–12 balanced; quire 5 adjusted balanced.

Navigation system: marginal notations to indicate readings (Ps. 3–27).

Ff. 1r–139v: Psalter [*Dawit*]. Cf. EMIP 1.
1. Ff. 1v–107r: Psalms of David.
2. Ff. 107v–119r: Biblical Canticles.
3. Ff. 119r–125v: Song of Songs, common version.
4. Ff. 125v–135v: Praises of Mary [*Wəddase Maryam*], laid out in one column. Arranged for the days of the week (Monday, f. 125v; Tuesday, f. 126v; Wednesday, f. 128v; Thursday, f. 130; Friday, f. 132r; Saturday, f. 133v; Sunday, f. 134v).
5. Ff. 136r–139v: Gate of Light [*Anqäṣä Bərhan*].

Miniatures:
1. F. ir: The Annunciation. Caption: "He announced."
2. F. iv(erso): Child being baptized, the mother, a priest, and a deacon. Caption: "He baptized." Caption on the book: "book of christening."
3. Picture of interwoven rope pattern: Caption: Ḥaräg.
4. F. iiv(erso): David Playing the Harp. Caption: "David."
5. F. 49v: Two Angels with Crowns and brandished Swords. Caption: "Angels."
6. F. 50r: Madonna and Child. Caption: "Maryam."
7. F. 50v: The Baptism of Jesus. Captions (top to bottom): "Dove" and "John baptized Jesus."
8. F. 60r: Two haloed men, possibly *Abunä* Täklä Haymanot and *Abunä* Ewosṭatewos.
9. F. 72r: Two flying angels with swords.
10. F. 140r: Mary raises the painter who fell from a scaffolding. Caption: "Mary raises the painter who fell from a scaffolding."
11. F. 140v: Mary and Joseph (on the flight to Egypt). Caption: "Mary and Joseph."

12. F. 141r: Martha and Salome carrying Jesus (on the journey to Egypt). Caption: "Martha, Jesus, Salome."
13. F. 141v: A priest blessing people with his hand cross. Caption: "He blessed with the cross."

Notes:
1. Decorative designs: ff. 107r, 139v (*haräg* using multiple colors); ff. 1r, 6v and 51r (*haräg* using black and red); f. 6r (*haräg* using red); ff. 6r, 17v, 19r, 19v, 28r, 28v, 36r, 125v, 134v, and 135v (dotted line using alternating black and red); f. 82v (dotted line using alternating black and red with blue marks added); ff. 21v and 96r (dotted line using black); ff. 67v, 93r, 101v, 105v, 119r (dotted line using red).
2. Columetric layout of text: f. 115v (tenth biblical canticle).
3. Overlooked words of text are written interlinearly (f. 138v).
4. The scribe regularly has to complete a line of text on another line. Much of the problem is addressed through the selection of an appropriate aspect ratio for the codex combined with an appropriate script size. But, where the line of text is still too long, the scribe completes the line of text above the end of the line (e.g., ff. 1v, 2v, 3r, 4v, etc.). This scribe will also reduce the font size at the end of lines to avoid having to go onto the next line (e.g., ff. 55v and 57v).

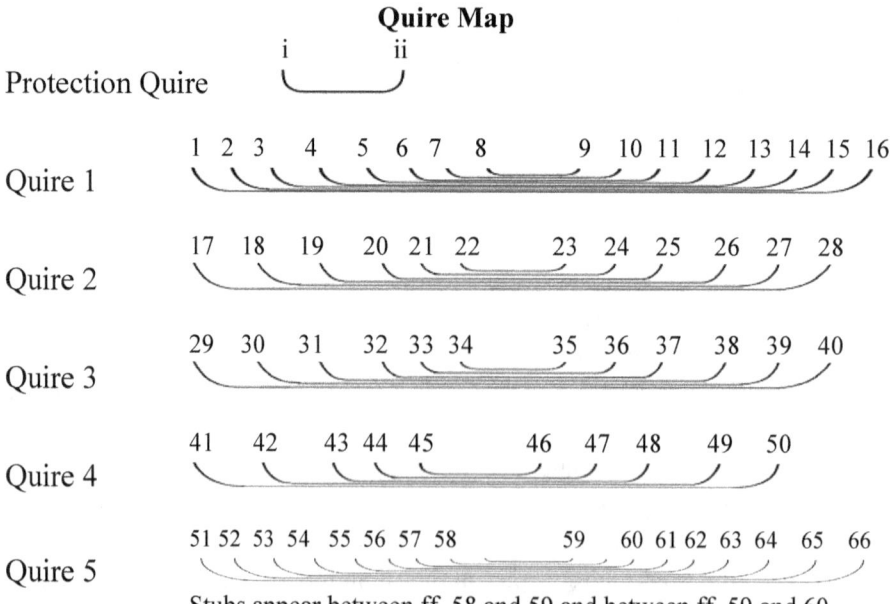

Stubs appear between ff. 58 and 59 and between ff. 59 and 60.

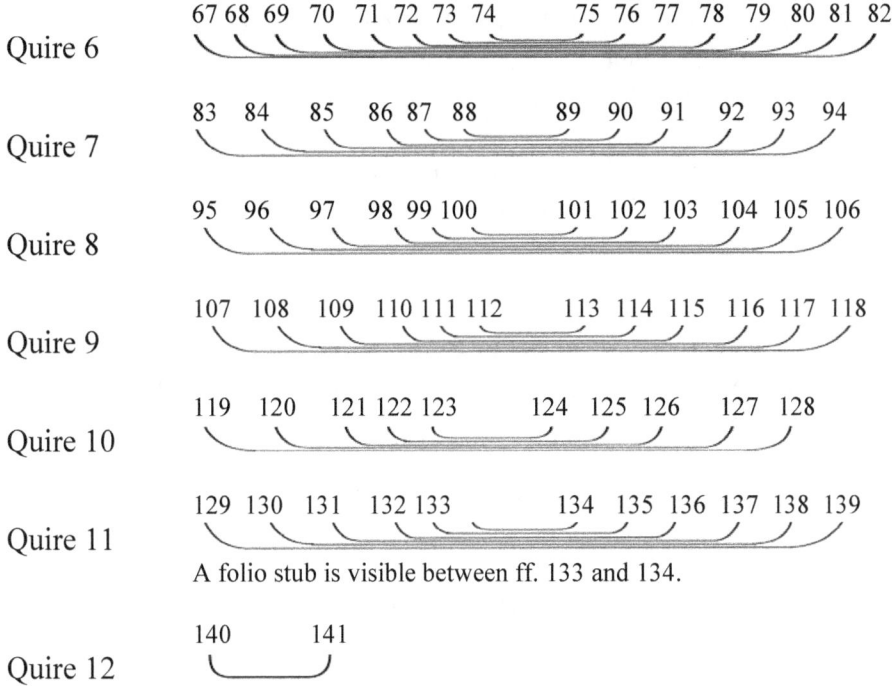

A folio stub is visible between ff. 133 and 134.

EMIP 74 – Mount Angel Codex 46
Image of Gabriel — The Mystagogia — Bandlet of Righteousness,
መልክዐ፡ ገብርኤል፡ — ትምህርተ፡ ኅቡአት፡ — ልfፈ፡ ጽድቅ፡

Parchment, 130 x 107 x 38 mm, four Coptic chain stitches attached with bridle attachments to rough-hewn boards covered with tooled leather over decorative linen patches visible inside the turn-ins on front and back cover, 8 full quires, quires 5 and 6 numbered (as 2, 3 respectively), 53 folios, 127 x 107 mm, top margin 8–12 mm, bottom margin 27–30 mm, fore edge margin 8–11 mm, gutter margin 7 mm, ff. 1v–10r one column, ff. 11r–51v two columns, Gəʿəz, 10–13 lines, 20th cent.

Quire descriptions: quires 2–5, 8 balanced; quires 1, 7 adjusted balanced; quire 6 unbalanced. Held in a library preservation box.

1. Ff. 1v–10r: Image of Gabriel, መልክዐ፡ ገብርኤል፡. EMIP 56, f. 63.
2. Ff. 11r–18v: The Mystagogia, ትምህርተ፡ ኅቡአት፡. EMIP 4, f. IIv (varia).
3. Ff. 19r–41v: Prayer of Mary at Golgotha. EMIP 52, f. 1r.
4. Ff. 42r–51v: Bandlet of Righteousness, ልfፈ፡ ጽድቅ፡. EMIP 69, f. 123r.

Notes:

1. Decorative designs: f. 18v (*haräg*-like feature using black); f. 41v (*haräg*-like feature using black and red).
2. Copied for Wäldä Gäbrə'el, f. 5v, and Gäbrä Kidan, f. 10r and 50v.
3. F. 52r–53v blank.
4. Overlooked words of text are written interlinearly (ff. 8r, 49v, 50rv); and overlooked lines of text are written interlinearly (ff. 5v, 7v, 9r, 47v).
5. The catalogue entry at Mount Angel includes these statements about provenance and date: "Dating is based on the script but also names in the various prayers, one of which can be plausibly identified with office holding in 1932; (cf. ff. 10, 18v, 19, 37, 41v)." "Ras Berru, governor of Tamben (Ethiopia), 1932." "Gabra Kidan Berru, original owner, n.d. (ca. 1925)."
6. The manuscript was donated to Mount Angel Library in 1980 by an "anonymous donor from Salem, Oregon."

Quire Map

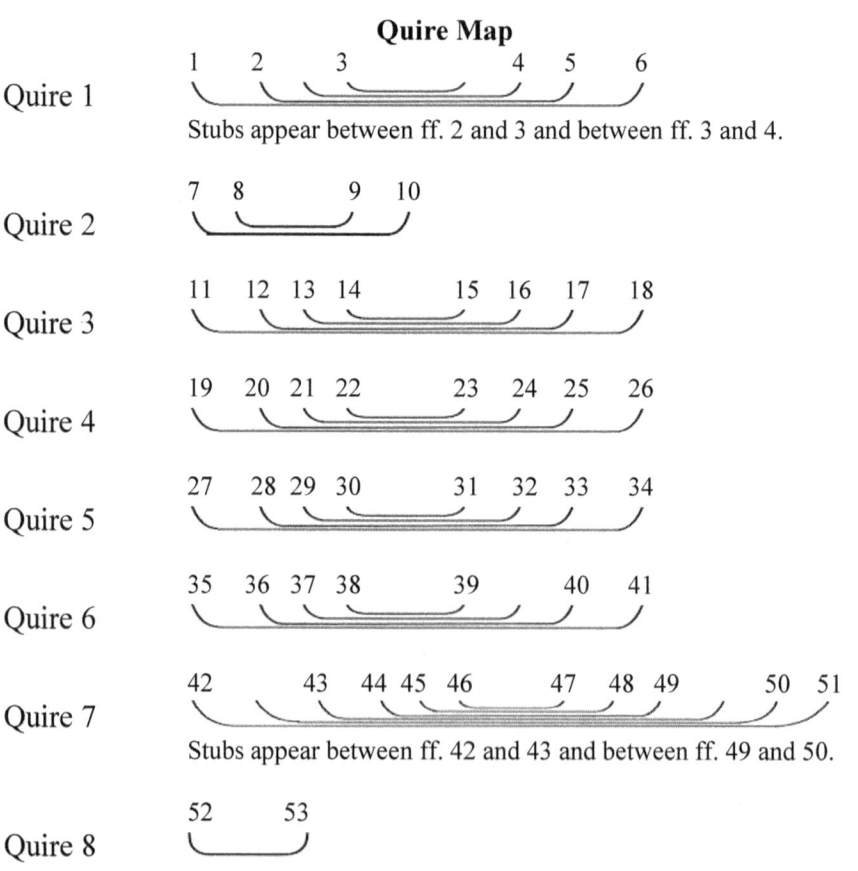

EMIP 75 – Weiner Codex 01
Accordion-fold Codex

Asmat Prayers, ጸሎት፡ በእንተ፡ ዓይነ፡ ጥላ፡ — ጸሎት፡ በእንተ፡ ሕማም፡ ዓይን፡

Parchment, 93 x 94 x 35 mm, accordion-fold codex, comprised of two strips sewn together and stitched to the end-boards; the back cover has three stitches so as to hold the broken board together and the parchment to the cover. 14 folios (numbered consecutively without reference to recto and verso), 94 x 90 mm, top margin 5–8 mm, bottom margin 10–12 mm, fore edge margin 8–10 mm, gutter margin 8–10 mm, one column, Gəʿəz, 12–13 lines, 19th/20th cent.

1. Ff. 1r–7r: *Asmat* prayer against evil eye and charm.
   በስመ፡ አብ፡ . . . ጸሎት፡ በእንተ፡ ዓይነ፡ ጥላ፡ ገርጋሪያ፡ (sic) ዓይነ፡ ባርያ፡ ወሌጌዖን፡ ዓይነ፡ ቡዳ፡ ወዓይነ፡ ጠቢብ፡ ዓይነ፡ መቅኛ፡ (sic) ወዓይነ፡ (sic) ወትንኩልኛ፡ (sic) መንኛ፡ (sic) ወጉኑሥምት፡ ወለሕማም፡ አሰውንውን፡ ወለሸንትምዕ፡ (sic) ወጉርጉሁ፡ ወጊርባ፡ ጆርባ፡ . . .

2. Ff. 7v–14r: The legend of Susənyos and the witch Wurzəlya. Or. 4865, Strelcyn, *British Library*, no. 77, p. 121.
   በስመ፡ አብ፡ . . . ጸሎት፡ በእንተ፡ ሕማም፡ ዓይን፡ ሾትላይ፡ (sic) ወሀሉ፡ ጅዱ፡ አምላክ፡ (sic) ብእሲ፡ ዘስሙ፡ ሱስንዮስ፡ . . .

Miniatures:

1. F. 1: Cross shape in a black box.
2. F. 3: Angel brandishing a Sword.
3. F. 4: Madonna and Child.
4. F. 5: Angel brandishing a Sword.
5. F. 8: Ethiopian Saint holding a prayer stick and a book.
6. F. 11–12: The Archangels Michael and Saraphim (f. 11), and Gabriel and Cherubim (f. 12).
7. F. 14: A panel with geometric shapes with the head of the watching guardian angel in a square box in the center.

Quire Map

This is an accordion-fold book

EMIP 76 – Weiner Codex 02
Image of the Savior of the World — Homiliary in Honor of Archangel Michael መልክዐ፡ መድኃኔ፡ ዓለም፡ — ድርሳነ፡ ሚካኤል፡

Parchment, 213 x 170 x 47 mm, four Coptic chain stitches attached with bridle attachments to rough-hewn boards covered with tooled leather, headband and tailband, one protection sheet + 10 full quires, ii + 88 folios, 208 x 165 mm, top margin 28 mm, bottom margin 40–42 mm, fore edge margin 18–23 mm, gutter margin 8–13 mm, two columns, Gəʿəz, 18–19 lines, 19th cent.

Quire descriptions: quires 1, 3–5, 7–10 balanced; quire 6 adjusted balanced; quire 2 complex composite. Navigation system: various colored string sewn into corners of folios 21, 26, 31, 57, 69, 74, 77 to mark content divisions.

1. Ff. 1r–7v, lacuna, 8r–88v: Homiliary for the Monthly Feast of the Archangel Michael, ድርሳነ፡ ሚካኤል፡. Cf. EMIP 16.
   Ḫədar: homily by Dämatewos, f. 1r, miracle, f. 6r, Synaxary entry (mission to Joshua), incomplete, f. 7v; **Taḫśaś**: homily, f. 15r, miracle, f. 20r, Synaxary entry (mission to Babylon), f. 21r, greeting, f. 21v; **Ṭərr**: homily, f. 21v, miracle, f. 25r, Synaxary entry (mission to Jacob), f. 25v, greeting, f. 26r; ; **Yäkkatit**: homily, f. 26r, miracle, f. 29v, Synaxary entry (mission to Samson), f. 30v, greeting, f. 31r; **Mäggabit**: homily, f. 31r, miracle, f. 45r, Synaxary entry (mission to Balaam, f. 46r, greeting, f. 46r; **Miyazya**: homily, f. 46v, miracle, f. 50r, Synaxary entry (mission to Jeremiah, f. 51v, greeting, f. 51v; **Gənbot**: homily, f. 52r, miracle, incomplete at the end, f. 53v; **Säne**: homily, f. 57r, miracle, f. 62r, Synaxary entry (The building of the church of the Archangel in place of a pagan temple in Alexandria), f. 63r, greeting, f. 69r; **Ḥamle**: homily, f. 69r, miracle, 73r, Synaxary entry (mission to the camp of Sennacherib), f. 73v, greeting, f. 74r; **Näḫase**: homily, f. 74r, miracle, f. 76v, Synaxary entry (mission to Emperor Constantine), f. 77r, greeting, f. 77v; **Mäskäräm**: homily, f. 77v, miracle, f. 79r, Synaxary entry (mission to Prophet Isaiah), f. 81r, greeting, f. 81r; **Ṭəqəmt**: homily, f. 81v, miracle, f. 84v, Synaxary entry (mission to Prophet Samuel), f. 85v, greeting, f. 86r.

2. Ff. 86v–88v and Ir–IIv: Image of the Savior of the World, መልክዐ፡ መድኃኔ፡ ዓለም፡. Chaîne, Répertoire, no. 164; MG 59, pp. 226ff. በስመ፡ አብ፡ . . . ሰላም፡ ለዝክረ፡ ስምከ፡ ዘአርከበ፡ ተፍጻሜተ፡፡ መላእክተ፡ ሰማይ፡ ወምድር፡ እለ፡ ለመዱ፡ ስብሐተ፡፡

Miniatures:
1. F. 55r: Saint George and the Dragon.
2. F. 55v: Madonna and Child.
3. F. 56r: Angel brandishing a sword.
4. F. 83v: The Lord on his throne holding an orb and the Four Living Creatures carrying the throne.

Varia:
1. F. 45r, list of numbers (1–10 and by tens thereafter) written in pencil in the center margin (between the two columns of text).
2. F. 54v: Record of purchase of land, date unclear.
3. F. 56rv: Prayer of Wäldä Mäsqäl for salvation with the *asmat* found in the *Dərsanä Mika'el* and the Hebrew letters found in Ps 118.

Notes:
1. Two sheets (9/24 and 10/23) wrap around two smaller quires. The first quire is made of two sheets (11/14 and 12/13); the second quire is made of four sheets (15/22, 16/21, 17/20 and 18/19).
2. Decorative designs: ff. 1r. (*haräg* with red and black ink); 21v, 26r, 63r, 77v, 79v, (rows of full-stop symbols, some with interspersed lines of alternating red and black dots); 69r (row of alternating red and black dots); 81r (rows of full-stop symbol above and below two lines made up of alternating red and black dots).
3. Note of ownership by Wäldä Mäsqäl and his wife Wälättä Iyyäsus, f/ 56r and *passim*.
4. Overlooked words of text are written interlinearly (ff. ir(ecto), 7v, 10v, 18r, 44r, 50r, etc.); and overlooked lines of text are written interlinearly (ff. 1r and 69r); and in the upper margin with a symbol (⊥) marking the location where the text is to be inserted (ff. 5r, line 19 and 15r, line 2).

Quire Map

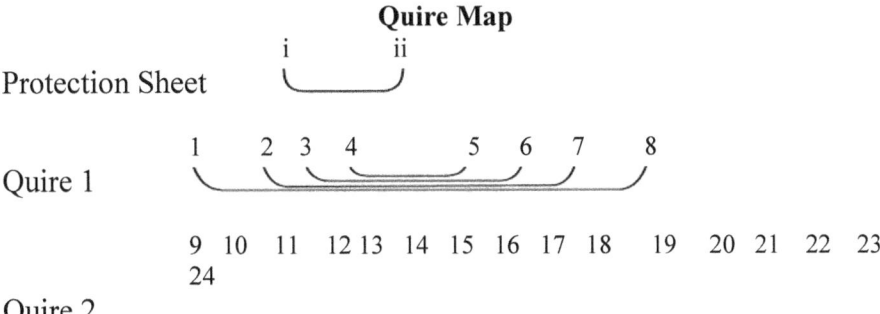

This is a complex, composite quire. Two sheets (9/24 and 10/23) wrap around two smaller quires. The first quire is made of two sheets (11/14 and 12/13); the second quire is made of four sheets (15/22, 16/21, 17/20 and 18/19).

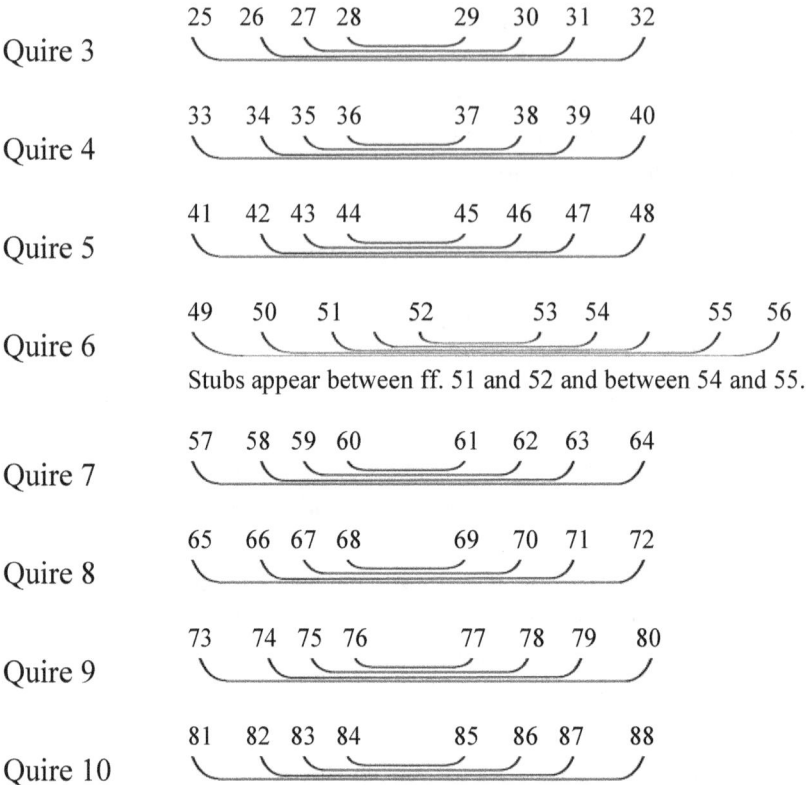

Stubs appear between ff. 51 and 52 and between 54 and 55.

EMIP 77 – The Bernhardt Codex
Anaphora of Our Lady Mary — Image of Mary — The Mystagogia,
ቅዳሴ፡ ማርያም፡ — መልክዐ፡ ማርያም፡ — ትምህርተ፡ ኅቡኣት፡

Parchment, 128 x 82 x 25 mm, two, secondary stitches attached to rough-hewn boards, one protection sheet + five quires, ii + 41 folios, 125 x 84 mm, top margin 5–7 mm, bottom margin 30 mm, fore edge margin 15 mm, gutter margin 7 mm, one column, Gəʿəz, 16 lines, reign of Metropolitan Matewos (1889–1926), f. 2v.

Quire descriptions: quires 1–5 balanced. Double-slip case with leather strap.

1. Ff. 1r–28r: Anaphora of Our Lady Mary ascribed to Cyriacus of Bəhənsa, $G^{w}\ddot{a}s\text{'}a$, **ቅዳሴ፡ ማርያም፡**.
2. F. 25r–30v: Image of Mary, **መልክዐ፡ ማርያም፡**. EMIP 27, f. 23r.
3. Ff. 31r–38v: The Mystagogia, **ትምህርተ፡ ኅቡኣት፡**. EMIP 4, f. IIv (varia).
4. Ff. 38v–39v: Prayer against demons with the *asmat* preserved in the *Dərsanä Mika'el*.

5. F. 40r: List of the sufferings of Jesus during Passion Week.
6. F. 40v–41v: Erased, but probably a certain *asmat* prayer.
7. F. 41v: The beginning of an Amharic letter, in a crude hand.

Varia:
1. F. IIr, Iv: Calendar of the feasts of the year, bound upside down.
2. F. IIv: *Asmat* prayer against evil eye.
   በስመ አብ . . . ጸሎተ፡ ነደራ፡ በዕንተ፡ ሕማመ፡ ዓይነት፡ አትሪኮን፡ በትሪኮንጶተሮ ፌሪኮን፡ አተርጋዎን፡ በኃይለ፡ ዝንቱ፡ አስማቲከ፡ አድህነን፡ እምሕማመ፡ ዓይነ፡ ሰብዕ፡ ለ . . .

Notes:
1. The protection quire is bound upside down into the codex.
2. The stitching has been done with two different types of string. One type, is a stiff parchment colored string made up of very thin strands of some type of animal (?) material. The other type, is a cotton based string. Green, orange, and light tan colored cotton strings have been used. Each quire of pages is bound using a different type/color of string, sometimes two. This mixture of string types and colors are probably the result of rebinding or repair efforts done over time. New string was added to replace or reinforce a worn or broken string or to bind in new quire of pages.
3. Most of the pages are water stained along their top outer edges. The water has caused some of the ink to run. The last page of the manuscript is heavily water damaged. The text on this page is almost completely washed off.
4. The lower and outer edges of many pages are darkened from use and from water stains.
5. F. Ir: What seems a proper name: Balä Ṭäkase (?).
6. F. Iv: Unintelligible words.
7. Provenance: Owned by Theodore Bernhardt Jr., Edgewater Park, New Jersey. Purchased June 25, 2002 (eBay Item #888884839) from Adam Langweiler, Amsterdam, the Netherlands. (Before 2002) Private collection of Coptic and Ethiopian manuscripts.
8. Publication: On-line presentation of the manuscript – August 30, 2002 to present (as of April 2006). Ethiopian Manuscript Prayer Book http://members.tripod.com/~palaeography/index.html. Note: This was the first Ethiopian manuscript codex to be presented in its entirety on the World Wide Web.

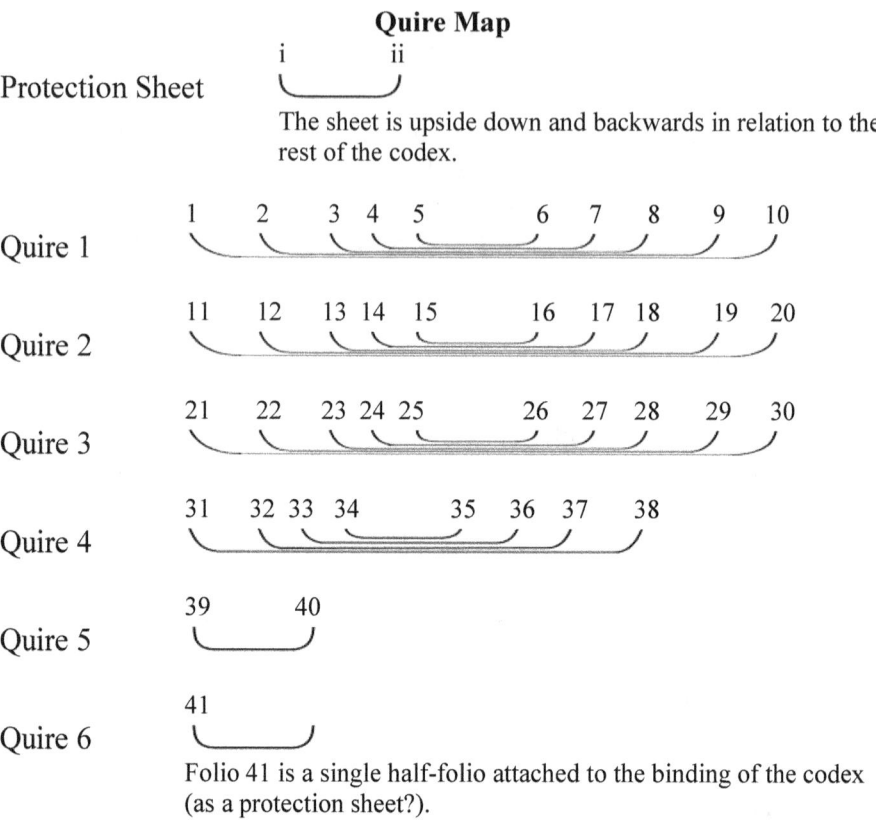

EMIP 78 – Eliza Codex 37

Gospel of John — Canticle of the Flower — Lamentation of the Virgin — Image of Mary, ወንጌለ፡ ዮሐንስ፡ — ማሕሌተ፡ ጽጌ፡ — ሰቆቃወ፡ ድንግል፡

Parchment, 165 x 127 x 62 mm, four Coptic chain stitches attached with bridle attachments to rough-hewn boards, 18 full quires, reinforcement strips around quires 1–18, quires 2–17 numbered, ii + 138 folios, 157 x 115 mm, top margin 13 mm, bottom margin 33–37 mm, fore edge margin 16–20 mm, gutter margin 6–10 mm, ff. iv(erso)–iir, 137r–138v one column, ff. 1r–136v two columns, Gəʿəz, 16–17 lines, 19th cent.

Quire descriptions: quires 1–18 balanced. Navigation systems: various colored string sewn into corners of folios 18, 23, 42, 50, 61, 77, and 112 to mark content divisions.

1. Ff. 1r–94r: Gospel of John, ወንጌለ፡ ዮሐንስ፡. Arranged for the days of the week (Saturday, f. 18v; Tuesday, f. 23v; Saturday, f. 42r; Wednesday, f.

Catalogue of the Ethiopic Manuscript Imaging Project · 207

50v; Thursday, f. 61r; Friday, f. 77v; Sunday, f. 87r; Everyday, f. 92r). Text, f. 1r; Conclusion, *Mäl'a*, f. 93v.
2. Ff. 94r–122r: Canticle of the Flower, ማኅሌተ፡ ጽጌ፡. Grohmann, *Marienhymnen*.
ጽጌ፡ አስተርአየ፡ ሠሪያ፡ እምዓዕመ፡፡
ለዘአምኃኪ፡ ጽጌ፡ ለገብርኤል፡ ምስለ፡ ሰላመ፡፡
3. Ff. 122r–132r: Lamentations of the Virgin, ሰቆቃው፡ ድንግል፡. EMIP 6, 21r.
4. Ff. 132v–135r: Image of Mary of Qʷəsqʷam, መልክዐ፡ ቀሉስቋም፡. EMIP 6, f. 34r.
5. Ff. 135v–136v: Reward for reading the Gospel regularly.
አአኃው፡ ስምዑ፡ ዘወሀበ፡ ተስፋ፡ እግ"፡ ለውሉደ፡ አዳም፡ ወዘያነብብ፡ ወንጌለ፡ እንበለ፡ አጽርዖ፡ . . .

Miniatures (all in a late twentieth-century hand):
1. F. 2r: Madonna and Child.
2. F. 5r: Saint George and the Dragon.
3. F. 9r: The Holy Trinity.
4. F. 25r: Jesus raising right hand.
5. F. 41r: The Resurrection, raising Adam and Eve.
6. F. 62r: Man pointing a dagger to the neck of another.
7. F. 80r: Man riding a horse spears a cow.
8. F. 115r: The Annunciation.
9. Recto side of rearguard flap: Crude drawing of face.

Varia:
1. Ff. Iv–IIr: Prayer for salvation from the sea of fire, hell, ድርሳን፡ ዘቀሌምንጦስ፡. Clement. . Our Lord's sufferings during Passion Week are invoked in the prayer.
በስመ አብ፡ . . . ድርሳን፡ ዘብፁዕ፡ ቀሌምንጦስ፡ ስምዕ፡ ኮሎ፡ ጊዜ፡ ከመ፡ ያውዕዕ፡ ነፍስተ፡ ፩አመሂ፡ ነፍስተ፡ ብዙኃ፡ ጸሎተ፡ እግዚአ፡ ዘኃደግነ፡ ለነ፡ ትእምርተ፡ ሕማማቲከ፡ ቅዱስ፡ ሰንዱን፡ በዘቡቱ፡ ተገንዘ፡ ሥጋከ፡ ቅዱስ፡ . . .
2. F. IIr: *Asmat* prayer to brighten the mind.
ሰድርቃኤል፡ አበድርቃኤል፡ አቅናፌድ፡ ዮሴዴ፡ አትሪኮን፡ ቦርፍሪኮን ፡ አተርጌያን፡ ስጥጥ፡ ግልባቤ፡ ልብየ፡ . . .
3. F. 136v: *Asmat* prayer whose purpose is not stated.
አልቅያኖስ፡ ዘሎሚ፡ ትሬትዕ፡ አቁም፡ በጠጁን፡ ዘሐጁን፡ ከረዙን፡ . . .
4. F. 137rv: Calendar of the Apostles and Evangelists.
5. F. 138r: Fragment of prayer against pestilence with the *asmat* preserved in the *Dərsanä Mika'el*.

Notes:
1. Decorative designs: f. 1r (*ḥaräg* using black and red); ff. 1r, 77v, and 122r (dotted line using alternating black and red); ff. 1r (5 full-stop symbols in red and black); f. 122r (4 full-stop symbols in red and black).
2. Verso of the rearguard leaf: an attempt to write the different forms of *h* (ሀ).
3. F. Ir blank.
4. Note of ownership by Gäbrä Mika'el, f. 1r, 135r and *passim*, and Wäldä Ḥsanna, f. 94r and *passim*.
5. Copied by Zewa Iyyäsus, ff. 1r, 94r and *passim*.
6. Overlooked words of text are written interlinearly (ff. 14v, 18v, 34v, 39v, 40r, 47v, 53r, etc.); and overlooked lines of text are written interlinearly (ff. 32v, 44v, 75v,); and in the upper margin with a symbol (+) marking the location where the text is to be inserted (f. 131v, line 14), and in another case where text was overlooked due to homoeoteleuton where the symbol (ᚺ) is used (f. 15r, line 11).
7. The codex was sold to Gerald Weiner in 2007.

Quire Map

	i	ii
Protection Quire	⌣	⌣

	1	2	3	4	5	6	7	8
Quire 1								

	9	10	11	12	13	14	15	16
Quire 2								

	17	18	19	20	21	22	23	24
Quire 3								

	25	26	27	28	29	30	31	32
Quire 4								

	33	34	35	36	37	38	39	40
Quire 5								

	41	42	43	44	45	46	47	48
Quire 6								

	49	50	51	52	53	54	55	56
Quire 7								

Catalogue of the Ethiopic Manuscript Imaging Project · 209

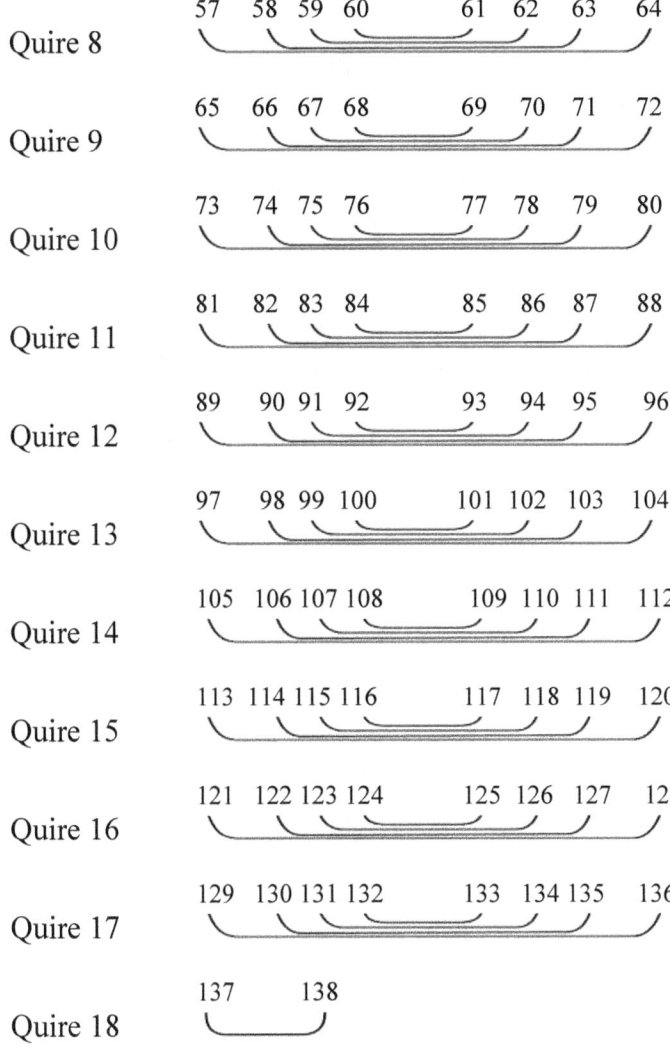

This quire has no number and is a single sheet, much smaller than the normal sheet size. It seems to come from another source. Ff. 137r and 138v contain text that is oriented as the rest of the folios in the codex. But ff. 137v and 138r are oriented 90 degrees to the clockwise. The sheet appears to have been cut in such a way as to preserve the text written on it (137v/138r), added to the codex and the outer folios used for additional writing.

EMIP 79 – Eliza Codex 38
Psalter, ዳዊት:

Parchment, 162 x 110 x 60 mm, four Coptic chain stitches attached with bridle attachments to rough-hewn boards, protection folio + 18 full quires, i + 171 folios, 160 x 109 mm, top margin 13–14 mm, bottom margin 25–28 mm, fore edge margin 12–15 mm, gutter margin 8–10 mm, ff. 1r–151v one column, ff. 152r–170r two columns, Gəʻəz, 21 lines, 20th cent.

Quire descriptions: quires 1–10, 12–18 balanced; quire 11 unbalanced. Navigation systems: 1) various colored string sewn into corners of ff. 15, 24, 35, 59, 65, 86, 100, 123, 130, 151, 165 to mark content divisions; 2) marginal notations to indicate readings.

Ff. 1r–170r: Psalter [Dawit]. Introduced with the first psalm of the Psalms of the Virgin, Mäzmurä Dəngəl. cf. EMIP 2.
1. Ff. 1r–130r: Psalms of David.
2. Ff. 130v–143v: Biblical Canticles.
3. Ff. 144r–151v: Song of Songs, common version.
4. Ff. 152r–165r: Praises of Mary [Wəddase Maryam], arranged for the days of the week (Monday, f. 152r; Tuesday, f. 153r; Wednesday, f. 155v; Thursday, f. 158r; Friday, f. 161r; Saturday, f. 162v; Sunday, f. 163v).
5. Ff. 165r–170r: Gate of Light [Anqäṣä Bərhan].

Miniatures, all in the late twentieth-century hand of the "beautiful painter," several painted over text:
1. F. 10v: Saint George and the Dragon.
2. F. 11r: Angel surrounded by crowd.
3. F. 119v: Jesus followed by a crowd.
4. F. 120r: The Resurrection, raising Adam and Eve.
5. F. 170v: An Angel standing.
6. F. 171r: Jesus Carrying the Cross.

Varia:
1. F. Iv: The first few words of the hymn to Mary, "The angels praise Mary."

Notes:
1. The general condition of the parchment is moderately dirty and relatively unworn. The parchment is fairly consistent and relatively thick.
2. Decorative designs: ff. 1r, 15v, 24r, 35r, 59r, 65v, 71v, 80rv, 86v, 100v, 113v, 117r, 123v, 130r, 143v, 151v (haräg using black and red); ff. 8r,

43r, 49v, 101v, 130v, 170r (*haräg* using black); ff. 1r, 49v, 71r, 80r, 105r, 113v, 117r, 143v, 144r, 152r, 153r, 155v, 158r, 160v, 162v, 165r, (dotted line using alternating black and red); f. 170r (dotted line using black ink).
3. Columetric layout of text: ff. 127r (Ps. 145), 128v (Ps. 148), 129v–130r (Ps. 150), 139v–140r (tenth biblical canticle).
4. F. 65v. A symbol and the word "half" mark the midpoint of the Psalms.
5. Note of ownership by Ləğ Yəggärämu, in a crude hand, f. 1r.
6. F. 151v: erased.
7. Note of ownership by Admaśu, f. 171r.
8. Overlooked words of text are written interlinearly (ff. 51v, 77v, 80v, 98r); and overlooked lines of text are written interlinearly (ff. 4r, 21r, 71r, 79rv, 85v, 108r, 121v).
9. The scribe regularly has to complete a line of text on another line. Much of the problem is addressed through the selection of an appropriate aspect ratio for the codex combined with an appropriate script size. But, where the line of text is still too long, the scribe completes the line of text above the end of the line (throughout). This scribe will also reduce the font size at the end of lines to avoid having to go onto the next line (e.g., ff. 43rv, 44r, 45rv, etc.).
10. The codex was sold to Gerald Weiner in 2007.

Quire Map

Protection Folio — i

Quire 1 — 1, 2, 3, 4, 5, 6, 7, 8, 9, 10

Quire 2 — 11, 12, 13, 14, 15, 16, 17, 18, 19, 20

Quire 3 — 21, 22, 23, 24, 25, 26, 27, 28, 29, 30

Quire 4 — 31, 32, 33, 34, 35, 36, 37, 38, 39, 40

Quire 5 — 41, 42, 43, 44, 45, 46, 47, 48, 49, 50

```
Quire 6    51  52  53 54 55       56  57  58    59  60

Quire 7    61  62  63 64 65       66  67  68    69  70

Quire 8    71  72  73 74 75       76  77  78    79  80

Quire 9    81  82  83 84 85       86  87  88    89  90

Quire 10   91  92  93 94 95       96  97  98    99 100

Quire 11  101     102 103 104    105 106 107   108 109
```
A folio stub is visible between ff. 101 and 102.
```
Quire 12  110 111  112 113 114   115 116 117   118 119

Quire 13  120 121  122 123 124   125 126 127   128 129

Quire 14  130 131  132 133 134   135 136 137   138 139

Quire 15  140 141  142 143 144   145 146 147   148 149

Quire 16  150 151  152 153 154   155 156 157   158 159

Quire 17  160 161  162 163 164   165 166 167   168 169

Quire 18  170     171
```

EMIP 80 – Eliza Codex 39
Psalter, ዳዊት፦

Parchment, 173 x 107 x 62 mm, four Coptic chain stitches attached with bridle attachments to rough-hewn boards, 16 full quires, 140 folios, 170 x 107 mm, top margin 15–17 mm, bottom margin 35–37 mm, fore edge margin 17–20 mm, gutter margin 9–10 mm, ff. 7r–126v one column, ff. 1r–6r, 127r–137r two columns, Gəʿəz, Psalms, Biblical Canticles and Song of Songs, 25–27 lines; Praises of Mary and Gate of Light, 27–32 lines, reign of Patriarch Yoḥannəs XIX (1928–1942), f. 6r.

Quire descriptions: quires 1–11, 13–15 balanced; quires 12, 16 adjusted balanced.

1. Ff. 1r–5r: Image of Phanuel, መልክዐ፦ ፋኑኤል፦. MG 59, pp. 376ff.
   በመለኮተ፦ አብ፦ ወወልድ፦ ወመንፈስ፦ ቅዱስ፦ ወጠነ፦፦
   ማኅሌተ፦ ክቡር፦ ፋኑኤል፦ በዘመልክዑ፦ ድርሳነ፦፦
   እመሰ፦ ላዕላዓ፦ ልሳንየ፦ ኮነ፦፦
   ነዓ፦ ፋኑኤል፦ ትርድአኒ፦ ወታድግነኒ፦ ፍጡነ፦፦
   እንዘ፦ ለስምከ፦ እገዝ፦ ወይዌጥን፦ (sic) አነ፦፦
   ሰላም፦ ለተፈጥሮትከ፦ ምስለ፦ መላእክት፦ ኅቡረ፦፦
   እንዘ፦ ኢትከውን፦ ቅድመ፦ ወኢትዴኃር፦ ድንረ፦፦

2. Ff. 5r–6r: Absolution of the Son, ፍትሐት፦ ዘወልድ፦. EMIP 10, f. IIr (varia).

3. Ff. 1r–178r: Psalter [*Dawit*]. Introduced with the first psalm of the Psalms of the Virgin, *Mäzmurä Dəngəl*. cf. EMIP 2.
   a. Ff. 7r–109r: Psalms of David.
   b. Ff. 109v–120r: Biblical Canticles.
   c. Ff. 120v–126v: Song of Songs, common version.
   d. Ff. 127r–136v: Praises of Mary [*Wəddase Maryam*]. Arranged for the days of the week (Monday, f. 127r; Tuesday, f. 127v; Wednesday, f. 129r; Thursday, f. 130v; Friday, f. 132r; Saturday, f. 133r; Sunday, f. 133v).
   e. Ff. 134v–137r: Gate of Light [*Anqäṣä Bərhan*].

Miniatures, all in twentieth-century hand:
1. F. 6v: Madonna and Child.
2. F. 137v: Madonna and Child.
3. F. 138r: Saint Yared and King Gäbrä Mäsqäl.
4. F. 138v: Saint George and the Dragon.
5. F. 139r: A man with a spear.
6. F. 139v: The Resurrection, raising Adam and Eve.
7. F. 140r: The Crucifixion.

Notes:

1. The general condition of the parchment is moderately dirty and relatively unworn. The parchment is fairly consistent and relatively thick.
2. Decorative designs: ff. 1v, 7r, 40v, 75r, 109r (*haräg* using black and red); ff. 5r, 6r, 12v, 25r, 34r, 46r, 49r, 53v, 63r, 70r, 96r, 98v, 104r, 120v, 134v, 137r (dotted line using alternating black and red); 19r, 86r, 126v (dotted line using black ink).
3. Columetric layout of text: ff. 108v–109r (Ps. 150), 116v–117v (tenth biblical canticle).
4. F. 58v: A small, red and black cross mark the midpoint of the Psalter.
5. Ff. 1r and 140v blank.
6. Overlooked words of text are written interlinearly (ff. 2r, 59v, 74r, 81r, 82v, 90v, 129r, 132v); and overlooked lines of text are written interlinearly (ff. 14v, 22r, 23r, 57v, 78r, 106r, 129v).
7. The scribe regularly has to complete a line of text on another line. Much of the problem is addressed through the selection of an appropriate aspect ratio for the codex combined with an appropriate script size. But, where the line of text is still too long, the scribe completes the line of text above the end of the line (throughout). This scribe will also reduce the font size at the end of lines to avoid having to go onto the next line (throughout).
8. The codex was sold to Gerald Weiner in 2007.

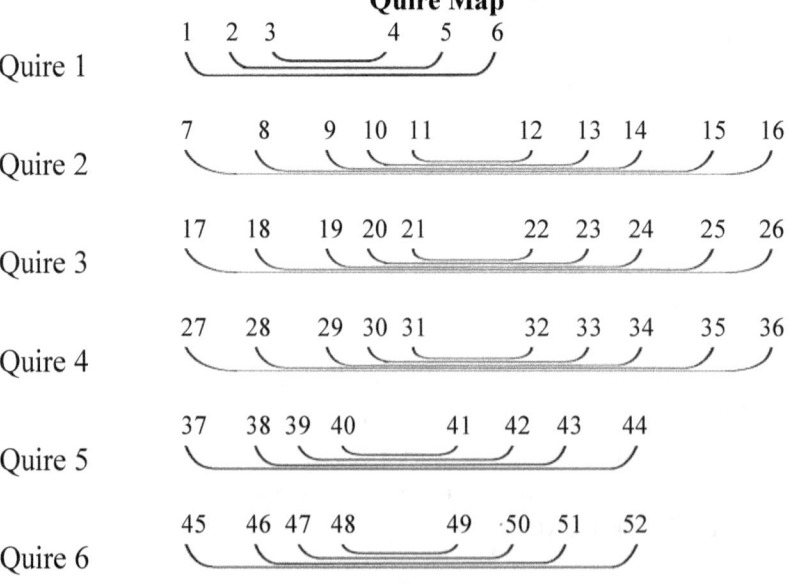

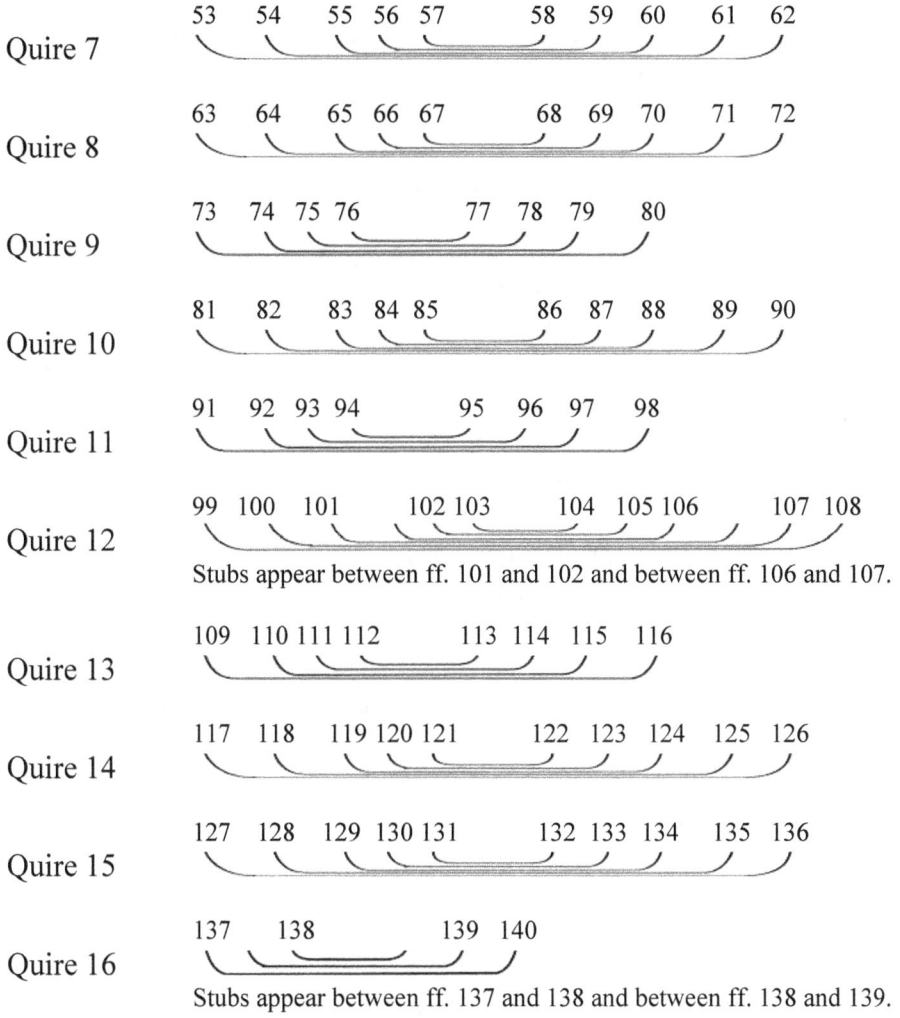

Stubs appear between ff. 101 and 102 and between ff. 106 and 107.

Stubs appear between ff. 137 and 138 and between ff. 138 and 139.

EMIP 81 – Eliza Codex 40
Psalter, ዳዊት፡

Parchment, 187 x 135 x 55 mm, four Coptic chain stitches attached with bridle attachments to rough-hewn boards, protection quire + 12 full quires, ii + 94 folios, 184 x 133 mm folio, top margin 12–15 mm, bottom margin 12–30 mm, fore edge margin 18–30 mm, gutter margin 8 mm, ff. 1r–86r one column, ff. 86v–93v two columns, Gəʿəz, 27–34 lines, reign of Yoḥannəs IV (1872–1889), f. 93r.

Quire descriptions: quires 1–12 balanced. Navigation system: brown yarn sewn into corners of folios to mark the location of miniatures.

Ff. 1r–93v: Psalter [*Dawit*]. A later crude hand has added the first psalm from the *Mäzmurä Dəngel* as an introduction; cf. EMIP 1 and EMIP 2.
1. Ff. 1r–74v: Psalms of David.
2. Ff. 74v–82v: Biblical Canticles.
3. Ff. 82v–86r: Song of Songs, common version.
4. Ff. 86v–90v (apparently since text was erased and painted over): Praises of Mary [*Wəddase Maryam*]. Arranged for the days of the week (Monday, f. 86v; Tuesday, f. 87r; Wednesday, f. 87v; Thursday, f. 88r; Friday, f. 89r; Saturday, f. 89v; Sunday, f. 90r).
5. Ff. 90v–93v: Gate of Light [*Anqäṣä Bərhan*].

Miniatures (1–6 are all in a twentieth-century hand akin to the "speckled garment artist," painted over text):
1. F. 3v: Madonna and Child.
2. F. 19r: The Crucifixion.
3. F. 38v: Saint George and the Dragon.
4. F. 49r: Moses with his brother and sister.
5. F. 69r: King David Playing the Harp.
6. F. 90v: The Striking of the Head (apparently painted over text showing the end of Praises of Mary and beginning of Gate of Light).
7. F. 94r: Crude drawing in blue pen of an insect with the face of a man.
8. F. 94v: Crude drawing of a woman.
9. Inside of back cover: a drawing of a partial image of a man.

Varia:
1. Ff. Ir–Vv: Excerpt from the *Dəggʷa* chant for the cross, Gabriel, Mary, Palm Sunday (*Hośa'na*) Michael and John the Baptist, with musical notations.
2. F. 94v: "In the name of the Father and the Son and the Holy Spirit, one."

Notes:
1. The general condition of the vellum is moderately dirty but relatively unworn.
2. In the Psalms of David, the scribe has placed a line of alternating red and black dots after every tenth Psalm. On these same folios someone has sewn red yarn into the upper fore edge.
3. Decorative designs: ff. iiir, (*haräg* using black and red); ff. 9r, 15v, 21v, 27r, 30v, 31rv, 50v 65v, 66r, 67rv, 70v (*haräg* using black); 31r (*haräg* using black, red and green); 43r, 47v, 51r (*haräg* using black,

gray and light blue); ff. 21v, 83rv, 84v, 86r, 93v (dotted line using alternating black and red).
4. Columetric layout of text: ff. 80rv (tenth biblical canticle).
5. Ff. Iv and 94r blank.
6. Overlooked words of text are written interlinearly (ff. 21v, 41v, 67r, 75v, 83r, etc.); and in the upper margin with a symbol (⊥) marking the location where the text is to be inserted (f. 17v, line 3,), and in another case where the symbol (+) is used (ff. 34v, line 10 and 38r, line 14).
7. The scribe regularly has to complete a line of text on another line. Much of the problem is addressed through the selection of an appropriate aspect ratio for the codex combined with an appropriate script size. But, where the line of text is still too long, the scribe completes the line of text above the end of the line (throughout).
8. The codex was sold to Gerald Weiner in 2007.

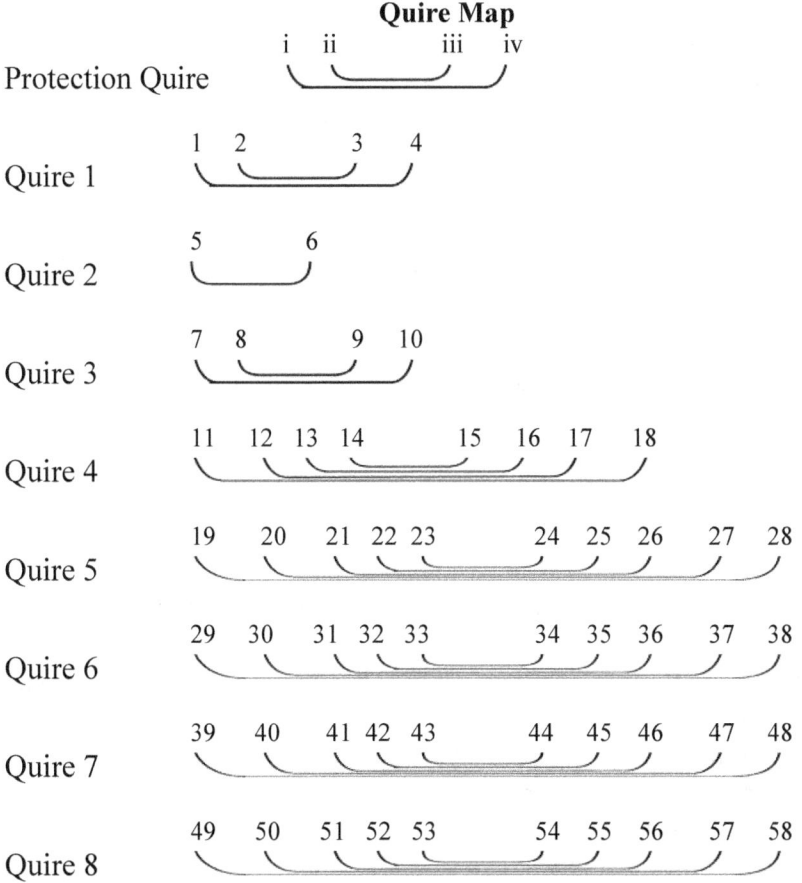

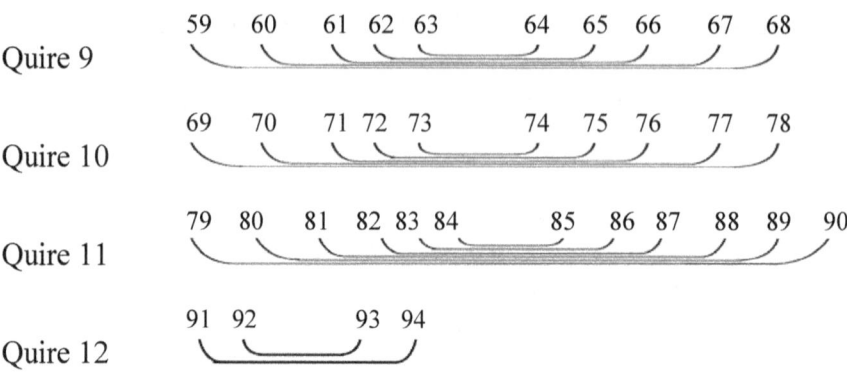

EMIP 82 – Eliza Codex 41
Prayer of Mary at Golgotha, Absolution of the Son, ጸሎተ፡ እግዝእትነ፡ ማርያም፡ ዘሰኔ፡ ጎልጎታ፡ — ፍትሐት፡ ዘወልድ፡

Parchment, 150 x 105 x 37 mm, four Coptic chain stitches attached with bridle attachments to rough-hewn boards covered with tooled leather, protection quire + 5 full quires, ii + 43 folios, 145 x 100 mm, top margin 12–17 mm, bottom margin 20–30 mm, fore edge margin 12–17 mm, gutter margin 8 mm, ff. 1r–42v one column, Gəʿəz, 15 lines, reign of Patriarch Yoḥannəs XIX (1928–1942), f. 41v.

Quire descriptions: quires 4, 5 balanced; quires 1, 2 adjusted balanced; quire 3 unbalanced. Navigation system: brown yarn sewn into corners of folios 1, 17, 36, 42 to mark the location of miniatures. Single-slip case with a strap of linen.

1. Ff. 1r–25v: Prayer of Mary at Golgotha, ጸሎተ፡ እግዝእትነ፡ ማርያም፡ ዘሰኔ፡ ጎልጎታ፡. Cf. EMIP 52.
2. Ff. 26r–35r: Introductory Rite from Muʿallaqa for the reading of the Miracles of Mary. EMIP 31, f. 1v and EMIP 36, f. 1v.
3. Ff. 36r–38v: One miracle of Mary: The governor Armatəyas against whom people brought false accusation. Budge, *Mary*, p. 297.
4. Ff. 38v–42: Absolution of the Son, ፍትሐት፡ ዘወልድ፡. EMIP 10, f. IIr (varia).

Miniatures, all in the late twentieth-century hand of the "speckled garment artist," painted over text:
1. F. iv(erso): Madonna and Child.
2. F. iir: Angel with Sword.
3. F. iiv(erso): Man with Book.
4. F: 16v: Angel with Sword.
5. F. 17r: God with Orb (Jesus?).

6. F. 35v: old man holds hand up to younger man; both have books; second old man in the rear.
7. F. 42v: Mary, haloed older man on her right; younger haloed man on her left.
8. F. 43r: The Last Supper.

Notes:
1. F. 1r: Unidentified figure.
2. Copied for Gäbrä Mädḫən, f. 36r and *passim*.
3. F. 43v blank.

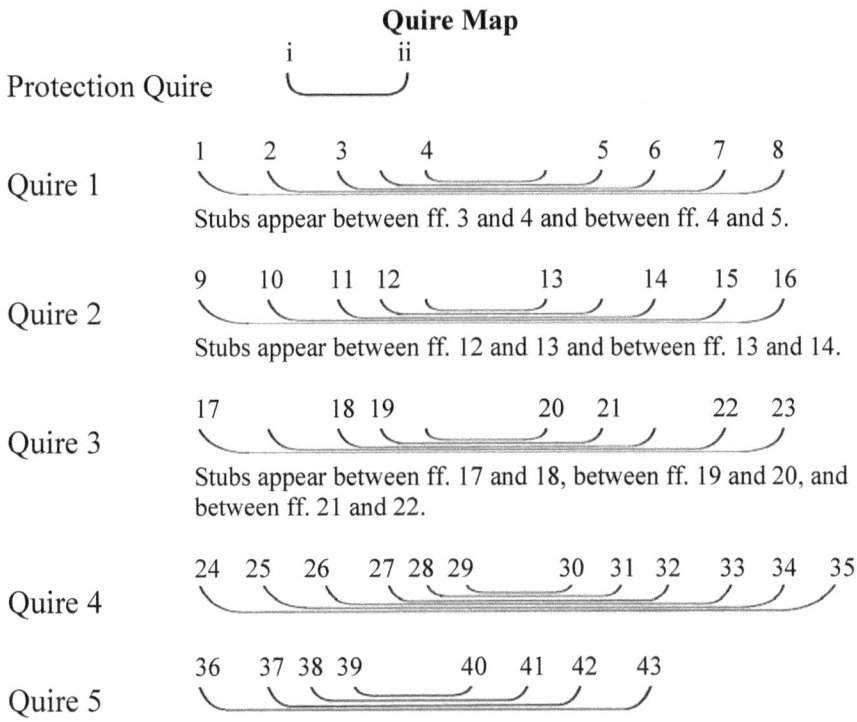

EMIP 83 – Weiner Codex 3
Psalter, ዳዊት፡

Parchment, 172 x 155 x 73 mm, four Coptic chain stitches attached with bridle attachments to rough-hewn boards, the entire codex covered with a decorative linen cover, protection quire + 24 full quires, quires 2–6 numbered, iii + 186 folios, 167 x 150 mm folio, top margin 21–23 mm, bottom margin 40–42 mm, fore edge margin 22–28 mm, gutter margin 10–14 mm, ff. 1r–163v one column, ff. 164r–182v two columns, Gə'əz, 19 lines, 18th cent.

Quire descriptions: quires 1–21, 23–24 balanced; quire 22 unbalanced. Navigation system: marginal notations to indicate readings. Double slipcase.

Ff. 1r–182v: Psalter [*Dawit*]. With the traditional spiritual meaning of the Hebrew letters of Ps 118 added; cf. EMIP 1.
1. Ff. 1r–141r: Psalms of David.
2. Ff. 141r–155v: Biblical Canticles.
3. Ff. 155v–163v: Song of Songs, common version.
4. Ff. 164r–177r: Praises of Mary [*Wəddase Maryam*]. Arranged for the days of the week (Monday, f. 164r; Tuesday, f. 165r; Wednesday, f. 167r; Thursday, f. 169r; Friday, f. 172r; Saturday, f. 174r; Sunday, f. 175r).
5. Ff. 177r–182v and 184r: Gate of Light [*Anqäṣä Bərhan*].

Miniatures, all in twentieth-century hand (with bright purple and red ink):
1. F. 87v: Crude drawing.
2. F. 94r: Crude drawing.
3. F. 100v: recent crude drawing in red ink of a person.
4. F. 126v: Crude drawing.
5. F. 155v: Crude drawing.
6. F. 163v: Crude drawing of three ornate crosses.
7. F. 185v: The Crucifixion (with cloth covering the illumination).
8. F. 186r: Madonna and Child.

Varia:
1. F. Irv: *Asmat* prayer, insufficiently legible.
2. F. Iv: *Asmat* prayer against the devil invoking the Trinity, Christ and the cross. The beginning is not there as the top margin is cut out.
3. Ff. Iv–IIr: *Asmat* prayer against the evil eye, *ḥəmamä ʽayn*. Cf. EMIP 9, f. IIIrv (varia).
4. F. IIv: Insufficiently legible *asmat* prayer.
5. F. IIIr: *Asmat* prayer against stomachache, copied for Kəflä Maryam and his wife Wälättä Samuʼel.
   ቁጼ፡ ቁፈት፡ ብያክ፡ ምሊ፡ መምሊ፡ . . .
6. F. IIIr: What seems a record of transaction of a certain item, insufficiently legible.
7. F. IIIv: Prayer to God of David for the protection of several names, in a crude hand.
8. F. 2r: Note of condolence by *Abba* Wube.
9. F. 163v: Prayer for the soul of many people whose names are copied replacing other names.
10. F. 183rv: Ps 44, obviously a rejected leaf from another Psalter.
11. F. 184rv: Nicene Creed.

Catalogue of the Ethiopic Manuscript Imaging Project · 221

12. F. 184v: *Asmat* prayer against the evil eye, *həmamä 'ayn*, incomplete at the end.
13. F. 185r: Ps 5:1–5, a rejected leaf from another Psalter.

Notes:
1. The general condition of the vellum is dirty and worn.
2. Decorative designs: ff. 1r, 8v, 17r, 26v, 38r, 47r, 64r, 77v, 87v, 94r, 95r, 110r, 115r, 123v, 141r, 155v, 164r, 182v (*haräg* using black and red); 163v (*haräg* using black and purple); 52r (*haräg* using black ink overwritten in red ink), 54r, 134r, 184r (*haräg* using black ink); 184v (a line of black dots).
3. Colūmetric layout of text: ff. f. 140v (Ps. 150), 151r–152r (tenth biblical canticle).
4. F. 71v: An erased symbol and an offset line of text mark the midpoint of the Psalter.
5. ?Ff. 161v and 162r, etc.: Text is written in the upper margin and a small cross indicates where in the text block it is to be inserted.
6. Note of ownership by Addis Ayyänäw, f. 185r.
7. Overlooked words of text are written interlinearly (ff. 41r, 49v, 132rv, 139v, 149r, etc.); and overlooked lines of text are written interlinearly (ff. 38v, 64r, 123r, 134r, 142r, etc.); and in the bottom margin with a symbol (⊥) marking the location where the text is to be inserted (f. 37r, line 16), and in another case where the symbol (+) is used in the upper margin (ff. 92r, line 3, 157r, line 9, 157v, line 6, 160v, line 4, 161r, line 16, 161v, line 3, 162r, line 5, 163v, line 8).
8. The scribe regularly has to complete a line of text on another line. Much of the problem is addressed through the selection of an appropriate aspect ratio for the codex combined with an appropriate script size. But, where the line of text is still too long, the scribe reduces the font size at the end of lines to avoid having to go onto the next line (throughout). This scribe also will complete the line of text above the end of the line (e.g., ff. 7v, 18v, 21r, 22v, 39v, etc.).

Quire Map

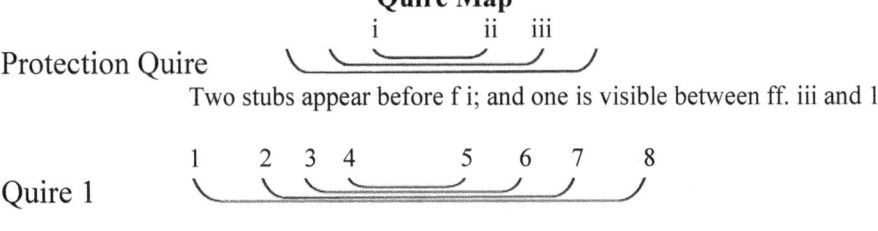

Protection Quire — Two stubs appear before f i; and one is visible between ff. iii and 1.

Quire 1 — 1 2 3 4 5 6 7 8

Quire 2 — 9 10 11 12 13 14 15 16

Quire 3: 17 18 19 20 21 22 23 24

Quire 4: 25 26 27 28 29 30 31 32

Quire 5: 33 34 35 36 37 38 39 40

Quire 6: 41 42 43 44 45 46 47 48

Quire 7: 49 50 51 52 53 54 55 56

Quire 8: 57 58 59 60 61 62 63 64

Quire 9: 65 66 67 68 69 70 71 72

Quire 10: 73 74 75 76 77 78 79 80

Quire 11: 81 82 83 84 85 86 87 88

Quire 12: 89 90 91 92 93 94

Quire 13: 95 96 97 98 99 100 101 102

Quire 14: 103 104 105 106 107 108 109 110

Quire 15: 111 112 113 114 115 116 117 118

Quire 16: 119 120 121 122 123 124 125 126

Quire 17: 127 128 129 130 131 132 133 134

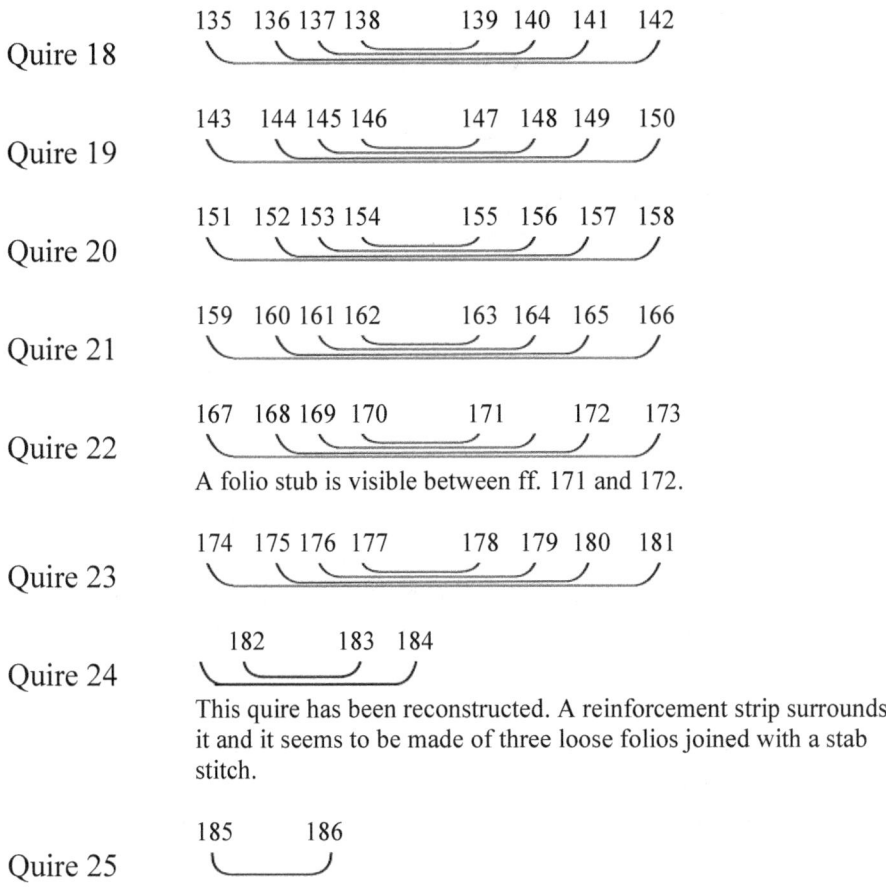

EMIP 84 – Delamarter Codex 2
The Bandlet of Righteousness, ልፋፈ: ጽድቅ:

Parchment, two Coptic chain stitches attached with bridle attachments to rough-hewn boards covered with tooled leather over decorative linen patches visible inside the turn-ins on front and back cover, 3 full quires, i + 23 folios, 65 x 49 mm, ff. 1r–22r one column, Gəʻəz, 4–5 lines, late 20th cent.

Quire descriptions: quires 1, 2 balanced; quire 3 adjusted balanced. Leather amulet case cut open at center.

Ff. 1r–22r: The Bandlet of Righteousness, ልፋፈ: ጽድቅ:. EMIP 69, f. 123r.

Notes:
1. Decorative designs: f. 22r (dotted line using alternating black and red).
2. F. Irv, 22r–23v blank
3. Purchased April, 2004 in Axum from a scribe.

Quire Map

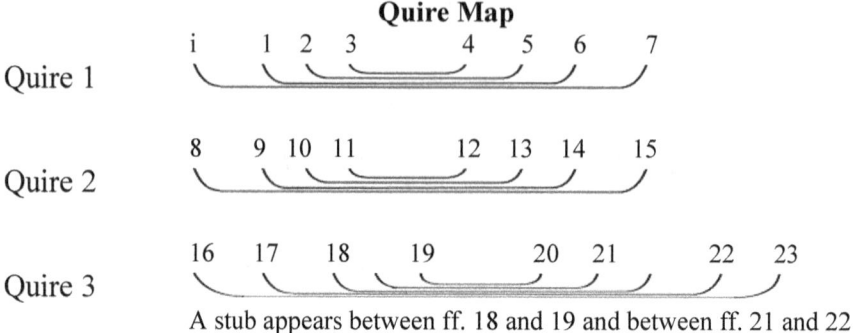

A stub appears between ff. 18 and 19 and between ff. 21 and 22

EMIP 85 – Trinity Western University Codex 4
The Bandlet of Righteousness, ለፋፈ: ጽድቅ:

Parchment, 54 x 45 x 25 mm, accordion-fold codex made up of two strips sewn together (5.4 x 158 cm) and attached with two leather strings to rough-hewn boards in three or four places (front cover loose), text written on both sides, i + 67 pages (i.e., numbered consecutively without reference to recto and verso), 54 x 45 mm, top margin 2 mm, bottom margin 4–5 mm, fore edge margin 0–3 mm, gutter margin 0–3 mm, ff. 1–67 one column, Gəʻəz, 9–11 lines, 20th cent.

1. Ff. 1r–45r: The Bandlet of Righteousness, ለፋፈ: ጽድቅ:. EMIP 69, f. 123r.
2. Ff. 45r–67r: Prayer for the journey to heaven. Part of the *Ləfafä Ṣədq*; cf. EMIP 85, f. 45r.

Notes:
1. Note of ownership by Šašit/Wälättä Śəllase, f. 30v and *passim*.
2. F. Ir not photographed
3. Ff. Iv and 34v blank.
4. Provenance: This codex was donated to Trinity Western University by Robert N. Thompson, who spent some years immediately following World War II in Ethiopia working with the Ministry of Education. Later, he served with the mission organization, SIM (then "Sudan Interior Mission," now "Serving In Ministry").

Quire Map
This is an accordion-fold book.

EMIP 86 – Marwick Codex 21
Prayer against the Tongue of People, ጸሎት፡ በእንተ፡ ልሳነ፡ ሰብእ፡

Parchment, two Coptic chain stitches attached with bridle attachments to rough-hewn boards, 3 full quires, 20 folios, 59 x 48 mm, ff. 1r, 2r–19v one column, Gəʿəz, 12–13 lines, 19th/20th cent.

Quire descriptions: quires 1–3 balanced. Amulet case cut open at center.

Ff. 2r–19v: Prayer against the Tongue of People, ጸሎት፡ በእንተ፡ ልሳነ፡ ሰብእ፡.

S. Grébaut, "L'Hymne-invocation Lesâna sab'e," *Aethiopica. Revue philologique*, vol. 3 (1936), pp. 6–12; MG 59, pp. 271ff.

በስመ፡ አብ፡ . . . ጸሎት፡ [በእንተ፡] ልሳነ፡ ሰብእ፡ ዘመድ፡ ወባዕድ፡ ምቀኛ፡ ወተንኮለኛ፡፡
ናሁ፡ ተማኅፀንኩ፡ ቡዖኒያተ፡ ስምከ፡ [ካፍ፡፡]
ወበቀዳማይ፡ የውጣ፡ ዘጥንት፡ ፊደሉ፡ (f. 2v) አሌፍ፡፡

Notes:
1. Note of ownership by Gäbrä Maryam, ff. 19v and 19r.
2. F. 20v not photographed
3. Ff. 19v–20r blank.

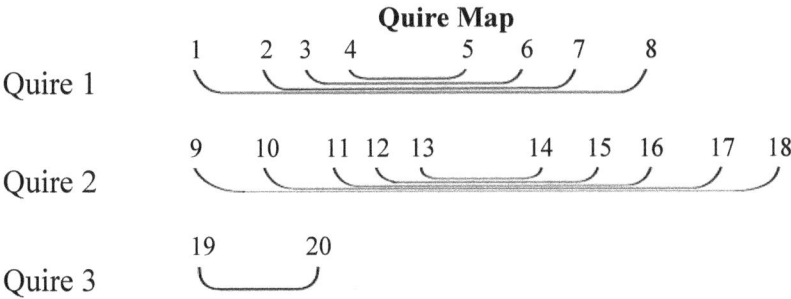

Quire Map

Quire 1: 1 2 3 4 5 6 7 8

Quire 2: 9 10 11 12 13 14 15 16 17 18

Quire 3: 19 20

EMIP 87 – Weiner Codex 4
Psalter, ዳዊት፡

Parchment, 131 x 87 x 48 mm, four Coptic chain stitches attached with bridle attachments to rough-hewn boards covered with tooled leather, headband and tailband, protection quire + 16 full quires, quires 3–16 numbered, iv + 166 folios, 125 x 84 mm folio, top margin 7–13 mm, bottom margin 15–24 mm, fore edge margin 8–14 mm, gutter margin 5 mm, ff. 1r–148r one column, ff. 149r–166v two columns, Gəʿəz, 20–22 lines, 20th cent. Double-slip case.

Quire descriptions: quires 1, 4–8, 10–16 balanced; quires 2–3, 9 adjusted balanced. Navigation system: red and green thread sewn into the upper fore edge of ff. 36, 72 to mark content.

Ff. 1r–165v: Psalter [*Dawit*]. Cf. EMIP 1.
1. Ff. 1r–126v: Psalms of David.
2. Ff. 127r–139v: Biblical Canticles.
3. Ff. 139v–148r: Song of Songs, Hebraic version.
4. Ff. 149r–160v: Praises of Mary [*Wəddase Maryam*]. Arranged for the days of the week (Monday, f. 149r; Tuesday, f. 150r; Wednesday, f. 151v; Thursday, f. 153v; Friday, f. 156r; Saturday, f. 158r; Sunday, f. 159r).
5. Ff. 160v–165v: Gate of Light [*Anqäṣä Bərhan*].

Miniatures, all in twentieth-century hand:
1. F. iiiv(erso): Madonna and Child.
2. F. ivr: Saint George and the dragon.
3. F. ivv(erso): Crown of Thorns (with evil Italians?).
4. F. 148v: The Crucifixion.
5. F. 166r: The Resurrection, raising Adam and Eve (Italian soldiers left in the grave?).

Varia:
1. F. Ir: "In the name of the Father and the Son and (the Holy) Spirit." (sic).
2. F. 1r: The name of the intermediary (in the purchase of the book?), Täšomä.
3. F. Iv: Record of settlement of dispute over property, dated Ḥamle 24, 1930 EC (July 31, 1938 AD.).
4. F. IIr: Will of *Ǝmmahoy* Dässəta Azagä, dated 1933 EC (1940/1 AD.).

Notes:
1. The textblock of most folios is unscathed and remains quite clear. The vellum is clean and worn only a little.
2. Decorative designs: ff. 1r, 8r, 25r, 26v, 45r, 51v, 61v, 72v, 87r, 114v, 127r, (*haräg* using black, yellow and red); ff. iiir (*haräg* using black and red); 16v, 36v, 87r, 100r, 127r, (*haräg* using black, yellow, red and orange); 36r, 51r, 72v, 126v, 139v, 148r, 165v (dotted line using alternating black and red); 111r, 114r, 120v (dotted line using red ink).
3. Columetric layout of text: ff. 135r–136r (tenth biblical canticle).
4. Note of ownership, effaced, f. 166v.
5. Ff. IIv–IIIr blank.

6. Overlooked words of text are written interlinearly (ff. 25v, 34r, 147r, 150r, 151v, 156v, etc.); and overlooked lines of text are written interlinearly (ff. 1r, 7r, 17v, 31v, 36v, 41v, 59v, 61r, etc.); and in the upper margin with a symbol (⊥) marking the location where the text is to be inserted (f. 155r, line 18).
7. The scribe regularly has to complete a line of text on another line. Much of the problem is addressed through the selection of an appropriate aspect ratio for the codex combined with an appropriate script size. But, where the line of text is still too long, the scribe completes the line of text above the end of the line (throughout). This scribe will also reduce the font size at the end of lines to avoid having to go onto the next line (throughout).

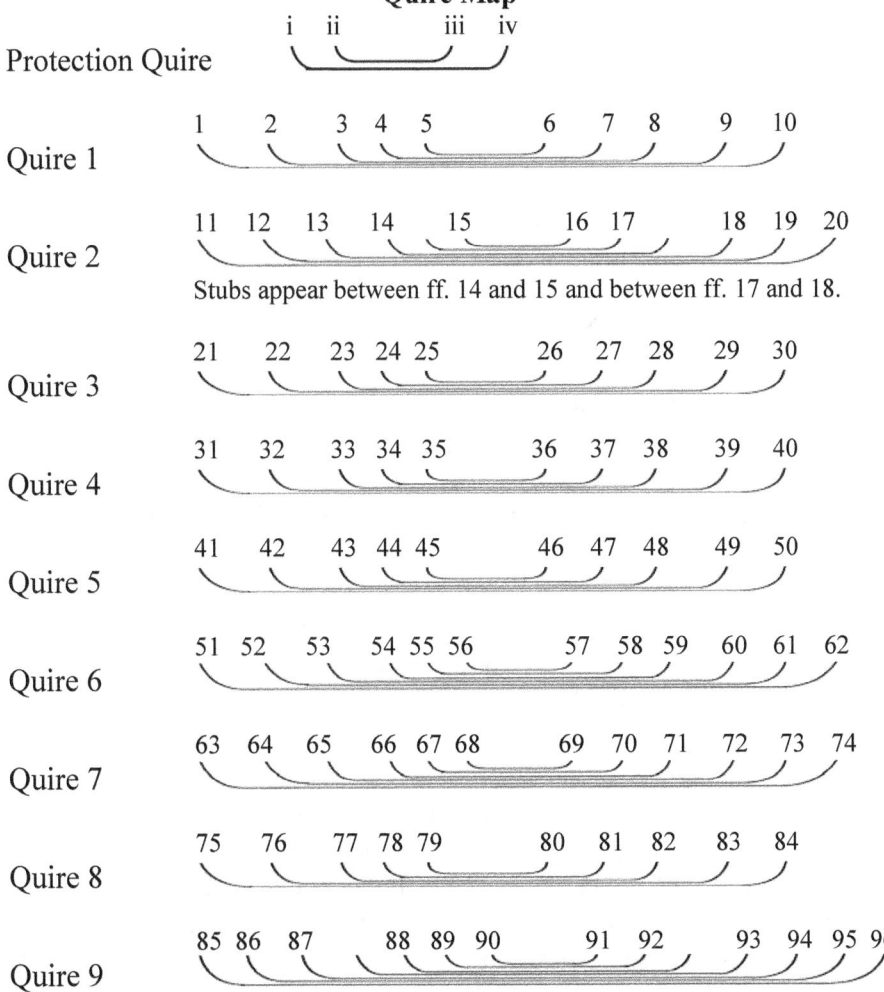

Stubs appear between ff. 87 and 88 and between 92 and 93.

Quire 10: 97 98 | 99 | 100 101 102 | 103 104 105 | 106 107 108

Quire 11: 109 110 | 111 | 112 113 114 | 115 116 117 | 118 119 120

Quire 12: 121 122 | 123 | 124 125 126 | 127 128 129 | 130 131 132

Quire 13: 133 | 134 | 135 136 137 | 138 139 140 | 141 142

Quire 14: 143 | 144 | 145 146 147 | 148 149 150 | 151 152

Quire 15: 153 | 154 | 155 156 157 | 158 159 160 | 161 162

Quire 16: 163 164 | 165 166

EMIP 88 – Weiner Codex 5
Psalter, ዳዊት፡

Parchment, 218 x150 x 58 mm, four Coptic chain stitches attached with bridle attachments to the wooden boards at four locations, wooden boards covered with tooled, Moroccan leather along with the spine, headband and tailband present or upper and lower folios sewn to spine to accomplish the same function, decorative linen patches are visible between the pastedowns on both the inside front and back covers, protection quire + 13 full quires, folios were numbered in two sets of numbers, neither of which seems accurate, ii + 126 folios, 212 x 147mm, top margin 15–20 mm, bottom margin 32–37 mm, fore edge margin 18–25 mm, gutter margin 10 mm, ff. 1r–114v one column, ff. 115r–125r two columns, Gə'əz, 25–28 lines, 20th cent.

Quire descriptions: quires 1–13 balanced. Navigation systems: 1) Brown yarn sewn into corners of folios to mark the location of miniatures.

Ff. 1r–125r: Psalter [*Dawit*]. Introduced with the psalm of the shorter *Mäzmurä Krəstos* "Psalms of Christ. Cf. EMIP 1 and EMIP 40.
  1. Ff. 1–99v: Psalms of David.

2. Ff. 100v–109v: Biblical Canticles.
3. Ff. 109v–114v: Song of Songs, common version.
4. Ff. 115r–126v: Praises of Mary [Wəddase Maryam]. Arranged for the days of the Week (Monday f. 115r, Tuesday f. 115v, Wednesday f. 116v, Thursday f. 118r, Friday f. 119r, Saturday f. 120r, Sunday f. 120v).
5. Ff. 121v–125r: Gate of Light [Anqäṣä Bərhan], incomplete.

Miniatures, all in the late 20th century hand of the "speckled garment artist," painted over text:
1. F. iv(erso): Madonna and Child.
2. F. iir: Saint George and the Dragon.
3. F. iiv(erso): King David Playing the Harp.
4. F. 31r: The Crucifixion.
5. F. 65v: The Resurrection, raising Adam and Eve.
6. F. 91r: The Ascension.
7. F. 125v: Jesus Carrying the Cross.
8. F. 126r: The Last Supper.

Varia:
1. F. 100r: The beginning of Amharic letter writing.
2. F. 100v: An unidentified chant of four paragraphs, with musical notation.

   ሙኑ: ሰብእ: ዘኢይዔብስ: ወሙኑ: ዘተወልደ: ዘኢሐደገ: ለሥርዓትከ: . . .

   ነሥአ: ሙሬተ: ወገብሮ: ለአዳም: እምድሬ: ፋጌ: . . .

   ዘኢትፌቅድ: ዝኃጥእ: (sic) ሞተ: አላ: ግብአተ: ወሚጠተ: . . .

   ዶሪዓሙ: (sic) ተዓጊሃሙ: ሙጠዉ: ነፍሶሙ: ለሞት: እለ: ሎሙ: ቀንዩ: በሕይወቶሙ: . . .
3. F. 126v: Two qəne poems.

Notes:
1. Two attempts have been made to foliate the codex. One set of numbers appears in the lower right corner of every page in purple ink. Another set appears in the upper right corner of every folio (recto side) in pencil. Neither system is completely accurate.
2. Decorative designs: black *harägs* on ff. 12r, 18r, 94v, 109r; red and black *harägs* on ff 6r, 26r, 32v, 37v, 45r, 54r, 61r, 66r, 76v, 80r, 86v, 89r, 101r, 115r; red, black and blue *haräg* on ff 1r.
3. Columetric layout of text: ff. 3r (Ps. 6), 6r (Ps. 10), 10v (Ps. 18), 11r (Ps. 19), 13v (Ps. 21), 16r (Ps. 27), 16v (Ps. 28), 17r (Ps. 29), 19r (Ps. 32), 22r (Ps. 36), 22v (Ps. 36), 34v (Ps. 55), 35r (Ps. 55), 35v (Ps. 56),

40v (Pss 65 & 66), 41r (Ps. 66), 44v (Ps. 70), 63v (Ps. 95), 79v (Ps. 117), 96v (Ps. 144), 97r (Ps. 145), 98r (Ps. 148), 99r (Ps. 150), 107rv (tenth biblical canticle).
4. F. Ir: Title of the book.
5. F. 114v: The name, Mulatu.
6. Overlooked words of text are written interlinearly (ff. 17v, 20v, 29v, 63r, 64v, etc.); and overlooked lines of text are written interlinearly (ff. 23r, 26r, 38r, 52r, 54r, etc.); and in the upper margin with a symbol (⊥) marking the location where the text is to be inserted (f. 24v, line 3).
7. This scribe has avoided the problem of lines of text too long to fit on one line by adopting an aspect ratio that leaves ample room for the width of most lines. Occasionally, the line would have been too long and the scribe finishes the end of the line with words written above or below the end of the line (e.g., ff. 1r, 20r, 27v, 28r, 31v, etc.).

Quire Map

Protection Quire: i, ii

Quire 1: 1, 2, 3, 4, 5, 6, 7, 8, 9, 10

Quire 2: 11, 12, 13, 14, 15, 16, 17, 18, 19, 20

Quire 3: 21, 22, 23, 24, 25, 26, 27, 28, 29, 30

Quire 4: 31, 32, 33, 34, 35, 36, 37, 38, 39, 40

Quire 5: 41, 42, 43, 44, 45, 46, 47, 48, 49, 50

Quire 6: 51, 52, 53, 54, 55, 56, 57, 58, 59, 60

Quire 7: 61, 62, 63, 64, 65, 66, 67, 68, 69, 70

Quire 8: 71, 72, 73, 74, 75, 76, 77, 78, 79, 80

Catalogue of the Ethiopic Manuscript Imaging Project · 231

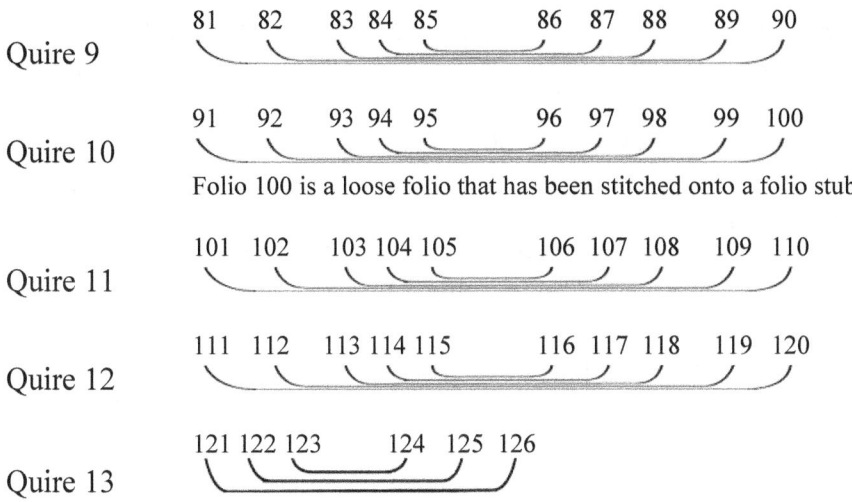

Folio 100 is a loose folio that has been stitched onto a folio stub.

EMIP 89 – Weiner Codex 6
Antiphonary for the year — *Dəggʷa* — *Məʿraf* — *Mäzmur*, ድጓ፡ — ምዕራፍ፡ — መዝሙር፡

Parchment, 235 x 190 x 68 mm, four altered Coptic chain stitches attached with bridle attachments to rough-hewn boards, 15 full quires, 113 folios, 225 x 188 mm, top margin 20–27 mm, bottom margin 40–50 mm, fore edge margin 22–32 mm, gutter margin 10 mm, ff. 81v–82v one column, f. 81r two columns, ff. 1r–80v, 83r–112r three columns, Gəʿəz, 25–30 lines, 18th cent.

Quire descriptions: quires 1–5, 7–12 balanced; quire 14 adjusted balanced; quires 6, 13, 15 unbalanced. Navigation system: brown yarn sewn into corners of folios 3, 29, 55, 67, 84, 94, 101, 112 to mark the location of miniatures.

1. Ff. 1r–83r: Antiphonary for the year, *Dəggʷa* (ድጓ፡). መጽሐፈ፡ ድጓ፡ ቅዱስ፡ ያሬድ፡ የደረሰው፡፡ Bərhanənna Sälam Press, Addis Ababa 1959 EC.
በስመ፡ ሥሉስ፡ ቅዱስ፡ አብ፡ ወወልድ፡ ወመንፈስ፡ ቅዱስ፡ ጸሐፍነ፡ ድጓ፡ ዘውእቱ፡ መሥዋእቱ፡ ለእ"፡ ምድር፡ በምልአ፡ ወእግ"፡ ነገሡ፡ ወይትባረክ፡ አርያም፡ ወመዝሙር፡ ዘአምላኪያ፡ ወአርባዕት፡ ዕዝል፡ ወይእዜ፡ ማኅሌት፡ ወስብሐት፡ ነግህ፡ Ö፡ ወሰላም፡ ዘበዓላት፡ ወዘሰንብት፡ ዘመዐው፡ ወጸደይ፡ [ወዘክረ]ምት፡ ወዘሐጋይ፡ ዘይፌጽም፡ ጥንቁቀ፡ ለለአውራኑ፡ ወለለሰንበቱ፡ ወለለኵሉ፡ በዓላት፡ ዘተሠርዓ፡ [. . .] ለወልደ፡ [. . .] በሥምረተ፡ ዝንቱ፡ መጽሐፍ፡፡

በፅ፡ ብፁዕ፡ አንተ፡ ዮሐንስ፡ ዘሀለወከ፡ ታእምር፡ ወተሐውር፡ ቅድመ፡ እግ"
ጸሊ፡ በእንቲአነ፡ ውስተ፡ ርእሰ፡ ዓውደ፡ አመት፡ ተጽሕፈ፡ ተዝካርከ፡ ባርከነ፡
. . .

Text, f. 1r; *Anqäṣä halleta*, f. 80v.

2. Ff. 84r–107r: *Məˈraf* chants. Velat, *Meˈerāf* I, and Velat, *Meˈerāf* II; AṢZ, pp. 103–246.
ምዕራፍ፡ ዘዮሐንስ፡ ወዘጌና፡ ቅዱስ፡ እግ"፡ ቅዱስ፡ ኃያል፡ . . . ወእምዝ፡
ተቀነይ፡ መዝሙር፡፡ መስተብቍዕ፡ በእንተ፡ እለ፡ ይነግፁ፡ በል፡፡ ለእግ"፡
ምድር፡ በምልዓ፡ ይቤ፡ ዮሐንስ፡ ዓለ፡ ለልየ፡ ወአነ፡ ሰግዕቱ፡፡ . . .

3. Ff. 109r–112r: *Zəmmare*, incomplete at the end. Cf. AṢZ, pp. 401–527.
ዝግሬ፡ እምዮሐንስ፡ እስከ፡ ዮሐንስ፡ ግዕዝ፡ [መጽአ፡] ኢየሱስ፡ እምገሲላ፡
ኀበ፡ ዮሐንስ፡ ከመ፡ ያጥምቆ፡ በፈለገ፡ ዮርዳኖስ፡ አጥመቆ፡ ዮሐንስ፡
ለኢየሱስ፡ ወገሠሦ፡ . . .

Miniatures, all in the late twentieth-century hand of the "speckled garment artist":

1. F. 4r: David Playing the Harp.
2. F. 30r: Madonna and Child.
3. F. 56r: Saint George and the Dragon.
4. F. 68r: Mary Enthroned.
5. F. 83v: Angel with Sword.
6. F. 95r: The Burial of Jesus.
7. F. 102r: The Crucifixion.
8. F. 114v: The Last Supper.

Notes:

1. This is one of the manuscripts that EMML/HMML had microfilmed. The pagination in stamped blue ink points in this direction. There is also a section of f. 113 that has been cut out. This area corresponds with the possible location of the signature stamp of the EMML project.
2. Decorative designs: f. 45r (*haräg*-like feature using black and red); ff. 3r, 4v, 7r, 8r, 10r, 10v, 13r, 16r, 17v, 20v, 22v, 23v, 25v, 28r, 29v, 30v, 31v, 32r, 32v, 33r, 34r, 35r, 35v, 36r, 38r, 39r, 41r, 43r, 45r, 47r, 47v, 48r, 48v, 49r, 50r, 50v, 51v, 52v, 53v, 55v, 57r, 57v, 59r, 60v, 62v, 63v, 66r, 67r, 67v, 69r, 70v, 71v, 73v, 74r, 74v, 75r, 76r, 77v, 79v, 83r, 85v, 94r, 94v, 105r (dotted line using alternating black and red); ff. 20v, 96v (dotted line using black); ff. 85v, 89v (stops connected by lines); f. 86v (red bars outlined in black).
3. Columetric layout of text: ff. 80v–83r.
4. F. 40rv, 45rv and 107v–108v blank.

5. Overlooked words of text are written interlinearly (ff. 70v, 78v, 87v, 88v, 94r, etc.).

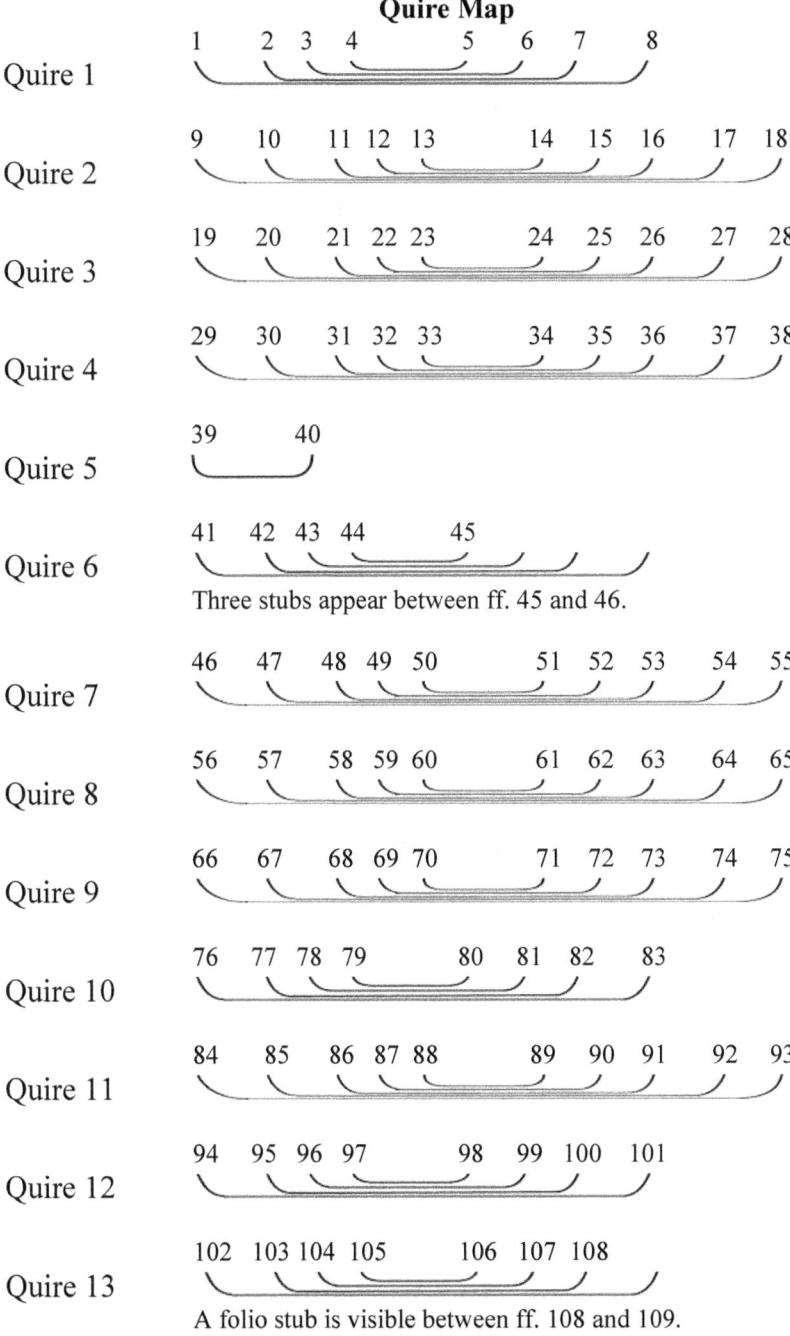

Quire 14   109 110   111 112
Stubs appear between ff. 109 and 110 and between ff. 110 and 111.

Quire 15   113
A folio stub is visible between ff. 112 and 113.

EMIP 90 – Weiner Codex 7
Images, መልክዐ፡ ጉባኤ፡

Parchment, 120 x 60 x 23 mm, three Coptic chain stitches attached with bridle attachments to rough-hewn boards covered with floral patterned linen (red with yellow), 3 full quires, i + 33 folios, 120 x 60 mm, top margin 2–10 mm, bottom margin 10–15 mm, fore edge margin 3–5 mm, gutter margin 5 mm, ff. 1r–32r one column, Gəʻəz, 17–22 lines, 20th cent. Quire descriptions: quires 1–3 balanced.

1. Ff. 1r–16r: Image of the Savior of the World, መልክዐ፡ መድኃኔ፡ ዓለም፡. EMIP 76, f. 86v.
2. Ff. 16r–20v: Image of George, George" መልክዐ፡ጊዮርጊስ፡. Chaîne, Répertoire, no. 208; MG 59, pp. 505ff.
   ሰላም፡ ለጽንስትከ፡ ወለልደትከ፡ ቡሩክ፡፡
   በበአለ፡ ቅድስት፡ ድንግል፡ ዘዮም፡ (sic) ወመስቀለ፡ ክርስቶስ፡ ክርስ፡ (sic) አምላክ፡፡
3. Ff. 21v–32r: Image of Michael, Michael" መልክዐ፡ ሚካኤል፡. Incomplete at the end; cf. EMIP 126, f. 92v.

Miniatures, all in a twentieth-century hand:
1. F. iiv(erso): The Crucifixion.
2. F. 12r: Resurrected Christ Displays His Wounds.
3. F. 24r: The Ascension.
4. F. 32v: Saint, in red hood, points to sky.
5. F. 33v: Saint, in gray hood, points to sky.

Notes:
1. Pen trial, f. 1r.
2. Copied for Wäldä Ṣadəq, f. 16r.
3. Overlooked words of text are written interlinearly (f. 26r).

Quire Map

Quire 1   i 1 2   3 4 5   6 7 8 9 10 11

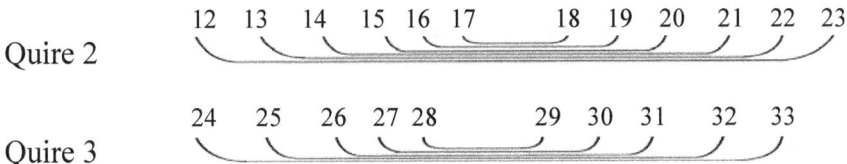

EMIP 91 – Weiner Codex 8
Asmat Prayers

Parchment, accordion-fold codex, 90 x 75 x 22 mm, accordion found book, two strips of parchment sewn together and attached to end boards, 14 folios (numbered consecutively without recto or verso), 85 x 75 mm, top margin 5–10 mm, bottom margin 5–10 mm, fore edge margin 5–10 mm, gutter margin 5–10 mm, one column, Gəʻəz, 10–11 lines, 20th cent.

Ff. 1–14: *Asmat* prayers for conception and against hemorrhage.

. . . ፩ አምላከ፡ ጸሎት፡ በእንተ፡ ሕማመ፡ ዕንስ፡ ወደም፡ አቁምላንስ፡ ሊሶ፡ አፍሊሶ፡ ፍለኪሶ፡ ወአሀዝ፡ ሚሎስ፡ . . .

Miniatures:
1. F. 1: A geometric pattern with a face at the center.
2. F. 2: Nine-box panel, each box containing text.
3. F. 3: Angel holding sword.
4. F. 4: Madonna and Child.
5. F. 5: Angel holding a sword.
6. F. 8: Ethiopian Dignitary with prayer stick.
7. F. 9: A geometric pattern with a face at the center.
8. F. 10: Ethiopian Dignitary with hand cross and book.
9. F. 12: Four Angels.
10. F. 14: A Cross.

Notes:
1. The general condition of the vellum is rather un-worn and clean.
2. Decorative designs: ff. 2, and 13 (nine-box table); ff. 6–7, and 11 (two black rectangular boxes surrounding the text filled with red ink in between).
3. Copied in a crude hand for Wälättä Iyyäsus, f. 11v.

Quire Map

This is an accordion-fold codex.

EMIP 92 – Weiner Codex 9
Asmat Prayers

Parchment, accordion-fold codex, 85 x 75 x 27 mm, accordion fold codex made of two parchment strips sewn together and attached to the end boards, 12 folios (numbered consecutively without recto or verso), 85 x 72 mm, top margin 5–10 mm, bottom margin 8 mm, fore edge margin 8 mm, gutter margin 6 mm, one column, Gə'əz, 9–11 lines, 20th cent.

Ff. 3v–12: *Asmat* prayer against evil eye and other evil spirits. Cf. EMIP 75, f. 1r.

በስመ፡ አብ፡ . . . ጸሎት በእንተ፡ ዓይነ ጥላ ገር ጋሪያ ዓይነ፡ ባርያ፡ ወሌጌዎን፡ ዓይነ ጥላ፡ ወጥላወጊ፡ ዓይነ፡ መቀኛ፡ ወዓይነ፡ ት(f. 4r)ንኩለኛ፡ መጋኛ ወጉሥምት፡ ፈሪ፡ ወንዳድ፡ . . .

Miniatures:
1. F. 1: Four petals with an eye in each and a square in the center.
2. F. 2: A woman with two children sitting on her lap and a cross above her head.
3. F. 5–6: Four heads of Angels.
4. F. 9: Seated man.
5. F. 11: A crowned man standing and a face on his right and left.
6. F. 12: Four petals with an eye in each and a square in the center.

Notes:
1. The general condition of the vellum is rather un-worn and clean.
2. Decorative designs: ff. 1–12 (two black rectangular boxes surrounding the text with red strips in between); f. 9 (*haräg* using black and red); f. 11 (*haräg* using black, red and yellow).
3. Copied crudely by the hand that copied EMIP 91 (Weiner Codex 8).

Quire Map

This is an accordion-fold codex.

EMIP 93 – Marwick Codex 23
Bandlet of Righteousness, ልፋፈ፡ ጽድቅ፡

Parchment, 75 x 58 x 24 mm, two Coptic chain stitches attached with bridle attachments to rough-hewn boards, one protection quire + 5 full quires, ii + 36 folios, 72 x 55 mm, top margin 6–8 mm, bottom margin 16–20 mm, fore edge margin 4–7 mm, gutter margin 5–6 mm, one column, Gə'əz, 8–9 lines, late 19th cent.

Quire descriptions: quires 1–5 balanced. Single-slip case with leather strap.

1. Ff. 1r–25v: Bandlet of Righteousness, ልፋፈ: ጽድቅ:. Cf. EMIP 69, f. 123r.
2. Ff. 25v–35v: Prayer for the journey to heaven. Part of the *Ləfafä Ṣədq*; cf. EMIP 69, f.126r, and EMIP 85, f.45r.

Miniatures, all in twentieth-century hand, painted over text:
1. F. iv(erso): Angel with sword.
2. F. iir: Madonna and Child.
3. F. 14r: Jesus debating (?).
4. F. 36r: Angel with a sword.
5. F. 34r: Jesus Carrying the cross.

Notes:
1. The general condition of the vellum is quite clean and relatively unworn.
2. Note of ownership by Wälättä Ṣəllase, f. 23r and *passim*.
3. F. Ir, IIv and 36v blank.

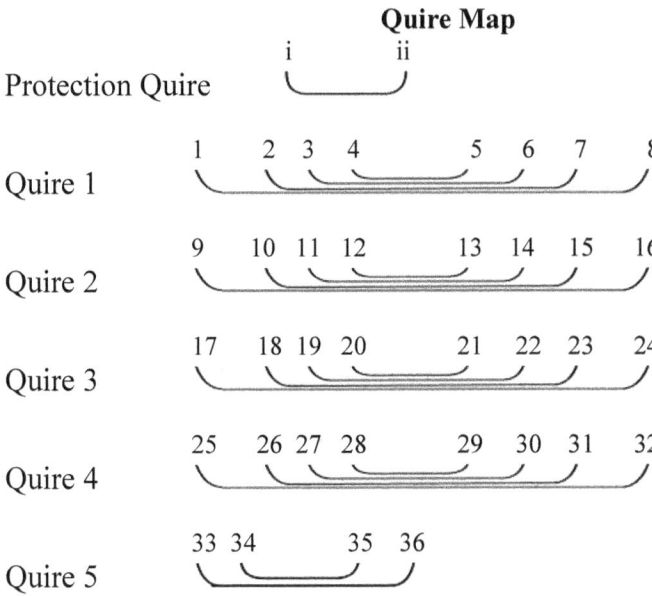

EMIP 94 – Weiner Codex 10
Psalter, ዳዊት:

Parchment, 262 x 192 x 75 mm, possible four Coptic chain stitches attached with bridle attachments to the wooden boards, rough-hewn boards covered with tooled leather over decorative linen patches (a brown colored cover is overlapped by a brighter red one that wraps around the binding), headband and tailband, protection quire + 17 full quires, quires 1–17 numbered, ii + 166 folios, 254 x 190 mm, top margin 25 mm, bottom margin 61 mm, fore edge margin 28–30 mm, gutter margin 15–18 mm, ff. 1r–147r one column, ff. 147v–164r two columns, Gəʿəz, 23 lines, 20th cent.

Quire descriptions: quires 1–15, 17 balanced; quire 16 adjusted balanced. Navigation system: Brown thread sewn into corners of ff. 40, 47, 76, 125, 147, and 164 to mark the location of miniatures. Modern conservation box.

Ff. 1r–164r: Psalter [*Dawit*]. Cf. EMIP 1.
1. Ff. 1r–125r: Psalms of David.
2. Ff. 125v–138v: Biblical Canticles.
3. Ff. 139r–147r: Song of Songs, common version.
4. Ff. 147v–158v: Praises of Mary [*Wəddase Maryam*], arranged for the days of the week (Monday f. 147v, Tuesday f. 148v, Wednesday f. 150r, Thursday f. 152r, Friday f. 154r, Saturday f. 156r, Sunday f. 157r).
5. Ff. 158v–164r: Gate of Light [*Anqäṣä Bərhan*].

Miniatures, original to the manuscript:
1. F. ir: The Holy Trinity with the Four Living Creatures.
2. F. iv: Adam and Eve Eating the Forbidden Fruit.
3. F. iir: Expulsion of Adam and Eve from Eden.
4. F. iiv(erso): King David Playing the Harp.
5. F. 40v: The Annunciation.
6. F. 47r: The Nativity.
7. F. 76r: Holy family and Salome in their flight to Egypt.
8. F. 76v: The Baptism of Jesus.
9. F. 77r: The miracle of feeding five thousand people with two fish and five loaves of bread.
10. F. 77v: Jesus heals the paralytic man.
11. F. 125r: Noah and his family.
12. F. 147r: Four chief priests.
13. F. 164r: The Foot Washing Ceremony (Jesus washes the feet of his disciples and Peter asks a question).
14. F. 164v: The Last Supper.
15. F. 165r: The Crucifixion.
16. F. 165v: "Jesus sets Adam and Eve free from bondage."

Varia:
1. Ff. 163v–164r: The hours of the days and nights in the different months.

Notes:
1. Repairs visible in ff. 154rv, 157rv, 158rv, 161rv.
2. The general condition of the vellum is quite clean and relatively unworn.
3. F. 62v: A small text in a box of alternating red and black symbols, as well as a line of text written fully in red ink, mark the midpoint of the psalms.
4. Psalm 118 contains the traditional headings to the twenty–two sections.
5. Decorative designs: f. 1r, (*haräg* with black, red, green, yellow and blue ink); no others appear, but there are several unfilled spaces left for additional *harägs* in the Psalms.
6. Columetric layout of text: ff. 134v–135r (tenth biblical canticle).
7. F. 166rv blank.
8. Overlooked words of text are written interlinearly (ff. 8r, 14v, 16r, 21r, 79r, etc.); and overlooked lines of text are written interlinearly (ff. 27r, 36v, 39v, 71v, 73r, 75r, etc.).
9. This scribe has avoided the problem of lines of text too long to fit on one line by adopting an aspect ratio that leaves ample room for the width of most lines. When the line would have been too long, the scribe finishes the end of the line with words written smaller so as to avoid leftover text (e.g., ff. 8r, 9v, 10r, 11v, 12r, etc.). Occasionally a line is still too long and has to be completed above or below the end of the line (e.g., ff. 18v, 59v, 100r, 120rv, 135v, 141v, 144r).

Quire Map

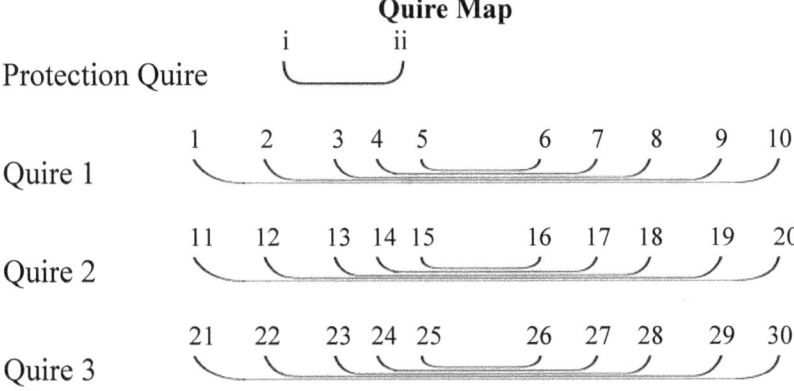

Quire 4: 31 32 33 34 35 36 37 38 39 40

Quire 5: 41 42 43 44 45 46 47 48 49 50

Quire 6: 51 52 53 54 55 56 57 58 59 60

Quire 7: 61 62 63 64 65 66 67 68 69 70

Quire 8: 71 72 73 74 75 76 77 78 79 80 81 82

Quire 9: 83 84 85 86 87 88 89 90 91 92

Quire 10: 93 94 95 96 97 98 99 100 101 102

Quire 11: 103 104 105 106 107 108 109 110 111 112

Quire 12: 113 114 115 116 117 118 119 120 121 122

Quire 13: 123 124 125 126 127 128 129 130 131 132

Quire 14: 133 134 135 136 137 138 139 140 141 142

Quire 15: 143 144 145 146 147 148 149 150 151 152

Quire 16: 153 154 155 156 157 158 159 160 161 162

Stubs appear between 156 and 157 and between ff. 159 and 160.

Quire 17: 163 164 165 166

EMIP 95 – Weiner Codex 11
Psalter, ዳዊት፡

Parchment, 142 x 95 x 58 mm, four Coptic chain stitches attached with bridle attachments to the wooden boards, rough-hewn boards covered with tooled leather over decorative linen patches visible inside the turn-ins on front and back cover, headband and tailband, protection quire + 22 full quires, iii + 177 folios, 139 x 93 mm folio, top margin 12–17 mm, bottom margin 20–27 mm, fore edge margin 8–12 mm, gutter margin 5 mm, ff. 1r –159v one column, ff. 160r–174v two columns, Ge'ez, 17–28 lines, late 19th cent. Double-slip *maḥdar*.

Quire descriptions: quires 1, 3–6, 9–10, 19, 21–22 balanced; quires 2, 8, 11, 13–15, 20 adjusted balanced; quires 7, 12, 16–18, unbalanced.

Navigation system: yellow thread sewn into corner of f. 67 to mark content.

Ff. 1r–174v: Psalter [*Dawit*]. Introduced with the first line of Ps 1 of the Psalter of the Virgin. Cf. EMIP 1 and EMIP 2.
1. Ff. 1r–139r: Psalms of David.
2. Ff. 139v–152r: Biblical Canticles.
3. Ff. 152v–159v: Song of Songs, common version.
4. Ff. 160r–170v: Praises of Mary [*Wəddase Maryam*]. Arranged for the days of the week (Monday, f. 160r; Tuesday, f. 161r; Wednesday, f. 163r; Thursday, f. 164v; Friday, f. 167r; Saturday, f. 168v; Sunday, f. 169v).
5. Ff. 170v–174v: Gate of Light [*Anqäṣä Bərhan*].

Varia:
1. Ff. Ir: Record of purchase of the manuscript by Wäldä Amanu'el and his wife Wälättä Śəllase, dated Gənbot 1901 EC (May/June 1909 AD).
2. F. Iv and IIv: Prayer against abortion of animals, in Amharic. ለጨንጋሬ፡ ከብት፡ እንዳይጨነግፍ፡ በደንገያ፡ ሰበር፡ ሜንገር፡ የእገሌ፡ ከብት፡ አትጨንግሬ፡ ያለወራትሽ፡ አትውለጂ፡ እያሉ፡
3. F. IIr: Unintelligible scribbling and the beginning of Amharic letter writing.
4. F. 174v: A better copy of f. Ir by Wäldä Ṣadəq.
5. Ff. 174v–175r: Medical prescription against python and snake (bite). ዘዝዱ፡ ወእባብ፡ የወገርት፡ የአጋም፡ የድግፃ፡ ገተም፡ . . . (f. 175r) እሊሀን፡ ወቅጠ፡ ይጠጡዋል፡ . . .
6. Ff. 175v–176r: Medical prescription against evil eye of Buda and Barya.

. . . ዘቡዳ፡ ዘባርያ፡ የሙጭል፡ ጥላ፡ ከማናቸው፡ ቆርጠ፡ ባለተ፡ (sic) ድንጋይ፡ ደቁሶ፡ . . .

7. F. 176v: Medical prescription for headache.
ለራስ፡ ፍልፀት፡ ዕፋራን፡ (sic) ቀለም፡ ሽንት፡ (sic) ዕፀ፡ ፍርስ፡ (sic) ፍሬ፡ ቦቱን፡ ደቁሰሀ፡ እራስክን፡ በጥተሀ፡ አግባ፡

8. F. 176v: Medicine for a person whom the enemy shut up.
ጸላት፡ አፉን፡ ስዘጋው፡ (sic) ዕፀ፡ መናኄ፡ ተቀጹላ፡ (sic) የገመሮ፡ ተቀ፡ [= ተቀጽላ፡] የምባሮሕ፡ ተቀ፡ . . .

9. F. 177rv: What to do when an enemy rises.
ጸላት፡ በተነሳበት፡ ከዳዊት፡ ግፍያሙ፡ ከቤተ፡ ግብር፡ ሐመድ፡ አምጽተሀ፡ ከትክል፡ ደንጊያ፡ . . .

Notes:
1. Original binding but additional and secondary stitching of the head and tail pieces.
2. The general condition of the vellum is dirty and stained but relatively unworn.
3. F. 73v: a small text enclosed in a box of alternating red and black dots marks the midpoint of the psalms.
4. Psalm 118 contains the spiritual meanings of the Hebrew letters.
5. Decorative designs: ff. 1r, 17r, 27r, 39v, 49r, 56v, 67r, 139v, 160r (*harägs* in black and red ink); 8v, 95r, 109v, 123r, 126r (*harägs* in red ink).
6. Columetric layout of text: ff. 148rv–149r (ninth and tenth biblical canticle).
7. F. IIIr erased.
8. F. IIIv blank save for the scrawls.
9. Overlooked words of text are written interlinearly (ff. 6r, 13v, 15v, 54r, 72r, 79v, etc.); and overlooked lines of text are written interlinearly (ff. 92r, 130v, 137r, 142v).
10. The scribe's chosen aspect ratio for the codex combined with the script size forces the scribe to complete the line of text above the end of the line (throughout).

Quire Map

Protection Quire i ii iii

A folio stub is visible between ff. i and ii.

Quire 1

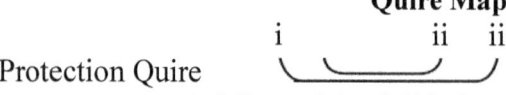

Catalogue of the Ethiopic Manuscript Imaging Project · 243

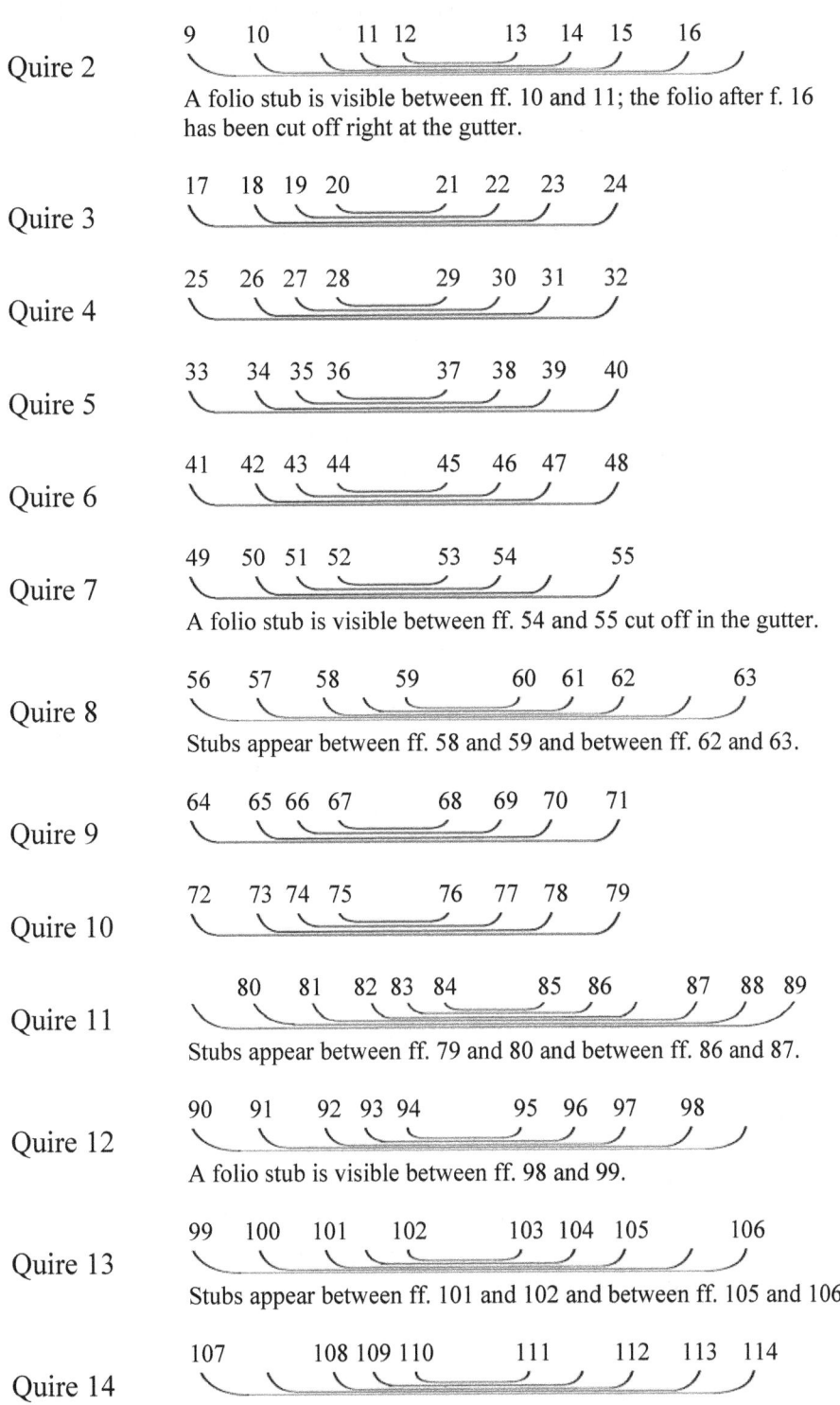

Stubs appear between ff. 107 and 108 and between ff. 111 and 112.

Quire 15: 115 | 116 117 118 | 119 | 120 | 121 122

Stubs appear between ff. 115 and 116 and between ff. 119 and 120.

Quire 16: 123 | 124 125 126 | 127 128 | 129

A folio stub is visible between ff. 128 and 129.

Quire 17: 130 | 131 132 133 | 134 135 | 136

A folio stub is visible between ff. 135 and 136.

Quire 18: 137 | 138 139 | 140 141 142 | 143

A folio stub is visible between ff. 137 and 138.

Quire 19: 144 | 145 146 147 | 148 149 150 | 151

Quire 20: 152 | 153 154 155 | 156 157 158 | 159

Stubs appear between ff. 152 and 153 and between ff. 159 and 160.

Quire 21: 160 | 161 162 163 | 164 165 166 | 167

Quire 22: 168 | 169 | 170 171 172 | 173 174 175 | 176 177

EMIP 96 – Weiner Codex 12
Psalter, ዳዊት፡

Parchment, 185 x 133 x 55mm, four Coptic chain stitches attached with bridle attachments to the wooden boards, rough-hewn boards covered with tooled leather over decorative linen patches, headband and tailband, protection quire + 11 full quires, ii + 112 folios, 182 x 130 mm folio, top margin 18–23 mm, bottom margin 23–29 mm, fore edge margin 15–20 mm, gutter margin 7–10 mm, ff. 1r–96v one column, ff. 97r–108v two columns, Gəʿəz, 27–30 lines, early 19th cent.

Quire descriptions: quires 1–12 balanced. Navigation systems: 1) various colored string sewn into corners of ff. 9r, 25r, 35r, 48r to mark content divisions; 2) marginal notations to indicate readings. Single-slip case.

Ff. 1r–108r: Psalter [*Dawit*]. Cf. EMIP 1.
1. Ff. 1r–81r: Psalms of David.
2. Ff. 81v–91v: Biblical Canticles.
3. Ff. 91v–96v: Song of Songs, common version.
4. Ff. 97r–104v: Praises of Mary [*Wəddase Maryam*]. Arranged for the days of the week (Monday, f. 97r; Tuesday, f. 97v; Wednesday, f. 99r; Thursday, f. 100r; Friday, f. 102r; Saturday, f. 103r; Sunday, f. 104r).
5. Ff. 104v–108r: Gate of Light [*Anqäṣä Bərhan*].

Miniatures, all in twentieth-century hand:
1. F. ir: *Abunä* Gäbrä Mänfäs Qəddus. Caption: "How *Abuna* Gäbrä Mänfäs Qəddus prayed for us."
2. F. iv(erso): drawing of King David Playing the Harp, unfinished.
3. F. iir: drawing of Madonna and Child, unfinished.
4. F. iiv: drawing of King David Playing the Harp, partially painted.
5. F. 110v: drawing of Madonna and Child.
6. F. 111r: drawing of woman holding looking glass.

Varia:
1. 111v: Receipt of money (borrowed?), insufficiently legible.

Notes:
1. The general condition of the vellum is a bit dirty and stained but relatively unworn.
2. F. 39r: A symbol in red and black and a short text, "here is half of Dawit," enclosed in a black-ink rectangle mark the midpoint of the psalms.
3. Psalm 118 contains the spiritual meanings of the Hebrew letters.
4. Ff. 108v–110r and 112rv blank.
5. Decorative designs: f. 1r (red, blue and black *haräg*); ff. 72r, 76v, 81v (red and black *haräg*); ff. 52v, 91v (black *haräg*). Columetric layout of text: ff. 80v–81r (Ps. 150), ff. 88v–89r (tenth biblical canticle).
6. Overlooked words of text are written interlinearly (ff. 10r, 14r, 19v, 23r, 35r, 41r, etc.); and in the upper margin with a symbol (+) marking the location where the text is to be inserted (ff. 44v, line 15, 58v, line 20, 63r, line 5, 67r, line 4, 89r, line 8, 104v, line 10).
7. The scribe regularly has to complete a line of text on another line. Much of the problem is addressed through the selection of an

appropriate aspect ratio for the codex combined with an appropriate script size. But, where the line of text is still too long, the scribe completes the line of text above or below the end of the line (throughout). This scribe will also reduce the font size at the end of lines to avoid having to go onto the next line (throughout).

Quire Map

```
                           i         ii
Protection Quire       _____/

                    1   2   3  4  5      6   7   8    9   10
Quire 1

                   11  12  13 14 15     16  17  18   19   20
Quire 2

                   21  22  23 24 25     26  27  28   29   30
Quire 3

                   31  32  33 34 35     36  37  38   39   40
Quire 4

                   41  42  43 44 45     46  47  48   49   50
Quire 5

                   51  52  53 54 55     56  57  58   59   60
Quire 6

                   61  62  63 64 65     66  67  68   69   70
Quire 7

                   71  72  73 74 75     76  77  78   79   80
Quire 8

                   81  82  83 84 85     86  87  88   89   90
Quire 9

                   91  92  93 94 95     96  97  98   99  100
Quire 10

                  101 102 103 104 105  106 107 108  109  110
Quire 11
```

Quire 12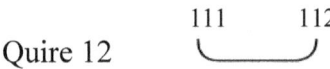

EMIP 97 – Weiner Codex 13
Psalter, ዳዊት፡

Parchment, 135 x 95 x 58 mm, four Coptic chain stitches attached with bridle attachments to the wooden boards, rough-hewn boards covered with tooled leather over decorative linen patches, headband and tailband, protection quire + 13 full quires, quires 2–13 numbered, ii + 156 folios, 128 x 90 mm folio, top margin 17 mm, bottom margin 23–25 mm, fore edge margin 10–13 mm, gutter margin 7 mm, ff. 1r–138v one column, ff. 139r–155v two columns, Gə'əz, 22 lines, 19th cent.

Quire descriptions: quires 1–13 balanced. Single-slip case.

Ff. 1r–155v: Psalter [*Dawit*]. Ps 1 of the Psalter of the Virgin copied on the top margin of f.1r; cf. EMIP 1 and EMIP 2.

1. Ff. 1r–119v: Psalms of David.
2. Ff. 120r–131v: Biblical Canticles.
3. Ff. 132r–138v: Song of Songs, common version.
4. Ff. 139r–150v: Praises of Mary [*Wəddase Maryam*]. Arranged for the days of the week (Monday, f. 139r; Tuesday, f. 140r; Wednesday, f. 142r; Thursday, f. 144r; Friday, f. 146r, Saturday, f. 147v; Sunday, f. 149r).
5. Ff. 150v–155v: Gate of Light [*Anqäṣä Bərhan*].

Miniatures, all in twentieth-century hand:
1. F. i: Angel Raphael brandishing a Sword. Caption: "Saint Raphael."
2. F. iv(erso): Angel Gabriel brandishing a sword. Caption: "Saint Gabriel."
3. F. iir: Gäbrä Mänfäs Qəddus Stands with arms outstretched. Caption: "How *Abuna* Gäbrä Mänfäs Qəddus prayed."
4. F. iiv(erso): Angel Michael brandishing a sword. Caption: "Saint Michael."
5. F. 138v: The face and wings of Angel Raguel. Caption: "Saint Raguel."
6. F. 156r: Madonna and Child. Captions (top to bottom): "Michael and Gabriel," "Virgin Mary."
7. F. 156v: Angel Standing with Sword uplifted in right hand.

Notes:

1. The general condition of the vellum is a bit dirty and stained but relatively unworn. Many folios are water stained around the perimeter and the text is smudged.
2. F. 62v: A black line surrounding a line of text marks the midpoint of the Psalms. The line appears to have been added later.
3. Ps 118 contains the spiritual meanings of the Hebrew letters.
4. Decorative designs: ff. 1r, 41r, 67v, 93v, 114r, 120r, 132r, 139r (*harägs* in black).
5. Columetric layout of text: ff. 119rv (Ps. 150), 128r–129r (tenth biblical canticle).
6. The name Gäbrä Iyyäsus, ff. 15r, 23r, 33r, 41r and *passim*.
7. Prayer of Wäldä Bərhan, f. 155v.
8. Overlooked words of text are written interlinearly (ff. 2v, 8r, 12r, 13r, 21v, 41v, etc.); and overlooked lines of text are written interlinearly (ff. 98r, 103r, 136r, 155r).
9. The scribe regularly has to complete a line of text on another line. Much of the problem is addressed through the selection of an appropriate aspect ratio for the codex combined with an appropriate script size. But, where the line of text is still too long, the scribe completes the line of text above the end of the line (throughout). This scribe will also reduce the font size at the end of lines to avoid having to go onto the next line (e.g., ff. 8v, 9v, 10v, 14v, 15v, etc.).

Quire Map

Protection Quire: i, ii

Quire 1: 1, 2, 3, 4, 5, 6, 7, 8, 9, 10, 11, 12

Quire 2: 13, 14, 15, 16, 17, 18, 19, 20, 21, 22, 23, 24

Quire 3: 25, 26, 27, 28, 29, 30, 31, 32, 33, 34, 35, 36

Quire 4: 37, 38, 39, 40, 41, 42, 43, 44, 45, 46, 47, 48

Quire 5: 49, 50, 51, 52, 53, 54, 55, 56, 57, 58, 59, 60

Quire 6: 61 62 63 64 65 66 | 67 68 69 70 71 72

Quire 7: 73 74 75 76 77 78 | 79 80 81 82 83 84

Quire 8: 85 86 87 88 89 90 | 91 92 93 94 95 96

Quire 9: 97 98 99 100 101 102 | 103 104 105 106 107 108

Quire 10: 109 110 111 112 113 114 | 115 116 117 118 119 120

Quire 11: 121 122 123 124 125 126 | 127 128 129 130 131 132

Quire 12: 133 134 135 136 137 138 | 139 140 141 142 143 144

Quire 13: 145 146 147 148 149 150 | 151 152 153 154 155 156

EMIP 98 – Abilene Christian University Codex 1

Prayer of Mary at Golgotha, ጸሎተ፡ እግዝእትነ፡ ማርያም፡ ዘሰኒ፡ ጎልጎታ፡
Parchment, 82 x 64 x 23 mm, two Coptic chain stitches attached with bridle attachments to rough-hewn boards, protection quire + 5 full quires, i + 43 folios, 80 x 63–64 mm, top margin 6–8 mm, bottom margin 3–9 mm, fore edge margin 6–10 mm, gutter margin 8–11 mm, ff. 1r–43r one column, Gəʻəz, 9–13 lines, 19th cent.
Quire descriptions: quires 1–4 balanced; quire 5 unbalanced.
Ff. 1r–42r: Prayer of Mary at Golgotha, ጸሎተ፡ እግዝእትነ፡ ማርያም፡ ዘሰኒ፡ ጎልጎታ፡. Cf. EMIP 52.

Varia:
1. F. 43r: Three lines of *asmat* prayer whose purpose is not stated.

Notes:
1. F. 1rv, f. 42v and 43v blank, save for some scrawls on f. 42v.
2. Copied for Ḥabtä Maryam, replaced by Wäldä Ḥəywät, f. 1v.
3. Overlooked lines of text are written interlinearly (f. 1v).

Quire Map

Protection Quire | i

This is a single, half-sheet sewed directly to the wood board.

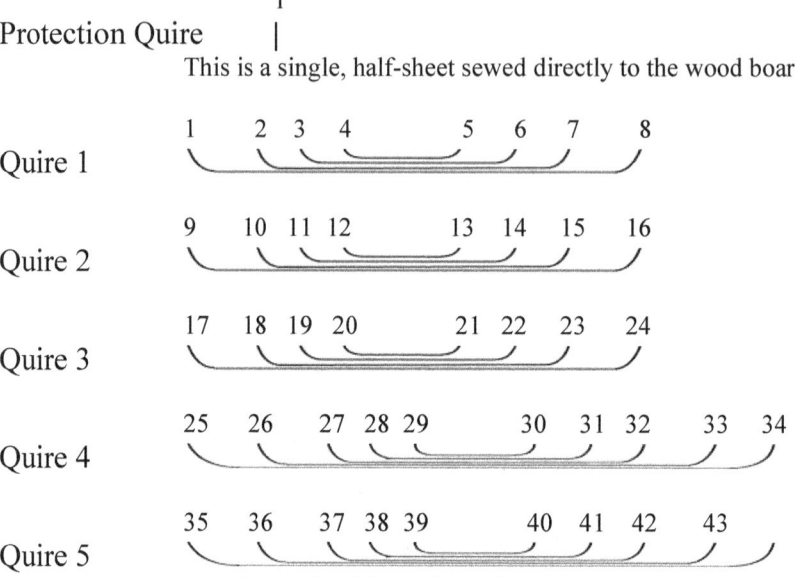

A folio stub is visible after f. 43.

EMIP 99 – Abilene Christian University Codex 2
Psalter with the Psalms of the Virgin, ዳዊት፡ ምስለ፡ መዝሙረ፡ ድንግል፡
Parchment, 235 x 205 x 82 mm, four Coptic chain stitches attached with bridle attachments to rough-hewn boards covered with tooled leather (a strip of plain white linen covers the spine), headband and tailband, 20 full quires, quires 2–19 numbered, 196 folios, top margin 32 mm, bottom margin 50 mm, fore edge margin 35 mm, gutter margin 12 mm, ff. 1r–182r one column, ff. 182v–197v two columns, Gəʻəz, 19–20 lines, 17th cent.

Quire descriptions: quires 1, 3, 5–10, 12–15, 17–19 balanced; quires 2, 4, 11, 16, 20 adjusted balanced. Navigation systems: 1) pink and red threads sewn into corners of folios 18, 28, 70, 102 and 157 to mark content divisions; marginal notation throughout, some of which may include insertions of overlooked text.

1. Ff. 2r–197r: Psalter [*Dawit*] with the *Mäzmurä Dəngəl*. Introduced with Ps 1 of the *Mäzmurä Krəstos*. Cf. EMIP 1; EMIP 2; EMIP 40.
    a. Ff. 2r–158r: Psalms of David. Supplied with commentary notes in Gəʻəz in the margins.
    b. Ff. 158v–174r: Biblical Canticles.
    c. Ff. 174v–182r: Song of Songs, common version.

Catalogue of the Ethiopic Manuscript Imaging Project · 251

    d. Ff. 182v–192v: Praises of Mary [Wəddase Maryam]. Arranged for the days of the week (Monday, f. 182v; Tuesday, f. 183r; Wednesday, f. 185r; Thursday, f. 186v; Friday, f. 189r; Saturday, f. 190r; Sunday, f. 191r).
    e. Ff. 192v–197r: Gate of Light [Anqäṣä Bərhan].
2. F. 197rv: Greeting to Church, ሰላም፡ ለኪ፡ ቤተ፡ ክርስቲያን፡ ሎሙ፡. EMIP 17, f. 40.

Varia:
1. F. 158r (at the end of the psalms): Record of purchase of the manuscript by *Qes* Ankore from *Qes* Kənfe Wäd(d)i.

Notes:
1. Decorative designs: many folios use dotted lines with alternating black and red dots.
2. F. 79v: A small cross-like symbol in the margin marks the midpoint of the Psalms.
3. The 118th psalm contains the spiritual meanings of the Hebrew letters.
4. Columetric layout of text: ff. 156v–157r (Ps. 150), 169r–170r (tenth biblical canticle).
5. The name of the original owner erased and replaced by Täsfa Giyorgis, end of the psalms.
6. This scribe has avoided the problem of lines of text too long to fit on one line by adopting an aspect ratio that leaves ample room for the width of most lines. On a few occasions, the line would have been too long and the scribe finishes the end of the line with words written smaller so as to avoid leftover text (e.g., ff. 30v, 32v, 33v, 36v, 38r, etc.). Occasionally a line is still too long and has to be completed above or below the end of the line (e.g., ff. 19v, 34v, 49v, 54r, 82r, etc.).

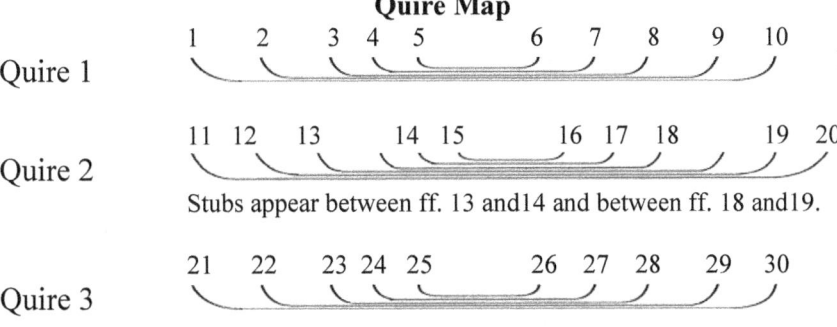

Quire 4: 31 32 33 34 35 36 37 38 39 40
Stubs appear between ff. 33 and 34 and between ff. 38 and 39.

Quire 5: 41 42 43 44 45 46 47 48 49 50

Quire 6: 51 52 53 54 55 56 57 58 59 60

Quire 7: 61 62 63 64 65 66 67 68 69 70

Quire 8: 71 72 73 74 75 76 77 78 79 80

Quire 9: 81 82 83 84 85 86 87 88 89 90

Quire 10: 91 92 93 94 95 96 97 98 99 100

Quire 11: 101 102 103 104 105 106 107 108 109 110
Stubs appear between ff. 102 and 103 and between ff. 107 and 108.

Quire 12: 111 112 113 114 115 116 117 118 119 120

Quire 13: 121 122 123 124 125 126 127 128 129 130

Quire 14: 131 132 133 134 135 136 137 138

Quire 15: 139 140 141 142 143 144 145 146 147 148

Quire 16: 149 150 151 152 153 154 155 156 157 158
Stubs appear between ff. 150 and 151 and between ff. 155 and 156.

Quire 17: 159 160 161 162 163 164 165 166 167 168

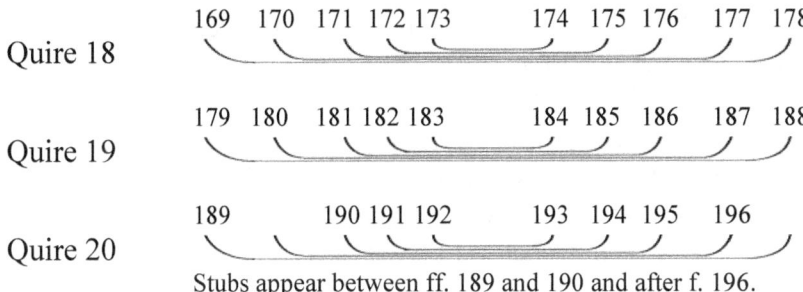

EMIP 100 – Weiner Codex 14
Psalter, ዳዊት፡

Parchment, 194 x 140 x 67 mm, four Coptic chain stitches attached with bridle attachments to rough-hewn boards, 1 protection quire + 16 full quires, 156 folios, 188 x 137 mm, top margin 20 mm, bottom margin 40 mm, fore edge margin 20 mm, gutter margin 7–10 mm, ff. 3r–139r one column, ff. 139v–154v two columns, Gə'əz, 21–22 lines, 19th cent.

Quire descriptions: quires 1–6, 8–12, and 15 balanced; quires 7 and 16 adjusted balanced; quires 13–14 unbalanced.

Ff. 3r–120r: Psalter [*Dawit*]. Introduced with Ps 1 of the Psalter of the Virgin; cf. EMIP 1 and EMIP 2.
1. Ff. 3r–120r: Psalms of David.
2. Ff. 120r–132r: Biblical Canticles.
3. Ff. 132v–139r: Song of Songs, common version.
4. Ff. 139v–149v: Praises of Mary [*Wəddase Maryam*]. Arranged for the days of the week (Monday, f. 139v; Tuesday, f. 140v; Wednesday, f. 142r; Thursday, f. 144r; Friday, f. 146r; Saturday, f. 147v; Sunday, f. 148v).
5. Ff. 150r–154v: Gate of Light [*Anqäṣä Bərhan*].

Miniatures, all in twentieth-century hand:
1. F. 2r: Crude drawing in ink: The Archangel Gabriel.
2. F. 2v: Resurrection, Raising Adam and Eve from the bondage of damnation, cf. 84, and f. 165v.
3. F.156r: The Ascension.
4. F. 156v: A holy man and a woman.

Notes:
1. F. 64r: The scribe possibly indicates the midpoint of the Psalms with a slight indent in the placement of the left margin for the midpoint line of text. All other lines are carefully placed on the left justified margin.

2. Psalm 118 contains the spiritual meanings of the Hebrew letters; each section is numbered.
3. Decorative designs: f. 49v (*haräg* in pencil and red); ff. 3r, 11r, 18v, 43v, 58r, 68v, 77r, 82r, 94r, 105r, 108r, 114r, 132r, 139r, 142r, 146r, 147v, and 148v (dotted line using alternating black and red); ff. 26r, and 120r (dotted lines with alternating black and red dots with additional full stop symbols); f. 149v (line of full stop symbols).
4. Columetric layout of text: ff. 119v (Ps. 150), and 128v–129r (tenth biblical canticle).
5. F. 155rv blank.
6. Overlooked words of text are written interlinearly (ff. 24v and 126r,).
7. The scribe regularly has to complete a line of text on another line. Much of the problem is addressed through the selection of an appropriate aspect ratio for the codex combined with an appropriate script size. But, where the line of text is still too long, the scribe completes the line of text above or below the end of the line (throughout). This scribe will also reduce the font size at the end of lines to avoid having to go onto the next line (e.g., ff. 10v, 26r, 33v, 35rv, 36v, etc.).

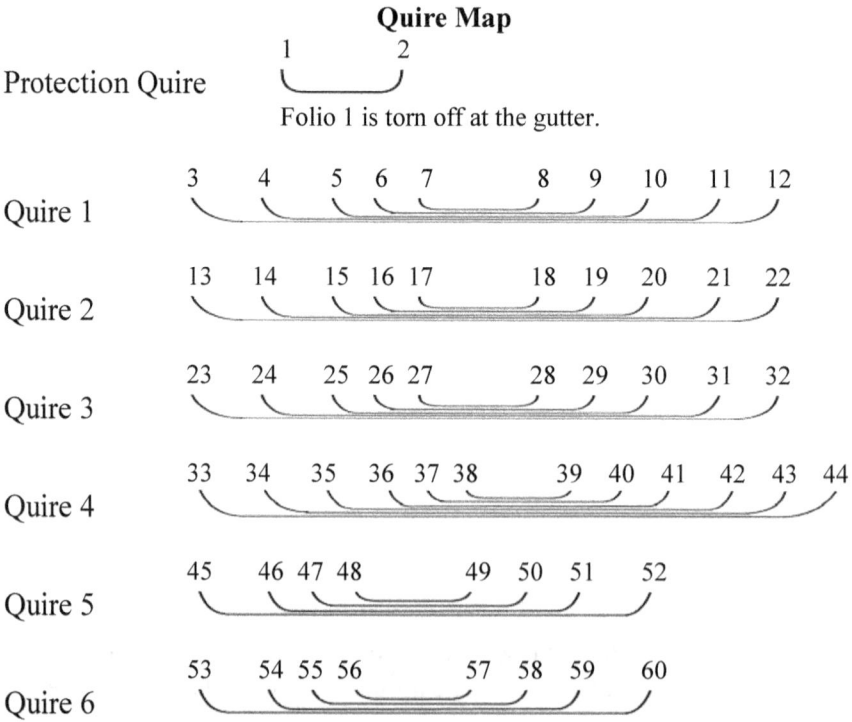

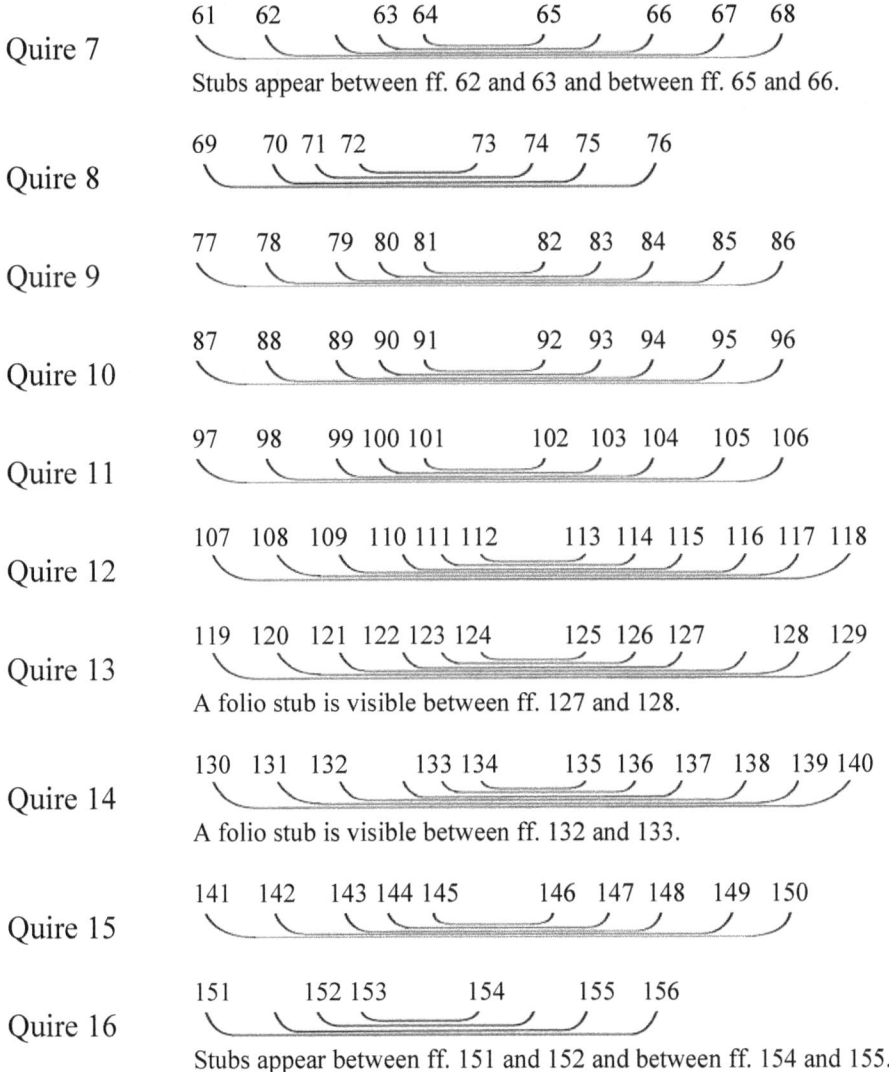

EMIP 101 – Weiner Codex 15
Psalter, ዳዊት:

Parchment, 162 x 142 x 74 mm, four Coptic chain stitches attached with bridle attachments to rough-hewn boards, one protection quire front, one in back + 18 full quires, 157 folios, 160 x 132 mm, top margin 14–16 mm, bottom margin 0–12 mm (trimmed), fore edge margin 15 mm, gutter margin 8 mm, ff. 4r–147r one column, ff. 148r–155v two columns, Gəʿəz, 23–25 lines, 19th cent.

Quire descriptions: quires 1, 3–6, 8–19 balanced; quires 2 and 7 unbalanced. Double-slip case.

Ff. 4r–155v: Psalter [*Dawit*]. Incomplete at the end, cf. EMIP 1.
1. Ff. 4r–127v: Psalms of David.
2. Ff. 128r–140r: Biblical Canticles.
3. Ff. 140r–147r: Song of Songs, common version.
4. Ff. 148r–155v: Praises of Mary [*Wəddase Maryam*] Only to the first half of Thursday. Arranged for the days of the week (Monday, f. 148r; Tuesday, f. 149r; Wednesday, f. 151v; Thursday, f. 154r.).

Notes:
1. Decorative designs: f. 4r (*haräg* using black and red, extending across top and down fore edge margin and gutter margin); ff. 46r, 88r, 128r, 140r, and 148r (*haräg* using black); ff. 11r, 19r, 27v, 63r, 74v, (dotted line using alternating black and red); ff. 16v, 38r, 66v, 82v, 101v, 105r, 113r, 116r, (line[s] of black dots); f. 69r (row of eight, red four-dot patterns [as though incomplete full-stop symbol]).
2. F. 69r: The midpoint of the Psalms is indicated by two lines of text written entirely in red ink (lines 12 and 14) and a row of partially completed full-stop symbols (line 16).
3. Psalm 118 contains the spiritual meanings of the Hebrew letters; each section is numbered.
4. Image for f. 126r is missing.
5. Columetric layout of text: ff. 126rv (Ps. 148), 127rv (Ps. 150), 136rv (tenth biblical canticle).
6. Note of ownership by Aläqa Adḥena Bärḫe, f. 156v.
7. Ff. 2r–3v, 8v, 147v, 156r, 157r–158r blank, mostly by erasure.
8. Overlooked words of text are written interlinearly (ff. 7r, 14r, 37v, 40v, 90r, 129v, etc.).
9. The scribe's chosen aspect ratio for the codex combined with the script size forces the scribe to complete the line of text above the end of the line (throughout).

Quire Map

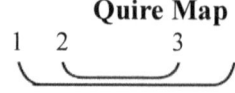

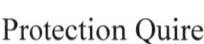

Folio 1 is a folio stub; another folio stub is visible between ff. 3 and 4.

Catalogue of the Ethiopic Manuscript Imaging Project · 257

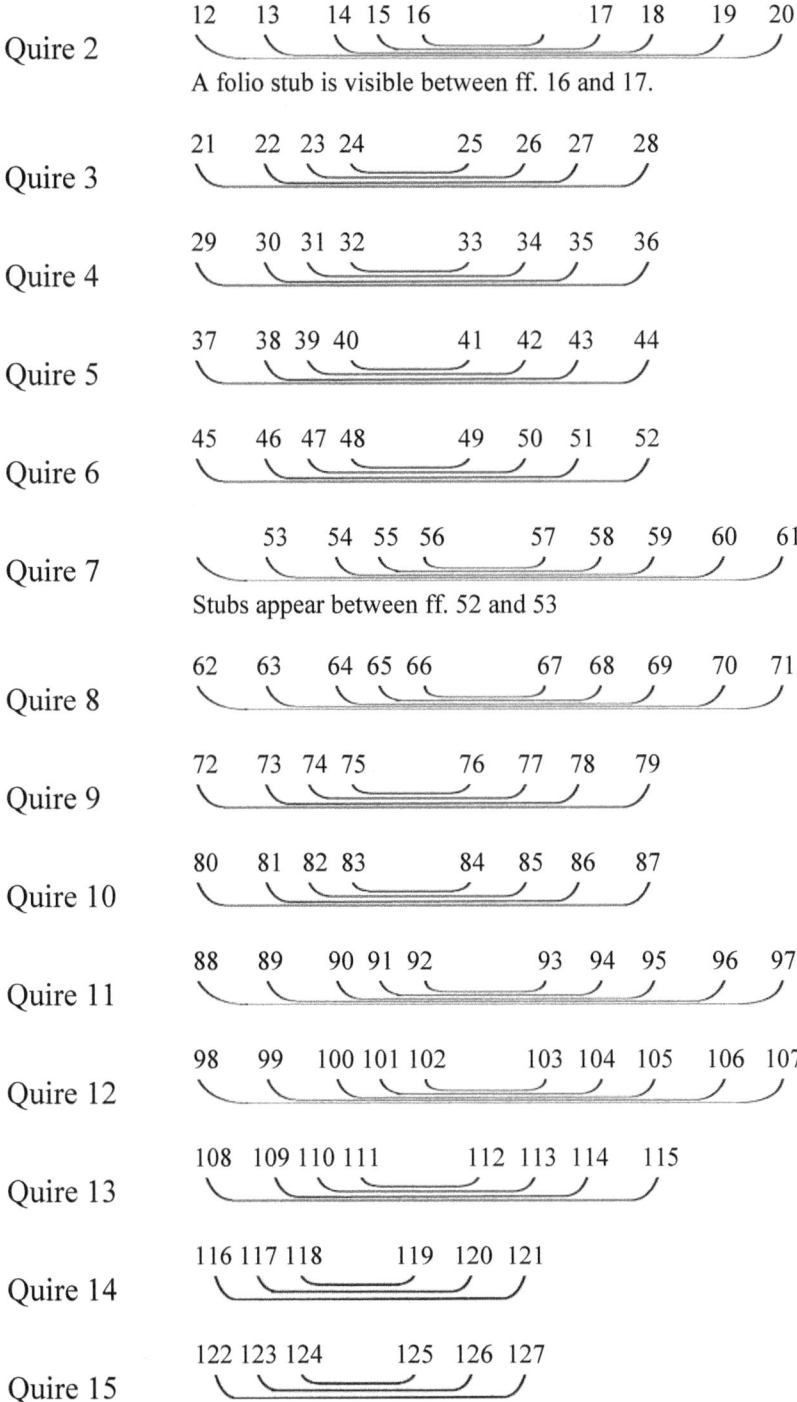

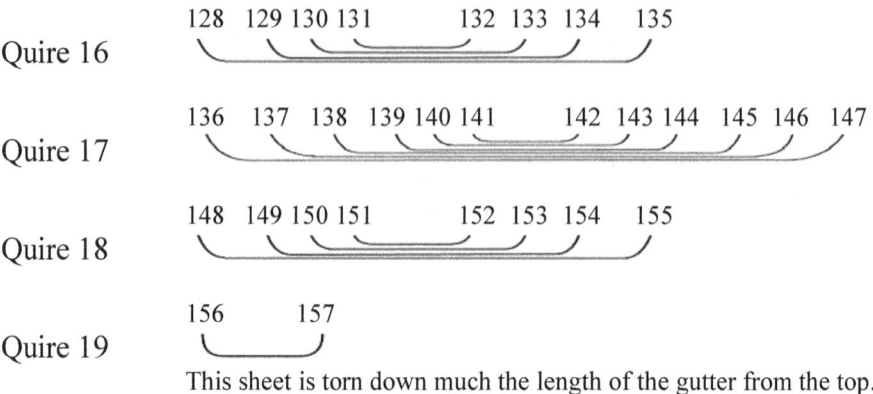

Quire 16: 128 129 130 131 | 132 133 134 135

Quire 17: 136 137 138 139 140 141 | 142 143 144 145 146 147

Quire 18: 148 149 150 151 | 152 153 154 155

Quire 19: 156 157

This sheet is torn down much the length of the gutter from the top.

EMIP 102 – Weiner Codex 16
Homiliary in Honor of the Archangel Michael, ድርሳነ፡ ሚካኤል፡

Parchment, 256 x 210 x 58 mm, four Coptic chain stitches attached with bridle attachments to rough-hewn boards, a protection sheet surrounds all the quires and covers the spine, 1 protection quire + 12 full quires, reinforcement strips around quires, quires 2–11 numbered (with ornate quire numbers in the top center of the first folio), i + 95 folios, top margin 30 mm, bottom margin 60 mm, fore edge margin 40 mm, gutter margin 15 mm, ff. 3r–93v in two columns, Gəʻəz, 17 lines, 18th cent.

Quire descriptions: quires 1–12 balanced. The name of Michael is rubricated throughout.

Ff. 3r–83v: Homiliary for the Monthly Feast of the Archangel Michael, ድርሳነ፡ ሚካኤል፡. Cf. EMIP 16.

Ḫədar: homily by Dämatewos, f. 3r, greeting, f. 10r, miracle, f. 10v; Taḫśaś: homily, f. 11r, miracle, f. 17v; Ṭərr: homily, f. 18v, greeting, f. 28v, miracle, 28v; Yäkkatit: homily, f. 29v, greeting, f. 33r, miracle, f. 33v; Mäggabit: homily by Archbishop of Antioch, f. 34v, greeting, f. 52v, miracle, f. 52v; Miyazya: homily by Rətuʻa Haymanot, f. 54r, miracle, f. 59r, greeting, f. 61r; Gənbot: homily by bishop of Ethiopia, f. 61v, greeting, f. 63r, miracle, f. 63r; Säne: homily, f. 65r, greeting, f. 71v, miracle, f. 72r; Ḥamle: homily, f. 73v, greeting, f. 78r, miracle, 78r; Näḫase: homily, f. 78v, greeting, f. 81v, miracle, f. 82r; Mäskäräm: homily, f. 82v, greeting, f. 85v, miracle, f. 85v; Ṭəqəmt: homily, f. 88r, prayer of the owner, Wäldä Maryam, and of Gäbrä Śəllus, in a rhyming hymn, f. 91v, miracle, f. 92r.

Miniatures, all in twentieth-century hand:
1. F. 2v: The Archangel Michael brandishing a sword. Caption: "Saint Michael."
2. F. 64r: Mary on a chair blessing a man who stands before her.
3. F. 94r: The Archangel Michael brandishing a sword. Caption: "Saint Michael."

Varia:
1. F. 1r: The beginning of the *Dərsan*.
2. F. 2r: The Amharic alphabet, with the numerical value of each letter.
3. F. 92r: The Amharic alphabet, with the numerical value of each letter.

Notes:
1. Decorative designs: ff. 3r, 11r, 29v, 34v, 54r space left for a *haräg* (and, on a few occasions, one is provided in pencil); ff. 10r, 17v, 26v, 28v (2x), 33r, 34v, 35v, 41r, 50v, 52v, 58r, 61v, 63r (2x), 65r, 78r, 78v, 82r, 82v, 85v (2x), 88r, 92r, 93v (line of alternating black and red dots and sometimes combined with full stop symbols); ff. 43r, 52r, 59r, 71v (multiple full stop symbols)
2. Lines written in red ink: f. 3r, both columns, lines 1, 2, 5, 6, 13, and 14; f. 11r, col. 2, lines 4 and 5; f. 17v, col. 1, lines 13 and 14; f. 26v, col. 2, lines 4 and 5; f. 28v, col. 2, lines 1 and 2; f. 29v, col. 1, lines 7 and 8; f. 33v, col. 1, lines 2 and 3; f. 34v, col. 2, lines 1 and 2; f. 35v, col. 2, lines 4 and 5; f. 41r, col. 2, line 13; f. 43r, col. 2, line 16; f. 50v, col. 1, lines 5 and 7; f. 52v, col. 1, lines 10 and 11; f. 54r, col. 1, lines 10 and 11; f. 58r, col. 1, lines 2 and 3; f. 59r, col. 1, lines 12 and 13; f. 61v, col. 1, lines 4 and 5; f. 63r, col. 2, lines 16 and 17; f. 65r, col. 1, lines 8 and 9; f. 72r, col. 1, lines 6 and 7; f. 73v, col. 1, lines 1 and 2; f. 78r, col. 1, lines 10 and 11; 78v, col. 2, lines 14 and 15; f. 82r, col. 1, lines 5 and 6; f. 82v, col. 2, lines 15 and 17; f. 85v, col. 2, lines 3 and 4; f. 88r, col. 1, lines 7 and 8; f. 92r, col. 1, lines 11 and 12.
3. Ff. Irv, 1v, and 95r blank.
4. Ff. 42r: note written in blue ink in bottom margin.
5. Ff. 53v, 54r, 73v: round stamp with cross in center in purple ink.
6. Copied for Wäldä Maryam, f. 3r and *passim*.

Quire Map
Front of Spine Strap

A sheet of parchment goes around all of the quires and under the boards, forming a strap to protect the spine. Under the front cover, the end of the sheet extends about 2 cm from the gutter. It is unfoliated.

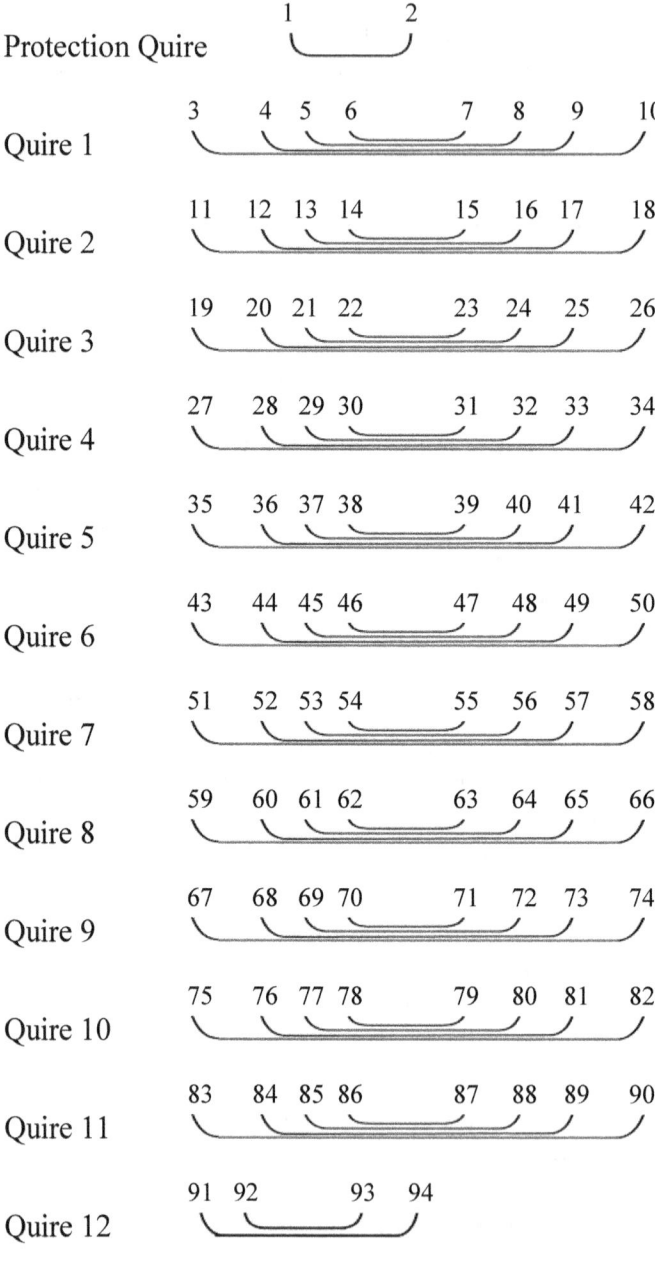

Back of Spine Strap   95

A sheet of parchment goes around all of the quires and under the boards, forming a strap to protect the spine. Under the back cover, the end of the sheet extends about 8 cm from the gutter. It is numbered as folio 95.

EMIP 103 – Weiner Codex 17
Table Blessing — Miracles of Jesus, በአልናከ፦ — ተአምረ፡ ኢየሱስ፡

Parchment, 275 x 182 x 32 mm, four Coptic chain stitches attached with bridle attachments to rough-hewn boards covered with tooled leather over decorative linen patches visible inside the turn-ins on front and back cover, 4 full quires, 32 folios, top margin 30 mm, bottom margin 55 mm, fore edge margin 25 mm, gutter margin 22 mm, ff. 4rv, 6rv, 8rv, 10rv, 12rv, 14rv, 16rv, 18v, 20rv, 22rv, 24rv, 26rv, 28rv, 29v, and 30v contain text in one column, the rest contain illuminations, Gəʿəz, 15–17 lines, 20th cent.

Quire descriptions: quires 1, 2, and 4 balanced; quire 3 adjusted balanced.
1. Ff. 4r–12r: Table blessing, በአልናከ፦. EMIP 17, f. 84r (varia).
2. Ff. 12v–30v: Miracles of Jesus, ተአምረ፡ ኢየሱስ፡.
   a. Ff. 12v–14r: The witness of John the Baptist, John 1:1–9.
   b. Ff. 14r–16v: How the child Jesus rode the ray of the sun.
   c. Ff. 16v–20r: How the child Jesus made real birds from mud.
   d. Ff. 20r–22r: Jesus on his first day in school.
   e. Ff. 22r–24v: The stolen calf, Grébaut, Jésus II, pp. 776–79.
   f. Ff. 24v–26v: Jesus ordered his followers to observe the Sabbath.
   g. Ff. 26v–28v: The choice of Mary to be the Mother of the Son.
   h. F. 28v: *Nunc dimittis*, Luke 2:29–32.
   i. Ff. 28v–30v: The story of the Nativity, Grébaut, Jésus I, pp. 583–89.

Miniatures, all in twentieth-century hand:
1. F. 1r: The watching eyes of the guardian angel in the middle of a cross.
2. F. 1v: A repeat of f. 1r.
3. F. 2r: A repeat of f. 1r and 1v, in a slightly different form.
4. F. 2v: The watching eyes of the guardian angel in the middle of an elaborated full-page frame.
5. F. 3r: A repeat of f. 1r, 1v and 2r in a slightly different form.
6. F. 3v: An angel stretching out his hands.
7. F. 5r: An elaborated cross.
8. F. 5v: An angel holding with his two hands a cross in a frame.
9. F. 7r: Two angels standing behind an elaborate cross.
10. F. 7v: A man holding a globe-shaped frame containing a cross.

11. F. 9r: The watching eyes of the guardian angel in the middle of two triangles surrounded with small crosses.
12. F. 9v: A repeat of f. 1r, 1v, 2r and 3r in a slightly different form.
13. F. 11r: An elaborate cross.
14. F. 11v: A repeat of f. 1r, 1v, 2r and 9v in a slightly different form.
15. F. 13r: An angel on whose wings each have a brandished sword.
16. F. 13v: Head in the middle of two crosses put on each other.
17. F. 15r: The watching eyes of the guardian angel in the middle of a cross in a frame. Other figures in the frame: two angels, an evil-looking angel (the devil?), and a cross.
18. F. 15v: A repeat of f. 1r, 1v, 2r and 9v in a slightly different form.
19. F. 17r: The watching eyes of the guardian angel in the middle of an elaborated full-page frame; cf. f. 2v.
20. F. 17v: Two angels guarding what looks like an elaborated jar, possibly a *mäsob* containing the Eucharistic bread.
21. F. 18r: The watching eyes of the guardian angel in the middle of an elaborated frame that looks like the figure on f. 17v.
22. F. 19r: A repeat of f. 1r, 1v, 2r and 9v in a highly elaborated form.
23. F. 19v: An angel with four wings and a book in his left hand.
24. F. 21r: magical figures, *ṭälsäm*.
25. F. 21v: The watching eyes of the guardian angel in the middle of a cross, and magical figures.
26. F. 23v: A cross in a frame.
27. F. 23v: Two crosses, each in a frame.
28. F. 25v: The watching eyes of the guardian angel in the middle of an elaborated cross.
29. F. 25v: Two triangles forming a cross and surrounded by small crosses.
30. F. 27r: An elaborated cross.
31. F. 27v: A repeat of f. 1r, 1v, 2r and 9v in a slightly different form.
32. F. 28r: A repeat of f. 1r, 1v, 2r and 9v in a slightly different form.
33. F. 30r: A repeat of f. 1r, 1v, 2r and 9v in a slightly different form.
34. F. 31r: A repeat of f. 1r, 1v, 2r and 9v in a markedly different form.
35. F. 31v: The watching eyes of the guardian angel on the right wing of a cross in a frame.
36. F. 32r: A repeat of f. 1r, 1v, 2r and 9v in a different form.
37. F. 32v: A repeat of f. 1r, 1v, 2r and 9v in a slightly different form.

Notes:
1. Lines written in red ink: f. 4r, lines 1 and 2; f. 12v, line 1; f. 28v, lines 2, 3, and 14;
2. Names of God, Mary and angels and saints rubricated throughout.

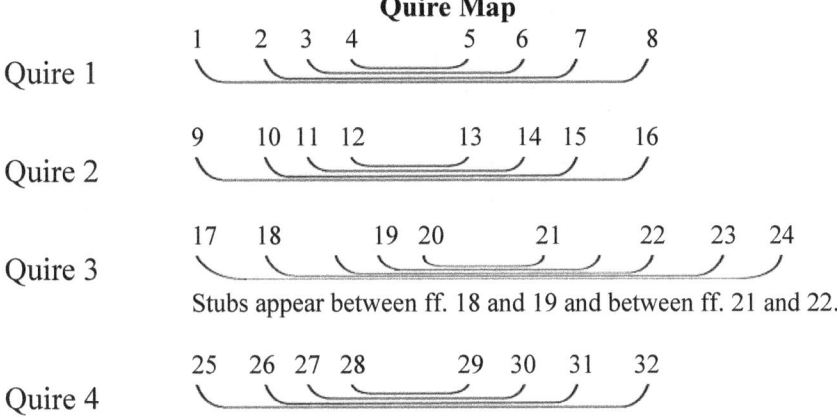

Stubs appear between ff. 18 and 19 and between ff. 21 and 22.

EMIP 104 – Weiner Codex 18
Images, መልክዐ፡ ጉባኤ፡

Parchment, 160 x 100–105 x 40 mm, three Coptic chain stitches attached with bridle attachments to rough-hewn boards of (non-traditional) soft wood, protection quire + 6 full quires, 60 folios, top margin 15 mm, bottom margin 32 mm, fore edge margin 15 mm, gutter margin 12 mm, ff. 3r–60v one column, Gəʿəz, 15 lines, 19th cent.

Quire descriptions: protection quire and quires 1–6 balanced. Navigation systems: 1) ff. 15, 42, 59 have colored string sewn into the fore edge indicating content; 2) f. 30r has a marginal notation to indicate content. Single-slip case with strap of embroidered and colorful heavy cloth.

1. Ff. 3r–15v: Image of Mary, መልክዐ፡ ማርያም፡. EMIP 25, f. 1r.
2. Ff. 15v–30r: Image of Jesus Christ, መልክዐ፡ ኢየሱስ፡. EMIP 26, f. 47r.
3. Ff. 30r–37v: Image of Arägawi/Zä-Mika'el, መልክዐ፡ አረጋዊ፡/ዘሚካኤል፡. Chaîne, Répertoire, no. 278.
በስመ፡ እግ"፡ እምግብጽ፡ ፍኖተ፡ ግዕዛን፡ ዘመርሐ፡፡
ለእግረ፡ እስራኤል፡ ሞቅሆ፡፡
እማዕሠረ፡ ቅኔ፡ ዘትፈትሐ፡፡
4. Ff. 37v–42r: Image of Gäbrä Mänfäs Qəddus, መልክዐ፡ ገብረ፡ መንፈስ፡ ቅዱስ፡. EMIP 20, 15r.
5. Ff. 42r–52v: Image of Michael, መልክዐ፡ ሚካኤል፡. EMIP 16, f. 92v.

6. Ff. 52v–59v: Image of Gabriel, መልክዐ፡ ገብርኤል፦ EMIP 56, f. 63r.
7. Ff. 59v–60v: Image of George, መልክዐ፡ ጊዮርጊስ፦ Incomplete at the end; Chaîne, Répertoire, no. 147.
   ሰላም፡ ለዝክረ፡ ስምከ፡ ዘሰሌዳ፡ ሞገስ፡ መጽሐፉ፦
   ዘየሜ(f. 60r)ኒ፡ (sic) ኩሎ፡ ወያስተሴፉ፦
   ጠዑመ፡ ዜና፡ ጊዮርጊስ፡ ለሐሊበ፡ እጐልት፡ ሱታፉ፦

Miniature, in a twentieth-century hand:
1. F. 2v: Saint George and the dragon.

Notes:
1. Decorative designs: ff. 3r (*haräg* using black and red); ff. 28r, (crosshatch lines using red and black); ff. 30r, 37v, 42r, 52v, (multiple full-stop symbols used as section dividers).
2. Lines written in red ink: f. 3r, lines 1, 2, 5 and 6; f. 42r, lines 12 and 13; f. 52v, lines 11, 12, and 15; f. 53r, line 1;
3. Names of God, Mary, angels and saints are rubricated throughout.
4. F. 2r: Pen trial.
5. F. 1rv blank.
6. Copied for Wäldä Zena Marəqos, f. 30r, 37r and *passim*.
7. Overlooked words of text are written interlinearly (ff. 7r, 9r, 14r, 16r, 18v, 30v, etc.) and with the symbol (⊥) marking the location where the text is to be inserted (f. 46r); and overlooked lines of text are written interlinearly (ff. 12v, 13v, 42r,); and in the bottom margin with a symbol (⊥) marking the location where the text is to be inserted (ff. 42r, line 13 and 47v, line 14).

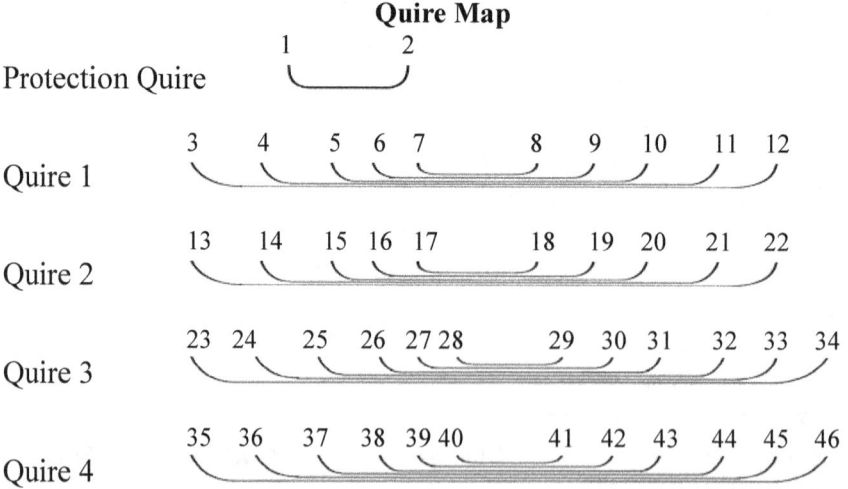

Quire Map

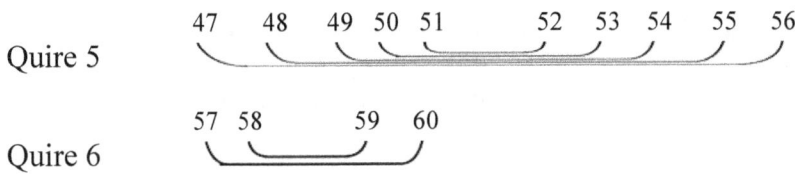

EMIP 105 – Weiner Codex 19
Book of Hours of *Abba* Giyorgis, መጽሐፈ፡ ሰዓታት፡ ዘአባ፡ ጊዮርጊስ፡

Parchment, 187 x 135 x 55 mm, four Coptic chain stitches (repaired) attached with bridle attachments to rough-hewn boards (both broken and both sewn together in two places), a parchment sheet extends around all the quires covering the spine, 13 full quires, 97 folios, reinforcement strips around quire 7, top margin 22 mm, bottom margin 35 mm, fore edge margin 15 mm, gutter margin 10 mm, ff. 3r–96v two columns, Gəʿəz, 23–25 lines, 19th cent.

Quire descriptions: quires 1–11, and 13 balanced; quire 12 unbalanced.

1. Ff. 3r–97v: Book of Hours of *Abba* Giyorgis, መጽሐፈ፡ ሰዓታት፡ ዘአባ፡ ጊዮርጊስ፡. MBB 52.
    a. Ff. 3r–45v: Horologium for Night Hours, ሰዓታት፡ ዘሌሊት፡., with musical notation on ff. 3r–16r, 26rv, 28v–29r, 32r–33r, 34rv, 35v–36v, and 45v. EMML 1362, f. 1a; EMML 2096, f. 84a; EMIP 42, f. 35r.
    በስመ፡ አብ፡ . . . እጽሕፍ፡ ሰዓታት፡ ዘሌሊት፡ ዘአባ፡ ጊዮርጊስ፡ በቂ፡ አአትብ፡ ወእትነሣእ፡ በስመ፡ አብ፡ ወወልድ፡ ወመንፈስ፡ ቅዱስ፡ ፩ቱ፡ አስግተ፡ ነኂእየ፡ እትመረጕዝ፡ እመኒ፡ ወደቁ፡ እትነሣእ፡ ወእመኒ፡ ሐርኩ፡ ውስተ፡ ጽልመት፡ እግዚአብሔር፡ ያበርህ፡ ሊተ፡ . . .
    b. Hymn to Mary, "The Angels praise Mary," ይዌድስዋ፡ መላእክት፡, f. 16v.
    c. Greeting to Mary, the Ark of Noah, ሰላም፡ ለኪ፡ ማርያም፡ ለኖኅ፡ ሐመሩ፡, f. 17r.
    d. Hymn to Jesus, "Glory to you in prostration," በስጊድ፡ ስብሐት፡, f. 19r.
    e. Image of the Icon, መልክዐ፡ ሥዕል፡, f. 21r. EMIP 42, f. 27r; Chaîne, Répertoire, no. 368.
    f. Hymn to Mary, "Rejoice, Mary, virgin in body and mind, ተፈሥሒ፡ ማርያም፡ ድንግልተ፡ ሥጋ፡ ወሕሊና፡, f. 23r.
    g. Hymn to Mary, "Rejoice, Mary, the Pasch of Adam," ተፈሥሒ፡ ማርያም፡ ለአዳም፡ ፋሲካሁ፡, f. 24r. Chaîne, Répertoire, no. 302.

h. Introductory rite from Muʻallaqa for the reading of the miracles of Mary, f. 27v.
i. Introductory exhortation to the Miracles of Mary, f. 30v, 32v and *passim*.
j. Miracles of Mary: The five dolors, f. 32v.
k. Rogation called "Glorification of the beloved," ስብሐተ፡ ፍቁር፡, f. 33r. (The sequence is 33r, 34r, not 33r, 33v. Also 34r does not follow 33v.)
l. Hymn to Jesus Christ, "O you who came down from heaven," አዘወረድከ፡ እምሰማይ፡ (Hammerschmidt, *Texte*, pp. 20–27), f. 34r.
m. Hymn to Mary, "You are blessed," ብፅዕት፡ አንቲ፡ ወንግሥተ፡ ጽድቅ፡ (EMIP 72, f. 42v.), f. 43r.

2. Ff. 46r–96v: Horologium for Daytime Hours, ሰዓታት፡ ዘመዓልት፡., with musical notation on ff. 46r, 47v–50r, 51r–52r, 55r–56v, 59r–61r, 62r–64r, 67r–68v, 71r–73r, 75v–76r, 78v–80v, 82r–83r, 84v–86r, and 87v–91v. MBB 52; EMML 1362, f. 32a; EMML 2096, f. 5a.
በስመ፡ አብ፡ . . . እጥን፡ ጽሐፊ፡ ሰዓታተ፡ መዓልት፡ ዘአባ፡ ጊዮርጊስ፡ በ፩ በጽሐ፡ አዕይንትየ፡ ለገይሥ፡ ከመ፡ እንብብ፡ ቃለከ፡ ስግዕ፡ እግዚአ፡ ቃልየ፡ ወለቡ፡ ጽራሕየ፡ . . .

   a. *Matins*, f. 46r.
      Miracle of Mary: The monk who had no virtue other than observing the fast of Mary, (Budge, *Mary*, p. 309), f. 51v.
   b. *Tierce*, f. 52v.
      ዘ፫፡ ሰዓት፡፡ በ፫፡ መኑ፡ ዘደመር፡ ለብርሃን፡ ምስለ፡ ጽልመት፡ ወለጽድቅኒ፡ ምስለ፡ ኃጢአት፡ . . .
      From the hymn, "Does not a man?" አኮኑ፡ ብእሲ፡ (EMIP 17, f. 26v), f. 58v.
      Miracle of Mary: The drunken monk whom Mary saved from a lion (Budge, *Mary*, p. 135), f. 59v.
   c. *Sext*, f. 60r.
      መዝሙር፡ በ፮፡ ሰዓት፡ በ፮፡ ትግሁ፡ እንከ፡ አኃውየ፡ ጻልዩ፡ ወሰአሉ፡ ከመ፡ ኢትባዑ፡ ውስተ፡ መንሱት፡ . . .
      Miracle of Mary: The thief for whom Mary begged forgiveness (Budge, *Mary*, p. 276), f. 67v.
   d. *None*, f. 68v.
      መዝሙር፡ በ፱ ሰዓት፡ በ፱ ኖላዊ፡ ዘመዓልት፡ ሐላዊ፡ ዘሌሊት፡ ኃይሎሙ፡ ለከዋክብት፡ አምላክነሰ፡ አምላከ፡ አድኅኖ፡ . . .
      Miracle of Mary: Märqorewos whose leprosy Mary cleansed (Budge, *Mary*, p. 71), f. 75r.

e. *Vespers*, 76v.
   ዘሥርk: መዘሙር: በ፪ ሀየኂ: እዴk: ትመርሐኒ: ወታነብረኂ: የማንk: አይቴኑ: አሐውር: እመንፈስk: . . .
   Miracle of Mary: How Mary wept for the sins of the world (Budge, *Mary*, p. 312), f. 82v.
f. *Compline*, f. 83v.
   ዘንዋም: በፅመኑ: ይትኤረዮ: ለእግ": በደመናት: ወመኑ: ይመስሎ: እምደቂቀ: አማልክት: . . .
   Miracle of Mary: The new George (Budge, *Mary*, p. 61), f. 88r.
g. Conclusion, f. 89r
   ዕዛል: ዘስብሐተ: ነግህ: ነአኮተk: እግዚአ: ወንሴብሐk: ንባርከk: ስቡሕ: ስምk: ኢይትሐሰው: ቃልk: . . .

Miniatures, all in twentieth-century hand:
1. F. 2v: Saint George and the dragon.
2. F. 15r: Christ enthroned.
3. F. 97r: The man with a stone foot, *Zä'ənb Ǝgru*, praying for Mary to heal him.
4. F. 96v: Drawing of human face in blue ink.

Varia:
1. F. 97v: Unintelligible text in a primitive hand.

Notes:
1. Decorative designs: ff.19r, 24r, 48r, 57r, 61v(?), 74r, 82r, 87v, (small box with interlaced pattern in red and black ink at beginning of section); ff. 31v, 33r (section divider using multiple full-stop symbols); ff. 9r, 10r, 20v, 22v, 57v, 65v, 80r, 85v, 91r, 92v (2x), (small dotted line using alternating black and red); ff. 26v, and 96v (multiple full-stop symbols with sets of three lines in red and black between); f. 88r (multiple full-stop symbols with line of alternating red and black dots connecting each).
2. Lines written in red ink: f. 3r, both cols., lines 1, 2, 5, 6, 13, 14, 21 and 22; f. 4v, col. 2, lines 1–2; f. 5r, col. 2, line 10; f. 14v, col. 2, lines 3 and 4; f. 16r, col. 1, lines 16 and 17, f. 17r, col. 2, lines 13 and 14; f. 26v, col. 1, lines 8–9 and 12–13; f. 29v, col. 2, lines 18 and 19; f. 31v, col. 2, lines 1 and 2; f. 33r, col. 1, lines 17–18 and 21; f. 34v, col. 1, lines 5 and 6; f. 35r, col. 1, lines 14 and 15; f. 35v, col. 1, lines 11–12; f. 36r, col. 1, lines 19 and 20; f. 38r, col. 2, lines 18 and 19; f. 39r, col. 2, lines 21 and 22; f. 40r, col. 2, lines 16 and 17; f. 41v, col. 1, lines 1 and 2, col. 2, lines 13 and 14; f. 43r, col. 1, lines 6–7, 10 and 11; f. 46r, both columns, lines 1–2, 5–6, 15 and 16; f. 50v, col. 2, lines 11 and 12; f.

51v, col. 1, lines 9–10; f. 58v, col. 2, lines 2 and 3; f. 60r, col. 2, lines 5 and 6; f. 66v, col. 1, lines 16 and 17; f. 75r, col. 1, lines 1 and 2; f. 75v, col. 2, line 5; f. 81v, col. 2, lines 9 and 10; f. 82v, col. 1, lines 1 and 2; f. 87r, col. 1, lines 9 and 10; f. 88r, col. 2, lines 8–9, 12, and 13;

3. F. 2r blank
4. Copied for Wäldä Maryam, f. 32r, 67r and *passim*.
5. Overlooked words of text are written interlinearly (ff. 6r, 10r, 52v, 56v, 69r, 78v, etc.); and in the upper margin with a symbol (⊥) marking the location where the text is to be inserted (ff. 25r, line 19, 56r, line 9, cf. 32r, line 20).

Quire Map

Front of Spine Strap 1

A sheet of parchment goes around all of the quires and under the boards, forming a strap to protect the spine. Under the front cover, the end of the sheet is cut very unevenly, extending about 8 cm from the gutter. It is numbers as folio 1.

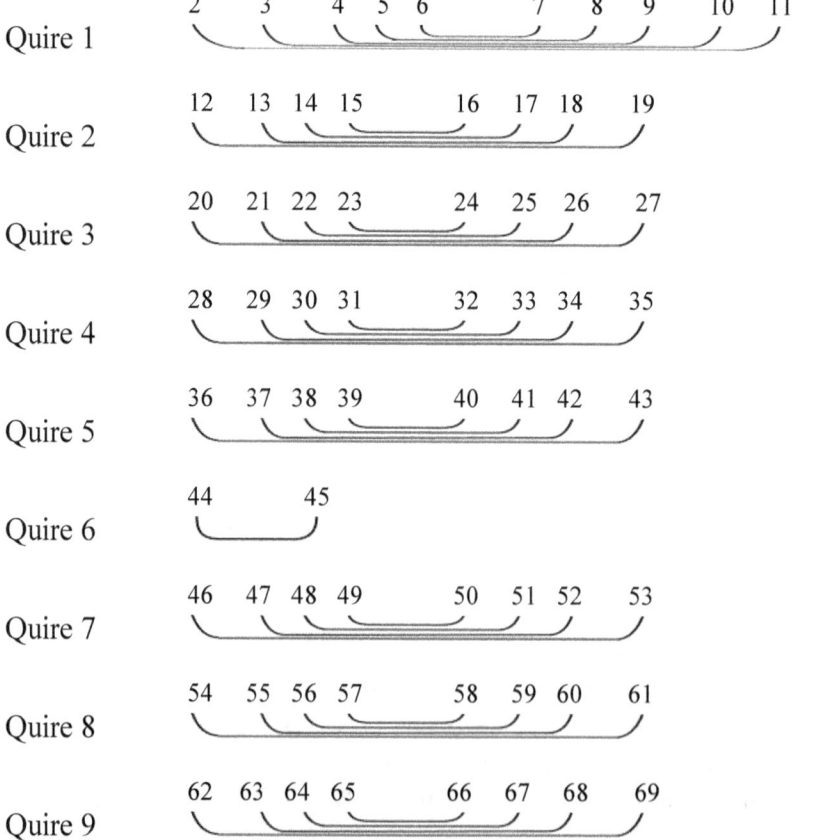

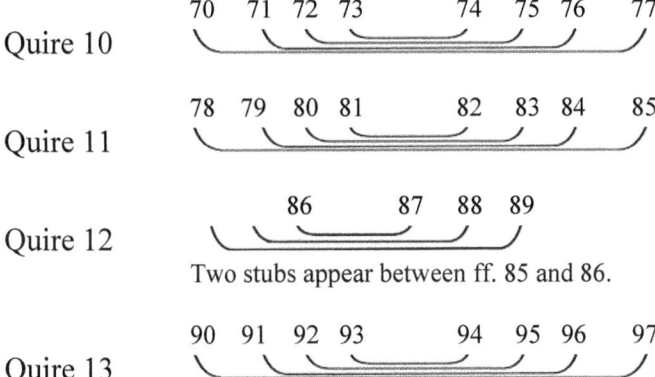

Quire 10

Quire 11

Quire 12

Two stubs appear between ff. 85 and 86.

Quire 13

Back of Spine Strap
    A sheet of parchment goes around all of the quires and under the boards, forming a strap to protect the spine. Under the back cover, the end of the sheet is cut quite unevenly extending at the top about 8 cm from the gutter and at the bottom about .5 cm from the gutter. It is un-foliated.

Catalogue of Scrolls of Ethiopian Spiritual Healing

EMIP MagSc 1 – Delamarter Magic Scroll 2
Parchment, 125 x 10.5 cm, one strip, one column, elaborate border of small horizontal strokes, Gəʿəz, 20th cent.
1. The opening prayer, "In the name of the Father…," unfinished.
   በስመ፡ አብ[፡] ወወል፡ ድወ፡ መን፡
2. The unfinished opening prayer, repeated.
   በስመ፡ አብ[፡] ወወልድ[፡] ወመንፈስቅ፡ ዱስ ፩፡ አም፡ ላክ፡ በቅዱስላሴ፡ እንዘ[፡] አአምን[፡] ወይትመፀ፡ እከደከ፡ ሰይጣን[፡] . . .
3. The unfinished opening prayer, repeated.
6. The unfinished opening prayer.
7. The Our Father, unfinished.

Miniatures and Magical Symbols:
1. Archangel Michael brandishing a sword.
2. An angel.
3. An angel.
4. An angel with the symbols and the text of the unfinished prayer.
5. An angel with head and wings only and his eyes closed.
6. Head of an angel.
7. Head of an angel with the symbols and the text of the unfinished prayer.

Copied in a crude hand of a semi-literate copyist.
Acquired on Zege, near Lake Tana, in the Spring of 2004.

EMIP MagSc 2 – Delamarter Magic Scroll 3
Parchment, 78.5 x 10 cm, one strip (bottom shows evidence of having been stitched to another strip at some time), one column, border, Gəʿəz, 20th cent.
Prayer against the demons Šotälay and Qotälay that kills infants, 68 lines; cf. Dobberahn, *Zauberrollen*, pp. 298–9.
   በስመ፡ አብ፡ . . . ጸሎት፡ በእንተ፡ ሕማም፡ ሾተላይ፡ ወቆቶላይ፡ ጋኔን፡ ዘትቀትል፡ ሕፃናተ፡ አምኃልኩከ፡ ወአውገዝኩከ፡ ወቄለዝኩከ፡ ወለገምከ፡

(sic) ወዓሠርኩኪ፡ ከመ፡ ኢትቅትል፡ ዘንተ፡ ሕፃነ፡ . . . በዝንቱ፡ አማተ፡
(sic) እግ"፡ መአጅን፡³ˣ መቀጅን፡³ˣ ፈቀጅን፡³ˣ . . . በኃይለ፡ ዝንቱ፡
አስማቲከ፡ ቀጥቅጦ፡ ወአርነቆ፡ . . . ወኢይቅትል፡ ሕፃናቲሃ፡ ለአመተ፡
እግ"፡ አመተ፡ ጸድቃን፡ ሰሎሞን፡³ˣ መሐፍሎን፡³ˣ ፖሎሞስ፡³ˣ ዮፍታሔ፡³ˣ
አምላከ፡ ጴጥሮስ፡ ወጳውሎስ፡ ብርስባሔል፡ ብርሃናኤል፡ የአየዊን፡³ˣ
ቆጻንዮስ፡ . . . ዕጴውእ፡ ስመ፡ ሳዶር፡ ጨ፡ አላዶር፡ ጨ[፡] ዳናት፡ ጨ፡
አዴራ፡ ጨ፡ ሮዳስ፡ ጨ፡ በኃይለ፡ ቅንዋተ፡ መስቀሉ፡ . . . አምኃልኩክሙ፡
ወአውገዝኩክሙ፡ ወለጐምኩክሙ፡ ወቄለፍኩክሙ፡ ወአሠርኩክሙ፡
በማዕሠረ፡ አብ፡ . . . አንተ፡ ሾተላይ፡ ወእንተ፡ ቆቶላይ፡ ጋኔን፡ ዘተቀትል፡
ሕፃናተ፡ ወኮልክሙ፡ መናፍስተ፡ ሥራይ፡ ኢትቅረቡ፡ ላዕሌሃ፡ ወላዕለ፡
ሕፃናቲሃ፡ (sic) ለአመተ፡ እግ"፡ አመተ፡ ጸድቃን፡

Miniatures and Magical Symbols:
 1. An angel with sword appearing from behind a curtain.

Copied for Amätä Ṣadqan.

Acquired in Addis Ababa in Spring 2004 from the Ethiopian Tourist Organization at the Institute of Ethiopian Studies.

EMIP MagSc 3 – Eliza Magic Scroll 1

Parchment, 159 x 5.5 cm, three strips sewn together, one column, no border, Gəʻəz, 20th cent.

1. Prayer against the evil eye of Barya: The story of the sorcerer at the Sea of Tiberias, 71 lines; cf. Strelcyn, *Lincei*, 32, 7, p. 109; Worrell, "Zauberwesen II," pp. 87f, 102f. and 111f; Six, *Handschriften*, 10, 3. p. 79; Dobberahn, *Zauberrollen*, pp. 285–7 and 307–8.
በስመ፡ አብ፡ . . . ጸሎት፡ በእንተ፡ ሕማም፡ ዓይን፡ ጥላ፡ ወዓይነ፡ ወርቅ።
ወእንዘ፡ የሐውር፡ እግዚእን፡ ውስተ፡ ባሕረ፡ ጥብርያዶስ፡ . . .

2. Prayer for binding demons, 35 lines.
ጸሎት፡ በእንተ፡ ማእሰረ፡ አጋንንት። ዮፍታሔ፡ ድንቃኤል፡ ቀርጥጥናኤል፡ የዝዮን፡ (sic) ወአትሮን፡ . . .

3. Prayer for conception, 14 lines.
ጸሎት፡ በእንተ፡ ዕ፡ (sic) ዕንስ። ይቤ፡ እግ"፡ ነዐርኩ፡ ኃቤኪ፡ ወይበዐብጽ፡ ከርሥኪ፡ ወይረስዮ ፡ ለደምኪ፡ ከመ፡ ይሰንር፡ ግብሮ፡ ለጋኔን፡ ዘእንበለ፡ ይብጻሕ፡ ጊዜሁ፡ ⌈ሰዓልናከ፡ ፈጣሪ፡ ሰዓልናከ፡ መሐሪ፡ (taken from the prayer for table blessing) . . .

4. Prayer for binding demons and against the evil eye, 22 lines.
በስመ፡ አብ፡ . . . ጸሎት፡ በእንተ፡ ማእሰረ፡ አጋንንት፡ ወዓይነ፡ ጥላ፡ ወዓይነ፡ ወርቅ፡ ወግርጋሪ፡ አሾቦር፡²ˣ ካሁ፡ ክሁ፡ ካሁ፡ ጋሁ፡ ግሁ፡ . . .

5. Prayer for binding demons and the evil hand, 37 lines.

ጸሎት፡ በእንተ፡ ማእሰሪ፡ አጋንንት፡ ወእጆ፡ ሰብእ፡ ወያጸልም፡ አዕይንቲሃ፡ ይ፡ (sic) ወየሀኪ፡ ግብተ፡ ወይመጽእ፡ ከመ፡ ጽላሉተ፡ ወሕልም፡ ወአውገዝኩከ፡ ወአምኃልኩከ፡ በፄቅንዋተ፡ መስቀሉ፡ . . .

6. Prayer against hemorrhage, in Gəʿəz and Amharic, 20 lines.
በስመ፡ አብ፡ . . . ጸሎት፡ በእንተ፡ ሕማመ፡ ደም፡ ሹች፡ አላሸች፡ አሸካላሹች፡ ብር.ጋ፡ ለደም፡ . . . ቁም፡ ወተከተር፡ በማርያም፡ ወላዲት፡ በኂዮርጊስ፡ ኮከበ፡ ክብር፡ በሩፋኤል፡ . . .

7. Prayer against hemorrhage, 6+10 lines. . . . ጸሎት፡ ል፡ (sic) ደም፡ አቅልያስ፡[3x] ዘሎምያስ፡[3x] ከምታሪ፡[3x] ኢታውርድ፡ ደግ፡ እምኃቤሃ፡ . . . (magical signs) ...

8. Prayer against hemorrhage, 10 lines.
ጸሎተ፡ ደም፡ ወሕማም፡ ያውሜሌር፡ ግድማሶር፡ ግምቶርም፡ ፈላታዎስ፡ አውዱን፡ . . . አድገና፡ እምሕማመ፡ ቡዳ፡ ወቁመኛ፡ ለአመትከ፡ . . . እስመ፡ አልቦ፡ ነገር፡ ዘይሰዓኖ፡ ለእግ"።። (Luke 1:37.)

Miniatures and Magical Symbols:
1. An angel brandishing a sword.
2. The watchful eyes of the guardian angel.
3. Apparently the woman for whom the scroll was copied, Səḫin (?).

Copied for Səḫin.

EMIP MagSc 4 – Eliza Magic Scroll 2

Parchment, 190.5 x 8.5 cm, three strips sewn together, one column, double border, Gəʿəz, 20th cent.

1. Prayer against demons of Zar, Barya, Legewon, Təgrida, Mäggañña, Ṭäbib, and Gudale, 38 lines; cf. Six, *Handschriften*, 37, a, 1, 1, p. 132.
በስመ፡ አብ፡ . . . ጸሎት፡ በእንተ፡ ሕማመ፡ ዛር፡ ወባርያ፡ ወሌጌዎን፡ ወትግሪዳ፡ መጋኛ፡ ወጠስምት፡ ፍልፀት፡ ወቁፀት፡ (sic) ፈሪ፡ ወንዳድ፡ ጠቢብ፡ ወጉዳሌ፡ አአትብ፡ ገጽየ፡ በትምዕተ፡ (sic) መስቀል፡ አአትብ ገጽየ ወኮለንታየ በስመ፡ አብ፡ . . . ፫ አስማተ፡ ነዛእየ፡ እመረጕዝ፡ (sic) እመኒ፡ ወደቁ፡ . . .

2. Prayer against hemorrhage and Šotälay, 32 lines; cf. Six, *Handschriften*, 10, 8, p. 79.
በስመ፡ አብ፡ . . . ጸሎት፡ በእንተ፡ ሕማመ፡ ደም፡ ወሾተላይ፡ አስማቲሁ፡ ለእግ"፡ ሊስ፡ አፍሊስ፡ መሊስ፡ መላሊስ፡ በኤዝሞስኤል፡ በኃይለ፡ ዝንቱ፡ አስማቲከ፡ . . . አጽንዕ፡ ፍሬ፡ ማኅፀና፡ ለአመትከ፡ . . . ሰንተም፡ ከንተም፡ ዘወጽአ ደም፡ እምገቦሁ፡ ለክርስቶስ፡ . . .

3. Prayer against hemorrhage and Šotälay, 25 lines.
በስመ፡ አብ፡ . . . ጸሎት፡ በእንተ፡ ሕማመ፡ ደም፡ ወሾተላይ፡ ወናሁ፡ ብእሲት፡ እንተ፡ ደም፡ ውኒዛ፡ (sic) ፪፡ (sic) አመተ፡ (Matt 9:20–22.)

4. Prayer for conception, to stop hemorrhage and against Šotälay, 39 lines.
በስመ፡ አብ፡ . . . ጸሎተ፡ መርግዔ፡ ደም፡ ወሾተላይ፡ ሐ ሐ ሐ፡ ቅ ቅ ቅ፡ ሊስ፡ አፍሊስ፡ መሊስ፡ መላሊስ፡ ማልኮስ፡[3x] ዘሀለት፡ ዘእርኃዕከ፡ ኃይለ፡ በረድ፡ ወነፋስ፡ ከማሁ፡ . . .

5. Prayer against all kinds of bodily and spiritual ailments, 30 lines.
በስመ፡ ሱሉስ፡ (sic) ቅዱስ፡ ነሐዩ፡ ኤፍራስን፡ ዳቴን፡ ሊሳ፡ ንዮን፡ ቆሬ፡ ሌዳጊዮን፡ . . . ዘንተ፡ አስማተ፡ ትብል፡ ሲድራ፡ ታኤል፡ የአፍታኤል፡ . . . በኃይለ፡ ዝንቱ፡ አስማቲከ፡ አድኅነኒ፡ እምሕማም፡ ውግዓት፡ ቅንዓት፡ (sic) ወምትሐት፡ ጽፍአት፡ ወርግዘተ፡ ገቦ፡ ወእምኮሉ፡ ሕማም፡ ሥጋ፡ ወነፍስ፡ ዘየሐቂ፡ (sic) ሐቂ፡ (sic) አቁያጽ፡ አዕጋሪ፡ ወአዕዳው፡ እምርእስ፡ እስከ፡ ሰኩና፡ አድኅነኒ፡ . . .

Miniatures and Magical Symbols:
1. An angel before a woman seated on a stool (large), above a design with four petals, each with an eye at the center.
2. Angel with sword and scabbard.
3. Large Panel with ornate cross design above a design with four petals, each with an eye or two at the center.
4. Talismanic symbol with many eyes.

Copied for Wälättä Iyyäsus Aškute.

EMIP MagSc 5 – Eliza Magic Scroll 3

Parchment, 204.5 x 7.5 cm, three strips sewn together, one column, no border, Gəʻəz, 20th cent.

1. Prayer against hemorrhage and Šotälay, 18 lines.
በስመ፡ አብ፡ . . . ጸሎት፡ በእንተ፡ ሕማም፡ ደም፡ ወሾተላይ፡ ዓርኃኤል፡[3x] ብጹእ፡ ብእሲ፡ (Ps 1:1–3) ኢይትነገፍ፡ ፍሬ፡ ማኀፀን፡ ለዓመትከ፡ . . .

2. Prayer against the evil eye, 37 lines; cf. Strelcyn, *Prières*, p. 4.
በስመ፡ አብ፡ . . . ጸሎት፡ በእንተ፡ ሕማም፡ ዓይነት፡ ፀዐ፡ በቀይሀ፡ ወጸሊም፡ ወበኩም፡ ወጸአ፡ እ፡ (sic) ዮሴፍ፡ እምሕሱም፡ ወእምሕቱም፡ ፌአንትአ፡ ኩሪ፡ ኩሪ፡ ይስድድከ፡ እግ" ዓቢይ አንተ፡ በስማይ፡. . . ዓዕ፡ ዓይነ፡ ክርስቲያናዊ፡ ወዓይነ፡ ዓረበዊ፡ (sic) ወዓይነ፡ አጋንንት፡ ወዓይነ፡ ሰይጣናት፡ አመሕለከ፡ (sic) በእግ" . . . አለሀ፡ ቃለ፡ አብ፡ . . . ሳዶር፡ አላዶር፡ . . . ዕቀባ፡ ወአድኅና፡ እምሕማም፡ ዓይነ፡ ርስ፡ ወዓይነ፡ ጥላ፡ እምሕማም፡ ባርያ፡ ወሌጌዎን፡ እምሕማም፡ ቡዳ ወቁመኛ፡ (sic) እምሕማም፡ ካይላ፡ ወሻንቅላ፡ እምሕማም፡ ዛር፡ ወዛሪት፡ ወቁራኛ፡ . . .

3. Prayer regarding the rampart of the Cross, ascribed to Jeremiah, 29 lines; cf. Strelcyn, *British Library*, 76, 3, p. 120; Grébaut, "Masqal"; and Lifchitz, *Textes*, p. 150.

ጸሎት፡ በእንተ፡ ሀዉረ፡ መስቀል፡ ዘጸሀፊ፡ ኤርምያስ፡ ነቢይ፡ ኅበ፡ ታቦተ፡ ማይ፡ (sic) ወያፉ፡ አጋንንት፡ መስቀል፡ መዋዔ፡ ፀር፡ መስቀል፡ መግረሬ፡ ፀር፡ መስቀል፡ ነሣቴ፡ ፀር፡ መስቀል፡ መግረሬ፡ ፀር፡ (again) መስቀል፡ ምርኩዝ፡ ለሐንካሳን፡ ... በዝ፡ ቃለ፡ መለኮት፡ ዕቀብ፡ ወአድኅን፡ እምሕማመ፡ አጋንንት፡ (sic) አየር፡ እኩያን፡ ወእምሰብእ፡ መሡርያን፡ ባርያ፡ ወሌጌዎን፡ ምቀኛ፡ ወተንኮለኛ፡ ...

Miniatures and Magical Symbols:
1. Angel with sword and scabbard (sword pointing down).
2. Baptism of Jesus by John the Baptist (dove hovers above).
3. Jesus, holding banner, points heavenward. Two men (showing only one eye) stand below and on either side.
4. Twelve-box panel (4 x 3) with faces in boxes 1, 4, 6, 7, 9, and 12.

Copied for Wälättä Śəllase/Wärqnäš.

EMIP MagSc 6 – Marwick Magic Scroll 1

Parchment, 121 x 9.5 cm, two strips sewn together, one column, no border, Gəʿəz, 20th cent.

1. Prayer against hemorrhage and for conception, 55 lines; cf. 4, 2 and 3.
    በስመ፡ አብ፡ ... ጸሎት፡ በእንተ፡ ሕማመ[፡] ደም፡ ዘርእ፡ ወፍሬ፡ ለአንስት፡ አእግዚእየ፡ ኢየሱስ፡ ክርስቶስ፡ ዘሐሎ፡ ወይኄሉ፡ አቢይ፡ ስሙ፡ ወመለከ፡ (sic) ምሕረት፡ ምክር ፡ ዘየአቅብ፡ (sic) ዘርእ፡ ወፍሬ፡ ለአንስት፡ በውስተ፡ ከርሡ፡ ድንግል፡ ... እንዘ[፡] ሀቢ፡ መስቀል፡ ወትቤ፡ አድራስ፡ አድራስ፡ ከሰለስ፡ (sic) አፍሊስ፡ (sic) መሊስ፡ መለሊስ፡ ዝዜሎን፡ ወዘዜናዊ፡ ዘአርጋእከ፡ ኃይለ፡ በረድ፡ ወነፋስ፡ ከገቡ፡ ...... እመኒ፡ ተባእተ፡ ወአንስተ፡ ይጽንዕ፡ በሕፀን፡ (sic) ኩሉ፡ ይትከሐለከ፡ ወአልቦ፡ ዘይሰአነከ፡ ስሙ፡ ለአብ፡. ... (Ps 1:1–3) ...

2. Prayer against hemorrhage, 22 lines; cf. 4, 2; Six, *Handschriften*, 10, 9a, p. 79; Six, "Zaubertexte," 314.
    በስመ፡ አብ፡ ... ጸሎት፡ በእንተ፡ ሕማመ[፡] ደም፡ ስንተም፡ ደም፡ ስም፡ ስንተረም፡ ደም፡ ስም፡ ስንተረም፡ ዘወጽአ፡ ደም፡ ወማይ፡ እምገቡሁ፡ ...

3. Greeting to Phanuel as prayer against nightmare; cf. Worrell, "Zauberwesen III," p. 113; *British Library*, 73, 2, p. 117; 82, 6, p. 129); see also Chaîne, Répertoire, no. 49.
    በስመ፡ አብ፡ ... ጸሎት፡ በእንተ፡ ሕልመ[፡] ሌሊት፡ ሰላም፡ ለከ፡ ሰዳዬ፡ ሰይጣናት፡ ፋኑኤል፡ ለእግ" እምጽርሁ፡ ኢይስክዩ፡ ሰብአ፡ እለ፡ ይኔስሩ፡ ..

4. Prayer against a piercing pain on the side, 27 lines; cf. Strelcyn, *Lincei*, 32, 10, p. 109; Six, *Handschriften*, 33, a, 15, 7, p. 123.

በስመ፡ አብ፡ . . . ጸሎት፡ በእንተ፡ በእንተ፡ (sic) ሕማመ፡ ዉግአት[፡] ምድምያስ፡[7x] ዘይትበወር፡[3x] ዘጌ፡[3x] ሀጋሌ፡ ...ዘአድኃንኮ፡ ለወልደ፡ ሰራቂ፡ (sic) ከማሁ፡ አድኅና፡ ለዓመትከ፡ . . .

5. Prayer against the evil eye, 38 lines.
በስመ፡ አብ፡ . . . ጸሎት፡ በእንተ፡ ሕማመ፡ ዓይን[፡]ጥላ፡ ወዓይነ፡ ወርቅ፡ በአሽማግ፡[3x] በአሽማደኤል፡ ቢያግኒ፡ በተክለ[፡] ወርሽል፡ ረሐቁ፡ ወተሰደዱ፡ አጋንንት፡ ወሰይጣናት፡ እኩያን፡ ወሰብ፡ (sic) መሰርያን፡ . . . ያሽርር፡[4x] ያሽቤርር፡ . . . በኃይለ፡ እሌ፡ አስማቲከ፡ አድኅና፡ እምዓይነ፡ አጋንንት፡ እኩያን፡ . . .

Miniatures and Magical Symbols:
1. Angel with sword.
2. Panel with three scenes. Top: ornate cross with an angel with a sword on either side. Middle: *talismanic symbol* with face in center. Bottom: small ornate cross with crude drawings on either side.

Copied for Wärq Yanṭəf.

EMIP MagSc 7 – Marwick Magic Scroll 2
Parchment, 174.5 x 11.5 cm, three strips sewn together, one column, double border, Gəʻəz, 20th cent.

1. Prayer for binding demons, 19 lines.
በስመ፡ አብ፡ . . . ጸሎት፡ በእንተ፡ ማዕሰሮሙ፡ ለአጋንንት፡ ወማዕሰሮሙ፡ ለሰይጣናት፡ መሰርያን፡ ወገባርያን፡ ኩርበት፡ አይኑት፡ ወዓይነ፡ ባርያ፡ ወሌጌዎን፡ ወገሩ፡ ዘፍጹም፡ በጽልመት፡ ፈርሃ፡ ወደንገጸ፡ ዲያብሎስ፡ ርዕዮ፡ ብሑተ፡ ልደት፡ በሥጋ፡ አምላክ፡ በሲአል፡ ሳዶር፡ አላዶር፡ . . .

2. Prayer regarding the rampart of the Cross, 29 lines; possibly a continuation of the preceding. See Grébaut, "Masqal."
በስመ፡ አብ፡ . . . መስቀል፡ መግረፊ፡ ፀር፡ መስቀል፡ መዋጌ፡ ፀር፡ መስቀል፡ ነሃቴ፡ ፀር፡ መስቀል፡ አንቅዕት፡ ለጽሙአን፡ . . .

3. Prayer of St. Susənyos and the story of his fight against Wərzəlya, the demon of infant mortality. See Worrell, "Zauberwesen" I, pp. 167–183; Basset, *Apocryphes* IV, pp. 38–42; Grébaut, "Sousneyos"; Dobberahn, *Zauberrollen*, pp. 291–95, 303–4 and 314–7.
በስመ፡ እግ"፡ ሕያው፡ ነባቢ፡ ወተናጋሪ፡ ጸሎቱ፡ ለቅዱስ፡ ሱስንዮስ፡ በእንተ፡ አሰስሎ፡ ደዊ፡ እምሕፃናት፡ . . . ወሀሎ፡ አሐዱ፡ ብእሲ፡ ዘስሙ፡ ሱስንዮስ፡ . . .

4. Prayer against illnesses caused by Barya, Legewon, and Zar, and for drowning demons, 110 lines.
በስመ፡ አብ፡ . . . ጸሎት፡ በእንተ፡ ሕማመ፡ ባርያ፡ ወሌጌዎን፡ ዛር፡ ወመስጥአጋመ፡ (sic) አጋንንት፡ ኤሰሶ፡ አሴ፡ ኤፓስ፡ አፓስ፡ ኤንክሞ፡

ካም፡ . . . θ³ˣ ዘተአመነ፡ θ²ˣ θ⁴ˣ ዘተአመነ፡ በጸሎቱ፡ ለቅዱስ፡ ሚካኤል፡ ሊቀ፡ መላዕክት፡ በጸሎታ፡ ወበእሊታ፡ . . . ታድኅነኒ፡ እመአተ፡ ወልዳ፡ ለዓመትከ፡ . . . ወበል፡ እሎንተ፡ አስማተ፡ አበይተ፡ በትሁት፡ ቃል፡ (from the Dərsanä Mika'el). . . . መስቀል፡ መግረሬ፡ ዐር፡ መስቀል፡ (as in 2 above) መስቀል፡ ኃይለነ፡ . . . አይሁድ፡ ክህዱ፡ ወነሕነሰ፡ አመነ፡ (from the daily prayer) . . . ወገጹ፡ ዘፍጹም፡ በጽልመት፡ (as in 1 above). Concluded with a magic symbol.

Miniatures and Magical Symbols:
1. Three crosses, crudely drawn.

Copied for Amätä Gäbrə'el.

EMIP MagSc 8 – Marwick Magic Scroll 3
Parchment, 185 x 9 cm, three strips sewn together, one column, no border, Gəʻəz, 20th cent.
1. Prayer of St. Susənyos against hemorrhage, Šätälay, the evil eye of Barya, and the story of his fight against Wərzəlya, the demon of infant mortality, 87 lines; cf. 7, 3.
   በስመ፡ አብ፡ . . . ጸሎት፡ በእንተ፡ ሕማም፡ ደም፡ ወሾተላይ፡ ወዓይነት፡ ባርያ፡ ወውርዝልያ፡ በስመ፡ እግ"፡ ሕያው፡ ነባቢ፡ ወተናጋሪ፡ ጸሎቱ፡ ለቅዱስ፡ ሱስንዮስ፡ በእንተ፡ አሰሰሎ፡ ደዌ፡ እምሕፃናት፡ . . .
2. Prayer with the *asmat* of Solomon that drive demons away, 15 lines.
   በስመ፡ አብ፡ . . . ጸሎት፡ በእንተ፡ አስማተ፡ ሰሎሞን፡ ሰዳዬ፡ አጋንንት፡ ሰባኬ፡ ሕገ፡ ቃራን፡ ወያሁራ፡ በሐቅለ፡ መግኑን፡ ዕልዋቁን፡ በዘረበሙ፡ ለአጋንንት፡ ወለነሀብተ፡ (sic) ሰሎሞን፡ ሎፍሐም³ˣ፡ ንምሎሽ³ˣ፡ ነዘይባር፡ (sic) ተዓሠር፡ . . .
3. Prayer for binding demons, Barya, and Legewon, 47 lines; cf. 7, 1.
   በስመ፡ አብ፡ . . . ጸሎት፡ በእንተ፡ ማእሥሮሙ፡ ለአጋንንት፡ ወለሰይጣናት፡ ባርያ፡ ወሌጌዎን፡ ወለዕብነ፡ (sic; for ወለሰብእ፡) ወቅኃሐኤል፡ ቱጅሽ፡ ተረ፡ አፈተሪ፡ አብተርኩክሙ፡ (?) ነባቢ፡ ወለነሀት፡ (sic) መጋኛ፡ ወጉሥምት፡ . . . በፈርዮን፡ ቀዛት፡ ቤዘትኩክሙ፡ ለኮልሙ፡ አጋንንት፡ . . . ኢታሕምሙኒ፡ ተመሲለክሙ፡ በንድፍት፡ ወበውግዓት፡ በፍልፀት፡ ወበቁርፀት፡ በዓይነት፡ ወበምትሐት፡ አምሐልኩክሙ፡ . . .
4. Prayer against hemorrhage, 11 lines.
   በስመ፡ አብ፡ . . . ጸሎት፡ በእንተ፡ ሕማም፡ ደም፡ አርዱማኖስ፡ ናኒማኖስ፡ አጀንራን፡ አሳዓል፡ አስማተ፡ ረቢከኒ፡ ወዘዜሚተቶር፡ ቶሮቆድ፡ አንተ፡ አስተጋባዕከሙ፡ ለአድባር፡ በኃይልከ፡ ከማሁ፡ አርግዕ፡ ወአቁም፡ ደማ፡ ወአጽንእ ፍሬሃ፡ በውስተ፡ ማኅፀና፡ . . .
5. Prayer against hemorrhage, 7 lines; cf. 4, 2.

ጸሎት: በእንተ: ሕማም: ደም: ሰንተም: ከንተም: ቀንተም: ሰንከሪም:
ሜሉስ: ደም: ዘወጽአ: እምገቦሁ: ለእግዚእን: . . . ክትር: ወአቁም: ደግ:
ለአመትከ: . . .
6. Prayer against hemorrhage, 6 lines.
ጸሎተ: ደም: ደም: ደም: ተንርነተር: (sic) ከበሳምባ: (sic) ስር: ወበስራስር:
ተመየጥ: ይብሉ: አብ: ወወልድ: . . . ደም: አመትከ: . . .
7. Prayer against hemorrhage, 9 lines.
ጸሎት: በእንተ: ሕማም: ደም: ሊስ:[3x] አፍሊፎሮስ:[3x] ሜሉስ: መልዮስ:[3x]
መላልዮስ: ዘእርግዕ: (sic) ወአቁም: ደግ: . . .
8. Prayer against illnesses caused by the evil eye, Barya, Mäggäñña, colic, Däsk, and Gudale, 31 lines.
በስም: አብ: . . . ጸሎት: በእንተ: ሕማም: ዓይነት: ባርያ: ወጽላ: ወጊ:
መጋኛ: ወቁርዐት: ደስክ: ወጉዳሌ: ወያጸልም: አዕይምተ: ወያብሐንን:
በሀለመ: ሌሊት: ወመዓልት: አምሕለከ: ወአዐግዘከ: በ፪ቅንዋተ: መስቀሉ:
ለእግዚእን: . . . ሳዶር: አላዶር: . . . እሉ: እሙንቱ: ማእሠሮሙ:
ለአጋንንት: ወለዓይነት: ወለቁርዐት: መጋኛ: ወጌኔ: ቀትር: ሾተላይ:
ወውርዝልያ: ነደሪ: ወቁመኛ: ወተያያ F: በሎፍሐም: ስምከ: . . . ወገጹ:
(as in 7, 1 above).

Miniatures and Magical Symbols:
1. Angel with sword and scabbard (large) below a twelve-box panel (4 x 3) with X-shape patterns.
2. *Talismanic symbol* with face in center.
3. Same

Copied for Wälätä Maryam/Yamrot.

EMIP MagSc 9 – Marwick Magic Scroll 4

Parchment, 149 x 11.5 cm, three strips sewn together, one column, border, Gəʽəz, 19th cent.
1. Prayer of St. Susənyos and the story of his fight against Wərzəlya, the demon of infant mortality, 44 lines; cf. 7, 3.
በስም: አብ: . . . በስም: እግ": ሕያው: ወተናጋሪ: ጸሎተ: ቅዱስ:
ሱስንዮስ: በእንተ: አሰስሎ: ደዌ: እምሕፃናት: . . .
2. Prayer against hemorrhage, 51 lines.
በስም: አብ: . . . ጸሎት: ዘደም: አፋሺ: አሸሿቱም: ሰፍም: ኬብዕ: ሰፍም:
ሸቱራን: ረበጥናክሙ: ለይትረጡ: (sic) ያሜሙማ: አንተ: ገብር: ሸፍሐም:
ቦሎም: ተአሡር: ከመ: ኢታውጽእ: ሕፃነ: ወደመ: እምከርሡ: ዓመትከ: . .
. ዘቀያ: ሰርከያ: ያመነሁ: . . .
በስሙ: ለአብ: በስሙ: ለወልድ: . . . ታአስ: ማስያስ: አክያስ:
አቅፎዬፎር: በስም: ሐራፒን: ሐራያንኮር: . . . በዝቃልከ: ውጉዝ:

ወበሰይፉ፡ ቃልከ፡ ስሐል፡ እሳተ፡ መለኮት፡ . . . መስቀል፡ መግረሬ፡ ፀር፡ መስቀል፡ (as in Strelcyn, *Prières*, p. 228–230; Six, *Handschriften*, 19, 1, 1, pp. 96–7; Six, "Zaubertexte," p. 313, and continued as in 7, 2 above) .

3. Prayer for binding demons, 17 lines.
በስመ፡ አብ፡ . . . ጸሎት፡ በእንተ፡ ማእሠሮሙ፡ ለአጋንንት፡ አሕያ፡ ሸራሕያ፡ አልሻዳይ፡ አልመክኑን፡ አልፉ፡ ወአ፡ ኢየሱስ፡ . . . ዘበመስቀልከ፡ አፅራእከ፡ ግብሮ፡ ለዲያብሎስ፡ ከማሁ፡ . . . ሕማም፡ ባርያ፡ ወለጌዎን፡ ወሥራይ፡ (sic) ደስክ፡ ወጉዳሌ፡ ቀኑርዐት፡ ወፍልዐት፡ ውግዐት፡ ወምትዐት፡ ዓይነተ፡ ባርያ፡ ቡዳ፡ ወነሀቢ፡ ፌራ፡ ወንዳድ፡ ድድቅ፡ ወጋኔነ፡ ቀትር፡ አርኑቅ፡ እምላእለ፡ . . . ወገጹ፡ ዘፍጹም፡ በጽልመት፡ (as in 7, 1 above; but see also Dobberahn, *Zauberrollen*, p. 285).

4. Prayer against filthy Legewon, 14 lines; cf. Strelcyn, *Manchester*, 29, 3, p. 77; Six, *Handschriften*, 15, 1, 2, p. 88; Six, "Zaubertexte," p. 321.
ጸሎት፡ በእንተ፡ ለጌዎን፡ ርኩስ፡ ዘይሰልብ፡ ልበ፡ ስንሰብእ፡ (sic) ወያጻልም፡ አእንተ፡ (sic) ... አምሕለከ፡ ወአወግዘከ፡ በ፫አስማት፡ ወበ፮መለኮት፡ ወበ፯ንዋተ፡ መስቀሉ፡ . . . ሳዶር፡ . . . በእሎንተ፡ (sic) አስማተ፡ (sic) አድናና፡ እምኮሎን፡ ደዊያት፡ . . .

5. The Net of Solomon for catching demons as prayer against Barya and Legewon, 25 lines; cf. Euringer, "Das Netz," ZS, vol. 6 (1928), pp. 76–100, 300–314, and vol.7 (1928), pp. 86–85; and Löfgren, "Wandamulette," pp. 109–116.
በስመ፡ አብ፡ . . . ጸሎት፡ በእንተ፡ ባርያ፡ ወለጊዎን፡ መርበብተ፡ ሰሎሞን፡ ዘከመ፡ ረበሞ፡ ለአጋንንት፡ ከመ፡ መርበብተ፡ ዓሣ፡ ዘባህር፡ ወመሳጤ፡ እምኔሁ፡ ወኢኮነ፡ ርእየቱ፡ ከመ፡ ርእየተ፡ ሰብእ፡ . . . የገጸ፡ ሰብእ፡ የገጸ፡ እንስሳ፡ የገጸ፡ አንበሳ፡ የገጸ፡ ላህም፡ የገጸ፡ አድግ፡ የገጸ፡ አፍራስ፡ የገጸ፡ ሆባይ፡ የገጸ፡ ሐለስትዮ፡ የገጸ፡ ከልብ፡ . . . እንዘ፡ ይብል፡ ሎፍሐም፡[3x] አዮሮስናዊ፡[3x] አውጽአ፡ ልሳኖ፡ . . . ወካዕበ፡ ይቤ፡ በስመ፡ አብ፡ . . . አአትብ፡ ገጽየ፡ . . .

6. Prayer against Barya and Legewon, 33 lines.
በስመ፡ አብ፡ . . . ጸሎት፡ በእንተ፡ ባርያ፡ ወለጌዎን፡ ዘይስልብ፡ ልበ፡ ሰብእ፡ ጀዘከመለህ፡ አንሰሉ፡ ኤላ፡ መዋጢኖ[፡]ኪን፡ አድብራኤል፡ ሰርቴን፡ . . . ወይቤ፡ አለፉ፡ አልፍ፡ ወለሐቀሐልዮት፡ ተቾቾ ተቾ ቱ ቾ ቾ . . . ጨዋሸጨ፡[4x] ጋፈረF፡ F ጋፈረF፡ ጋፈረF፡ ለከፋውራትን፡ . . . አጀርማድር፡ እምቤተ፡ አቡሁ፡ ወእሙ፡ አድጋና፡ እምባርያ፡ ወለጌዎን፡ ጨዋትኩካኤል፡

Miniatures and Magical Symbols:
1. Angel with sword and scabbard.
2. Talismanic symbol with face in center.

3. Same.
4. Same.
Copied for Wätättä Ḥəywät.

EMIP MagSc 10 – Marwick Magic Scroll 5
Parchment, 115 x 8 cm, three strips sewn together, one column, border, Gə'əz, 20th cent.
1. Prayer against the evil eye, the evil eye of Barya, Legewon, Zar and Təgrida, 22 lines.
በስመ፡ አብ፡ . . . ጸሎት፡ በእንተ፡ ሕማመ፡ አነት፡ (sic) ወአነጥላኛ፡ (sic) ወአናባርያ፡ (sic) ወሌጌዎን፡ ዛር፡ ወቄራኛ፡ ወ፡ ወትግሪዳ፡ ወነወርቅ፡ (sic) ወበትግ፡ (sic) በስሙ፡ ለአብ፡ መናቴር ፡ . . . ሳዶር፡ አላዶር፡ . . . በጄ፡ ቅንዋተ፡ መስቀሉ፡ . . . እቀብ፡ ወአድሕን፡ ቅሕማመ[፡] አነባርያ፡ (sic) ወሌጌዎን፡ ዛር፡ ወትግሪዳ፡ ወነወርቅ፡ (sic) ቡዳ፡ ወቀሙመኛ፡ መነሽ፡ (sic) ወተዛዋሪ፡ ምቀኛ፡ ወተንኮለኛ፡ አነጥላ፡ (sic) ወ፡ (sic) ወግርጋሪ፡ . . .
2. Prayer against illnesses caused by Barya and Legewon, 25 lines.
በስመ፡ አብ፡ . . . ጸሎት፡ በእንተ፡ ሕማመ[፡] ባርያ[፡] ወሌጌያን፡ አአትብ፡ ገጽየ፡ ወ፡ (sic) ካበትምርተ፡ (sic) መስቀል፡ በስመ፡ አብ፡ . . . አአትብ፡ አባልየ፡ ሕፅሪኒ፡ በሐፀመስቀልክ፡ (sic) ከልለኒ፡ . . . ንሲራን፡ ወጢጢባሳሳን፡ ክሽጁን፡ . . .
3. Prayer of St. Susənyos and the story of his fight against Wərzəlya, the demon of infant mortality.
በስመ፡ አብ፡ . . . ጸሎት፡ በስመ፡ እግ"፡ ሕያው፡ ነባቢ፡ ወተናጋሪ፡ ⌐ቅዱስሱን ዮስ፡ (sic) በእንተ፡ አሰስሎ፡ ደዌ፡ እም ሕፃናት፡ . . . ወሀሎ፡ አሐዱ፡ ብእሲ፡ ዘስሙ፡ ሱስንዮስ፡ . . .
4. Prayer for binding demons and the evil hand, 18; cf. 3, 5.
በስመ፡ አብ፡ . . . ጸሎት፡ በእንተ፡ ማእሰረ፡ አጋንንት፡ እኩያን፡ ወሰብአመሰርያን፡ (sic) ወሰይጣናት፡ ዝልጉሣን፡ ወያጸልሙ፡ አእይንት፡ ወያመጽኡ፡ (sic) ጽላሎት፡ ወአመልኩሐክሙ፡ ወአውገዝኩክሙ፡ . . .

Miniatures and Magical Symbols:
1. Ornate cross (large).
2. Eight-box panel (2 x 4) with triangle patterns.
3. Two cross-shaped patterns with circles on each point and two circles between.

Copied with insufficient care for Yälfne/Wälättä Maryam.

EMIP MagSc 11 – Marwick Magic Scroll 6
Parchment, 142 x 9 cm, three strips sewn together, one column, border, Gə'əz, 20th cent.

1. Prayer for binding Satan (*ḫaṭi'at* for *säyṭanat*) and against the evil eye of Zar, 18 lines. በስም፡ አብ፡ . . . ጸሎት፡ በእንተ፡ ማዕሠረ፡ ሐጢአት፡ (sic) ጸሎት፡ በእንተ፡ አይን፡ ዘርወአይን፡ (sic) ርቅ፡ (sic) ቀዳሚሁ·ቃል፡ (sic) ውእቱ፡ ቀል፡ (sic) ወንጌል፡ ዘዮሐንስወሀሎ (sic) አፀብእሲ፡ ቀዳሚሁ፡ ቃል፡ ውእቱ፡ ቃል፡ (copied carelessly from John 1:1–5).
2. Prayer against illnesses caused by Barya, Legewon, and the evil eye of Šotälay: the story of the fight of St. Susǝnyos against Wǝrzǝlya, the demon of infant mortality. Prayer: against illnesses caused by Barya, Legewon, and the evil eye of Šotälay"
በስም፡ አብ፡ . . . ጸሎት፡ በእንተ፡ ሕማመ፡ ባርያ፡ ወሌጌዎን፡ ወአይን፡ ሶተላይ፡ (sic) ጸሎቱ፡ ወስእለተ፡ (sic) ለቅዱስ፡ ሱስንዮስ፡ በስም፡ እግ"፡ አብ፡ ሕያው፡ ነባቢ ወተናጋሪ፡ ጸሎቱ፡ ወበረከቱ፡ ለቅዱስ፡ ሱስንዮስ፡ በእንተ፡ አስስሎ፡ ደውየ፡ (sic) እምሕጻናት፡ . . .
3. Prayer for binding demons, and for driving Satan, 30 lines. ስም፡ አብ፡ . . . ጸሎት፡ በእንተ፡ ማእሠሮሙ፡ ለአጋንንት፡ ወበእንተ፡ ሰደዱሙ፡ (sic) ለሰይጣናት፡ ሕቡዕ፡ ስሙ፡ ለእግ" አስፉ፡ (sic) ኤኬስ፡ ኢ.በንኸ፡ . . . ኤ.ጋ፡ ኤ.ፖ.ስ፡ አውጻአ፡ (sic) ወኩሎ ዘይጸሐር፡ (sic) ለዝንቱ፡ አስማት፡ ወኢይነብሮ፡ (sic) ውስተ፡ መካን፡ ሕሱም፡ . . . (a corrupt text).

Miniatures and Magical Symbols:
1. Nine-box panel (3 x 3) with face in center box and X-shaped patterns in the rest.
2. Same.
3. Nine-box panel (3 x 3) with X-shaped patterns in all the boxes.
4. Same.

Copied corruptly for Q^{w}adi/Wälättä Iyyäsus.

EMIP MagSc 12 – Marwick Magic Scroll 7

Parchment, 199 x 9.5 cm, four strips sewn together, one column, border of wavy line, Gǝ'ǝz, early 20th cent.

1. Prayer for drowning demons, and against illnesses caused by Barya, Qumäñña, the eye of Šanqǝlla, Däbas, Zar, Täzawarit, Šotälay, and others, 40 lines.
ስም፡ አብ፡ . . . ጸሎት በእንተ፡ መስጥመ፡ ለአጋንት፡ ባርያ፡ ወዓይነ፡ ጽላ፡ ቋመኛ፡ ወዓይነ፡ ሻንቅላ፡ ወዓይነ፡ ወርቅ፡ ወደ ባስ፡ (sic) ዛር፡ ወተዛዋሪት፡ ደም፡ ወሾተላይ፡ ነቲጣይ፡ ወአሲደኛ፡ ዛር፡ ወቸንፈር፡ ወኩሎሙም፡ መናፍስተ፡ ርኩሳን፡ ወታሰድዶሙ፡ አጋንት፡ በሰይፈ፡ ሥላሴ፡ ተሰደዱ፡ (follored by Mark 1:23–28) . . . በዝ፡ ቃለ፡ ወንጌልከ፡ ቅዱስ፡ አድገና፡ . . .

2. Prayer for drowning demons, against Barya, Čänäfär, the noontime demon, for binding and terrorizing demons, and against Barya and the noontime demon, 37 lines.
ስመ፡ አብ፡ . . . ጸሎት፡ በእንተ፡ መስጥም፡ ለአጋንት፡ (sic) ባርያ፡ ወቸንፈር፡ (sic) ወጋኔነ፡ ቀትር፡ ጸሎት፡ በእንተ፡ ማዕሠሮሙ፡ ወመደንግጾሙ፡ ለአጋንት፡ ባርያ፡ ወጋኔነ፡ ቀትር፡ ተሰቅለ፡ ወሐመ፡ ዘእንበ፡ ኃጢአት፡ ተረግዘ፡ ገቦሁ፡ ዘእንበለ፡ ደዌ፡ . . . በኃይለ፡ መስቀልከ፡ አድኅነ፡ . . .

3. Prayer against demons and for undoing charm, 46 lines.
ስመ፡ አብ፡ . . . ጸሎት፡ በእንተ፡ መፍትሔ፡ ለአጋንት፡ (sic) ወመፍትሔ፡ ሥራይ፡ (John 1:1–5) ዘየአምን፡ በወልድ፡ ቦሕይወት፡ ዘለዓለም፡ አእግዚአ፡ በቃለ፡ ወንጌልከ፡ አድኅነ፡ እምህማም፡ ዓይነ፡ ጽላ፡ ወዓይነ፡ ወርቅ፡ ወሾተላይ፡ ወጋላ፡ ዛር፡ ወውርዛ፡ ወቸንፈር፡ (sic) ወኩሎሙ፡ መናፍስተ፡ ርኩሳን፡ አድኅነ፡ ለአመትከ፡ አድኅነ፡ እምህማም፡ ባርያ፡ ወሌጌዎን፡ ወዓይነ፡ ጽላ፡ ወቁራኛ፡ ቡዳ፡ ወቁመኛ፡ ወመጋኛ፡ ተላዋሽ፡ ወዓይነት፡ ወዓይነ፡ ወርቅ፡ ደስክ፡ ወጉዳሌ፡ ወቁመኛ፡ ወፍልጠት፡ ወፈንጻያ፡ ወፈራ፡ ወቁርጥማን፡ ወእራስ፡ ፍልጠት፡ ወሾተላይ፡ ወኩሎሙ፡ መናፍስተ፡ ርኩሳን፡ አድኅነ፡ ለአመትከ፡ . . .

4. Prayer against a piercing pain on the side and Qumäñña, 74 lines; cf. 6, 4, but possibly also Six, *Handschriften*, 33, b, 12, 13a, p. 124.
በስመ፡ አብ፡ . . . ጸሎት፡ በእንተ፡ በእንተ፡ (sic) ሐማም፡ ቁመኛ፡ ሐማግ፡ ውግአት፡ ምድምያስ፡[7x] የሐቂ፡[6x] የሐብራስቂ፡[6x] በስመ፡ አድኅንኩ፡ ለወልደ፡ ከራሳቂ፡ (sic) አውላላኤል፡[6x] . . . አአብዪድ፡ አብዪድ፡ ምሐመድ፡ አላሁማግ፡ አላሁማግ፡ አላሁ፡ አላሁማግ፡ ይብልያኤል፡ . . . ስድዶሙ፡ ለአጋንት፡ ከመ፡ ኢትረቡ፡ አጋንት፡ ዛር፡ ወውላጄ፡ ወሾተላይ፡ ወዓይነ፡ ጥላ፡ ወግርጋር፡ ዛር፡ ወቸንፈር፡ ወኩሎሙ፡ መናፍስተ፡ ርኩሳን፡ ከመ፡ ኢትቅትሎሙ፡ ለሕፃናት፡ ከመ፡ ኢትቅረቡ፡ ኀበ፡ ነፍሳ፡ ወሥጋሃ፡ . . .

5. Prayer against illnesses caused by Šotälay, Galla, and Zar, 30 lines; possibly related to Six, *Handschriften*, 14, b, 3, p. 98.
በስመ፡ አብ፡ . . . ጸሎት፡ በእንተ፡ ሐማም፡ ሾተላይ፡ ወጋላ፡ ዛር፡ አስማቲሆሙ፡ ለ፲ወ፪ ነቢያት፡ ፲ወ፪ ሐዋርያት፡ እሉ፡ እሙንቱ፡ ራኩን፡ ራፍን፡ ጺስ፡ አፍሊስ፡ . . . በኃይለ፡ ዝንቱ፡ አስማቲከ፡ አድኅነ፡ እምህማም፡ አየረ፡ አጋንት፡ ወባርያ፡ ወኩሎሙ፡ መናፍስተ፡ ርኩሳን፡ ወሾተላይ፡ ዳሙን፡ ዛር፡ ውላጄ፡ ወቸንፈር፡ ጋላ፡ አምሐራ፡ ከመ፡ ኢትቅረቡ፡ ኀበ፡ ነፍሳ፡ ወሥጋሃ፡ . . .

Miniatures and Magical Symbols:
1. Angel with sword and holding handkerchief in other hand; two figures behind.
2. Panel with angel-wing (?) patterns.

3. Panel with four triangular spaces, each with the head (and wings of an angel?). All the heads face outward from the center, i.e., the top head appears upside down, the left head appears 90 degrees clockwise, etc. Copied for Amätä Mika'el/Wäynitu Fä(n)taye.

EMIP MagSc 13 – Marwick Magic Scroll 8
Parchment, 199 x 9.5 cm, three strips sewn together, one column, border, Gəʿəz, 19th cent.

1. Prayer for binding demons, and for terrorizing satans the eye of the filthy Legewon, 27 lines.
በስመ፡ አብ፡ . . . ጸሎት በእንተ፡ ማዕሠረ፡ አጋንንት፡ ወመደንግፀ፡ ሰይጣናት፡ ወመደንግፀ፡ ዓይነ፡ ጥላ፡ ወዓይነ፡ ሌጌዎን፡ ርኩስ፡ ዘይሰልብ፡ ልቡ፡ ሰብእ፡ ወያጸልም፡ አእይንተ፡ ወይመጽእ፡ ከመ፡ ጽላሎት፡ ወሕል(ም፡) አምሕለከ፡ ወአዐግዘከ፡ በእግ" አብ፡ ወበክርስቶስ፡ ወልድ፡ . . . ወበእግዝእትነ፡ ማርያም፡ . . . በሚካኤል፡ ወገብርኤል፡ . . . ወበ፯ንዋተ፡ መስቀሉ፡ ለእግዚእን፡ ኢየሱስ፡ ክርስቶስ፡ ዘውእቶሙ፡ ሳዶር፡ አላዶር፡ ዳናት፡ አዴራ፡ ሮዳስ፡ ዘበመ፡ ለስሐ፡ ሕምዙ፡ ለሞት፡ ወተቀጥቀጠ ኃይለ፡ ሰይጣን፡ ከማሁ፡ ይልሳሕ፡ ኅምዞሙ፡ ወይትቀጥቀጥ፡ ኃይሎሙ፡ . . .

2. Prayer of St. Susənyos and the story of his fight against Wərzəlya, the demon of infant mortality; cf. 7, 3.
በስመ፡ እግ" ሕያው፡ ነባቢ፡ ወተናጋሪ፡ ጸሎት፡ ዘዱስ፡ ሱስንዮስ፡ በእንተ፡ አሰስሎ፡ ደዌ፡ እምሕፃናት፡ . . . ወሀሎ፡ አሐዱ፡ ብእሲ፡ ዘስሙ፡ ሱስንዮስ፡ . . .

ጸሎተ፡ ነድራ፡ ወእንዘ፡ የ(ጎ)ልፍ፡ እግዚእነ፡ ውስተ፡ (ባሕ)ረ፡ ጥብርያዶስ፡ . . .

3. The Net of Solomon for catching demons as prayer against the evil eye of Barya, 29 lines.
ጸሎት፡ በእንተ፡ ሕማመ፡ ዓይነ፡ ባርያ፡ ዘእንበለ፡ መጥባሕት ዘይበልዕ፡ ሥጋ፡ . . . ወዘእንበለ፡ ጽዋዕ፡ ዘይሰቲ፡ ደመ፡ ማዕሠረ፡ አጋንት፡ ዘበመ፡ ረበቦሙ፡ ለአጋንት፡ ከመ፡ መርበብተ፡ አሳ፡ ዘውስተ፡ ባሕር፡ እንዘ፡ ይብል፡ ሰዱቃኤል፡[3x] ኢያታኤል፡[3x] . . . አስግተ፡ ሰሎሞን፡ ወትሑር፡ ሸሸት፡ አጠላት፡ ብርስግሐል፡ ስሙ፡ ለፈጣሬ፡ አለማት፡ ኢየሱስ፡ ክርስቶስ፡ ለጁጅ፡ ወለጁጅ፡ ለ(?) ወለነገሥታተ፡ አጋንንት፡ አምሕልኩክሙ፡ በሰይፈ፡ ቃሉ፡ ለመለኮት፡ ዝንቱ፡ ደም፡ ይርገዕ፡ ሕፃኑ፡ እስከ፡ አመ፡ ይትወለድ፡ በዕድሜሁ፡ ለዓመትክ፡ . . . ባርያ፡ ቀይሓን፡ ወባርያ፡ ጸሊማን፡ ወሰብአ፡ መሠርያን፡ አሠርኩክሙ፡ ወአውግዘኩክሙ፡ በ፫ዋ ሰናስለ እሳት፡ . . . ከመ፡ ኢትቅርቡ፡ . . .

4. Prayer of St. Susənyos against hemorrhage, 11 lines.

ጸሎት፡ በእንተ፡ ሕማመ፡ ደም፡ ዘቅዱስ፡ ሱስንዮስ፡ ሠየ፡³ˣ ሰሐ፡³ˣ ሶቤ . . .
ሊስ፡³ˣ አፍሊስ፡³ˣ አፍለስኪስ፡³ˣ አቅሊስ፡³ˣ ዘአርጋዕከ፡ ኃይለ፡ በረድ፡ ወነፋስ፡
ከማሁ፡ . . .

5. Prayer against a piercing pain and rheumatism, 9 lines; cf. 6, 4; 12, 4;
and Dobberahn, *Zauberrollen*, p. 288.
ጸሎት፡ በእንተ፡ ሕማመ፡ ውግዓት፡ ወቁርጥማት፡ ምድምያስ፡⁷ˣ የሐቂ፡³ˣ
የሐብረስቂ፡³ˣ በከመ፡ አድኅንኮ፡ ለወልደ፡ ከራስቂ፡ ከማሁ፡ . . .

6. Prayer against colic, 8 lines.
ጸሎት፡ በእንተ፡ ሕማመ፡ ቀርጻት፡ ቄጼቤ፡³ˣ ቄፌኑ፡³ˣ ብያክ፡²ˣ ሞሊ፡³ˣ
መሞሊ፡³ˣ ዘአርጋዕከ፡ ኃይለ፡ በረድ፡ ወነፋስ፡ . . .

7. Greeting to Phanuel as prayer for binding demons, incomplete at the end,
54 lines; see Strelcyn, *British Library*, 81, 4, p. 128. The greeting is the
first stanza of is Image, መልክአ፡ ፋኑኤል፡ ድርሳነ፡ ራጉኤል፡ ወድርሳነ፡
ፋኑኤል፡ መልክአ፡ ራጉኤል፡ ወመልክአ፡ ፋኑኤል፡ Täsfa Press 1964 EC, p.
60.
ጸሎት በእንተ፡ ማዕሠረ፡ አጋንንት፡ ሰላም፡ ለተፈጥሮትከ፡ ምስለ፡ መላእክት
ንቡረ፡ . . .

Miniatures and Magical Symbols:
1. Angel.
2. Seventeen-box panel. There is a top and bottom row of four boxes (4 x 1)
with X-shaped patterns. The nine boxes in between are in a 3 x 3 layout.
A face is in the center box. X-shaped patterns are in boxes 2, 4, 6, and 8.
Eyes are in boxes 1, 3, 7, and 9.

Copied carefully for Wälättä Iyyäsus.

EMIP MagSc 14 – Marwick Magic Scroll 9
Parchment, 188.5 x 7.5 cm, three strips sewn together, one column, double
border, Gəʻəz, 19th cent.

1. Prayer against the evil eye of Barya Legewon and all filthy spirits, 37
lines; cf. 5, 3.
በስመ፡ አብ፡ . . . ጸሎት፡ በእንተ፡ ዓይነ፡ ባርያ፡ ወሌጌዎን፡ ወኩሎሙ፡
አጋንንት፡ ርኩሳን፡ በስመ፡ ለአብ፡ በስመ፡ ለወልድ፡ በስመ፡ ለመንፈስ፡
ቅዱስ፡ ታአስ፡ አዝየስ፡ ወስምክያስ፡ ኤቅዴፍርር፡ በስመ፡ ወበዕንተ፡ ሐውረ፡
መስቀል፡ ዘጸሐፈ፡ ኤርምያስ፡ ነቢይ፡ ውስተ፡ ኩኩሕ፡ ንበ፡ ታቦተ፡ በይ፡
(sic).

2. Prayer against hemorrhage, 38 lines; cf. 4, 2; 4, 4; 8, 4.
ጸሎት፡ በእንተ፡ ሕማመ፡ ደም፡ ሊስ፡ አፍሊስ፡ ሜሎስ፡ መሊስ፡ መላልዮስ፡ .
. . ⌐ሰተም፡ ከተም፡³ˣ ⌐መሊሃ፡ እልመሊሃ፡³ˣ በዝ፡ ቃል፡ አርጎዕ፡ ደማ፡ . . .
ወአንከረም፡ ዘወጽአ፡ ደም፡ እምገቦሁ፡ ለክርስቶስ፡ . . .

Catalogue of the Scrolls of Ethiopian Spiritual Healing · 285

3. Greeting to Phanuel, driver of demons, 59 lines; cf. 6, 3.
ሰላም፡ ለከ፡ ሰዳዴ፡ አጋንንት፡ ፋኑኤል፡ ለእግ" እምጽርሐ፡ . . .

Miniatures and Magical Symbols:
1. Figure (angel?) standing (large).
2. Three small designs at the end of the scroll.

Copied for Asnaqäy/Amätä Maryam.

EMIP MagSc 15 – Marwick Magic Scroll 10

Parchment, 198.5 x 9.5 cm, three strips sewn together, one column, colored border, Gəʽəz, 19th cent.

1. Prayer for cleansing sin, 42 lines.
በስመ፡ አብ፡ . . . ጸሎት፡ መንጽሔ፡ ኃጢአት፡ ወመድኃኒተ፡ ሥጋ፡ ወነፍስ፡ ወንጌል፡ ዘማቴዎስ፡ መስደዴ፡ አጋንንት፡ ወሕማም፡ ባርያ፡ ወለ (sic, followed by Matt 8:28–34) በዝንተ፡ (sic) ቃለ፡ ወንጌል፡ ተዓሥሩ፡ አጋንንት፡ ወሰይጣናት፡ ዓይነ፡ ዛር፡ ወተዛዋሪ፡ ወዓይነ፡ ጥላ፡ ተቀራሪ፡ (sic) ወእምኩሉ፡ ዓይነ፡ ጸላኢ፡ ዕቀብ፡ ወአድኅን፡ . . .

2. Prayer against illnesses caused by Barya, Legewon, Zar, and Mäggäñña other illnesses, and for binding demons, 50 lines; cf. 8, 8.
በስመ፡ አብ፡ . . . ጸሎት፡ በእንተ፡ ባርያ፡ ወሌጌዎን፡ አይነ፡ ጥላ፡ ወዛር፡ መጋኛ፡ ወጉሥምት፡ ፍልፀት፡ ወቁርፀት፡ ቁርጥማት፡ ምትዓት፡ ወጽፍዓት፡ ዓይነ፡ ባርያ፡ ወማዕሡረ፡ አጋንንት፡ ዘይሰልቡ፡ ልብ፡ ሰብእ፡ ወያጸልም፡ (sic) አእይንተ፡ ከመ፡ ጽላሎት፡ ወያበሕንኑ፡ በሕልመል፡ (sic) ሌሊት፡ በስመ፡ እግ"፡ ኢያዝሐጥ፡ ⌐ሉፍሐም፡ ዕሥር፡⌐[3x] ሉፍሐም፡ ኢያዝሐጥ፡ ሉፍሐም፡ ዕሥር፡ በማዕሡረ፡ ዕደ፡ አጋንን፡ እደ፡ አጋንንት፡ እደ፡ ሌጌዎን፡ ሐራብድው፡ ሐራባFርርት፡ . . . ወገጹ፡ ዘፍጹም፡ በጽልመት፡ (as in 7, 1 above).

3. Prayer of St. Susənyos for binding demons, Mäggäñña, Šotälay, Buda, Qumäñña and different kinds of illnesses, and the story of his fight against Wərzəlya, the demon of infant mortality; cf. 7, 3.
በስመ፡ አብ፡ . . . ጸሎት፡ በእንተ፡ ማዕሡረ፡ አጋንንት፡ ወመጋኛ፡ ወጉሥምት፡ ፌራ፡ ወንዳድ፡ ዓይነት፡ ፍልፀት፡ ወቁርፀት፡ ቁርጥማት፡ ዛር፡ ደጋሚ፡ ወረጋሚ፡ ወሾተላይ፡ ቡዳ፡ ወቁመ[ኛ፡] በስመ፡ እግ" ሕያው፡ ነባቢ፡.
. .
በስመ፡ አብ፡ . . . እግ"፡ ዕጉሥ፡ ወንጉሥ፡ ዘፈኖከ፡ ላቲ፡ ⌐ወჃመላእክተ፡ ብርሃን፡ ከመ፡ ታርግበ፡ ፍሬ፡ ማኅፀና፡ ወውኅዘተ፡ ደማ፡ . . .

Miniatures and Magical Symbols:
1. Ornate cross.
2. Angel standing.

3. Talismanic symbol with face in center below 3 x 1 panel with X patterns and above another 3 x 1 panel with X patterns. Below these are two more boxes with X patterns and text.
Copied for Wälättä Sämaʿt.

EMIP MagSc 16 – Marwick Magic Scroll 11

Parchment, 176.5 x 10.2 cm, three strips sewn together, one column, colored double border, Gəʿəz, 18th cent.

1. Prayer of St. Susənyos and the story of his fight against Wərzəlya, the demon of infant mortality; cf. 7, 3.
በስመ፡ እግ"፡ ሕያው፡ ፈጣሪ፡ ነባቢ፡ ወተናጋሪ፡ ጸሎቱ፡ ለቅዱስ፡ ሱስንዮስ፡ በእንተ፡ አሰሰሎ፡ ደዌ፡ እምሕፃናት፡ . . . ወሀሎ፡ አሐዱ፡ ብእሲ፡ ዘስሙ፡ ሱስንዮስ፡ . . .

2. Prayer against Barya and Legewon, 19 lines; cf. 3, 5; 8, 8; 17, 6.
ጸሎት፡ በእንተ፡ ባርያ፡ ወሌጌዎን፡ ዘይሰልብ፡ ልብ፡ ሰብእ፡ ወይመጽእ፡ ከመ፡ ጽላሎት፡ ወሕልም፡ አምሕለክ፡ በ፪መለኮት፡ ወበ፫አካላት፡ ወበ፭ቅንዋተ፡ መስቀሉ፡ ለእግዚእነ፡ . . . ሳዶር፡ አላዶር፡ . . . እሉ፡ እሙንቱ፡

3. Prayer against the demon Šotolawi who causes infant mortality, 24 lines; Six, *Handschriften*, 20, 1, 2a, p. 98; Six, "Zaubertexte," p. 312.
በስመ፡ አብ፡ . . . ጸሎት፡ በእንተ፡ ሕማሙ፡ ሾቶላዊ፡ አእንተ፡ ሾቶላዊ፡ ዘትቀትል፡ ሕፃናተ፡ እንዘ፡ ትጐጸጉጽ፡ ከርሡ፡ ወትፈነቅል፡ አዕፅምተ፡ ወትጠዊ፡ አጋዕተ፡ አምሐልኩከ፡ . . . ወካዕበ፡ አሰርኩከ፡ አእንተ፡ ሾቶላዊ፡ በዝቱ አስማት፡ መንጆን፡ መቃጆን፡ ፈታጆን፡ . . . ፈውስ፡ ወመሐር፡ በኃይለ፡ ዝንቱ፡ አስማት፡ አርሐቆ፡ ወስድዶ፡ ለዝንቱ፡ ሕማም፡ ቆሌ፡ ዛር፡ ተዛዛሪ፡ ወጋኔን፡ ተፃሪ፡ ዓይን፡ ሰብእ፡ እኩያን፡ እለ፡ ይትሜሰሉ፡ በሕማም፡ ቀርፀት፡ ወፍልፀት፡ ወቀርጥማት፡ ወሕማም፡ ውግዓት፡ ወቀርፀት፡ ወቀርጥማት፡ መንገኛ፡ (sic) . . . አድናና . . .

4. Prayer against the evil eye and for binding demons that Alexander uttered before Gog and Magog, 30 lines; cf. Six, *Handschriften*, 31, 1, 2, p. 117.
በስመ፡ አብ፡ . . . ጸሎት፡ በእንተ፡ ሕማም፡ ዓይነ፡ ጥላ፡ ወጽላ፡ ወጊ፡ ወዓይነ፡ ወርቅ፡፡ ወማዕሠሮሙ፡ ለአጋንንት፡ ዘተናገር፡ እስክንድር፡ ንጉሥ፡ በቅድመ፡ ጎግ፡ ወማጎግ፡ እንዘ፡ ይብል፡ ንፍሣጨር፡ ንጉሥ፡ አጋንንት፡ ተናጨር፡ ንጉሥ፡ ምች፡ ኖባ፡ ንጉሥ፡ ዛር፡ ተለዋፅ፡ ቆርሽ፡ ንጉሥ፡ ችነፈር፡ ጅናኤል፡ ንጉሥ፡ ብድብድ፡ ቁልጭልጭ፡ ንጉሥ፡ ፈራ፡ ጋሙራ፡ ንጉሥ፡ ትግሪዳ፡ ራውል፡ ንጉሥ፡ ፈለግ፡ ታውስ፡ ንጉሥ፡ ቀትር፡ ኖፌ፡ ንጉሥ፡ ሐመድ፡ ጨመፍሐሲ፡ ንጉሥ፡ አየር፡ ወጨሽ፡ ዶቃኤል፡ ንጉሥ፡ ውቅያኖስ፡ ኩልክሙ፡ መሠርያን፡ ዘዘግርክሙ፡ ምድረ፡ ፋቱራ፡ ረሐቀ፡ ወተሰደዱ፡ ወሰስሉ፡ በሠራዊትክሙ፡ አጋንንት፡ . . . አኸያ፡ ሸራህያ፡ . . . ሩጋል፡ ያሸኩት፡ ጋዬን፡ ዓምደ፡

ብርሃን፤ . . . አርእየኒ፤ ኃይለ፤ ግርማ፤ ⌜ንጉሡ፤ ስብሐት፤ (cf. last hymn of Tuesday's Praises of Mary) ፈጣሪ፤ ኢይርአዩ፤ ገጹየ፤ ወኢይስምዑ፤ ድምጹየ፤ ለዓመትከ፤ . . .

5. Greeting to Phanuel, as prayer against Barya and filthy Legewon, 28 lines; cf. 6, 3.
ጸሎት፤ በእንተ፤ ባርያ፤ ወሌጌዎን፤ ርኩስ፤ ዘይመጽእ፤ ከመ፤ ጽላሎት፤ ወሕልም፤ ሰላም፤ ለከ፤ ፋኑኤል፤ ሰዳዬ፤ ሰይጣናት፤ ለእግ" እምጽርሑ፤ . . .

Miniatures and Magical Symbols:
1. Angel with sword and scabbard, above a row of seven eyes.
2. Talismanic symbol (in nine-box panel) with face in center.
3. Small symbols with triangles and circles at end of scroll.

Copied for Wälättä Ḥǝywät.

EMIP MagSc 17 – Marwick Magic Scroll 12

Parchment, 173 x 10.3 cm, three strips sewn together, one column, colored double border, Gǝʽǝz, 19th cent.

1. Prayer for binding demons, Barya and Legewon, 16 legible lines; cf. 11, 1.
   . . . (the text in red ink is illegible) ወማዕሠረ፤ ሰይጣን፤ ወባርያ፤ ወሌጌዎን፤ ወጌሌ፤ ዘፀሐንስ፤ (John 1:1–5) ዘየአምን፤ በወንጌል፤ . . . በዝቃለ፤ ወንጌል፤ ዕቀቦ፤ . . .

2. Prayer for binding demons, and illnesses caused by Barya, Legewon, Däsk, Legewon, Mäggäñña, Zar, Buda, Tǝgrida, Šotolay, and Wǝrzǝlya, 21 legible lines; Six, *Handschriften*, 15, 3. 7, p. 88, Six, "Zaubertexte," p. 313.
   . . . (the text in red ink is illegible) ወማዕሠረ፤ አጋንንት፤ አብ፤ እሳት፤ ወልድ፤ እሳት፤ . . . ፩ውእቱ፤ እሳት፤ ሕይወት፤ በዝንቱ፤ አስማት፤ ዘአጽራዕከ፤ ግብር፤ ለዲያብሎስ፤ ከማሁ፤ አጽርዕ፤ ሕማመ፤ ባርያ፤ ወሌጌዎን፤ ደስክ፤ ወሌጌዎን፤ (again) ወዓይነ፤ ሰብእ፤ ዓይነ፤ አጋንንት፤ ምትሐት፤ ወጽፍዓት፤ መጋች፤ ወጉሥምት፤ ዛር፤ ወቸንፈር፤ ፈሪ፤ ወንዳድ፤ ቡዳ፤ ወትግሪዳ፤ ወሾቶላይ፤ ወውርዝልያ፤ ⌜እመሂ፤ ፍልፀት፤ ወቀርፀት፤²ˣ እመሂ፤ ውግዓት፤ ወቀርጥዓት፤ እድ፤ ወእግር፤ እመሂ፤ ደስግ፤ ባርያ፤ ወሌጌዎን፤ ወነገርጋር፤ አምሐልኩክሙ፤ ፳፻፻ (sic) ሰናስለ፤ እሳት፤ (cf. 13, 3).

3. . . . (the text in red ink is illegible) The Net of Solomon for catching demons, 22 legible lines.
   ... መርበብተ፤ ሰሎሞን፤ ሰሎጋዊ፤ አርበምን፤ አርክምን፤ ፍልቸልሚኤል፤ ፍልፋል፤ ⌜ሜሎስ፤ ገጸ፤ ፍርቃና፤²ˣ ሜሎስ፤ ጋዬን፤ ስሙ፤ ዘያደንግያሙ፤ ለአጋንንት፤ ለደስግ፤ ወለማግርት፤ ዳዊን፤ ሐርናቂ፤ . . . ዝንቱ፤ ማዕሰሮሙ፤ ለአጋንንት፤ ለባርያ፤ ወሌጌዎን፤ ለደስክ፤ ⌜ወለሌጌዎን፤ ለደስክ፤ (again)

ወለማሪት፡ ያይቀርናሃ፡ ሽርኮሽ፡ አሕርኩሽ፡ . . . አወግዘከ፡ እንተ፡ ሰይጣን፡ በፚወፚ ጸጸሳት፡ በፚ (sic) ቀሳውስት፡ በፚወፚመነኮሳት፡ በፚወፚ (sic) ዲያቆናት፡ በፚወፚ (sic) ነገሥታት፡ ተአሰር፡ ወተወገዝ፡ ከመ፡ ኢትግበር፡ ሕሱመ፡ በላዕለ፡ ገብርከ፡ ኃይለ፡ ሥላሴ፡ . . .

4. Prayer regarding the rampart of the Cross for binding demons, 30 legible lines; cf. 7, 2.
   (The first three limes in red ink are illegible) ፀር፡ መስቀል፡ መግፌሬ፡ አጋንንት፡ መስቀል፡ መዋዔ፡ ፀር፡ መስቀል፡ ነግቴ፡ ፀር፡ መስቀል፡ ቀጥቃጤ፡ ፀር፡ መስቀል፡ ሰዳዴ፡ ፀር፡ . . . ተሰቅለ፡ ሐመ፡ (cf. 12, 2.) . . . ወሰይጣን፡ ተአሰረ፡ በኃይለ፡ መስቀሉ፡ ለእግዚእን፡ . . . ከማሁ፡ ይትአሰሩ፡ ባርያ፡ ወሌጌዎን፡ አጋንንት፡ ጸዋጋን፡ ወመናፍስት፡ ርኩሳን፡ ከመ፡ ኢይቅርቡ፡ . . .

5. Greeting to Phanuel as prayer for terrorizing demons and Barya, 25 lines; cf. 6, 3; 14, 3.
   በስመ፡ አብ፡ . . . ጸሎት፡ በእንተ፡ መደንግፀ፡ አጋንንት፡ ወባርያ፡ ሰላም፡ ለከ፡ ሰዳዴ፡ አጋንንት፡ ፋኑኤል፡ ለእግ": እምጽርሐ፡ . . .

6. Prayer against filthy Legewon, 20 lines; cf. 13, 1. "
   በስመ፡ አብ፡ . . . ጸሎት፡ በእንተ፡ ሌጌዎን፡ ርኩስ፡ ዘይሰልብ፡ ልብ፡ . . . ሉፍሐም፡[3x] እስር፡ በማዕሰረ፡ ሰሎሞን፡ . . .

7. Prayer against filthy spirits, 37 lines; cf. Six, *Handschriften*, 22, 1, 1, p. 101.
   በስመ፡ አብ፡ . . . ጸሎት፡ በእንተ፡ መንፈስ፡ ርኩስ፡ አአምን፡ በአብ፡ አአምን፡ በወልድ፡ አአምን፡ በመንፈስ፡ ቅዱስ፡ በ፬አካላት፡ ወበ፮መለኮት፡ ከመ፡ ኢትቅርበኒ፡ ወኢትልክፈኒ፡ አንተ፡ ጋኔን፡ ይልሳሕ፡ ሕምዘከ፡ ወይትቀጥቀጥ፡ አእጽምቲከ፡ በዝንቱ፡ አስማተ፡ ሔማጅ፡[3x] ...ፎሎጅ፡[3x] አምሐልኩከ፡ . . . ካን፡ ብርኻን፡ ለሸድቃን፡ . . . ኢየሱስ፡ ክርስቶስ፡ ወልደ፡ እግ" ሕያው፡ በአብ፡ አስቆሮታዊ፡ ነበልባለ፡ እሳት፡ ከመ፡ ይጥፍኡ፡ ኩሎሙ፡ መናፍስት፡ ርኩሳን፡ ባርያ፡ ጸሊማን፡ ወባርያ፡ ቀይሐን፡ ደስክ፡ ወሌጌዎን፡ መጋኛ፡ ወጉሥምት፡ ዓይነት፡ ወውግአት፡ ፍልፀት፡ ወቁርፀት፡ ምታት፡ ወጽፍአት፡ ምት፡ ወተላዋሽ፡ ፌራ፡ ወንዳድ፡ ግብጥ፡ ወዛርት፡ መዋቂ፡ ወነቀጥቃጥ፡ ሾተላይ፡ ወውርዝልያ፡ ወቁርጥማተ፡ እድ፡ ወእግር፡ ሐቄ፡ ወዘገን፡ ወኮሉ፡ አባለ፡ ሥጋ፡ ቡዳ፡ ወነሀቢ፡ ወበዓለ፡ ግብር፡ ወጠበብት፡ ሸንፈር፡ ወነገርጋር፡ ድድቅ፡ ወጋኔ፡ ቀትር፡ ጅን፡ ወውላጅ፡ አምኃልኩሙ፡ . . .

8. Prayer against the evil eye, 20 lines; cf. Strelcyn, *Prières*, p. 4.
   በስመ፡ አብ፡ . . . ጸሎት፡ በእንተ፡ ሐጋም፡ ዓይነት፡ ውፃዕ፡ በጸሊም፡ ወበቀይሐ፡ ዮሴፍ፡ በከመ፡ ወጽአ፡ እምሕሱም፡ ፌአንታ፡ አበሱን፡ ዘበሹን፡ ስቡን፡ ስቡሐን፡ ሐፉራን፡ መራዛን፡ አርጽቡ፡ ጤቃ፡ ቤቃ፡ ሐናጽኤል፡ ካፍ፡ . . . ውፃዕ፡ በጸሊም፡ ወበቀይሐ፡ አንተ፡ ሐጋም፡ ዓይነት፡ ወዓይነ፡ እስላም፡ ወክርስቲያን፡ ዓይነ፡ ሕዝባዊ፡ ወዓይነ፡ ኩሉ፡ ፍጥረት፡ ፺ወ፡ ወተሰደዱ፡

ኩልክሙ፡ አጋንንት፡ ባርያ፡ ወሰይጣናት፡ አምኃልኩክሙ፡ ወአውገዝኩክሙ፡ ከመ፡ ኢትቅረቡ፡ ኀበ፡ ነፍሱ፡ ወሥጋሁ፡ ለገብረ፡ እግ"፡ . . .

Miniatures and Magical Symbols:
1. Angel with sword and scabbard.
2. Twelve-box panel (3 x 4): top nine boxes contain an talismanic symbol with face inside. Boxes 1, 3, 10, and 12 have eyes in them.
3. Ornate cross, with moon on the left and sun on the right.

Copied for Ḫaylä Śəllase. Other names: Wälättä Mika'el and *Ləǧ* Amməḫay (?).

EMIP MagSc 18 – Marwick Magic Scroll 13

Parchment, 199.5 x 8.5 cm, three strips sewn together, one column, elaborate "candy-cane" borders, Gəʿəz, 19th cent.

1. Prayer against the eye of Barya, Legewon, the eye of Zar, Šotolay, Täyayaž, the eye of Dədq, noontime demon, and other demons, 47 lines.
በስመ፡ አብ፡ . . . ጸሎት፡ በእንተ፡ ዓይነ፡ ባርያ፡ ወሌጌዎን፡ ዓይነ፡ ዛር፡ ወዓይነ፡ ተያ[..፡ ወን]ይነ፡ ሰብእ፡ ወሾቶላይ፡ ወዓይነ፡ ድድቅ፡ ወጋኔነ፡ ቀትር፡ ዓይነ፡ ጥላ፡ ወጥላ፡ ወጊ፡ ወዓይነ፡ ፍርቅቃት፡ ወሥቅሥቃት፡ ዓይነ፡ አስወ[..]ውን፡ ወለህማም፡ (sic) ወቁርፀት፡ ውግአት፡ ወቀርጥማት፡ መጋኛ፡ ወጒሥምት፡ ቡዳ፡ ወጠቢብ፡ መንሾ፡ ወዳባሽ፡ ጕርገሃ፡ ⌜ወጀርባ፡ ወደዊ፡ (probably ወጀርባ፡ ደዊ) ወለሽንት፡ ማዕ፡ ወለመናፍስት፡ ርኩሳን፡ አድኅነ፡ . . . ድሜጥሮስ፡^{3x} ጋይስጠስ፡^{3x} ሳቁታው፡^{3x} ተአሰሩ፡ አጋንንት፡ ሸ^{7x} ቸ^{7x} ጨ^{7x} ሸር፡^{7x} በኃይለ፡ ዝንቱ፡ አስማቲከ፡ ይትአሰሩ፡ አጋንንት፡ . . . ምድምያስ፡^{3x} . . .

2. The two Greetings to Phanuel as prayer for binding and driving away demons, 42 lines; cf. 13, 7; 16, 5.
ሰላም፡ ለተፈጥሮትከ፡ ምስለ፡ መላእክት፡ ሀቡራ፡ . . .
ሰላም፡ ለከ፡ ሰዳዬ፡ አጋንንት፡ ፋኑኤል፡ ለእግ"፡ እምጽርሑ፡ . . .

3. Prayer of St. Susənyos and the story of his fight against Wərzəlya, the demon of infant mortality; cf. 7, 3.
በስመ፡ እግ"፡ ህያው፡ ነባቤ፡ ሐይወት፡ ወተናጋሬ፡ መለኮት፡ በእንተ፡ አሰስሎ፡ ደዊ፡ እምሕፃናት፡ . . . ወሃሎ፡ ፩ ብእሲ፡ ዘስሙ፡ ሱስንዮስ፡ . . .

4. Hymns to St. George, 59 lines; cf. EMML 1214, ff. 38a–40a; includes Chaîne, Répertoire, no. 380).
ወአፍጡነ፡ ሬድኤት፡ ለጅኑአ፡ ወለድኩም፡ . . . (followed by John 1:1–5).

5. Prayer against colic, 9 lines; cf. Strelcyn, *Prières*, p. 331; Six, *Handschriften*, 10, 6a, p. 79.

ጸሎት፡ በእንተ፡ ሕማመ፡ ቍርፀት፡ ሄርሄርኩሹ፡ ሄርኬሹ፡ ኪሹ፡^{3x} ኪሸ፡^{3x} አርኪሸ፡ . . . ክርስቶስ፡ ኩና፡ ወአድኅና፡ እምሕማመ፡ ባርያ፡ ወሌጌዎን፡ ወእምሕማመ፡ ቍርፀት፡ ለአመትከ፡ . . .

Miniatures and Magical Symbols:

1. Angel with sword and scabbard (large).
2. Talismanic symbol with face in center.
3. Four-petal symbol with eye in each petal.

Copied for Wälättä Gäbrəʾel, but owned also by Ḥanna whose name has been copied several times on and around the first picture, and by Wälättä Maryam, whose name has been copied on the last image.

EMIP MagSc 19 – Marwick Magic Scroll 14

Parchment, 148.5 x 9.2 cm, three strips sewn together, two columns, elaborate colored double border and "candy-cane" margin between columns, Gəʿəz, 20th cent.

A1. The Net of Solomon for catching demons as prayer against illnesses caused by Barya and Legewon, 121 lines; cf. 9, 5; 16, 3.
በስመ፡ አብ፡ . . . ጸሎት፡ በእንተ፡ ሕማመ፡ ባርያ፡ ወለጌዎን፡ አስማተ፡ መርበብቱ፡ ለሰሎሞን፡ ንጉሥ፡ ከመ፡ መርበብተ፡ ዓሣ፡ ዘያወጽእ እምባሕር፡ ዘረበቦሙ፡ ወአጽያሙ፡ ለአጋንንት፡ እንዘ፡ ይብል፡ ሰዳቃኤል፡ አዳቃኤል[፡] ናክርሚል፡ አልመረም፡ . . . ወይሰዓር፡ ሥራይከ፡ ወይልሳሕ፡ ሕምዝከ፡ ወ፩ወ፲ ጽጽስና፡ ወ፩ወ፲ ንግሥና፡ ወ፩ወ፲ቅስና፡ አምሐለከ፡ በጸሎሙ፡ (sic) ወበስዕለቶሙ፡ ለአባ፡ ጳንጠሌዎን፡ . . . ወካዕበ አውገዝኩክሙ፡ ወአምሐልኩክሙ፡ . . .
በስመ፡ እግ"፡ ዲና፡ ቂና፡ ሸራጎር፡ ግምየለ፡ ዳዜን፡ በበአራእዩ፡ አብጥልአምዕ፡ . . .

A2. Prayer for binding demons, 58 lines.
በስመ፡ እግ"፡ ብርሃን፡ [ጸሎት፡] በእንተ፡ ማዕሠሮሙ፡ ለሰይጣናት፡ አስማተ፡ ኃይል፡ ዘስሙ፡ ሸፒራ፡ አለሸፒራ፡ ቃስያን፡^{4x} ቃራሳን፡^{3x} ካራን፡^{3x} ዳራን፡^{3x} ጫራን፡^{3x} . . . አድኅነኒ፡ እምዓይነ፡ ባርያ፡ ወኅማመ፡ ደም፡ ወሾተላይ፡ አድኅና፡ . . .

A3. Prayer for binding demons, 21 lines.
ጸሎት፡ በእንተ፡ ማዕሠረ፡ አጋንንት፡ ወይቤ፡ ደዘኩምላህ፡ አንሰሪፋኤል፡ . . . ወይቤ፡ አልፋ፡ አልፍ፡ መርበቤኩም፡ ገጋጋ፡ . . . በዝንቱ፡ ቃል፡ ተአሠሩ፡ አጋንንት፡ ጸዋጋን፡ ወመናፍስት፡ ርኩሳን፡ . . .

A4. Prayer of St. Susənyos and the story of his fight against Wərzəlya, the demon of infant mortality, 34 lines, incomplete at the end; cf. 7, 3; 10, 3; 16, 1.

በስመ፡ እግ"፡ ሕያው፡ ነባቢ፡ ወተናጋሪ፡ ጸሎቱ፡ ወበረከቱ፡ ለቅዱስ፡ ሱስንዮስ፡ በእንተ፡ አሰስሎ፡ ደዌ፡ እምወራዙት፡ ወሕፃናት፡ ዘይጸርሮሙ፡ ሕማም፡ ሾተላይ፡ ለእመ፡ ይትአመንዎ፡ ወያጽሕፍዎ፡ ወይጸውርዎ፡ . . . ወሀሎ፡ ፱ ብእሲ፡ ወአውሰበ፡ . . .

B1. Prayer against illnesses caused by the eye of Barya, Täyayaž, Šotälay, Mäggäñña, Buda, Ṭäbib, Qumäñña, and other illnesses, 31 lines.

በስመ፡ አብ፡ . . . ጸሎት፡ በእንተ፡ ሕማም፡ ዓይን፡ ባርያ፡ ወተያያF፡ ወሾተላይ፡ ወድርጎኛ፡ መጋኛ፡ ወጉሥምት፡ ፌራ፡ ወንዳድ፡ ፍልፀት፡ ወቁርጻት፡ ውግዓት፡ ወቁርጥማት፡ ወረርሽኝ፡ ተቅማጥ፡ ቡዳ፡ ወጠቢብ፡ ቁመኛ፡ ወቁረኛ፡ ውላጅ፡ ጆን፡ ስቅስቃት፡ ወፍርቅቃት፡ በጆድ፡ ውግዓት፡ እጆበጅ፡ አቸን፡ አትቻን፡ . . . በዝአስማት፡ ተሰደድ፡ አንተ፡ ዓይነ፡ ባርያ፡ . . .

B2. Prayer against colic, 45 lines.

ጸሎት፡ በእንተ፡ ሕማም፡ ቀርጻት፡ በኮፓኮስ፡ ስምከ፡ በብርያዋስ፡ ስምከ፡ በንቡዕ፡ ስምከ፡ . . . ጆር፡[3x] ሸር፡[3x] . . . ለአርጋዬ፡ ነፋሳት፡ ከማሁ፡ . . .

B3. Prayer against punching pain, 17 lines.

ጸሎት፡ በእንተ፡ ሕማም፡ ቀርጻት፡ በኮፓኮስ፡ ... ጉሥምት፡ በንቡዕ፡ ቃልከ፡ አድኃንኮ፡ ኮግያ፡ ፔናዊ፡ ማስጋኖን፡ ኬዊፌዊ፡ ዳሌጥ፡ . . .

B4. Prayer against headache, 18 lines.

በስመ፡ አብ፡ . . . ጸሎት፡ በእንተ፡ እራስ፡ ውግዓት፡ ወፍልጸት፡ ሐጌሴንዮስ፡ አቃራጥንዮስ፡ ጽስታንዮስ፡ ስብደልማሩያል፡ ማሉናት፡ . . .

B5. Prayer against rheumatism, 22 lines. Full text:

ጸሎት፡ በእንተ፡ ቀርጥማት፡ ክንፍራ፡ ደለዊ፡ ዘይፈቅዕ፡ መልያልP፡ እግዚእ፡ ዘፈወስከ፡ ቁስሎ፡ ለኢዮብ፡ ምሕረታዊስ፡ ድንረታዊ፡ ፈውሰኒ፡ ሾውድን፡ ሾማድን፡[3x] ተከላቤት፡ ከላዬ፡ ይኩን፡ ማንተማ፡ ለንጉሥከ፡ መንግሥት፡ ኢትንክስ፡ ወኢትቆርጥም፡ አባላቲሃ፡ አድኅና፡ እምሕማም፡ ሾተላይ፡ ለአመትከ፡ (name erased).

B6. Prayer against hemorrhage, in Gəʿəz and Amharic, 15 lines; cf. 8, 7; 14, 2.

ጸሎት፡ በእንተ፡ ደም፡[:] ለት፡ ሻት፡[3x] መልዮስዮስ፡ (sic) መልዮስ፡ መላልዮስ፡ ዘአተረ ⌈ደም፡ ደም፡[2x] እንደ፡ ሰማይ፡ እራቅ፡ እንደ፡ ምድር፡ ጥበቅ፡ አለሀ፡ ቃለ፡ አብ፡ . . .

B7. Prayer against hemorrhage, 14 lines; cf. 14, 2.

ጸሎት፡ በእንተ፡ ደም፡ ሊስ፡ አፍሊስ፡ አፍሊስ፡ ሊስ፡ አፍሊስ፡ ሜሎስ፡[3x] ገለውዴያስ፡[3x] በላዬ፡ በረድ፡ ወነፋስ፡ . . .

B8. Prayer for binding demons, and against Qedar, Carpenters (Nähabt) and Gärgar, 41 lines.

በስመ፡ አብ፡ . . . በእንተ፡ ማዕሥሮሙ፡ ለአጋንንት፡ ወበእንተ፡ ቄዳር፡ ወነሀብት፡ ዓይነት፡ ወምትአት፡ ወጽፍአት፡ ወነገርጋር፡ አአትብ፡ ገጽዮ፡

በስመ፡ ፫አስማት፡ ወበጀመለኮት፡ . . . አግንፀንኩ፡ በሎፍሐም፡ ስምከ፡ ከመ፡ ታድኅና፡ እምባርያ፡ ጸሊማን፡ ወመናፍስት፡ ርኩሳን፡ ወሰብአ፡ መሡርያን፡ ወደጋምያኒ፡ (sic) ፅፅ፡ . . .

Miniatures and Magical Symbols:
1. Angel with sword and scabbard.
2. Talismanic symbol with face in center.
3. Another talismanic symbol with face in center.

The name of the original owner erased and replaced by Bällätäč/Wälättä Ḥəwät.

EMIP MagSc 20 – Marwick Magic Scroll 15

Parchment, 145.5 x 9.5 cm, two strips sewn together, one column, colored double border, Gəʿəz, 18th/19th cent.

1. Prayer for binding demons, Barya, and Legewon, 45 lines.
   በስመ፡ አብ፡ . . . ጸሎት፡ በእንተ፡ ማዕሠረ፡ አጋንንት፡ ባርያ፡ ወሌጌዎን፡ ጬትኮትኤል፡^{3x} ሽትኮትኤል፡^{3x} ጀትኮትኤል፡^{3x} ቸትኮትኤል፡^{3x} ኘትኮትኤል፡^{3x} Fትኮክትኤል፡ C Fትኮትኤል^{2x} ያሽምክት፡ ያሽኪት፡ ያምንሁ፡ መጠጬት ያወልጭዕ፡ አልህያ፡ ያልህብ፡ ምያብሐር፡ ያወንጌዝ፡ ያእቱF፡ ያሽኪት፡ . . . በእሉ፡ ቃላቲከ፡ ወበእሉ፡ አስምቲከ፡ አድኅና፡ እምሕማመ፡ ዓይነት፡ ወዓይነ፡ ጽላ፡ ባርያ፡ ወሌጌዎን፡ ሾተላይ፡ ወተላዋሽ፡ መጋኛ፡ ጉሥምት፡ ቁመኛ፡ ወተንኮለኛ፡ እደ፡ ሰብእ፡ ወጸላ፡ (sic) ወጊ፡ ቡዳ፡ ወጠቢብ፡ ፌራ፡ ወንዳድ፡ ደስክ፡ ወጉዳሌ፡ ለገብርከ፡ (sic) ለዓመትከ፡ ያይን፡ ዋጋ፡ ሃሀለ፡ ማርያም፡

2. Rampart of the Cross, 55 lines.
   በስመ፡ አብ፡ . . . ጸሎት፡ በእንተ፡ ሐፀረ፡ መስቀል፡ (sic) ክርስቶስ፡ መርሆሙ፡ መምርኩዞሙ፡ (sic) ለሐንካሳን፡ . . . ተፈጸመ፡ ዝንቱ፡ ሐፀረ፡ መስቀል፡ . . .

3. Prayer for binding demons, Barya and Legewon, 30 lines.
   በስመ፡ አብ፡ . . . በእንተ፡ ማዕሠረ፡ አጋንንት፡ ባርያ፡ ወሌጌዎን፡ አካዕ፡^{4x} ቤቃ፡^{3x} ጼቃ፡ ቤቃ፡^{2x} ፌቃ፡^{2x} ኤቃ፡ አሌፍ፡^{4x} አልፋኤል፡ . . . ሐርበ፡ ደጀን፡ ክሎከ፡ ሎፍሐም፡ ምርታዬ፡ በእሉ፡ አስምቲከ፡ አድኅና፡ እምሕማመ፡ ዛር፡ ወዓይነ፡ ጸላ፡ (sic) ወቁራኛ፡ ለዓመትከ፡ . . .

4. Prayer against the evil eye of demons, and different ailments, 25 lines.
   በስመ፡ አብ፡ . . . ጸሎት፡ በእንተ፡ ሕማመ፡ ዓይነ፡ ጥላ፡ ወዓይነ፡ ወርቅ፡ ወዓይነ፡ ርእስ፡ ክርስቶስ፡ ጸድቅ፡ ወማዕምር፡ ⌜አበ፡ ምራቅከ፡ (sic; for አበ") ከሥትከ፡ አዐይንተ፡ ዕውራን፡ . . . በስመ፡ እግ" አዶናይ፡ አልፋዊ፡ ሜሎሳዊ፡ ታያሳዊ፡ ዘጸሐፈ፡ ኤርምያስ፡ ነቢይ፡ በታሕተ፡ ሰማይ፡ ወበምድር፡ . . .

Miniatures and Magical Symbols:
1. Face above "torso" of four petal shapes.
2. Angel with sword and scabbard.
3. Small *haräg* -like panel.

Copied for Yayn Waga/Śahlä Maryam.

EMIP MagSc 21 – Marwick Magic Scroll 16

Parchment, 147.5 x 8.5 cm, three strips sewn together, one column, colored border, Gəʻəz, 20th cent.

1. Prayer of St. Susənyos against the evil eye, Zar, the eye of Buda, Təgrida, Legewon, Muslims and Christians, and the story of his fight against Wərzəlya, the demon of infant mortality; cf. 7, 3.
   በስመ፡ አብ፡ . . . ጸሎት ፡ በእንተ፡ ሱስንዮስ፡ በስመ፡ እግ"፡ ሐያው፡ ነባቢ፡ ወተናጋሪ፡ ጸሎቱ፡ ለቅዱስ፡ ሱስንዮስ፡ በእንተ፡ አሰስሎ፡ ደዌ፡ እምሕፃናት፡ . . . ወሀሎ፡ አሐዱ፡ ብእሲ፡ ዘስሙ፡ ሱስንዮስ፡ . . . አአምላከ፡ ሱስንዮስ፡ ዕቀበኒ፡ ወአድኅነኒ፡ እምዓይነ፡ ጥላ፡ ወዛር፡ ወቸነፈር፡ እምዓይነ፡ ቡዳ፡ ወትግሪዳ፡ እምዓይነ፡ [..]ን፡ ወሌጌዎን፡ እምዓይነ፡ እምዓይነ፡ (sic) እስላም፡ ወክርስቲያን፡ . . .

2. Prayer against the evil spirit of Gergesenes, i.e., Legewon (Mark 5:1–17; Luke 8:26–37), 69 lines.
   በስመ፡ አብ፡ . . . ጸሎት፡ በእንተ፡ ጌርጌስሮን፡ ወጺአ፡ ማዕዶተ፡ ጌርጌሴንዎን፡ (sic) . . . በዝ[፡] ቃለ፡ ወንጌልከ፡ ዕቀበኒ፡ . . .

3. Prayer against the evil spirit of Luke 4:31–36, 27 lines.
   ወንጌል፡ ዘሉቃስ፡ ወሀሎ፡ ፩ብእሲ፡ እምኮራብ፡ . . .

4. Prayer against evil spirit, 34 lines.
   በስመ፡ አብ፡ . . . ጸሎት፡ በእንተ፡ ሕማም፡ ዓይነ፡ ጥላ፡ ዘፀሐድር፡ በረድኤተ፡ ልዑል፡ ዘይነብር፡ ውስተ፡ ጽላሎት፡ (Ps 90:1–11) . . . ከማሁ፡ እቀበኒ፡ . . .

Miniatures and Magical Symbols:
1. Sixteen-box panel (4 x 4) with X-shaped patterns in boxes 1–5, 7, 10, 13 and 15 and faces in boxes 6, 9, 11, and 14.
2. Angel with sword and scabbard (large).

Copied for Wälättä Mika'el. There is also the name Wälättä Arägawi Adina.

EMIP MagSc 22 – Marwick Magic Scroll 17

Parchment, 171 x 9.5 cm., three strips sewn together, one column, no border, Gəʻəz, 19th cent.

1. Prayer against charm, taken from the Eighty-One (Canonical) Books, 38 lines; cf. Strelcyn, *Prières*, pp. 30–38 and 58–60.

በስመ፡ አብ፡ . . . ጸሎት፡ በእንተ፡ መፍትሔ፡ ሥራይ፡ ዘተቀድሐ፡
እምፂወ፩ መጻሕፍት፡ በዝንቱ፡ ጠልሰም፡ ተፈትሁ፡ መሰርያን፡
ብዙኃን፡ ነባብያን፡ ሐሰት፡ እለ፡ ይገብሩ፡ ዕፀ፡ ሥራይ፡ ወአስማተ፡ ዕፀ
ሰቢሮሙ፡ አሙ፡ ነቂሎሙ፡ ሰግዖ፡ ነጺሮሙ፡ ወምድረ፡ ኮኢቶሙ፡
(sic) ታቦተ፡ ገሲሶሙ፡ ስመ፡ ፀዊያሙ፡ ሐመደ፡ ዘሪዎሙ፡ ሰርዶ፡
ጠምጢሞሙ፡ በዕንቄቀሎ፡ ዶርሆ፡ ድፍንተ፡ ቀቢሮሙ፡ ወለመብልዕ፡
ወለመስቴ፡ እስላም፡ ደጊሞሙ፡ በአድግ፡ ወበእንገደ፡ (sic) ልጅ፡
ወገመል፡ ወቶት፡ ወፍኔ፡ አልጉም፡ ወልጉሞሙ፡ ሥራየ፡ ብእሲ፡
ወብዕሲ፡ (sic) ወብእሲት፡ ዘገብረት፡ በሃርሰም፡ ፀጉር፡ ወጌጉት፡
ደም፡ ወፍቁራ፡ እስላም፡ ደጊሞሙ፡ ሥራየ፡ ካህናት፡ ፍታሕ፡
ተፈታሕ፡ . . . (a text from the *Dəggʷa*, identical to the oldest
known manuscript, Vat. etiop. 28, f. 30b, Silvanus Grébaut et
Eugenius Tisserant, *Codices Aethiopci Vaticani et Borgiani
Barberinianus Orientalis 2 Rossianus 865*, Vatican 1935, pp. 134–
5, follows):
ተሰቅለ፡ ወሐመ፡ ዘእንበለ፡ ንጢአት፨
ተረግዘ፡ ገቦሁ፡ ዘእንበለ፡ ደዌ፤
እስመ፡ መለኮቱ፡ ኢሐመ፨
ተሰቅለ፡ ከመ፡ እቡስ፡ ማእከለ፡ ፪ፈያት፨
ወኮርዕዎ፡ ርእሶ፡ በሐለት፤
ረገዝዎ፡ ገቦሁ፡ በኩናት፤
ለአምላክ፡ ምሕረት፨
ለንጉሥ፡ ስብሐት፨
ሰፍሐ፡ እደዊሁ፡ ቅዱሳት፤
ዲበ፡ ዕፀ፡ መስቀል፡ ወተቀነወ፡ በቅንዋተ፡ መስቀል፡ ከመ፡ ያግዕዘነ፡
እምንጢአት፨
. . . ዕቀበኒ፡ ለአመትከ፡ . . . ጅር፡ አቅፋጅር፡ ሸር፡ ተአሸር፡ . . .

2. *Asmat* prayer of the Qəmant (MS: Qämawənt) against charm, 20 lines.
በስመ፡ አብ፡ . . . ጸሎተ፡ አስማተ፡ ሥራይ፡ ዘቀማውንት፡ ድንድጋሰኒ፡
አግማኒ፡ አቅማኒ፡[3x] አቅማኛሆኝ፡ . . .

3. Prayer against the evil eyes, 30 lines.
በስመ፡ አብ፡ . . . አንተ፡ በሰማይ፡ ወአንተ፡ በምድር፡ ሐራስ፡ ወንዋም፡
ዘኢይመጽአከ፡ ወአንተ፡ ንጉሥ፡ ሰማይ፡ ወአንተ፡ ንጉሥ፡ ምድር፡ . . .
ውጻዕ፡ አንተ፡ ዓይን፡ ሥራይ፡ ወጸልዋኔ፡ (sic) ዓይን፡ ብእሲ፡ ወብእሲት፡
ዓእስላማዊ፡ ወአረማዊ፡ ዓይን፡ ክርስቲያናዊ፡ ወአይሁዳዊ፡ ዓሰይጣናት፡
ወአጋንንት፡ በኃይለ እግ" . . .

4. Prayer against charm, 19 lines.
በስመ፡ አብ፡ . . . ፍታሕ፡ ሥራየ፡ አጋንንት፡ ወባርያ፡ ሥራየ፡ ኪን፡
ወካህናት፡ ወዲያቆናት፡ ሥራየ፡ ቅርጥናኤል፡ ክፍትጥናኤል፡ አዝዮስ፡

አስፍቃፍ፡ ቃስታፍስ፡ . . . በዝንቱ፡ አስማቲክ፡ . . . (includes John 1:1–5).
5. Prayer against hemorrhage, 52 lines.
በስሙ፡ ለእ"፡ አብ፡ በስሙ፡ ለእ"፡ ወልድ፡ በስሙ፡ ለእ"፡ ወመንፈስ፡ ቅዱስ፡ ዘአርግአ፡ ማየ፡ በሥልጣኑ፡ . . . ከማሁ፡ ይርጋዕ፡ ወይጽናዕ፡ ወይትዓቄር፡ በሰፋድለ፡ ሐይወት፡ ደም፡ ትክቶሃ፡ ለአመትክ፡ . . .

Miniatures and Magical Symbols:
1. Talismanic symbol with face in center.
2. Another talismanic symbol with face in center.
3. Another talismanic symbol with face in center.
4. (Incomplete) talismanic symbol.

Originally copied for Aster; replaced with Wälättä Ḥəywät.

EMIP MagSc 23 – Marwick Magic Scroll 18
Parchment, 171 x 8 cm, three strips sewn together, one column, elaborate "sawtooth" and crosses border, Gəʿəz, 19th cent.
1. Prayer of St. Susənyos against illnesses caused by Mäggäña, Buda, Carpenter, Šotolay, and the story of his fight against Wərzəlya, the demon of infant mortality; cf. 7, 3.
በስመ፡ አብ፡ . . . ጸሎት፡ በእንተ፡ አስ (sic) ሕማም፡ መጋኛ፡ ቡዳ፡ ወነሀቢ፡ ሾቶላይ፡ በስሙ፡ እግ"፡ ነባቢ፡ ወተናጋሪ፡ ቃለ፡ መለኮቱ፡ ለእ"፡ ጸሎቱ፡ ወበረክቱ፡ ለቅዱስ፡ ሱስንዮስ፡ በእንተ፡ አሰስሎ፡ ደዌ፡ እምሕፃናት፡ . . .
2. Prayer against the evil eye and for binding demons, Satan, Buda, Carpenter, Käyla, Fäläša that Alexander uttered before Gog and Magog, 35 lines; cf. 16, 4.
በስመ፡ አብ፡ . . . ጸሎት፡ በእንተ፡ ማዕሠሮሙ፡ ለአጋንንት፡ ወለሰይጣን፡ ለቡዳ፡ ወለነሀቢ፡ ለከይላ፡ ወለፋላሻ፡ ለምቀኛ፡ ለተንኮለኛ፡ ለሥራየኛ፡ ወሟለርተኛ፡ ለመጋኛ፡ ወለኩራኛ፡ ዘተናገሮ፡ እስክንድር፡ ንጉሥ፡ በዕለተ፡ ዓርብ፡ በቅድመ፡ ጎግ፡ ወማጎግ፡ እንዘ፡ ይብል፡ አልፍ፡ . . .
3. Prayer against the evil eye of Barya, Legewon, Däsk and Gudale, 21 lines.
በስመ፡ አብ፡ . . . ጸሎት፡ በእንተ፡ ዓይነተ፡ ባርያ፡ ወሌጌዎን፡ ደስክ፡ ወጉዳሌ፡ ኢያስከይን፡ ደርር፡ መያጠር፡ ሸፉን፡ ሸፍሸፉን፡ . . .
4. Prayer for binding demons, Buda and Carpenter (Nähabi), 46 lines; cf. 7, 1; and 9, 3.
በስመ፡ አብ፡ . . . ጸሎት፡ በእንተ፡ ማዕሠሮሙ፡ ኮነ፡ ለአጋንንት፡ ወለሰይጣናት፡ ለቡዳ፡ ወለነሀቢ፡ አህያ፡ ሸራህያ፡ አልመክቱን፡ አልፋ፡ ቤጋ፡ . . . ዘመስቀልከ፡ አጽራዕከ፡ ግብሮ፡ ለዲያብሎስ፡ . . .

Miniatures and Magical Symbols:
1. Angel with sword and scabbard.
2. Talismanic symbol with face in center.
3. Cross-shaped pattern at the end of the scroll.

Copied for Wälättä Kidan.

EMIP MagSc 24 – Marwick Magic Scroll 19

Parchment, 165 x 8 cm, three strips sewn together, two column, no border, diamond patterned margin between columns, Gəʻəz, 20th cent.

A1. Prayer against the evil eye and Legewon: The story of the sorcerer at the Sea of Tiberias, all col. A and 9 lines of col. B; cf. 3, 1.
በስመ፡ አብ፡ . . . ጸሎት፡ በእንተ፡ ሕማመ፡ ዓይነት፡ (sic) ወርቅ፡ ወዓይነ፡ ጥላ፡ ወሌጌዎን፡ ርጉም፡ ወተፃራሪ፡ አፍጠለሽም፡ . . . ጸሎተ፡ ንድራ፡ ወእንዘ፡ የሐውር፡ እግዚእነ፡ ኢየሱስ፡ ክርስቶስ፡ ውስተ፡ ባሕረ፡ ጥብርያዶስ፡ . . .

B1. Prayer against hemorrhage, 24 lines; cf. 4, 2; 14, 2.
በስመ፡ አብ፡ . . . ጸሎት፡ በእንተ፡ ደም፡ ዘውህዘ[፡] ሐፍረ፡ ብእሲት፡ ዘወጽአ፡ እምአረቢ፡ ሊስ፡[3x] አፍሊስ፡[3x] መሊስ፡[3x] መርግኤ፡ ደም፡ ክርስቶስ፡ አርግዕ፡ ደጋ፡ በማኅፀን፡ ለአመትከ፡ . . .

B2. Prayer against Täyayaž which brings nightmare, 27 lines.
ጸሎት፡ በእንተ፡ ተያያዝ፡ ዘሌሊት፡ ወዘመዓልት፡ ወዘያበሐን፡ በሕልመ፡ ሌሊት፡ አብ፡ ወወልድ፡ . . .

B3. The Net of Solomon for catching demons as prayer against the evil eye of Barya, Zar Balaho, and others, 42 lines.
ጸሎት፡ በእንተ[፡] ዓይነ፡ ባርያ[፡] ወዛር፡ ወባላሆ፡ ወውላጅ፡ ወተላዎሽ[፡] መርበብት[፡] ሰሎሞን፡ . . . ነጋ፡ ኄሎየ፡ ገብርኤል፡ ነበባለ፡ እሳት[፡] ነቡዕ፡ ውእቱ፡ . . .

Miniatures and Magical Symbols:
1. Cross shape with many geometric patterns.
2. Angel with sword.
3. Talismanic symbol with face in center.
4. Angel with sword.

The last ten lines are insufficiently legible.

Copied probably for Wälättä Gäbrə'el, but the name is replaced with Wälättä Iyyäsus.

EMIP MagSc 25 – Marwick Magic Scroll 20

Parchment, 154 x 9 cm, three strips sewn together, one column, colored border, Gəʿəz, 18th cent.

1. Prayer against the evil eye of Barya, Legewon, Zar, Zarit, Təgrida, Mäggäñña, Buda, Fälaša…, 32 lines.
   The beginning has been damaged, but there is the claim that the *asmat* are from the *Dərsanä Mikaʾel*: . . . እሉ፡ እሙንቱ፡ ክቡታት፡ ወኀቡኣት፡ አስማቲሁ፡ ለእ"፡ ዘተረክቡ፡ በእደ፡ ቅዱስ፡ ሚካኤል፡ ሊቀ፡ መላእክት፡ መግረሬ፡ ፀር፡ ወጸላእት፡ . . . አድኀና እምሕማም፡ ዓይነ፡ ጽላ፡ ወጽላ፡ ወጊ፡ ባርያ፡ ወሌጌዎን፡ ዛር፡ ወዛሪት፡ ወትግሪዳ፡ ፍልፀት፡ ወቀኑርፀት፡ መጋኛ፡ ወጉሥምት፡ ..ፈዲ፡ ንዳድ፡ ቡዳ፡ ወፈላሻ፡ ዓይነት፡ ወዓይነ፡ ናስ፡ ወዓይነ፡ ወርቅ፡ ዓይነ፡ ጸላኢ፡ ወዓይነ፡ አጋንንት፡ ለዓመተ፡ እግ"፡ . . .

2. Prayer of St. Susənyos and the story of his fight against Wərzəlya, the demon of infant mortality; cf. 7, 3.
   በስመ፡ እግ"፡ ሐያው፡ ነባቢ፡ ወተናጋሪ፡ ጸሎቱ፡ ለቅዱስ፡ ሱስንዮስ፡ በእንተ፡ አሰስሎ፡ ደዌ፡ እምሕፃናት፡ . . . ወሀሎ፡ ጀብእሲ፡ ዘስሙ፡ ሱስንዮስ፡ . . .

3. Prayer against the evil eye and for binding demons, Barya, Legewon, and Mäggäñña, invoking the name of the cross, 47 lines.
   በስመ፡ አብ፡ . . . ጸሎት፡ በእንተ፡ ሕማም፡ ዓይነ፡ ጽላ፡ ወጽላ፡ ወጊ፡ ማዕሡረ፡ አጋንንት፡ ዕቀበኒ፡ ክርስቶስ፡ በመስቀልኽ፡ መስቀል፡ ሰዳዬ ፀር፡ መስቀል፡ መዋዔ፡ ፀር፡ መስቀል፡ መግረሬ፡ ፀር፡ መስቀል፡ መዋዔ፡ ፀር፡ መስቀል፡ መልዕልተ፡ ኮሉ፡ ነገር፡ መስቀል፡ ለቤተ፡ ክርስቲያን፡ ዓምዳ፡ ወድዳ፡ . . . መስቀል፡ ዘዘበጦ፡ ለሰይጣን፡ ከማሁ፡ ዝብጠሙ፡ ለሰይጣናት፡ ወለዓይነ፡ ጽላ፡ ለባርያ፡ ወለጌዎን፡ ለፍልፀት፡ ወለቀኑርፀት፡ ወለቀኑርፀት፡ (sic) ለመጋኛ፡ ወለጉሥምት፡ ለፈሪ፡ ወለንዳድ፡ ከመ፡ ኢይቅርቡ፡ . . .

4. Prayer against the evil eye, incomplete, 18 lines.
   በስመ፡ አብ፡ . . . ጸሎት፡ በእንተ፡ ሕማም፡ ዓይነት፡ ይትነሣእ፡ እግ" ወይዘረዉ፡ ወይኮይዩ፡ ጸላእቱ፡ እምቅድሙ፡ ገጹ፡ (Ps 68:1) መርከብዮን፡ መሐፍርኪን፡ ፈፍራን፡ መልጎሙ፡ እሳት፡ . . .

Miniatures and Magical Symbols:
1. Angel with sword and scabbard.
2. Nine-box panel: talismanic symbol with face in center.
3. Another talismanic symbol with face in center.

Copied for Wälättä Yoḥannəs Ṭəruyyä; the name Yaṭenaš/Amätä Maryam added later.

26. Marwick Magic Scroll 21

Parchment, 176.5 x 10.5 cm, three strips sewn together, one column, colored border, Gəʿəz, late 19th cent.

1. Prayer against illnesses caused by the evil eye, Barya, etc., 12 lines.
   በስመ፡ አብ፡ . . . ጸሎት፡ በእንተ፡ ሕማመ፡ ዓይነ፡ ጽላ፡ ወባርያ፡ ዛር፡ ወቍራኛ፡ ከሪስ፡ ዐጕር፡ ወእግር፡ ጥፍር፡ አለሁ፡ ውፃዕ፡ አለሁ፡ ቃለ፡ አብ፡ . . . በእንተ፡ ሕማም፡ ምትዓት፡ (sic) ያኤርር፡³ˣ ያሽባኤርር፡²ˣ . . .
2. Prayer against punching pain, 7 lines; cf. Six, *Handschriften*, 22, 2, 8, p. 102.
   ጸሎት፡ በእንተ፡ ሕማመ፡ [ቁርፀት?]፡ ወጉሥምት፡ ዘተፈነዎ፡ (sic) እም[..] ከመ፡ ይፃዕ፡ ወይቤዙ፡ ውሉደ፡ እንለ፡ እመሕያው፡ . . .
3. Prayer with *Asmat* of Solomon, for catching demons, taken from The Net of Solomon for catching demons, 8 lines. Prayer: *Asmat* of Solomon"
   ጸሎት፡ በእንተ፡ ሕማመ፡ ዓይነ፡ ጽላ፡ ወማዕሠረ፡ አጋንንት፡ ዘረበቦሙ፡ ለአጋንንት፡ ከመ፡ መርበብተ፡ ዓሣ፡ . . .
4. Prayer against Barya and Däsk, 14 lines
   ጸሎት፡ በእንተ፡ ባርያ፡ እኩይ፡ ወደስክ፡ ወንጌል፡ ዘዮሐንስ፡ ቀዳሚሁ፡ ቃል፡ (John 1:1–5).
5. Greeting to Phanuel as prayer for binding demons, 41 lines; cf. 13, 7.
   ጸሎት፡ ማዕሠረ፡ አጋንንት፡ ሰላም፡ ለከ፡ ሰዳዬ፡ አጋንንት፡ ፋኑኤል፡ ለእግ"፡ እምጽርሑ፡ . . .
6. Prayer of St. Susənyos against illnesses caused by Barya and Legewon, and the story of his fight against Wərzəlya, the demon of infant mortality; cf. 7, 3.
   ጸሎት፡ በእንተ፡ ሕማመ፡ ባርያ፡ ወሌጌዎን፡ . . . በስመ፡ እግ"፡ ሕያው፡ ነባቢ፡ ወተናጋሪ፡ ለቅዱስ፡ ሱስንዮስ፡ በእንተ፡ አሰስሎ፡ ደዊ፡ እምሕፃናት፡ . . . ወሀሎ፡ አሐዱ፡ ብእሲ፡ ዘስሙ፡ ሱስንዮስ፡ . . .
7. Prayer against hemorrhage as Gabriel announced to Mary, 103 lines.
   ዜነዎ፡ ገብርኤል፡ ለማርያም፡ ገብርኤል፡ በዮግና፡ ወሩፋኤል፡ በጸጋህ፡ በዝ፡ ዐንዑ፡ ሰግያት፡ ወምድር፡ ከማሁ፡ አጽንዕ፡ ደማ፡ . . . ሰዓልናከ፡ መሐሪ፡ . . . በስመ፡ ጥምቀትከ፡ ድማኄል፡ አማኑኤል፡ ሊስ፡ አፍሊስ፡ . . . ደም፡ ደማጊት፡ በምንት፡ ትነብር፡ በአጽም፡ ወበአጽንት፡ አቁም፡ አለሁ፡ ቃለ፡ አብ፡ . . . ጸሎተ፡ ሰንተም፡ ሰንከተም፡ ስንቀራም፡ ዘከተሮ፡ ለሰይጣን፡ ከማሁ፡ ክትር፡ ደማ፡ . . . ፍካሬ፡ ዘጻድቃን፡ (Ps 1:1–3). ወገፀ፡ ዘፍጹም፡ በጽልመት፡ . . .
   This section could be more than one prayer.

Miniatures and Magical Symbols:
1. Talismanic symbol with face in center.
2. Angel with sword and scabbard.
3. Another talismanic symbol with face in center.
4. Ornate-letter symbols at the end of the scroll.

Copied for Wälättä Giyorgis.

EMIP MagSc 27 – Marwick Magic Scroll 22

Parchment, 182.5 x 8.5 cm, three strips sewn together, one column, colored border, Gəʻəz, 19th cent.

1. Prayer of St. Susənyos against illnesses caused by Šotälay, and the story of his fight against Wərzəlya, the demon of infant mortality, 67 lines; cf. 7, 3.
   ጸሎት፡ በእንተ፡ ዓይነ፡ ጥላ፡ ወሕማም፡ ሾተላይ፡ በስመ፡ እግ"፡ ሕያው፡ ነባቢ፡ ወተናጋሪ፡ ጸሎቱ፡ ለቅዱስ፡ ሱስንዮስ፡ በእንተ፡ አሰሰሎ፡ ደዌ፡ እምሕፃናት፡ . . . ወሀሎ፡ ጎብእሲ፡ ዘስሙ፡ ሱስንዮስ፡ . . .

2. Prayer for binding demons, Barya, the filthy Legewon, and the evil hand, 26; cf. 3, 5; 8, 8; 9, 4; 15, 2.
   በስመ፡ አብ፡ . . . ጸሎት፡ በእንተ፡ ዓይነ ዓይነ ጥላ፡ ባርያ፡ ወሌጌዎን፡ ርኩስ፡ ዘይሰልብ፡ ልበ፡ ሰብእ፡ ወያጻልም፡ አእይንተ፡ ወያመጽእ፡ ከመ፡ ጸላሎት፡ በመዓልት፡ ወበሌሊት፡ አምሐልኩክሙ፡ በጅየየቅንዋተ፡ (sic) መስቀሉ፡ . . .

3. Prayer against the evil eye and for drowning the Zar, 40 lines; it has some similarity with 16, 4.
   በስመ፡ አብ፡ . . . ጸሎት፡ በእንተ፡ ዓይነ፡ ዓይነ (sic) ጥላ፡ ዛር፡ ወመስጥም፡ ዛር፡ ዘአብርኮሙ፡ (sic) ለአእዋፈ፡ ሰማይ፡ በመዓጥር፡ እጥር፡ . . . ተናጨር፡ ንቱው፡ አጋንንት፡ ደሌፍ፡ ንቱው፡ ቆሪፍ፡ ንቱው፡ ዛር፡ . . . አምሐልኩክሙ፡ ወአውገዝኩክሙ፡ በአምያዝ፡ (sic) መልአከ፡ ምክርከ፡ . . .

4. Prayer against the evil eye, 21 lines. Prayer: against the evil eye"
   በስመ፡ አብ፡ . . . ጸሎት፡ በእንተ፡ ዓይነ፡ ዓይነ፡ ጥላ፡ ጥላ፡ (sic) በስመ [፡] ፒስ፡ አላፒስ፡ አላሽዊራ፡ ቃራን፡ ዳራን፡ ካራን፡ ሜራን፡ . . .

5. Prayer for binding demons, using the Greeting to Phanuel, badly copied, 49 lines.
   ጸሎት፡ በእንተ፡ ማዕሡረ አጋንንት፡ ወማዕሡረ[፡] አሰይጣናት፡ (sic) ሰላም፡ ለከ፡ አጋንንተ፡ ስድድ፡ እምላዕሌየ፡ እግዚአ፡ ፋኑኤ[ል፡] እግዚአ፡ ፋኑኤል[፡] አንተ፡ ለተራድአ፡ . . . ሰዳዬ፡ አጋንንት፡ ለእግ"፡ እምጽርሁ፡ . . . ወገዑ፡ ዘፍዑም፡ በጽልመት፡ ፈርህ፡ ወዲንገዐ፡ ዲያብሎስ[፡] ርእዮ፡ ብሁተ፡ ልደት፡ በሥጋ[፡] አምላክ፡ በሲአል፡ እስመ፡ አልቦ፡ ነገር፡ ዘይሰአኖ፡ ለእግ"፡

Miniatures and Magical Symbols:
1. Angel with sword and scabbard.
2. Talismanic symbol with face in center.
3. Ornate cross.
4. Three crosses.
5. Illegible pattern.

Copied for Wälättä Maryam Fälqa, replace with Wälättä Gäbrel.
Note of ownership by Sisay Därräbä.

EMIP MagSc 28 – Marwick Magic Scroll 23

Parchment, 182 x 9.3 cm, three strips sewn together, one column, colored border, Gəʽəz, 20th cent.

1. Prayer against Barya, Legewon, hemorrhage, the evil eye and Šotälay, 33 lines.
   በስመ፡ አብ፡ . . . ጸሎት፡ በእንተ፡ ባርያ፡ ወሌጌዎን፡ ወደም፡ ወጽላዊጊ፡ (sic) ወሶተላይ፡ (sic) ቀዳሚሁ፡ ቃል፡ ውእቱ፡ (John 1:1–5) . . .
2. Prayer against Barya, Legewon, and the evil eye, 45 lines; cf. 27, 2.
   በስመ፡ አብ፡ . . . ጸሎት፡ በእንተ፡ ባርያ፡ ወሌጌዎን፡ ወዓይነ፡ ጽላ፡ ዘይሰልብ፡ ልበ፡ ሰብእ፡ . . .
3. Glorification of the angels as prayer against Barya and Legewon, 89 lines.
   በስመ፡ አብ፡ . . . ጸሎት፡ በእንተ፡ ባርያ፡ ወሌጌዎን፡ ስብሐታተ፡ መላእክት፡ እንዘ፡ ይብሉ፡ በአርያም፡ ሃሌ፡ ሉያ፡ ለአብ፡ . . . ሐርዲቴን፡ ዘተጸውዓ፡ እምቅድመ፡ ዓለም፡ አናያ፡ ሸራያ፡ (sic) በስሙ፡ ለእግ"፡ አብ፡ . . . ታአስ፡ አዝዮስ፡ ማስያስ፡ . . . ተሰቅለ፡ ወሐም፡ ዘእንበለ፡ ደዌ፡ ተረግዘ፡ ገቦሁ፡ ዘእንበለ፡ ንጢአት፡ እስመ፡ መለኮቱ፡ ኢሐመ፡ (cf. 22, 1). . . .
4. Prayer against hemorrhage, 54 lines; cf. 4, 2.
   በስመ፡ አብ፡ . . . ጸሎት፡ በእንተ፡ መርግዔ፡ ደም፡ ሰንታም፡ ቀንታም፡ ሰንከሬም፡ . . .
5. Prayer against a piercing pain on the side, 16 lines; cf. 6, 4.
   በስመ፡ አብ፡ . . . ጸሎት፡ በእንተ፡ ሐጋመ፡ ውግዓት፡ ምድምያስ፡[7x] የሐቂ፡[3x] . . .
   The last four lines are illegible.

Miniatures and Magical Symbols:
1. Angel with sword and scabbard.
2. Talismanic symbol with face in center.

Copied for Wälättä Maryam/Mänän.

EMIP MagSc 29 – Marwick Magic Scroll 24

Parchment, 186.5 x 9.3 cm, three strips sewn together, one column, colored double border, Gəʽəz, 19th cent.

1. The Net of Solomon for catching demons as prayer against illnesses caused by Barya, Legewon, Zar, and Fora, 70 lines.
   በስመ፡ አብ፡ . . . ጸሎት፡ በእንተ፡ ሐጋመ፡ ባርያ፡ ወሌጌዎን፡ ዛር፡ ወፎራ፡ አስማት፡ አስማተ፡ ሰሎሞን፡ ዘረበሙ፡ ለአጋንንት፡ ከመ፡ መርበብተ፡ ዓሣ፡ ዘባሕር፡ ሰደቃኤል፡ ሰደታኤል፡ ኤናኤል፡ ርክማኤል፡ . . .

Catalogue of the Scrolls of Ethiopian Spiritual Healing · 301

2. Prayer against illnesses caused by Barya and Legewon, 50 lines; cf. Strelcyn, Manchester, 31, 7, p. 79.
በስመ፡ አብ፡ . . . ጸሎት፡ በእንተ፡ ሕማመ፡ ባርያ፡ ወሌጌዎን፡ በስመ፡ ለአብ፡ እግ"፡ በስመ፡ ለወልድ፡ እግ"፡ . . . ታዓስ፡ (sic) አዝዮስ፡ ወሌምክያስ፡ . . .ያቂ፡ ወያቂ፡ አንተ፡ ባርያ፡ ወሌጌዎን፡ አንተ፡ ዛር፡ ወወራዛ፡ ወዓይነ፡ ጥላ፡ ወጥላወጊ፡ ወእደ፡ ሰብእ፡ አንተ፡ ውጋት፡ ወቁርጥማት፡ አንተ፡ መጋኛ፡ ወጉስምት፡ አንተ፡ ተያF፡ ወቁራኛ፡ ወእደሰብእ፡ አንተ፡ ምትአት፡ ወጽፍአት፡ አንተ፡ ፍልፀት፡ ወቁርፀት፡ አንተ፡ ፈራ፡ ወንዳድ፡ አንተ፡ ደስክ፡ ወጉዳሌ፡ ወበርደሌ፡ ዘትትሜሰሉ፡ በብዙኅ፡ ያታ፡ አህያ፡ ሸራክያ፡ . . .

3. Prayer against the evil eye: The story of the sorcerer at the Sea of Tiberias, 30 lines; cf. 3, 1; 24, 1.
ጸሎተ፡ ነድራ፡ ወእንዘ፡ የሐውር፡ እግዚእነ፡ ኢያሱስ፡ ክርስቶስ፡ ውስተ፡ ባሕረ፡ ጥብርያዶስ፡ . . .

4. Prayer for binding demons, 33 lines; cf. 17, 1 and 7.
ጸሎት፡ በእንተ፡ ማዕሠረ፡ አጋንንት፡ አአምን፡ ወእትአመን፡ በ፫ቱ፡ አካላት፡ ወበ፩መለኮት፡ አብ፡ እሳት፡ . . . followed by John 1:1–5.

5. Prayer against a piercing pain on the stomach and heart, with a greeting to the pierced side of Jesus, 10 lines; cf. 93, 3.
ጸሎት፡ በእንተ፡ ሕማመ፡ ውግአተ፡ ከርሥ፡ ወልብ፡ ለገብርከ፡ ካህ፡ ሰላም፡ ለገቦከ፡ ኮይተ፡ (sic) ለንጊኖስ፡ ዘወግአ፡ ሳዶር፡ ወአምአዘተ፡ ማይ፡ ከርሥከ፡ ለደመ፡ ስርአት፡ እንተ፡ አንቅአ፡ አላዶር፡ ሐዋርያ፡ አብ፡ ክርስቶስ፡ ዘፈጸምከ፡ ግበረ፡ ተሰብአ፡ . . .

6. Prayer against illnesses caused by Barya, Legewon, Zar, invoking the name of the cross, 63 lines; cf. 4, 2.
በስመ፡ አብ፡ . . . ዓአትብ፡ ወእትአመን፡ በ፫አካላት፡ ወእትነሣእ፡ ፫ተ፡ አስማተ፡ ነሲዕየ፡ እትመረጐዝ፡ እመኒ፡ ወደቁ፡ . . . ያቂ፡ ወያቂ[፡] አንተ፡ ባርያ፡ ወሌጌዎን፡ አንተ[፡] ሰይጣን፡ ወጋኔን፡ አንተ፡ ዛር፡ ወወራዛ፡ ወዓይነ፡ ጥላ፡ ወጥላወጊ፡ ወእደ፡ ሰብእ፡ አንተ፡ ምትአት፡ ወጽፍአት፡ አንተ፡ ፍልፀት፡ ወቁርፀት፡ አንተ፡ መጋኛ፡ ወጉስምት፡ አንተ፡ ተያF፡ ወቁራኛ፡ አንተ፡ ፍልፀት፡ ወቁርፀት፡ አንተ፡ ፈራ፡ ወንዳድ፡ አንተ፡ ደስክ [፡] ወጉዳሌ፡ ወበርደሌ፡ ዘትትሜሰሉ፡ በብዙኅ፡ ያታ፡ አህያ፡ ሸራክያ፡ . . . (see 2 above).

7. Prayer against rheumatism, 25 lines.
ጸሎት፡ በእንተ፡ ሕማመ፡ ቁርጥማት፡ ሽምደንተክል፡ (?) ሸርታን፡ ሐውልተ፡ ስምዕ፡ ዘጊጊሃጋሌ፡ ኖብ፡ ንጉሥ፡ ክወብ፡ ከድ፡ ወርቀ፡ (sic) ንግሥትከ፡ ኢትንክስ፡ ወኢትቄርጥም፡ . . . ለገብርከ፡ ካህ፡ ጸሎት፡ በእንተ፡ ሕማመ፡ ቁርጥማት፡ የስየመ፡ (?) ኸ፡[7x] ሸ፡[7x] ፍርደሳዊ፡ ምሕረታዊ፡ . . .

Miniatures and Magical Symbols:
1. Angel (with sword?) (effaced).

2. Talismanic symbol with face in center.
3. Ornate cross with two figures, one on either side.
Copied for Kaśa/Gäbrä Naryam; other names in pencil: Wäldä Sänbät and Gäbrä Iyyäsus/Wasehun.

EMIP MagSc 30 – Marwick Magic Scroll 25
Parchment, 143.5 x 9.5 cm, three strips sewn together, one column, colored double border, Gəʻəz, 19th cent.
1. Prayer of St. Susənyos for binding demons and the story of his fight against Wərzəlya, the demon of infant mortality; cf. 7, 3; 16, 1.
በስመ፡ አብ፡ . . . ጸሎት፡ በእንተ፡ ማዕሠረ አጋንንት፡ [. . .] ጥላ፡ ጸዉዑ፡ አስማተ፡ ሥላሴ፡ ንቡአተ፡ ያሮክ፡ ታሮክ፡ ሳሮክ፡ ቤቁሮስ፡ አዳርስ፡ . . . በእሉ፡ አስማተ፡ ሥላሴ፡ ረሐቁ፡ ወታሰዱ፡ . . . በስመ፡ አብ፡ . . . ወሀሎ፡ አሐዱ፡ ብእሲ፡ ዘስሙ፡ ሱስንዮስ፡ . . ., followed by John 1:1–5.
2. Prayer against hemorrhage, 54 lines; cf. 4, 2.
በስመ፡ አብ፡ . . . ጸሎት፡ በእንተ፡ ሕማም፡ ደም፡ ሊስ፡ አፍሊስ፡ መሊስ፡ ሜሌያስ፡ ኢየሱስ፡ ክርስቶስ፡ ንይለ፡ በረድ፡ . . . ሰንተም፡ ከተም፡ ዘወጽአ፡ ደም፡ እምገቦሁ፡ ለእግዚእን፡ ኢየሱስ፡ ክርስቶስ፡ በከመ፡ ከተሮ፡ ለብርያል፡ ከማሁ፡ . . . followed by Ps 1:1–3.
3. Prayer of the rampart of the cross, written by Jeremiah, 32 lines; cf. 5, 3.
በስመ፡ አብ፡ . . . ጸሎት፡ በእንተ፡ ሐጹረ፡ መስቀል፡ ዘጸሐፎ፡ ኤርምያስ፡ ነቢይ፡ በውስተ፡ ኮኮሕ፡ እንዘ፡ ይብል፡ መስቀል፡ መግረሪ፡ ዐር፡ . . .
4. Greeting to Phanuel as prayer to terrorize demons, 63 lines; cf. 14, 3; 16, 5; 26, 5.
በስመ፡ አብ፡ . . . ጸሎት፡ በእንተ፡ መደንግጺ፡ አጋንንት፡ ወዓይነ፡ ጥላ፡ ሰላም፡ ለከ፡ ሰዳዬ፡ አጋንት[፡] ፋኑኤል፡. . .

Miniatures and Magical Symbols:
1. Angel with sword and scabbard.
2. Nine-box panel (3 x 3) with faces in boxes 1, 3, 5, 7, and 9 and X patterns in the other boxes.
3. Ornate cross.
Copied for Šiwäqet/Wälättä Mika'el.

EMIP MagSc 31 – Marwick Magic Scroll 26
Parchment, 168.5 x 9.3 cm, three strips sewn together, one column, wavy-line border, Gəʻəz, 19th cent.
1. Prayer of St. Susənyos and the story of his fight against Wərzəlya, the demon of infant mortality; cf. 7, 3; 16, 1.

[በስመ፡ አብ፡ . . .] አምላክ፡ በስመ፡ እግ" ነባቢ፡ ወተናጋሪ፡ ቅዱስ፡ ሱስንዮስ፡ በእንተ፡ አሰስሎ፡ ደዌ፡ . . . ጸሎቱ፡ ለቅዱስ፡ ሱስንዮስ፡ . . .
(*incipit* of the story has been damaged).
2. Prayer against the evil eye: The story of the sorcerer at the Sea of Tiberias, 102 lines; cf. 3, 1; 24, 1.
ጸሎት፡ በእንተ፡ ንድራ፡ ዘውእቱ፡ አይነት፡ ወእንዘ፡ የሐውር፡ እግዚእነ፡ ውስተ፡ ባሕረ፡ ጥብርያዶስ፡ . . .
3. Prayer against Barya and Legewon, 23 lines; cf. 15, 2. .
[ጸሎት፡ በእንተ፡] ሕማም፡ ባርያ፡ ወሌጌዎን፡ ዘይሰልብ፡ ልብ፡ ሰብእ፡ ወያጸልም፡ አእይንተ፡ . . .

Miniatures and Magical Symbols:
1. Angel.
2. Angel.

Name of the original owner erased and replaced with Wälättä Libanos and Wälättä Sänbät.

EMIP MagSc 32 – Marwick Magic Scroll 27

Parchment, 186 x 8 cm, three strips sewn together, one column, colored border, Gəʿəz, 19th cent.
1. The beginning of the prayer of St. Susənyos against infant mortality and The Net of Solomon for catching demons, 42 lines.
በስመ፡ አብ፡ . . . በስመ፡ እግ" ሕያው፡ ነባቢ፡ ወተናጋሪ፡ ፈጣሪ፡ (sic) ለቅዱስ፡ ሱስንዮስ፡ በእንተ፡ አሰስሎ፡ ደዌ፡ . . . ጸሎቱ፡ ለቅዱስ፡ ሱስንዮስ፡ . . . በስመ፡ አብ፡ . . . ጸሎት፡ በእንተ፡ መርበብተ፡ ሰሎሞን፡ ዘረበቦሙ፡ ለአጋንንት፡ ከመ፡ መርበብተ፡ ዓሣ፡ ዘባሕር፡ እንዘ፡ ይብል፡ ሰደቃኤል፡ አዳታኤል፡ ኪናኤል፡ . . .
2. Prayer against eye disease and headache, 52 lines.
በስመ፡ አብ፡ . . . ጸሎት፡ በእንተ፡ ሕማም፡ ዓይን፡ ወርስ፡ (sic) ፍልፀት፡ አምላክዬ፡ (sic) በደዊ፡ አብያቴር፡ ዛርዮን፡ መእንዝር፡ . . . በስመ፡ ሸገር፡ ጋላ[፡] ጆር፡ ኦኔር፡ ሐኢር፡ . . .
Concluded with a short prayer invoking the name of the cross.
3. Prayer against the evil eye, the evil eye of Barya and the story of St. Susənyos fighting Wərzəlya, the demon of infant mortality; cf. 7, 3; 16, 1.
በስመ፡ አብ፡ . . . ጸሎት፡ በእንተ፡ ዓይነ፡ ጥላ፡ ወዓይነ፡ ባርያ፡ ወዓይነ፡ ወርቅ፡ ድርሳን፡ ዘብዱስ፡ ወብጹእ፡ ሱስንዮስ፡ መስተጋድል፡ በቂዊን፡ ስም፥፡ በእንተ፡ ስም፡ እግዚእነ፡ ኢየሱስ፡ ክርስቶስ፡ ጸሎት፡ በእንተ፡ አሰስሎ፡ ደዌ፡ . . . ወሀሎ፡ ጂብሲ፡ ዘስሙ፡ ሱስንዮስ፡ . . . Concluded with John 1:1–5.
4. Prayer for binding demons, quoting Mark 1: 23–28, 40 lines.

በስመ፡ አብ፡ . . . ጸሎት፡ በእንተ፡ ማዕሠረ፡ አጋንንት፡ ወንጌል፡ ዘማርቆስ፡ ወሀሉ፡ ፪ብእሲ፡ ውስተ፡ ምኩራብ፡ ዘቦቱ፡ ጋኔን፡ እኩይ . . .
5. Prayer against the evil eye, Barya, Legewon, hemorrhage, 16 lines; cf. 4, 2.
በስመ፡ አብ፡ . . . ጸሎት፡ በእንተ፡ ህማም፡ ዓይነ፡ ጥላ፡ ወባርያ፡ ወሌጌዎን፡ ወህማም፡ ደም፡ ሊስ፡^{7x} አፍሊስ፡^{3x} መሊስ፡^{3x} መላሊስ፡^{3x} . . .
6. Prayer against illnesses caused by Šotälay, 19 lines, with the last three lines partly cut out; cf. 26, 7.
ጸሎት፡ በእንተ፡ ሕማመ፡ ሾተላይ፡ ሰርክተም፡^{5x} ሰንክተም፡

Miniatures and Magical Symbols:
1. Angel with sword and scabbard.
2. Ornate cross.
Copied for Wäynitu/Wälättä Mika'el.

EMIP MagSc 33 – Marwick Magic Scroll 28

Parchment, 177.5 x 8.6 cm, three strips sewn together, one column, colored border, Gǝʽǝz, 19th cent.

1. Prayer against illnesses caused by Barya, and the evil eye, 15 lines; cf. 27, 2; 28, 2.
በስመ፡ አብ፡ . . . ጸሎት፡ በእንተ፡ ሕማመ፡ ባርያ፡ ወአይነ፡ ጽላ፡ ዘይሰልብ፡ ልበ፡ ሰብእ፡ . . .
2. Prayer against eye disease and headache, 12 lines.
በስመ፡ አብ፡ . . . ጸሎት፡ በእንተ፡ ሕማመ፡ ርእስ፡ ፍልፀት፡ የሸለት፡ ያሸለት፡፡ ያሸለትት፡^{5x} አድገና፡ . . .
3. Prayer against illnesses caused by Barya and Legewon, and the story of St. Susǝnyos fighting Wǝrzǝlya, the demon of infant mortality.
በስመ፡ አብ፡ . . . ጸሎት፡ በእንተ፡ ሕማመ፡ ባርያ፡ ወሌጌዎን፡ በስመ፡ እግ'' ሕያው፡ ነባቢ፡ ወተናጋሪ፡ ጸሎቱ፡ ለቅዱስ፡ ሱስንዮስ፡ በእንተ፡ አሰሰሎ፡ ደዊ፡ . . . ወሀሉ፡ ፪ብእሲ፡ ዘስሙ፡ ሱስንዮስ፡ . . .
4. Prayer against hemorrhage and Šotälay, 29 lines; cf. 4, 3.
በስመ፡ አብ፡ . . . ጸሎት፡ በእንተ፡ ሕማመ፡ ደም፡ ወሾተላይ፡ ወወመጽአት፡ ብእሲት፡ እንተ፡ ደም፡ ይውኂዛ፡ እም ፲ወ ፪፡ አውራኅ፡ (Matt 9:20–22). . . . ሊስ፡^{3x} አፍሊስ፡^{3x} ሜልዮስ ሊስ፡^{3x} ኢየሱስ፡ ክርስቶስ፡ . . . ዘለብሶ፡ ለአዳም፡ መዊቶ፡ ሐይወ፡ ወዓርገ፡ . . .
5. Prayer against illnesses caused by Barya and Legewon, 25 lines; cf. 27, 2; 28, 2.
በስመ፡ አብ፡ . . . ጸሎት፡ በእንተ፡ ሕማመ፡ ባርያ፡ ወሌጌዎን፡ ዘይሰልብ፡ ልበ፡ ሰብእ፡ ወያጸልም፡ አዕይንተ፡ ወይመጽእ፡ ከመ፡ ጽላሎት፡ አመሕለኮ፡

(sic) ወአወግዘኩ፡ (sic) በሯ ቅንዋተ፡ መስቀል፡ . . . only longer than 1 above.
Miniatures and Magical Symbols:
1. Angel with sword and scabbard.
2. A stack of seven *asmat* face symbols.

Copied for Wälättä Arägay; (Wälättä) Mädḫən added later.

EMIP MagSc 34 – Marwick Magic Scroll 29

Parchment, 172 x 9.5 cm, three strips sewn together, one column, Gəʿəz, colored wavy-line border, early 20th cent.

1. Prayer of St. Susənyos and the story of his fight against Wərzəlya, the demon of infant mortality; cf. 33, 3.
በስመ፡ አብ፡ . . . በስመ፡ እግ" ሕያው፡ ነባቢ፡ ወተናጋሪ፡ ጸሎቱ፡ ለቅዱስ፡ ሱስንዮስ፡ በእንተ፡ አሰስሎ፡ ደዌ፡ . . . ወሀሎ፡ ፯ብእሲ፡ ዘስሙ፡ ሱስንዮስ፡ . . .

2. Prayer against charm, 58 lines
በስመ፡ አብ፡ . . . ጸሎት፡ በእንተ፡ መፍትሔ፡ ሥራይ፡ ብድሁድ፡^{5x} ማምሮን፡^{4x} . . .
Almost every possible *asmat* and their origin are listed.

3. Prayer against *Qämäñña* (sic) ... and for binding demons, insufficiently legible, 19 lines.
በስመ፡ አብ፡ . . . ጸሎት፡ በእንተ፡ ቀመኛ፡ ወተ[..፡] ቁርጥማት፡ ወፍልጸት፡ [. . .] ማዕሡረ፡ አጋንንት፡ ዘስሙ፡ አልአሹርዋእ፡ . . .(?)

4. Prayer against the evil eye, Barya, Legewon, Zar, Tägrda and Šalay, Buda, and Fälaša, 20 lines.
በስመ፡ አብ፡ . . . ጸሎት፡ በእንተ፡ ዓይነ፡ ጥላ፡ ወዓይነ፡ ባርያ፡ ወጊዎን፡ (sic) ዛር፡ ወተግርዳ፡ ወሾቶላይ፡ ቡዳ፡ ወፍላሻ፡ ዓዕ፡^{3x} በስሙ፡ ለእግዚእነ፡ ኢየሱስ፡ ጨጨር፡^{3x} ጊጊር፡^{3x} . . .

Miniatures and Magical Symbols:
1. Angel with sword and scabbard.
2. Talismanic symbol with face in center.
3. Angel (damaged).

Copied crudely for Copied for Wälättä Tənśaʾe.

EMIP MagSc 35 – Marwick Magic Scroll 30

Parchment, 126.5 x 8.8 cm, four strips sewn together, one column, colored border, Gəʿəz, 19th cent.

1. Prayer against illnesses caused by Barya, Legewon, 36 lines; cf. 27, 2; 28, 2.

በስመ፡ አብ፡ . . . ጸሎት፡ በእንተ፡ ሕማም፡ ባርያ፡ ወሌጌዎን፡ ዘይሰልብ፡ ልብ፡ ሰብእ፡ ወያጸልም፡ አእይንተ፡ ከመ፡ ጽላሎት፡ ወያበሀንን፡ በሀለመ፡ ሌሊት፡ . . . ሎፍሐም፡ በማዕሰረ፡ ኮሼኩሪ፡ አጀአ፡ በዝ፡ አስማት፡ . . . followed by John 1:1–5.

2. Prayer against the evil eye: The story of the sorcerer at the Sea of Tiberias, 71 lines; cf. 3, 1; 24, 1.
ጸሎተ፡ ነደራ፡ ወእንዘ፡ የሐውር፡ እግዚእ፡ ኢየሱስ፡ ምስለ፡ አርዳኢሁ፡ ብሐሪ፡ (sic) ጥብርያዶስ፡ . . . followed by the Greeting to Phanuel: ሰላም፡ ለተፈጥሮትከ፡ ምስለ፡ መላእክት፡ ኅቡረ፡ . . . and concluded with: ወገጹ፡ ዘፍጹም፡ በጽልመት፡ ፈርሃ፡ ወደንገጸ፡ ዲያብሎ[ስ፡ ርዕየ:] ብሁተ[፡] ልደት፡ በሥጋ፡ አምላክ፡ በሲአል፡ በዝ፡ ቃልከ፡ ወበዝ፡ ስምከ፡ አድህን፡ . . .

Miniatures and Magical Symbols:
1. Angel.
2. Figure with face with assortment of geometric shapes (squares, circles, dots, etc.) including face in box.
3. Set of circles at end of scroll.

Copied for Wälättä Mika'el.

EMIP MagSc 36 – Marwick Magic Scroll 31
Parchment, 179 x 9.8 cm, four strips sewn together, one column, Gəʿəz, colored border, early 20th cent.

1. Prayer against charm, the Jealous, Buda, and Qumäñña, 29 lines.
በስመ፡ አብ፡ . . . ጸሎት፡ በእንተ፡ መፍትሔ፡ ሥራይ፡ ወእጀ፡ ሰብእ፡ ወምቀኛ፡ ቡዳ፡ ወቁመኛ፡ ባዕድ፡ ወዘመድ፡ ወእምኮሉ፡ ሕማም፡ ወአልጉም፡ ፍታሕ፡ ወዘርዝር[፡] ሥራያቲሆሙ፡ ለመሠርያን፡ ፍታህ፡ ዘገሙ፡ ወዘረጉሙ፡ በመብልዕ፡ ወበልብስ፡ ፍታህ፡ በጥፍር፡ ወበእግር፡ ጥፍር፡ ፍታህ፡ በልብስ፡ ወበመስቴ፡ ፍታህ፡ በራስ፡ ፀጉር፡ ወበአይን፡ ምድር፡ ፍታሕ፡ ዘደገሙ፡ በካህን፡ ወበዲያቆን፡ ወበመሃይምን፡ ፍታሕ፡ ዘደገሙ፡ በእስላም፡ ቱቅራ፡ ወእምኮሉ፡ ፍታሕ፡ ሡዓር፡ ወዘርዝር፡ ሥራያቲሆሙ፡ ለመሠርያን፡ ሰብእ፡ ኢትቅረቡ፡ . . .

2. Prayer for driving away evil spirits, 22 lines.
በስመ፡ አብ፡ . . . ጸሎት፡ በእንተ፡ ዘንግዶሙ፡ (sic) ይሰደዱ፡ መላእክተ፡ ጽልመት፡ በአላዊ፡ ስምከ፡ በከቦራዊ፡ ስምከ፡ በሕያው፡ ስምከ፡ በናአስ፡ ስምከሂ፡ በዳፈር፡ ስምከ፡ ሰንተው፡ ቀንተው፡ . . . ስድድ፡ ዓይነ፡ ጽላ፡ ወዓይነ፡ ባርያ፡ ወዓይነ፡ ሾተላይ፡ ስድድ፡ ሕማም፡ ደም፡ ወተያያF፡ ወሕማም፡ ቁርፀት፡ ወፍልፀት፡ ወነሀብት፡ . . .

3. Prayer against the evil eye and miscarriage, 28 lines.
በስመ፡ አብ፡ . . . ጸሎት፡ በእንተ፡ ሕማም፡ ዓይነት፡ ወሕማም፡ ዕንስ፡ ክርስቶስ፡ ብርሃን፡ ክርስቶስ፡ መድኅን፡ ክርስቶስ፡ ምእመን፡ ክርስቶስ፡ ፀወን፡

... ቴስፍያታዊ፡ ሜስያዊ፡ ታርባዊ፡ ከቦራዊ፡ ዘጸሐፈ፡ ኤርምያስ፡ ነቢይ፡ ኀበ፡ ታቦተ፡ ማይ፡ ...

4. Greeting to Phanuel as prayer for binding demons with the, 46 lines.
በስመ፡ አብ፡ ... ጸሎት፡ በእንተ፡ ማእሠሮሙ፡ ለአጋንንት፡ ሰላም፡ ለከ፡ ሰዳዬ፡ አጋንንት፡
ፋኑኤል ለእግ" እምጽርሑ፡ ...

5. Prayer against the evil eye: The story of the sorcerer at the Sea of Tiberias, 64 lines; cf. 3, 1; 24, 1; 35, 2.
በስመ፡ አብ፡ ... .በእንተ፡ ሕማም፡ ዓይነት፡ ነጺራ፡ (sic) ወእንዘ፡ ዘውእቱ፡ ሕማም፡ እኩይ፡ ወእንዘ፡ የሐውር፡ እግዚእ፡ ውስተ፡ ባሕረ፡ ጥብርያዶስ፡ ... . ጸሎት፡ በእንተ፡ ሕማም፡ ቡዳ፡ ወቀመኛ፡ ወገጹ፡ በጽልመት፡ ፈርሀ፡ ወደንገፀ፡ ዲያብሎስ፡ ርእዮ፡ ...

Miniatures and Magical Symbols:
1. Angel with sword and scabbard.
2. Ornate cross.
3. Angel with sword and scabbard.

Copied for Wälättä Maryam.

EMIP MagSc 37 – Marwick Magic Scroll 32

Parchment, 130 x 8.5 cm, two strips sewn together, one column, colored border, Gəʻəz, early 20th cent.

1. The Net of Solomon for catching demons, 45 lines.
በስመ፡ አብ፡ ... ጸሎት፡ በእንተ፡ አስማተ፡ ሰሎሞን፡ ዘረበቦሙ፡ ለአጋንንት፡ ከመ፡ መርበብተ፡ አሣ፡ ... እንዘ፡ ይብል፡ ሰዳካኤል፡[3x] አደታኤል፡[3x] ኪያስ፡[3x] አድናኤል፡ ለመርብብ፡ ኪያስ፡ ጸለዎ፡ በሱራፌል፡ ከንፍ፡ (sic) ዕቀብ፡ ወልድነ፡ እምሕ"መ፡ ባርያ፡ ወሌጌዎን፡ ቀርፀት፡ ወፍልፀት፡ መገኛ፡ ወጕሥምት፡ ፌራ፡ ወንዳድ፡ ፈጌን፡ ወአልጉም፡ ወጽላ፡ ወጊ፡ ውግአት፡ ፍርቅቃት፡ ወቀርጥማት፡ ወጋኔን፡ ቀትር፡ ምች፡ ወምታት፡ እቀባ፡ ... ሀላዊ፡ (sic) ሀላዊሁ፡ (sic) ንንዕድ፡ ለሰሎሞን፡ ...

2. *Asmat* by which Solomon was saved from the Carpenters (*Nähabt*), obviously a continuation of 1 above, but with a clear division, 31 lines.
በስመ፡ አብ፡ ... በዝንቱ፡ አስማት፡ ድኅነ፡ ሰሎሞን፡ እምእዴሆሙ፡ ለነገብት፡ እምድኅረ፡ አነዝም፡ ወአንበርም፡ እስከ፡ ይከውን፡ ዖለተ፡ በአምሳለ፡ ንዋም፡ ኀበ፡ ንጉሥ፡ በሌሊት፡ ...

3. Prayer against illnesses of Täyayaž, Qʷərañña, Šotälay and hemorrhage, 22 lines.
[...] ፪አምላክ፡ ጸሎት፡ በእንተ፡ ሕማም፡ ታያF: (sic) ወቊራኛ፡ (sic) ወመርግዔ፡ ደም፡ ወፆተላይ፡ በዓዊን፡ በጋዲን፡ በጆርዳን፡ በዳታኤል፡ ... ፫አስጋተ፡ (sic) ወበ፬መለኮት፡ ይትአሰር፡ ደም፡ ...

4. Prayer against piercing pain caused by Šotälay and the wicked Legewon. Full text:
በስመ: አብ: . . . ጸሎት: በእንተ: ሕማም: ውግአት: ጸሉቱ: ወበከቱ: (sic) የሀሉ: ምስሌነ: ለዓለም: ዓለም: ሾተላይ: ወሌጌዎን: እኩይ: እግ": ንጉሥ: ወንጉሥሙ[:] ዝ: (sic) ፈኖክ: (sic) ለሐዋን: ፲ወ፪መላእክተ: ምሕረት: ወሣህል: አድኅና: ለአመትከ: . . .

5. Prayer against illnesses caused by Barya, Legewon and Šotolay. Full text, save for the last two illegible lines:
በስመ: አብ: . . . አብ: እሳት: ወልድ: እሳት: . . . በዝንቱ: አስግኔቲከ: ዘአጽራኪ: (sic) ግብር: ለዲያብሉስ: ከማሁ: አዕርዕ: (sic) ሕማም: ባርያ: ወሌጌዎን: ወሾቶላይ ዘይሰልብ: ልበ: ሰብእ: ወየሐንቅ: ክሳደ: ወያበሃን: በሀልም: (sic) ሌሊት: ወመዓልት: አምህልከ: (sic) በ፫አካላት: ወበ፪መለኮት: ድምናኤል:⁷ˣ አድናኤል:⁵ˣ አሽርምናኤል: (sic) ሸርምናኤል:⁶ˣ ጋዬዎን:⁷ˣ . . .

Miniatures and Magical Symbols:
1. Angel with sword.
2. Panel of three lines of geometric patterns.
3. Panel with one larger cross and two smaller crosses and cryptic S-shape patterns.
4. Panel with three diamond-shaped patterns and eight small circles.

The name of the original owner has been replaced by Wälättä Sänbät.

EMIP MagSc 38 – Bowerman-Hall Magic Scroll 1
Parchment, 206.5 x 11.5 cm, three strips sewn together, one column, colored border, Gəʿəz, 19th cent.
1. Prayer for driving away evil spirit, 32 lines; cf. Six, *Handschriften*, 31, 1, 1, 4a, p. 118.
በስመ: አብ: . . . በስሙ: ለእግ" አብ: በስመ: ለእግ" ወልድ: በስመ: ለእግ": መንፈስ: ቅዱስ: ታአስ: አዝዮቶስ: ማሲ: ማስያስ: አቅዳፈር: . . . በሰይፈ: ሚካኤል: ይትገዘም: ወይዐዕ: . . .
2. Prayer against Šotälay, Mäggañña, the eye of Barya, Legewon, Däsk, Gudale, Buda, etc. and the story of St. Susənyos fighting Wərzəlya, the demon of infant mortality; cf. 33, 3.
በስመ: እግ" ሕያው: ነባቢ: ወተናጋሪ: ጸሎት: ዘቅዱስ: ሱስንዮስ: በእንተ: አሰስሉ: ደዌ: . . . ወሀሉ: ፯ብእሲ: ዘስሙ: ሱስንዮስ: . . .
3. Prayer against Šotälay which causes infant mortality, possibly a continuation of 2; 47 lines.

Catalogue of the Scrolls of Ethiopian Spiritual Healing · 309

ጸሎት፡ በእንተ፡ ሾተላይ፡ አንተ፡ ሾተላይ፡ አንተ፡ ሾተላይ፡ ወሾተላዊ፡ ጋዬን፡
ዘትቀትል፡ ኀፃናተ፡ ወትጠዊ፡ አንFተ፡ ወትቄርዕ፡ አማዑተ፡ . . .
አምሐልኩከ፡ ወአውገዝኩከ፡ በፅቅንዋተ፡ . . . concluded with Mark 5:1–8.

Miniatures and Magical Symbols:
1. Row of four boxes with four-petal patterns in them above nine-box talismanic symbol with face in center.
2. Talismanic symbol with face in center.
3. Talismanic symbol with face in center.
4. Talismanic symbol with face in center.

Copied for Wälättä Rufa'el.

EMIP MagSc 39 – Bowerman-Hall Magic Scroll 2

Parchment, 186.5 x 10.3 cm, two strips sewn together, one column, colored double border, Gəʿəz, 20th cent.

1. Prayer for conception and against Šotälay, 26 lines.
   በስመ፡ አብ፡ . . . ጸሎት፡ በእንተ፡ ዘዘርን፡ ብእሲት፡ አእግዚእየ፡ ኢየሱስ፡
   ክርስቶስ፡ ዐቢይ፡ ኃይሉ፡ ዘየዓቅብ፡ ዘርን፡ ወፍሬ፡ ለእንስ፡ እመሕያው፡ ኀበ፡
   ውሉደ፡ (sic) ከመ፡ ትለድ፡ ትባዕተ፡ (sic) ወአንስተ፡ ወኢይቤልዋ፡ መካን፡
   በከመ፡ ሰማዕከ፡ ጸሎታ፡ ወስእለታ፡ ለሐና፡ እመ፡ ሳሙኤል፡ እ፡ ወሐና፡
   እመ፡ ማርያም. . . ሊስ፡ አፍሊስ፡ መለልዮስ፡ . . . በስመ፡ አብ፡ . . .
   ጸሎት፡ በእንተ፡ ሾተላይ፡ ፯^{7x} ሾተላይ፡ ከርተሃ፡ ሾተላይ፡ አናላይ፡ አንተ፡
   ውእቱ፡ ዘተቀኁዕ፡ (sic) አማዑተ፡ ወትጠዊ፡ ሐንFተ፡ ወተጌጸገጹ፡
   ሐንብርተ፡ ወተቀትል፡ ሕፃናተ፡ ተኃቅ፡ . . .

2. Prayer of St. Susənyos against infant mortality, actually for conception and against hemorrhage and Mäggañña, 31 lines.
   በስመ፡ እግ" ሕያው፡ ፈጣሪ፡ ወተናጋሪ፡ ነባቢ፡ መለኮት፡ ናሁ እጽሕፍ
   ጸሎት፡ ዘቅዱስ፡ ሱስንየስ፡ በእንተ፡ አሰስሎ፡ ደዌ፡ . . . በስመ፡ አብ፡ . . .
   ጸሎት፡ በእንተ፡ ደም፡ ወመጋኛ፡ በሰሎሜ፡ አቡን፡ ዘበሰማያት፡ ይሴብሑ፡
   ካህናት፡ ይሰድዱ፡ አጋንንት፡ ይወርዱ፡ መላእክት፡ ጻድቃን፡ ወሰማዕት፡
   ነቢያት፡ ወሐዋርያት፡ ዐቢይ፡ ስም፡ መልአከ፡ ምክር፡ . . . በከመ፡ ወሀብካ፡
   ለሐና፡ ሳሙኤልሃ፡ ወለሳራ፡ . . . ደም፡ ደም፡ ደም ኖሪ፡ (ጥሪ?) በዝ፡
   መሐፍለ (?) . . . ክትር፡ ቃለ፡ አብ፡ . . .

3. Greeting to Phanuel as prayer for binding demons, 17 lines.
   በስመ፡ አብ፡ . . . ጸሎት፡ በእንተ፡ ማዕሡረ፡ አጋንንት፡ ሰላም፡ ለከ፡ ስዳዬ፡
   አጋንንት፡ ፋኑኤል፡ . . .

4. Prayer of St. Susənyos and the story of his fight against Wərzəlya of infant mortality, 72 lines.
   ወሀሎ፡ ፩ብእሲ፡ ዘስሙ፡ ሱስንዮስ፡ . . .

5. Prayer against filthy Legewon, the demon that brings nightmare, 22 lines; cf. 3, 5; 8, 8; 9, 4; 15, 2; 26, 6.
  በስመ፡ አብ፡ . . . ጸሎት፡ በእንተ፡ ሌጌዎን፡ ርኩስ፡ ዘይሰልብ፡ ልበ፡ ሰብእ፡ ወያጸልም፡ አዕይንተ፡ ወይመጽእ፡ ከመ፡ ጽላሎት፡ ወሕልም፡ አምኀለከ፡ ወአወግዘከ፡ በ፫ቅንዋተ፡ መስቀሉ፡ . . .
6. Prayer for casting out evil spirit, 22 lines; cf 38, 1.
  በስመ፡ ለእግ" አብ፡ በስመ፡ ለእግ" ወልድ፡ በስመ፡ ለእግ"፡ መንፈስ፡ ቅዱስ፡ ታአስ፡ አዝዮስ፡ ማሲ፡ ማስያስ፡ አቅደፌር፡ . . . በሰይፈ፡ ሚካኤል፡ ይትገዝም፡ ወይዋዕ፡ . . .
7. Prayer to subjugate evil spirits, and unbind charm, 16 lines.
  በስመ፡ አብ፡ . . . ጸሎት፡ በእንተ፡ ምቅናዮሙ፡ ለአጋንንተ፡ ጸዋጋን፡ ዘሳሳተ፡ ቃላቲሆሙ፡ እሳት፡ አዕይንቲሆሙ፡ ወቀራንብቲሆሙ፡ . . . ድድያስ፡ ዕንጌ፡ በያቴር፡ በዝንቱ፡ አስጋተ፡ እስክንድር፡ ወሰሎሞን፡ ነገሥተ፡ መክብብ፡ ከማሁ፡ ክብበሙ፡ ወእስሮሙ፡ . . . ፍታሕ ሥራየ፡ አስገታ፡ . . .
8. Prayer against colic, 24 lines.
  ጸሎት፡ በእንተ፡ ኅማመ፡ ቀርፀት፡ አምላከ፡ አናንያ፡ ወአዛርያ፡ ወሚሳኤል፡ ዘአድኃንከሙ፡ . . . ይትመየጥ፡ ወይሰስል፡ ዝንቱ፡ ኅማመ፡ ከብድ፡ ወቀርፀት፡ . . .

Miniatures and Magical Symbols:
1. Angel with sword.
2. Talismanic symbol with face in the center.
3. Nine-box panel (3 x 3) with talismanic symbol with face in the center; four-petal symbol with eyes in boxes 1, 3, 7, and 9.
4. Panel with elaborate symbol with two boxes with X shapes in the center.

Copied for Wälättä Mika'el; Wälättä Haymanot added later.

EMIP MagSc 40 – Weiner Magic Scroll 1
Parchment, 160 x 9.7 cm, two strips sewn together, one column, double border, Gəʻəz, early 20th cent.
1. Prayer for conception, 17 lines.
  በስመ፡ አብ፡ . . . ጸሎት፡ በእንተ፡ አንስት፡ መካናት፡ እለ፡ ይ[ፈ]ቅዳ፡ ወሊደ፡ ወትብል፡ ከመዝ፡ (two lines in red are insufficiently legible) [..]ሌም፡ ወነሥአ፡ ፩እምአጽሙ፡ ገቦሁ፡ ወፈጠራ፡ ለሔዋን፡ ወይቤሎሙ፡ ብዝኁ፡ . . . ወይእዜኒ፡ እግ"፡ አምላክነ፡ . . .
2. Prayer against hemorrhage, 8 lines
  በስመ፡ አብ፡ . . . ጸሎት፡ በእንተ፡ አርግኤ፡ ደም፡ ሊስ፡ አፍሊስ፡ ሊስ፡ ዓፍሊስ፡ ሊስ፡ ዓፍሊስ፡ አስትር፡ (sic) ደመ፡ ዓመትከ፡ . . .
3. Prayer for drowning demons, 10 lines.

ጸሎት፡ በእንተ፡ መስጠም፡ አጋንንት፡ ይደሃይኖባ፡ (sic) ብስላምን፡ አመነሁ፡ ወይኩር፡ ሸይጣን፡ . . .
4. Prayer for binding Satan and Nägärgar, 14 lines.
ጸሎት፡ በእንተ፡ ማዕሡፉ፡ ለሡይጣን፡ ወለ፡ ነገርጋር፡ ዘሰሙ፡ ቶፒራ፡³ˣ አሸፒራ፡³ˣ አስፒራ፡ አሸፒራ፡ ጨርጨቤ፡³ˣ መስተቤ፡ . . .
5. Prayer against the evil eye of Barya: The story of the sorcerer at the Sea of Tiberias, 36 lines; cf. 3, 1; 24, 1.
ጸሎት፡ በእንተ፡ አይነተ፡ ባርያ፡ ጸሎተ፡ ነደራ፡ ዘውዕቱ፡ ዓይን ዕኩይ፡ ወእንዘ፡ የሐልፍ፡ እግዚእነ፡ ኢየሱስ፡ ውስተ፡ ባህረ፡ ጥብርያዶስ፡ . . .
6. Prayer against Barya, 26 lines.
ጸሎት፡ በእንተ፡ ባርያ፡ አሌፍ፡ ነፋጨር፡ ንጉሡ፡ አጋንንት፡ ቆርጨር፡ ንጉሡ፡ ባርያ፡ (two lines in red are insufficiently legible) . . . ሸ፡⁵ˣ ቀነሸ፡ አቅማን፡ በዝንቱ፡ አስማት፡ ይሡፉ፡ አጋንንት . . .
7. Prayer against filthy Legewon, the demon that brings nightmare, 29 lines; cf. 3, 5; 8, 8; 9, 4; 15, 2.
ጸሎት፡ በእንተ፡ ሌጌዎን፡ ርኩስ፡ ዘይሡልብ፡ ልበ፡ ሰብ፡ (sic) ወያጸልም፡ ዓዕይንተ፡ ወይመጽእ፡ ከመ፡ ጽላሎት፡ ወሕልም፡ . . . በቬቅንዋተ፡ መስቀሉ፡ . . .
8. Prayer of St. Susənyos and the story of his fight against Wərzəlya, the demon of infant mortality, 58 lines.
በሰመ፡ አብ፡ . . . ጸሎት፡ ወአስተብቁዓት፡ ሰበ፡ ጸለየ፡ ቅዱስ፡ ሱስንዮስ፡ በእንተ፡ አሰስሎ፡ ደዌ፡ እምሕፃናት፡ . . . ወሀሎ፡ ፩ብእሲ፡ ዘስሙ፡ ሱስንዮስ፡ . . .
9. Prayer against Buda and Carpenters (Nähabt), 15 lines.
ጸሎት፡ በእንተ፡ ነንብት፡ (sic) በለሶን፡³ˣ ወሰሶን፡³ˣ ሆለፐርኒስ፡ . . . ሎፍሐም፡³ˣ መሐፍሎም፡³ˣ ሰለማን፡ በኃይለ፡ ዝንቱ፡ አስማቲከ፡ . . .
10. Prayer for binding demons, 26 lines.
በስመ፡ አብ፡ . . . ጸሎት፡ በእንተ፡ ማዕሡሮሙ፡ ለአጋንንት፡ አህያ፡ ሸራኽያ፡ አልሻዳይ፡ . . . በዝንቱ፡ አስማት፡ ቃልከ፡ ውጉዝ፡ . . .

Miniatures and Magical Symbols:
1. Talismanic symbol with face in the center.
2. Angel with sword and hand cross.
3. Ornate cross.

Copied for Wälättä Ananya and her husband Askalä Maryam.

EMIP MagSc 41 – Weiner Magic Scroll 2

Parchment, 164.5 x 12.5 cm, three strips sewn together, one column, colored double border, Gəʻəz, late 20th cent.

1. Prayer against infertility, 118 lines; possibly several prayers, including some against hemorrhage, but without the usual break signs. The instructions, deciphered in bold, are in code.
   በስመ፡ አብ፡ . . . ጸሎት፡ በእንተ፡ መካናት፡ ⌈ሀብር፡ ጣብር፡³ˣ ወንጌል፡ ዘማቴዎስ፡ (sic, for Mark 5:25–32). ከማሃ፡ አሕይዋ፡ ለአመትከ፡ . . . ቆቆሆሂን፡ ቆቆሆሊን፡ ቆቆሆሒን፡ ቆቆሆሚን፡ ቆቆሆሚን፡ ቆቆሆሪን፡ ቆቆሆሲን፡ ቆቆሆቢን፡ [note the alphabet embedded in the *asmat* in their right order: ሂ ሊ ሒ ሚ ሚ ቂ ሲ ቢ] በዝ፡ ስእለት፡ ይትረኘው፡ ማንፀና፡ ለአመትከ . . . ዘተዐፀወ፡ በመልጉሙ፡ አጋንንት፡ እንዘ፡ እኑዛን፡ በመዋቅንት፡ ኀቡአ፡ ስሙ፡ ማስያስ፡ ትስቡቋሮን፡ እብኖዲ፡ ሙአግያ፡ ሙኪርያ፡ አንቲሲልያሱ፡ በዝንቱ፡ ስምክ፡ ወአስማጥኪ፡ ይፃእ፡ እምውስተ፡ ከርሣ፡ ⌈ይማፀብ፡ ቶትስት፡ ዓዛፍ፡ ቿክሊዘ፡ [i. e. በግይ፡ ትስትቶ፡ ፍዛፃ ዘለከፍ] ፌኑ፡ ብርሃንከ፡ . . . . . .
   በስመ፡ እግ"፡ ድግም፡ ⌈ያስትአ፡ ብሐፀትው፡ [i. e. **አስትያ፡ ወትትሐፀብ፡**] አሕያ፡ ሽራሒያ፡ አልሻዳይ፡ አልመክኑን፡ አልፋ፡ ወአ፡ ኢየሱስ፡ ክርስቶስ፡ እግ" ሒያው፡ ወወልደ፡ ማርያም፡ . . . ሳዶር፡ አላዶር፡ . . . ሊስ፡ አፍሊስ፡ መላሊስ፡ . . .ሸረክሸ፡ አንዋጢም፡ ዱንቴም፡ ብርስባሔል፡ . . . ግርግ፡ መለኮት፡ ብዑድ፡ ሰይፈ፡ መለኮት፡ መርዕድ፡ . . . ቁም፡ ተከተር፡ አንተ፡ ደም፡ አኒዝባ፡ ያዝነሉሙ፡ . . . ዘአቀምከ፡ ነቅዓ፡ ደግ፡ ለብእሲት፡ . . . ስንታም፡ ቀንታም፡ ሶተራም፡ ሊስ፡ አፍሊስ፡ ሜሎስ፡ ሜልዮስ፡ ቤልዮስ፡ . . . ደም፡ ደም፡ ዘትነብር፡ በሳምባ፡ ስር፡ በስራስር፡ እንደ፡ ወሐ፡ ተከተር፡ እንደ፡ ሐፀር፡ ተሐፀር፡ አሉህ፡ አብ፡ . . .
   ጸሎት፡ ጽኑዓት፡ (sic) ጽኑሳት፡ አንስት፡ እግ" ንጉሥ፡ ዘፈኖክ፡ ለሐዋን፡ ፲ወፀተ መላእክተ፡ ኃያላን፡ (sic) ወጽኑዓን፡ (sic) ከማሁ፡ አጽዕፅ፡ ውሕዘተ፡ ደግ፡ ለአመትከ፡ . . . አህያ፡ ሽራሁያ፡ ሴራህያ፡ አልሻዳይ፡ እልመክኑን፡ ኢየሱስ፡ ክርስቶስ፡ ወልደ፡ እግ"፡ ሒያው፡ . . . ዘበመስቀልከ፡ አጽራዕከ፡ ግብሮ፡ ለዲያብሎስ፡ ከማሁ፡ . . .
2. Prayer against Barya and Legewon, 32 lines.
   ጸሎት፡ በእንተ፡ ባርያ፡ ወሌጌዎን፡ ደም፡ ሌጌዎን፡ ዘንተ፡ አልፋ፡ ጎድር፡ ሽጎድር፡ አሽጎድር፡ ሡናየ፡ ዘርአ፡ ሥጋያ፡ በውስተ፡ ከርሣ፡ ለአመትከ፡ . . . አፍሊስ፡ መሊስ፡ መላሊስ፡ ሜልዮስ፡ ዘአርጋከ፡ ኃይለ፡ በረየ፡ ወነፋስ፡ ከማሁ፡ አርግዕ፡ ውሕዘተ፡ ደግ፡ . . . ዘዙኤል፡ ቤል፡ ወዘላል፡ ብርጋምዜል፡ . . . እአምላከ፡ ደም፡ ዘፈቅጠር፡ ደም፡ ዘጊዮርጊስ፡ ደም፡ ዘመርቆሬዎስ፡ ደም፡ ዘፋሲለደስ፡ . . . ደም፡ ቁም፡ አሉህ፡ አብ፡ . . .

Miniatures and Magical Symbols:
1. Man (angel?) standing.
2. Nine-box panel with faces in boxes 1, 3, 5, and 7, and X patterns in the other boxes.
3. Talismanic symbol with face in the center.

Copied for Wälädä Kidan.

EMIP MagSc 42 – Weiner Magic Scroll 3
Parchment, 214.5 x 10.8 cm, three strips sewn together, one column, no border, Gəʿəz, 19th and 20th cent.

1. Prayer against the evil eye: The story of the sorcerer at the Sea of Tiberias, confused with the story in the prayer titled "The Net of Solomon".
   በስመ፡ አብ፡ . . . ከመ፡ ወርቅ፡ ቀይን፡ አዕዳዊሃኒ፡ ወአዕጋሪሃኒ፡ ከመሡረገላ፡ ወይወጽእ፡ እምአፉሃ፡ ነበልባለ፡ እሳት፡ . . . አውግዞሙ፡ ወለጉምኩክሙ፡ (sic) አጋንንት፡ በደራ፡ ፈንቋት፡ በደራ፡ ነጋሽ፡ ወ$^\cap$ቃለ፡ (probably በወለቃ) ነጋሽ፡ በዱር፡ ነጋሽ፡ በገደል፡$^{,2\bar{\eta}}$በባሕር፡ ነጋሽ፡ በበቅል፡ (በበቅላ?) ነጋሽ፡ አውገዝክሙ፡ (sic) ይሰስል፡ ሌጌዎን፡ ሊቅክሙ፡ . . .

2. Prayer against piercing pain and other illnesses.
   በእግ"፡ አብ፡ ጸሎቱ፡ (sic) አብ፡ እሳት፡ ወልድ፡ እሳት፡ . . . ሳዶር፡ አላዶር፡ ዳናት፡ አዲራ፡ ሮዳስ፡ በ፫ቅንዋተ፡ . . . በስመ፡ ስሉስ፡ ቅዱስ፡ ነጋዬ፡ ኤር፡ ቀንደቂን፡ . . . ዘንተ፡ አስማተ፡ እንዘ፡ ትብሉ፡ ሲድራታኤል፡ ያአፍታኤል፡ (sic) ኢታኢኤል፡ . . . ቡዪለ፡ ዝንቱ፡ አስማቲክ፡ አድኅነኒ፡ እምሕማም፡ ወግዓት፡ (sic) ወምታት፡ ወጽፍዓት፡ ወርግፀት፡ ገቦ፡ ወእምነ፡ ኮሉ፡ ሕማም፡ . . . ክርስቂ፡ ከርስ፡ ኪስ፡ ስርዋዝ፡ ምድምያስ፡^{3x} የሐቂ፡ . . .

3. Prayer against hemorrhage.
   ቀነጹ፡^{3x} ጥርሜሐስን፡ ሡራዊ፡ ሡራዊን፡ ሊስ፡ አፍሊስ፡ መሊስ፡ ዘኬዎስ፡ ቡኃይለ፡ ዝንቱ፡ አስግቲክ፡ አርግዕ፡ ደግ፡ በውግዘተ፡ ደም፡ ለገብከ፡ (sic)…

4. Prayer against hemorrhage.
   ጸሎት፡ በእንተ፡ ነከራም፡ (?) ዘይወጽእ፡ እምገቡሁ፡ ለእግዚእነ፡ . . . ዘአርጋዕከ፡ ኀይለ፡ በረድ፡ . . . በስመ፡ ዚአከ፡ ይስግዕ፡ (sic) ሞት፡ ወደዊ፡ አጋንንት፡ ይደንግፁ፡ እለ፡ ይበጽብጹ፡ (sic) ማነፀነ፡ . . . አውገዝኩክሙ፡ ወለጉምኩክሙ፡ በመለኮቱ፡ ለ፫ቱ፡ አካላት፡ . . . አእግዚእየ፡ ኢየሱስ፡ ክርስቶስ፡ አቅም፡ ደግ፡ . . . ጥራኤል፡ ሸራኤል፡ ሸሻራኤል፡ አማኑኤል፡ ቡኃይለ፡ ዝንቱ፡ አስግቲክ፡ ዘአርጋዕከ፡ ኀይለ፡ በረድ፡ ወነፋስ፡ ከማሁ፡ . . . አሊስ፡ አፍሊስ፡ አክሊስ፡ መ$^\Lambda$ክሊስ፡ መልኪልስ፡ . . .

5. The Net of Solomon for catching demons, Däsk, Gudale, Legewon, and Barya, but here without title.
   ዘረበሙ፡ ለአጋንንት፡ ከመ፡ መርበብተ፡ አሳ፡ እንዘ፡ ይብል፡ ሰዱቃኤል፡ አደታኤል፡ ከርሜል፡ አናታኤል፡ . . . አስግተ፡ ሰሎሞን፡ ወካዕበ፡ አያስ፡ ባአስ፡ አያቀልም፡ ዘእንበለ፡ ም፡ (sic) ዝቃል፡ ዘወረደ፡ እምላዕለ፡ ኀቡዕ፡ ቃለ፡ ለአብ፡ . . . ወሀሎ፡ ሰሎሞን፡ ሸተከለሸ፡ አለሸ፡ ሸተሸር፡ . . . በዝንቱ፡ አስማተ፡ ድኅነ፡ ሰሎሞን፡ . . . ወእዝብጠሙ፡ ወእቅትሎሙ፡ ወእኩን፡ ፀሮሙ፡ ለአጋንንት፡ ወለደስክ፡ [ወለጉ]ዳሌ፡ ወለጌዎን፡ (sic) ወለባርያ፡ ከመ፡

ኢትቅትሉኒ፡ ነፍስየ፡ ወሥጋየ፡ ወለዉሉድየ፡ ወብእሲትየ፡ ወእንስሳየ፡ ወኮሎ፡ ዘአጥረይኩ፡ . . .

Miniatures and Magical Symbols:
1. Small panel with geometric shapes and (perhaps) three small crosses.
2. Small panel with geometric shapes, and crosses.
3. Man standing (faded and stained).

The first half is copied (20th cent) in a crude hand; *incipit* and division signs not copied. About ten lines from bottom are insufficiently legible.
Copied for Gäbrä Kiros.

EMIP MagSc 43. Weiner Magic Scroll 4

Parchment, 214 x 9.4 cm, three strips sewn together, one column, colored double border, Gəʻəz, 20th cent.

1. Prayer for binding demons, 24 lines.
   በስመ፡ አብ፡ . . . ጸሎት፡ በእንተ፡ ማዕሠሬ፡ አጋንንት፡ ወሰይጣናት፡ ሊቃኖስ፡ ብሂል፡ [. . .]፡ ነገር፡ ሰዱቃኤል፡ ብሂል፡ ስዱቱ፡ (sic) ለሰይጣን፡ በእንተ፡ ገባቶን፡ መስቀል፡ ብሂል፡ ኑሳቴ አጋንንት፡ መስቀል፡ ብሂል፡ መዋዔ፡ ፀር፡ መስቀል፡ ብሂል፡ መግረሬ፡ ፀር፡ . . . ምድያስ፡[3x] የሐቂ፡[3x] ይበርስቂ፡[3x] አክርስቂ፡ ወልደ፡ በሩስቂ፡ አጎና፡ (sic) ለዓመትከ፡ . . .

2. Prayer against the evil eye of Buda, artisans and Qumäñña, 110.
   በስመ፡ አብ፡ . . . ጸሎት፡ በእንተ፡ ሕማም፡ ቡዳ፡ ወእጀሰብእ፡ አስኮራችሲ፡[4x] አስኮራጽስ፡[3x] አህኺያ፡ (sic) አኺያ፡ . . . አልፋ፡ ወቤጣ፡ ጼቃ፡ ቤቃ፡ ቤጋ፡ ደልጋ፡ አዶናይ፡ . . . ሎፍሐም፡[4x] ነገርኩሙ፡ ኢያኤል፡ ያጥፍዕ፡ እግ"፡ ሕማም፡ እኩይ፡
   ስሙ፡ ለእግ"፡ አቅደ ቀጀር፡ አቅደቀጀር፡ ኢታንስሐስ፡ እደዊከ፡ ወንገሪከ፡ ተአሥር፡ በስመ፡ ሳዶር፡ አላዶር፡ . . . አላሁ"ግ፡[4x] ወያኑሬሐጀ፡ ረጀ፡ ሐቀበረጀ፡ በሐቅለ፡ ማግየር፡ . . .

3. Prayer against the evil eye, and Šotälay, and the story of St. Susənyos fighting Wərzəlya, the demon of infant mortality, 20 lines (!)
   ጸሎት፡ በእንተ፡ ዓይነ፡ ጥላ፡ ወሾቶላይ፡ ድርሳን፡ ዘቡፅዕ፡ ወንፉይ፡ ዘቅዱስ፡ ሱስንዮስ፡ መስተጋድል፡ ወነበረት፡ አሐቲ፡ ብእሲት፡ ወቀተለቶ፡ ለወልደ፡ አረጊት፡ ወይእቲ፡ ነገረቶ፡ . . .

4. Prayer against the evil eye and the evil eye of Barya and others: The story of the sorcerer at the Sea of Tiberias, 34 lines; cf. 3, 1; 24, 1.
   ጸሎት [፡] በእንተ፡ ዓይጥላ፡ ጸሎተ፡ ወአይነተ [፡] ባርያ፡ ወአይነ፡ ሰብእ፡ ጸሎተ[፡] ንደራ፡ ወእንዘ [፡] የሐውር፡ እግዚእ፡ ኢየሱስ [፡] ክርስቶስ፡ ውስተ [፡] ባሕረ፡ ጥብርያዶስ፡ . . .

Miniatures and Magical Symbols:
1. Angel with sword.

Catalogue of the Scrolls of Ethiopian Spiritual Healing · 315

2. Angel with sword.
3. Angel with sword.
4. Angel with sword.

Copied for Wälättä Yoḥannəs.

EMIP MagSc 44 – Weiner Magic Scroll 5

Parchment, 156 x 14.3 cm, three strips sewn together, two columns, colored double border, elaborate margin between columns with faces and interlaced rope patterns, etc., Gəʻəz, 20th cent.

1. Prayer against the evil eye, the evil eye of Barya, Legewon, Zar, Täyayaž, Šotälay and Mäggañña, 51 lines; cf. 47, 1.
በስመ: አብ: . . . ጸሎት: በእንተ: ዓይነ: ባርያ: ወሌጌዎን: ዓይነ: ዛር: ወአይነ: ተያዦ: (sic) ዓይነ: ሰብእ: ወሾተላይ: ዓይነ: ጥላ: ወጥላ: ወጌ: ዓይነ: ሥትሥታት: ወፍርቅቃት: ዓይነ: አስወንውን: ወለህማመ: መገኛ: ወጉሥምት: ወለሐማመ: ቁርፀት: ወፍልጸት: ጠቢብ: መንሾ: ወለሸንት: ምፅ: ወጕርጕሖ: ወጀርባ: ደዊ: ወመናፍስት: . . . አጋንንት: ፀዋጋን: ባርያ: ፀሊማን: ባርያ: ቀይሖን: እደ: ሰብእ: . . . ምድምያስ:[4x] ምድር: ቆቅት: ላይ: በባህር: ዝትነብር: (sic) . . .

2. Prayer against infant mortality and the story of St. Susənyos fighting Wərzəlya, the demon of infant mortality.

Miniatures and Magical Symbols:
1. Madonna and Child with angel on either side and ornate cross on either side.
2. Elaborate four-petal pattern with face in box in center and angel in each quadrant.
3. Talismanic symbol with face in center.
4. Eighteen-box panel (6 x 3) with faces in the even-numbered boxes and four-petal patterns in the odd-numbered boxes.

Copied crudely.

EMIP MagSc 45 – Weiner Magic Scroll 6

Parchment, 205 x 7.8 cm, three strips sewn together, one columns, colored border, Gəʻəz, 19th cent.

1. Prayer, using the name of the Trinity, against illnesses caused by Zar and demons, and for drowning demons, Legewon, Wəllaǧ, and illnesses caused by Təgərtya, 63 lines.
በስመ: አብ: . . . ጸሎት: በእንተ: ሕማመ: ዛር: ወሕማመ አጋንንት: ወመስጦም: አጋንንት: ወሌጌዎን: ወውላጅ: ወሕማመ: ትግርትያ: ዝንቱ ስመ: [ሥላሴ: . . . ለጸድቃ]ን: ማንተመ: መንሱት: ለረሚያን: ዝንቱ ስመ:

ሥላሴ፡ [ሕመም፡] ሲያጣን [. . . ሰ]ዳዲሆሙ፡ ለአጋንንት፡ ወለሰብእ፡ እኩያን፡ ወመሠርያን፡ ዝንቱ፡ ስመ፡ ሥላሴ፡ . . .

2. Prayer against terror that God gave to Adam, 18 lines.
በስመ፡ አብ፡ . . . ጸሎተ፡ ድንጋዔ፡ ዘወሀቦ፡ እግ" ለአቡነ፡ አዳም፡ አመ፡ ወጽአ፡ እምገነት፡ ከመ፡ ኢደንግ[.]ፅ፡ ልቡ፡ ወይቤሎ፡ ለቡ፡ ቤግ፡ በፈግ፡ በፍያም፡ በድልሰቅያም፡ ከዘዚህ፡ ወባርያ፡ ወበዝ፡ አስማት፡ እእትት፡ እምላዕሌሃ፡ ሕግመ፡ መጋኛ፡ ወሸተላይ፡ ለአመትከ፡ . . .

3. Prayer against terror that God gave to Noah, 38 lines.
በስመ፡ አብ፡ . . . ጸሎተ፡ ድንጋዔ፡ ዘወሀቦ፡ እግ" ለአቡነ፡ ኖኅ፡ አመ፡ ነትገ፡ ማየ፡ አይኀ፡ ወሰበ፡ ሰምዓ፡ ድምፀሙ፡ ለፄአጋንንት፡ ዘተዓሥሩ፡ በፈለገ፡ ጤግሮስ፡ እንዘ፡ ይብሉ፡ ጽምጽማኤል፡ ቆርሽ፡ ቆኖሽር፡ ወበነሺር፡ ተዓሡሩ፡ በከመ፡ ተዓሡረ፡ ዲያብሎስ፡ ብርያል፡ . . . ወገጹ፡ ዘፍጹም፡ በጽል[.]መት፡ ፈርሁ፡ ወደንበፀ፡ ዲያብሎስ፡ ርእዮ፡ . . .

4. Prayer against illnesses caused by Barya, Legewon, Šotälay, the evil eye and child killer, 35 lines; the latter half, copied in red, is illegible.
በስመ፡ አብ፡ . . . ጸሎት፡ በእንተ፡ ሕግመ፡ ባርያ፡ ወሌጌዎን፡ ወሸተላይ፡ ወዓይነ፡ ወርቅ፡ ልጅ፡ ገዳይ፡ ኀቡዕ፡ ስሙ፡ ለእግ"፡ ዘጽሑፍ፡ ውስተ፡ ክነፈሁ፡ ለቅዱስ፡ ሚካኤል፡ ሊቀ፡ መላእክት፡ ኢኮስ፡ . . .

5. Prayer against the evil eye, the evil eye of Šotälay, and the eye of child killer: The story of the sorcerer at the Sea of Tiberias, 48 lines; cf.3, 1.
በስመ፡ አብ፡ . . . ጸሎት፡ በእንተ፡ ዓይነ፡ ወርቅ፡ ወዓይነ፡ ጥላ፡ ወዓይነ፡ ሸተላይ፡ ዓይነ፡ ልጅ፡ ገዳይ፡ ጸሎተ፡ ነድራ፡ እንዘ፡ የሐውር፡ እግዚእነ፡ ውስተ፡ ባሕረ፡ ጥብርያዶስ፡ . . .

Miniatures and Magical Symbols:
1. Angel with sword and scabbard (large).
2. Talismanic symbol with face in center.
3. Man with sword and scabbard.
4. A few, small cryptic s-shaped patterns at the end of the scroll.

Copied for Wälättä Mädḫan; Wälättä Iyyäsus/Təblät added later.

EMIP MagSc 46 – Weiner Magic Scroll 7

Parchment, 194 x 9.2 cm, three strips sewn together, one columns, (faintly) colored border, Gəʽəz, late 20th cent.

1. Title is insufficiently legible, but looks like a prayer for drowning/binding demons and against Barya and *Nähabi*, and hemorrhage, similar to 38, 1; 39, 6; 56 lines.
[በስሙ፡ ለእግ"፡ አብ፡ በስሙ፡ ለእግ"፡ ወልድ፡ በስሙ፡ ለእግ"፡ መንፈስ ቅዱ]ስ፡ ማስ፡ ማስያስ፡ አክያስ፡ አቁዬፈር፡ በስሙ፡ ለጋራቡ፡ . . .
ያሽኩት፡ ሊሃለ፡ በዝ፡ አስማት፡ ቃልከ፡ ኢየሱስ፡ ወለደ፡ ማርያም፡ ድንግል፡

ወበሰይፈ፡ ሚካኤል፡ ይትገዘም፡ ወይዳእ፡ መንፈስ፡ ርኩስ፡ . . . የሐቂ፡³ˣ
አንተ፡ ባርያ፡ ወአንተ፡ ነሀቢ፡ . . . (cf. 29, 2.)
2. Prayer against filthy Legewon, 38 lines; cf. 9, 4; 13, 1.
ጸሎት፡ በእንተ፡ ሌጌዎን፡ ርኩስ፡ ዘይሰልብ፡ ልብ፡ ሰብእ፡ ወያጸልም፡
አዕይንተ፡ ወይመጽእ፡ ከመ፡ ጽላሎት፡ ወሕልም፡ አምሕለከ፡ ወአውግዘከ፡
በጽቅንዋተ፡ መስቀሉ፡ ለእግዚእነ፡ ኢየሱስ፡ ክርስቶስ፡ ሳዶር፡ አላዶር፡ ዳናት፡
አዴራ፡ ሮዳስ፡ . . . አድኅና፡ ለአመትከ፡ . . . እምባርያ፡ ዘቤት፡
ወዘማገርት፡ ዘማይ፡ ወዘዱር፡ እምሕማም፡ አጋንንት፡ ዘያበሐንን፡
ወያመነምን፡ ወያተኩስ፡ ወያሰለሰል፡ . . . ባርያ፡ (sic) ዘይነብር፡ በምሰሶ፡
ባርያ፡ ዘይነብር፡ በንር፡ ባርያ፡ ዘይነብር፡ በማጆት፡ ባርያ፡ ዘይነብር፡ በቆጥ፡
ባርያ፡ ዘይጥህር፡ ባርያ፡ (sic) ዘይወጽእ፡ እምውስተ፡ ባሕር፡ ወይሰብር፡
አስነን፡ ወይዘረዝር፡ ምራቀ፡ እምዝንቱ፡ ኩሉ፡ . . .
3. The Net of Solomon for catching demons, 94 lines; cf. Six, *Handschriften*, 41, 3, 8 , p. 138.
አስግተ፡ ሀላዌሁ፡ ለሰሎሞን፡ ዘረበቦሙ፡ ለአጋንንት፡ ከመ፡ መርበብተ፡ ዓሣ፡
ዘባሕር፡ እንዘ፡ ይብል፡ ሱፉቃኤል፡ ኤል፡ አገታኤል፡ ኪአስ፡ ኪሚስ፡ . . .
በዝንቱ፡ ስመ፡ ለእግ" ድነን፡ ሰሎሞን፡ እምእዴሆሙ፡ ለነሀብት፡ እምድንረ፡
አጋዝፕ፡ ወአንበርፕ፡ እስከ፡ ፫ዕለት፡ በአምሳለ፡ ንዋም፡ ወአቀምፕ፡ ቅድመ፡
ንጉሥሙ፡ በሌሊት፡ ወአዘዘሙ፡ ኅቡዕ፡ ንጉሥ፡ ለነሀብት፡ ያምጽኡ፡
መጥባሕተ፡ . . .

Miniatures and Magical Symbols:
1. Angel with sword and scabbard.
2. Talismanic symbol with face in center.
3. Sixteen-box panel (4 x 4) with X shapes in every box.
4. Talismanic symbol (no face in center box).

Copied for Ṣädalä Maryam.

EMIP MagSc 47 – Weiner Magic Scroll 8

Parchment, 158 x 9.2 cm, two strips sewn together, one column, colored border with continuous half-circles, Gə'əz, 20th cent.

1. Prayer against the evil eye, Gärgari, the evil eye of Barya, Legewon, Buda, Ṭäbib, Mäggañña and others, 39 lines; cf. 44, 1.
በስመ፡ አብ፡ . . . ጸሎት፡ በእንተ፡ ሕማም፡ ዓይን፡ ጥላ፡ ገርጋሪ፡ ዓይን፡
ባርያ፡ ወሌጌዎን፡ ዓይን፡ ጥላ፡ ወጊ፡ ዓይን፡ ቡዳ፡ ወዓይን፡ ጠቢብ፡ ዓይን፡
መተኛ፡ (sic) ወዓይን፡ ተንኩለኛ፡ መገኛ፡ ወጉሥምት፡ ወለሕማም፡
አስወንውን፡ ወለሽንት፡ ምዕፅ፡ (sic) ወጐርጉሃ፡ ወጌርባ፡ . . . ንሴብሐ፡ (Ex 15:1) . . . ወገጹ፡ በጽልመት፡ ፈርሃ፡ ወደንገፀ፡ ዲያብሎስ፡ ርእዮ፡ . . .
2. Prayer against miscarriage and hemorrhage, 21 lines.

በስመ፡ አብ፡ . . . ጸሎት፡ በእንተ፡ ሕማም፡ ዕንስ፡ ወደም፡ አቀምላንስ፡ ሊስ፡ አፍሊስ፡ ፋላኪስ፡ ወዘዘ፡ ሜሎስ፡ ወዘዘ፡ ሚካኤል፡ ደም፡ በምንት፡ ትነብር፡ በርእስ፡ በበዓይን፡ በአንፍዕ፡ (sic) ወበክናፍር፡ በአስናን፡ በእድ፡ ወበዕግር፡ በጉረሮ፡ ዎጭ፡ (sic) አለህ፡ ቃለ፡ አብ፡ . . .

3. Prayer against the eye of Šotälay, and the story of St. Susənyos fighting Wərzəlya, the demon of infant mortality; cf. 7, 3; 33, 3.
በስመ፡ አብ፡ . . . ጸሎት፡ በእንተ፡ ሕማም፡ ዓይነ፡ ሾተላይ፡ ወሀሎ፡ ጀብእሲ፡ ዘስሙ፡ ሱስንዮስ፡ . . .

4. Prayer against charm, taken from the Eighty-One (Canonical) Books, 36 lines; Six, *Handschriften*, 61, 1, b, 6, p. 173.
በስመ፡ አብ፡ . . . ጸሎት፡ በእንተ፡ መፍትሔ፡ ሥራይ፡ ንወጥን፡ በረድኤተ፡ እግ" ልዑል፡ ወክቡር፡ መጽሐፈ፡ መፍትሔ፡ ሥራይ፡ ዘተቀድሐ፡ እምሥወዱ መጸሕፍት፡ ፍታሕ፡ ሥራየ፡ እስላም፡ ወሥራየ፡ አምሐራ፡ ፍታሕ፡ ሥራየ፡ ቤት፡ ወሥራየ፡ ጕረቤት፡ ፍታሕ፡ ሥራየ፡ ዘመድ፡ ወሥራየ፡ ባዕድ፡ ፍታህ፡ ሥራየ፡ በጌምድር፡ ፍታህ፡ ሥራየ፡ ጎንደር፡ ወሥራየ፡ ጐጃም፡ ፍታሕ፡ ሥራየ፡ በለግ፡ ወሥራየ፡ ቂሊሳ፡ ፍታሕ፡ ሥራየ፡ ስሜን፡ ወሥራየ፡ ጸለምት፡ ፍታሕ፡ ሥራየ፡ ትግሬ፡ ወአቡርጊሬ፡ (sic) ፍታሕ፡ ሥራየ፡ ዕንድርታ፡ ወሥራየ፡ ገረአልታ፡ ፍታህ፡ ሥራየ፡ አገው፡ ወሥራየ፡ በለው ፍታህ፡ ሥራየ፡ ዲንጋይ፡ (sic) ወሥራየ፡ ንቋይ፡ (?) ተፈታህ በአብ፡ . . . ለእመ፡ ደገምክሙ፡ ኩልክሙ፡ እመኒ፡ ቀሲስ፡ . . .

Miniatures and Magical Symbols:
1. Angel with sword and scabbard.
2. Small row of four boxes with faces in boxes 1 and 4 and four-petal patterns with eyes in the other boxes.
3. Twenty-box panel with faces in the odd-numbered boxes and four-petal patterns with eyes in the other boxes.
4. Same as number two above.
5. Variation of talismanic symbol with face in center.

Copied crudely with the place for the name of the owner left blank; prepared apparently for sale.

EMIP MagSc 48 – Weiner Magic Scroll 9

Parchment, 147.5 x 8.3 cm, two strips sewn together, one column, colored border, Gəʻəz, 18th cent.
1. Prayer against illnesses caused by Barya and Legewon and for binding demons, that King Alexander uttered before Gog and Magog, 32 lines; cf. 16, 4.
በስመ፡ አብ፡ . . . ጸሎት፡ በእንተ፡ ሕማም፡ ባርያ፡ ወሌጌዎን፡ ወማዕሠሩ፡ ለጋኔን፡ ዘተናገሮ፡ እስክንድር፡ ንጉሥ፡ በቅድመ፡ ጎግ፡ ወማጎግ፡ እዝ ይብል፡

አሌፍ፡ አሌፍ፡ ንጉሡ፡ ባርያ፡ ወአጋንንት፡ ተናጨር፡ ንጉሡ፡ ባርያ፡ ዳሊፍ፡
ንጉሡ[፡] ምች፡ ኖቢ፡ ንጉሡ፡ ሐሡር፡ ጨመረሐለ፡ (sic) ጉሡ፡ (sic) ሐመድ፡[፡]
ኖባዊ፡ ጉሡ፡ (sic) ቸነፈር፡ ዳንኤል፡ ንጉሡ፡ ብድብድ፡ ጋሙር፡ ንጉሡ፡
ትግሪዳ፡ ራውል፡ ንጉሡ፡ ፈለግ ቁልጭልጭ፡ ንጉሡ፡ ፌራ፡ ወተላሽ፡ (sic)
ቃውዛ፡ ንጉሡ፡ ቀትር፡ ኖፌ፡ ንጉሡ፡ ዛር፡ ወተላዋሽ፡ ቆረሽ፡ ንጉሡ፡ የዓር፡
(sic) ወጢስ፡ ደቃሊ፡ ንጉሡ፡ ውቅያኖስ፡ ኮልክሙ፡ ምድረ፡ ፋትራ፡
ሀገርክሙ፡ ርሐቁ፡ . . .

2. Prayer for binding and drowning demons, 17 lines.
 በስመ፡ አብ፡ . . . ጸሎት፡ በእንተ፡ ማዕሠረ፡ ወመጥመ፡ (sic) አጋንንት፡
 እኩያን፡ ቸመላቸ፡:7x ታዲሉን፡:6x ለዜፍ፡:2x ታዲሉን፡ ለዜፍ፡:5x ቅርም፡ . . .
 ከግሁ፡ ሕትም፡ መናሥግቲሆሙ፡ ለመሡርያን፡ . . .

3. Prayer for binding and drowning (demons), 46 lines.
 በስመ፡ አብ፡ . . . ጸሎት፡ በእንተ፡ መስጥም፡ ወማዕሠር፡ ወግ፡ (sic) ጬ፡ ጬ፡
 ጬ፡ ጬ፡ (with a T-like sign on them, (as in ሟ) አሥሉስ፡ ቅዱስ፡ አብ፡ . .
 . ተማኀፀንኩ፡ ከመ እድኃን፡ እምበላያነ፡ ሥጋ፡ ወእምሰያታእያነ፡ (sic)
 ደም፡ . . . ሐራፔን፡:5x ቀጥራሹሂት፡ አውራሹን፡ . . .

4. Prayer against charm, 56 lines.
 በስመ፡ አብ፡ . . . በስሙ፡ ለእግ"፡ አብ፡ በስሙ፡ ለእግ"፡ ወልድ፡ . . .
 ፍታሕ፡ ወዘርዝር፡ መፍትሔ፡ ሥራይ፡ በሥልጣነ፡ አብ፡ በሥልጣነ፡ ወልድ፡
 ፍታሕ፡ ወዘርዝር፡ ሠዓር፡ ወመንዝር፡ ኮሉ፡ ሥራየ፡ መሡርያነ፡ ታእስ፡
 አዝዮስ፡ ማስያስ፡ . . .

5. The Net of Solomon for catching demons, 25 lines.
 በስመ፡ አብ፡ . . . ጸሎት፡ በእንተ፡ ሐማም፡ መርበብተ፡ ሰሎሞን፡ ዘረበበሙ፡
 ከመ፡ መርበብተ፡ አሣ፡ ዘባሕር፡ አላሁማ፡:4x ወኑር፡ ኃጅ፡ ረጅ፡:3x በኃቅለ፡
 ረጅ፡ በኃቅለ፡ መግኑን፡ እልባቆን፡ . . .

6. Prayer against the evil eye with the *asmat* of the Archanel Michael, 18 lines.
 በስመ፡ አብ፡ . . . ጸሎት፡ ወስዕለት፡ ዘቅዱስ፡ ሚካኤል፡ ዘተጽሕፈ፡ በዞጋም፡
 እዱ፡ ኢኮስ፡ አስሌ፡ ኤጋ፡ ኤጋስ፡ . . . ወገጹ፡ ዘፍጹም፡ በጽልመት፡ ፈርሃ፡
 ወደንጉጹ፡ ዲያብሎስ፡ ርዕዮ፡ . . .

Miniatures and Magical Symbols:
1. Ornate cross with figure standing on either side (Mary and John?) (large).

Name of original owner erased and replaced with Wälättä Śəllase.

EMIP MagSc 49 – Weiner Magic Scroll 10

Parchment, 170 x 10.1 cm, three strips sewn together, one column, (colored?) borders, Gəʻəz, 19th cent.

1. Prayer for binding demons, [Legewon], Buda, Ṭäbib, Täyayaž, Dədq, and noontime demon. The first six lines in red are insufficiently legible, 37 lines; cf. 18, 1; but also 44, 1; 46, 2.
 . . . [ሌጌዎን፡] ዘይስልብ፡ ልቡ፡ ሰብእ፡ ወያጸልም፡ አዕይንተ፡ ወይመጽእ፡ ከመ፡ ጽላሎት፡ በመዓልት፡ ወበሊሊት፡ አምሐልኩክሙ፡ በ፷ቅንዋተ፡ መስቀሉ፡ . . . ይትመሰሉ፡ በምትዓት፡ ወበሬራ፡ ወበጉሥምት፡ ወንዳድ፡ ወበዉዳ፡ ወጠቢብ፡ [ወበ]ተያF: (sic) ወጽላ፡ ወጊ፡ ድድቅ፡ ወጋኔነ፡ ቀትር፡ ወውጋት፡ ወንፍሐተ፡ ከርሥ፡ በት[..]፡ ⌈ወታየ፡ አይሰድ፡ (Amharic) በዓይነት፡ ወቁርጥማት፡ ወቁርዐት፡ ወፍልፀት፡ በትኩሳት፡ ወበልብ፡ በጉርጉሀ፡ ወምች፡ በጅን፡ ወደባስ፡ በመንሾ፡ ወበምች፡ ሰዱር፡ በንስር ወንጀL: በማነቅ፡ ወበውጋት፡ በሕማመ፡ ግብጥ፡ ወማቄ፡ ወተቅማጥ፡ [. . .]ት፡ በጀርባ፡ ደዌ፡ ወሰአል፡ በሕም[መ?]ት፡ ወበሕበጥ፡ ወበቁስል፡ በሸውሸው[ታ፡] ወጅውጅውታ፡ ወመበሐነን፡ ቢድንጋዬ፡ ወድጋም፡ ወተንኩል፡ በመድኃኒት፡ ወነስናሽ፡ ወሾተላይ፡ ወቆላይ፡ በዓይን፡ ወርቅ፡ ወውላጅ፡ ገዳይ፡ መጋኛ፡ ወቁራኛ፡ በቀናተኛ፡ ወምቀኛ፡ በአስማተኛ፡ ወበደለኛ፡ ወተኮስኛ፡ ወቁመኛ፡ በዝ፡ ኩሉ፡ አምሐልኩክሙ፡ . . .

2. Prayer against Barya, a drowner (of Barya):
   a. Monday, its guardian angel is the Archangel Michael, and its star, Gəzakumullah, 17 lines.
      ጸሎት፡ በእንተ፡ ሐማም፡ ባርያ፡ መስጥም፡ ዘዕለተ፡ ሰኑይ፡ ዓቃቢሁ፡ ሚካኤል፡ ሊቀ፡ መላእክት፡ ወከክቡኒ፡ ጅዛኩሙላሁ፡ (54, 2: ቀመር፡ ኢላሂ፡ ካዛኩም፡) አንስሩፋኤል፡ ኢስመወጠኪን፡ አጅብርኤል፡ ሩሀኒን፡ . . .
   b. Tuesday, its guardian angel is Gabriel, and its star, Almäriš, 13 lines.
      ጸሎት፡ በእንተ፡ መስጥም፡ ዘዕለተ፡ ሰሉሥ፡ ዓቃቢሁኒ፡ ገብርኤል፡ ወከክቡኒ፡ አልመሪሽ፡ (54, 2: አልመኒሽ፡) ማምሮን፡ በድሁድ፡ጋLCH፡ ራግርF፡ ጊልግድን፡[3x] አሸግድን፡
   c. Wednesday, its guardian angel is Surafel (Seraphim), and its star, Aṭarəd, 40 lines.
      ጸሎት፡ በእንተ፡ መስጥም፡ ዘዕለተ፡ ረቡዕ፡ ዓቃቢሁኒ፡ ሱራፌል፡ ወከክቡኒ፡ አማርድ፡ ጬትኩታኤል፡[3x] ሸዛኩታኤል፡[3x] ትትኩታኤል፡[7x] . . . (The list of the *asmat* of this day is longer than in the other days.)
   d. Thursday, its guardian angel is Rufa'el (Raphael), and its star, Almäštäri, 26 lines.
      [ጸሎት፡ በእንተ፡ መስጥም፡] ዘዕለተ፡ ሐሙስ፡ ዓቃቢሁኒ፡ ሩፋኤል፡ ወከክቡኒ፡ አልመሸተሪ፡ ሸኩክሌ[፡] መሐጀሽ፡ ሬድ፡ ስልሁማግኢቂቲ፡ ቄደቀነልናሁ፡ ጸናት፡ . . .
   e. Friday, its guardian angel is Afnin, and its star, Alzähra, 24 lines.

Catalogue of the Scrolls of Ethiopian Spiritual Healing · 321

ጸሎተ፡ መስጥም፡ ዘዕለተ፡ ዓርብ፡ ዓቃቢሁኒ፡ አፍኒን፡ ወከኮቡኒ፡
አልዘገራ፡ አርካሁ፡[3x] ኮናንን፡[3x] . . .

f. Saturday, its guardian angel is Ura'el (Uriel), and its star, Zaḫl, 16 lines.
[ጸሎተ፡] መስጥም፡ ዘዕለተ፡ ቀዳሚት፡ አቃቢሁኒ፡ ኡራኤል፡ ወከኮቡኒ፡
ዛኀል፡ ኢሰይና፡ ሲአርደድ፡ . . .

g. Sunday, its guardian angel is Saqu'el, and its star, Šämäša, 33 lines.
ጸሎተ፡ መስጥም፡ ዘዕለተ፡ እሁድ፡ ዓቃቢሁኒ፡ ሳቁኤል፡ ወከኮቡኒ፡
ሸመሻ፡ አላሁ·ግ፡ ያችናችጅ፡ እለመለኪ፡ ወያኑራ፡ ዋቂራ፡ . . .

Miniatures and Magical Symbols:
1. Sixteen-box panel (4 x 4) with faces in boxes 1, 3, 6, 8, 9, 11 and 15 and X-shaped patterns in the others.
2. Angel with sword and scabbard (large)
3. Talismanic symbol with face in center.
4. Geometric patterns and lines above eighteen-box panel (6 x 3) with faces in several of the boxes.

EMIP MagSc 50 – Weiner Magic Scroll 11
Parchment, 158 x 10 cm, three strips sewn together, one column, border, Gəʿəz, 18th cent.

1. Prayer for binding demons and terrorizing Satan, Barya and Legewon, Buda, Anṭəräñña, Qumäñña, and Təgərtya, 20 lines.
በስመ፡ አብ፡ . . . ጸሎት፡ በእንተ፡ ማዕሡሮሙ፡ ለአጋንንት፡ ወመደንግጸ፡
ሰይጣናት፡ ባርያ፡ ወልጋን፡ (sic) መጉሸት፡ (sic) ቡዳ፡ ወአንጥረኛ፡
ወቁመኛ፡ ወበዓለ፡ ግብር፡ ወትግርትያ፡ ወሐማም፡ መንሽ፡ ወተላዋሽ፡
ወሐማም፡ ፈጸንት፡ ወነቀጥቃጥ፡ በዝ፡ ቃለ፡ መለኮት፡ ወበጀቅንዋተ፡ . . .
ሳዶር፡ አላዶር፡ . . .

2. Prayer for binding Satan and against charm, 27 lines.
በስመ፡ እግ"፡ . . . በእንተ፡ ማዕሡሩ፡ (sic) ለሰይጣናት፡ ለሥራይ፡ ወለዓይን፡
ሰብእ፡ ዕኩያን፡ አስግተ፡ ኃይል፡ ዘስሙ፡ (sic) ሸፐጸራ፡ ሸሸፐጸራ፡
ሸሸሳላሸሽ፡ ጨርጨር፡ . . .

3. Prayer against hemorrhage, 9 lines.
ጸሎት፡ በእንተ፡ ደም፡ ምንሁብ፡[3x] ቁርስጥንትያ፡[6x] አንተ፡ ባርያ፡ . . .

4. *Asmat* prayer of Solomon against the evil eye, Zar, Qurañña, Buda, and Qumäñña 31 lines.
በስመ፡ አብ፡ . . . ጸሎት፡ በእንተ፡ ዓይነ፡ ጥላ፡ ወዓይነ፡ ወርቅ፡ ዛር፡
ወቁራኛ፡ ቡዳ፡ ወቁመኛ፡ ደም፡ . . . አአትብ፡ ገጽየ፡ በትእምርተ፡ መስቀል፡
. . . ሰሎሞን፡ ዘከመ፡ ረበሙ፡ ለአጋንንት፡ . . . ሎፍሐም፡ . . .

5. Prayer against the evil eye, and for binding demons, Barya, Legewon, and Šotälay, 28 lines.
በስመ፡ አብ፡ . . . ጸሎት፡ በእንተ፡ ሕማመ፡ ዓይንት፡ ኢ.ቋያኖምንን፡ አቋያንስ፡ አብያዋ፡ ኪ.ብርያ፡ . . . አንተ፡ ባርያ፡ ወሌጌዎን፡ ወአንተ፡ ሾተላይ፡ . . .

Miniatures and Magical Symbols:
1. Angel with sword and scabbard (large)
2. Eighteen-box panel (3 x 6) with face in center box.
3. Angel with sword and scabbard.

Copied for Wälättä Mädḫən.

EMIP MagSc 51 – Weiner Magic Scroll 12

Parchment, 191 x 9.4 cm, three strips sewn together, one column, colored border, Gəʿəz, 20th cent.

1. The *Mystagogia*.
   Hammerschmidt, *Texte*, pp. 48–72; Lifchitz, *Textes*, pp. 40–52; Velat, *Meʿerǟf* I, pp. 215–7; MG 59, pp. 9ff.
   በስመ፡ አብ፡ . . . ጸሎት፡ በእንተ፡ ትምኅርተ፡ ኅቡዓት፡ ቅድመ፡ ዘትትነገር፡ እምጽርስፌራ፡ ለምእመናን፡ . . .
2. Prayer for binding demons and against charm, 24 lines; cf. 50, 2.
   በስመ፡ አብ፡ . . . ጸሎት፡ በስመ፡ እግ"፡ ብርሃንት፡፡ (sic) በእንተ፡ ማዕሠሩ፡ ለሰይጣን፡ አስማተ፡ ኃይል፡ ዘስሙ፡ ሽፌራ፡ አጨርጨቤ፡ መሽቸቤ፡ ጋቡርፉበርፉ፡ (sic) . . . ፍጡነ፡ ያሽብሮሙ፡ ለአጋንንት፡ . . .
3. Prayer of the rampart of the cross against illnesses caused by Barya, Legewon, Zar, and Təgərtya, 43 lines.
   በስመ፡ አብ፡ . . . ጸሎት፡ በእንተ፡ ሐፁረ፡ መስቀል፡ አንያ፡ ሽራንያ፡ . . . አልፉ፡ ወን፡ (sic) . . . በኃይለ፡ ዝንቱ፡ ዘአጽራዕከ፡ ግብሮ፡ ለዲያብሎስ፡ ከማሁ፡ አጽርኽ፡ ሕማመ፡ ባርያ፡ ወሌጌዎን፡ ዛር፡ ወትግርትያ፡ ፍልፀት፡፡ ወቀርፀት፡ ዓልሻ፡ ወጉሥምት፡፡ . . . ends with greeting to the Guardian Angel, Chaîne, Répertoire, no. 39: ሰላም፡ ለከ፡ መልአከ፡ ዑቃቤ፡ ቃውም፡ . . .

Miniatures and Magical Symbols:
1. Angel with sword and scabbard (large)
2. Angel with sword and scabbard (large)
3. Ornate cross

The blank space for the name of the owner is filled with three names in three different hands: Bäyyänäčč/Wälättä Sänbät, Yäzabnäš/Wälättä Maryam and Wälättä Kiros.

EMIP MagSc 52 – Weiner Magic Scroll 13

Parchment, 148 x 8.6 cm, three strips sewn together, one column, elaborate colored border with hour-glass and diamond shapes, Gəʿəz, 20th cent.

1. Prayer for binding and drowning (demons), 32 lines.
   በስመ፡ አብ፡ . . . ጸሎት፡ በእንተ፡ መስጦመ፡ አጋንንት፡ አርኩህ፡[3x] አርኩ፡ ክናንሁ፡[3x] እምኛ፡ ሸርሁ፡ . . .

2. Prayer against charm, with a stanza from the Image of Jesus, መልክዐ፡ ኢየሱስ፡, 56 lines; Chaîne, Répertoire, no. 123; and Strelcyn, *Lincei*, 35, 1, e, p. 112; Strelcyn, *Prières*, p. 110.
   በስመ፡ አብ፡ . . . ጸሎት፡ በንተ፡ (sic) መፍትሄ፡ ሥራይ፡ ዘጋኔን፡ . . . ሰላም፡ ለስእርተ፡ ርእስከ፡ ዘስሙር፡ አብቂሉ፡ ሳዶር፡ ወጽፉቅ፡ ጥቀ፡ ለአርዘ፡ ሊባኖስ፡ ቄጽሉ፡ አላዶር፡ . . .

3. Prayer for drowning filthy demons, 28 lines.
   በስመ፡ አብ፡ . . . ጸሎት፡ በእንተ፡ ማዕሠሮሙ፡ ለአጋንንት፡ ወለኩሎሙ፡ መናፍስት፡ ርኩሳን፡ ገባርያነ፡ እኩይ፡ እኮ (?) ኢነላሁ፡ ስማዕተ፡ ረጀዉ፡ (ረጀሁ፡?) አንተ፡ ዙላ፡ ወይላን፡፡ ዘልታን፡ . . .

4. Prayer against terror, 35 lines.
   በስመ፡ አብ፡ . . . ጸሎት፡ በእንተ፡ ድንጋፄ፡ አውላኩኤል፡ ጐጤ፡ ቶራካኤል፡ ቅሩፋሪኩን፡ በዝ፡ ስምከ፡ . . .

5. Prayer against a piercing pain on the side, 12 lines; cf. 6, 4; 28, 5.
   በስመ፡ አብ፡ . . . ጸሎት፡ በእንተ፡ ሕማመ፡ ውግዓት፡ ምድምያስ፡[2x] የሐቂ፡[4x] . . .

Miniatures and Magical Symbols:
1. Talismanic symbol with face in center.
2. Angel with sword and scabbard (large).
3. Small four-box panel (1 x 4) with face in box three.

Copied for Wälättä Ǝgzi'.

EMIP MagSc 53 – Weiner Magic Scroll 14

Parchment, 156 x 9.4 cm, three strips sewn together (third is very small), one column, colored (red) border, Gəʿəz, 19th cent.

1. Prayer against Gärgari, the evil eye, and the story of St. Susənyos fighting Wərzəlya, the demon of infant mortality; cf. 7, 3; 16, 1.
   በስመ፡ አብ፡ . . . ጸሎት፡ በእንተ፡ ዓይነ፡ ጥላ፡ ገርጋሪ፡ ወልሳን ተናጋሪ፡ ወእምእኩይ፡ ተገራሪ፡ ዕቀብ፡ . . . ወሀሎ፡ ፩ብእሲ፡ ዘስሙ፡ ሱስንዮስ፡ . . . በስመ፡ እግ"፡ ሕያው፡ ነባቢ፡ ወተናጋሪ፡ ጸሎቱ፡ ለቅዱስ፡ ሱስንዮስ፡ [በእንተ፡] አሰስሎ፡ ደዌ፡ እምሕጻናት፡ . . .

2. Prayer against Šotälay and hemorrhage, 38 lines.

በስመ፡ አብ፡ . . . ጸሎት፡ በእንተ፡ ሾተላይ፡ ወደም፡ ሽንታም፡ ቀንታም፡ ሰንኮራም፡ ማይ፡ ዘወጽአ፡ እምገቦሁ፡ . . . ሊስ፡ አፍሊስ፡ ሚልዮስ፡ . . .

3. Prayer against the evil eye, Gärgari, Legewon and the eye of a Muslim, 49 lines.
በስመ፡ አብ፡ . . . ጸሎት፡ በእንተ፡ ዓይነ፡ ጥላ፡ ወገርጋ፡ (sic) ወለጌዎን፡ (sic) ወዓይነ፡ እስላም፡ ይቁም፡ ዕደ፡ ወዕግረ፡ ወኮሎ፡ (sic) ኅባለ፡ ሥጋሁ፡ አኪ፡ (አኬ?) አብ፡ ድርሰት፡ አጨጨ[፡] ሰንቦራ፡ ጨ፡[4x] ሮዳስ፡ . . .

Miniatures and Magical Symbols:
1. Angel with sword and scabbard (large).
2. Twelve-box panel (3 x 4) with faces in boxes five and eight
3. Effaced symbol (face?)

Copied for Wälättä Maryam.

EMIP MagSc 54 – Weiner Magic Scroll 15

Parchment, 180 x 10.3 cm, four strips sewn together, one column, no border, Gəʻəz, 20th cent.

1. Prayer for drowning demons, Barya, Legewon Ǧänn, Däbas, Gudale, Zar, Təgrida, Mäggäñña, Šotälay, and others, 29 lines.
በስመ፡ አብ፡ . . . ጸሎት፡ በእንተ፡ መስጠመ፡ አጋንንት፡ ወሰጣናት፡ (sic) ባርያ፡ ወለጌዎን፡ ጀን፡ ወደባስ፡ ደስክ፡ ወጉዳሌ፡ ዛር፡ ወትግዲ፡ (sic) መገኛ፡ ወሾተላይ፡ ንዳድ፡ ወመንሽ፡ ምትሐት፡ ወጽፍዓት፡ ጉስማት፡ ወፍርቃቃት፡ ውግአት፡ ወሰቅሰቃት፡ ኤልክሻካሽ፡ ወተላካሽ፡ ቡዳ፡ ወቂመኛ፡ አልጉም[፡] ፌራ፡ ወቸነፌር፡ ፍልጸት፡ ወቁርጸት፡ ወቁርጥማት፡ ዓይነ፡ ባርያ፡ ወዓይነ፡ ወርቅ፡ እደ፡ ሰብእ፡ ፍኔን፡ ወስራይ፡ ዝ፡ ውእቱ፡ መጽሐፍ፡ ዘወሀቦ፡ ቅዱስ፡ ሚካኤል፡ ለሰሎሞን፡ ንጉሥ፡ ከመ፡ ያንገሎሙ፡ ለአጋንንት፡ . . . ወይቤ፡ ሊቆሙ፡ ዘስሙ፡ ጋቡር፡ ንኅሥአ፡ ለሰብእ፡ ወንንጽሐ፡ ውስ፡ (sic) ሐመድ፡ . . . ወይቤ፡ ዕርነ፡ ዘስሙ፡ ፌቂጠር፡ ሜራ፡ ማሜራ፡ ፒፓፒሎ፡ አማኑኤል፡ . . .

2. Prayers for the days of the week for terrorizing and drowning demons; cf. 49, 2.
በስመ፡ አብ፡ . . . ጸሎት፡ በእንተ፡ መደንግጸ፡ አጋንንት፡ ወመሥጥሞሙ፡ ለአጋንንት፡ ጸዋጋን፡ ዘይትነብብ፡ በዕለተ፡ ሱይ፡ ወአቃቢሁኒ፡ ቅዱስ፡ ሚካኤል፡ . . .

3. Prayer against evil spirits, and the story of St. Susənyos fighting Wərzəlya, the demon of infant mortality.
በስመ፡ አብ፡ . . . በስመ፡ እግ" ሕያው፡ ነባቢ፡ ወተናጋሪ፡ ጸሎቱ፡ ወበረከቱ፡ ለቅዱስ፡ ሱስንዮስ፡ በእንተ፡ አሰስሎ፡ ደዌ፡ . . . ወሀሎ፡ ጂብእሲ፡ ዘስሙ፡ ሱስንዮስ፡ . . .

Catalogue of the Scrolls of Ethiopian Spiritual Healing · 325

Miniatures and Magical Symbols:
1. Angel with sword and scabbard (large).
2. Small panel with three faces: face on left rotated 90 degrees counter-clockwise; face on right rotated 90 degrees clockwise.
3. *Haräg* in rectangular box.
4. Talismanic symbol with face in center.
5. Small ornate cross.

Copied for Wäldä Gäbrə'el in a crude hand.

EMIP MagSc 55 – Weiner Magic Scroll 16

Parchment, 160 x 10.2 cm, two strips sewn together, one column, colored (yellow) double border, Gə'əz, 19th cent.
1. Prayer against Šotolay, the demon of infant mortality, 54 lines.
በስመ፡ አብ፡ . . . ጸሎት፡ በዕንተ፡ ሾቶላይ፡ አንተ፡ ሾቶላይ፡ አንተ፡ ሾቶላይ፡ ዘትቀትል፡ ህፃናተ፡ ወ[.]በይት፡ ወተሀንቅ፡ ክሳዳተ፡ ወታበርር፡ ነፍስ፡ (sic) . . . አምሐልኩክሙ፡ ወአውገዝኩክሙ፡ . . . አንተ፡ ሾቶለይ፡ (sic) ወመገኛ፡ በዝንቱ፡ አስማት፡ እንዘ፡ እብል፡ መአጅን፡^{3x} መቃፈጅን፡ . . . ኢትቅረቡ፡ ለአመትከ፡ . . . ሰሎሞን፡ ሰሎሞን፡ ሎፍሐም፡ መሐፍሎን፡ . . .
2. Prayer for driving away evil spirits, 25 lines.
በስመ፡ አብ፡ . . . ቅዱስ፡ አአምን፡^{3x} ወንትአመን፡ በ፫አካላት፡ ወበ፩መለኮት፡ ረሁቁ፡ ወትሰድድ፡ (sic) ከመ፡ ኢትቅረብኒ፡ አንተ፡ ጋኔን፡ ወትግርዳ፡ . . . በዝንቱ፡ አስማት፡ ወበዝንቱ፡ ቃላት፡ ወበዝንቱ፡ ቀለም፡ ወበዝንቱ፡ ጠልሰም፡ . . . ሎንጅ፡ . . . ሎጅ፡ መጅን፡ መንጅን፡ . . .
3. Prayer against evil spirits, and the story of St. Susənyos fighting Wərzəlya, the demon of infant mortality.
በስመ፡ እግ" ሕያው፡ ነባቢ፡ ወተናጋሪ፡ ጸሎቱ፡ ዘቅዱስ፡ ሱስንዮስ፡ በዕንተ፡ አስሩሎ፡ ደዌ፡ . . . ወሀሎ፡ ፩ብእሲ፡ ዘስሙ፡ ሱስንዮስ፡ . . .

Miniatures and Magical Symbols:
1. Torn top edge: remains of colorful *haräg*.
2. Angel standing (large).
3. Four faces in clover-shaped arrangement.

Copied for Wälättä Kidan; other names in the same hand: Wälättä Mika'el and (Wälättä A)rägawi.

EMIP MagSc 56 – Weiner Magic Scroll 17

Parchment, 178 x 11.5 cm, three strips sewn together, two columns, colored (yellow) border and margin between columns, Gə'əz, 20th cent.

A1. Prayer against the evil eye of Barya, illnesses caused by Šotolay, and Mäggañña, and the story of St. Susənyos fighting Wərzəlya, the demon of infant mortality.
በስመ፡ አብ፡ . . . ጸሎት፡ በእንተ፡ ዓይነ፡ ባርያ፡ ወሕማም፡ ሾቶላይ፡ ወመጋኛ፡ በስመ፡ እግ" ሕያው፡ ነባቢ፡ ወተናጋሪ፡ ጸሎቱ፡ ወበረከቱ፡ ለቅዱስ፡ ሱስንዮስ፡ በእንተ፡ አሰሥሎ፡ ደዊ፡ . . . ወሀሎ፡ ፩ብእሲ፡ ዘስሙ፡ ሱስንዮስ፡ . . .

A2. Prayer against the eye of Barya and demons with the *asmat* of the *Dərsanä Mika'el*, 69 lines.
በስመ፡ አብ፡ . . . ጸሎት፡ በእንተ፡ ዓይነ፡ ባርያ፡ ወአጋንንት፡ ድርሳን፡ ዘቅዱስ፡ ሚካኤል፡ ሊቀ፡ መላእክት፡ ወትብል፡ በትሑት፡ ቃል፡ እሉንተ፡ አስማተ፡ ዓቢያተ፡ ዓቢይ፡ አሜዕ፡ ቤኪ፡ ኢንካ፡ . . .

A3. Prayer against the evil eye of Barya, and charm, with "*asmat* extracted from the Eighty-One (Canonical) Books," 22 lines.
በስመ፡ አብ፡ . . . ጸሎት፡ በእንተ፡ ዓይነ፡ ባርያ፡ ወመፍትሔ፡ ሥራይ፡ ዘተቀድሐ፡ እም፹ወ፩ መጻሕፍት፡ መጨጨ፡ ኤልክስፋድስ፡[3x] በስመ፡ አብ፡ . . . ውፀዕ፡ እንተ፡ ትግርትያ፡ ወሌጌያን፡ ወዛር፡ . . . ⌈ወአብሮ፡ አደግ፡ ተያዝ፡ አይሰድ፡ (Amharic) ወርደሌ፡ ነስናሽ፡ ክትር ደም፡ ትክቶ፡ ሃ፡ ለአመትከ፡ . . .

B1. Prayer against the evil eye of Barya and illnesses caused by Šotolay, 28 lines.
በስመ፡ አብ፡ . . . ጸሎት፡ በእንተ፡ ዓይነ፡ ባርያ፡ ወሕማም፡ ሾቶላይ፡ ጸሎቱ፡ አልጊሆ፡ ያሽነጅ፡ ባሕቱ፡ ምስኪን፡ ብልቁን፡ በከክ፡ ንቅጥ፡ ፋጎን፡ . . . ቦጋለ፡ ዝንቱ፡ አስማቲከ፡ . . .

B2. Prayer against the evil eye of Barya: The story of the sorcerer at the Sea of Tiberias; cf. 3, 1; 24, 1.
በስመ፡ አብ፡ . . . ጸሎት፡ በእንተ፡ ዓይነ፡ ባርያ፡ ጸሎተ፡ ነደራ፡ ዘውእቱ፡ እግዚእነ፡ ኢየሱስ፡ ክርሶስ፡ ውስተ፡ ባሕር፡ (sic) . . .

B3. Prayer against the evil eye of Barya: The prayer of *Abunä* Kiros that God may release him from his illness.
በስመ፡ አብ፡ . . . ጸሎት፡ በእንተ፡ ዓይነ፡ ባርያ፡ በይዕቲ፡ ሰአተ[፡] ሌሊት፡ ጸለየ፡ አቡነ፡ ኪሮስ፡ ኀበ፡ እግ" ከመ፡ ይስአሮ፡ እምውእቱ፡ ደዊ፡ ወግብ፡ ወግት፡ (sic) መጽአ፡ መጽአ[፡] እግዚእ፡ . . . (There are no *asmat* in this prayer.)

B4. Prayer against hemorrhage, 11 lines. Full text:
ጸሎት፡ ሰንተራም፡ ወእስንተራም፡ ደም፡ ወማይ፡ ዘውጽአ፡ እምገቦሁ፡ ለእግዚእነ፡ ወአምላክነ፡ ወመድኃኒነ፡ ኢየሱስ፡ ክርስቶስ፡ በስመ፡ ከተርኩ፡ ለሰይጣን፡ ከማሁ፡ ክትር፡ ደም፡ ትክቶሃ፡ ለመትከ፡ (sic) ወ፡ (sic) ፍሬ፡ ማርያም፡

B5. Prayer against hemorrhage and miscarriage; cf. third paragraph of 41, 1.
ስመ፡ አብ፡ . . . ጸሎት፡ በእንተ፡ ዓርጋጌ፡ ደም፡ . . . ቅልያስቃም፡ መቅር[፡] እግዚእ፡ ይትፈታሕ፡ ፍሬ፡ ወ፡ (sic) በውስተ[፡] ማሕፀን፡ ለአመትከ፡ ፍጽንስ፡ (sic) ለጽኑሳን፡ አምላኪየ፡ ዘፈነውካ፡ ላቲ፡ ለሔዋን፡ . . . concluded with the Greeting to Phanuel: ሰላም፡ ለተፈጥሮትከ፡ ምስለ፡ መላእክት፡ ሕቡረ፡ . . .

Miniatures and Magical Symbols:
1. Angel with sword and scabbard (large).
2. Four-petal pattern with eye in each petal.
3. Angel holding curved knife and scabbard; standing beside ornate cross. Text written on left and right.

Copied for Fre Maryam.

EMIP MagSc 57 – Weiner Magic Scroll 18
Parchment, 148 x 10.8 cm, four strips sewn together, one column, colored (black) border, Gəʿəz, 20th cent.

1. Prayer against illnesses caused by the evil eye of Barya, Zar, Nägärgar, Dədq, noontime demon, and charm, 35 lines; cf. 55, 2.
    በስመ፡ አብ፡ . . . ጸሎት፡ በእንተ፡ ሀማም፡ ዓይነተ፡ ባርያ[፡] ቁርጻት፡ ፍልፀት[፡] ውግአት፡ ወቁርጥማት፡ ዘር፡ (sic) ወነገርጋር[፡] ድድቅ፡ ወጋኔን፡ ቀትር፡ . . . አአምን፡ በአብ፡ . . . አወግዞሙ[፡] ለአጋንንት፡ . . .
2. Prayer against illnesses caused by the evil eye of Barya and charm, 20 lines.
    በስመ፡ አብ፡ . . . ጸሎት፡ በእንተ፡ ሀማ (sic) ዓይነተ፡ ባርያ፡ ወጽላ፡ ወጊ፡ ዘያባሕንን፡ ወዘያንቀጠንቅጥ፡ ወዘያመነምን፡ ዘያደቅቅ፡ ወዘያንቀጠቅጥ፡ ኤኮስ፡ አስሌ፡ ኤጻስ፡ . . .
3. The Net of Solomon for catching demons.
    በስመ፡ አብ፡ . . . ጸሎት፡ በእንተ፡ ሀማም፡ (sic) ማእሠሮሙ፡ ለአጋንት፡ (sic) አስገተ፡ ሰሎሞን፡ ዘረበሙ[፡] ለአጋንንት፡ አም፡ (sic) መርበብተ፡ አሣ፡ . . . ሠደቃኤል፡ አደታኤል፡ . . . ሎፍሐም፡^{3x} . . . በስሙ፡ ለእግ"፡ . . .

Miniatures and Magical Symbols:
1. Angel with sword and scabbard (large).
2. Ornate cross (large).
3. Small X-shaped and semi-circular patterns in red and black ink.

Copied for Ǝmmukäy (እሙኸይ); later in pencil: Wälättä Səllase.

EMIP MagSc 58 – Weiner Magic Scroll 19

Parchment, 147 x 14.4 cm, three strips sewn together, two columns, elaborate woven-rope border and interlacing-rope pattern in margin between columns, Gəʻəz, 20th cent.

Another copy of EMIP MagSc 44 – Weiner Magic Scroll 5, in the same crude hand.

Miniatures and Magical Symbols:
1. Ethiopian dignitary before a throne and holding a prayer stick; an angel hovers on either side.
2. Three angels, side by side.
3. Fifteen-panel box (5 x 3) with faces in boxes 1, 3, 5, 7, 9, 11, 13, and 15.
4. Talismanic symbol with face in center; faces in each corner of the surrounding panel.

EMIP MagSc 59 – Weiner Magic Scroll 20

Parchment, 149 x 13.5 cm, three strips sewn together, two columns, elaborate woven-rope border and elaborate swirl pattern in margin between columns, Gəʻəz, 20th cent.

Another copy of EMIP MagSc 44 – Weiner Magic Scroll 5, in the same crude hand.

Miniatures and Magical Symbols:
1. Ethiopian dignitary before a throne and holding a prayer stick; an angel hovers on either side.
2. Seven angels standing side by side with swords drawn.
3. Twenty-box panel (5 x 4) with faces in every other box and X-shaped patterns in the others.
4. Large panel with talismanic symbol and face in center.

EMIP MagSc 60 – Weiner Magic Scroll 21

Parchment, 189 x 9.4 cm, four strips sewn together, one column, colored (bright yellow) border, Gəʻəz, late 19th cent.

The Net of Solomon for catching demons; cf. 46, 3.

በስመ፡ አብ፡ . . . ጸሎት፡ በእንተ፡ መርበብተ፡ ሰሎሞን፡ ዘረበበሙ፡ ለአጋንንት፡ ከመ፡ መርበብተ፡ ዓሣ፡ ዘባሕር፡ ኤል፡ ኪአ፡ አናሜስ፡ አናምያስ፡ አናሜኤ፡ . . . ወካዕበ፡ ዓዲ፡ ጸሎት፡ ዘሰሎሞን፡ እስከ፡ ህላዌ፡ አስገቲሁ፡ ለሰሎሞን፡ ንዑዳን፡ አስግቲሁ፡ አስጋት[፡] አኽያ፡ ሸራኽያ፡ . . . ወረደ፡ ዝቃል፡ ኀበ፡ ሰሎሞን፡ ሸተላሹ፡ ሸተከላሹ፡ . . . ወካዕበ፡ ዓዲ፡ ጸሎት ፡ ዘሰሎሞን፡ አላሻር፡ ርሹር፡ ሸርታን፡ . . . ሎፍሐም፡^{3x} ሎፍሎ፡^{3x} ወዘንተ፡ አስግተ፡ እንዘ፡ ይብል፡ ተሰጥመ፡ ነቢ፡ ውስተ፡ ባሕር፡ . . .

Miniatures and Magical Symbols:
1. Ornate cross (large).
2. Tall panel with geometric designs and three faces in center.
3. Talismanic symbol with face in center.

Copied for 'Ayne/Wälättä Iyyäsus.

EMIP MagSc 61 – Weiner Magic Scroll 22

Parchment, 265 x 11.6 cm, four strips sewn together, one column, elaborate border of woven-rope pattern (one red, the other white), Gəʿəz, 19th century, leather amulet case.

1. From the beginning of Friday's Sword of Trinity, *Säyfä Śəllase*, 42 lines; cf. EMML 1170, ff. 50a–60a, vol. 4, p. 103–4.
   በስመ፡ አብ፡ . . . አይ፡ ልሳን፡ ወአይ፡ ነቢብ፡ . . .
2. From the Sword of Divinity, 72 lines; Grébaut, *Sayfa malakot*; also published in Ethiopia in 1967 EC by Täsfa Press.
   በስመ፡ አብ፡ . . . መብረቀ፡ መብረቀ፡ (sic) መለኮት፡ መደንግፅ፡ ፍህመ፡ መለኮት፡ ብቁጽ . . . ዘበአግን፡ በትር፡ ዘዘበጦ፡ ለሰይጣን፡ ውእቱ፡ ኢየሱስ፡ ክርስቶስ፡ . . . አውግዞሙ፡ ለአጋንንት፡ ዕኩያን፡ ወለሰብእስ፡ መሰርያን፡ ከመ፡ ይርኃቁ፡ እምኔየ፡ በአብ፡ እትኬለል፡ . . . ሳድር፡ አላድር፡ . . .
3. The Net of Solomon for catching demons, 50 lines.
   በስመ፡ አብ፡ . . . አስግተ፡ ሰሎሞን፡ ዘረበሙ፡ ለአጋንንት፡ ቆመ፡ (sic) መርበብተ፡ አጋ፡ እንዘ፡ ይብል፡ ሰዳቃኤል፡ አዶናይ፡ አዳዳኤል፡ . . . ወካዕበ፡ አስግተ፡ ሀላዊሁ፡ ለሰሎሞን፡ ንዑደ፡ አጋሁ፡ ዘአንደዱ፡ አብያስ፡ ይልቅሱም፡ . . . ወረደ፡ ዝቃል፡ ጎበ፡ ሰሎሞን፡ ዘወረደ፡ እምላዕለ፡ ጎበዕ፡ ቃሉ፡ ለአብ፡ . . . ሸታ፡ ከለሹን፡ ሸራሱን፡ . . . ወመጽአ፡ ነሀቢ፡ ዘስሙ፡ መሲሕ፡ ፈቀደ፡ ይነርዱ፡ ወደገመ፡ አስግተ፡ እንዘ፡ ይብል፡ ሎፍሐም፡ . . .
4. Prayer against fever, *gəbṭ* and shivering, 19 lines.
   በስመ፡ አብ፡ . . . ጸሎት፡ በእንተ፡ ሕጋመ፡ ነዳድ፡ (sic) ሕጋመ፡ ግብጥ፡ ወነቀጥቃጥ፡ አንፍሕም፡ ወልድ፡ ፍሕም . . . አብ፡ ነበልባል፡ . . . አብ፡ እሳት፡ . . . ጎብስተ፡ ሥጋሁ፡ እሳት፡ ጽዋዓ፡ ደሙ፡ እሳት፡ ቅድሜሁ፡ እሳት፡ የማነ፡ ገቦሁ፡ እሳት፡ ድኅሬሁ፡ እሳት፡ መንበሩ፡ እሳት፡ . . . አምሐልኩክሙ፡ እኩያን . . .
5. A collection of excerpts from different prayers for binding and driving away demons, 67 lines.
   በስመ፡ አብ፡ . . . ጸሎት፡ በእንተ፡ ማዕሠሮሙ፡ ለአጋንንት፡ ወስደቶሙ፡ ለሰይጣናት፡ ጸሎት፡ በእንተ፡ ቅዱስ፡ ስንስዮስ፡ (sic) ዘአሰረቶ፡ እምሕፃናት፡ ዓዲ፡ ይበቁዓ፡ ለብእሲት፡ ትጽሕፍ፡ ወትስቅሎ፡ . . . አምላኮሙ፡ ስንስዮስ፡ አድገኖ፡ እምባርያ፡ ወለጌዎን፡ አምላኮሙ፡ ለአብርያም፡ . . . ወለዘሂ፡ ሰመየ፡ ወልዶ፡ ወለቶ፡ በስምኪ፡ አነ፡ እሁቦ፡ . . ., followed by stanzas from

the different images, e. g., Image of the Savior of the world, Chaîne, Répertoire, no. 164: ሰላም፡ ለቃልከ፡ በላዕለ፡ መስቀል፡ ዘከልሃ፡ . . .
Miniatures and Magical Symbols:
1. Small panel with three angels' faces.
2. Angel with sword and scabbard (large).
3. Angel standing above three objects with eyes.
4. Four round faces.

Copied for Gäbrä Tənśa'e, Wälättä Śəllase, Wälättä Giyorgis, and Ḫaylä Maryam.

EMIP MagSc 62 – Weiner Magic Scroll 23
Parchment, 202 x 9.4 cm, three strips sewn together, one column, (faint yellow?) border, Gə'əz, early 20th cent.
1. Prayer against the evil eye of Barya, demons and Legewon, 35 lines; cf. Six, *Handschriften*, 14, a, 1, pp. 86–87.
   በስመ፡ አብ፡ . . . አልቦ፡ ስም፡ በታሕተ፡ በታሕተ፡ (sic) ሰማይ፡ ዘእንበለ፡ ስም፡ እግ"፡ ጸሎት፡ በእንተ፡ ዓይነ፡ ባርያ፡ ወአጋንንት፡ ወለጌዎን፡ እኩይ፡ ዘይሰልብ፡ ልበ፡ ሰብእ፡ ወይመጽእ፡ ከመ፡ ጽላሎት፡ ወያበሕንን፡ በሕልም፡ ወየሐንቅ፡ ክሣደ፡ ወያጠዊ፡ አንፈተ፡ ወአግዑተ፡ ደስክ ፡ ወጋኔነ፡ ቀትር፡ አሌፍ፡ ንጉሡ፡ ንሻጨር፡ . . .
2. Prayer against the evil eye of Barya demons and Legewon, 15 lines.
   ጸሎት፡ በእንተ፡ ዓይነ፡ ባርያ፡ ወለጌዎን፡ ትብል፡ አራህድ፡^{3x} አህያ፡ ሸራህያ፡ ይምርኤል፡ ኃይል፡ እግ" አዱናይ፡ . . .
3. Prayer against the evil eye of demons, 26 lines; cf. Six, *Handschriften*, 13, 1, 2a, p. 86; Six, "Zaubertexte," p. 313.
   በስመ፡ አብ፡ . . . ጸሎት፡ በእንተ፡ ዓይነ፡ ለአጋንንት፡ ወሰይጣናት፡ ወትብል፡ አልፉ፡^{3x} ዓዕ፡^{3x} ወመጺአከ፡ ኢትግባዕ፡ ዝየ፡ ዳግመ፡ ይቤለከ፡ . . .
4. Prayer for binding demons and against the eye of Barya, 30 lines.
   በስመ፡ አብ፡ . . . ጸሎት፡ በእንተ፡ ማዕሰረ፡ አጋንንት፡ ወዓይነ፡ ባርያ፡ አህያ፡ ሸራህያ፡ አልሻዳይ፡ ፀባያት፡ . . . ዘበመስቀልከ፡ አጽራዕከ፡ ግብር፡ ለሰይጣን፡ ከማሁ፡ . . . በስሙ፡ ለአብ፡ በስሙ፡ ለወልድ፡ . . . ታአስ፡ አዝዮስ፡ ማስያስ፡ አቅዳፌር፡ . . . በኃይለ፡ ዝንቱ፡ አስፓቲክ፡ ወበቃልከ፡ ኢየሱስ፡ ክርስቶስ፡ በሰይፈ፡ ሚካኤል፡ ወገብርኤል፡ ይትገዘም፡ ወይዓዕ፡ እምኔየ፡ ለዓመትከ፡ . ..
5. The Net of Solomon for catching demons and Näḥabt, 49 lines. This and the next section are given as one piece in Dobberahn, *Zauberrollen*, see p. 289.
   በስመ፡ አብ፡ . . . ጸሎት፡ በእንተ፡ መርበብተ፡ ሰሎሞን፡ ወነሀብት፡ አላሁማን፡ ወያኑራህ፡ ሽምራድ፡ እልዋዋቆን፡ መብሽሾን፡ ጠብሽሾን፡ . . .

Catalogue of the Scrolls of Ethiopian Spiritual Healing · 331

ዘረበሙ፡ ለአጋንንት፡ እንዘ፡ ይብል፡ ሎፍሐም፡ መሐፍሎም፡ . . .
Concluded with Mark 1:23–28 . . . በዝ፡ ቃለ፡ ወንጌልh፡ ዐቀባ፡ . . .
6. Greeting to Phanuel as prayer for binding demons.
በስመ፡ አብ፡ . . . ጸሎት፡ በእንተ፡ ማዕሠረ፡ አጋንንት፡ ሰላም፡ ለከ፡ ሰዳዬ፡ አጋንንት፡ ፋኑኤል፡ እምገጸ፡ ፈጣሬ፡ ልዑል፡ ከመ፡ ኢይስክዩ፡ ሰብአ፡ በነገረ፡ ኃጉል፡ ሰላም፡ ለከ፡ ሰዳዬ፡ አጋንንት፡ ፋኑኤል፡ ለእግ" እምጽርሑ፡ . . .

Miniatures and Magical Symbols:
1. Talismanic symbol with face in center.
2. Same.
3. Talismanic symbol with upside down face in center.
4. Talismanic symbol with face in center.
5. Person standing beside ornate cross.

Copied for Wälättä Kidan/Wälättä Maryam, Gäbrä Ḥəywät, Ḥaylä Maryam, and Wäldä Gäbrə'el.

EMIP MagSc 63 – Weiner Magic Scroll 24

Parchment, 175 x 9.1 cm, three strips sewn together, one column, elaborate woven-rope border, Gəʻəz, 20th cent.

1. Prayer against all kinds of illnesses, introduced with John 1:1–5; 38 lines.
   በስመ፡ አብ፡ . . . ወንጌል፡ ዘዮሐንስ፡ ቀማ፡ (sic) ቀዳሚሁ፡ . .
   .ወጽልመትኒ፡ ኢይረክቦ፡ ወኢይርህቦ፡ ዘየአምን፡ በወልድ፡ ቦሕይወት፡ ዘለዓለም፡ በማቴዎስ፡ ወንጌል፡ ተማሕፀንኩ፡ በማርቆስ፡ ወንጌል፡ ተማሕፀንኩ፡ . . .
2. Greeting to Phanuel as prayer for binding demons.
   በስመ፡ አብ፡ . . . ጸሎት፡ በእንተ፡ ማእሰረ፡ አጋንንት፡ ሰላም፡ ለከ፡ ሰዳዬ፡ ሰይጣናት፡ ለእግ" እምጽርሑ፡ . . .
3. Prayer against the evil eye of Barya and Legewon: The story of the sorcerer at the Sea of Tiberias.
   በስመ፡ አብ፡ . . . ጸሎት፡ በእንተ፡ ዓይነ፡ ባርያ፡ ወለጌዎን፡ ጸሎት፡ ንድራ፡ ወእንዝ፡ የሐውር፡ እግዚእነ፡ ኢየሱስ፡ ክርስቶስ፡ ውስተ፡ ባሕረ፡ ጥብርያዶስ፡ . . .
4. Prayer against charm.
   በስመ፡ አብ፡ . . . ጸሎት፡ በእንተ፡ መፍትሔ፡ ሥራይ፡ አካኤል፡[3x] ስራካኤል፡[5x] አልሲደክኤል፡[5x] . . . ፍታሕ፡ ስአር፡ . . .

Miniatures and Magical Symbols:
1. Persons (Mary and John?) standing on either side of an ornate cross (large).

2. Nine-box panel with face in center box and upside down faces in boxes 1 and 3 and right side up faces in boxes 7 and 9.
3. Talismanic symbol with face in center.

Copied for Abäbay, replaced with Ṣähaynäši, in pencil.

EMIP MagSc 64 – Weiner Magic Scroll 25

Parchment, 151 x 11.2 cm, two strips sewn together, one column, colored (brown) border, Gəʿəz, 19th cent.

1. Prayer against the evil eye of Barya, 13 lines.
   በስመ፡ አብ፡ . . . ጸሎት፡ በእንተ፡ ዓይነ፡ ባርያ፡ ዘይሰልብ፡ ልብ፡ ሰብእ፡ ወያሐኝክ፡ ክሣዴ፡ እንዘ፡ [. . .] ጽላሎት፡ በስመ፡ ሳዶር፡ . . . በ፷ቅንዋተ፡ መስቀሉ፡ . . . . . . በዝንቱ፡ አስማቲከ፡ አምሐልኩከ፡ . . .
2. Prayer for drowning demons, Barya, Təgərtya, Däsk, Wərzəlya, Legewon, Mäggañña, Gudale, and Ṭäfänt, 15 lines.
   ጸሎት፡ በእንተ፡ መስሳጠም፡ (sic) አጋንንት፡ በአብ፡ አስቆሮታዊ፡ ነበልባል፡ እሳት፡ ከመ፡ ይጥፍዑ፡ በውእቱ፡ ስምከ፡ ኩሎሙ፡ መናፍስት፡ ርኩሳን፡ ባርያ፡ ጸሊግን፡ ወትግርትያ፡ ቀይሐን፡ ወሰብእ፡ መሰርያን፡ ደስክ፡ ወውርዝልያ፡ ወሌጌዎን፡ መጋኛ፡ ወጉሥምት፡ ጉዳሌ፡ ወጠፈንት፡ ዓይነት፡ ወውግዓት፡ . . .
3. Prayer of St. Susənyos and the story of his fight against Wərzəlya, the demon of infant mortality.
   በስመ፡ አብ፡ . . . በስመ፡ እግ"፡ ጎያው[፡] ነባቢ፡ ወተናጋሪ፡ ልዑል፡ ጸሎቱ፡ ለቅዱስ፡ ሱስንዮስ፡ በእንተ፡ አሰሰሎ፡ ደዌ፡ እምሕፃናት፡ . . . ወሀሎ፡ አሐዱ፡ ብእሲ፡ ዘስሙ፡ ሱስንዮስ፡ . . .
4. Prayer against Mäggañña and miscarriage, 9 lines.
   በስመ፡ አብ፡ . . . ጸሎተ፡ መጋኛ፡ ድሜጥሮስ፡[3x] ጋይጦስ፡[3x] [...] ጨር፡[3x] ኝር፡[3x] ሸር፡[3x] ሰቆታው፡[3x] . . . ዝጋዔን፡ ይትኃረድ፡ . . . followed by the full prayer of በስመ፡ አብ፡, and: ተማኅፀንኩ፡ በ፫ግጽ[፡] በ፩መለኮት፡ . . . አዕንዕ፡ ሕፃነ፡ በማኅፀን፡ . . .
5. Prayer against hemorrhage and miscarriage, 37 lines.
   ጸሎት፡ በእንተ፡ አርግ[ያ፡] ደም፡ ወአጽንያ፡ ጽንስ፡ በእንተ፡ ፈሪሆተ፡ ስምከ፡ እግዚአ፡ ፀነስኒ፡ ሃመምነሂ፡ ወወለድነ፡ እስመ፡ መካን፡ ወለደት፡ ፯ተ፡ ይልሳሲት፡ ሹሸር፡ . . . ሊስ፡ አፍሊስ፡ . . . ደም፡ ደም፡ ዘትነብር፡ በስር፡ ወበሥራስር፡ . . .

Miniatures and Magical Symbols:
1. Angel with sword and scabbard (large).
2. Two panels: upper panel contains three people side by side; lower panel contains two persons with swords on either side of ornate cross with face at intersection of cross pieces.
3. Ornate cross.

Copied for Amätä Krəstos.

EMIP MagSc 65 – Weiner Magic Scroll 26

Parchment, 135 x 9 cm, two strips sewn together, one column, elaborate colored (brown) sawtooth border, Gəʿəz, 20th cent.

1. Prayer against the evil eye of Barya, Legewon and charm, 44 lines.
   በስመ፡ አብ፡ . . . ጸሎት፡ በእንተ፡ ዓይነ፡ ባርያ፡ ወሌጌዎን፡ ወመፍትሄ፡ ስራይ፡ አርከሁ፡[3x] ክናንሁ፡[2x] ከህክናንሁህ፡ (sic) እምኛርሁ፡[3x] ጐፍትሃ፡[2x] . . . በዝ፡ መስጥመ፡ አጋንንት፡ አርሀቅ፡ . . .

2. Prayer against the evil eye of Barya, Legewon, and against terror, 19 lines.
   ጸሎት፡ በእንተ፡ ዓይነ፡ ባርያ፡ ወሌጌዎን፡ ወጸሎት፡ ድንጋጼ፡ ባርክ፡ ባርከኒ፡ ወርድአኒ፡ ክርስቶስ ባርክ፡ እምፍርሃት፡ ወእምድንጋጼ፡ አጋንንት፡ ዘመአልት፡ ወዘሌሊት፡ ዘቀትር፡ ወዘምሴት፡ እመሂ፡ ባርያ፡ ወእመሂ፡ ሌጌዎን፡ ይቤ፡ ወቤት፡ ወቤተ፡ ጦቢት፡ ማሪ፡ ወማሪት፡ . . .

3. Prayer against the evil eye of Barya, Legewon and charm, 21 lines; for the *asmat*, cf. Six, *Handschriften*, 22, 2, 6, p. 102.
   ጸሎት፡ በእንተ፡ ዓይነ፡ ባርያ፡ ወሌጌዎን፡ ክ፡ (sic) ወመፍትሔ፡ ስሥራይ፡ (sic) ከሙናዝር፡[3x] ስፉሐዝር፡[5x] ኤልናዝር፡[4x] አቅፌናዝር[፡][3x] . . .

4. Prayer against the evil eye of Barya and Legewon, 19 lines.
   በስመ፡ አብ፡ . . . ጸሎት፡ በእንተ፡ ዓይነ፡ ባርያ፡ ወሌጌዎን፡ ፈቀጅ፡ መሐመጅ፡ መታቅጅ፡ ፍጆና፡ መከመች፡ . . . ድፍድሮስ፡ ዘአውዓእከ፡ ልቦ፡ ለዲያብሎስ፡ ዘአውዓእከ፡ ንጉሥ፡ (sic) ሁዝ፡ ፌዝ፡ ያፌዝ፡ . . .

5. Prayer against the evil eye of Barya and Legewon, 40 lines.
   በስመ፡ አብ፡ . . . ጸሎት፡ በእንተ፡ ዓይነ፡ ባርያ፡ ወሌጌዎን፡ ሃይወክን፡ ሃሳሊ፡ ሃዛሊዎን፡ ዝውእቱ፡ ሰይፈ[፡] ቃሉ፡ ሉ፡ (sic) ለእግ፡ ዘቦቱ፡ ይቀስፎሙ፡ ለዓይነ፡ አጋንንት፡ . . . ዘይነብር፡ በመቃብር፡ ወዓይነ፡ ባሕር፡ ወደባስ፡ ወዓይነ፡ ፈለግ፡ ወቀላያት፡ ወዓይነ፡ አድባር፡ ወአውግር፡ ወዓይነ፡ ከተማ፡ ወእድ፡ ወአይነ፡ አንስት፡ ወእድ፡ ወአይነ፡ አእሩግ፡ ወሕፃናት፡ ወአይነ፡ አ፡ (sic) ወዲያቆናት፡ ወአይነ፡ ዘመድ፡ ወባእድ፡ ወአይነ፡ ፀር፡ ወፀላኢ፡ ወዓይነ፡ ሐማም፡ (sic) ባርያ፡ ወሌጌዎን፡ ወዓይነ፡ እስላም፡ ወአረሚ፡ ወዓይነ፡ ጋላ፡ ወሻቅላ፡ (sic) ወአይነ፡ አረብ፡ ወሽናሽ፡ ወዓይነ፡ ትሁሪር፡ ወዓይነ፡ ፈፈረጅ፡ (sic) ቡዳ፡ ወቄመኛ፡ . . .

Miniatures and Magical Symbols:
1. Angel with sword and scabbard (large).
2. Twelve-box panel (3 x 4) with upside down angel faces in boxes 1 and 3, face in box 5, angel faces in boxes 7 and 9 and eyes in panels 10–12.
3. Talismanic symbol with face in center.

The name of the original owner is effaced and replaced with Ṭayitu Abägaz.

EMIP MagSc 66 – Weiner Magic Scroll 27

Parchment, 158 x 11.2 cm, four strips sewn together, one column, colored (yellow) border, Gəʻəz, 19th cent.

1. Prayer for disgracing the arrogant, *ǝbbuy*, apparently against a person called Gäbrä Mäsiḥ Mammo, and/or Wändəmmenäh, 132 lines.
    በስመ፡ አብ፡ . . . ወአንሥሮ፡ ለዕቡይ፡ አውሉግዮስ፡ አውጌዶስ፡ ጌርዮስ፡ ጌራዮስ፡ ግዮስ፡ አግዮስ፡ ዝዮስ[፡] አዝዮስ፡ ፓንዋግ፡ ንጦን፡ አላቲኖን፡ አንኮሪሶን፡ መሐዋሲል፡ (or ”ሊል፡) አብሳላንዲስ፡ ሮሐድ፡ መንበሊስ[፡] . . . አፍጺ፡ ደገና፡ ቢቶና፡ ⌈ደም፡ ጠጭ፡ ገብረ፡ መሲሕ፡ ማሞ፡ (!) ገብር፡ ማሞ፡ (Amharic) . . . ⌈ቢስሚላ፡ ለህሊላ፡ ክፍርላ፡ (Arabic). . . አንትሙ፡ ኮልክሙ፡ አጋንንት፡ ምስለ፡ ብራኤል፡ ንጉሥክሙ፡ አመሐልኩክሙ፡ . . . መጥምጥማኤል፡ ንጉሥክሙ፡ . . .
2. Prayer for drowning demons, 59 lines.
    ጸሎት፡ በእንተ፡ መስጥመ፡ አጋንንት፡ ጆዘላህ፡ እምዕሬፉ፡ ኢለግዋጥኪን፡ አጅብራኤል፡ ስዊቲኪን፡ ሰርዮቲን፡ ሰርዮቲን፡ ሬፉኑን፡ . . . አሸታን፡ አሸሸታን፡ ዓሸታን፡ አሸሸታን፡ አሸታን፡ አሸሸታን፡ . . . አህላወሳህላ፡ . . . በዝንቱ፡ ስምከ፡ በከመ፡ አንሣእኮ፡ ለአልአዛር፡ . . .
3. Prayer against the eye that causes piercing pain, 22 lines.
    በስመ፡ አብ፡ . . . ጸሎት፡ በእንተ፡ ዓይን፡ ውግአት፡ እምአምን፡ አንዳኮርሔቦር፡ በርጦሜያር፡ ዓይን፡ ዘገጸወር፡ እዮር፡ መጣሰረው፡ ውግዓት፡ ሰረመጋኝ፡ ወጉሥምት፡ ፈፈተናይ፡²ˣ ቀቀተናይ፡²ˣ . . .
4. Prayer against the evil eye, with a *dərsan* of Solomon and prayer of Mary, 65 lines.
    በስመ፡ አብ፡ . . . ጸሎት፡ በእንተ፡ አይነ፡ ጥላ፡ ድርሳን፡ ዘሰሎሞን፡ ንስግድ፡ ወናስተባርክ፡ ከመ፡ ሞገደ፡ ባሕር፡ ማእከለ፡ እናጉንስጢስ፡ ወመዘምራን፡ አአሩግ፡ ወሕጻናት፡ ኩሎሙ፡ ሕዝባውያን፡ ፍና፡ መልእክቱ፡ ለአርእስተ፡ አማሊስ፡ አውጹእ፡ አጋንንተ፡ . . . ወቃለ፡ አረቡን፡ ወኢለላሁ፡ ለአዲን፡ መርመጁን፡ ሲ/ሊአኣን፡ ወቃለ፡ ረአኩን፡ መሐመድ፡ ሰይዲና፡ (!) . . . ወትቤ፡ ማርያም፡ በነገረ፡ ዕብራይስተ፡ ፈላሳምዮስ፡ ቀኖስብያኤል፡ . . .
    Concluded with greeting to Səbəstəyanos (Sebastian): ሰላም፡ ለከ፡ ስብስትያኖስ፡ ሰማዕተ፡ ወልድ፡ ዘንዱፍ፡ በአሕፃ፡ ወእሱር፡ በጎንድ፡ . . .

Miniatures and Magical Symbols:
1. Talismanic symbol with face in center.
2. Angel with sword grasping demon by arm; animal below (large).
3. Equestrian saint with spear above bearded leopard; an angel is in the upper right.
4. Four-petal pattern with eyes, with diamond shape in the background.

5. Four-petal shape with circle in center.
Copied by two different hands for Mänän, with the name Abbäbäčč inserted later.

EMIP MagSc 67 – Weiner Magic Scroll 28
Parchment, 220 x 9.5 cm, three strips sewn together, one column, elaborate but crude colorful border of intertwined jagged lines, Gəʿəz, 19th cent.

1. The Net of Solomon for catching demons as prayer against the evil eye of Barya, Šätolay, demons and hemorrhage, 56 lines; cf. 9, 5.
በስመ፡ አብ፡ . . . ጸሎት፡ አልቦ፡ ስም፡ በታሕተ፡ ሰማይ፡ ዘእንበለ፡ እግ"፡ ጸሎት፡ በእንተ፡ ዓይነ፡ ባርያ፡ ወሸቶላይ፡ ወመርግዔ፡ ደም፡ ወሰዳዴ፡ አጋንንት፡ አስማተ፡ ሰሎሞን፡ ዘረፆሙ፡ (sic) ለአጋንንት፡ ርኩሳን፡ ከመ፡ መርበብተ፡ ዓሣ፡ ዘባሕር፡ በምስጢር፡ ንቡዕ፡ እምኔነ፡ ወኢኮነ፡ አርአዮሙ፡ በአሐቲ፡ ርእየተ፡ ሰብእ፡ . . . ወካዕበ፡ ደገመ፡ ሰሎሞን፡ እንዘ፡ ይብል፡ ሎፍሐም፡ . . . ወዓተብ፡ ገጾ፡ በትእምርተ፡ መስቀል፡ እንዘ፡ ይብል፡ ያፎ፡³ˣ ያፎ፡ ማሬ፡²ˣ . . .

2. Prayer against hemorrhage, 53 lines.
በስመ፡ አብ፡ . . . ጸሎት፡ በእንተ፡ መርግዔ፡ ደም፡ አንሰ፡ እብል፡ አግጽኤል፡ አዳኤል፡ በዘድንገ፡ ሰሎሞን፡ እምእደዊሆሙ፡ ለአጋንት፡ (sic) ወእምድንረ፡ አኀዝዎ፡ ለሰሎሞን፡ አንበርዎ፡ ቅድመ፡ ንጉሥሙ፡ (sic) . . . ወካዕበ፡ ደገመ፡ ሰሎሞን፡ እንዘ፡ ይብል፡ ሎፍሐም፡ . . . ውእተ፡ ጊዜ፡ መተረ፡ ጉርዔሁ፡ ለጌ ነቢ፡ ዘስሙ፡ መስሐይ፡ . . .

3. Prayer against *Nähabt*, and Artisans (*Ṭäbbäbt*), 21 lines; cf. *Six, Handschriften*, 38, 2, a, 4a, p. 133.
በስመ፡ አብ፡ . . . ጸሎት፡ በእንተ፡ ነሀብት፡ ወጠበብት፡ አላሁማ፡ ወያኑሪ፡ ሸምረጅ፡ እልዋቁን፡ መብሸሽን፡ ጠብሸሽን፡ ዘረፆሙ፡ ለአጋንንት፡ እንዘ፡ ይብል፡ ሎፍሐም፡ መሐፍሎም፡ . . .

4. Prayer and the story of St. Susǝnyos fighting Wǝrzǝlya, the demon of infant mortality.
በስመ፡ አብ፡ . . . በስመ፡ እግ"፡ ሐያው፡ ነባቢ፡ ወተናጋሪ፡ ጸሎት፡ ለቅዱስ፡ ሱስንዮስ፡ በእንተ፡ አሰስሎ፡ ደዌ፡ እምሕጻናት፡ . . . ወሀሎ፡ አሐዱ፡ ብእሲ፡ ዘስሙ፡ ሱስንዮስ፡ . . . ጸሎቱ፡ ለቅዱስ፡ ሱስንዮስ፡ ተያስቅያስ፡ ክርያስ፡ ልብትያል፡ ፩ አብ፡ ቅዱስ፡ ፩ ወልድ፡ ቅዱስ[፡] ቅዱ[ስ፡] (sic) መንፈስ፡ ቅዱስ፡

5. Prayer against charm, 47 lines; it could be part of the preceding section.
ጸሎት፡ በእንተ፡ መፍትሔ፡ ሥራይ፡ ስመናዝር፡ አሙናዝር፡ . . . ዘፍጹም፡ በጽልመት፡ ፈርህ፡ ወደንገጸ፡ ዲያብሎስ፡ ርእዮ፡ . . . Concluded with John 1:1–5, and 23 lines of make-Arabic symbols.

Miniatures and Magical Symbols:
1. Panel with two talismanic symbols side by side with face in center of each.
2. Angel with sword and scabbard.
3. Panel with box in center with face.
4. Angel with sword and scabbard.
5. Twenty-panel box (4 x 5) with face in center.

Some of the spaces left blank for the name of the owner are still blank and some are filled with … Wände, Wälättä Maryam, and Haftä Maryam.

EMIP MagSc 68 – Weiner Magic Scroll 29
Parchment, 198 x 9.7 cm, three strips sewn together, one column, border, Gə'əz, 19th cent.
1. Prayer for drowning demons, Barya, Legewon Ǧänn, Däbas, Däsk, Gudale, Zar, Təgrida, Mäggäñña, Šotälay, Buda, Qimäñña, and others, 34 lines; cf. 54, 1.
   በስመ፡ አብ፡ . . . ጸሎት፡ በእንተ፡ መስጠም፡ አጋንንት፡ ወሰይጣናት፡ ባርያ፡ ወሌጌዎን፡ ጃን[፡] ወደባስ፡ ደስክ፡ ወጉዳሌ፡ ዛር፡ ወትግሪዳ፡ መገኛ፡ ወሾተላይ፡ ንዱድ፡ ወምትሐት፡ ወጽፍዓት፡ ጉሥመት፡ (sic) ወፍርቅቃት፡ ውግዓት፡ ወስቅስቃት፡ ኤልክሻክሽ፡ ወተላካሽ፡ ቡዳ፡ ወቂመኛ፡ አልጉም፡ ፌራ፡ ወቸነፈር፡ ፍልጸት፡ ወቁርጥማት፡ ዓይነ፡ ባርያ፡ ወዓይነ፡ ወርቅ፡ ፍጌን፡ ወእደ፡ ሰብእ፡ ወሥራይ፡ ዝውእቱ፡ መጽሐፍ፡ ዘወሀበ፡ ቅዱስ፡ ሚካኤል፡ ለሰሎሞን፡ ንጉሥ፡ ከመ፡ ያንገሉሙ፡ ለአጋንንተ፡ ሰማይ፡ ወምድር፡. . . ወይቤ፡ ሊቆሙ፡ ዘስሙ፡ ጋውል፡ ንሥእ፡ ለሰብእ፡ ወንጽሐ፡ ውስተ፡ ሐመድ፡ . . . ወይቤ፡ ፀርነ፡ ዘስሙ፡ ጋውል፡ ፈቅጦር፡ ሜራ፡ ማሜራ፡ ፒፒሎ፡ አማኑኤል፡ . . .
2. Prayers for the days of the week for terrorizing and drowning demons; cf. 49, 2; 54, 2.
   በስመ፡ አብ፡ . . . ጸሎት፡ በእንተ፡ መሥጠም፡ ለአጋንንተ፡ ዘይትነብብ፡ በዕለተ፡ ሰኑይ፡ ወአቃቢሁኒ፡ ቅዱስ፡ ገብርኤል፡ (sic) . . .

Miniatures and Magical Symbols:
1. Angel with sword.
2. Panel with simple geometric designs with box and face in center.
3. Ornate cross with text around it.
4. Simple box with face in center.

The spaces left blank for the name of the owner are filled with Wälättä Täklä Haymanot, Mänbärä Səllase, and Wälättä Mika'el.

EMIP MagSc 69 – Weiner Magic Scroll 30

Parchment, 193 x 11.4 cm, three strips sewn together, two columns, colored (yellow) border and margin between columns, Gəʻəz, 19th cent.

A1. Prayer against evil spirits, and the story of St. Susənyos fighting Wərzəlya, the demon of infant mortality.
በስመ፡ አብ፡ . . . በስመ፡ እግ" ሕያው፡ ነባቢ፡ ወተናጋሪ፡ ጸሎቱ፡ ወበረከቱ፡ ለቅዱስ፡ ሱስንዮስ፡ በእንተ፡ አሰሰሎ፡ ደዌ፡ . . . ወሀሎ፡ ፩ብእሲ፡ ዘስሙ፡ ሱስንዮስ፡ . . .

A2. Prayer against the evil eye, related to "Joseph who came out of a wicked fever," 27+13 lines; cf. Strelcyn, *Prières*, p. 4.
በስመ፡ አብ፡ . . . ጸሎት፡ በእንተ፡ ሕማም፡ ዓይነት፡ ት፡ (sic) በቀይሕ፡ ወበጸሊም፡ በከመ፡ ወጽአ፡ ዮሴፍ፡ እምሕሱም፡ ፈጸንታ፡ ፈጸንታ፡ (sic) ይበላሹ፡ አብሹን፡ ሕዱራን፡ አዜይሹን፡ በገቡዕ፡ . . . ቤቃ፡ ቤቃ፡ ሐፌጽ፡ አላፍክፍ፡ ስድንቅዱ፡ አፍልዮን፡ . . . በስመ፡ አብ፡ . . . [አ]ርእስተ፡ ዲያኮሮስ፡[3x] በኮሉ፡ ወበውስተ፡ ኮሉ፡ ይስድድከ፡ እግ"፡ በጽንአ፡ ሰማይ፡ ወምድር፡ ዓቢይ፡ አንተ፡ ሰይጣን፡ (!) ርጉም፡

A3. Prayer against Barya and the evil eye, 64 lines.
በስመ፡ አብ፡ . . . ጸሎቱ፡ ባርያ፡ ወዐይነት፡ ውጭ፡ ጆባጅር፡[2x] ሔኢል፡ ተክለ፡ ሰርዝን፡ (or ሸርዝን፡) አደንዝር፡ ፍታሕ፡ ወዘርዝር፡ . . . ጸሎተ፡ ስንተራም፡ ወእምስንተራም፡ ወማይ፡ ዘወጽአ፡ ዕምገቦሁ፡ . . . አፍሊስ፡ መሊስ፡ . . .

B1. Prayer(s) for binding demons, begins with John 1:1–5; 101 lines.
በስመ፡ አብ፡ . . . ጸሎት፡ በእንተ፡ ማዕሠሮሙ፡ ለአጋንንት፡ ወንጌል፡ ዘዮሐንስ፡ ቀዳሚሁ፡ . . . ወጽልመቱኒ፡ ኢያድክቦ፡ ወኢይቀርባ፡ አጋንንት፡ ጸዋጋን፡ . . . በስመ፡ ረበሙ፡ ሰሎሞን፡ (sic) ሰሎሞን፡[2x] ሎፍሐም፡[3x] መሐፍሎን፡[3x] ዮፍታሔ፡[3x] . . . አማኑኤል፡ እብዎዲ፡ ተስፋጣ፡ ታአስ፡ ማስያስ፡ ሳዶርጬ፡ አላዶርጬ፡ ዳናትጬ፡ . . . በቅንተ፡ መስቀሉ፡ . . . በስመ፡ አብ፡ አብ፡ (sic) አአምን፡ በስመ፡ ወልድ፡ አአምን፡ . . . በ፫አካላት፡ ወበ፩መለኮት፡ ከመ፡ ኢትቅረቡ፡ ገቢ፡ . . .

B2. Prayer against the evil eye of Barya and charm, 18 lines.
ጸሎት፡ በእንተ፡ ዓይን፡ ባርያ፡ ወመፍትሔ፡ ሥራይ፡ መጨጨ፡[2x] ወዣውንዚላ፡ ይሊካ፡[2x] ምንቀለቢካ፡ ወሊአ፡ ኢላያ፡ በሚነ፡ በሂሚን፡ አረቢኩም፡ ወፈውላሂ፡ ዘመደቱም፡ . . . በዝ፡ ቃለ፡ አረቢ፡ ወበዝ፡ ጠለሰም፡ ፍታሕ፡ . . .

B3. Prayer against stomachache, 8 lines.
ጸሎት፡ ከርሡ፡ ዘይጉጸጉጽ፡ ገቦዋተ[፡] ወያደቅቅ፡ ዓዕጽመተ፡ ወይጠዊ፡ ዓንጀተ፡ ወአማዑተ፡ ደር[ደ]ር፡ ከመ፡ ታድገና፡ . . .

B4. Prayer against the evil eye of Barya: The story of the sorcerer at the Sea of Tiberias.
ጸሎት፡ በእንተ፡ ዓይን፡ ባርያ፡ ጸሎተ፡ ነደራ፡ ዝውእቱ፡ እግዚእን፡ ኢየሱስ፡ ክርስቶስ፡ ውስተ፡ ባሕረ፡ ጥብርያደስ፡ . . .

B5. Greeting to Phanuel, as prayer against evil spirits.
በስመ፡ አብ፡ . . . ሰላም፡ ለተፋጥሮትከ፡ ምስለ፡ መላእክት፡ ሕቡራ፡ . . .
B6. Prayer against headache, 8 lines. Full text:
ጸሎት፡ በእንተ፡ ሕማመ፡ ፍልፀት፡ መቶ፡ ቀሬ፡ ቀሬ፡ ተቃረብ፡ መቶ፡ ቀሬ፡
ተቃረብ፡ አድኅና፡ እምህማመ፡ ፍልፀት፡ ለአመትከ፡ ወለተ፡ አረጋዊት፡

Miniatures and Magical Symbols:
1. Angel with sword and scabbard.
2. Ornate cross with persons on either side.
3. Talismanic symbol with face in center.

Copied for Wälättä Arägawit, replaced with Amätä Mika'el.

EMIP MagSc 70 – Weiner Magic Scroll 31

Parchment, 182 x 9.2 cm, four strips sewn together, one column, colored (yellow) border, Gəʿəz, 18th cent.

1. Prayer against Barya, Legewon, the evil eye, Zar, Təgrida, and others, and for binding demons, 43 lines.
በስመ፡ አብ፡ . . . ጸሎት[፡] በእንተ[፡] ባርያ፡ ወሌጌዎን[፡] ወሕማመ[፡]
ጽላዐጊ፡ ዛር[፡] ወትግሪዳ፡ [. . ...] ዘአየረ[፡] አጋንንት፡ [..]ረኛ፡ ወተላዋሽ፡
በስመ[፡] እግ"፡ ብርሃን[፡] በእንተ[፡] ማዕሠ[ረ ፡] ሰይጣን፡ አስማተ[፡] ኃይል፡
ዘስሙ[፡] ሽፒራ[፡] ሽዊራ፡ ሽዊ፡ አሽዊራ፡ አሽቲር፡ በባላሹገር፡ ጬርጭቢ…(?)
. . . [. . .]ሞን፡ ግራኤል፡ ግራኤል፡ . . . ያገር፡ ያገርር፡ . . . መፍቅደ[፡]
ልብየ፡ ዘተነ[ብአ፡ ወዘ]ተከሥተ፡ ወዘተሰወረ፡ . . . The words in red are insufficiently legible. Also the left margin is cut out in one spot.
2. Prayer against Barya, Legewon, and the evil eye, 23 lines.
[ጸሎት፡] በእንተ[፡] ባርያ፡ ወሌጌዎን[፡] ወዓይን፡ ጽላዐጊ፡ ክልቂዶን፡[3x]
በኅይለ፡ በዝንቱ[፡] አስማቲከ፡ ዘአንሣእኮ፡ ለአልአዛር፡ . . .
3. Prayer for drowning demons and Barya, 19 lines.
በስመ፡ አብ፡ . . . ጸሎት[፡] በእ[ን]ተ[፡] መስጠመ[፡] አጋንንት[፡] ወባርያ[፡]
ዘተሰብር[፡] አጽመ [፡] ወዘተሐንቅ[፡] ክንዴ፡ ወትቀጠ (sic) አባላተ[፡]
ወትስቲ[፡] ደመ፡ ወይትቀነይ[፡] በውስጢ[፡] ደም፡ አብድናዝር፡ በጽና፡
ገራፍ[፡] ተገረፍ፡ በጥምቀተ[፡] እሳት፡ ተጠመቅ፡ በረምሃ[፡] ጊዮርጊስ፡
ተረገዝ፡ በሰይፈ[፡] ሚካኤል[፡] ወገብርኤል፡ ተቀሰፍ፡ በሥልጣነ፡ አብ[፡]
ወወልድ . . .
4. Prayer for drowning demons, 19 lines.
ጸሎት[፡] በእንተ[፡] መስጠመ[፡] አጋንንት፡ በቡፊሒም፡ ቁረሽን፡
ሩስለተሽንጥ፡ ወሰይፌ[፡] አራብ፡ ፈዘል[፡] በልደቱ፡ እለዚ፡ አመጠሒም፡
ምንጆኢን፡ ወአመነሁ፡ ምንሽጠራን፡ የሚወምጥ[፡] ባርያ፡ የሚያመነምን[፡]
ባርያ፡ የሚታገል[፡] ባርያ፡ የሚለውስ[፡] (?) ባርያ፡ የሚያለከለኩ፡ (sic)
ባርያ፡ . . .

Catalogue of the Scrolls of Ethiopian Spiritual Healing · 339

5. Prayer of St. Susənyos against infant mortality, prayer against illnesses caused by Barya, Legewon, the evil eye, and for drowning demons, 64 lines; cf. Six, *Handschriften*, 42, 3, 3, p. 138.
   በስመ፡ አብ[፡] . . . ጸሎ[ት፡] ዘቅዱስ፡ ሱስንዮስ፡ በእንተ፡ . . .ዓእ[፡] ሰይጣብውጥ[፡] (sic) በዓዲ፡ ለብእሲት፡ ትጽሕፍ[፡] . . . ጸሎት [፡] በእንተ[፡] ሕማም[፡] ባርያ[፡] ወሌጌዎን[፡] ወዓይን[፡] ጽላዊ፡ ወመስጥመ[፡] አጋንንት፡ በስመ[፡] ለአብ፡ ሙራኤል[፡] በስመ፡ ለወልድ[፡] መናቴር፡ . . . ሳዶር[፡] አላዶር፡ . . . በስሚላሂ[፡] እሮሕማን[፡] እሮሒም፡ አላለሽን ጠፈላሽን፡ አብሽር፡ ሽር፡ መሐትም[፡] አጋንንት፡ ዘተነሳገሮሙ፡ እስክንድር[፡] ንጉሥ፡ በዕለተ[፡] ዓርብ፡ በጊዜ[፡] ምጽአቱ፡ ለሶበደአት፡ (sic) በጽንፉ[፡] ባሕር[፡] እንዘ[፡] ይብል፡ መግረሩማን፡ ማገለፍማን፡ መጀርማን፡ ከለዳው፡ ናማር፡ አብረሂም፡ ፈላረም[፡] ወበቃለ[፡] ሙሴ፡ . . . አምሐልኩክሙ፡ እለቡደያጆ፡ እለቀንጨ፡ እለአጥማጆ፡ እለቆራጨ፡ እለደመጠጮ፡ እለቀባብር፡ እለሶቢሶቢ፡ አለጅብ፡ አለጅብጋሳቢ፡ እለሬሳ ጐታች፡ እለመቃብር[፡] ከፋች፡ እለምግቡ፡ አለቀለቡ፡ እለሰወበላ፡ እለጅብ[፡] ፈረሱ፡ እለሳውል፡ እለክነፍሱ፡ እለአይላብስ፡ እለጠቢሶ፡ እለንጉሡ[፡] አቦላው[፡]ንጉሥ፡ እለስር[፡] እለስር[፡] (sic) ማሽ፡ እለሰው የምትገለ፡ እለየምታጋደለ፡ እለበሰው የሚተናኮሉ፡ ይሰአር ሥራያቲክሙ፡ ወይልሳሕ ሕምዝክሙ፡ . . . (ቸ and ጨ represent also ች and ጭ, respectively.)

6. The story of St. Susənyos fighting Wərzəlya, the cause of infant mortality.
   ወሀሎ፡ ፩ብእሲ፡ ዘስሙ፡ ሱስንዮስ፡ ወአውሰበ፡ . . .

Miniatures and Magical Symbols:
1. Panel with two strips above, main panel and one strip below. Two strips above: the top has geometric patterns with diamond shapes; the lower has six eyes. The main panel: three ornate crosses with triangle face at the cross piece of each; four heads of people below and between. The lower strip is as the second strip above (eyes).
2. Angel standing with sword and scabbard.
3. Talismanic symbol with face in center.

Copied for Däbritu/Wälättä Kidan.

EMIP MagSc 71 – Weiner Magic Scroll 32

Parchment, 100 x 12.5 cm, one strip (a seam shows at the top indicating the loss of an earlier strip), one column, colored (yellow) border, Gəʿəz, 20th cent.

1. Greeting to Phanuel, as prayer against evil spirits. The beginning is apparently cut out.

መልአከ፡ [. . .] ሰላም፡ ለከ፡ ሰዳዬ፡ አጋንንት፡ ፋኑኤል፡ ለእግ"፡ እምጽርሑ፡ . . .
2. Prayer against the evil eye of Barya: The story of the sorcerer at the Sea of Tiberias.
ጸሎት፡ በእንተ፡ ሕማመ፡ ዓይነ፡ ባርያ፡ ጸሎተ፡ ነደራ፡ ወእንዘ፡ የሐውር፡ እግዚእነ፡ ኢየሱስ፡ ክርስቶስ፡ ውስተ፡ባሕረ፡ ጥብርያደስ፡ . . .
3. Prayer against piercing pain, with a greeting to the pierced side of Jesus, 48 lines.
ጸሎት፡ በእንተ፡ ሕማመ፡ ውግዓት፡ ምድምያስ፡³ˣ የሐቂ፡³ˣ የሐብራስቂ፡³ˣ . . . ሰላም፡ ለገቦከ፡ ኩናት፡ (sic) ለንጊኖስ፡ ዘወግየ፡ ሳድር፡ . . . ወትብል፡ በትሑት፡ እሎተ፡ (sic) አስማተ፡ አኪዕ፡ አሜዕለኪ፡ ኢንካ፡ . . .

Miniatures and Magical Symbols:
1. Angel with sword.
2. Talismanic symbol with face in center.

Copied for Wälättä Mika'el, replaced with Wälättä Iyyäsus.

EMIP MagSc 72 – Weiner Magic Scroll 33

Parchment, 157 x 6 cm, three strips sewn together, one column, colored (red) double border, Gəʽəz, early 20th cent.
1. Prayer against the evil eye, Barya, Gudale, Däsk, Zar, Šotälay, and Quränña, 36 lines.
በስመ፡ አብ፡ . . . ጸሎት፡ በእንተ፡ ሕማመ፡ ዓይነ፡ ጥላ፡ ወዓይነ፡ ወርቅ፡ ባርያ፡ ወጉዳሌ፡ ደስከ፡ ወጉዳሌ፡ ዛር፡ ወሾተላይ፡ ቁሬኛ፡ (sic) ወተፃራሪ፡ . . . ዘይሰልብ፡ ልበ፡ ወያጸልም፡ አዕይንተ፡ ወያሐንቅ፡ ክሣደ፡ . . . አምሐለከ፡ ወአውግዘከ፡ በስምከ፡ ሳድር፡ (!) . . .
2. Prayer of St. Susənyos, and the story of his fight against Wərzəlya of the infant mortality.
በስመ፡ እግ"፡ ሐያው፡ ነባቢ፡ ወተናጋሪ፡ ጸሎቱ፡ ወበረከቱ፡ ለቅዱስ፡ የሀሉ፡ ምስሌነ፡ . . . ድርሳን፡ ዘብፁዕ፡ ወቅዱስ፡ ሱስንየስ፡ መስተጋድል፡ በኪዊን፡ ስምዕ፡ በእንተ፡ ስሙ፡ እግዚእነ፡ ኢየሱስ፡ ክርስቶስ፡ ዝንቱ፡ ሱስንዮስ፡ ጸሎት፡ በእንተ፡ አሰስሎ፡ ደዊ፡ . . . ወሀሎ፡ ጂብእሲ፡ ዘስሙ፡ ሱስንዮስ፡ . . .
3. Prayer against hemorrhage, 17 lines.
በስመ፡ አብ፡ . . . ጸሎት፡ በእንተ፡ ሕማመ፡ [ደም፡ ሊ]ስ፡ አፍሊስ፡²ˣ ሊስ፡ አፍሊስ፡ ሊስ፡ መሊስ፡ መላሊስ፡ መላሊያስ፡ ዘአርጋዕከ፡ ኃይለ፡ በረድ፡ . . .
4. Prayer for binding demons, the evil eye of Zar, Wəllağ, the eye of Buda, Ṭäbib, the eye of jealous people, the eye of Muslim and Christian, the eye of Wärǧ, Färänǧ and against all their evil eyes, 31 lines.
በስመ፡ አብ፡ . . . ጸሎት፡ በእንተ፡ ማዕሠሮሙ፡ ለአጋንንት፡ ወዓይነ፡ ጥላ፡ ወዓይነ፡ ሠይጣናት፡ ዓይነ፡ ዛር፡ ወውላጅ፡ ዓይነ፡ ቡዳ፡ ወጠቢብ፡ ዓይነ፡

Catalogue of the Scrolls of Ethiopian Spiritual Healing · 341

ወምቀኛ፡ ወተንኮላኛ፡ ዓይነ፡ እሳላም፡ ወክርስቲያን፡ ዓይነ፡ ወርጅ፡
ወፈረንጅ፡ ወዓይነ፡ ኵሎሙ፡ . . . ዘይሰልብ፡ ልበ፡ ወያጸልም፡ አዕይንተ፡
ወያሐንቅ፡ ክሣደ፡ . . .

Miniatures and Magical Symbols:
1. Angel with sword.
2. Panel with face in center.

Two names compete for ownership: Wälättä Iyyäsus/Yalganäš and Wälättä Säsnbät.

EMIP MagSc 73 – Weiner Magic Scroll 34

Parchment, 205 x 9 cm, three strips sewn together, one column, no border, Gəʿəz, 20th cent.

1. Prayer against hemorrhage and for conception, using the letters of the Hebrew alphabet from Aleph to Heth as given in Ps 119, 15 lines.
   በስመ፡ አብ፡ . . . ጸሎት፡ በእንተ፡ ደም፡ ወዕንስ፡ ወዘተድግም፡ (sic, probably for ወውዝተ፡ ደም፡) ኦርጌ፡ ደግ፡ አሌፍ፡ ስምከ፡ ኦርጌ፡ ደግ፡ በግንፀን፡ ቤተ፡ ኦርጌ፡ ደግ፡ በግንፀን፡ ለክዊነ፡ ጎዳን፡ ጋሜል፡ . . .

2. Prayer against *Aq^{w}yaṣat* and charm, 108 lines; cf. Six, *Handschriften*, 43, 1, 2a, p. 139.
   በስመ፡ አብ፡ . . . ጸሎት፡ በእንተ፡ አቁያጸት፡ ወአቃብያን፡ ሥራይ፡ እለ፡ ይቀትሉ፡ ነፍሰ፡ ወእለ፡ ቦሙ፡ ዕፀ፡ መሰውር፡ ይመስሉ፡ በሕልም፡ ወበአርኣያ፡ መዓልት፡ እለ፡ ይመስሉ፡ ዝእቢ፡ ወቀናጽለ፡ ነምረ፡ ወአረረ፡ ቆፍ፡ (?) ወሆባይ፡ ሐረሳ፡ (sic) ወሐርማዝ፡ አንበሳ፡ ወሰገኖ፡ ወጸሐፍ፡ ጽንዕልያት፡ (sic) ወጽንዕንያ፡ እለ፡ ይትመሰሉ፡ በጸዕዕ፡ እለይመሰሉ፡ (sic) እሳተ፡ ወጸልመተ፡ (sic) ወእለ፡ ይትመሰሉ፡ ፈፈስ፡ ወበቅለ፡ ኦርገ፡ (sic) ወእንሰ፡ ወገመለ፡ ወእለ፡ ይትመሰሉ፡ ከይሲ፡ . . . ወይዌልጡ፡ ኦርአያ፡ ሥጋ፡ ሰብአ፡ ዘዚሎሙ፡ ይትሜሰሉ፡ እንዘ፡ ውእቶሙ፡ ሰብአ፡ ዘከማነ፡ ወዘንተ፡ ብሔሉ፡ (sic) ተሰአሎ፡ ሰሎሞን፡ ለእግ" ዘቦሉ፡ ጥበባተ፡ መሁብከ፡ ምክረ፡ ወኪዳነ፡ . . . ወይቤሎ፡ እግ"፡ ለሰሎሞን፡ አነ፡ እሁብከ፡ ዕፀ፡ ዘይመውዕ፡ ኵሎ፡ መናፍስተ፡ . . . አልፋ፡ ቤካ፡ ክስብኤል፡ ተማንፀንኩ፡ በአስግቲከ፡ ቅዱሳት፡ . . . አውገዝኩክሙ፡ በአስጢፋኖስ፡ ቀዳሜ፡ ስምዕት፡ ወበዘካርያስ፡ ካህን፡ ወዮሐንስ፡ . . .

3. Prayer against Barya, Legewon, and the evil eye, and for binding demons, 11 lines.
   በስመ፡ አብ፡ . . . በእንተ፡ ባርያ፡ ወሌጌዎን፡ ወዓይነ፡ ጥላ፡ ጸሎት፡ ወማዕሥረ፡ አጋንንት፡ አመሐልኩክሙ፡ ወአውገዝኩክሙ፡ በአብርሃም፡ በይስሐቅ፡ ወያዕቆብ፡ በፀወንጌላውያን፡ . . .

4. Prayer against hemorrhage, 14.

በስመ፡ አብ፡ . . . ጸሎት፡ በእንተ፡ ደም፡ አቁም፡ ደግ፡ በገግዐና፡ ሰንተም፡ ከንተም፡ ሰንተም፡ አላቲራም፡ በከመ፡ ወጽአ፡ ደም፡ እምገቦሁ፡ . . .

5. Prayer for binding demons, 28 lines.

በስመ፡ አብ፡ . . . ጸሎት፡ በእንተ፡ ማዕሠሬ፡ አጋንንት፡ አመሐልኩክሙ፡ ወአውገዝኩክሙ፡ በልደቱ፡ ወበጥምቀቱ፡ ወበአስተርዮቱ፡ (sic) . . . ወረገሞሙ፡ ዘከመ፡ ይቤሎ፡ ሰሎሞን፡ ለአጋንንት፡ ወለመሠርያን፡ . . .

6. Greeting to Phanuel as prayer as prayer against nightmare.

በስመ፡ አብ፡ . . . ጸሎት፡ በእንተ፡ ሕማም፡ ባርያ፡ ወሕልመ፡ ሌሊት፡ ሰላም፡ ለከ፡ ሰዳዴ፡ ሰይጣናት፡ ፋኑኤል፡ ለእግ" እምጽርሑ፡ . . .

7. Prayer against hemorrhage and Šotälay, 47 lines.

በስመ፡ አብ፡ . . . በእንተ፡ ደም[፡] ወሾተላይ፡ ሡት፡ አላሡት፡ አክላሡት፡ . . . ሰተሪም፡ ሽንተሪም፡[6x] ዘወጽአ፡ ማይ፡ ወደም፡ እምገቦሁ፡ . . . አናይ፡ ሽራንየ፡ አልሻዳይ፡ . . .

8. Prayer against hemorrhage, Šotälay, and menstruation, 16 lines.

በስመ፡ አብ፡ . . . በእንተ፡ ደም[፡] ወሾተላይ፡ ወደም፡ ትክቶሃ፡ ሰተናዊ፡ ለተናዊ፡ ቀተናዊ፡ ተንከተም፡ ወወጽአ፡ ወደም፡ እምገቦሁ፡ . . .

Miniatures and Magical Symbols:
1. Angel with sword.
2. Face with four wings (variation on talismanic symbol?).
3. Man wearing cross.

Copied for Wälättä Ḥanna/Ṭəruyyä.

EMIP MagSc 74 – Weiner Magic Scroll 35

Parchment, 196 x 6 cm, three strips sewn together, one column, (narrow) colored (yellow) border, Gəʻəz, 20th cent.

1. Prayer against illnesses caused by Barya and Legewon, and for binding demons, 32 lines.

በስመ፡ አብ፡ . . . ጸሎ[ት፡] በእንተ፡ ሕመ፡ (sic) ባርያ፡ ወሌጌዎን፡ አዝያጥ፡ (sic) ሎፍሐም፡ እሥር፡ በማዕሠረ፡ ኮሽት፡ እደ፡ አጋንንት፡ ወእደ፡ ሌጌዎን፡ ሐርበደው፡ ሐርበፈት፡ FG፡ ሰሎሞን፡ በርሃቅ፡ ዓይን፡ ጡጡ፡ አንተ፡ ቁም፡ ንጉሥሙ፡ ለአጋንንት፡ ሰተን፡ ሰተናዊ፡ . . .

2. Prayer for drowning Barya, Legewon, and Nägärgar, 20 line.

በስመ፡ አብ፡ . . . መስጥም፡ ዘባርያ፡ መስጥም፡ ዘሌጌዎን፡ መስጥም፡ ዘነገርጋር፡ ጃዝኩም፡ ላህ፡ አንሰራፉ፡ ኤላም፡ ፍጢኪን፡ ዘባርያል፡ . . .

3. Prayer against the evil eye: The story of the sorcerer at the Sea of Tiberias.

በስመ፡ አብ፡ . . . ጸሎት፡ በእንተ፡ ነደራ፡ ዝውእቱ፡ ሕማ፡ መ፡ (sic) ዓይነት፡ እኩይ፡ እንዝ፡ ይ፡ (sic) የሐውር፡ እግዚእነ፡ ኢየሱስ፡ ክርስቶስ፡ ውስተ፡ ሀገረ፡ (sic) . . .

4. Prayer of St. Susənyos, and the story of his fight against Wərzəlya of the infant mortality.
በስመ፡ አብ፡ (sic) እግ"፡ ሐያው፡ ነባቢ፡ ወተናጋሪ፡ ጸሎተ፡ ቅዱስ፡ ስ (sic) ዘንተ፡ ነገረ፡ በእንተ፡ አሰስሎ፡ ደውየ፡ (sic) . . . ወሀሎ፡ ፩ብእሲ፡ ዘስሙ፡ ሱስንዮስ፡ . . .

5. Prayer against hemorrhage, using the letters of the Hebrew letters from Aleph to He as given in Ps 119, 23 lines; cf. 73, 1.
በስመ፡ አብ፡ . . . ጸሎት፡ በእንተ፡ ውዝዐት፡ በእንተ፡ ውዝዘተ፡ ደም፡ አሌፍ፡ ስምከ፡ አርግዕ፡ ደማ፡ በማሕፀን፡ ቤት፡ አርትዕ፡ ደማ፡ ለከዊነ፡ ሕፃን፡ . . . (followed by John 1:1).

6. Prayer against piercing pain and colic, 14 lines. Full text:
ጸሎት፡ በእንተ፡ በእንተ፡ (sic) ውግአአት፡ (sic) ምድምያስ፡ የሐቂ፡ የሐብራስቂ፡ በእንተ፡ ሕማመ፡ ቁርጸት፡ ፀፍልል፡ ፀፍልል፡ ወጉሥምት፡ በእንተ፡ ዕንስ፡ ለከ፡ ሐ፡ (sic) ሰላም[፡] ለተፈጥሮትከ[፡] ምስለ፡ መላእክት፡ ንቡረ፡ እንዘ፡ ይትከውን፡ (sic) ቅድመ፡ ወ (sic)

Miniatures and Magical Symbols:
1. Nine-box panel with face in center and four faces in the corners.
2. Box with geometric designs with face in center.
3. Ornate cross with face in box at the intersection of the cross pieces.
4. Angel.

Copied for Ṭäǧǧətu.

EMIP MagSc 75 – Weiner Magic Scroll 36
Parchment, 146 x 9.2 cm, three strips sewn together, one column, colored (yellow) border, Gəʻəz, early 18th cent.
1. Prayer against the evil eye of Barya, Qurañña, the eye of Buda, Ṭäbib, Dədq and noontime demon, 95 lines.
በስመ፡ አብ፡ . . . ጸሎት፡ በእንተ፡ አይነ፡ ባርያ፡ ወቁራኛ፡ ወአይነ፡ ጥላ፡ አይነ፡ ቡዳ፡ ወቡዳ፡ መሥርይ፡ ወጠቢብ፡ ወዓይነ፡ ወርቅ፡ ፍልፀት፡ ወቁርፀት፡ ወቀሩጥማት፡ ወስቅስቃት፡ ድድቅ፡ ወጋኔነ፡ ቀትር፡ ወመናፍስት፡ ርኩሳን፡ ውግዓት፡ ወጉስምት፡ ወጀርባ፡ ደዌ፡ ወለሸንት ማዕ፡ እምዝ፡ ኮሉ፡ አድኅኖ፡ ለገበርከ፡ ገብረ ኪሮስ፡ ገብሬ፡፡ መርበብተ፡ ሰሎሞን፡ ረበቦሙ፡ ለአጋንንት፡ ከመ፡ መርበብተ፡ ዓሣ፡ ዘያወጽእ፡ እምባሕር፡ ከማሁ፡ አውጽአሙ፡ ለሠራዊተ፡ አጋንንት፡ ነዓ፡ ገብርኤል፡ መልአክ፡ ንቡዕ፡ ውእቱ፡ ወቀጥቅጥ፡ ኃይሎሙ፡ ለመናፍስት፡ (sic) ርኩሳን፡ ለደስክ፡ ወለጉዳሌ፡ ወይመጽኡ፡ መላእክት፡ ሚሌስ፡ ወይዘረዉ፡ ማንበረ አጋንንት፡ ዳና፡ ቁዳ፡ ሐርናል፡ ሕምምያሽ፡ ዳዳዚር፡ በአርዶ፡ አብጦ፡ ግም፡ አሸቂቲ፡ አልዚዲ፡ ዝውቱ፡ ማዕሠሮሙ፡ ለአጋንንት፡ ⌐ዳና፡ ቁዳ፡ ሐርናል፡ ሕርምምያሽ፡ ደዳዚር፡ በአርዶ[፡] አብጦ፡ ግም፡ አሸቂቲ፡ አልዜዲ፡ ዝውእቱ፡ ማዕሠሮሙ፡ ለአጋንንት፡ (repeated)

ያቀርነሐሽ፡ ኮሽ፡ አሕራኮሽ፡ ብዬሃ፡ የሐብድ፡ ያሜኻን፡ (ኻ without its leg, i.e. the vowel sign placed on top of መ, not on ኅ) . . . በስመ፡ ለእግ" ወልድ፡ . . . ታያስ፡ ማስያስ፡ አዝዮስ፡ አቅጹፍር፡ በስመ፡ ለሐራፒን፡ ሐራፌክር፡ . . . (cf. Six, *Handschriften*, 19, 1, 1, pp. 96–7.)
2. Prayer against piercing pain, with a greeting to the pierced side of Jesus, 15 lines; cf. 29, 5; 71, 3.
ጸሎት፡ በእንተ፡ ውግዓት፡ ሰላም፡ ለገቦከ፡ . . . አድኅነኒ፡ በመስቀልከ፡ . . . ምድያስ፡³ˣ የሐቂ፡²ˣ የሐበረቂ፡ በከመ፡ አድኃንኮ፡ ለወልደ፡ ኮርሶቂ፡ . . .
3. Prayer against the evil eye, 13 lines; cf. 5, 2; 17, 8, 69, A2.
ጸሎት፡ በእንተ፡ ዓይን፡ ጥላ፡ በቀይሕ፡ ወጸሊም፡ ውፃእ፡ በከመ፡ ወጽአ፡ የሴፍ፡ እምሕሱም፡ ፈኖንታ፡ አበሹን፡ ቀሐቡን፡ . . .
Miniatures and Magical Symbols:
1. Angel with sword.
2. Box with X-shaped design in center.
Copied for Gäbrä Kiros Gäbre.

EMIP MagSc 76 – Weiner Magic Scroll 37
Parchment, 199 x 9.5 cm, three strips sewn together, one column, colored (yellow?) border, Gəʽəz, early 19th cent.
1. Prayer of St. Susənyos, and the story of his fight against Wərzəlya of the infant mortality.
በስመ፡ አብ፡ . . . ጸሎት፡ በእንተ፡ ቅዱስ፡ ስንዮ (sic) በስመ፡ እግ"፡ ሕያው፡ ፈጣሪ፡ ነባቢ፡ ወተናጋሪ፡ ጸሎተ፡ ሱስንዮስ፡ በእንተ፡ አሰስሎ፡ ደወያታት፡ (sic) . . . ወሀሎ፡ ጽብእሲ፡ ዘስመ፡ ሱስንዮስ፡ . . .
2. Prayer for conception and against hemorrhage 32 lines.
በስመ፡ አብ፡ . . . ጸሎተ፡ ዕንስ፡ ወውኃዘተ፡ ደም፡ ስንተም፡²ˣ ቀንተም፡³ˣ ስንከራም፡ ደግ፡ ኅርጥ፡ በቃለ፡ አብ፡ . . . ዘወጽአ፡ ደም፡ እምገቦሁ፡ . . . ይቤላ፡ መልአክ፡ ለሔዋን፡ እምነ፡ አጽዕዕ፡ እዴየ፡ በላዕሌከ፡ ትፀንሲ፡ ወትወልዲ፡ . . .
3. Prayer for binding demons, against Šotälay, Mäggäñña, Zar, and hemorrhage.
ጸሎት፡ [ዘ]ማዕሥረ፡ አጋንንት፡ ወዓይነ፡ ጥላ፡ ወሾተላይ፡ ወውኃዘተ፡ ደም፡ ወመጋኛ፡ ወዛር፡ አንሣእኩ፡ አዕይንትየ፡ followed by Ps 120/1; and Greeting to Phanuel: ሰላም፡ ለከ፡ ሰዳዬ፡ አጋንንት፡ ፋኑኤል፡ እምገጸ፡ ፈጣሪ፡ ልዑል፡ . . .
4. Prayer for conception, 11 lines.
ጸሎተ፡ በእንተ፡ ጽንስ፡ ያኻኘሆ፡³ˣ ያሐሸብጥአ፡³ˣ . . . ዘዓርጋዕከ፡ ኃይለ፡ በረድ፡ ወነፋስ፡ . . .
5. Prayer for binding demons and the eye of Barya, 43 lines; cf. 16, 2.

Catalogue of the Scrolls of Ethiopian Spiritual Healing · 345

ጸሎት፡ በእንተ፡ ማዕሠረ፡ አጋንንት፡ ወዓይነ፡ ባርያ፡ ወይሰልቡ፡ ልበ፡ ሰብእ፡
. . . ወገጹ፡ ዘፍጹም፡ በጽልመት፡ ፈርሃ፡ ወደንጸ፡ ዲያብሎስ፡ . . .

Miniatures and Magical Symbols:
1. Angel with sword.
2. Nine-box panel with geometric designs.
3. Flower shape with face in center.
4. Talismanic symbol with face in center surrounded by four faces in the corners.

Copied for Wälättä Kidan.

EMIP MagSc 77 – Weiner Magic Scroll 38

Parchment, 172 x 7 cm, three strips sewn together, one column, (narrow) colored border, Gəʿəz, 20th cent.

1. The Net of Solomon for catching demons, 46 lines.
   በስም፡ አብ፡ . . . ጸሎት፡ በእንተ፡ መርበብተ፡ ሰሎሞን፡ ዘረበሙ፡
   ለአጋንት፡ (sic) ከመ፡ መርበ^ብተ፡ ዓሣ፡ በቅድመ፡ አንበሪ፡ ከመ፡ ጠሊ፡
   በቅድመ፡ ነ^ምብር፡ ከመ፡ በግዕ፡ በቅድመ፡ ተኩላ፡ ከመ፡ ነፋስ፡ (or ነፍስ፡)
   በቅድመ፡ አውሎ፡ ከመ፡ ጸበል፡ በቃለ፡ አካክ፡ ክስብኤል፡ ራፍን፡ ራኮፐን፡ . . .
   . በዝንቱ፡ ስምከ፡ ወበዝንቱ፡ አስማቲከ፡ አሥብሮሙ፡ . . .
2. Prayer against …, Barya, and filthy Legewon, 20 lines.
   በስም፡ አብ፡ . . . ጸሎት፡ በእንተ፡ ሕማም፡ ንዴት፡ (?) ባርያ፡ ወሌጌዎን፡
   ርኩስ፡ ዘይሰልብ፡ ልበ፡ ሰብእ፡ ወቤልዖ፡ (sic, for ወይበልዑ፡) አዕንይተ፡ (sic)
   ወያበሓን፡ (sic) በሕልመ፡ ሌሊት፡ . . .
3. Prayer of St. Susənyos, and the story of his fight against Wərzəlya of the infant mortality, badly copied.
4. Prayer for terrorizing demons.
   በስም፡ አብ፡ . . . አፍዝዝሙ፡ ወአደንግጾሙ፡ ወስልብ፡ ልቦሙ፡ ወአጽልም፡
   (sic) አእይንቲሆሙ፡ አልሕም፡ (?) ኮሉታሆሙ፡ (sic) ለአጋንት፡ (sic). . .
   ሽር፡^{3x} ሽርሽሮን፡^{3x} . . . በዝንቱ፡ አስማቲከ፡ ምስለ፡ ኖብ፡ ንጉሥከሙ፡
   ወምስለ፡ ወለተ፡ ወርቅ፡ ንግስትክሙ፡ ሐተምኩክሙ፡ ወአውገዝኩክሙ፡ . . .
5. Title of a prayer against evil spirit.

Miniatures and Magical Symbols:
1. Variation of talismanic symbol with face in box in center.
2. Angel with sword and scabbard above a nine-box panel (large).
3. Nine-box panel with designs in boxes.

Copied for Däbritu.

EMIP MagSc 78 – Weiner Magic Scroll 39

Parchment, 202 x 10 cm, four strips sewn together, one column, no border, Gəʿəz, 20th cent.

1. Prayer against the evil eye, Gärgari, Barya, Legewon, and the eye of Barya, 29 lines.
   በስመ፡ አብ፡ . . . ጸሎት፡ በእንተ፡ ዓይን፡ ጥላ፡ ወዓይነ፡ ወርቅ፡ ወገርጋሪ፡ ባርያ፡ ወሌጌዎን፡ ወዓይነ፡ ባርያ፡ ንሆጀን፡ ንሆሻሽን፡ ወኮሬብ፡ (sic) ስሙ፡ ለአብ፡ መፍርሁ፡ ወመደንግፅ፡ ስሙ፡ ለወልድ፡ ግሩም፡ ወነጉድንድ፡ ስሙ፡ ለመንፈስ፡ ቅዱስ፡ ነዓዲ፡ ቶንዲን፡ ቴቴርቴር፡ ፌፌዲሆን፡ . . . በዝንቱ፡ ቃለ፡ አረቢ፡ አስተናግሮሙ፡ ለቡዳ፡ ወመሠርይ፡ ወሌጌዎን፡ እኩይ፡ ኤኮስ፡ አሜ፡ ኤሌኬ፡ ኢንኽ፡ . . .

2. Prayer against the eye of Barya, Legewon, demons, and the wicked Legewon; cf. 61, 1.
   በስመ፡ አብ፡ . . . አልቦ፡ ስም፡ ዘያሐዩ፡ በታሕተ፡ ሰማይ፡ ዘእንበለ፡ ስመ፡ እግ፡ ጸሎት፡ በእንተ፡ ዓይነ፡ ባርያ፡ ወአጋንንት፡ ወለጌዎን፡ እኩይ፡ ዘይሰልብ፡ ልበ፡ ሰብእ፡ ወይመጽእ፡ ከመ፡ ጽላሎት፡ ወያበሕን፡ በሕልም፡ ወሐንቅ፡ ክማደ፡ ወያጠዊ፡ አንF ተ፡ ወአማዑተ፡ ደስክ፡ ወጋኔን፡ ቀትር፡ አሌፍ፡ ንጉሡ፡ ንሻጨር፡ . . .

3. Prayer by which Solomon was saved from evil sprits; cf. 46, 3; 67, 2.
   በስመ፡ አብ፡ . . . እንዘ፡ ዕብለ፡ አቅብኤል፡ አዳኤል፡ በዘድንን፡ ሰሎሞን፡ እምእደዊሆሙ፡ ለአጋንንት፡ ወእድግሪ፡ (sic) አጋዝዎ፡ ለሰሎሞን፡ አንበርዎ፡ ቅድመ፡ ንጉሥሙ፡ . . .

4. Prayer against the evil eye, with a greeting to the pierced side of Jesus.
   በስመ፡ አብ፡ . . . ጸሎት፡ በእንተ፡ ሕማም፡ ዓይንት፡ ፌራንኩኪ፡ ሕማም፡ ዓይንት፡ ሰብ፡ እቤለኪ፡ አንቲ፡ (sic, for አይቴ፡) ተሐውሪ፡ ወትቤልኒ፡ አነ፡ አሐውር፡ ከመ፡ እብላዕ፡ ሥጋ፡ እንበለ፡ መጥባሕት፡ ወእስተይ፡ ደመ፡ እንበለ፡ ጸዋዕ፡ (sic) አምሐልኩኪ፡ ሕማም፡ ዓይነት፡ በእግ፡ አብ፡ . . . ሰላም፡ ለገቦከ፡ ኮናተ፡ ለንጊኖስ፡ ዘወግያ፡ ምድያስ፡[3x] የሐቂ፡[3x] . . . followed by Greeting to Phanuel: ሰላም፡ ለከ፡ [ሰዳዴ፡ አጋንንት፡, not copied] ፋኑኤል፡ ለእግ፡ እምጽርሁ፡ . . .

Miniatures and Magical Symbols:
1. Talismanic symbol with face in center.
2. Angel with sword.
3. Forty-box panel (6 x 5 above and 5 x 2 below) with geometric designs and eyes.

Copied for Wäldä Giyorgis; Ḥirutä Śəllase added later, probably in the same hand.

Catalogue of the Scrolls of Ethiopian Spiritual Healing · 347

EMIP MagSc 79 – Weiner Magic Scroll 40

Parchment, 120 x 10 cm, two strips sewn together, one column, colored (yellow) border, Gəʻəz, 19th cent.

1. Prayer to terrorize and bind demons, incomplete at the beginning, 28 lines.
   [. . .]አዊ፡ አርክምና፡ ፍልናግሎስ፡ ገጸ (or ገጽ፡) ፍርቀና፡ ወጋዲን፡ ስሙ፡ ከመ፡ ያደንግያሙ፡ ለሥራዊተ፡ አጋንንት፡ ዳና፡ ቲና፡ ኒርና፡ ቂስር፡ . . .
   ዝውእቱ፡ ማዕሠሮሙ፡ ለአጋንንተ፡ ያቀርን፡ አሽርኩሶ፡ አሐራኩሲ፡ . . .
   ወይመርዓከ፡ ወይመርሐከ፡ ወይስዓር፡ ሥራይከ፡ ወይልስን፡ ኃምዝከ፡
   አውግዝከ፡ (sic) . . .

2. Prayer of St. Susənyos, and the story of his fight against Wərzəlya of the infant mortality.
   በስመ፡ አብ፡ . . . ጸሎት፡ በእንተ፡ ቅዱስ፡ ሱስንዮስ፡ በእንተ፡ አሰስሎ፡ ደዊ፡ . . . ወሀሎ፡ ጅብእሲ፡ ዘስሙ፡ ሱስንዮስ፡ . . .

Miniatures and Magical Symbols:
1. Angel.
2. Face enclosed in circle.

Copied for Wälättä Maryam.

EMIP MagSc 80 – Weiner Magic Scroll 41

Parchment, 107 x 12 cm, two strips sewn together, one column, colored (yellow) border, Gəʻəz, 19th cent.

1. Prayer of St. Susənyos, and the story of his fight against Wərzəlya of the infant mortality, the first half is missing and 13 lines are partially torn out.

2. The Net of Solomon for catching demons; cf. 28, 1; 32, 1.
   በስመ፡ አብ፡ . . . ጸሎት፡ በእንተ፡ ማዕሠሮሙ፡ ለአጋንንት፡ መርበብተ፡
   ሰሎሞን፡ ዘረበቦሙ፡ ለአጋንንተ፡ በመርበብተ፡ አሃ፡ ዘባሕር፡ እንዘ፡ ይብል፡
   ሰደቃኤል፡ አደታኤል፡ ኪያስ፡ ኪርናሚል፡ . . .

3. Prayer against hemorrhage, with a greeting to Thomas and the greeting to the pierced side of Jesus.
   በስመ፡ አብ፡ . . . ጸሎት፡ በእንተ፡ አርጋኤ፡ ደም፡ ስንተራም፡[3x] ኢያሩዝ፡
   ጅክኤል፡ ዝብድናክኤል፡ ምዝርናክኤል፡ ወጸሎት፡ አመ፡ ቀኃጸረታ፡ ዘነገርካ፡
   ገብርኤል፡ ለሐና ከማሁ፡ አርጎዕ፡ ደማ፡ . . .
   ሰላም፡ ለቶማስ፡ እንዘ፡ ይገብር፡ መድምም፡
   እምላዕለ፡ ብእሲ፡ ወብእሲት፡ አግኒሶ፡ ትድምርተ፡ ጋኔን፡ ኃሡም፡
   መጥዎ፡ መጠዋ፡ ሥጋ፡ ወደም፡
   አኮኑ፡ ትቤሎ፡ ነቢኒ፡ ማንተሙ፡
   ከመ፡ ላዕሌየ፡ ኢዕባዕ፡ ጻጋም፡

ሰላም፡ ለገቦክ፡ ኩኑተ፡ ለንጊኖስ፡ ዘወግዖ፡ . . .
Miniatures and Magical Symbols:
1. Box with four-petal design with eyes.
2. Nine-box panel with face in center.
Copied for 'Amätä Maryam.

EMIP MagSc 81 – Weiner Magic Scroll 42
Parchment, 155 x 11.5 cm, three strips sewn together, one column, colored (yellow) border, Gəʿəz, 19th cent.
1. Prayer against Barya and Legewon, 21 lines.
   በስመ፡ አብ፡ . . . ጸሎት፡ በእንተ፡ ባርያ፡ ወለጌዎን፡ ⌜ሰዱ፡ ቃኤል፡[2x] ሰዱቃኤል፡ ክስብኤል፡[2x] ሽከተላሸሁ፡ ለሜ፡ ሽከተላሹ፡ አላ፡ ሹሹት፡ . . .
2. Prayer against Barya, 11 lines.
   ጸሎት፡ በእንተ፡ ባርያ፡ አላኮማት፡ ዝኤል፡ መላኪያስ፡ ይ[ስረ?] ይ..አረ፡ ወይሹሩ፡ ፐፐፓር፡ ዓቅም፡ ምሕ፡ ን/ነብት፡ ከው፡ . . .
3. Prayer against Barya, Legewon, and Təgrida, 28 lines.
   በስመ፡ አብ፡ . . . ጸሎት፡ በእንተ፡ ባርያ፡ ወለጌዎን፡ በዱሐም፡ ይሰደዱ፡ ትግሪዳ፡ በሺሐልል፡ ይትአሰሩ፡ ትግርትያ፡ በሽንላል፡ ይትአሰሩ፡ በዱሐም፡ ፍዘዙ፡ በዱሐም፡[2x] ድኅሪተ፡ ተአሰዘዙ፡ (sic) በዱሐም፡ . . .
4. Prayer against Barya and the demon Legewon, 58 lines. Prayer: "
   በስመ፡ አብ፡ . . . ጸሎት፡ በእንተ፡ ባርያ፡ ወለጌዎን፡ ጋኜን፡ ዘትሠርቅ፡ በዓይነ፡ ጠባይዕ፡ እሳታዊ፡ ኢትስግር፡ በሥራይ፡ ተመሰለ፡ ይቤለክ፡ ቃለ፡ እግ"፡ . . . ያውሽ፡ ያድሬውንክሽያ፡ በኃይለ፡ ዝንቱ፡ አስግተክ፡ . . . ቀቶቶቤቶ፡ በኃይለ፡ ዝንቱ፡ አስግተክ፡ አድግን፡ እምባርያ፡ ወእምኪርያ፡ ወእምኮሉ፡ . . . ቃሽን፡ ሄንና፡ ሄንፍና፡ ርቃቃርት፡ ዮስ፡ ታምን፡ ያምር፡ ፌሪ፡ አይመወ፡ በኃይለዝ፡[2x] አስግተክ፡ አድነኖ፡ . . .
Miniatures and Magical Symbols:
1. Angel with sword.
2. Talismanic symbol with face in center with an angel in each upper corners.
3. Haloed man (Jesus) standing above prostrate donor.
Copied for Mäzgäbä Śəllase.

EMIP MagSc 82 – Weiner Magic Scroll 43
Parchment, 175 x 9 cm, three strips sewn together, one column, no border, Gəʿəz, 19th cent.
1. Prayer of St. Susənyos, and the story of his fight against Wərzəlya of the infant mortality.

2. Prayer against the evil eye of Barya: The story of the sorcerer at the Sea of Tiberias.
በስመ፡ አብ፡ . . . ጸሎት፡ በእንተ፡ መደንግፀ፡ ሕማመ፡ ዓይነ፡ ባርያ፡ ወአይነ፡ ወርቅ፡ ወአይነ፡ ነደሪ፡ ውእቶሙ፡ ሕማመ፡ ዓይነ፡ አጋንንት፡ ወእንዘ፡ የሐውር፡ እግዚእነ፡ ኢየሱስ፡ . . .

3. Prayer, with *asmat* of Solomon, against the eye of Barya, wicked people, Šotälay, and hemorrhage, insufficiently legible, 39.
ስመ፡ አብ፡ . . . ጸሎት፡ በእንተ፡ ሕማመ፡ ዓይነ፡ ባርያ[:] ወዓይነ፡ ሰብእ፡ እኩይ፡ ሾቶላይ፡ ወደም፡ ዘይበጽብጹ፡ አግዑተ፡ ወያደቅቅ፡ አእፅምተ፡ ተአስግተ፡ ሰሎሞን፡ . . . ሊስ፡ አፍሊስ፡ . . . ለዘፈነውከ፡ ላቲ፡ ሰሎሞን፡ ፲ወ፪ መላእክተ፡ ምህረት፡ ፲ወ፪ መላእክተ፡ ግሀል፡ . . .

4. The Net of Solomon for catching demons, as prayer against the eye of Barya and wicked people, 22 lines; cf. 80, 2.
ጸሎት፡ በእንተ፡ ሕማመ፡ ዓይነ፡ ባርያ፡ ወአይነ፡ ሰብእ፡ እኩይ፡ ዘይበልእ፡ ሥጋ፡ ዘእንበለ፡ መጥባሕት፡ ወይሰቲ፡ ደም፡ ዘእንበለ፡ ጽዋ፡ (sic) መርበብተ፡ ሰሎሞን፡ ዘከመ፡ ረበቦሙ፡ ከመ፡ መርበብተ፡ ዓሣ፡ ውስተ፡ ባሕር፡ እንዘ፡ ይብል፡ ሰዱቃኤል፡ . . .

5. Prayer against illnesses caused by red and black Barya.
ጸሎት፡ በእንተ፡ ሕማመ፡ ባርያ፡ ቀይሐን፡ ወጸሊማን፡ ቅድመ፡ ሠራርያን፡ አሰርኩክሙ፡ በ፷፺፻ ነበልባለ፡ እሳት፡ በ፷፺፻ ሠናስለ፡ እሳት . . . አሠርኩክሙ፡ ወአውገዝኩክሙ፡ ከመ፡ ኢትቅረቡ፡ . . . ወገጹ፡ ዘፍጹም፡ በጽልመት፡ ፈርሃ፡ ወደንግፀ፡ ዲያብሎስ፡ ርዕዮ፡ . . .

Miniatures and Magical Symbols:
1. Face of angel (wings behind?).
2. Face.

Copied for Amätä Ṣəyon.

EMIP MagSc 83 – Weiner Magic Scroll 44

Parchment, 162 x 8 cm, two strips sewn together, one column, border, Gəʿəz, early 20th cent.

1. Prayer to remove illnesses found from head to feet, against hemorrhage caused by the Zar, Quränña, Täyayaž, eye of Barya, Legewon, Təgərtya, Mäqawəzi, Mäggañña, Šotälay and others, and for conception, 41 lines.
በስመ፡ ለእግ"፡ አብ፡ . . . ጸሎት፡ በእንተ፡ አስስሎ፡ ደዌ፡ ዘሀሎ፡ እምርእሳ፡ እስከ፡ እግሪ፡ ወደም፡ ዘደውንዝ፡ እምፀብአ፡ ዘር፡ (sic) ቁራኛ፡ ተያየK፡ ዓይነ፡ ባርያ፡ ጋኔን፡ ወሌጌዎን፡ ወእምኮሉ፡ ዘይትቃረና፡ ወትግርትያ፡ ወመቃውዚ፡ መጋኛ፡ ወሾተላይ፡ ወአርግፅ፡ ደግ፡ ወአብቁሌ፡ ፍሬ፡ በግነፀና፡ ለዓመትከ፡ . . . ጸሎት፡ በእንተ፡ ሕማመ፡ ደም፡ ሠራቅያን፡ አርጋዔ፡ ደም፡ ሰርከተም፡[2x]

ሰርተም፡ እንተ፡ ይውኅዝ፡ ደም፡ ሳትር፡ ቀንትር፡ ተከንተር፡[2x]. . . ሊስ፡ አፍሊስ፡ . . .

2. Prayer for drowning illness-causing demons, 24 lines.
   ስም፡ አብ፡ . . . ጸሎት፡ በእንተ፡ መሥጠም፡ ደዊ፡ ወሕማም፡ ፍልፀት፡ ወቀኅርፀት፡ ወገኀስምት፡ ፌሪ፡ ወንዳድ፡ ተላሻሽ፡ ተዛዋሪ፡ ወተቃራኒ፡ ዘይሰቲ፡ ደም፡ ወይበልዕ፡ ሥጋ፡ ዘእንበለ፡ መጥባሕት፡ አብ፡ እሳት፡ . . . አኽያ፡ ሸራኽያ፡ . . . ወበፄቅንዋተ፡ (sic) መስቀሉ፡ . . .

3. Prayer of St. Susənyos, and the story of his fight against Wərzəlya of the infant mortality.

4. Prayer against hemorrhage, about 22 lines.
   ጸሎት፡ በእንተ፡ ሕማም፡ ደም፡ ዘሠራቅያን፨ ፍያት፡[3x] ሐኩ፡ . . . ሊስ፡[3x] አፍሊስ፡ ደማሊስ፡ . . .

Miniatures and Magical Symbols:
1. Angel with sword.
2. Panel with face in center.
3. Variation on talismanic symbol with face in center and wings protruding in various directions.

Owner's name, Wälättä (?) has been replaced with Wälättä Gäbr'əl.

EMIP MagSc 84 — Weiner Magic Scroll 45

Parchment, 175 x 9.5 cm, three strips sewn together, one column, colored (yellow) border, Gəʿəz, 20th cent.

1. Prayer against illnesses caused by filthy demons, Barya, Legewon and filthy demon of the sea, 46 lines; cf. 83, 2.
   ጸሎት፡ በእንተ፡ ሕማም፡ ጋኔን፡ ርኩስ፨ ወሕማም፡ ባርያ፡ ወሌጌዎን፨ ዘባሕር፡ ጋኔን፡ ርኩስ፨ ዘይሰልብ፡ ልባ፡ ለቦሳን፡ ወልበ፡ ሕፃን፡ ወያጸልም፨...

2. Prayer for drowning demons, 29 lines.
   በስም፡ አብ፡ . . . ጸሎት፡ በእንተ፡ መሥጥም[፡] ዘአጋንንት፡ ጆFኩላሁ፨ እምሰፈፍ፡ ኢላግጢኪን፡ ሰዊቲኪን፡[3x] ሰርዮቲኪን፡ ረኑኑን፡[3x] ወህውቅ፨ አሽተተ፨ አሽታን፡ ⌈አህላ፡ ወሣህላ፡ (These two words—*alhan wa-sahlan*—indicate that the prayer is heavily influenced by Arabic) አዝብ፡ ወአክሮም፡ ሳምሮን፡ ሎፍሐም፡ . . .

3. Prayer against illnesses and charm of different demons, including Zar and Qurañña, 61 lines.
   ስም፡ አብ፡ . . . ጸሎት፡ በእንተ፡ መፍትሔ፡ ሕማማት፨ ወሥራየ፡ አጋንንት፡ ወዓይን፡ ሰብእ፡ ዛር፡ ተዛዋሪ፨ ወዓይን፡ ጥላ፡ ተጸራሪ፨ ቁረኛ፡ ዘእናት፡ ወዘአባት፡ ይከሽር፡ ያፈክትር፡ መቅልም፡[3x] . . . በዝስም፡ በከመ፡ አንሣእኩ፡ ለአዛር፡ (sic) . . .

Miniatures and Magical Symbols:

1. Angel with sword and scabbard.
2. Square with X shape pattern and small cross at center.

Copied for Bosäna/Wälättä Iyyäsus and her mother 'Amätä Iyyäsus.

EMIP MagSc 85 – Weiner Magic Scroll 46

Parchment, 115 x 9 cm, three strips sewn together, one column, colored (yellow) border, Gə'əz, 19th cent.

Prayer against demons, Barya, Legewon, the evil eye, Gärgari, Buda, Qumäñña, Fəgen, and others, 96 lines; cf. 28, 3; 38, 1.

[ስመ፡ አብ፡ . . . ጸሎት፡ በ]እንተ፡ አጋንንት፡ ወሰይጣናት፡ ባርያ፡ ወሌጌዎን፡ ዓይነ፡ ጥላ፡ ወዓይነ፡ ወርቅ፡ ወእደ፡ ሰብእ፡ ተዛዋሪ፡ ወገርጋሪ፡ ቡዳ፡ ወቁመኛ፡ ፍጌን፡ ወአልጉም፡ ኑሁን፡ አኑሁን፡ አስተፋን፡ ሀብረፋን፡ . . . በስሙ፡ ለእግ"፡ አብ፡ . . . ታአስ፡ አዝዮስ፡ . . . ምንዓድላሁ፡ አምር፡ አሴ[.]፡ ፈያኩን፡ ቀውለከ፡ ወአንሰራሁ፡ አን[..]፡ ዕልመልአክ፡ . . . በዝንቱ፡ አስማተ፡ ቃልከ፡ . . .

Miniatures and Magical Symbols:
1. A small strip of patterns with five eyes.
2. Nine-box panel with face in center box, faces in the four corner boxes, and X-shaped patterns in the other four boxes. Above and below is a small strip of patterns with five eyes (as in 1 above).
3. Same as 2, except that there are no faces in the four corner boxes.

Copied for Zällaläw.

EMIP MagSc 86 – Weiner Magic Scroll 47

Parchment, 90 x 7 cm, two strips sewn together, one column, colored (yellow or brown) border, Gə'əz, 19th cent.

Prayer of St. Susənyos, and the story of his fight against Wərzəlya of the infant mortality. The beginning is wanting.

Miniatures and Magical Symbols:
1. Angel with sword and scabbard.
2. Variation on talismanic symbol with face at center, wings protruding in various directions.

EMIP MagSc 87 – Weiner Magic Scroll 48

Parchment, 187 x 8.5 cm, three strips sewn together, one column, colored (yellow) double border, Gə'əz, 19th cent.

1. Prayer against Barya Təgərtya, and Šotolay, 26 lines; cf. Strelcyn, *Lincei*, 66, 1, p. 180.

በስመ፡ አብ፡ . . . ጸሎት፡ በእንተ፡ ባርያ፡ ወትግርትያ፡ ወሾቶላይ፡ ዘትቀትሉ፡ ሕፃናተ፡ ወታወሕዙ፡ (sic) ደም፡ አመሐልኩክሙ፡ ወአውገዝኩክሙ፡ ወአሰርኩክሙ፡ ወቄለፍኩክሙ፡ ወለጐምኩክሙ፡ በግሕተመ፡ አብ፡ . . . በዝንቱ፡ አስማት፡ መዓጁን፡[2x] መአጁን፡ መሐጅር፡[3x] . . .

2. Prayer against hemorrhage, Šotolay, Təgərtya, and Belbab, 22 lines.
ጸሎት፡ በእንተ፡ አርጋኤ፡ ደም፡ ወሸቶላይ፡ ወትግርትያ፡ ቤልበብ፡ (sic) መሐለቲ፡ ነውሳል፡ ነውሻል፡ ቄሐቤል፡ ከሐእFምእን፡ ካፍ፡[2x] ሐበነብእፍ፡ . . . ዘከተሮሙ፡ ለሰይጣናት፡ ወለመናፍስት፡ ርኩሳን፡ . . .

3. Prayer against Barya, Legewon, and hemorrhage, 40 lines; cf. 83, 2.
ጸሎት፡ በእንተ፡ ባርያ፡ ወለጌዎን፡፡ ወአርጋኤ፡ ደም፡ ዘያወሕዝ፡ (sic) ደም፡ ወይቀትል፡ ሕፃናተ፡ ወይመጹ፡ ከመ፡ ጽላሎት፡ ወሕልም፡ አምሕለከ፡ ወአወግዘከ፡ በፈቅንዋተ፡ መስቀሉ፡ . . .

4. Prayer of St. Susənyos, and the story of his fight against Wərzəlya of the infant mortality.
5. Prayer against Šätolay, Šätolawit, and hemorrhage, 13 lines; probably Six, *Handschriften*, 16, b, 3, 10, A, p. 91; see also here 106, 3; 117, 7.
ጸሎት፡ በእንተ፡ ሸቶላይ፡ ወሸቶላዊት፡ ወአርጋኤ፡ ደም፡ ሰንተም፡ ቀንተም፡ አጅር፡ መጅር፡ . . .

Miniatures and Magical Symbols:
1. Angel with sword and scabbard.
2. Ornate cross with a person on either side.
3. Nine-box panel with face in center.
4. Talismanic symbol with face in center.

Copied for Wälättä Krəstos.

EMIP MagSc 88 – Weiner Magic Scroll 49

Parchment, 183 x 8.5 cm, two strips sewn together, one column, colored (yellow) double border, Gə'əz, 19th cent.

1. Prayer against Barya, Təgərtya, and Belbab, 23 lines; cf. 87, 2.
ጸሎት፡ በእንተ፡ ባርያ፡ ወትግርትያ፡ ቤልባብ፡ መሕቦቲ፡ ነውሻል፡ . . . ዘከተሮሙ፡ ለሰይጣናት፡ ወለመናፍስት፡ ርኩሳን፡ . . .

2. Prayer against piercing pain, illnesses caused by Zar, demons of the air, and Legewon, 21 lines.
በስመ፡ አብ፡ . . . ጸሎት፡ በእንተ፡ ሕማመ፡ ውግአት፡ ወሕማም፡ ዝር፡ (sic) ወአየረ፡ አጋንንት፡ ወለጌን፡ (sic) አብ፡ እሳት፡ ወልድ፡ እሳት፡ . . . አብ፡ ፍሕም፡ . . . አምሐልኩክሙ፡ እኩያን፡ አጋንንት፡ ከመ፡ ኢትቅረቡ፡ . . .

3. Prayer against colic, 13 lines; cf. 69, B3; Dobberahn, *Zauberrollen*, p. 298; and Strelcyn, *Lincei*, 66, 5, p. 180, and 67, 13, p. 182.

ጸሎት፡ በእንተ፡ ቁርጻት፡ ዘተፈነወ፡ እምነበ፡ አብ፡ ወወልድ፡ . . . ይርዳዕ፡
ወይቤዙ፡ ውሉደ፡ እጓለ፡ እመሕያው፡ እንዘ፡ ይበጽብጽብጽ፡ (sic) ከርሰ፡
ወይጐጻጉጽ፡ ገቦዋተ፡ ወይጠዊ፡ አንፍተ፡ ወይቄርጽ፡ አማዑተ፡ ቄጼቤ፡[3x]
ቄፌኑ፡[3x] ሸገር፡[3x] በኃይለ፡ ዝንቱ፡ አስማቲከ፡ አድኅኖ፡ . . .

4. Prayer against piercing pain, 9 lines.

ጸሎት፡ በእንተ፡ ሕማመ፡ ውግአት፡ ምድያምስ፡[2x] የሐቂ፡[3x] በከመ፡ አድኃንኮ፡
ለወልደ፡ መበለት፡ ሰራቂ፡ ከማሁ፡ አድኅኖ፡ . . .

5. Prayer against charm, taken from the Eighty-One (Canonical) Books, 24 lines.

በስመ፡ አብ፡ . . . ጸሎት፡ በእንተ፡ መፍትሔ፡ ሥራይ፡ ዘተቀድሐ፡ በ፹ወ፩
መጻሕፍት፡ በንብረ[፡] ደጀን፡ ምርዳታ፡[3x] አክሎክ፡[2x] ኢፍዛዜምር፡ . . .

6. Prayer against illnesses caused by charm, 17 lines; cf. 22, 1.

በስመ፡ አብ፡ . . . ጸሎት፡ በእንተ፡ ሕማመ፡ ⌐ ሥራይ፡ ዮፍታሔ[፡]²ˣ
ዮፍታሔ[፡] እመሂ፡ ዘገብሩ፡ ሥራያተ[፡] አስማተ፡ ሰማየ፡ ነጺሮሙ[፡] ምድረ፡
ረጊያሙ፡ . . .

7. Greeting to Phanuel as prayer to drive away demons.

ሰላም፡ ለከ፡ ሰዳዬ፡ አጋንንት፡ ፋኑኤል፡ ለእግ"፡ እምጽርሑ፡ . . .

8. Prayer against Barya, Təgərtya, and Legewon, 38 lines; cf. 87, 2.

ጸሎት፡ በእንተ፡ በርያ፡ (sic) ወትግርትያ፡ ወለጌዎን፡ ዘይሰልብ፡ ልበሰብ፡
(sic) ወያጸልም፡ ዓዕይንተ፡ ወይመጽእ፡ ከመ፡ ጽላሎት፡ ወሐልም፡ አምሕልከ፡
ወአውግዘከ፡ (sic) በፒአካላት፡ ወበ፪መለኮት፡ በ፫ቅንዋተ፡ መስቀሉ፡ . . .

9. Prayer against illnesses caused by Buda, Ṭäbib, Anṭäräñña, and Fälaša (?), 24 lines, cut out at the end; cf. Six, *Handschriften*, 18, a, 4, 5, p. 95.

በስመ፡ አብ፡ . . . ጸሎት፡ በእንተ፡ ሕማመ፡ ቡዳ፡ ወጠቢብ፡ ወአንጠረኛ፡
ወፈላንሳ፡ (possibly for ወፈላሻ፡) አላሁመ፡ ወያነሩ፡ ተዋቂራ፡ ኃጀረጅ፡
ወበሕቀለ፡ ረጅ፡ እልበቆን፡ መበሹን፡ ዘረበሙ፡ ለአጋንንት፡ ሎፍሐም፡ በዝ፡
አስማት፡ ወበዝ፡ በቃላት፡ በኃይለ፡ መስቀሉ፡ . . . አስተናግር፡ ለቡዳ፡
መሰርይ፡ ወለጌዎን፡ . . . ይትናገር፡ ፈለሹን፡ ሁሁዳን፡ ሸ ሸ ላካ፡ ራቂ፡
ሰሙ፡ ለእግ"፡ መፍርሕ፡ ወመደንግዕ፡ ወልድ፡ . . .

Miniatures and Magical Symbols:
1. Angel with sword and scabbard.
2. Ornate cross with a person on either side.
3. Talismanic symbol with face in center.
4. Nine-box panel with elaborate patterns and face in center.

Three lines of writing on the back.
Copied for Gäbrä Maryam.

EMIP MagSc 89 – Weiner Magic Scroll 50
Parchment, 155 x 10.5 cm, three strips sewn together, one column, colored (yellow) border, Gəʿəz, 19th cent.
1. Prayer against Barya, the evil eye, Zar, Quräñña, Mäggañña, Täyayaž, Ṭäbib, Qumäñña and several illnesses, 130 lines.
በስመ፡ አብ፡ . . . ጸሎት፡ በእንተ፡ ባርያ፡ ወዓይ[፡] ነጥላ፡ ዛር፡ ወቁረኛ፡ ፍልጠት፡ ወቁርጠት፡ መጋኛ፡ ወጉሥምት፡ ስቅስቃት፡ ወቁርጥግት፡ ተያF፡ ወጠምዛF፡ ዓይነ፡ ጥላ፡ ወዓይነ፡ ወርቅ፡ ጠቢብ፡ ወዓይነ፡ ዛር፡ ወቁመኛ፡ ዓይነ፡ ቋመኛ፡ ወተግባሪኛ፡ ዓይነ፡ ሰብእ፡ ወዓይነ፡ ዘመድ፡ ወዐዕድ፡ ዓይነ፡ ካህናት፡ ወዲያቆናት፡ ባርያ፡ ዘአየር፡ ባርያ፡ ዘዲስማር፡ ባርያ፡ ዘባሕር፡ ባርያ፡ ዘሐመድ፡ ባርያ፡ ዘጉድንድ፡ ባርያ፡ ዘአሥር፡ ዘይትሜሰል፡ በከልብ፡ ወበዝሕብ፡ (sic) ዘይትሜሰል፡ በአንበሳ፡ ወነምር፡ ዘይትሜሰል፡ በሆባይ፡ ወበድም፡ (sic) ዘይትሜሰል፡ በተመን፡ ወበጕሎን፡ ዘይትሜሰል፡ በሶር፡ ወበአግ፡ ዘይትሜሰል፡ በበግዕ፡ ወበጠሊ፡ ዘይመጽእ፡ በመአልት፡ ወይመጽእ፡ በሌሊት፡ ወይመጽእ፡ በብርሃን፡ ወይመጽእ፡ በጽልመት፡ ለዝኮሉ፡ ዘይትሜሰሉ፡ ተማኅፀንኩ፡ በዝ፡ ስምከ፡ አብ፡ ወወልድ፡ ወመንፈስ፡ ቅዱስ፡ ጨትኩታኤል፡:7x ዘአብርርከሙ፡ ለአዕዋፈ፡ ሰማይ፡ በመጥአጥር፡ አጥበርብር፡ አድርመዓምዕ፡:7x አምፌውስት፡:7x . . . አብ፡ እሳት፡ ወልድ፡ እሳት፡ . . . በእሉ፡ አመሐልኩክሙ፡ አጋንንት፡ . . . ፀዐ፡ መንፈስ፡ ርኩስ፡ በስሙ፡ ለኢየሱስ፡ ክርስቶስ፡ ኪርኪሹ፡:7x አካዐ፡:7x ቤቃ፡ ክስብኤል፡ . . . በስሙ፡ ለእግ"፡ አብ፡ . . . ታአስ፡ አዝዮስ፡ ወሲማክያስ፡ አቅጼፍር፡ ወበስሙ፡ ለሐራሱን፡ ሐራሱን፡:5x . . . አልፉ፡:3x ፀእ፡ . . . ያቀ፡:2x ወያቀ፡ ያቀ፡:4x አድገና፡ . . .
2. The prayer titled "Rampart of the Cross," 18 lines.
ጸሎት፡ በእንተ፡ ሐውረ፡ መስቀል፡ መስቀል፡ ነጋቴ፡ ፀር፡ መስቀል፡:2x መዋዒ፡ ፀር፡ መስቀል፡ መድኃኒቶሙ፡ ለሕሙማን፡ መስቀል፡ . . .

Miniatures and Magical Symbols:
1. Robed man holding up hand cross in his left hand and holding handkerchief in his right hand.
2. Roman cross.
3. Robed man standing, left hand raised.
4. Small cross at end of the scroll.

Copied beautifully for Wälättä Maryam, to which the name ʿAmättä Wäld, with her picture, is added.

EMIP MagSc 90 – Weiner Magic Scroll 51
Parchment, 203 x 9.5 cm, three strips sewn together, one column, (wide) sawtooth border, Gəʿəz, 19th cent.

1. Prayer against illnesses caused by the evil eye of Barya and Šotolay that is the prayer of St. Susənyos against Wərzəlya of the infant mortality, 22 lines.
 በስመ፡ አብ፡ . . . ጸሎት፡ በእንተ፡ ሕማም፡ ዓይነ፡ ባርያ፡ ወሾቶላይላይ፡ (sic) በስሙ፡ ለእግ"፡ ሕያው፡ . . .
2. Prayer for drowning demons, 22 lines.
 በስመ፡ አብ፡ . . . ጸሎት፡ በእንተ፡ መስጥም፡ አጋንንት፡ ገባሮን፡ (?) አርያሰ፡ ሰውር፡ (sic) ስሙ፡ አጆናጦር፡ . . . ዘይሰልብ፡ ልብ፡ ሰብእ፡ ወይመጽእ፡ . . .
3. Prayer of St. Susənyos, and the story of his fight against Wərzəlya of the infant mortality.
4. Prayer against the evil eye, Barya, and Šotolay causing hemorrhage, 15 lines.
 በስመ፡ አብ፡ . . . ጸሎት፡ በእንተ፡ ዓይነ፡ ጥላ፡ ባርያ፡ ወሾቶላይ፡ በስመ፡ ባራት፡[5x] አድሮን፡[5x] በኃይለ፡ ዝንቱ፡ አስማት፡ ዘእርጋዕከ፡ ደግ፡ ለእንተ፡ ደም፡ ይውኅዝ፡ . . .
5. Prayer against piercing pain, 10 lines; cf. Dobberahn, *Zauberrollen*, pp. 305–5.
 በስመ፡ አብ፡ . . . ጸሎት፡ በእንተ፡ ውግዓት፡ ምድምያኖስ፡[5x] የሐቂ፡[3x] . . . በሰመ፡ አድኃንኮ፡ ለወልደ፡ ከርሡቂ፡ . . .
6. Prayer against stomachache, 14 lines.
 በስመ፡ አብ፡ . . . ጸሎት፡ በእንተ፡ ሕማም፡ ቀርጸት፡ ዘተፈነወ፡ ወልድ፡ ከመ፡ ይቤዙ፡ ወይርዳዕ፡ ዕጓለ፡ እመ፡ ሕያው፡ እምዘይበጽብጸ፡ ከርሡ፡ ወያደቅቅ፡ አእጽምተ፡ ወይጠዊ፡ አንጌተ፡ ወአገዉተ፡ ሽግር፡[3x] በኃይለ፡ ዝንቱ፡ አስማቲከ፡ ዕቀብ፡ . . .

Miniatures and Magical Symbols:
1. Three figures with swords; two figures above. Faded and worn.
2. Angel with sword and scabbard.
3. Two people, one large and one small, side by side.
4. Angel with sword and scabbard.
5. Small panel with face at the end of the scroll.

Copied for Wälättä Śəllase.

EMIP MagSc 91 – Weiner Magic Scroll 52

Parchment, 207 x 9.5 cm, bottom 30 centimeters are water stained and the text is faded, four strips sewn together, one column, colored (yellow) and hatched line border, Gəʿəz, 19th cent.

1. Prayer for drowning and binding demons, 33 lines; cf. 13, 1.

በስመ፡ አብ፡ . . . ጸሎት፡ በእንተ፡ መሥጠም፡ አጋንንት፡ ወማዕሠረ፡ አጋንንት፡ ንን (sic) አርያኖስ፡ ሰውር፡[3x] ሥመር፡[3x] አግናጦር፡ አውተደናብልጥ፡ ዘይሰልብ፡ ልብ፡ ወያጸልም፡ አዕይንተ፡ ወይመጽእ፡ ከመ፡ ጽላሎት፡ በመዓልት፡ ወበሌሊት፡ ሕልም፡ አምሐልኩክሙ፡ ወአውገዝዙክሙ፡ በ፫ቅንዋተ፡ መስቀሉ፡ ለእግዚእን፡ ኢየሱስ፡ ክርስቶስ፡ ሳዶር፡ አላዶር፡ ዳናት፡ አዴራ፡ ሮዳስ፡ ጤቃ፡ ቤቃ፡ በንቡዕ፡ᵚᵃᵏʰᵘᵃᵗ ስምከ፡ . . . ይልሳሕ፡ ሕምዞሙ፡ ወይትቀጥቀጥ፡ ኃይሎሙ፡ . . .

2. Prayers for the days of the week for drowning demons; cf. 49, 2; 54, 2; 68, 2.
The list of classes of evil spirits, listed as እለ in the prayer for Sunday, is longer than in 70, 5: እለ፡ ኖባ፡ ወኖብ፡ ወእለ፡ አፌ፡ ጋም፡ ወእለ፡ ባም፡ ወእለ፡ አፌ፡ ሰይፍ፡ ሰዲፍ፡ እለ፡ ጆናን፡ እለ፡ ቆራማ፡ እለ፡ ቆጋጥ፡ እለ፡ ናጥፍ፡ እለ፡ ቀኡልጵልጭ፡ እለ፡ አይጋይ፡ እለ፡ ኮርንጁ፡ እለ፡ ከልከሉስ፡ እለ፡ ጉማን፡ እለ፡ ኮብሽ፡ እለ፡ ሳይቀስስ፡ (?) እለ፡ አይመል፡ (sic) እለ፡ ሌጌዎን፡ እለ፡ ቦሊስ፡ እለ፡ ደልቃንሽ፡ እለ፡ መጆ[.]፡ እለ፡ ባሮ፡ እለ፡ ጥቁሮ፡ እለ፡ ስንዝሮ፡ እለ፡ ማጬር፡ እለ፡ ቀበን፡ እለ፡ ከፌላ፡ እለ፡ ኑኤላ፡ እለ፡ ደባሽ፡ እለ፡ ጋውር፡ እለ፡ ዳውር፡ እለ፡ መዓት፡ እለ፡ ቆሚጥ፡ እለ፡ ሸመላይ፡ እለ፡ ሜዳድ፡ እለ፡ ጨምዳድ፡ እለ፡ መዝሐብ፡ እለ፡ ሙዕጆን፡ እለ፡ ሙራን፡ እለ፡ አሕመር፡ እለ፡ በቄን፡ እለ፡ ሸምሐሮሽ፡ እለ፡ ሙሰፍይ፡ ነጋር፡ እለ፡ ጆቆር፡ እአ (sic) ጋምሬ፡ እለ፡ አህልያ፡ እለ፡ ወለተ፡ ወለተ፡ (sic) ወርቅ፡ እለ፡ ዓይን፡ ወርቅ፡ እለ፡ አረጊት፡ እለ፡ ዓይን፡ ጥላ፡ ᵃᵃዓይን፡ አፍጆጆ፡ አሰቡሽ፡ እለ፡ ቀቦቲ፡ እለ፡ ደርቦን[፡] እለ፡ አምሐሊ፡ እለ፡ አጋሬ፡ እለ፡ አብራሪ፡ እለ፡ አጦሊ፡ (አጣሊ፡?) እለ፡ አዋጊ፡ (አዋጊ፡?) እለ፡ ሰዳቢ፡ ወአሰዳቢ፡ አለ፡ አሀልዮማ፡ እለ፡ ሳቢ፡ እለ፡ ድቆን፡ እለ፡ ደም፡ ጠጭ፡ እለ፡ ጸም፡ (?) ሐዲስ፡ ወኮልክሙ፡ ሰብእ፡ መሠርያን፡ እለ፡ ቀናተኛ፡ ወምቀኛ፡ እለ፡ ቡዳ፡ ወጠቢብ፡ ወቀኡማኛ፡ እለ፡ ቀኡንጣጭ፡ ወጥማጭ፡ ወቀኡራጭ፡ እለ፡ ቀብሮ፡ ሳቢ፡ እለ፡ ጆብ፡ ጋባቢ፡ እለ፡ ሬሳ፡ ጕታች፡ እለ፡ መቃብር፡ ከፋኪ፡ (sic) እለ፡ ምግቡ፡ ወቀለቡ፡ ሰው፡ እለ፡ ጆብ፡ ፈረሱ፡ እለ፡ አይውል፡ ተነፍሱ፡ እለ፡ አይለብሱ፡ እለ፡ እኣይጠብሱ፡ (sic) እለ፡ ንጉሥ፡ አቦላ፡ እለ፡ አይጠብሱ፡ (sic, again) እለ፡ ሥር፡ በማሽ፡ እለ፡ ሰው፡ የምትበሉ፡ እለ፡ ሰው፡ የምትገድሉ፡ እለ፡ ሰው፡ የምትተናኮሉ፡ ይሡዓር፡ ሥራያቲክሙ፡ . . . በዝ፡ መሥጥም፡ ወበዝ፡ አስማተ፡ ጠልሰም፡ ወበዝ፡ ቃለ፡ አስግት፡ ወበዝ፡ ቃላት፡ ኩኑ፡ [ዕ]ቡዳን፡ ወድንጉጻን፡ ከመ፡ ኢትቅረቡኒ፡ . . .

3. Prayer for driving away demons, and subduing satanic spirits.
በስመ፡ አብ፡ . . . ጸሎት፡ ዘመስደዴ፡ አጋንንት፡ ወመማግረሬ፡ ሰይጣናት[፡] ከመ፡ ይሰደዱ፡ ሕገም፡ ኪር፡ ወብድብድ[፡] ማቁ፡ ወንዳድ፡ ዛር፡ ወዛሪት፡ ጉዳሌ፡ ወነሀብት፡ ወቄዳር፡ ባርያ፡ ወነገርጋር፡ ሮሓቅ፡ እምኔየ፡ ወኢትቁሙ፡ ንበ፡ ዓዕድየ፡ ወኢትልክፉኒ፡ ኪያየ፡ ወኮሎ፡ ዘኮነ፡ ዘዚአየ፡ ከመዝ፡ እብል፡ አምሐለክሙ፡ . . .

Miniatures and Magical Symbols:
1. Angel with sword and scabbard.
2. Nine-box panel with face in center; strip of five small boxes with X-shaped patterns above and strip with interlacing rope pattern and five eyes below.
3. Box with four-petal pattern and eyes in each.

About 22 lines at the end are stained with water, affecting legibility.
Copied for Gäbrä Śəllase and (his wife) Wälättä Ḥəywät.

EMIP MagSc 92 —Weiner Magic Scroll 53

Parchment, 148 x 9.5 cm, two strips sewn together, one columns, colored (yellow) border with sawtooth pattern, Gəʻəz, 19th cent.

1. Prayer of St. Susənyos against illnesses caused by evil eye, Šätolay, and others, and against hemorrhage, with an abbreviated story of the saint's fight against Wərzəlya of the infant mortality, 32 lines.
   በስመ፡ አብ፡ . . . ጸሎት፡ በእንተ፡ ሕማም፡ ዓይነ፡ ሰብእ፡ ሸቶላይ፡ ወመርግጌ፡ ደም፡ መቀኛ፡ ዐይቅ (sic) ወሥራይ፡ ፍልፀት፡ ወቀኍርፀት፡ በስመ፡ እግ"፡ ሕያው፡ . . . ወሀሎ፡ ብእሲ፡ ዘስሙ፡ ሱስንዮስ፡ . . .
2. Prayer against the evil eye, Šätolay, Mäggañña, Anṭärañña, Marit, Zarit, Gudale, Təgrida, and Šätolawit others, 13 lines.
   በስመ፡ አብ፡ . . . ጸሎት፡ በእንተ፡ ሕማም፡ ዓይነት፡ ወሸቶላይ፡ መገኛ፡ (sic) ወአንጠረኛ፡ ወማሪት፡ ዛሪት፡ ጉዳሌ፡ ወጉዳሌ፡ (sic) ትግሪደ፡ (sic) ወሸቶላዊት፡ በስመ፡ ፒራ፡ ወአስወሪራ፡ ቀራሽን፡[3x] ከራን፡[3x] ደራን፡[2x] ጨጨሪር፡[2x] በዝንቱ፡ አስማት፡ ስድዱሙ፡ . . .
3. Prayer against the evil eye, Šätolay, and against hemorrhage, 14 lines.
   በስመ፡ አብ፡ . . . ጸሎት፡ በእንተ፡ ሕማም፡ ዓይነት፡ ሸቶላይ፡ ወመርግጌ፡ ደም፡ መቃጅን፡[2x] መአጅን፡ ዓዲስ፡ ወንጌል፡ ዘዮሐንስ፡ ወይቀውማ፡ (John 19:25–27) . . .
4. Greeting to Phanuel as prayer to drive away demons, 37 lines.
   ሰላም፡ ለከ፡ ሰዳዬ፡ አጋንንት፡ ፋኑኤል፡ ለእግ" አምጽርሑ፡ . . .
5. Prayer against the evil eye, the evil eye of Barya, Legewon, different illnesses, and charm,
   በስመ፡ አብ፡ . . . ጸሎት፡ በእንተ፡ ሕማም፡ ዓይን[ት]፡ ወዓይን፡ ባርያ፡ ወለጌዎን፡ ምትዓት፡ ወውጋት፡ ወቁርጥማት፡ ወፍልፀት፡ ወመፍት[ሔ፡] ሥራይ፡ ወእሙ፡ ኢየሱባ፡ (!) ፍታሕ፡ በአቡነ፡ ገብር፡ መንፈስ፡ ቅዱስ፡ ዘትኤዝዞሙ፡ . . . አሜን፡ F: [እ]ምኮ[ሉ፡ ደ]ዌንት፡ ሕማም፡ ኮሪ፡ [ወኮሪት፡] ዘሪ፡ ወዘሪት፡ ጉዳሌ፡ ወጥጥፍነት፡ ወቁደር፡ ወነገርጋር፡ እለ፡ ይመጽኡ፡ በሕቡዕ፡ ወበክሡት፡ ሰዓር፡ ወመንዝር፡ . . .
6. Prayer against the evil eye, unfinished. The 7 lines in full:

በስመ፡ አብ፡ . . . ጸሎት፡ በእንተ፡ ሐማም፡ ዓይነት፡ ጆጆቢ፡ ረረቢ፡ ከፈሹማግ፡ ዘደገመ፡ ፍታሕ፡ ምድረ፡ ረጊጾሙ፡ ሰማየ፡ነጺሮሙ፡ ባሕረ፡ በጽቢጾሙ፡ ዕብነ፡ ወር[ዊ]ሮሙ፡ . . . (99, 4 has the full text.)

Miniatures and Magical Symbols:
1. Remains of panel (broken off at top); five-box panel (5 x 2), top row all have faces in them, the bottom row of boxes all have quarter circles in each corner.
2. Angel with sword and scabbard.
3. Four-box panel (2 x 2) with faces in the top two boxes and with quarter circles in each corner of the lower boxes.

Copied for Wälättä Tənśa'e.

EMIP MagSc 93 – Weiner Magic Scroll 54

Parchment, 162 x 10 cm, two strips sewn together, one column, colored (yellow or brown) border with line on inside and outside of border, Gəʻəz, 18th cent.

1. Prayer of St. Susənyos, and the story of his fight against Wərzəlya of the infant mortality.
2. Prayer against charm, the evil eye, Fəgen, Fälaša, the evil eye of Zar, Təgrida, and Mäggañña.
   በስመ፡ አብ፡ . . . ጸሎት፡ በእንተ፡ መፍትሔ፡ ሥራይ፡ ወጽላዋጊ፡ ፍጌን፡ ወፈላሻ፡ ዓይነ፡ ዛር፡ ወትግሪዳ፡ ዓይነ፡ ቁራኛ፡ ወተጸሪሪ፡ ወተሻጋሪ፡ ወመጋኛ፡ followed by a chart of 10 times 12 square places each filled with a letter of *asmat* (Dobberahn, *Zauberrollen*, p. 322) በእሉ፡ አስማተ፡ እግ"፡ ፍታሕ፡ ወዘርዝር፡ ሡጻር፡ ወመንዝር፡ . . .
3. Greeting to the pierced side of Jesus, prayed against hemorrhage.
   ሰላም፡ ለገቦከ፡ ኵናተ፡ ለንጊኖስ፡ ዘወግዖ፨
   እምዓቅተ፡ ማይ፡ ክርሦከ፡ [በደሙ፡] ሥርዓት፡ እንተ፡ አንቀዖ፨
   [ሐቀ]ርያ፡ አብ፡ ክርስቶስ፡ ዘፈጸምከ፡ ግብረ፡ ተሰብአ፨
   አድኅነኒ፡ በመስቀልከ፡ ለመአከ፡ ሞት፡ (no 75, 2: ጽልመት፡) ዘሞዖ፨
   ከመ፡ ኖላዊ፡ የዓቅብ፡ እምተኵላ፡ በግዖ፨
   ምድምያስ፡[3x] የሐቂ፡[3x] ያብራስቂ፡ ዘጊ፡[3x] በከመ፡ አድኃንክ፡ ለወልደ፡ በራስቂ፡ (!) ከጎሁ፡ . . .
4. Prayer against colic; cf. 88, 3.
   በስመ፡ አብ፡ . . . ጸሎት፡ በእንተ፡ ሐማም፡ ቁርፀት፡ ፈነወ፡ (sic, for ተፈነወ፡) ወልድ፡ እምነበ፡ አቡሁ፡ ከመ፡ ይርዳዕ፡ . . .
5. Greeting to Phanuel as prayer against illnesses caused by the eye of Barya, and to drive away demons and bind them.

በስመ፡ አብ፡ . . . ጸሎት፡ በእንተ፡ ሕማም፡ ዓይን፡ ባርያ፡ ወማዕሥሮሙ፡ ለአጋንንት፡ ሰላም፡ ለቱ፡ ሰዳዴ፡ አጋንንት፡ ፉኑኤል፡ ለእግ" አምጽርሐ፡ . . .

6. Prayer for binding demons.
በስመ፡ አብ፡ . . . ጸሎት፡ በእንተ፡ ማዕሥረ፡ አጋንንት፡ ስድዶሙ፡ እምየግንየ፡ ወእምፀጋምየ፡ ይርጓቂ፡ እምኔየ፡ . . . ቀዳሚሁ፡ ቃል፡ ውእቱ፡ (John 1:1–5) በዝ፡ ቃለ፡ ወንጌልከ፡ አድኅና፡ . . . በስመ፡ አብ፡ . . . አምሐልኩክሙ፡ ወአውገዝኩክሙ፡ መናፍስት፡ ርኩሳን፡ በፀእንሳ፡ በጀወፀ ካህናተ፡ ሰግይ፡ በሚካኤል . . . ወገጹ፡ ዘጹጹም፡ በጽልመት፡ ፈርሃ፡ ወደንገፀ፡ ዲያብሉስ፡ (written upside down) ርእዮ፡ ብሑተ፡ ልደት፡ በሥጋ፡ አምላክ፡ በሲኦል፡ በዝ፡ ቃለ፡ መለከ[ት]ከ፡ ዕቀብ፡ . . .

Miniatures and Magical Symbols:
1. Six-box panel (3 x 2) with face in box two, X patterns in boxes 1, 3, and 5 and concentric circles in boxes 4 and 6 (faded).
2. Talismanic symbol with face in the center, surrounded with geometric designs.
3. Magical table of letters.
4. Angel with sword and scabbard (pointing up).
5. Panel with geometric designs (faded).

Copied carefully, but some of the words in red are illegible.
Copied for Wälättä Täklä Haymanot.

EMIP MagSc 94 – Weiner Magic Scroll 55
Parchment, 198 (with securing tab that extends another 10cm) x 12 cm, three strips sewn together, one columns, colored (red) border, Gəʻəz, 18th/19th cent.

1. Prayer, with *asmat* of Solomon that Michael gave him, for drowning demons, Barya, Legewon (,) Ğənn, Däbas, Däsk, Gudale, Zar, Təgrida, Mäggäñña, Šotolay, Buda, and Mänšo; cf. 54, 1.
በስመ፡ አብ፡ . . . ጸሎት፡ በእንተ፡ መሥጠም፡ አጋንንት፤ ወሰይጣናት፡ ባርያ፡ ወሌጌዎን፡ ጅን፡ ወደባስ፡ ደስክ፡ ወጉዳሌ፡ ዛር፡ ወትግሪዳ፡ መገኛ፡ ወሾቶላይ፡ ንዳድ፡ ወመንሾ፡ ምትሐት፡ ወጽፍዓት፡ ጉስግት፡ ወፍርቃቃት፡ ውግዓት፡ ወሰቅስቃት፡ ኤልክሻካሽ፡ ወተለካሽ፡ ቡዳ፡ ወቂመኛ፡ አልጉም፡ ፈሪ፡ ወንዳድ፡ ወቸንነፈር፡ ፍልፀት፡ ወቁርጥማት፡ . . . ዝውእቱ፡ መጽሐፍ፡ ዘወሀቦ፡ ቅዱስ፡ ሚካኤል፡ ለሰሎሞን፡ ንጉሥ፡ ከመ፡ ይᑎጉሎሙ፡ ለአጋንንት፡ . . .
2. Prayer for Monday, taken from prayers of the seven days of the week, for terrorizing and drowning demons; cf. 49, 2; 68, 2; 91, 2.

Miniatures and Magical Symbols:
1. Twelve-box panel (3 x 4) with faces in boxes 5, 7, 9, and 11.

2. Angel (large).
3. Angel (large).
4. Large panel made of three sections. In the top is a dog representing Judas (of Iscariot); in the middle is a four-box panel (2 x 2) with faces in each box; at the bottom is an animal and a serpentine design.
Copied for Wälättä Iyyäsus.

EMIP MagSc 95 – Weiner Magic Scroll 56

Parchment, 194 x 10 cm, three strips sewn together, one column, Gəʻəz, colored (yellow) border, 20th cent.

1. Prayer against demons; cf. 38, 1; 29, 2 and 6.
   በስሙ፡ ለእግ" አብ፡ በስሙ፡ ለእግ" ወልድ፡ በስሙ፡ ለእግ"፡ መንፈስ፡ ቅዱስ፡ ታአስ፡ አዝዮስ፡ ማሲ፡ ማስያስ፡ አቅዳፌር፡ . . . በሰይፈ፡ ሚካኤል፡ ይትገዘም፡ ወይፃዕ፡ . . . አሜን፡ አንተ፡ ሰይጣን፡ የሐቂ፡[3x] አንተ፡ ባርያ፡ ወአንተ፡ ነሀቢ፡ አንተ፡ ፍጌን፡ ወአንተ፡ ጽላዎጊ፡ አንተ፡ ምታት፡ ወአንተ፡ ውግዓት፡ አንተ፡ ቀርጸት፡ ወአንተ፡ ፍልፀት፡ አንተ፡ ቡዳ፡ ወአንተ፡ ምች፡ ወአንተ፡ መጋኛ፡ ወአንተ፡ ዝግልፍታ፡ ዘትትሜሰል፡ በብዙኅ፡ ጸታ፡ አሕያ፡ ሸራህያ፡ . . . ልፍ፡[3x] አልፍ፡ አልአ፡ ፃእ፡[3x] ወዒኣከ፡ ኢትግባእ፡ ይቤሉከ፡ አብ፡ . . .

2. Prayer against filthy Legewon; cf. 9, 2; 46, 2.
   ጸሎት፡ በእንተ፡ ሌጌዎን፡ ርኩስ፡ ዘይሰብብ፡ ልቡ፡ ሰብእ፡ ወያጸልም፡ አዕይንተ፡ . . . አምሕለከ፡ ወአውግዘከ፡ በ፬ቅንዋተ፡ መስቀሉ፡ . . . ሳዶር፡ . . . በኃይለ፡ ዝንቱ፡ አስማቲከ፡ አድኅናን፡ . . . ባርያ፡ ዘይነብር፡ በቆጥ፡ . . .

3. The Net of Solomon for catching demons; cf. Strelcyn, Lincei, 125, XIX, b, p. 312.
   ጸሎት፡ አስማተ፡ ሀላዌሁ፡ ለሰሎሞን፡ ዘረበበሙ፡ ለአጋንንት፡ ከመ፡ መርበብተ፡ ዓሣ፡ ዘዛሕር፡ እንዘ፡ ይብል፡ ሰዳቃኤል፡ አደታኤል፡ ኪአስ፡ ኪ.ማስ፡ ኪናሚስ፡ . . . አስማተ፡ ሀላዌሁ፡ ለሰሎሞን፡ ንዓድ፡ አስማተ፡ ንውደ፡ አያስ፡ አያያስ፡ . . . ዘወረደ፡ ነበ፡ ሰሎሞን፡ እንዘ፡ ይብል፡ ሸብለሺ፡ ሸተለን፡ ሸርታን፡ ሸላሆም፡[3x] . . . ሎፍሐም፡ መሐፍሎን፡ ንምሉስ፡ በዝንቱ፡ ስሙ፡ ለእግ"፡ ድንነ፡ ሰሎሞን፡ . . .

Miniatures and Magical Symbols:
1. Angel with sword and scabbard.
2. Talismanic symbol: nine-box panel with face in center.
3. Twelve-box panel (3 x 4) with geometric and X shapes.
4. Talismanic symbol: nine-box panel with face in center.

Copied for Wälättä Yoḥannəs.

EMIP MagSc 96 – Weiner Magic Scroll 57

Parchment, 137 x 8 cm, four strips sewn together, one column, narrow colored (yellow or brown) border, Gəʿəz, 1865–1913 (reign of Menelik).

1. Prayer to terrorize the enemy and against charm, with much Arabic and Amharic.
    [. . .] በእንተ፡ ስመ[፡ . .]ሁ፡ በእንተ፡ ስመ፡ ወላሁ፡ [ቢስ]ሚላሂ፡ ቢስሚላሂ፡ ቢስሚ[ላሂ፡ ቢስ]ሚላሂ፡ ቢስሚላሂ፡³ˣ አፈርዝም፡⁷ˣ ⌐በላ፡ በሂ፡⁷ˣ አንበርብር፡ ወአሽብር፡ . . . በእንተ[፡ ስ]መ፡ አብ፡ አቁኤል፡ በእንተ፡ ስመ፡ ወ[ል]ድ፡ ናምሩድ፡ በእንተ፡ ስመ፡ መ[ን]ፈስ፡ ቅዱስ፡ አዙኤል፡ አንበርብሩ፡ ወአሽብሩ፡ ፀርየ፡ ወጸላእትየ፡ . . . ሰግየ ጠቂስክሙ፡ ወምድረ፡ ከፈተክሙ፡ ባሕረ፡ በጽቢዘክሙ፡ (sic) ምስለ፡ ብርያል፡ ንጉሥክሙ፡ አመሓልኩክሙ፡ ወአውገዝኩክሙ፡ በጥምጥማኤል፡ ንጉሥክሙ፡ (The list of "their" kings is long) . . .

2. Prayer against Buda, Fälaša, and Qumäñña, 10 lines.
    በስመ፡ አብ፡ . . . ጸሎት፡ በእንተ፡ ቡዳ፡ ወፈላሻ[፡ .]ጉም፡ ወቁመኛ፡ አላሁ፡ አላሁም፡⁷ˣ አኑሬሪጅ፡ በሐጅ፡ . . .

3. The Net of Solomon, as prayer for binding demons, 15 lines; a different manuscript whose beginning has been lost.
    ዘረበሙ፡ ለአጋንንት፡ ሎፍሐም፡ መሐፍሎን፡ በዝ፡ አስማት፡ ወበዝ፡ ቃላት፡ በኃይለ፡ መስቀሉ፡ ለኢየሱስ፡ ክርስቶስ፡ አስተናግር፡ ለቡዳ፡ መሰርይ፡ ወ^ሌጌወን፡ (sic) እኩይ፡ ወለአሎም፡ አጋዝአም፡ እጅ፡ ሰብእ፡ ሐመም[፡] ለሕሙም፡ ይትናገር፡ ፈላሹን፡ ነሆነሆጅን፡ ነሸሾን፡ . . .

4. Prayer of Our Lady Mary which she prayed when they made her drink the bitter water (Mum 5:11–31), 21 lines.
    ጸሎተ፡ እግዝእትነ፡ ማርያም፡ ያስርህ፡ ሮህ፡ ሮዲዲ፡ ያዲኬ፡ አሶሶር፡ ሩኤ፡ (?) ዘንተ፡ ብሂላ፡ አመ፡ ስትየት፡ ማየ፡ ዘለፉ፡ ኮነ፡ . . .

5. Prayer against illnesses caused by Barya, incomplete at the end, 6 lines.
    ጸሎት፡ በእንተ፡ ሕማም፡ ባርያ፡ ቦቶል፡ አነቶል፡ . . .

Miniatures and Magical Symbols:
1. Angel with sword and scabbard(?) (torn and repaired at this point).
2. Angel surrounded by geometric patterns and wavy lines

Words at the margin are not always legible. A few lines from the beginning are faded.
Copied for Ṭəru.

EMIP MagSc 97 – Weiner Magic Scroll 58

Parchment, 150 x 8.5 cm, three strips sewn together, one column, colored (yellow or brown) border, Gəʿəz, 19th cent.

1. Prayer of St. Susənyos for binding demons and against the eye of Barya, filthy Legewon, Mäggäñña, Šotälay, Buda, Carpenter (*Nähabi*), Zar, and the story of his fight against Wərzəlya of the infant mortality, finished in a different hand.
በስመ፡ አብ፡ . . . ጸሎት፡ [በእ]ንተ፡ ማዕሠሮሙ፡ አጋንንት[፡] ዓይነ፡ ባርያ፡ ወሌጌዎን፡ ርኩስ[፡] መጋኛ፡ ወሾተላይ፡ ቡዳ፡ ወነሀቢ[፡] ዛር፡ ተንኮለኛ፡ ዘየኃዉ፡ ጉርጌ[፡] ወዘይለጉም፡ አፈ፡ ውግዓት፡ ወቀኑርጥማት፡ ፍልፀተ፡ ርእስ፡ ወ[ሕ]ማም፡ ዓይን፡ ምች፡ ወተላዋሽ[፡] ምታት፡ ወጽፍዓት፡ ወኮሉ፡ አባለ፡ ሥጋ፡ ዘያውዒ፡ ዕቀብ፡ . . . በስመ፡ አብ፡ . . . ጸሎት፡ ዘቅዱስ፡ ሱስንዮስ፡ ነባቢ፡ ወተናጋሪ፡ . . . ወሀሎ፡ ፩ብእሲ፡ . . .

2. Prayer against Buda and Carpenter (*Nähabi*), apparently a continuation of 1 above.
ጸሎት፡ በእንተ፡ ቡዳ፡ ወነሃቢ፡ በሉፍሃም[፡] ስምከ፡ በኢዮአስ፡ ስምከ፡ ኢዮስያስ፡ ስምከ[፡] በዓማንኤል[፡] (sic) ስምከ፡ በማስያስ፡ ስምከ፡ . . .

Miniatures and Magical Symbols:
1. Panel with upper and lower sections: upper section depicts an angel (the top is torn off); the lower section is a six-box panel (3 x 2) with a face in box two and X-shaped patterns in the rest of the boxes.
2. Panel divided with an X into four quadrants, each containing a face.
3. Ornate cross (bottom torn off).

Finished by a different hand.
Copied for Wälättä Mädḫən.

EMIP MagSc 98 – Weiner Magic Scroll 59
Parchment, 202 x 8 cm, three strips sewn together, one column, narrow colored (yellow) border, Gəʻəz, 20th cent.

1. Prayer against the evil eye: The story of the sorcerer at the Sea of Tiberias.
በስመ፡ አብ፡ . . . ጸሎተ፡ ነደራ፡ ዘውእቱ፡ አይነት፡ ወእንዘ፡ የሐውር፡ እግዚእ፡ ኢየሱስ፡ ወስተ፡ (sic) ባሕረ፡ ጥብርያደስ፡ (sic) ናሁ፡ መጽኡ፡ ፲ወ፪ አርዳኢሁ፡ . . .

2. Prayer, with the *asmat* of the Archangel Michael, against Barya, Təgərtya, and different illnesses.
በስመ፡ አብ፡ . . . ጊቡዕ፡ ስሙ፡ ለሚካኤል፡ ዓቢይ፡ ክእ፡ እጌእ፡ ሌክ፡ ሌንክ፡ . . . በእሉ፡ አስማት፡ አድህን፡ እምብርያ፡ (sic) ወእምትግርትያ፡ . . . followed with the greeting to the pierced side of Jesus; cf. 93, 3.

3. Prayer against charm by people, demons, Fälaša, Gudale, Ṭäfinǧ, Buda, Carpenter (*Nähabi*), Dobbi, Dobbit, Zar, Zarit, Muslims, and Christians.

ጸሎት፡ በእንተ፡ ፍትሐተ፡ ሥራይ፡ ዘሰብእ፡ ወዘአጋንንት፡ ወዘፈላሻ፡ ወጉደሌ፡ ወጠፈንጀ፡ ወቡዳ፡ ወነሀቢ፡ ሥራየ፡ ብእሲ፡ ወብእሲት፡ ሥራየ፡ ዶቢ፡ ወዶቢት፡ ሥራየ፡ ዛር፡ ወዛሪት፡ ሥራየ፡ እስላም፡ ወክርስቲያን፡ ዘገብሩ፡ ሰግየ፡ ነኂሮሙ፡ . . . አድኅና፡ . . . በስሙ፡ ለአብ፡ በስሙ፡ ለወልድ፡ በስሙ፡ ለመንፈስ፡ ቅዱስ፡ ታአስ፡ አራአስ፡ ማስያስ፡ አቅዳፌር፡ በስሙ፡ ለሐራፕን፡ ሐራፕን፡ . . . ያቁ፡³ˣ አልፋ፡³ˣ ዓዐ፡³ˣ ይቤለከ፡ . . .

4. Prayer against colic.
ጸሎት፡ በእንተ፡ ሕማም፡ ቀርጸት፡ ሸው፡ ለአውሸትር፡ ከለዓውሸ፞ር፡ አውለለኤል፡ ሰራድኤል፡ ብርሱባሔል፡ አግኑኤል፡ ቤቃ፡ ወሴቃ፡ . . . ዘአድኃንኮሙ፡ ለአናንያ፡ . . . አዝረቢ፡ በኒሲ፡ ታአስ፡ ምድምያስ፡³ˣ የሐቂ፡³ˣ የሐብረስቂ፡ . . . ለወልደ፡ ሠራቂ፡ (sic).

Miniatures and Magical Symbols:
1. Panel with diamond shape and four petals; above and below are strips with sawtooth patterns.
2. Nine-box panel with face in center; above and below are strips with sawtooth patterns.
3. Nine-box panel with designs; above and below are strips with colorful C-shaped patterns.

Copied for Wälattä Maryam, replaced with 'Amätä Maryam.

EMIP MagSc 99 – Weiner Magic Scroll 60

Parchment, 172 x 8.5 cm, four strips sewn together, one column, double border (line at edge of parchment and about a half cm from the edge), Gəʻəz, 20th cent.

1. Prayer of St. Susənyos against the evil eye, Barya, Legewon, Šätolay, Anṭärañña, Mäggañña, and others, against hemorrhage, and an abbreviated story of his fight against Wərzəlya of the infant mortality; cf. 92, 1.
በስመ፡ አብ፡ . . . ጸሎት፡ በእንተ፡ ዓይነ፡ ሰብ፡ (sic) ወዓይነ፡ ጥላ፡ ወባርያ፡ ወሌጌዎን፡ ሾቶላይ፡ ወመርግዬ፡ ደም፡ መቀኛ፡ ወአንጠረኛ፡ መገኛ፡ ዐይቅ፡ (sic) ወሥራይ፡ ፍልፀት፡ ወቀሥፀት፡ በስሙ፡ እግ"፡ ሕያው፡ . . . ወሀሉ፡ ብእሲ፡ ዘስሙ፡ ሱስንዮስ፡ . . .
2. Greeting to Phanuel and Mary as prayer to drive away demons, against the evil eye, Mäggäñña, and Anṭärañña, 37 lines.
በስመ፡ እግ"፡ አብ፡ ሕያው፡ ነባቢ፡ ወተናጋሪ፡ ጸሎቱ፡ ወበረከቱ፡ የሀሉ፡ ምስለ፡ ዓመቱ፡ . . . በስመ፡ አብ፡ . . . ጸሎት፡ በእንተ፡ ሕማም፡ ዓይነ፡ ሰብእ፡ መገኛ፡ ወአንጠረኛ፡ ሰላም፡ ለከ፡ ሰዳዬ፡ አጋንንት፡ ፋኑኤል፡ ለእግ" አምጽርሐ፡ . . . ሰላም፡ ለኪ፡ መቅደሰ፡ አሪት፡ ዘቦእኪ፡ ማርያም፡ እምነ፡ ወእሙ፡ ለእግዚእነ፡ . . .

3. Prayer against the evil eye and Šätolay and against hemorrhage, Mäggäñña, Anṭäräñña, Zar, and Təgrida, and against charm; cf. 92, 5.
በስመ፡ አብ፡ . . . ጸሎት፡ በእንተ፡ ሕማመ፡ ዓይነት፡ ሸቶላይ፡ ወመርግዔ፡ ደም፡ መገኛ፡ ወእንጠረኛ፡ ዛር፡ ወትግሪዳ፡ ወመፍትሔ፡ ወእሙ፡ ኢየሉጣ፡ ፍታሕ፡ በአቡነ፡ ገብረ፡ መንፈስ፡ ቅዱስ፡ ዘትእዝዞሙ፡ . . . አሜን። F: እምኮሉ፡ ደዌንት፡ (sic) ሕማመ፡ ኮሪ፡ ወኮሪት፡ ዘሪ፡ ወዘሪት፡ ጉዳሊ፡ ወጉዳሊት፡ ወጥጥፍነት፡ ወቄደር፡ ወነገርጋር፡ እለ፡ ይመጽኡ፡ በንቡዕ፡ ወበክሡት፡ ሰአር፡ ወመንዝር፡ . . .
4. (Prayer against the evil eye), untitled, but see 92, 6; 50 lines.
ጆጆቢ፡ ጆጆቢ፡ ረረቢ፡ ከፈሹግ፡ ዘደገመ፡ ፍታሕ፡ ምድረ፡ ረጊጸሙ፡ ሰግየ፡ ነጺሮሙ፡ በእንቀ፡ ወበእንቁላል፡ ወበኖጭ፡ ዕጣን፡ ዘተደገመ፡ ፍታሕ፡ . . . The list is long.
5. Prayer against the evil eye, 25 lines.
በስመ፡ አብ፡ . . . ጸሎት፡ በእንተ፡ ሕማመ፡ ዓይነት፡ ኢከስ፡ አሜሊክ፡ ኢንካ፡ ካዜዕ፡ . . .
6. Prayer against Buda, 15 lines.
በስመ፡ አብ፡ . . . ጸሎተ፡ ቡዳ፡ ኢጢሚስር፡[3x] ግድግር፡ ግምትርም፡ . . . ናግለከፍን፡ አኽያ፡ ሽራኽያ፡ . . .

Miniatures and Magical Symbols:
1. Twelve-box panel (4 x 3) with two rows of patterns above.
2. Angel with sword and scabbard.
3. Four-box panel (2 x 2) with set of eyes (bottom torn off).

Copied for Gäbrä Ḥəwät and Wälättä Rufa'el.

EMIP MagSc 100 – Weiner Magic Scroll 61

Parchment, 212 x 9.5 cm, three strips sewn together, two columns, double border and lined margin between columns of text, Gəʿəz, 20th cent.

A1. Prayer against illnesses caused by Quräñña, Täyaž, Zar, Təgrida, and others, and different illnesses, insufficiently legible, 62 lines of a single col.
[በስ]መ፡ አ[ብ፡] . . . [ጸ]ሎት[፡ በ]እንተ፡ [ሕማመ፡ . . .] ቁራኛ፡ ወተያF[፡ ዛ]ር[፡] ወትግሪዳ፡ ወጉሥምት፡ ውግዓት፡ ወቁርጥማት፡ ፌሪ፡ ወንዳድ፡ ጆን፡ ወውላጅ፡ አንትሙ፡ አምሐልኩክሙ፡ . . . The *asmat* are insufficiently legible.

A2. Prayer to win the love of authorities. Full text:
በስመ፡ አብ፡ . . . ጸዋእኩ[፡] ስመከ፡ እግዚእ፡ አምላኪየ[፡] ወአድኅነኒ፡ በእንተ፡ ምሕረትከ፡ እስመ፡ አንተ፡ መሐሪ፡ ወመስተሳህል፡ ወብዙኅ፡ ምሕረት፡ ወኢትርሐቅ፡ አምኔየ፡ ሮፎኮር[፡][3x] ክዝዮን፡[3x] ሰቢላ፡[2x] ሰጊላ፡[2x] ዘወህብክሙ፡ ለዳዊት። ወለሰሎሞን፡ ወለኢያሱ[፡] በቃለ፡ ቀን፡ (sic)

ወለሐዋርያት[፡] በገሪ (sic) ሰላም፡ ለዘይጸልዑኒ፡ ያፍቅሩኒ[፡] ነገሥት፡ ወመኳንንት፡ ሊተ፡ ባዕድ፡ ወዘመድ፡ ሊተ፡ ለአመትከ[፡] . . .

A3. Prayer against the evil eye, Gärgari, Šotälay, Ǧənn, Wəllaǧ, Täyaž, the eye Zar, the eye of Buda, Fälaša, and the eye of Nas.

በስመ፡ አብ፡ . . . ጸሎት፡ በእንተ፡ ዓይነ፡ ጥላ፡ ወገርጋሪ፡ ወሾተላይ፡ ጅን፡ ወውላጅ፡ ወተያሪ፡ ኃኔን፡ ወተያF፡ ወጽላ፡ ወጊ፡ ወእጅ፡ (sic) ወዓይነ፡ ዛር፡ ወዓይነ፡ ቡዳ፡ ወፈላሻ፡ ወዓይነ፡ ናስ፡ አንትሙ፡ አውገዝኩክሙ፡ አሌሁሙን፡^{2x} አሸር፡^{2x} አሸሙሄር፡^{2x} አሸማር፡ ፍታሕ[፡] ሕዝብ፡ . . .

A4. Prayer of St. Susənyos, and the story of his fight against Wərzəlya, the demon of infant mortality. It begins in the middle of the story:

በስመ፡ አብ፡ . . . ቅዱስ፡ ሱስንዮስ[፡] አንተ፡ ንሳእ፡ ወልታ፡ ጽንዕ፡ ወኃይል፡ ቦቱ፡ አመ፡ ተንኣ፡ (sic) ረሲአ፡ ምግባር፡ ወመአትም፡ ለጽድቅ፡ ወለሠናይ፡ ኢይሐልያ፡ ወኢይነሥአ፡ ከመ፡ ወድቀት፡ በትር፡ ውስተ፡ ዕደው፡ አሜሃ፡ ተንስአ፡ ወአንሥአ፡ ኮናቶ፡ . . .

B1. Prayer against demons.

በስመ፡ አብ፡ . . . ጸዋእኩ፡ ስመከ፡ እግዚአብሔር፡ ዕንዘ፡ (sic) ሰዱቃኤል፡ ክርኤል፡^{3x} ጋጋታኤል፡ አዳታኤል፡ አሌላ፡ አልፍ፡ . . . ጸልሰኒ፡ ወአድግነኒ፡ . . .

B3. The first part of the story of the fight of St. Susənyos against Wərzəlya.

በስመ፡ አብ፡ . . . በስመ፡ እግ"፡ ሕያው፡ ነባቢ፡ ወተናጋሪ፡ በመለኮት፡ አብ፡ ወወልድ፡ . . . ጸሎቱ፡ ወበረከቱ፡ የሀሉ፡ ምስለ፡ አመቱ፡ ወሀሎ፡ ፯ብእሲ፡ ዘስሙ፡ ሱስንዮስ፡ . . .

Miniatures and Magical Symbols:
1. Angel standing (very faded and worn)
2. Panel with designs.
3. Panel with designs.

Bottom dirty and worn.
Copied for Wälättä Maryam.

EMIP MagSc 101 – Weiner Magic Scroll 62

Parchment, 205 x 9.5 cm, three strips sewn together, one column, colored (yellow) double border, Gəʿəz, 18th cent.

1. The Net of Solomon for catching demons, combined with the story of the fight of St. Susənyos against Wərzəlya. The words in red, including the beginning of the prayer, are insufficiently legible.

[በስመ፡ አብ፡ . . . ጸሎት፡ በእንተ፡ ሕማመ፡ ዓይነት..ጽላ፡] ወጊ፡ ወሾተላይ፡ አስገተ፡ ሰሎሞን፡ ዘረበሙ፡ ለአጋንንት፡ ከመ፡ መርበብተ፡ ዓሣ፡ ዘባሕር፡ እንዘ፡ ይብል፡ [. . . .ጸሎተ፡] ቅዱስ፡ [ሱስንዮስ፡ በእንተ፡ አሰስሎ፡] ደዌ፡ እምሕጻናት፡ [. . . .] ወመጽአ፡ ቃል፡ እምሰማይ፡ [. . . .] እቅመ[.]ሹን፡

በዝንቱ፡ [ድኅነ፡ ሰሎሞ]ን፡ እምዕደ፡ ነሃብት፡ ወከማሁ፡ . . . ወይቤሎ፡ ሰሎሞን፡ ኃይለ፡ እግ" ኢ.ይ[..] እምእዴየ፡ ዘፈቀድኩ፡ እገብር፡ . . . ወመጽአ፡ ነሃቢ፡ ዘስሙ፡ ሱስንዮስ፡ (!) . . .

2. Prayer for unstated purpose, but possibly for driving away demons, 17 lines; cf. 104, 3.
በስሙ፡ ለእ"፡ አብ፡ በስሙ፡ ለእግ" ወልድ፡ እሳት፡ በስሙ፡ ለእግ"፡ መንፈስ፡ ቅዱስ፡ እሳት፡ በሥጣን፡ አብ፡ በሥጣን፡ ወልድ፡ በሥጣን፡ መንፈስ፡ ቅዱስ፡ ታእስ፡ አዝዮስ፡ ሜልዮስ፡ አቅዬፍር፡ በስመ፡ ሐራሹን፡ ሐራፌክር፡ በጠጁን፡ . . . በስመ፡ ሳዶር፡ . . .

3. Prayer for conception, 17 lines.
በስመ፡ አብ፡ . . . ጸሎት፡ በእንተ፡ [አር.ጋዬ፡ ደ]ም፡ ወ[አዕንፅ]፡ ዕንስ፡ ወበእንተ፡ ሕማም፡፡ (sic) ፈሪሆተ፡ ስምከ፡ እግዚአ፡ ፀንስነ፡ ሐመምነሂ፡ ወወለድነ፡ እስመ፡ መካን፡ ወለደት፡ ሹር፡⁴ˣ ወአቁም፡ ዘንተ፡ ለአመትከ፡ . . . በሰይፈ፡ ሚካኤል፡ ይትገዘሙ፡ . . .

4. Prayer against illnesses caused by Buda and the noontime demon.
በስመ፡ አብ፡ . . . ጸሎት፡ በእንተ፡ ሕማም፡ ቡዳ፡ ቢጋኔ፡ (sic) ቀትር፡ አልሁግ፡ ወያኑራ፡ [. .]ረጅ፡ በጠቅለ፡ መግኑን፡ ዕልዋቆን፡ መበሽሹን፡ ጠበሽሹን፡ ዘረበበሙ፡ ለአጋንንት፡ ሎፍሐም፡ ሙንፍሎን፡ በዝ፡ አስማት፡ . . .

5. Prayer against illnesses caused by Šotälay and 'Urde, 9 lines. Full text:
በስመ፡ አብ፡ . . . ጸሎት፡ በእንተ፡ ሕማም፡ ሾተላይ፡ ዑርዴ፡ ኒሥራን፡ የሐ፡ Fን፡ ቢ.ያ፡²ˣ ያልሽኩን፡²ˣ ያልሽኩታን፡ አድገና፡ እምሕማም፡ ሾተላይ፡ ወዑርዴ፡ ለአመትከ፡ . . .

6. Prayer against illnesses caused by Šotälay that causes stomach upset, 9 lines. Full text:
በስመ፡ አብ፡ . . . ጸሎት፡ በእንተ፡ ሕማም፡ ሾተላይ፡ ዘይበጸብጽ፡ ክርማ፡ ወይቆርጽ፡ አማዑታ፡ ኩላሳሂም፡²ˣ ኩልሂም፡³ˣ ቆልሂም፡³ˣ ቆላሂም፡³ˣ በዝአስማት፡ አር.ጋዕ፡ (sic) ለአመትከ፡ . . .

7. Prayer against hemorrhage, 30 lines.
በስመ፡ አብ፡ . . . ጸሎት፡ በእንተ፡ ሕማም፡ ዓር.ጋዬ፡ ደም፡ ሰተም፡³ˣ ሰንከረም፡³ˣ ሰንቀረም፡³ˣ ሰርክተም፡³ˣ ተመሰርክተም፡³ˣ . . . ደም፡ ወማይ፡ ይውኅዝ፡ ከመ፡ ፈልፈለ፡ ማይ፡ . . . ጸሎት፡ ትርጉ[..]፡ ይልባብ፡ . . .

Miniatures and Magical Symbols:
1. Angel with sword and scabbard (dirty and worn).
2. Three men, center one holding hand cross and book.
3. Cross (crudely drawn).

Copied for Amätä Maryam/Birarra.

EMIP MagSc 102 – Weiner Magic Scroll 63

Parchment, 109 x 9 cm, two strips sewn together, one column, colored (yellow or brown) double border, Gəʻəz, 19th cent.

1. Prayer against the evil eye, Barya, and Legewon, 20 lines.
   በስመ፡ አብ፡ . . . ጸሎት፡ በእንተ፡ ዓይነጽላ፡ ወጽላዊጊ፡ (sic) ወባርያ፡ ወሌጌዎን፡ በስመ፡ ፫፡ አስማት፡ አብ፡ እሳት፡ ወልድ፡ እሳት፡ . . . የማነ፡ ገቦሁ፡ እሳት፡ . . . በዝንቱ፡ አስማት፡ ይዘርዝ[ር፡] ም[ክር]ሙ፡ ለሰይጣናት፡ ወለአ[ጋ]ንንት፡ ለደስክ፡ ወለዓይነት[፡] ለምትዓት፡ . . . አምሐልኩክሙ፡ ወአውገዝኩክሙ፡ ፀሎ፡ ወተሰደዱ፡ መናፍስት፡ ርኩሳን፡ አድኅና፡ እምሕማም፡ ባርያ፡ ወዓይነጽላ[፡] ቡዳ፡ ወቁመኛ፡ ሊተ፡ ለዓመትከ፡ ፋጢማ፡

2. Prayer for binding demons, 24 lines.
   በስመ፡ አብ፡ . . . ጸሎት፡ በእንተ፡ ማዕሰረ፡ ዓጋንንት፡ ዘይስልብ፡ ልብ፡ ሰብዕ፡ ወያጸልም ዓይንተ፡ ወየሐቂ፡ አስኖ፡ ወየሐንቅ፡ ክሣደ፡ ወይቀጠቅጥ፡ አእጽምተ፡ ወይመጽኤ፡ ከመ፡ ጽላሎት፡ በመዓልት፡ ወበሌሊት፡ በሕቡዕ፡ ወበክሱት፡ በ፫፡ ፻፡ ፶፡ ሰናስለ እሳት፡ በ፫፡ ፻፡ ፶፡ መሐፒለ፡ እሳት፡ በ፫፡ ፻፡ ፶፡ ሥጉንጥረ፡ እሳት፡ በ፫፡ ጋጋ፡ እሳት፡ በ፫፡ ፻፡ ፶፡ ኮሬባዊ፡ እሳት፡ ዘሐሰርከ፡ ለብርያል፡ ንጉሥ፡ . . . ወአመልሕክሙ፡ (sic) ወአውገዝኩክሙ፡ ፀሎ፡ ወተሰደዱ፡ መናፍስት፡ ርኩሳን፡ አድኅና፡ እምሕማም፡ ባርያ፡ ወዓይነ[፡] ናስ፡ ሊተ፡ ለዓመትከ፡ ፋጢማ፡

3. Prayer of St. Susənyos against hemorrhage and the story of his fight against Wərzəlya.
   በስመ፡ አብ፡ . . . ጸሎት፡ በእንተ፡ ውሕዘተ፡ ደም፡ በስመ፡ እግ"፡ ሕያው፡ . . . ጸሎቱ፡ ዘቅዱስ፡ ሱስንዮስ፡ በእንተ፡ አሰስሎ፡ ደዌ፡ እምሕፃናት፡ . . . ወሀሎ፡ ፩፡ ብእሲ፡ ዘስሙ፡ ሱስንዮስ፡ . . . followed by 9 lines of a prayer for binding demons, without *asmat*.

Miniatures and Magical Symbols:
1. Angel with sword and scabbard.

Copied for Faṭima.

EMIP MagSc 103 – Weiner Magic Scroll 64

Parchment, 150 x 8.5 cm, three strips sewn together, one column, narrow colored (yellow) border, Gəʻəz, 18th cent.

1. Prayer for binding demons, Šätolay and Šätolawit, 52.
   በስመ፡ አብ፡ . . . ጸሎት፡ በእንተ፡ ማእሰሮ፡ (sic) ለአጋንንት፡ ወሸቶላይ፡ ወሸቶላዊት፡ ዘትቀተል፡ ሕፃናተ፡ አምሐልኩክ፡ ወአውገዝኩክ፡ ላጉምኩክ፡ (sic) ወእሰርኩክ፡ . . . በማንቱም፡ አብ፡ . . . ወካዕበ፡ አሰርኩክ፡ በዝንቱ፡ አስማት፡ መአጅን፡[4x] መቃጅን፡[3x] መሐጅር፡[3x] መአጅር፡[3x] . . . የሐቅይ፡[3x] ኡ፡[7x] ጨ፡[7x] . . . ሰሎሞን፡[3x] ሎፍም፡ (sic) ሎፍሐም፡[2x] መሐምፍሎም፡ (sic) መሐፍሎም፡[3x] . . . ዮፍታሔ፡[3x] አአምላከ፡ ጴጥሮስ፡ ወጳውሎስ፡ . . .

2. Prayer against demons and Šotälay, 18 lines.
በስመ፡ አብ፡ ... አአምን፡³ˣ ወአአምን፡ ወእትአምን፡ (sic) ከመ፡ ኢይቀርቡኒ፡ ወኢይልክፉኒ፡ አጋንንት፡ ወሾተላይ፡ ... በዝንቱ፡ አስማት፡ ሒማጅ፡³ˣ ፊለጅ፡³ˣ ... ፖየ፡ ሾቶላይ፡ ፀርተሃ፡ ሾተላይ፡ አነላይ፡ ብርተሃ፡ ሾተላይ፡ አንተ፡ ውእቱ፡ ዘተቁረፅ፡ (sic) አማዑተ፡ ወትበፀብፅ፡ አንጀተ፡ ሸገር፡ ወትቀትል፡ ሕፃናተ፡ ...

3. Prayer for binding demons, Šotälay and Təgərtya, 22 lines.
በስመ፡ አብ፡ ... ጸሎት፡ በእንተ፡ ማእሰሙ፡ (sic) ለአጋንንት፡ ወሾቶላይ፡ ወትግርትያ፡ ተሰደዱ፡ በሰሐለል፡ ትግርትያ፡ በሎኤል፡ ተአሰሩ፡ ትግርትያ፡ ትወገዙ፡ (sic) በኢያኤል፡ ትግርትያ፡ በአኩናኤል፡ ተለጉሙ፡ (sic) ትግሙ፡ (sic) ትግርትያ፡ ... ሽሽሽ፡ መሐፍሎን፡ ቶቶቶ፡ (or ቾቾቾ) ንምሎስ፡ ኽኽኽ፡ ሰሎሞን፡ ...

4. Prayer for conception and against hemorrhage, 28 lines; related to Six, *Handschriften*, 16, b, 13, p. 91.
በስመ፡ አብ፡ ... ጸሎት፡ በእንተ፡ ጽንሰት፡ ወደም፡ ድማሌስ፡³ˣ ሊስ፡³ˣ አፍሊስ፡ መሊሊስ፡ ዝንቱ፡ ስንቱ፡ አክርም፡ ዘወፅአ፡ የማነ፡ (sic) ገቡሁ፡ ለክርስቶስ፡ ክትር፡ ... ዘፈነዋ፡ ላቲ፡ እግ"፡ ለሔዋን፡ ...

5. The introductory part of the prayer of St. Susənyos.

Miniatures and Magical Symbols:
1. Large panel with multiple sections. A top strip has three boxes with geometric patterns in all three. Below that is a large, single box with various patterns in it. At the bottom is a nine-box panel with X patterns in boxes 1–6 and other patterns in boxes 7–9.
2. Panel with four-petal pattern with square in center. Three-box strip below.
3. Panel with face and diamond-shaped body (and angel wings?).
Copied for Wälättä Mädḫən.

EMIP MagSc 104 – Weiner Magic Scroll 65
Parchment, 157 x 10 cm, three strips sewn together, one column, colored (yellow) border, Gə'əz, 17th cent.
1. Prayer against the eye of Barya, Legewon, Qurañña, Mäggäñña, and filthy spirits, Dədq and noontime demon, 16 lines.
በስመ፡ አብ፡ ... ጸሎት፡ በእንተ፡ አይነ፡ ባርያ፡ ወለጌዎን፡ ቁራኛ፡ ወመገኛ፡ ወመናፍስተ፡ ርኩሳን፡ ድድቅ፡ ወጋኔነ፡ ቀትር፡ ዘይመጽእ፡ ከመ፡ ጽላሎት፡ ተመሲሎ፡ በመዓልት፡ ወበሌሊት፡ ...

2. The Net of Solomon for catching demons, 51 lines.
መርበብተ፡ ሰሎሞን፡ ዘረበቦሙ፡ ለአጋንንት፡ ከመ፡ መርበብተ፡ ዓሣ፡ ዘያወጽእ፡ እምባሕር፡ ከማሁ፡ አውጽአሙ፡ ለሠራዊተ፡ አጋንንት፡ ወሰይናት፡

(sic) ነጋ፡ ገብርኤል፡ መልአክ፡ ንቡዕ፡ ወቀጥቅጥ፡ ኃይሎሙ፡ ለመናፍስተ፡ ርኩሳን፡ ለደስክ፡ ወለጉዳሴ፡ ወይ[መጽ]ኡ፡ መላእክ[ተ፡ ቀር]ሜሎስ፡ ወይዘ[ርዉ፡] ማህበረ፡ አጋንንት[፡ ..] ቅዳሔ፡ ርናል፡ ሕም[፡ ..]ያዳዚር፡ በአብ[..]ገም፡ አሽቂተ፡ . . . [. . .]ርነሐሽ፡ ኩሽ፡ አህራኩስ፡ ብዶሃ፡ የሐብድ፡ ያሜምን፡ . . .

3. Prayer for driving away demons, 26 lines.
በስሙ፡ ለእግ"፡ አብ፡ . . . ታያስ፡ አዝዮስ፡ ማሲ፡ ማስያስ፡ አቅጼፍር፡ ⌈በስሙ፡ ለሐራፒን፡ ሐራፌክር፡⌉³ˣ . . . አኸያ፡ ሸራኸያ፡ ወአ፡ ወለደ፡ እግ"፡ ሕያው፡ በሰይፈ፡ ሚካኤል፡ ወገብርኤል፡ ይትገዘሙ፡ ወይፃእ፡ መንፈስ፡ ርኩስ፡ . . .

4. Prayer against the eye of Barya and filthy spirits, 24 lines.
በስሙ፡ አብ፡ . . . ጸሎት፡ በእንተ፡ አይነ፡ ባርያ፡ ወመናፍስተ፡ ርኩሳን፡ ውግዓት፡ ወቀኑርጥማት፡ ሎልዮን፡³ˣ ሌዎንልዮን፡³ˣ አዊን፡³ˣ ጋዬን፡³ˣ ሶብራቅ፡ ሰይፈ፡ እሳተ፡ . . .

Miniatures and Magical Symbols:
1. Angel with sword and scabbard.
2. Nine-box panel with face in center box.

Many lines are stained with water; scroll is torn at bottom.
Copied for Ǝgzi' Ḫaräya.

EMIP MagSc 105 – Weiner Magic Scroll 66

Parchment, 207 x 9.5 cm, three strips sewn together, one column, parchment prepared with lines for text, narrow border, Gəʻəz, 19th cent.

1. Prayer of St. Susənyos, and the story of his martyrdom and fight against Wərzəlya.
    a. History of his martyrdom; cf. F. M. Pereira, *Acta Martyrum I*, CSCO, vol. 37, script. aeth. t. 20, reprint, 1962, pp. 259–275.
    በስመ፡ አብ፡ . . . ጸሎት፡ በእንተ፡ ቅዱስ፡ ሱስንዮስ፡ ሱሲ፡ ወልደ፡ ሱሲ፡ ፊጥሮስ፡ ወኮነ፡ አቡሁ፡ እምወዓልያነ፡ ንጉሥ፡ ዲዮቅልጥያኖስ፡፡ . . .
    b. His prayer and story of his fight against Wərzəlya.
    በስመ፡ አብ፡ . . . በስመ፡ እግ"፡ ሕያው፡ ነባቢ፡ ወተናጋሪ፡ ጸሎቱ፡ ለቅዱስ፡ ሱስንዮስ፡ በእንተ፡ አስስሎ፡ ደዌ፡ እምሕፃናት፡ . . . ወሀሎ፡ ፩ ብእሲ፡ ዘስሙ፡ ሱስንዮስ፡ . . .
2. How Our Lady Mary drove away demons and healed the sick, 16 lines.
    በስመ፡ አብ፡ . . . ዘከመ፡ ሰደደቶሙ፡ እግዝእትነ፡ ማርያም፡ ለአጋንንት፡ ወፈወሰት፡ ዱያነ፡ በጸውዓ፡ ዝንቱ፡ ስምዔል፡ አርማሴፍ፡ ፖፖሮን፡ አግኑኤል፡ ሜሎስ፡ ልምልያኖስ፡ . . .
3. *Asmat* prayer of Solomon and the story of his fight with the carpenters, *nähabt*; cf. 46, 3; 61, 3; 95, 3.

በስመ፡ አብ፡ . . . አስማተ፡ ሀላዌሁ፡ ለሰሎሞን፡ ንዑድ፡ አያስ፡ አያበዓስ፡ አድዳኤል፡ ዝቃል፡ ዘወረደ፡ ዘወረደ፡ (sic) . . . ወዘንተ፡ ኩሎ፡ አርአየ፡ ለሰሎሞን፡ ወጸፍየ፡ ወባረከ፡ ወዳግም፡ ይቤሎ፡ ሎፍሐም፡[3x] መሐፍሎን፡[3x] ንምሎስ፡[3x] ሰሎሞን፡[3x] አዊን፡[3x] . . . ወዘንተ፡ እንዘ፡ ይብል፡ ሰሎሞን፡ ወአውጽአ፡ ልሳኖ፡ . . .

4. Prayer against colic. Full text:
በስመ፡ አብ፡ . . . ጸሎት፡ በእንተ፡ ሕማም፡ [ቁ]ርጸት፡ ኢየሱስ፡ ክርስቶስ፡ ሞዓዊ፡ ኢየሱስ፡ ክርስቶስ፡ ናዝራዊ፡ ኢየሱስ፡ ክርስቶስ፡ መለኮታዊ፡ ⌈ውኃ፡ ቀውትል፡[7x] ቦኃይለ፡ ዝንቱ፡ አስማቲክ፡ ዝጋኔን፡ ይትኃረድ፡[7x] ዘሀሎ፡ በውስተ፡ ከርሡ፡ (sic) አድኅና፡ ለዓመትከ፡ . . .

5. Prayer against illnesses caused by (the eye of) *Näḥabt*, 7 lines.
በስመ፡ አብ፡ ወ (unfinished) ዱስ[፡] ፱ አምላክ፡ ጸ(unfinished) ሕማም[፡] ነሀብት፡ ሐረፖሮስ፡[3x] አልዩጽ/ድ፡ አልሕምዩድ፡ ሴድስየር፡ ፱ ጊዜ፡ ሔቅ፡ ነሥኩክሙ፡ (sic) በአብ፡ አውገዝኩክሙ፡ . . . ከመ፡ ኢትሕምምዋ፡ . . .

6. Prayer against colic, 8 lines; cf. 88, 3.
በስመ፡ አብ፡ . . . ጸሎት፡ በእንተ፡ ሕማም፡ ቁርፀት፡ ዘተፈነወ፡ እምነበ፡ አብ፡ ወወልድ፡ . . . ይርዳዕ፡ ወይቤዙ፡ ለውሉደ፡ ሰብእ፡ እንዘ፡ ይበብጽ፡ ከርሡ፡ (sic) ወያጠዊ፡ አማዑተ፡ . . . ሸገር፡፡ ቦኃይለ፡ ዝንቱ፡ አስማቲከ፡ አድኅና፡ . . .

Miniatures and Magical Symbols:
1. Angel with sword and scabbard.
2. Talismanic symbol with face in center.

Top of the scroll is mutilated.
Copied for Wälättä Iyyäsus, with the name Gäbrä Mika'el Ayyalew added later.

EMIP MagSc 106 – Weiner Magic Scroll 67

Parchment, 180 x 10 cm, three strips sewn together, one column, colored (yellow or brown) double border, Gəʻəz, 19th cent.

1. Prayer against Barya, Təgərtya, hemorrhage, Šotälay and Belbab; cf. 88, 1.
በስመ፡ አብ፡ . . . ጸሎት፡ በእንተ፡ ባርያ፡ ወትግርትያ፡ ወአርጋኤ፡ ደም፡ ወሸቶላይ፡ ቤልባብ፡
መሕቦ[ቲ፡] ነውሻል፡[3x] . . . ዘከተሮሙ፡ ለሰይጣናት፡ ወለመናፍስት፡ ርኩሳን፡ . . .

2. Prayer against Barya and Legewon.
ጸሎት፡ በእንተ፡ ባርያ፡ ወለጌዎን፡ ዘይሰልብ፡ ልበ፡ ሰብእ፡ ወያጸልም፡ አዕይንተ፡ ወያውሕዝ፡ ደም፡ ወየሐንቅ፡ ክሳደ፡ ሕጻናት፡ ወይመጽአ፡ ከመ፡ ጽላሎተ፡ ወሕልም፡ አምሕለከ፡ ወአውግዘከ፡ በፀቅንዋተ፡ መስቀሉ፡ . . .

3. Prayer against Šotälay and hemorrhage.
ጸሎት፡ በእንተ፡ ሕማመ፡ ሸቶላይ፡ ወአርጋኤ፡ ደም፡ ስንታም፡ አጅር፡ መጅር፡ ጁሐም፡ ተአሰር፡ አንተ፡ ባርያ፡ ወሸቶላይ፡ ወሸቶላይት፡ ወትግርትያ፡ [. .]ህከ፡ ሁር፡ ያቅደረድር፡ ዱራዱር፡ ስንተም፡ ከን፡ ብርካን፡ መቲርካን፡ . . . ደም፡ ዘወጽአ፡ እምገቦሁ፡ . . .

4. Prayer against hemorrhage.
ጸሎት፡ በእንተ፡ አርጋኤ፡ ደም፡ እግዚእየ፡ ኢየሱስ፡ ክርስቶስ፡ ዘከተሮ፡ ለሰይጣን፡ በጅ፡ ቅንዋት፡ ሳዶርቅ፡ አላዶርቅ፡ ዳናትቅ፡ . . . በዝ፡ አስማት፡ ዘወሀብኮን፡ ዘርኣ፡ ለሳራ፡ ይስሐቅሃ፡ ወለሐና፡ ሳሙኤልሃ፡ ከማሆን፡ ሀባ፡ ፍሬ፡ ማኅፀና፡ . . .

5. Prayer against Šotälay, Šätolayt, and hemorrhage, 30 lines.
ጸሎት፡ በእንተ፡ ሸቶላይ፡ ወሸቶላይት፡ ወአርጋኤ፡ ደም፡ አንትሙ፡ ሸቶላይ፡ ወሸቶላይት፡ ዘታውሕዙ፡ ደመ፡ ወትቀትሉ፡ ጓፃተ፡ አመሐልኩክሙ፡ ወአውገዝኩክሙ፡ ወአሰርኩክሙ፡ ወቄለፍኩክሙ፡ ወለጐምኩክሙ፡ ወሐተምኩክሙ፡ በማሕተመ፡ አብ፡ ወወልድ፡ . . . በዝንቱ፡ አስማት፡ ማአጁን፡[3x] መሐጅር፡[3x] . . . ፈውሳ፡ ወአሕይዋ፡ ወአርግዐ፡ ደግ፡ ለአመትከ፡ . . .

6. Prayer against illnesses caused by Buda, Ṭäbib, Anṭäräñña, and Fälaša, 17 lines; cf. Strelcyn, *Prières*, p. 85.
ጸሎት፡ በእንተ፡ ሕማመ፡ ቡዳዳ፡ (sic) ወጠቢብ፡ ወአንጠረኛ፡ [ወ]ፈላንሻ፡ (sic) አላሁማ፡ ወያኑራ፡ [ወ]ዋቂራ፡ ኋጅረጅ፡ ወበሐቅለ፡ ረጅ[፡] አልበቆን፡ መበሹን፡ ዘረበሙ፡ ለአጋእንት፡ ሎፍሐም፡ በዝአስማት፡ ወበዝ፡ ቃላት፡ በኃይለ፡ መስቀሉ፡ . . .

7. Prayer of St. Susənyos, and the story of his fight against Wərzəlya.
በስመ፡ እግ"፡ ሕያው፡ ነባቢ፡ ወተናጋሪ፡ ጸሎቱ፡ ወበረከቱ፡ የሐሉ፡ ለቅዱስ፡ ሱስንዮስ፡ በእንተ፡ አሰሰሎ፡ ደዌ፡ ወሕፃናት፡ (sic). . . ወሀሎ፡ ፩፡ ብእሲ፡ ዘስሙ፡ ሱስንዮስ፡ . . .

Miniatures and Magical Symbols:
1. Angel with sword and scabbard.
2. Ornate cross with two people (angels?) standing, one on either side.
3. Talismanic symbol with face in center.

Copied for Wälättä Kidan.

EMIP MagSc 107 – Weiner Magic Scroll 68

Parchment, 174 x 7.5 cm, three strips sewn together, one column, narrow colored (yellow) border, Gəʿəz, 18th/19th cent.

1. Prayer against illnesses caused by Barya and Legewon, 21 lines.
ጸሎት፡ በእንተ፡ ሕማመ፡ ባርያ፡ ወሌጊዎን፡ አያዝጠ፡ ሎፍሐምጠ፡ ዕሦር፡ (sic) በማዕሡረ፡ ኮሸር፡ እደ፡ አጋእ³ንት፡ ወእደ፡ ሌጊዎን፡ ሐርLት፡ ሐርበደው፡

FC: FC: ሰሎሞን፡ ብርሃቅጥ፡ ዓይን፡ ጡጡ፡ አንተ፡ ንጉሥሙ፡ ለአጋንንት፡ ሰተና፡ አሽተና፡ . . . ይትዓሠሩ፡ አጋንንት፡ በመዓጥሎኤን፡ ስሙ፡ ይትዓሠሩ፡ አጋንንት፡ በመንፈስ፡ ቅዱስ፡ ስሙ፡ ይትዓሠሩ፡ አጋንንት፡ ደስ፡ ይምንን፡ . . . . ይትዓሠሩ፡ አጋንንት፡ እለ፡ ያበሃንት፡ በሀልም፡ ወያስተራግር፡ (sic) ባርያ፡ ቀይሐን፡ ወባርያ፡ ጸሊማን፡ ድድቅ፡ ወጋዼን፡ ቀትር፡ ሊተ፡ ለዓመተ፡ . . .

2. Prayer for binding Satan, 28 lines.
በስመ፡ አብ፡ . . . በስመ፡ እግ"፡ ብርሃን፡ በእንተ፡ ማዕሠሩ፡ ለሰይጣን፡ አስማተ፡ ኃይል፡ ዘስሙ፡ ሸፒራ፡ አሸፒራ፡ ሸለላ፡ ሹጬር፡ ቢሚሽ፡ ተሚFቡC፡ Fሙአቱና፡ ፈጨፈጨን፡ ዘቁርዓ፡ ይቀጠቅጥ፡ ያጀጅ፡ ያመሽብር፡ ያሸባር፡ አላ፡ ፈርዳን፡ አዚዝፈርዳን፡ ዋጀቢል፡ . . . ጤግሮስ፡^{3x} ግፋኤል፡^{4x} ዘየአቅድ፡ የአቅድ፡^{5x} ይትአ/ዓቅድ፡^{3x} ዘየአስር፡ የዓ/አስር፡^{3x} ይትዓሠር፡^{4x} ዝጋዼን፡ ዘብርት፡ ወዘል"ኩት፡ ዘተኃባእ፡ (sic) ወዘተሰወረ፡ በዱሃም፡ ፍዘዘ፡ በዱሃም፡ ቅዘዘ፡ በዱሃም፡ ንበቡ፡ ያመከቺር፡ ያፈክቺር፡ መቅስም፡ . . .

3. The Prayer *Säyfä Mäläkot* "Sword of Divinity;" see 61, 2.
በስመ፡ አብ፡ . . . በስመ፡ እግ"፡ ቀዳማዊ፡ ዘእንበለ፡ ዮም፡ . . .

4. Prayer of St. Susənyos and the story of his fight against Wərzəlya.

5. Prayer against Barya, Legewon, and the evil eye.
ጸሎት፡ በእንተ፡ ባርያ፡ ወሌጊያን፡ ወዓይነት፡ አጊ፡ ፋኢ፡ ኃድ፡ ረቢ፡ ኃታኪን፡ ድብፍጢ፡ አኮስ፡ ኢንኩስ፡ ከመ፡ ጌሉ፡ አሲ፡ ያብሲት፡ አልካኪፍ፡ አማኮቢስ፡ . . . አግዮስ፡ ሜልዮስ፡ ሰይፈ፡ ጽዋዕ፡ ዝንቱ፡ ቃል፡ ዘተጽሕፈ፡ በደሙ፡ ለእግዚእን፡ . . . አድናና፡ እምሕማም፡ ባርያ፡ ወሌጊያን፡ ወዓይነት፡ ለዓመትከ፡ . . . ተሰደድ፡ ባርያ፡ ጸሊማን፡ አዕመ፡ ዘትስብር፡ ወዘተኃንቅ፡ ክሳደ፡ ወዘታባሃንት፡ በሀልመ፡ . . .

6. Prayer against colic, 13 lines; cf. 69, B3.
ጸሎት፡ በእንተ፡ ሳዕለ፡ ክብድ፡ ዘፈነው፡ (sic) እምአብ፡ ወወልድ፡ . . . ዘቤዘው፡ እንለ፡ እመሕያው፡ እንተ፡ ይበጽብጽ፡ ከርሡ፡ ወያጠዊ፡ አንFተ፡ ወአግዑተ፡ . . . ሸገር፡^{7x} አቁም፡ ዘርአ፡ ውስተ፡ ከርሃ፡ ተመልተ፡ አትራም፡ ዘወጽአ፡ ደም፡ . . . አአንተ፡ አአንት፡ በሸለሸ፡ ደኪቅ፡ ጽድዋም፡ አርሸዲቦራ፡ ቡኃለ፡ ዝንቱ፡ . . .

7. Prayer against the evil eye: The story of the sorcerer at the Sea of Tiberias.
ጸሎት፡ ነዲራን፡ ወእመ፡ መፍርሂት፡ ወመደንግዕተ፡ ጥቀ፡ ቀነፀ፡ እግዚእን፡ ኢየሱስ፡ ክርስቶስ፡ እንዘ፡ የሐውር፡ ውስተ፡ ባሕረ፡ ጥብርያዴስ፡ . . .

Miniatures and Magical Symbols:
1. Nine-box panel with faces in boxes 2, 4, 6, and 8 and X-shaped patterns in the others.
2. Variation on talismanic symbol with face in center; wing-shapes protruding in various directions.

Catalogue of the Scrolls of Ethiopian Spiritual Healing · 373

3. Angel with sword and scabbard.
4. Ornate cross with a person on either side.

Dirty and worn at the very bottom.
Copied for Tayyäčč/Faṭima, with the name Alganäš/Wälättä Gäbrə'el added later in pencil in a crude hand.

EMIP MagSc 108 – Weiner Magic Scroll 69

Parchment, 169 x 8.5 cm, three strips sewn together, one column, colored (yellow) border, Gəʿəz, 19th cent.

1. Prayer against the evil eye, Zar, filthy demons, Gudale, Barya, Legewon, and other demons.
   ጸሎት፡ በእንተ፡ ሕማመ፡ ዓይነጥ፡ (sic) ወዓ[ይነ፡ ወ]ርቅ፡ ወተዓራሪ፡ ዛር፡ ወ[. . . ወ]ተዓራሪ፡ ሕማም[፡ ወአጋንን]ት፡ ርኩሳን፡ ወጉዳ[ሌ፡ ወባ]ርያ፡ ወሌጌዎን፡ ወዓይነ[፡] ምትዓት፡ ዓይነ፡ እጋንንት፡ ጸዋጋን፡ ዓነጸሊማን፡ (sic) ወቀይሐን፡ ግዘተ፡ አጋንንት፡ አወግዘከ፡ ሰይጣን፡ በስሙ፡ ለእግ" . . . አወግዘከ፡ ሰይጣ፡ (sic) ወለኩሎሙ፡ (sic) መላእክቲከ፡ ወኩሎሙ፡ (sic) ጣዖታቲከ፡ . . .

2. Prayer for refuge (against evil spirits), 27 lines.
   ጸሎተ፡ ተማኅጽና፡ ተማኅፀንኩ፡ በሥርግዋን፡ መላእክቲከ፡ ተማኅፀንኩ፡ በፀንሳ፡ ጸዋርያነ፡ መንበር፡ በሡረገላሁ፡ ለእግ"፡ . . . አድኅነኒ፡ . . . ዕቀብ፡ ወአድኅና፡ . . .

3. Prayer for driving away demons, 76 lines.
   በስመ፡ አብ፡ . . . ጸሎተ፡ አውቅያ፡ ገጽገተ[፡] (sic) ሥራይ፡ ዘመሐሉ፡ ወተሰደዱ፡ አጋንንት፡ ወሰይጣናት[፡] ኮርዳል፡ ረጓቁ፡ እምኔየ፡ በስወወልድ፡ (sic) ፪አምላክ፡ አምሕለከ፡ ወአወግዘከ፡ ወአፈልስከ፡ አንተ፡ ኮርዴል፡ . . . በእግ"፡ ፈጣሪ፡ በክርስቶስ፡ ወልድ፡ ወበሳልጋይ፡ መንፈስ፡ ቅዱስ፡ ወነሡተ፡ እረፍተ፡ (sic) እንተ፡ ማእከለ፡ ጸላኢ፡ በግቲሁ፡ (sic) ወበሞቱ፡ ወጸራቅሊጦስ፡ በሊሁ፡ አፉሁ፡ . . . አወግዘከ፡ ሰይጣን፡ በውግዘት፡ እግዝእትነ፡ ማርያም፡ . . . አወግዘከ፡ ሰይጣን፡ በውግዘት፡ ሚካኤል፡ ወገብርኤል፡ በሱራፌል፡ ወኪሩቤል፡ . . .

4. Prayer against hemorrhage,
   በስመ፡ አብ፡ . . . ጸሎተ፡ ደም፡ ሊስ፡[7x] አፍሊስ፡[7x] አናሊስ፡[7x] መሊስ፡[7x] መልዮስ፡ ደዴክ፡ ዘዓርጋዕስ፡ ኃይለ[፡] በረድ፡ ከግሁ፡[፡] አርጎዕ፡ ደሙ፡ ትክቶሃ፡ ወደመ፡ ወሊድ፡ . . . ቀዳሚሁ፡ ቃል፡ ሥጋ[፡] ኮነ፡ ወነ (sic) ወነደረ፡ ላዕሌነ፡ ወርኢነ፡ ስብሓቲሁ፡ ከመ፡ ስብሐት[፡] (sic) ፩ እስመ፡ አልቦ፡ ነገር፡ ዘሰአኖ፡ (sic) ለእግ"፡

Miniatures and Magical Symbols:
1. Face above eight-box panel (4 x 2), each with an X-shaped pattern.
2. Rectangle containing nine-box panel with parallel-line designs.

Copied for Wälättä Iyyäsus/Yäši

EMIP MagSc 109 – Weiner Magic Scroll 70

Parchment, 170 x 8.5 cm, three strips sewn together, two columns, border (outlined in red ink) and margin between columns (outlined in black ink), Gəʿəz, 1958 EC (=1965/6 AD.).

A. Prayer against illnesses caused by Šotälay, Qurañña, Zar, Zarit, Nähabi, Ṭəfnät, and Gudale.

በስም፡ አብ፡ . . . ጸሎት፡ በእንተ፡ ሕማም፡ ሾተላይ፡ ወቁራኛ፡ ፍልጸት፡ ወቁርፀት፡ ው፡ግእት፡ ወቁርጥማት፡ ወቸነፈር፡ ዘር፡ (sic) ወዘሪት፡ (sic) ነሀቢ፡ ወጥፍነት፡ ወጉደሊ፡ (sic) በስሙ፡ ለአብ፡ በስሙ፡ ለወልድ፡ . . . ታፖስ፡ አዝዞስ፡ ማሲ፡ አቅዳፈር፡ ወበስም፡ ለሐሹዮን፡ አቅዳፈር፡ ሐፈፈኪር፡ በጠጅን፡ ዘሐጅን፡²ˣ ዋሀ፡ ፈልማኤል፡ በስም፡ ሳዶር፡ . . . በዝ፡ አስግት፡ ወበስም፡ . . . አልፋ፡³ˣ ጸዕ፡ ወጊአከ፡ ኢትግባእ፡ ዳግም፡ ይቤለከ፡ ኢየሱስ፡ . . ., finished on col. B.

B1. Prayer against the evil eye, illnesses caused by Šotälay, other illnesses, and the story of the fight of St. Susənyos against Wərzəlya; finished on col. A and back on col. B.

B2. (Prayer against the evil eye) untitled, but see 92, 6; 99, 2.

ጆጆቢ፡³ˣ ረቢ፡³ˣ ከፈሹማ፡ ዘደገሙ፡ ፍታሕ፡ ምድረ፡ ረጊዖሙ፡ በሕረ፡ (sic) በጽቢጸሙ፡ ሰማየ፡ ነጺሮሙ፡ ስረ፡ መዝሚዞሙ፡ . . .

Miniatures and Magical Symbols:
1. Nine-box panel with faces in boxes 1, 3, 5, 7, and 9; above is a sixth face.
2. Angel with sword and scabbard(?).

The red ink is smeared in many places.
Copied for Wälättä Giyorgis and Wälättä Yoḥannəs.

EMIP MagSc 110 – Weiner Magic Scroll 71

Parchment, 152 x 8.5 cm, three strips sewn together, one column, no border, Gəʿəz, 19th cent.

1. Prayer for binding demons (and) filthy Legewon.

በስም፡ አብ፡ . . . ጸሎት፡ በእንተ፡ ማዕሰሮሙ፡ ለአጋንንት፡ ለጌዎን፡ ርኩስ፡ ዘይሰልብ፡ ልቡ፡ ሰብእ፡ ወያጸልም፡ አእይንተ፡ ወይመጽእ፡ ከመ፡ ጽላሎት፡ በመዐልት፡ ወበሌሊት፡ አምሳለከ፡ ወአውግዘከ፡ (sic) በፈቅንዋተ፡ መስቀሉ፡ . . .

2. Prayer against evil spirits, wicked demons, Dədq, noontime demon, Buda, and *Nähabi*, 14 lines.

በስመ፡ አብ፡ . . . ወንጌል፡ ዘዮሐንስ፡ ቀዳሚሁ፡ ቃል፡ (John 1:1–5). ከማሁ፡ ኢ.ይርክብዎ፡ ወኢ.ይቅረብዎ፡ መናፍስት፡ ርኩሳን፡ ወአጋንንት፡ ጸዋጋን፡ ድድቅ፡ ወጋኔነ፡ ቀትር፡ ቡዳ፡ ወነሀቢ፡ ወውግአት፡ ወቅርጥማት፡ ቁርፀት፡ ወፍልፀት፡ አድነዎ፡ . . .

3. Prayer against piercing pain, with a greeting to the pierced side of Jesus.
ጸሎት፡ በእንተ፡ ሕማመ፡ ውግአት፡ ምድምያስ፡^{3x} የሐቂ፡^{4x} የሐብራስቂ፡ በ/ዘከመ፡ አድነንኮ፡ ለወልደ፡ ከራስቂ፡ ከማሁ፡ አድነኖ፡ እምሕማመ፡ ውግአት፡ ለገብርከ፡ ወልደ፡ አምላክ፡ ሰላም፡ ለገቦከ፡ ኩናተ፡ ለንጊዎስ፡ ዘወግዖ፡ . . .

4. Prayer against piercing pain and colic.
ጸሎት፡ በእንተ፡ ሕማመ፡ ውግአት፡ ወቁርፀት፡ እልፍሉል፡^{3x} እልፍሉሌ፡^{3x} ቀጌቤ፡^{3x} ቄፌኑ፡ ብኬያምሌ፡^{3x} ዘእርጋእከ፡ ኃይለ፡ ነፋስ፡ ወበረድ፡ ከማሁ፡ . .

5. Prayer for binding demons; cf. 7, 1; 9, 3; Dobberahn, *Zauberrollen*, p. 285.
በስመ፡ አብ፡ . . . ጸሎት፡ በእንተ፡ ማዕሰሮሙ፡ ለአጋንንት፡ አህያ፡ ሸራሁ፡ (sic) አልሻዳይ፡ እልማክኑን፡ (sic) አልፋ፡ ወአ፡ . . . ዘበከመ፡ አጸራእከ፡ ግብሮ፡ ለዲያብሎስ፡ . . .

6. Prayer against charm; cf. Strelcyn, *Prières*, p. 40.
በስመ፡ አብ፡ . . . ጸሎት፡ በእንተ፡ መፍትሔ፡ ሥራይ፡ ዘተቀድሐ፡ እምዢ፡ ወፅ መጻሕፍት፡ ፍታሕ፡ ዮፍታሔ፡ ድንጥኤል፡ ክፍትናኤል፡ ግቶን፡ ያዝሕዝዖን፡ በለ.ስ፡ (sic) [.]ፍርዮን፡ ቀበለስቲሮስ፡ ኪራ፡ ኮናዎስ፡ . . . ከመ፡ ኢ.ይመአኒ፡ (sic) ሞት፡ ወተግባረ፡ ሰብእ፡ ዘእንበለ፡ ጊዜሁ፡ ለገብርከ፡ . . . ከመ፡ ይትፌታሕ፡ ኮሎ፡ (sic)ሥራይ፡ እመሂ፡ ሕማመ፡ ማ[.]ት፡ ወጠአት፡ (sic) ወነገርጋር፡ ወቄያጸት፡ በብሩር፡ ዘብርዕ፡ እመሂ፡ ዘረገሙ፡ ሰማዖ፡ ነጺሮሙ፡ . . . The list of the means is long,

7. Prayer against *Nähabt*; cf. 105, 5.
ጸሎት፡ በእንተ፡ ነሀብት፡ ብት፡ (sic) ሐረፖሮስ፡^{3x} [.]ርክ፡ ሕምዩድ፡ አልዩድ፡ ናሻር፡ [. . .] ቼቄቀኑነስ፡ አመግዘከሙ፡ ነሀብት፡.. እከለክለክሙ፡ አንትሙ፡ ጠበብት፡ . . . ወገጹ፡ ዘፍፁም፡ በጽልመት፡ ፌርህ . . .

Miniatures and Magical Symbols:
1. Angel with sword and scabbard.
2. Fifteen-box panel (5 x 3) with faces in boxes 2, 4, 6, and 8 and four-petal patterns with eyes in the other boxes.
3. Nine-box panel with face in center.

Copied for Wäldä Amlak, with Gäbrä Kidan added later.

EMIP MagSc 111 – Weiner Magic Scroll 72

Parchment, 155 x 10 cm, three strips sewn together, one column, colored (yellow) double border, Gəʿəz, 20th cent.

1. First half of the Greeting to Phanuel as prayer against the evil eye and illnesses caused by Barya and filthy Legewon, 21 lines.
   በስመ፡ አብ፡ . . . ጸሎት፡ በእንተ፡ ሕማም፡ አይነት፡ ባርያ፡ ወለጌዎን፡ ርኩስ፡ ጸሎት፡ በእንተ፡ ሕማም፡ አጋንንት፡ ሰላም፡ ለከ፡ ሰዳዬ፡ አጋንንት፡ ወሰይጣናት፡ ፋኑኤል፡ ለእግ"፡ እምጽርሁ፡ . . .

2. Second half of the Greeting to Phanuel as prayer for binding demons, a continuation of the preceding, 21 lines.
   በስመ፡ አብ፡ . . . ጸሎት፡ በእንተ፡ ማዕሰሮሙ፡ ለአጋንንት፡ ወሰይጣናት፡ እግዚአ፡ ወአድሕዎተ፡ ፋኑኤል፡ ትጉሕ ለተራድአ፡ ወአድሕዎተ፡ (sic) እስመ፡ ብየ፡ ሕገ፡ ተሰብአ፡ ወ፡ (sic) ሰላም[፡] ለከ፡ ነሁብ፡ ለለ፡ ጌሴሙ፡ (sic) ስብሓት፡ ፋኑኤል፡ ግበር፡ ኮሎ፡ እለተ፡ . . .

3. Prayer against colic and headache, 31 lines.
   በስመ፡ አብ፡ . . . ጸሎት፡ በእንተ፡ ሕማም፡ ቅርፀት፡ (sic) ወፍልፀት፡ ቄዜቤ፡⁷ˣ ቀፀብከ፡ ሞሞሊ፡⁷ˣ ⌜ብእያሚ፡ ሞሊ፡³ˣ ብእያ፡ በከመ፡ አርጋእከ፡ ኃይልከ፡ ኃለ፡ (sic) በረድ፡ . . .

4. Prayer to terrorize demons, 32 lines.
   በስመ፡ አብ፡ . . . ጸሎት፡ በእንተ፡ መሽብር፡ (sic) አጋንንት፡ አሽብሮሙ፡ ወአደንግፖሙ፡ ለሰረዊተ፡ (sic) ዲያብሎስ፡ ቀሀሹን፡ ሸንሾን፡ ሎፎሐም፡ (sic) መሐፍሎን፡ . . .

5. Prayer related to the story of St. Susənyos fighting Wərzəlya, 35 lines.
   በስመ፡ አብ፡ . . . ጸሎት፡ ከያ፡ ቹ፡³ˣ ሹ፡³ˣ ጆ፡³ˣ ወለተ፡ ወሰ፡ (sic) ወሰአለ፡ ኀበ፡ እግ"፡ አምላከሙ፡ (sic) እንዘ፡ ይብል፡ . . . በለተ፡ ውርዝልያ፡ ወቆመት፡ ወትቤሎ፡ . . .

6. Prayer against the eye of Barya, the eye of Buda (?), and thunderstorm, void of *asmat*, 7 lines. Full text:
   በስመ፡ አብ፡ . . . ጸሎት፡ አይነት፡ ባርያ፡ ወአይነተ፡ ባዳ፡ (sic) ወነጐድጋድ፡ (sic) በክብደ፡ (?) ዝናብ፡ (sic) በበርቅ፡ (sic) ወበነጐድጋድ፡ (sic) አድሕኖ፡ ለገብርከ፡ ገብረ፡ ማርያም፡

7. Prayer for safety, *adhḫənno*, of the owner of the scroll, void of *asmat*, 7 lines.

Miniatures and Magical Symbols:
1. Five boxes (one atop the next) with a face in the top box.
2. Two large circle patterns.
3. Talismanic symbol with face in the center.

Copied, very badly, for Gäbrä Maryam.

EMIP MagSc 112 – Weiner Magic Scroll 73

Parchment, 192 x 10 cm, three strips sewn together, one column, colored (yellow) border, Gəʻəz, 20th cent.

1. Prayer against charm, 17 lines.
   በስመ፡ አብ፡ . . . ጸሎት፡ በእንተ፡ መፍትሔ፡ ሥራይ፡ አራፎን፡ አራኮን፡ ፍታህ፡ ፈታሒ፡ ፍታህ፡ ገሀኤል፡:3x ጋሐኤል፡:2x ገሐኤል፡ ጋሐኤል፡ ፍታህ፡ ሰንተው፡ ፍታህ፡ ቀንተው፡ ፍታህ፡ ቀነለው፡ ፍታህ፡ ቀሐዲል፡ አማኑኤል፡ ፍታህ፡ ወዘርዝናኤል፡ ፍታህ፡ ዘፈታህከሙ፡ ለጴጥሮስ፡ ወለጻውሎስ፡ . . . ⌈አፍናዝር፡ ሰፍናዝር፡:3x . . .

2. Prayer against charm, 7 lines.
   በስመ፡ አብ፡ . . . ስሙናዝር፡ ክሙናዝር፡ ወኤልናዝር፡ ፍታህ፡ ወዘርዝር፡ አስግተ፡ ሥራይ፡ . . .

3. Prayer against charm, 43 lines; cf. Strelcyn, *Prières*, p. 12.
   በስመ፡ አብ፡ . . . ጸሎት፡ በእንተ፡ መፍትሔ፡ ሥራይ፡ መፍታሒ፡ ፍታህ፡ ወርዝር፡ ሰዓር፡ ወመንዝር፡ አስግተ፡ ሥራየ፡ አጋንንት፡ ወሰይጣናት፡ ሥራየ፡ ባሬ፡ ወሌጌዖን፡ ባሬ፡ ጺሊማን፡ ወቀይሐን፡ ፍታህ፡ ሥራየ፡ እስላም፡ ወክርስቲያን፡ ፍታህ፡ ሥራየ፡ ጋላ፡ ወሻንቅላ፡ ፍታህ፡ ሥራየ፡ አገው፡ ወፈላሽ፡ ፍታህ፡ ሥራየ፡ ቱርክ፡ ወፈረጅ፡ . . .
   (Others included are: ዋድላ፡ ደላንታ፡ ላስታ፡ የጁ፡ ዳጆ፡ አምብላል፡ (sic) ሳይንት፡ አምሐራ፡ ጐጃም፡ በጌምድር፡ ምጽግና፡ ሸዋ፡ ይፋት፡ መሪቤቴ፡ ግድም፡ ገምዛ፡ አንጾኪያ፡ ደብር (?) ዜመ (sic) ላሊግ (sic) ቆቦ፡ ዞብል፡ ኮረም፡ ማይ፡ ጨው፡ አላሳ፡ ሀንጣሎ፡ ቦራ፡ ሰለዋ፡ እንደርታ፡ ተምቤን፡ ሽሬ፡ አድቦ፡ አስገደ፡ ጠለምት፡ ወልቃይት፡ ጸገዴ፡ አርማጭሆ፡ ዛና፡ አዲት (sic) አድዋ፡ አኩስም፡ ሐማሴን፡ አጋሚ፡, followed by a list of the means).

4. (Prayer against charm) untitled, 31 lines; cf. 48, 4.
   በእግ¨ ፡ አብ፡ ወበክርስቶስ፡ ወልድ፡ ወበማልሳይ፡ መንፈስ፡ ቅዱስ፡ ወበማርያም፡ ወላዲተ፡ አምላክ ፡ ፍታህ፡ ተፈታህ፡ በፀባዖት፡ ስምከ፡ በማስያስ፡ ስምከ፡ . . . ይትነሣእ፡ እግ¨ ፡ ወይዘረው፡ ጸሩ፡ (Ps 67:2–3/68:1–2.) አንትሙ፡ ካህናት፡ አይሁድ፡ ተአሰሩ፡ ተከንተሩ፡ ፍዙዛን፡ ኩት፡ ድንዙዛን፡ ኩት፡ እንቡዛን፡ ኩት፡ አንትሙ፡ ካህናት፡ ወሰይጣናት፡ በዘትገብሩ፡ ብርእሰ፡ ወትቀንዑ፡ በንብረትየ፡ . . .

5. The Net of Solomon for catching demons, 85 lines.
   በስመ፡ አብ፡ . . . ጸሎት፡ በእንተ፡ መርበብተ፡ ሰሎሞን፡ ዘረበሙ፡ ለአጋንንት፡ ከመ፡ መርበብት፡ ዓሣ፡ ዘባህር፡ እንዘ፡ ይብል፡ ሰዱቃኤል፡ አዳታኤል፡ ቅርኬል፡ ክርሜኤል፡ . . . ወካዕበ፡ አስግተ፡ ዘሰሎሞን፡ ድድርያስ፡ አያስ፡ አየበአስ፡ አአያስ፡ ዘንበለ፡ ቀለም፡ ዘወረደ፡ እምላዕሉ፡ ሐቡዕ፡ ቃሉ፡ ለአብ፡ እምቅድመ፡ ማርያም፡ ሐደረ፡ ዝቃል፡ ኀበ፡ ሰሎሞን፡ እንዘ፡ ይብል፡ ሸት፡ ክላሸ፡ አላሽ፡ . . . ወመጽአ፡ ፄነሐቢ፡ መዛጢ ነህቢ፡

ወፈቀደ፡ ከመ፡ ይሕርዱ፡ ወደገመ፡ ሰሎሞን፡ እንዘ፡ ይብል፡ ሉፍሐም፡:⁵ˣ
ሰሎሞን፡ . . .
6. Greeting to Phanuel prayed for drowning demons, about 5 lines at the end are illegible.
በስመ፡ አብ፡ . . . ጸሎት፡ በእንተ፡ መስጠመ፡ አጋንንት፡ ሰላም፡ ለከ፡ ሰዳዬ፡
አጋን³ት፡ ፋኑኤል፡ ለእግ"፡ እምጽርሁ፡ . . .

Miniatures and Magical Symbols:
1. Angel with sword and scabbard.
2. Angel with sword and scabbard.
3. Talismanic symbol with face in center and surrounded by eyes.

Bottom 5 cm dirty and faded.
Copied clearly for Yaṭenäš/Wälättä Tǝnśa'e, also Wälättä Kidan, in the same hand.

EMIP MagSc 113 – Weiner Magic Scroll 74

Parchment, 128 x 10 cm, two strips sewn together, one column, elaborate colored (yellow) border with woven-rope pattern, Gǝ'ǝz, 18th/19th cent.
1. Prayer against the evil eye of Barya and for drowning demons, 16 lines.
   በስመ፡ አብ፡ . . . ጸሎት፡ በእንተ፡ ዓይነ፡ ባርያ፡ ወመስጠመ፡ አጋንንት፡
   ጸሎተ፡ አልሆግ፡ ያሽነጅ፡ ባሕቱ፡ ምስኪን፡ (sic) በልቁን፡ በከክ፡ ንቅጥ፡ . .
   .
2. (Prayer against charm) untitled, 51.
   በስመ፡ አብ፡ . . . በስሙ፡ ለእግ"፡ አብ፡ በስሙ፡ ለእግ"፡ ወልድ፡ በስሙ፡
   ለእግ"፡ መንፈስ፡ ቅዱስ፡ ታያስ፡ አዝዮስ፡ ወበማክያስ፡ አቅጼፍር፡ በስሙ፡
   ለሐራሹን፡ . . . በዝንቱ፡ አስማተ፡ ቃልከ፡ . . . አኺያ፡ ያቁ፡:²ˣ አንተ፡ ቡዳ፡
   አንተ፡ ባርያ፡ . . .
3. Prayer against demons that cause stomachache and other illnesses, 15 lines.
   በስመ፡ አብ፡ . . . ጸሎት፡ (sic) ከርሥ፡ ዘጎጽጉጽ፡ (sic) ገበዋተ፡ ወያደቅቅ፡
   አእዕምተ፡ ወያጠዊ፡ አንጀተ፡ ወአማዑተ፡ ደር፡:⁴ˣ ከመ፡ ታድኅኖ፡
   እምሕማመ፡ ውር[?]ት፡ ለገብርከ፡ . . . እልፍሉል፡:³ˣ ቀጼቤ፡:³ˣ ቀፈኑ፡:³ˣ . .
   .
4. Prayer against colic, void of *asmat*, 7 lines.
5. Prayer against illnesses caused by Barya, 14 lines.
   በስመ፡ አብ፡ . . . ጸሎት፡ በእንተ፡ ሕማመ፡ ባርያ፡ ዘይቀትል፡ እግ"፡
   ይቀጠቅጥ፡ ፀብዓ፡ ወእግ"፡ ስሙ፡ እሳት፡ ወልድ፡ ወልድ፡ እሳት፡ . . .
   ጋዲን፡ እሳት፡ ፍሕም፡ እሳት፡ . . .
6. Prayer against the eye of Barya, 14 lines.

በስመ፡ አብ፡ . . . እሳት፡ ደ[?]፡ አርደድ፡ [illegible] ቃለ፡ ዓረቢ፡ ሽርሐፍ፡ .
. . [illegible].
7. Prayer against charm, 35 lines.
በስመ፡ አብ፡ . . . ጸሎት፡ በእተ፡ (sic) መፍትሔ፡ ሥራይ፡ በመብልዕ፡
ወበመስቴ፡ ተፈታሕ፡ . . . [ወገጹ፡] ዘፍጹም፡ በጽልመት፡ ፈርሃ፡ ወደንጋጸ፡
ዲያብሎስ፡ . . .

Miniatures and Magical Symbols:
1. Angel with sword (presumably) and scabbard (top is torn and damaged).
2. Talismanic symbol (nine-box panel) with face in center.

Bottom 10 cm damaged and shrunken. Insufficiently legible.
Owned by Ḥaylä Maryam.

EMIP MagSc 114 – Weiner Magic Scroll 75

Parchment, 178 x 9.3 cm, four strips sewn together, one column, colored (yellow) double border with dashed line between the two inner lines of the border, Gəʻəz, 18th/19th cent.

1. Prayer for binding the evil eye and Zar; cf. 26, 4; 28, 1.
በስመ፡ አብ፡ . . . ጸሎት፡ በእንተ፡ ማእሠረ፡ ዓይነ፡ ጽላ፡ ወዛር፡ ቀዳሚሁ፡
ቃል፡ (John 1:1–5)።
2. Prayer against headache, stomachache, piercing pain, Barya, demons, and others. The prayer is mostly from the liturgy.
በስመ፡ አብ፡ . . . ጸሎት፡ ወስእለት፡ ወአስተብቁዖት፡ አአምን፡ ወእትአመን፡
በስመ፡ ፫አስማት፡ ወበ፩መለኮት፡ አብ፡ እሳት፡ . . . ኢየሱስ፡ ክርስቶስ፡
ኅብስተ፡ ሕይወት፡ ወጽዐ፡ (sic) መድኃኒት፡ አድኅን፡ ዘንተ፡ ሕማመ፡
ፍልፀት፡ ወቁርፀት፡ ውግዓት፡ ወጉሥምት፡ ጽፍዓት፡ ወምትአት፡ ባርያ፡
ወአጋንንት፡ እደ፡ ሰብእ፡ ወሥራያተ[፡] በኃይለ፡ ዝንቱ፡ አስማንቲከ፡ . . .
ሠራዊተ፡ መላእክቲሁ፡ ለመድኃኔ፡ ዓለም፡ . . . ሳድር፡ አላዶር፡ . . .
followed by a stanza from the image of the Archangel Michael, Chaîne, Répertoire, no. 119: ሰላም፡ እብል፡ ለኩሎን፡ መልእክ፡ . . .
3. Prayer for protection.
በስመ፡ አብ፡ . . . በስሙ፡ ለአብ፡ በስሙ፡ ለወልድ፡ በስሙ፡ ለመንፈስ፡
ቅዱስ፡ ወአሕስር፡ ለእቡይ፡ አውሎጊያስ፡[7x] አውሎጊዶስ፡[7x] ርዶስ፡[7x]
ጌርዮስ፡[7x] ግዮስ፡[14x] አዝዮስ፡[7x] አዝያስ፡[7x] . . .
4. Prayer for binding demons and Zar.
በስመ፡ አብ፡ . . . ጸሎት፡ በእንተ፡ ማእሰረ፡ አጋንንት፡ ወዛር፡ ዘዖንድር፡
በረድኤተ፡ ልዑል፡ ወይነብር፡ ውስተ፡ ጽላሎቱ፡ (Ps 90:1–16) ስብሐት፡
ለአብ፡. . ርእዮ፡ ብሕቱ፡ ልደት፡ በሥጋ፡ ወሬዱ፡ በሲኦል፡ ፈርሃ፡
ወደንጋጸ፡ ዲያብሎስ፡፡ እስመ፡ አልቦ፡ . . .

Miniatures and Magical Symbols:
1. Plant-shaped patterns.
2. Angel with sword and scabbard.
3. Ornate cross.
4. Man (angel?) with sword and scabbard.

10 cm fastening strip attached to top.
Copied clearly for Wälättä Kidan/Däbritu Ǝ(n)guday, "daughter of Täwabäčč."

EMIP MagSc 115 – Weiner Magic Scroll 76

Parchment, 174 x 7 cm, three strips sewn together, one column, colored (yellow) border, Gəʿəz, 18th cent.
1. Prayer of St. Susənyos and the story of his fight against Wərzəlya.
በስመ፡ አብ፡ . . . ጸሎት፡ በእንተ፡ (sic) በስመ፡ እግ"፡ ሕያው፡ ነባቢ፡ ወተናጋሪ፡ ጸሎቱ፡ ወበረከቱ፡ የለቅዱስ፡ (sic) ሱስንዮስ፡ በእንተ፡ አሰሰሎ፡ ደዊ፡ እምሕፃናት፡ . . . ወሀሎ፡ ጎብእሲ፡ ዘስሙ፡ ሱስንዮስ፡ . . .
2. Prayer against hemorrhage and for conception.
በስመ፡ አብ፡ . . . ጸሎት፡ በእንተ፡ ደም፡ ወአቋም፡ ለንስ፡ ሊስ፡^{2x} ፍለኪስ፡ ሜሎስ፡ ኢየሱስ፡ ክርስቶስ፡ ወወአዘ፡ (sic) ዘሚካኤል፡ በኃይለ፡ ዝንቱ፡ አስግተክ፡ ዘአርጋዕካ፡ እግህፀን፡ ለከዊነ፡ ህፃን፡ ደም፡^{3x} በምን፡ ትነብር፡ በርእስ፡ በከንፈር፡ . . .
3. Prayer against colic.
በስመ፡ አብ፡ . . . ጸሎት፡ በእንተ፡ ሔርፀት፡ (sic) ኬለኮርኪስ፡^{8x} አርዋሸ፡ አድሃን፡ ወፈውሳ፡ ለዓመትከ፡ . . . ወገጹ፡ ዘፍጹም፡ ጽልመት፡ ፈርህ፡ ወደንገጸ፡ ዳቢሎስ፡ (sic) . . .

Miniatures and Magical Symbols:
1. Angel with sword and scabbard.
2. Variant talismanic symbol with face in center with wings protruding in various directions.
3. Panel with stars above and criss-cross pattern below.

EMIP MagSc 116 – Weiner Magic Scroll 77

Parchment, 171 x 7 cm, four strips sewn together, one column, narrow border, Gəʿəz, 20th cent.
1. Prayer for binding demons.
በስመ፡ አብ፡ . . . ጸሎት፡ በእንተ፡ ማዕሠረ፡ አጋንንት፡ [. . .]ርያንስ፡ ሥዋር፡ አዋር፡ ስዋር፡ አግና[..] አግናጠስ፡ መናጥር፡ . . . ዘይሰልብ፡ ልበ፡ ወያጸልም፡ አዕይንተ፡ ወይመጽእ፡ ከመ፡ ጽላሎት፡ በመዓልት፡ ወበሌሊት፡

አምሐልኩክሙ፡ ወአውገዝኩክሙ፡ በጸቅንዋተ፡ መስቀሉ፡ . . . ሴቃ፡ ቤቃ፡ ክስብኤል፡ . . .
2. Prayers for the days of the week for drowning demons; cf. 49, 2; 91, 2.
በስመ፡ አብ፡ . . . ጸሎት፡ ወመሥጥም፡ ዘዕለተ፡ ሱኑይ፡ ዓቃቢሁ፡ ቅዱስ፡ ሚካኤል፡ . . . The prayer for Sunday includes one of the two Greetings to Phanuel: ሰላም፡ ለሬፋጥሮትከ፡ ምስለ፡ መላእክት፡ ኀቡረ፡ . . .
3. Prayer of St. Susənyos and the story of his fight against Wərzəlya, followed by a panel of 49 boxes (7 x 7) each filled with a letter from the name Cyprianus and others and concluded with Ps 1:1–3.

Miniatures and Magical Symbols:
1. Angel with sword and scabbard.
2. Rectangle with border of red and white woven-rope pattern. The rectangle contains a nine-box panel with heart shapes in the four corner boxes and a cross shape in the center box.
3. Table (7 x 7) of letters.
4. Face above nine-box panel above three-box panel (barely legible)
Copied with care but the ink has faded.

EMIP MagSc 117 – Weiner Magic Scroll 78

Parchment, 197 x 9.5 cm, three strips sewn together, one column, colored (yellow) double border, Gəʿəz, 20th cent.
1. Prayer against Barya and filthy Legewon; cf. 27, 2; 31, 3; 88, 8.
በስመ፡ አብ፡ . . . ጸሎት፡ በእንተ፡ ባርያ፡ ወለጌዎን፡ ርኩስ፡ ዘይሰልብ፡ ልብ፡ ሰብእ፡ ወያጸልም፡ አእይንተ፡ ወይመጽእ፡ ከመ፡ ጽላሎት፡ ወሕልም፡ አምሐለከ፡ ወአገግዘከ፡ በጸቅንዋተ፡ መስቀሉ፡ ዘውእቶሙ፡ . . .
2. Prayer against Šätolay, Šätolawit, Təgərtya, and Belbab; cf. Six, *Handschriften*, 16, 3, 4, p. 90.
በስመ፡ አብ፡ . . . ጸሎት፡ በእንተ፡ ሸቶላይ፡ ወሸቶላዊት፡ ወትግርትያ፡ ቤልባብ፡. መሐቢቲ፡ ነውሻል፡[3x] ቆሐቤል፡[3x] . . . አምነልኮከ፡ ወአውገዝኮከ፡ ከመ፡ ኢትቅርብ፡ . . .
3. Prayer against hemorrhage. Full text:
በስመ፡ አብ፡ . . . ጸሎት፡ በእንተ፡ አርጋኤ፡ ደም፡ ጸሎሉኪር፡[2x] ኪን፡ ኪንዋግ፡ አሸዋሃ፡ ያአድያአ፡ ያአKʾአ፡ የአጅያአ፡ ያአKያአ፡ በነይለ፡ ዝንቱ፡ አስማቲከ፡ አርጋእ፡ ደግ፡ ወኢትቅትል፡ ሀፃናቲሃ፡ ለአመትከ፡ . . .
4. *Asmat* prayer that Gabriel told Mary regarding her conception of Jesus Christ, 19 lines.
ዝንቱ፡ አስማት፡ ዘነገረ፡ ገብርኤል፡ ለማርያም፡ በእንተ እግዚእነ፡ ኢየሱስ፡ ክርስቶስ፡ ቁዕረተ፡ ወገብርኤል፡ ዘምሉእርምርያም፡ (sic) ኤሎም፡ ዘኢረከበ፡

ለዝንቱ፡ አስማት፡ ኅበ፡ ወልድ፡ ዝንቱ፡ ቅንዋተ፡ መስቀሉ፡ . . . ሊሰርስ፡ ጸፌና፡ ኪቢሬዎን፡ መፈጢዎን፡ . . .
5. Prayer of St. Susənyos and the story of his fight against Wərzəlya.
6. Prayer for conception.
በስመ፡ አብ፡ . . . ጸሎት፡ በእንተ፡ ዕንስ፡ ወንጌል፡ ዘማርቆስ፡ (Mark 5:25–29) ከማሁ፡ አህያዋ፡ ወአርግእ፡ ደማ፡ ወኢትቅትል፡ ህፃንቲሃ፡ . . .
7. Prayer against hemorrhage.
በስመ፡ አብ፡ . . . ጸሎት፡ በእንተ፡ አርጋኤ፡ ደም፡ ሰንተም፡² ቀንተም፡²ˣ አጀር፡ መጀር፡²ˣ ጀሐም፡ ተአሰር፡ ጅም፡ ተሰደድ፡ እንተ፡ ባርያ፡ ሽቶላይ፡ ወሽቶላዊት፡ ዘተቀትል፡ ሕፃንት፡ . . .
8. Prayer for conception.
በስመ፡ አብ፡ . . . ጸሎት፡ በእንተ፡ ጽንስ፡ ዘፈነወ፡ እግ"፡ ንጉሥ፡ ወእጉሥ፡ ዘፈነወ፡ ላቲ፡ ለሄዋን፡ ከመ፡ ይእቀብዋ፡ በመዋእለ፡ ጽንሳ፡ ፯ወ፱ መላእክተ፡ ምህረት፡ . . .

Miniatures and Magical Symbols:
1. Angel with sword and scabbard (large).
2. Ornate cross with two figures, one on either side.
3. Talismanic symbol with face in center.

Copied clearly for Wälättä Ḥaywät.

EMIP MagSc 118 – Weiner Magic Scroll 79

Parchment, 155 x 11 cm, two strips sewn together, one column, narrow colored (yellow) border, Gəʿəz, 19th cent.

1. Prayer against the eye of Barya and for binding demons; cf. 113, 1. Prayer: against the eye of Barya and for binding demons"
በስመ፡ አብ፡ . . . ጸሎት፡ በእንተ፡ ዓይነ፡ ባርያ፡ ወማእሠረ፡ አጋንንት፡ ጸሎተ፡ አልሆግ፡ ያሽጅ፡ ባሕቱ፡ ምስኬባብልቁን፡ (sic) በከክ፡ ንቅንጥ፡ . . .
2. Prayer of St. Susənyos and the story of his fight against Wərzəlya.
3. Prayer against demons that cause stomachache and other illnesses; cf. 113, 3. Full text:
ጸሎት፡ በእንተ፡ ሕማመ፡ ከርሥ፡ ዘይጐጸጉጽ፡ አግዐተ፡ ወያደቅቅ፡ አእጽምተ፡ ወያጠዊ፡ ዓንጀተ፡ ወአግዐተ፡ ዶር፡³ˣ ከመ፡ ታድኅና፡ እምሕማመ፡ መጋኛ፡ ወሽቶላይ፡ ለዓመትከ፡ . . . እመሂ፡ ሥጋ፡ ዘይበልዕ፡ ወእመሂ፡ ደመ፡ ዘይሰቲ፡ በውስተ፡ ከርሥ፡ ዘይትወነይ፡ እምኮሉ፡ መናግቱሁ፡ (sic) ለሰይጣን፡ አእግዚአ አድኅን፡ እምሕማመ፡ ቁርጸት፡ ወመጋኛ፡ ለዓመትከ፡ ወለተ፡ ሕይወት፡
4. Prayer against the eye of Barya and charm, unfinished. Full text:

በስመ፡ አብ፡ . . . ጸሎት፡ በእንተ፡ ዓይን፡ ባርያ፡ ወመፍትሔ፡ ሥራይ፡ [.]ጨጨ፡ አንተ፡ በሰማይ፡ ወአንተ፡ በምድር፡ ወአንተ፡ ተሐዩ፡ ወአንተ፡ ትቀትል፡ ሐራስ፡ ወንጎም፡ በዘይመጽአከ፡

5. Prayer against the eye of Barya and piercing pain, 7 lines.

በስመ፡ አብ፡ . . . ጸሎት፡ በእንተ፡ ዓይን፡ ባርያ፡ ወሕግመ፡ ውግዓት፡ ዱዳ፡ ወራዳ፡ ለደም፡ ደም፡ ወፈቅዓ፡ በለምለም፡ በ፯ እስትንፋስ፡ ይምሕረከ፡ እመንፈስ፡ ቅዱስ፡ ከመ፡ ይፃዕ፡ . . .

6. Prayer against hemorrhage (?), 8 lines; cf. 3, 6.

ጸሎት፡ በእንተ፡ [ደ]ም፡ ሸት፡ አእላሹት፡ አሸሕት፡ ወታይ፡ ድለለም፡ ቅም፡ (sic) አለሀ፡ . . .

7. Prayer against hemorrhage, 9 lines.

ጸሎት፡ ዘይምወጋኛ፡ (sic) ለተምከተም፡ ከተተምህን፡ [.]ዘወጽዋደም፡ (sic) ወማይ፡ እምገቦሁ፡ ለእግዚእነ፡ ኢየሱስ፡ ክርስቶስ፡ . . .

Miniatures and Magical Symbols:
1. Angel with sword and scabbard.
2. Four-petal pattern with face in the center.
3. Box-shaped face and various designs below.

Bottom 20 cm stained and faded. Some writing exercise in blue ink.
Copied clearly for Wälättä Ḥəywät

EMIP MagSc 119 – Weiner Magic Scroll 80

Parchment, 198 x 7.5 cm, three strips sewn together, one column, colored (yellow or brown) border, Gəʿəz, 19th cent.

1. Prayer against the evil eye (?), Zar and Ṭäbib; the beginning is illegible, 12 lines.

[በስመ፡ አብ፡ . . . ጸሎት፡ በእንተ፡ . . .] ዛር፡ [ወ]ጠቢብ፡ ነገሪ፡ (sic) ወተዛዋሪ፡ ሬጓቁ፡ በቃለ፡ እግ"፡ አልቦ፡ ስም፡ በታሕት፡ ሰማይ፡ ወምድር፡ ዘእንበለ፡ እግዚእነ፡ ኢየሱስ፡ ክርስቶስ፡ ጋኔን፡ ዘትሬኢ፡ በዓይን፡ ጠባይ፡ መሬታዊ፡ ተአሰር፡ ይቤለክ፡ . . .

2. Greeting to Phanuel as prayer against illnesses caused by Barya, Legewon, Zar, and Ṭäbib.

[. . .] ጸሎት፡ በእንተ፡ ሕግመ፡ ባርያ፡ ወሌጌዎን፡ ዛር፡ ወጠቢብ፡ ነገሪ፡ ወተዛዋሪ፡ ሬጓቁ፡ በቃለ፡ እግ"፡ ሰላም፡ ለከ፡ ሰዳዬ፡ ሰይጣናት፡ ፋኑኤል፡ ለእግ" እምጽርሁ፡ . . . መቅደስ፡ ኦሪት፡ ዘቦዕኪ፡ ማርያም፡ እምነ፡ ወእሙ፡ ለእግዚእነ፡ . . .

3. Prayer against illnesses (hemorrhage, etc.) caused by Barya, Legewon, Zar, and Ṭäbib.

በስመ፡ አብ፡ . . . ጸሎት፡ በእንተ፡ ሕግመ፡ ባርያ፡ ወሌጌዎን፡ ዛር፡ ወጠቢብ፡ ነገሪ፡ ወተዛዋሪ፡ ደም፡ ወከተላይ፡ (sic) ⌈ሊስ፡ አፍሊስ፡[8x]

መሊስ፡[8x] መሌያስ፡[8x] መላሴያስ፡[8x] በላኪስ፡[8x] ወዘዘሎማኤል፡[5x] ሶር፡[7x] ክትር፡[7x] . . . ዘወጽአ፡ ደም፡ እምገቦኪ፡ (sic) አድገና፡ እምሕማመ፡ ደም፡ . . .

4. Prayer against Šätäle, Täyayaž and other demons.
በስመ፡ አብ፡ . . . ጸሎት፡ በእንተ፡ ሕማመ፡ ሸተሌ፡ ወ[ተያ]ያF፡ ነዋሪ፡ ወተዛዋሪ፡ ረጓቁ፡ በቃለ፡ እግ"፡ የአሪቅፍ፡[7x] አይሁትስ፡[6x] ሐረቁ፡ . . . እንተ፡ እምሕማመ፡ ሸተሌ፡ (sic) ወተያያF፡ ነዋሪ፡ ወተዛዋሪ፡ ረጓቁ፡ በቃለ፡ እግ"፡ . . .

5. Prayer against illnesses caused by Barya, Legewon, Zar, and Ṭäbib and for drowning them, 43 lines of *asmat*.
በስመ፡ አብ፡ . . . ጸሎት፡ በእንተ፡ ሕማመ፡ ባርያ፡ ወሌጌዎን፡ ዛር፡ ወጠቢብ፡ ነዋሪ፡ ወተዛዋሪ፡ ረጓቁ፡ በቃለ፡ እግ"፡ መሥምጥም፡ (sic) ዘባርያ፡ መሥጥም፡ ዘሌጌዎን፡ መሥጥም፡ ዘነገርጋር፡ ጆዝኩም፡ ላህ፡ አንስራፉ፡ ኤላም፡ . . .

6. Prayer of St. Susǝnyos against illnesses caused by Barya, Legewon, Zar, Ṭäbib, and the story of his fight against Wǝrzǝlya.
በስመ፡ አብ፡ . . . ጸሎት፡ በእንተ፡ ሕማመ፡ ባርያ፡ ወሌጌዎን፡ ዛር፡ (sic) ወጠቢብ፡ ነዋሪ፡ ወተዛዋሪ፡ ረጓቁ፡ በቃለ፡ እግ"፡ በስመ፡ እግ"፡ ፈጣሪ፡ ጸሎተ፡ ቅዱስ፡ ሱስንዮስ፡ . . .

7. John 1:1–5 as prayer to drive away demons.
በስመ፡ አብ፡ . . . ዮሐንስ፡ ወን፡ (sic) ቀዳሚሁ፡ . . . ኢይቀርቦ፡ ባርያ፡ ወሌጌዎን፡ ዛር፡ (sic) ወጠቢብ፡ ነዋሪ፡ ወተዛዋሪ፡ ረጓቁ፡ በቃለ፡ እግ"፡ አድገና፡ . . .

8. Prayer against colic, piercing pain, Täyayaž and other demons, 13 lines.
በስመ፡ አብ፡ . . . ጸሎት፡ በእንተ፡ ሕማመ፡ ቁርፀት፡ ወውግዓት፡ ወተያያF፡ ነዋሪ፡ ወተዛዋሪ፡ ረጓቁ፡ በቃለ፡ እግ"፡ እልፍሉስ፡[3x] ሸገር፡[3x] ቀጸቤ፡[3x] ቀፌኑ፡[3x] . . .

9. Prayer against illnesses caused by Barya, Legewon, Zar, Ṭäbib, and for binding them.
በስመ፡ አብ፡ . . . ጸሎት፡ በእንተ፡ ሕማመ፡ ባርያ፡ ወሌጌዎን፡ ዛር፡ ወጠቢብ፡ ወተያያF፡ ማዕሠረ፡ ባርያ፡ ወሌጌዎን፡ አዝያጥ፡ (sic) ሎፍሐም፡ ዕሥር፡ በማዕሰረ፡ አጋንንት፡ ወዕደ፡ ሌጉዋን፡ (sic) ሐርበደው፡ ሐርበF፡ ሰሎሞን፡ በርሃ፡ ቅጥ፡ ዓይነ፡ ጡጡ፡ ሰተና፡ ሸተናዊ፡ . . .

Miniatures and Magical Symbols:
1. Twelve-box panel with faces in the even-numbered boxes and crosses in the odd-numbered boxes.
2. Angel with sword and scabbard.
3. Ornate cross with figure on either side; above and below strip containing twelve eyes.

Catalogue of the Scrolls of Ethiopian Spiritual Healing · 385

4. Roman cross shape.

The name of the original owner is replaced with Kiros (and) Ḥaylä Maryam.

EMIP MagSc 120 – Weiner Magic Scroll 81

Parchment, 197 x 10 cm, three strips sewn together, one column, elaborate colored (yellow or brown) border made of interlinking crescent-shaped lines, Gəʿəz, 19th cent.

1. Prayer for binding demons; cf. 30, 1.
   በስመ፡ አብ፨ . . . ጸሎት፡ በእተ፡ (sic) ማእሰረ፡ አጋንንት፡ ያሮክ፡ ሳሮክ፡ ጤቄሮስ፡ አደሮስ፡ ያሳድር፡ አዊን፡ አውብይ፨ ትያኤል፡ አአ፤ አውላኤል፡ የሐፍር፡ ይመቀድር፡ . . . በዝ፡ አስግተኪ፡ አድኅኒ፨ . . .

2. Prayer to subjugate demons, Däsk and Gudale.
   ጸሎት፡ በእተ፡ (sic) ምቅናየ፡ አጋንንት፡ ገሃ፡ ነሃ፡ ድርድርያኖስ፤ ሳጦር፡ (!)፤ አላጦር፤ (!) አግናጦር፡ አውተደናብጦል፡ (sic) በዝቱ፡ (sic) አስግተ፤ አጋንት፡ (sic) ያበርደስክ፡ (sic) ወጉዳሌ፡ ለእለ፡ ይትሜሰሉ፤ በምታአት፤ (sic) ወፍልጸት፡ . . .

3. The Net of Solomon for catching demons.
   በስመ፡ አብ፨ . . . አስግተ፡ ሰሎሞን፡ ዘረበሙ፡ ለአጋንንት፡ ከመ፡ መርበብተ፤ አሃ፡ ዘባሕር፡ እ᎒ዘ፡ ይብል፤ ሰድራኤል፡ አዳታኤል፡ ኩርሜል፡ . . . ካይዕበ፡ (sic, for ካዕበ፡ ይቤ፡) አዲ፡ ሰሎሞን፡3x ኢያኤስ፡3x . . . ወበዝ፡ ስምከ፡ አድኅኖ፨ . . . followed by the Greeting to Phanuel: ሰላም፡ ለከ፡ ሰዳዬ፡ አጋንንት፡ ፋኑኤል፡ እምገጸ፡ ፈጣሪ፡ ልዑል፡ ኢያስተዋደዮ፡ ሰብአ፡ ሐጉል፤ . . .

4. John 1:1–5 as prayer against Barya, Legewon, Zar, Šotälay, and the evil eye.
   ቀዳሚሁ፡ ቃል፡ . . . ወኢይረክቦ፡ ዘየአምን፡ በወልድ፡ በሕይወት፡ ዘለአለም፡ በዝ፤ ቃለ፡ ወንጌልከ፡ አድኅና፡ እምነማመ፤ ባርያ፡ ወሌገወን፡ (sic) ወሾተላይ፡ (sic) . . .

5. Prayer against hemorrhage.
   በስመ፡ አብ፨ . . . ጸሎት፤ በእተ፡ (sic) ደም፤ ቆርቆታኤል፤ ቆርቆታኤል፤6x ወደራቅኤል፨7x እርወነA ርወነA6x ራኪራ፤ እራኪራ፨ ራኪራA5x ዘአቆምከ፡ ደግ፤ አንተ፡ (sic) ደም፤ ይውህዝ፡ (sic) አመ፡ (sic) ፲ወ፪ ክረምታ፡ ከግሁ፡ አቁም፤ ደግ፡ . . . ሊስ፡ አፍሊስ፤ መሊስ፤ መላሊስ፤ ሜሌዕስ፤ ዘአርጋእስ፡ ደመ፤ በዝ፡ ከግሁ፡ አቁም፤ ደግ፤ ለአመትከ፡ . . . አንቸርዊ፡7x ⌜አንተ፡ ደም፤2x አፍሊስ፡ በጥራስ፡ ጥራሲሳ፡ ተአሰር፡ በቃለ፡ አብ፡ . . . ሰንታም፡ ከተማስን፡ ዘወጽአ፡ ደም፡ ወማይ፤ እምገቦሁ፡ . . . ሳዖር፤ አላዳር፡ (sic) . . .

6. Prayer against hemorrhage.

በስመ፡ አብ፡ . . . ጸሎት፤ በእተ፡ (sic) ደም፤ ሰንታም፡ ቀንታም፡ ሰንከራም፤ ዘወጽአ፡ ደም፤ እምየማነ፡ ገቦሁ፡ . . . ዘከተሮ፤ ለሰይጣን፤ ከማሁ፡ ስትር፡ (sic) ደማ፡ . . . ሊስ፡³ˣ አፍሊስ፡ ሜለልዮስ፡ ኢታውጽአ፡ (sic) ደም፡ ደሞ፡ ግባ፡ (sic) ድጎሬከ፡ በሰላጣነ፡ አብ፡ . . . ያሽያፍታዉ፡⁷ˣ ሜጢጣዊ፡⁹ˣ . . . በዝ፡ ቃልከ፤ አድኅን፡ . . .

Miniatures and Magical Symbols:
1. Angel (large)
2. Panel with face in center and designs above and below (variation on talismanic symbol with face in center?)
3. Ornate cross.

Widely spaced lines.
Copied for Abbäbčč/Wälättä Mika'el.

EMIP MagSc 121 – Weiner Magic Scroll 82
Parchment, 178 x 9 cm, three strips sewn together, one column, colored (yellow or brown) sawtooth border, Gəʻəz, 19th/20th cent.
1. Prayer for binding demons and against headache, 32 lines.
   በስመ፡ አብ፡ . . . ጸሎት፡ በእንተ፡ ማዕሰረ፡ አጋንንት፡ ወደዊ፡ ርእስ፡ ዘይሰልብ፡ ልበ፡ ሰብእ፡ ወያፀልም፡ አዕይንተ፡ ወይቀጠቅጥ፡ ርእስ፡ ወላ፡ (sic) ወሐቂ፡ (sic) ስነነ፡ ወይመጽኡ፡ ከመ፡ ጽላሎት፡ ሳዶር፡ አላዶር፡ ዳናት፡ አዴራ፡ ሮዳስ፡ በፄንዋተ፡ መስቀሉ፡ . . . ዘበመስቀልከ፡ አጽራእከ፡ ግብሮ፡ ለዲያብሎስ፡ . . . በስመ፡ አብ፡ . . . በአፓሮስ፡ ስምከ፡ በዳፌል፡ ስምከ፡ በሁሩያኖስ፡ ስምከ፡ በጽፁኤል፡ ስ፡ (sic) በሕቡእ፡ ስምከ፡ ዘኢተናገር፡ (sic) ወበክሱት፡ ስምከ፡ ዘኢትፌከር፡ (sic) እስመ፡ ተማኅፀንኩ፡ . . .
2. Prayer against stomachache, 13 lines.
   በስመ፡ [አብ፡ . . .] ጸሎት፡ በእንተ፡ ሕማም፡ ከርሥ፡ ዘርጉጉ፡ (sic) ገበዋት፡ (sic) ወያወዊ፡ (sic) አንጀተ፡ ወአማዐተ፡ ዘይሰልብ፡ ኮልያተ፡ ቄጼቤጀር፡ ቄ፡ ቄጼ፡ ⌈ቄጼ፡ ቄ፡²ˣ ቄፈኑ፡⌉ ቄፈኑ፡ ብያክ፡ ቄፈ፡ ⌈ቄ፡ ብ፡³ˣ . . . አርጋኢ፡ (sic) ነፋስ፡ ወበረድ፡ ከማኩ፡ አርጌ፡ . . . እስመ፡ አልቦ፡ ነገር፡ ዘይሰአኖ፡ ለእግ"፡
3. Prayer for binding Satan and demons. Full text: Prayer: for binding Satan and demons"
   በስመ፡ አብ፡ . . . ጸሎት፡ በእንተ፡ ማዕሰሩ፡ ለሰይጣን፡ ወዓጋንንት፡ አካስ፡ አሜኬ፡ ኤንክ፡ ከዚእ፡ አርናኤም፡ ካዝቦን፡ ጌኩ፡ ጌሎ፡ አስኢሌቅ፡ አስኢ፡ ከለፌውስ፡ ያብሴት፡ ፓፓስዬር፡ ኪፍፍ፡ አርሐላ፡ አውጽ፡ ወአኮ፡ በዝንቱ፡ አስማቲክ፡ አድኅና፡ ወፈውሳ፡ ለአመትክ፡ ወለተ፡ ተክለ፡ ሃይማኖት፡
4. Prayer for binding Satan and against the evil eye and the evil eye of Barya, 13 lines.

በስም፡ አብ፡ ... ጸሎት፡ በሰሩ፡ (sic, obviously for በእንተ፡ ማእሰሩ፡) ለሰይጣን፡ ጸሎት፡ በእንተ፡ ዓይነት፡ ወዓይነ፡ ጥላ፡ ወዓይነ፡ ባርያ፡ ወዓይነ፡ ወርቅ፡ ዝንቱ፡ አስማት፡ ኢኮስ፡ ኢታአጋ፡ ኢጋስ፡ ኢንክስ፡ ... በዕሉ፡ አስማት፡ ...

5. Prayer for binding Satan and Legewon, 35 lines.

በስም፡ አብ፡ ... ጸሎት፡ በእንተ፡ ማዕሰሩ፡ ለሰይጣን፡ ወሌጋን፡ (sic) አስማተ፡ ኃያል፡ አሽፒሬ፡²ˣ ጉፕልሽን፡ መፒራ፡ Fሁር፡ Fመንቱ፡ ወጭር፡ ... ዘብርት፡ ወዘልሕኮት፡ ኩሎሙ፡ መናፍስተ፡ ርኩሳን፡ መፍድየ፡ በዘተሓብአ፡ ወተሰወረ፡ ይትከሰት፡ ገሃደ፡ በዝንቱ፡ አስማት፡ አድኅና፡ እምኩሉ፡ መከራ፡ ወእምኩሉ፡ መስገርት፡ ለአመትከ፡ ... ቃል፡ ከትር፡ ያፌሽትር፡ መቅስም፡ ...

6. Prayer for binding demons: Mark 5:1–13.
7. Greeting to Phanuel as prayer for binding demons; cf. 62, 4.

Miniatures and Magical Symbols:
1. Five faces in two rows: two above, three below.
2. Angel with sword.

Widely spaced lines. End of scroll torn off.
Copied for Wälättä Täklä Haymanot.

EMIP MagSc 122 – Weiner Magic Scroll 83

Parchment(?), 144 x 14.5 cm, two strips sewn together, two columns, elaborate hatched double borders (including red line) and woven-ropes pattern between the two columns of text, Gəʻəz, 20th cent.

1. Prayer against the eye of Barya, Legewon, eye of Zar, eye of Täyaž, Šotälay, Mäggäñña, Buda, Ṭäbib, Mänšo, and other illnesses.

በስም፡ አብ፡ ... ጸሎት፡ በእንተ፡ ዓይነ፡ ባርያ፡ ወለጌዋን፡ (sic) ወዓይነ፡ ዘር፡ ወአይነ፡ ተያዦ፡ ዓይነ፡ ሰብእ፡ ወሾተላይ፡ ዓይነ፡ ጥላ፡ ወጽ (sic) ወጊ፡ ዓይነ፡ ሥትሥታ፡ (sic) ወፍርቅቃት፡ ዓይነ፡ አስወንዉን፡ ወለህጋመ[፡] ቁርፀት፡ ወፍልፀት፡ መገኛ፡ ወጉሥምት፡ ወቡዳ፡ ጠቢብ፡ ወመንሾ[፡] ወለሸንት[፡] ምዕ፡ ወጉርጉሆ፡ ወጆርዐ[፡] ደዌ፡ ወመናፍስተ፡ ርኩሳን፡ አድኅና፡ ለአመትከ፡ ዕገሊት፡ ... በኃይለ፡ ዝንቱ፡ አስማቲከ፡ ይትአሰሩ፡ አጋንንት፡ ፀዋጋን፡ ... ምድምያስ፡³ˣ ምጽር፡ ቆቅት፡ ...

2. Prayer against the eye of Šotälay and the story of St. Susənyos fighting Wərzəlya, the demon of infant mortality; cf. 33, 3.

በስም፡ አብ፡ ... ጸሎት፡ በእንተ፡ ሐማመ፡ ዓይነ፡ ሾተላይ፡ ወሀሎ፡ ፩ብእሲ፡ ዘስሙ፡ ሱስንዮስ፡ ...

Miniatures and Magical Symbols:
1. Angel (above) stabbing with a sword a monster (below).

2. Two boxes (side by side) with four-petal shape, faces in a box in the center, and diamond shapes in the four quadrants.
3. Talismanic symbol with face in center.
4. Twenty-box panel (5 x 4) with faces in the odd-numbered boxes and four-petal shape with eyes in the even-numbered boxes.

Another copy of 44 by the same bad copyist of 47.

EMIP MagSc 123 – Weiner Magic Scroll 84

Parchment(?), 153 x 14 cm, three strips sewn together, two columns, elaborate double border (with orange strip) and woven-rope pattern in margin between columns of text, Gəʻəz, 20th cent., thin strip of parchment 40-cm long sewn into one end.

1. Prayer against illnesses caused by the eye of Šotälay and the story of St. Susənyos fighting Wərzəlya, the demon of infant mortality; cf. 33, 3.
   በስመ፡ አብ፡ . . . ጸሎት፡ በእንተ፡ ሕማመ፡ ዓይነ፡ ሾተላይ፡ ወሀሎ፡ ፩ብእሲ፡ ዘስሙ፡ ሱስንዮስ፡ . . .
2. Prayer against the evil eye, the evil eye of Barya, Legewon, …; cf. 122, 1, with the *asmat* of the Archanel Michael. Prayer: against the evil eye, the evil eye of Barya, Legewon"

Miniatures and Magical Symbols:
1. Two angels, side by side, with swords and scabbards.
2. Panel with four small boxes (one in each corner) with a face in each. Inside is an talismanic symbol with a face in the center.
3. Three hovering angels, side by side.
4. Fifteen box panel (5 x 3) with faces in the odd-numbered boxes and four-petal patterns with eyes in the even-numbered boxes.

Copied by the same bad copyist of 37, 47 and 122.

EMIP MagSc 124 – Weiner Magic Scroll 85

Parchment, 162 x 9.5 cm, three strips sewn together, one column, double border, Gəʻəz and some Amharic, 20th cent.

1. Prayer for binding demons; probably related to Six, *Handschriften*, 23, 2, 4. p. 102. Full text:
   በስመ፡ አብ፡ . . . ጸሎት፡ በእንተ፡ ማዕሠረ፡ አጋንንት፡ በስሙ፡ ለአብ፡ ሙራኤል፡ በስሙ፡ ለወልድ፡ ምናቴር፡ በስሙ፡ ለመንፈስ፡ ቅዱስ፡ አብያቴር፡ ዓዕ፡ ዓይነ፡ ባርያ፡ ወሌጌዎን፡ ዛር፡ ወግሪዳ፡ (sic) ዉጋት፡ (sic) ወቁርጥማት፡ መጋኛ፡ ወጉሥምት፡ ዘኢይትረአይ፡ በመአልት፡ ወበሌሊት፡ እምላእለ፡ ዓመትከ፡ ተዋበች፡

2. Prayer of Alexander that he uttered on a Friday against illnesses caused by Barya, Legewon, for biding demons, against charm, Mäggañña, Mari, and Marit, 73 lines; cf. 16, 4.
በስመ፡ አብ፡ . . . ጸሎት፡ በእንተ፡ ሕማመ፡ ባርያ፡ ወሌጌዎን፡ ዓይነ፡ ጥጹ፡ ወማእሠረ፡ አጋንንት፡ ዓይነ፡ ጽላ፡ (again) ወገቤታ፡ ወተያያሾ፡ ወዓይነ፡ ወርቅ፡ ወቁመኛ፡ ወእጆ፡ ሰብእ፡ ወመፍትሔ፡ ሥራይ፡ ወመጋኛ፡ ወማሪ፡ ወማሪት፡ ወበእንተ፡ እስክንድር፡ ንጉሥ፡ ዘተናገረ፡ በእለተ፡ ዓርብ፡ አልፋ፡ ንጉሥ፡ ናጨር፡ ንጉሥ፡ ንፋሽር፡ . . . ንዑ፡ ኩልክሙ፡ (sic) አጋንንት፡ ወዛራት፡ . . . እኔን፡ ተነካችሁ፡ እላንተም፡ ታስነካችሁኝ፡ እግ"፡ ብርሃነ፡ ሕይትን፡ (sic) ባርክ፡ ኩለንታየ፡ . . .

3. Three prayers against hemorrhage and for conception.
በስመ፡ አብ፡ . . . ጸሎት፡ በእንተ፡ ውኅዘተ፡ ደም፡ ወዘኒሰ፡ ጽንስ፡ አሌፍ፡ ስምከ፡ አርድዕ፡ ዳሌጥ፡ አጥግዕ፡ ደግ፡ በግንፀና፡ ቤት፡ አርትዕ፡ ደግ፡ ለከዊየ፡ ሕፃን፡ ጋሜል፡ . . . (cf. 73, 1).
ጸሎት፡ በእ[ንተ፡] ውኅዘተ፡ ደም፡ ሰተም፡:[7x] ቀንታም፡ ቀንቀታም፡፡ ስንክራም፡ ዘወጽአ፡ ደም፡ እምገቦሁ፡ . . .
ጸሎት፡ (sic) ደም[፡] ሊስ፡ አፍሊስ፡ መላሊስ፡[2x] በለኬስ፡ ወዘዘሎሜጌ/ኤል፡ በኃይለ፡ ዝንቱ፡ አስማቲከ፡ ዘአርጋዕኩ፡ ኃይለ፡ (sic) በረድ፡ ወነፋስ፡ ከማሁ፡ . . . ኤሎስ፡[3x] አፍሊስ፡ ሊስ፡ መላልዮስ፡ ኢየሱስ፡ ክርስቶስ፡ "አርጋዕ"ኃይለ፡ በረድ፡ ወነፋስ፡ ፰:[7x] ፫:[7x] . . . በኃይለ፡ ዝንቱ፡ ጠልሰም፡ ዓርግዕ፡ ውኅዘተ፡ ደግ፡ ወአጽንዕ፡ ፍሬ፡ ማኅፀና፡ . . . እስመ፡ አልቦ፡ ነገር፡ ዘይሰአኖ፡ ለእግ"፡፡

4. The Net of Solomon for catching demons, as prayer against illnesses caused by Barya and Legewon, 17 lines.
በስመ፡ አብ፡ . . . ጸሎት፡ በእንተ፡ ሕማመ፡ ባርያ፡ ወሌጌዎን፡ አስግተ፡ ለሰሎሞን፡ ዘረበበሙ፡ ለአጋንንት፡ ከመ፡ መርበብተ፡ አሣ፡ ዘባሕር፡ እንዘ፡ ይብል፡ ሰዱቃኤል፡ አዳታኤል፡ ርክም፡ እልመርም፡ አፍ፡ ጸላ፡ እግዚኡ፡ እምዓይነ፡ ፀላኢ፡ ወፀር፡ ወሰውራ፡ እምዓይነ፡ ባርያ፡ ወሌጌዎን፡ . . .

5. Prayer against illnesses caused by Barya and Legewon and for binding demons and Satan, in Gəʿəz and some Amharic.
ጸሎት፡ በእንተ፡ ሕማመ፡ ባርያ፡ ወሌጌዎን፡ ወበእንተ፡ ማእሠረ፡ አጋንንት፡ ወሰይጣናት፡ ስሙ፡ ለአብ፡ ሰዳዴ፡ ፀር፡ ስሙ፡ ለወልድ፡ መግሬ፡ ፀር፡ ወስሙ፡ ለመንፈስ፡ ቅዱስ፡ መዋዒ፡ ፀር፡ ወከማሁ፡ አድኅና፡ . . . በስመ፡ ሰፒራ፡ አላ፡ ሻሜራ፡ ቃስያስ፡ ከቃራን፡ ካራን፡ ዳራን፡ . . . ተሰደድ፡ ገብር፡ በርሻን፡ ወበሻፍር፡ እለ፡ ሲዞ፡ እለ፡ ደለጮ፡ እለ፡ ጨኑት፡ ⌈እለ፡ ሐመዱት፡:⌉[2x] እለ፡ ባሔ፡ እለ፡ ተፍታ፡ ከደረሳችሁ፡ እለ፡ ቆሪፍ፡ እለ፡ ዝንጆር፡ እለ፡ ደበስ፡ እለ፡ ሙርጃን፡ እለ፡ መቀስ፡ እለ፡ ሽምላ፡ እለ፡ ወለተ፡ ወርቅ፡ እለ፡ ውርዝልያ፡ ከደረሳችሁ፡ በሥልጣነ፡ አብ፡ ወወልድ፡ ወመንፈስ፡ ቅዱስ፡ ውጉዛን፡ ኩኑ፡ ከመ፡ አርዮስ፡ ወበሳልዮስ፡ (sic) ወመቅደንዮስ፡ (sic) ያድርጋችሁ፡ followed by the greeting to the kidneys of the Archangel

Michael, from the Archangel's image, Chaîne, Répertoire, no. 119:
ሰላም፡ ለኮልያቲከ፡ እግ"፡ ዘሰቀሎ፡ . . . and the Greeting to Phanuel:
ሰላም፡ ለከ፡ ሰዳዬ፡ አጋንንት፡ ፋኑኤል፡ ለእግ" እምጽርሁ፡ . . . እስመ፡
አልቦ፡ ነገር፡ ዘይሰአኖ፡ ለእግ"፡

Miniatures and Magical Symbols:
1. Angel with sword.
2. Angel with sword.
3. Variation on talismanic symbol with face in center.

EMIP MagSc 125 – Weiner Magic Scroll 86

Parchment, 143 x 10 cm, three strips sewn together, one column, colored (yellow) border, Gəʿəz and some Amharic, 20th cent, amulet case.

1. The Net of Solomon for catching demons as prayer against illnesses caused by Barya, Legewon, Däsk and Gudale.
   በስመ፡ አብ፡ . . . ጸሎት፡ በእንተ፡ ሕማም፡ ባርያ፡ ወሌጌዎን፡ ደስክ፡
   ወጉዳሌ፡ አስግብት፡ ለሰሎሞን፡ ዘረበሙ፡ ለአጋንንት፡ ከመ፡ መርበብት፡ አኃ፡
   ዘይወጽእ፡ እምባህር፡ እንዘ፡ ይብል፡ ስዱቃኤል፡ አዳታኤል፡ ርክም፡
   እልመሪም፡ አፍ፡ ጸላ፡ እግዚአ፡ እምዓይን፡ ጸላኢ፡ ወጸር፡ ወሰውራ፡
   እምዓይን፡ እኩይ፡ ሊተ፡ ለአመትከ፡ . . . (cf. 124, 4.)
   አብ፡ እሳት፡ በአካለ፡ ወልድ፡ እሳት፡ በካለ፡ ወመንፈስ፡ ቅዱስ፡ በዝንቱ፡
   አስግት፡ ዘአፅራዕከ፡ ግብሮ፡ ለዲያብሎስ፡ ከማሁ፡ . . . አምሐልኩክሙ፡
   ወአውገዝኩክሙ፡ በከመ፡ አሰር፡ ለብርያል፡ በ፷፻፻ መሐፒለ፡ እሳት፡ . . .
   (cf. 17, 2.)
2. Prayer of St. Susənyos and the story of his fight against Wərzəlya, the demon of infant mortality.
3. Prayer against colic, 8 lines.
   ጸሎት፡ በእንተ፡ ሕማም፡ ቁርጻት፡ ሄርኪሹ፡[6x] ኪሹ፡[3x] ኪስ፡[3x] አርኪስ፡[3x]
   ራግራይ፡ ራማኪስ፡ ፀሃያት፡ ኢየሱስ፡ ክርስቶስ፡ ኩን፡ ወአድኃን፡ . . .
4. Prayer against piercing pain, 6 lines.
   ጸሎት፡ በእንተ፡ ሕማም፡ ውጋት፡ (sic) ምድምያስ፡[3x] የሃቂ፡[3x] የሐብራስቂ፡
   አእግዚአ፡ በከመ፡ አድኅንከ፡ ለወልደ፡ ኮራስቂ፡ ከማሁ፡ ዕቀብ፡ . . .
5. Two prayers against hemorrhage, each 7 lines; the first is mostly in Amharic.
   ጸሎት፡ በእንተ፡ ሕማም፡ ያም፡ (sic) ደም፡ ሄት፡ ትነብር፡ ባርቅ፡ ጋብስ፡
   ሰርገላ፡ ንጉሥ፡ ከወሃቦ፡ ከወረድሁ፡ የወፃ፡ የወረደ፡ አለሁ፡ ቃለ፡ አብ፡ . . .
   ዕቀብ፡ ወአድኅን፡ እምሕማም፡ ደም፡ . . .
   ጸሎት፡ በእንተ፡ ሕማም፡ ደም፡ ⌐ሊስ፡ አፍሊስ፡ መሊስ፡ መላሊስ፡[3x] ሜልዮስ፡
   ዘአርጋዕከ፡ ኀይለ፡ ነፋስ፡ . . .
6. Prayer against rheumatism, 6 lines; cf. Six, *Handschriften*, 10, 7, p. 79.

Catalogue of the Scrolls of Ethiopian Spiritual Healing · 391

ጸሎት፡ (sic) ሕማመ፡ ቁርጥማት፡ ቁርጥማትየስ፡ ያመከድሽድሽ፡
ካፉራድላዊ፡ ሲድራቃዊ፡ ዘይፈቅዕ፡ አፅመ፡ ቁስሉ፡ ለኢዮብ፡ መሬታዊ፡
ዕቀብ፡ ወአድኅን፡ እምሕማመ፡ ቁርጥማት፡ . . .

7. Prayer against the evil eye, 2 lines, perhaps unfinished. Full text:
ጸሎት፡ በእንተ፡ ሕማመ፡ ዓይነት፡ ውፃዕ፡ ዓይነት፡ በቀይህ፡ ወበጥቁር[፡]

8. Prayer against terror caused by demon of the day, night, *Sext*, and *None*, Šotälawi, Zar, Qurañña, Barya, and Legewon, 18 lines.
በስመ፡ አብ፡ . . . ጸሎት፡ በእንተ፡ ሕማመ፡ ድንጋጼ፡ ዕቀበኒ፡ ክርስቶስ፡
እምአጋንንት፡ ዘመዓልት፡ ወዘመዓልት፡ (sic) ወዘሌሊት፡ ዘቀትር፡ ወዘሰአት፡
እምንስቲቲ፡ ሙኪርያ፡ አንቲ፡ . . . በዝ፡ ቃለ፡ ሰቆቃው፡ ዕቀብ፡ ወአድኅን፡
እምሕማመ፡ ዓይነ፡ ጥላ፡ ሾተላዊ፡ ጋኔን፡ ዛር፡ ወቁራኛ፡ ባርያ፡ ወሌጌዎን፡
ፍልጸት፡ ወቁጸት፡ (sic) . . .

9. Prayer for binding demons, Barya, Legewon, Däsk and Gudale, 13 lines.
በእንተ፡ ማዕሠረ፡ አጋንንት፡ ⌜ያሮክ፡ ሳሮክ፡ ታሮክ፡³ˣ ጤቁሮስ፡ አዳሮስ፡
ያስድር፡ . . . በእሉ፡ አስማቲከ፡ ዕቀበኒ፡ ወአድኅነኒ፡ እምሕማመ፡ ዓይነ፡
ጥላ፡ ወዓይነ፡ ወርቅ፡ ባርያ፡ ወሌጌዎን፡ ደስክ፡ ወጉዳሌ፡ ፍልጸት፡ ወቁርጸት፡
. . .

10. Prayer against Barya, Legewon, Däsk and Gudale, 13 lines.
ጸሎት፡ በእንተ፡ ባርያ፡ ወሌጌዎን፡ ደስክ፡ ወጉዳሌ፡ ወገጹ፡ ዘፍጹም፡
በጽልመት፡ ፈርሃ፡ ወደንጋጿ፡ ዲያብሎስ፡ ርእዮ፡ ብሑተ፡ ልደት፡ በሥጋ፡
አምላክ፡ በሲኦል፡ በዝ፡ ቃለ፡ መለኮትከ፡ ዕቀብ፡ ወአድኅን፡ እምሕማመ፡
ባርያ፡ ወሌጌዎን፡ ደስክ፡ ወጉዳሌ፡ ፍልጸት፡ . . . እስመ፡ አልቦ፡ ነገር፡
ዘይሰአኖ፡ ለእግ":

Miniatures and Magical Symbols:
1. Angel with sword and scabbard.
2. Six-box panel (3 x 2) with faces in boxes 1, 3, and 5.
3. Ornate cross.

Copied for Yälfəññ.

EMIP MagSc 126 – Weiner Magic Scroll 87

Parchment, 159 x 8.5 cm, three strips sewn together, one column, elaborate colored (yellow or brown) double border of interlocking crescent-shaped lines, Gəʿəz, 20th cent.

1. Prayer for binding the evil eye and Zar Qarsa (?). Prayer: for binding the evil eye and Zar"
ጸሎት፡ በእንተ፡ ማእሰረ፡ ዓይነ፡ ጽላ፡ ወዘር፡ ቃርሳ፡ ወእጀ፡ ሰብእ፡ ወንጌል፡
ዘዮሐንስ፡ (John 1:1–5) ዘየአምን፡ በወልድ፡ ቦሕይወት፡ ዘለዓለም፡ በዝ፡ ቃለ፡
ወንጌልከ[፡] አድኅነኒ፡ . . .

2. Prayer for binding demons, Legewon, and Barya, Täyayaž.

ጸሎት፡ በእንተ፡ ማእሰረ፡ አጋንንት፡ ወሌጌዎን፡ ባርያ፡ ወተያያF፡ ቃል፡ ዘሙሻ፡ የአጄ፡ ሞአጄ፡ አሳሂ፡ ሩብ፡ አባጀን፡ የአይ፡ አዝርር፡ ወይኩን፡ በበዳ፡ ነጋሽ፡ ቢሐቅ፡ አስተብርር፡ ሰሎሞን፡ ሐርሞሐ፡ ሰሎሞን፡ በጽሐ፡ ሰሎሞን፡ ፍሥሐ፡ አቂያቴር፡[7x] ምቅናዮሙ፡ ወማእሰሮሙ፡ ወማንተሞሙ፡ ለባርያ፡...

3. Prayer to subjugate the enemy and Šotälay, nine lines. Prayer: to subjugate the enemy and Šotälay"

ጸሎት፡ በእንተ፡ መግረሬ፡ ዐር፡ ወሾተላይ፡ ድርሳን፡ ዘቅዱስ፡ ሚካኤል፡ ሳዶር፡ አላዶር፡...

4. Prayer for binding Šotälay and others demons.

በስመ፡ አብ፡... ጸሎት፡ በእንተ፡ ማእሰረ፡ ሾተላይ፡ ወአናቂ፡ በጥባጭ፡ ወአስፈጣጭ፡ ቀጥቃጭ፡ ወአማጭ፡ ኑዙኤልA[7x] ሱዙኤልA[7x] ኩዙኤልA[7x] ምድምያስA[7x] ያሐቂA[7x] ያብራስቂ፡[7x] ቦኃይለ፡ ዝንቱ፡ አስግቲከ፡ በከመ፡ አድኃንከ፡ ለወልደ፡ ኮራስቂ፡ እምሕማም፡ ውግዓት፡ ወጒሥምት፡...

5. Prayer for binding Barya and Legewon, with the glorification of the Cross; cf. MD, 59, p. 461.

ጸሎት፡ በእንተ፡ ማእሰረ፡ ባርያ፡ ወሌጌዎን፡ መስቀል፡ ኃይለነ፡... አይሁድ፡ ክሕዱ፡ ወንሕነስ፡ አመነ፡...

Miniatures and Magical Symbols:
1. Six strips containing various geometric shapes.
2. Angel with sword and scabbard.
3. Ornate cross with animal on the left side.

Copied for Wälättä Kidan/Däbritu Ǝ(n)guday, "daughter of Täwabäčč;" cf. 114.

EMIP MagSc 127 – Abilene Christian University Magic Scroll 1

Parchment, 155 x 7.5 cm, four strips sewn together, one column, colored (yellow) border, Gəʽəz, 20th cent.

1. The Net of Solomon for catching demons.

በስመ፡ አብ፡... እጽሕፍ፡ ፡ መርበብተ፡ ሰሎሞን፡ ዘረበቦሙ፡ ለአጋንንት፡ ከመ፡ መርበብተ፡ ዓሣ፡ ዘባሕር፡ አውዳታኤል፡ ገቡዕ፡ መለኮት፡ ሹሪ፡ አፍ፡ አስላፍ፡ ማኒ፡ ቃዲ፡ ኢያስ፡ አስላፍ፡ ጸልኒ፡ ወሰውሪኒ፡ እምዓይን፡ እዬሆሙ፡ ለነሃብት፡ ወለአጋንንት፡... ድንገ፡ አንዘዎ፡ ለሰሎሞን፡ አንበርዎ፡ እስከ፡ ሡሉስ፡ መዋዕል፡ ወእስከ፡ ሡሉስ፡ ለያልይ፤ ዝንቱ፡ ውእቱ፡ አስግተ፡ እዬሁ፡ ለሰሎሞን፡ ኢያስ፡[3x] ሜሎስ፡ ሜሎስ፤ እሳት፡ ሰይፈ፡ እሳት፡ ጋዴን፡ እሳት፡ ወዝ፡ ውእቱ፡ ዘወሀብ፡ ለእግዝእትነ፡ ማርያም፡... እምቅድመ፡ ይትወለድ፡ እምኔሃ፡ በዝንቱ፡ ድንኅ፡ ሰሎሞን፡ እምኤሆሙ፡ ለነሐብት፡... ወደገም፡ ሰሎሞን፡ እንዝ፡ ይብል፡ በስመ፡ አብ፡... ሰሎሞን፡[3x] መሐፍሎን፡[3x] ሎፍሐም፡[3x] ንምሎስ፡[3x] አምያታሪ፡[3x] አሜሃ፡ ተመትረ፡ ጉርዔሆሙ፡ ለጀ (or ጄ, not clear) ነሓብት፡...

2. Greeting to Phanuel as prayer to drive away demons.
ሰላም፡ ለከ፡ ሰዳዬ፡ አጋንንት፡ ፋኑኤል፡ ለእግ" እምጽርሑ፡ . . .
Miniatures and Magical Symbols:
1. Angel with sword and scabbard.
2. Twelve-box panel (3 x 4) with faces in boxes 1, 3, 5, 7, 9 and 11 and geometric patterns in the others.
3. Ornate cross.

Copied for Ǝgzi' Ḥaräya.

EMIP MagSc 128 – Abilene Christian University Magic Scroll 2

Parchment, 149 x 8.5 cm, two strips sewn together, one column, colored (red jagged line on yellow) border, Gǝ'ǝz, 20th cent.

1. Prayer of St. Susənyos against the evil eye, illnesses caused by Buda and the story of his fight against Wǝrzǝlya, the demon of infant mortality; cf. 7, 3.
በስም፡ አብ፡ . . . ጸሎት፡ (sic) እምሕጸናት፡ በእንተ፡ ዓይነት፡ ወሀጋም፡ ቡዳ፡ ወዓይነ፡ ወርቅ፡ ጸሎቱ፡ ለቅዱስ፡ ሱስንዮስ፡ ህያው፡ ወተናጋሪ፡ በእንተ፡ አሰሰሎ፡ ደዌ፡ እምሕጸናት፡ . . . ወሀሎ፡ አሐዱ፡ ብእሲ፡ ዘስሙ፡ ሱስንዮስ፡ . . .
2. Prayer against the evil eye, the evil eye of Barya, Legewon, Zar, and Təgrida: The story of the sorcerer at the Sea of Tiberias.
በስም፡ አብ፡ . . . ጸሎት፡ በእንተ፡ ዓይን፡ ወዓይነተ፡ ባርያ፡ ወለጌዎን፡ ዛር፡ ወትግሪዳ፡ ወእንዘ፡ የሀውር፡ እግዚእ፡ ኢየሱስ፡ ወመጽኡ፡ ምስሌሁ፡ Ṭወፀአርዳኢሁ፡ ወርእዩ፡ . . .
3. Prayer against the evil eye and the evil eye of Barya. Full text:
ጸሎት፡ በእንተ፡ ዓይነ፡ ጥላ፡ ወዓይነተ፡ ባርያ፡ ለጀርኒ፡ መጀርኒ፡ ወ፡ (sic) ፈያኒ፡ ቀታኒ፡ ሀያኒ፡ እልኮማትኒ፡ ወገጹ፡ ዘፍጹም፡ በጽልመት፡ ፈርሃ፡ ወደንገፀ፡ ዲያብሎስ፡ ርእዮ፡ ብሑት፡ ልደት፡ በሥጋ፡ እምላክ፡ በሲኣል፡ እስሙ፡ አልቦ፡ ነገር፡ ዘይሰእኖ፡ ለእግ"፡ ወከማሁ፡ አድኅና፡ ለአመትከ፡ . . .
Miniatures and Magical Symbols:
1. Angel with sword (with an atypical representation and dark blue and bright red and pink colors).
2. Square panel with three faces side by side.
3. Square panel with face in the center.
4. Cross.

EMIP MagSc 129 – Abilene Christian University Magic Scroll 3

Parchment, 143 x 6.7 cm, three strips sewn together, one column, double border with "candy cane" red and black line pattern, Gǝ'ǝz, 20th cent.

1. Prayer against the evil eye of Barya, Gärgari, Zar, Mäggañña, all types of stomachache, and the demon Ǧuḥa, 48 lines.
   በስመ፡ አብ፡ . . . ጸሎት፡ በእንተ፡ ዓይነተ[፡] ባርያ፡ ወገርጋሪ፡ ዘዘር፡ ወመጋኛ፡ ወኮሉ፡ ሕማም፡ ከርሥ፡ ወጋኔን፡ ዘስሙ፡ ጁሐ፡ ዘዘይነብር፡ (sic) በፀድፍ፡ ወበዋሻ፡ ወበባሕር፡ ዘኢይነጽፍ፡ በግድፍ፡ ዘየሐምማ፡ ለብእሲት፡ ወይጼልባ፡ ከመ፡ ደመና፡ ይነውም፡ ምስሌሃ፡ ወይቀንዕ፡ በእሲሃ፡ በብዕላ፡ ወበፍሥሐሁ፡ በክብሪ፡ ወበሞገሳ፡ . . . ወጸውዕ፡ ዓቢየተ፡ አስማተ፡ ሊስ፡ አሊፍ፡ ላፍ፡ ካፍ፡ ጸላ፡ ወሠውሪ፡ . . . አስካአሜኤሊኪ፡ ካዜእርና፡ ኪምክዮንሀሊ፡ አስሌ፡ ቤቃ፡ . . .
2. Prayer against terrorizing demons and the evil eye of Barya, the evil eye of Zar, 35 lines. Prayer: against terrorizing demons and the evil eye of Barya, the evil eye of Zar".
   በስመ፡ አብ፡ . . . ጸሎት፡ በእንተ፡ መደንግጸ፡ አጋንንት፡ ወዓይነተ፡ ባርያ፡ ወዓይን፡ ዛር፡ ወኮሉ፡ ፀብእ፡ አጋንንት፡ እለዘ፡ (sic) ወመለኪ፡ ወያኑሪ፡ እልበረጀ፡ ወመጀኑን፡ እላሃ፡ እለመንሙናበ፡ መለርፉ፡ በሹኒ፡ ንሀም፡ መሽተራሚ፡ ቃለ፡ ሆሼቤን፡ ወለጀላንትሽንድናሂ፡ በዝ፡ አስማት፡ ወበዝ፡ ቃላት፡ አድኀና፡ እምዓይነተ፡ ባርያ፡ ወሌጌያን፡ ለዓመትከ፡ . . . አላኩ፡ . . . ወዝ፡ ውእቱ፡ አስማቲሆሙ፡ ለአብ፡ . . . ጀር፡[2x] ኢይምጽኡ፡ አጋንንት፡ በሀልም፡ ሌሊት፡ ወመዓልት፡ አምህልኩክሙ፡ ወአውገዝኩክሙ፡ በጀቅንዋተ፡ መስቀሉ፡ ለእግዚእነ፡ . . . ሳድር፡ አላዶር፡ . . . በዝንቱ፡ አስማት፡ አድኀና፡ . . . ወገጹ፡ ዘፍጹም፡ በጽልመት፡ ፈርህ፡ ወደንገጸ፡ ዲያብሎስ፡ ርኢዮ፡ ብሑተ፡ ልደት፡ በሥጋ፡ አምላካ፡ (sic) በሲኤል፡
3. The Net of Solomon for catching demons, 36 lines.
   በስመ፡ አብ፡ . . . አስማተ፡ ሰሎሞን፡ ዘረበበሙ፡ ለአጋንንት፡ ከመ፡ መርበብተ፡ ዓሣ፡ ዘባሕር፡ እንዘ፡ ይብል፡ ሰሎሞን፡[2x] ንቡር፡ መናትዮን፡ ጉጀ፡ በኃያለ፡ ዝንቱ፡ አስማቲክ፡ ፈቀጀ፡ ያትብው፡ ጀበጀር፡ አጀብ፡ በስመ፡ እግ"፡ ብርሃን፡ በእንተ፡ ማዕሡሩ፡ ለሰይጣን፡ ሶጺራ፡ አስጺራ፡ ጉጉባክን፡ ጨርጨቢ፡[2x] ደመዓቱ፡ ፈጮራጨጀጀያ፡ (sic) መሽብረ፡ አጋንንት፡ በፍጡን፡ ያሽሐብር፡ ያዘዋብል፡ ሰይጣናተ፡ በጼቃ፡ ፍዘዘ፡ ወበሲቃ፡ ሀዘዘ፡ ጀበሆም፡ ንበቡ፡ ጠበጁሐም፡ (sic) ተናገሩ፡ ኮልክሙ፡ . . .
4. The prayer titled "Rampart of the Cross," 22 lines.
   በስመ፡ አብ፡ . . . ጸሎት፡ በእንተ፡ ሐፁረ፡ መስቀል፡ አአትብ፡ በስመ፡ አብ፡ ወወልድ፡ ወመንፈስ፡ ቅዱስ፡ ፫አስማተ፡ ነዊእየ፡ እትመረጎዝ፡ እሙኒ፡ ወደቁ፡ እትነሣእ፡ . . .
5. Prayer against illnesses caused by the evil eye of Barya, and the evil eyes of others, which is a prayer against the evil eye of the sorcerer at the Sea of Tiberias, unfinished and the last few lines are insufficiently legible.

በስመ፡ አብ፡ . . . ጸሎት፡ በእንተ፡ ሕማመ፡ ዓይነተ፡ ባርያ፡ ወዓይነ፡ ጽላ፡ ዘውእቱ፡ ጸሎተ፡ ንድራ፡ ወእንዘ፡ ይነብር፡ (sic)እግዚእን፡ ወመድኃኒነ፡ ምስለ፡ Ī ወክልኤቱ፡አርዳኢሁ፡ ርኢዮ፡ . . .

Miniatures and Magical Symbols:
1. Panel with diamond-shaped face with eyes; *haräg* below.
2. Two panels: upper, talismanic symbol with face in the center; lower, angel with sword and scabbard.
3. Talismanic symbol with face in the center.

Copied for Wälättä Giyorgis

EMIP MagSc 130 – Weiner Magic Scroll 88

Parchment, 197 x 8.3 cm, three strips sewn together, one column, colored (yellow) border, Gəʿəz, 20th cent.

1. Prayer of St. Susənyos against Barya, Legewon, Däsk, Gudale, and the story of his fight against Wərzəlya.

በስመ፡ አብ፡ . . . ጸሎት፡ በእንተ፡ ባርያ፡ ወሌጌዎን፡ ደስክ፡ ወጉዳሌ፡ ወያበሐንን፡ (sic) ወበሕልመ፡ ሌሊት፡ ወመአልት፡ በስመ፡ እግ"፡ ሕያው፡ . .

2. Prayer related to the rampart of the cross that the Lord gave to the Disciples against fear before kings.

በስመ፡ አብ፡ . . . ጸሎት፡ በእንተ፡ ሐጹረ፡ መስቀል፡ ዘ፻፡ ሐፁሩ፡ (sic) በእንተ፡ ዘተመንደቡ፡ በእንተ፡ ፍርሐተ፡ ንጉስ፡ አሕዛበ፡ ምድር፡ ዘወሀበ፡ እግ"፡ ለአርዳኢሁ፡ ከመ፡ ይባኡ፡ በዝንቱ፡ ስምከ፡ ከመ፡ ይባዙ/ፁ፡ (?) በላእሌሆሙ፡ አጋንንት፡ . . .

3. Prayer related to the rampart of the cross for acquiring grace before kings and rulers as Paul before God.

በስመ፡ አብ፡ . . . ጸሎት፡ በእንተ፡ ሐጹረ፡ መስቀል፡ በቅድመ፡ ነገስተ፡ ምድር፡ ወመኳንንት፡ በከመ፡ ጳውሎስ፡ ሞገሰ፡ በቅድመ፡ እግ"፡ ከማሁ፡ ሀቦ፡ በዝንቱ፡ ሐጹረ፡ መስቀል፡ . . . በዝንቱ፡ ሐፁረ፡ መስቀል፡ ክርስቶስ፡ ወልዑል፡ . . . እቀብኒ፡ . . . በዝንቱ፡ ስምከ፡ ዘተአመነ . . .

Miniatures and Magical Symbols:
1. Angel with sword and scabbard.
2. Ornate cross with two people, one on each side.
3. Square panel with face in the center.
4. Small strip with sawtooth design.

Copied carelessly for Dässəta; other names, one of which could be Dässəta's:
    Wälättä Iyyäsus, Muluyyä Wälättä Səllase, Amätä Iyyäsus/Dässəta

EMIP MagSc 131 – Weiner Magic Scroll 89

Parchment, 173 x 8.5 cm, three strips sewn together, one column, colored (yellow) border, Gəʿəz, 20th cent.

1. Prayer for binding filthy demons, 23 lines.
   በስመ፡ አብ፡ . . . ጸሎት፡ በእንተ፡ ማእሰረ፡ አጋንንት፡ ርኩስ፡ ዘይሰልብ፡ ልቡ፡ ሰብእ፡ ወያጻልም፡ አዕይንተ፡ ወያበሐንን፡ በሕልም፡ ሌሊት . . . ወአመሐልኩክሙ፡ ወአውገዝኩክሙ፡ በ፫ቅንዋተ፡ መስቀሉ፡ . . .
2. Prayer of St. Susənyos for binding demons, and the story of his fight against Wərzəlya.
3. The prayer titled, Rampart of the Cross, 11 lines.
4. Prayer against hemorrhage, 23 lines.
   በስመ፡ አብ፡ . . . ጸሎት፡ በእንተ፡ ሐጋመ፡ ደም፡ ቀተም፡ ሰተም፡ ሳንዕልእም፡ ዘወጽአ፡ ደም፡ እምገቦሁ፡ . . . ሊስ፡ አፍሊስ፡ መልዮስ፡ . . . ወገጹ፡ ዘፍጹም፡ በጽልመት፡ . . .
5. Prayer for binding filthy demons, 50 lines; cf. 39, 6.
   በስመ፡ አብ፡ . . . ጸሎት፡ በእንተ፡ ማእሰረ፡ አጋንንት፡ በስሙ፡ ለእግ"፡ አብ፡ . . .

Miniatures and Magical Symbols:
1. Angel with sword and scabbard (large).
2. Ornate cross (large).
3. Nine-box panel with geometric designs and patterns.

1 and 2 copied for Wälättä Maryam but replaced with Wälättä Kidan/Adanäñña; the rest copied carefully for ʿƎnkʷäy Lul.

EMIP MagSc 132 – Weiner Magic Scroll 90

Parchment, 206 x 7.4 cm, three strips sewn together, one column, no border, Gəʿəz, 20th cent.

1. Greeting to Phanuel as prayer binding and driving away demons, cf. 6, 3.
   በስመ፡ አብ፡ . . . ጸሎት፡ በእንተ፡ ማዕሡረ፡ አጋንንት፡ ወስዳዴ፡ ሰይጣናት፡ ፋኑኤል፡ ለእግ"፡ እምጽርሑ፡ . . . ሰላም፡ ለኪ፡ መቅደሰ፡ አሪት፡ . . .
2. Prayer against hemorrhage; cf. 114, 2.
   በስመ፡ አብ፡ . . . ጸሎት፡ በእንተ፡ ሐጋመ፡ ደም፡ ሠራዊተ፡ መላእክቲሁ፡ . . .
3. Prayer for drowning Barya and Legewon, 59 lines; cf. 89, 1.
   በስመ፡ አብ፡ . . . ጸሎት፡ ሐጋመ፡ በእንተ፡ መሡጥ[መ፡] ባር፡ (sic) ወሌጌዎን፡ Fዛk፡ ምላህ፡ አንሰሩፉ፡ ድሁᶰድ፡ ሐሙ፡ . . . ጬተኩታኤል፡ ዘአብረከሙ፡ ለአዕዋፌ፡ ሰማይ፡ በመጥር፡ አጥበርብር፡ ወአድበርብር፡ . . .

Miniatures and Magical Symbols:
1. Angel with sword

2. Talismanic symbol with face in the center, above and below are two boxes side by side with X-shaped patterns.
3. Cross (painted brown) with face above. Above and below are two boxes side by side with X-shaped patterns.

Copied for Marsa/Wälättä Maryam.

EMIP MagSc 133 – Weiner Magic Scroll 91

Parchment, 202 x 8.3 cm, three strips sewn together, one column, colored (yellow or brown) border, Gəʿəz, early 20th cent.

1. Prayer for binding filthy demons and defiled spirits, cf. 124, 5.
   በስመ፡ አብ፡ . . . ጸሎት፡ በእንተ፡ ማዕሰረ፡ አጋንንት፡ ወመናፍስተ፡ ርኩሳን፡ ስሙ፡ ለአብ፡ ሰዳዬ፡ ፀር፡ . . .
2. Prayer for binding filthy demons and defiled spirits, 8 lines.
   በስመ፡ አብ፡ . . . ጸሎት፡ በእንተ፡ ማዕሰረ፡ አጋንንት፡ ወመፍስተ፡ (sic) ርኩሳን፡ ሳዶር፡ አላዶር፡ . . .
3. Prayer against the evil eye, Barya and Legewon, 33 lines.
   በስመ፡ አብ፡ . . . ጸሎት፡ በእንተ፡ አይነ፡ ጥላ፡ ወባርያ፡ ወሎግዮን፡ (sic) ደርብዮን፡ መርከብዮን፡ መፍርሃከን፡ ጉዳሌ፡ ደስክ፡ በፌያ፡ መሐዊለ፡ እሳት፡ . . . በአብ፡ እትዌከል፡ ወበወልድ፡ እትኬለል፡ ወበመንፈስ፡ ቅዱስ፡ እኤለል፡ ሳዶር፡ አላዶር፡ . . .
4. Prayer against hemorrhage.
   በስመ፡ አብ፡ . . . ጸሎት፡ በእንተ፡ ሀማመ፡ ደም፡ አብረሬ፡ አሽሬ፡ በአብራሀክም፡ ፈጠፈጠሀክም፡ በፖልሽም፡ መሐጅም፡ . . . ሊስ፡ አፍሊስ፡ መሊስ፡ መላሊስ፡ ሞሉስ፡ . . .
5. Prayer against charm; cf. 22, 1.
   በስመ፡ አብ፡ . . . ጸሎት፡ በእንተ፡ መፍትሔ፡ ሥራይ፡ ዘተደገመ፡ ወዘተገብረ[፡] በሰው፡ ፀጉር፡ ወበሰው፡ አዕንት፡ . . .
6. Prayer of St. Susənyos against illnesses caused by Barya and Šotälay, and the story of his fight against Wərzəlya.

Miniatures and Magical Symbols:
1. Angel with sword and scabbard.
2. Two men with long processional crosses.
3. Talismanic symbol with face in the center.

Copied for Wälättä Ṣadəq.

EMIP MagSc 134 – Weiner Magic Scroll 92

Parchment, 115 x 8.8 cm, two strips sewn together, one column, no border, Gəʿəz, 20th cent.

1. Prayer against the evil eye, the evil eye of Nas, Buda, Wägi, Zar, . . ., 24 lines.
   በስመ፡ አብ፡ . . . ጸሎት፡ በእንተ፡ ዓይነ፡ ጽላ፡ ወዓይነ፡ ወርቅ፡ ወዓይነ፡ ናስ፡ ወዓይነ፡ ቡዳ፡ ወዓይነ፡ ወጊ፡ ወዓይነ፡ ሰብእ፡ ወእጀ፡ ሰብእ፡ ወጽላ፡ ወጊ፡ ወዓይነ፡ ዛር፡ ወዓይነ፡ ውግዓት፡ ወቁርጥማት፡ ፍልጠት፡ ወቁርፀት፡ ፈሪ፡ ወንዳድ፡ ባርከኒ፡ ክርስቶስ፡ . . . በስሙ፡ ለአብ፡ ሙራኤል፡ በስሙ፡ ለወልድ፡ አብያቴር፡ . . . ፱ቱ፡ መናፍስተ፡ ርኩሳን፡ . . .

2. Net of Solomon; cf. 13, 3; 29, 1; 37, 1.
   በስመ፡ አብ፡ . . . ጸሎት፡ በእንተ፡ መርበብተ፡ ሰሎሞን፡ ከመ፡ መርበብተ፡ ዓሣ፡ ዘባሕር፡ ነዓ፡ ጎቤየ፡ ገብርኤል፡ እንዘ፡ ይብል፡ በደመና፡ ሰማይ፡ እንተ፡ ይእቲ፡ ወክድንት፡ ይእቲ፡ መርመሪ፡:³ˣ አብቴሪ፡:³ˣ ነዓ፡ ጎቤየ፡ ገር፡ (sic) ገብርኤል፡ ወነዓ፡ ፍቁርየ፡ ሚካኤል፡ መልአክ፡ እንዘ፡ ይብል፡ ሰዱቃኤል፡:⁷ˣ አዳታኤል፡:⁷ˣ . . .

3. Prayer regarding the rampart of the cross, ascribed to Jeremiah; cf. 5, 3.

Miniatures and Magical Symbols:
1. Three faces with wings, leafed *haräg* above and below.
2. Talismanic symbol with four faces, leafed *haräg* above and below.
3. Two faces with wings (lower upside down), leafed *haräg* above and below.

Copied for Mäsärät/Wälättä Sänbät

List of the Manuscripts by EMIP Number and Owner Number

Codices

EMIP 1 = Herron Codex
EMIP 2 = Eliza Codex 1
EMIP 3 = Eliza Codex 2
EMIP 4 = Eliza Codex 3
EMIP 5 = Marwick Codex 1
EMIP 6 = Marwick Codex 2
EMIP 7 = Marwick Codex 3
EMIP 8 = Marwick Codex 4
EMIP 9 = Marwick Codex 5
EMIP 10 = Marwick Codex 6
EMIP 11 = Marwick Codex 7
EMIP 12 = Marwick Codex 8
EMIP 13 = Marwick Codex 9
EMIP 14 = Marwick Codex 10
EMIP 15 = Marwick Codex 11
EMIP 16 = Marwick Codex 12
EMIP 17 = Marwick Codex 13
EMIP 18 = Marwick Codex 14
EMIP 19 = Marwick Codex 15
EMIP 20 = Marwick Codex 16
EMIP 21 = Marwick Codex 17
EMIP 22 = Marwick Codex 18
EMIP 23 = Marwick Codex 19
EMIP 24 = Marwick Codex 20
EMIP 25 = Eliza Codex 4
EMIP 26 = Eliza Codex 5
EMIP 27 = Eliza Codex 6
EMIP 28 = Eliza Codex 7
EMIP 29 = Whisnant Codex 1
EMIP 30 = Whisnant Codex 2
EMIP 31 = Earl Codex
EMIP 32 = Delamarter Codex 1
EMIP 33 = Eliza Codex 8
EMIP 34 = Eliza Codex 9
EMIP 35 = Eliza Codex 10
EMIP 36 = Eliza Codex 11
EMIP 37 = Eliza Codex 12
EMIP 38 = Eliza Codex 13
EMIP 39 = Eliza Codex 14
EMIP 40 = Eliza Codex 15
EMIP 41 = Eliza Codex 16
EMIP 42 = Eliza Codex 17
EMIP 43 = Eliza Codex 18
EMIP 44 = Eliza Codex 19
EMIP 45 = Eliza Codex 20
EMIP 46 = Eliza Codex 21
EMIP 47 = Eliza Codex 22
EMIP 48 = Eliza Codex 23
EMIP 49 = Eliza Codex 24
EMIP 50 = Eliza Codex 25
EMIP 51 = Eliza Codex 26
EMIP 52 = Eliza Codex 27
EMIP 53 = Eliza Codex 28
EMIP 54 = Eliza Codex 29
EMIP 55 = Trinity Western University Codex 1
EMIP 56 = Trinity Western University Codex 2
EMIP 57 = Trinity Western University Codex 3

EMIP 58 = Tsunami Codex
EMIP 59 = Kahan Codex
EMIP 60 = Eliza Codex 30
EMIP 61 = Eliza Codex 31
EMIP 62 = Eliza Codex 32
EMIP 63 = Eliza Codex 33
EMIP 64 = Eliza Codex 34
EMIP 65 = Eliza Codex 35
EMIP 66 = Eliza Codex 36
EMIP 67 = Focanti Codex 1
EMIP 68 = Focanti Codex 2
EMIP 69 = Focanti Codex 3
EMIP 70 = Marwick Codex 22
EMIP 71 = University of Oregon Museum of Natural and Cultural History, 10–845
EMIP 72 = University of Oregon Museum of Natural and Cultural History, 10–843
EMIP 73 = University of Oregon Museum of Natural and Cultural History, 10–844
EMIP 74 = Mount Angel Codex 46
EMIP 75 = Weiner Codex 1
EMIP 76 = Weiner Codex 2
EMIP 77 = Bernhardt Codex
EMIP 78 = Eliza Codex 37
EMIP 79 = Eliza Codex 38
EMIP 80 = Eliza Codex 39

EMIP 81 = Eliza Codex 40
EMIP 82 = Eliza Codex 41
EMIP 83 = Weiner Codex 3
EMIP 84 = Delamarter Codex 2
EMIP 85 = Trinity Western University Codex 4
EMIP 86 = Marwick Codex 21
EMIP 87 = Weiner Codex 4
EMIP 88 = Weiner Codex 5
EMIP 89 = Weiner Codex 6
EMIP 90 = Weiner Codex 7
EMIP 91 = Weiner Codex 8
EMIP 92 = Weiner Codex 9
EMIP 93 = Marwick Codex 23
EMIP 94 = Weiner Codex 10
EMIP 95 = Weiner Codex 11
EMIP 96 = Weiner Codex 12
EMIP 97 = Weiner Codex 13
EMIP 98 = Abilene Christian University Codex 1
EMIP 99 = Abilene Christian University Codex 2
EMIP 100 = Weiner Codex 14
EMIP 101 = Weiner Codex 15
EMIP 102 = Weiner Codex 16
EMIP 103 = Weiner Codex 17
EMIP 104 = Weiner Codex 18
EMIP 105 = Weiner Codex 19

Scrolls

EMIP MagSc 1 = Delamarter MagSc 2
EMIP MagSc 2 = Delamarter MagSc 3
EMIP MagSc 3 = Eliza MagSc 1
EMIP MagSc 4 = Eliza MagSc 2
EMIP MagSc 5 = Eliza MagSc 3

EMIP MagSc 6 = Marwick MagSc 1
EMIP MagSc 7 = Marwick MagSc 2
EMIP MagSc 8 = Marwick MagSc 3
EMIP MagSc 9 = Marwick MagSc 4
EMIP MagSc 10 = Marwick MagSc 5

EMIP MagSc 11 = Marwick MagSc 6
EMIP MagSc 12 = Marwick MagSc 7
EMIP MagSc 13 = Marwick MagSc 8
EMIP MagSc 14 = Marwick MagSc 9
EMIP MagSc 15 = Marwick MagSc 10
EMIP MagSc 16 = Marwick MagSc 11
EMIP MagSc 17 = Marwick MagSc 12
EMIP MagSc 18 = Marwick MagSc 13
EMIP MagSc 19 = Marwick MagSc 14
EMIP MagSc 20 = Marwick MagSc 15
EMIP MagSc 21 = Marwick MagSc 16
EMIP MagSc 22 = Marwick MagSc 17
EMIP MagSc 23 = Marwick MagSc 18
EMIP MagSc 24 = Marwick MagSc 19
EMIP MagSc 25 = Marwick MagSc 20
EMIP MagSc 26 = Marwick MagSc 21
EMIP MagSc 27 = Marwick MagSc 22
EMIP MagSc 28 = Marwick MagSc 23
EMIP MagSc 29 = Marwick MagSc 24
EMIP MagSc 30 = Marwick MagSc 25
EMIP MagSc 31 = Marwick MagSc 26
EMIP MagSc 32 = Marwick MagSc 27
EMIP MagSc 33 = Marwick MagSc 28
EMIP MagSc 34 = Marwick MagSc 29
EMIP MagSc 35 = Marwick MagSc 30
EMIP MagSc 36 = Marwick MagSc 31
EMIP MagSc 37 = Marwick MagSc 32
EMIP MagSc 38 = Bowerman Hall MagSc 1
EMIP MagSc 39 = Bowerman Hall MagSc 2
EMIP MagSc 40 = Weiner MagSc 1
EMIP MagSc 41 = Weiner MagSc 2
EMIP MagSc 42 = Weiner MagSc 3
EMIP MagSc 43 = Weiner MagSc 4
EMIP MagSc 44 = Weiner MagSc 5
EMIP MagSc 45 = Weiner MagSc 6
EMIP MagSc 46 = Weiner MagSc 7
EMIP MagSc 47 = Weiner MagSc 8
EMIP MagSc 48 = Weiner MagSc 9
EMIP MagSc 49 = Weiner MagSc 10
EMIP MagSc 50 = Weiner MagSc 11
EMIP MagSc 51 = Weiner MagSc 12
EMIP MagSc 52 = Weiner MagSc 13
EMIP MagSc 53 = Weiner MagSc 14
EMIP MagSc 54 = Weiner MagSc 15
EMIP MagSc 55 = Weiner MagSc 16
EMIP MagSc 56 = Weiner MagSc 17
EMIP MagSc 57 = Weiner MagSc 18
EMIP MagSc 58 = Weiner MagSc 19
EMIP MagSc 59 = Weiner MagSc 20
EMIP MagSc 60 = Weiner MagSc 21
EMIP MagSc 61 = Weiner MagSc 22
EMIP MagSc 62 = Weiner MagSc 23
EMIP MagSc 63 = Weiner MagSc 24
EMIP MagSc 64 = Weiner MagSc 25
EMIP MagSc 65 = Weiner MagSc 26
EMIP MagSc 66 = Weiner MagSc 27
EMIP MagSc 67 = Weiner MagSc 28
EMIP MagSc 68 = Weiner MagSc 29
EMIP MagSc 69 = Weiner MagSc 30
EMIP MagSc 70 = Weiner MagSc 31
EMIP MagSc 71 = Weiner MagSc 32
EMIP MagSc 72 = Weiner MagSc 33
EMIP MagSc 73 = Weiner MagSc 34
EMIP MagSc 74 = Weiner MagSc 35
EMIP MagSc 75 = Weiner MagSc 36
EMIP MagSc 76 = Weiner MagSc 37
EMIP MagSc 77 = Weiner MagSc 38
EMIP MagSc 78 = Weiner MagSc 39
EMIP MagSc 79 = Weiner MagSc 40
EMIP MagSc 80 = Weiner MagSc 41
EMIP MagSc 81 = Weiner MagSc 42
EMIP MagSc 82 = Weiner MagSc 43
EMIP MagSc 83 = Weiner MagSc 44
EMIP MagSc 84 = Weiner MagSc 45
EMIP MagSc 85 = Weiner MagSc 46
EMIP MagSc 86 = Weiner MagSc 47

EMIP MagSc 87 = Weiner MagSc 48
EMIP MagSc 88 = Weiner MagSc 49
EMIP MagSc 89 = Weiner MagSc 50
EMIP MagSc 90 = Weiner MagSc 51
EMIP MagSc 91 = Weiner MagSc 52
EMIP MagSc 92 = Weiner MagSc 53
EMIP MagSc 93 = Weiner MagSc 54
EMIP MagSc 94 = Weiner MagSc 55
EMIP MagSc 95 = Weiner MagSc 56
EMIP MagSc 96 = Weiner MagSc 57
EMIP MagSc 97 = Weiner MagSc 58
EMIP MagSc 98 = Weiner MagSc 59
EMIP MagSc 99 = Weiner MagSc 60
EMIP MagSc 100 = Weiner MagSc 61
EMIP MagSc 101 = Weiner MagSc 62
EMIP MagSc 102 = Weiner MagSc 63
EMIP MagSc 103 = Weiner MagSc 64
EMIP MagSc 104 = Weiner MagSc 65
EMIP MagSc 105 = Weiner MagSc 66
EMIP MagSc 106 = Weiner MagSc 67
EMIP MagSc 107 = Weiner MagSc 68
EMIP MagSc 108 = Weiner MagSc 69
EMIP MagSc 109 = Weiner MagSc 70
EMIP MagSc 110 = Weiner MagSc 71
EMIP MagSc 111 = Weiner MagSc 72
EMIP MagSc 112 = Weiner MagSc 73
EMIP MagSc 113 = Weiner MagSc 74
EMIP MagSc 114 = Weiner MagSc 75
EMIP MagSc 115 = Weiner MagSc 76
EMIP MagSc 116 = Weiner MagSc 77
EMIP MagSc 117 = Weiner MagSc 78
EMIP MagSc 118 = Weiner MagSc 79
EMIP MagSc 119 = Weiner MagSc 80
EMIP MagSc 120 = Weiner MagSc 81
EMIP MagSc 121 = Weiner MagSc 82
EMIP MagSc 122 = Weiner MagSc 83
EMIP MagSc 123 = Weiner MagSc 84
EMIP MagSc 124 = Weiner MagSc 85
EMIP MagSc 125 = Weiner MagSc 86
EMIP MagSc 126 = Weiner MagSc 87
EMIP MagSc 127 = Abilene Christian University MagSc 1
EMIP MagSc 128 = Abilene Christian University MagSc 2
EMIP MagSc 129 = Abilene Christian University MagSc 3
EMIP MagSc 130 = Weiner MagSc 88
EMIP MagSc 131 = Weiner MagSc 89
EMIP MagSc 132 = Weiner MagSc 90
EMIP MagSc 133 = Weiner MagSc 91
EMIP MagSc 134 = Weiner MagSc 92

List of Dated or Datable Manuscripts

1706 – 8 (reign of Täklä Haymanot I): EMIP 72
1720 – 1743 (reign of Metropolitan Krestodolu): EMIP 46
1747 – 1761 (reign of Iyyo'as): EMIP 20
1770 – 1803 (reign of Metropolitan Yosab): EMIP 27
1855 – 1868 (reign of Tewodros): EMIP 43
1872 – 1889 (reign of Yoḥannəs IV): EMIP 81
1889 – 1926 (reign of Metropolitan Matewos): EMIP 77
1923: January 29 (Ṭərr 21, 1915): EMIP 11
1923/24 (1916 EC): EMIP 37
1928 – 1942 (reign of Patriarch Yoḥannəs XIX): EMIP 80 and 82
1940: November 5 (Ṭəqəmt 27, 1933 EC): EMIP 31
1930 – 1974 (reign of Haile Sellasie): EMIP 59
2000: December 2 (Ḫədar 23, 1993EC): EMIP 38

List of Undated and Composite Manuscripts

16th Century
    16th century: EMIP 15 (composite), 42 (composite).

17th Century
    17th century: EMIP 57 and 99.
    Late 17th century: EMIP 1, 12, and 19.

18th Century
    Early 18th century: EMIP 13, 18, and 24.
    18th century: EMIP 2, 6, 9, 29, 30, 34, 42 (composite), 53, 60, 66, 68, 69, 83, 89, and 102.
    Late 18th century: EMIP 7 and 33 (composite).
    18th/19th century: EMIP 64.

19th Century
    Early 19th century: EMIP 21, 36, and 96.
    19th century: EMIP 8, 14, 10 (composite), 15 (composite), 16, 23, 33 (composite), 35, 39, 45, 50, 56 (composite), 67, 76, 78, 97, 98, 100, 101, 104, and 105.
    Late 19th century: EMIP 28, 93, and 95.
    19th/20th century: EMIP 5, 40, 51, 52, 54, 55, 58, 62, 75, and 86.

20th Century
    Early 20th century: EMIP 48 and 65.
    20th century: EMIP 4, 10 (composite), 17, 22, 25, 26, 41, 47, 49, 56 (composite), 61, 63, 70, 71, 73, 74, 79, 85, 87, 88, 90, 91, 92, 94, and 103.
    Late 20th century: EMIP 3, 32, 37 (composite), 44, and 84.

Bibliography

Basset, René. *Les Apocryphes éthiopiens traduit en français I–XI*. Paris: Bibliotheque de la Haute Science, 1803–1909.

Budge, E. A. Wallis. *One Hundred and Ten Miracles of Our Lady Mary*. London: Oxford University Press, 1933.

Cerulli, Enrico. *Il libro etiopico dei Miracoli di Maria e le sue fonti nelle letterature del medio evo latino*. Studi orientali, v. 1. Roma: G. Bardi, 1943.

Chaîne, Marius. "Répertoire des salam et de malk'e contenus dans les manuscrits éthiopiens des bibliothèques d'Europe." *ROC*, 2e série, 8 18 (1913) 183–205 and 337–57.

Conti Rossini, Carlo. "Manoscritti ed opera abissine in Europa" In *Rendiconti della Reale Accademia dei Lincei. Classe di scienze morali, storiche e filologiche*, 5, 8 (1899) 606–37.

Conti Rossini, Carlo. "Notice sur les manuscrits éthiopiens de la collection d'Abbadie." Extrait du *JA* (1912–1914) Paris 1914.

Delamarter, Steve. "Catalogues and Digitization for Previously Uncatalogued Ethiopian Manuscripts in the United States." In *Proceedings of the Sixteenth International Conference of Ethiopian Studies*. Forthcoming.

Delamarter, Steve. "More Ethiopian Manuscripts in North America." *SBL Forums*, November, 2007. Online: http://www.sbl-site.org/publications/article.aspx?ArticleId=736.

Delamarter, Steve. "The SGD Digital Collection: Previously Unknown and Uncatalogued Ethiopian Manuscripts in North America." *SBL Forums*, February 2007. Online:http://www.sbl-site.org/Article.aspx?ArticleId=622.

Delamarter, Steve, and Demeke Berhane. *A Catalogue of Previously Uncatalogued Ethiopic Manuscripts in England: Twenty-Three Manuscripts in the Bodleian, Cambridge University and John Rylands University Libraries and in a Private Collection*. Journal of Semitic Studies 21. Oxford: Oxford University Press on behalf of the University of Manchester, 2007.

Dillmann, Augustus. *Chrestomathia Aethiopica*. 1866. Reprint Darmstadt: Wissenschaftliche Buchgesellschaft, 1967.
Daoud, Marcos, and H. E. Blatta Marsie Hazen. *The Liturgy of the Ethiopian Church*. Cairo: Egyptian Book Press, 1959.
Dobberahn, Friedrich Erich. *Funf Athiopische Zauberrollen: Text, Ubersetzung, Kommentar. Vorgelegt Von Friedrich Erich Dobberahn*. Bonn: Rheinische Friedrich-Wilhelms-Universitat, 1976.
Euringer, Sebastian. "Das Netz Salomons." *ZS* 6 (1928) 76–100, 179–199 and 300–314; and 7 (1929) 68–85.
Euringer, Sebastian. "Die Binde der Rechtfertigun (Lefâfa ṣedek)." *Or* NS 9 (1940) 76–99 and 244–59.
Fries, Karl. "The Ethiopic Legend of Socinius and Ursula." In *Actes du Huitème Congrès International des Orientalistes*, I, 2, Leiden (1893) 55–70.
Getatchew. *The Epistle of Humanity of Emperor Zär'a Ya'əqob (Ṭomarä Təsbə't)*, CSCO, text vol.522, script. aeth. 95; tr. vol. 523, script. aeth. 96 (1991).
Getatchew. *The Gə'əz Acts of Abba Ǝsṭifanos of G^wəndag^wənde*, CSCO, vol. 619/620, forthcoming.
Grébaut, Sylvain. "La prière de Marie au Golgotha." *JA* 226 (1935) 273–86.
Grébaut, Sylvain. "Les miracles de Jésus. Texte éthiopien publié et traduit." *PO* 12 (1919) 551–649 (I); 14 (1920) 767–840 (II); and 17 (1923) 783–854 (III).
Grébaut, Sylvain. "Petit Ḥaṣoura Masqal." *Æthiops*, 6me année, no. 1 (1938) 12–13.
Grébaut, Sylvain. "La prière *Sayfa malakot*," *Aethiopica* 4 (1936) 1–6.
Grébaut, Sylvain. "La légend de Sousneyos et de Werzelyâ d'après de ms. Éthiopien Griaule n° 297," *Or* NS, VI (1937) 177–183.
Grohmann, Adolf. *Aethiopische Marienhymnen*. Abhandlungen der Philologisch-Historischen Klasse der Sächsischen Akademie der Wissenschaften 33,4. Leipzig: Teubner, 1919.
Guerrier, Louis. *Le Testament en Galilée de Notre-Seigneur Jésus-Christ: texte éthiopien, édité et traduit en français*. PO, t. 9, fasc. 3. Paris: Firmin-Didot, 1913.
Hammerschmidt, Ernst. *Aethiopische liturgische Texte der Bodleian Library in Oxford*. Veröffentlichung, Nr. 38. Berlin: Akademie, 1960.
Harden, J. M. *The Ethiopic Didascalia*. London: SPCK, 1920.

Krestos Samra, and Enrico Cerulli. *Atti di Krestos Samra. CSCO*, v. 163–164. Scriptores Aethiopici, t. 33–34. Louvain: Durbecq, 1956.

Lifchitz, Déborah, and Sylvain Grébaut. *Textes éthiopiens magico-religieux*. Paris: Institut d'ethnologie, 1940.

Littmann, Enno. "Arde'et: The Magic book of the Disciples." *JAOS*. 25 (1904) 1–48.

Löfgren, Oscar. "Äthiopische Wandamulette." *Orientalia Suecana* 11 (1962) 95–120.

Mercier, Jacques. *Zauberrollen aus Äthiopien: Kultbilder magischer Riten*. Munich: Prestel, 1979.

Pankhurst, Richard. "A Serious Question of Ethiopian Studies: Five Thousand Ethiopian Manuscripts Abroad, and the International Community," *Addis Tribune*, 17 December 1999; available online at http://www.afromet.org/Archives/AddisTribune/17-12-99/Five.htm.

Pereira, F. M. Esteves. *Acta Martyrum I, CSCO*, vol. 37, script. aeth. t. 20, reprint, 1962, 259–75.

Six, Veronika. *Äthiopische Handschriften, Teil 3: Handschriften Deutscher Bibliotheken, Museen und Privatbesitz*. Stuttgart: Steiner, 1994.

Six, Veronika. "Kategorien der äthiopischen Zaubertexte." *ZDMG* 139 (1989) 310–17.

Strelcyn, Stefan. *Catalogue of Ethiopian Manuscripts in the British Library Acquired since the Year 1877*. London: British Museum Publications, 1978.

Strelcyn, Stefan. *Catalogue des manuscrits éthiopiens de l'Accademia Nazionale dei Lincei: Fonds Conti Rossini et Fonds Caetani 209, 375, 376, 377, 378*. Rome: Accademia Nazionale dei Lincei, 1976.

Strelcyn, Stefan. *Catalogue of Ethiopic Manuscripts in the John Rylands University Library of Manchester*. Manchester: Manchester University Press, 1974.

Strelcyn, Stefan. *Prières magique éthiopiens pour délier les charmes (maftəḥ šəray)*. Rocznik orientalistyczny, t. 18, Warsaw: Panstwowe Wydawnictwo Naukowe, 1955.

Strelcyn, Stefan. "Catalogue of Ethiopic Manuscripts of the Wellcome Institute of the History of Medicine in London." *Bulletin of the School of Oriental and African Studies*, University of London 35 (1972) 27–55.

Trumpp, Ernst. *Das Hexaëmeron des Pseudo-Epiphanius*. Abhandlungen der philosophisch-philologischen Classe der Königlich Bayerischen

Akademie der Wissenschaften, 16. Bd., 2. Abt., [5]. Munich: Franz, 1882.

Velat, Bernard. *Me'erāf.Commun del'office divin éthiopien pour toute l'année*. PO 34 (1966) I–XV and 1–413. Paris: Firmin-Didot et Cie, 1966.

Velat, Bernard. *Étude sur le Me'erāf. Commun del'office divin éthiopien. Introduction, traduction française, commentaire litugique et musica*. PO 33 (1966). Paris: Didot, 1966.

Wendt, Kurt. *Das Maṣḥafa Milād (Liber Nativitatis) und Maṣḥafa Sellāsē (Liber Trinitatis) des Kaisers Zar'a Yā'qob*. CSCO 41. Louvain: Secr. du CorpusSCO, 1962.

Worrell, William Hoyt. "Studien zum Abessinischen Zauberwesen." *Zeitschrift für Assyriologie und verwandte Gebiete* 23 (1909) 149–83, 24 (1910) 59–96, and 29 (1914) 85–141.

Index of Works in the Codices

Absolution of the Father, 105
Absolution of the Son, 26, 52, 213, 218
Acts of *Abunä* Tärbu, 172
Admonition, 144
Alphabet, Amharic, 52, 259
Alphabet, Gəʿəz, 3, 6, 27
Anaphora
    of Athanasius the Apostolic, 76, 193
    of Basil, 193
    of Cyril of Alexandria, 159, 193
    of Dioscorus, 76, 159, 193
    of Epiphanius, 76, 159, 193
    of Gregory (I), 159
    of Gregory of Armenia, 193
    of Həryaqos, 76
    of James of Sarug, 76, 159, 193
    of John Chrysostom, 76, 159, 193
    of John, Son of Thunder, 76, 159, 193
    of Our Lady Mary, 74
    of Our Lady Mary ascribed to Cyriacus of Bəhənsa, 150, 157, 159, 193, 204
    of Our Lord Jesus Christ, 76, 105, 109, 159, 193
    of the 318 Orthodox Fathers, 76, 193
    of the Apostles, 76, 129, 159, 193

Antiphonary for the year, *Dəgg^{w}a*, 231
Antiphony for the Fast of Lent, 19
Arabic words transliterated into Amharic letters, 22
Asmat prayer, 77, 114, 136, 150, 161, 172, 205, 220, 249
    against charm, 120
    against epidemics and dysentery, 15
    against evil eye, 205
    against evil eye and charm, 201
    against evil eye and other evil spirits, 236
    against evil spirits, 176
    against fever and pestilence, 172
    against hemorrhage, 93, 194
    against pestilence, 207
    against rinderpest, 62
    against stomachache, 93, 220
    against the devil, 220
    against the enemy, 14, 54
    against the evil eye, 220, 221
    against the serpent, 174
    against thieves and robbers, 35
    for conception and against hemorrhage, 235

for help in learning, 77, 161, 194
for the days of the week, 177
for the revelation of divine matters, 106
of Jeremiah against the evil eye, 132
that God gave to Peter, 178
to brighten the mind, 207
to Jesus Christ against eye disease and headache, 161
to protect domestic animals from wild animals, 3, 39, 112
whose purpose is not stated, 207
Bandlet of Righteousness, 185, 199, 223, 224, 237
Baptismal Ritual, 89
Bible (besides Psalter)
   1 John, 98, 120
   General Epistles through Revelation, 34
   Gospel of John, 8, 69, 109, 119, 172, 206
   Gospel of Matthew 25, 161
Blessing of *Abunä* Yared, 90
Book of Hours of *Abba* Giyorgis, 265
Booklet of prayer that came down from heaven, 49, 91
Calendar
   of some feast days, 82
   of the Apostles and Evangelists, 71, 150, 161, 188, 207
   of the Archangel Michael's twelve feast days of the year, 35
   of the days of the year on which heaven is open to receive prayers, 107, 179
   of the feast days of the year, 111, 181, 205
   of the holy days of the year, 168
   of the year, 27, 39
   the lucky days of the year, 22
   time table for the use of the different anaphoras, 111
Canticles of Flower, 207
Catechism or Christian theology in modern Amharic, 29
Chant, 229
Chant for Easter, 98
Chants, *Mə'raf*, 232
Commentary on Hail Mary, Amharic, 144
Commentary on Our Father, Amharic, 128, 144, 170
Computus, 117, 119
Computus, excerpt, 71
Dəgg^{w}a, excerpt, 216
Five Pillars of Mystery, 144
Funeral Ritual, 184
Funeral Ritual, directory, 15
Gate of Light (see also, Psalter), 65, 123, 174
Genealogy of the early Shoan dynasty, 10
Glorification of the Trinity, 126
Good wishes for the teacher by the student, 52
Greek Names of the Nails of the Cross, 62
Greeting
   of the *Dərsanä Mika'el*, 61
   to Abib, 60
   to Abunafər, of Säne 16, 62

to Church, 251
to Mary, 111, 265
to Täklä Haymanot, 61
to the Archangel Michael, 16
to the Archangel Phanuel, 62
to the love of the Trinity, 18
to the suffering of Jesus Christ, 51
to the tongue, words and breath of the Archangel Raphael, 22
Halleluiatic hymn to Jesus Christ, 80
Halleluiatic hymn to the Trinity, 111, 117
History of Priest Yared, 91
History of the book and the benefit of praying with it, 50
Homiliary for the Monthly Feast of the Archangel Michael, 42, 202, 258
Horologium, 119
Horologium for Daytime Hours, 266
Horologium for Night Hours, 120, 194, 265
Hymn
Does not a man?, 266
God Reigns, 148
of the Nativity, 117
praising what Iyyo'as did for the monastery of *Abunä* Täklä Haymanot, 62
the first hymn of the Praises of Mary, 174
to Jesus Christ, 193
to Saint George, 193
to the Archangel Michael, 66
to the Martyr George, 111
to the Trinity, 193
Wise of the Wise, 14
Your power has been known, 51
Hymn to God
All spiritual hosts of angels, 144
Hymn to Jesus Christ
For the sake of your Trinity, 193
Glory to you in prostration, 265
I prostrate before your conception, 52
O you who came down from heaven, 266
Hymn to Mary, 36, 51
All hosts of heaven glorify you, 144
fragment, 22
I prostrate before you, 101, 120
Image of Edom, 50, 60
In heaven and on earth, 52
In the name of the Father and the Son, 112
Peace to you, Mary, 124
Rejoice Mary, the Pasch of Adam, 50
Rejoice, Mary, the Pasch of Adam, 265
Rejoice, Mary, virgin in body and mind, 265
Rejoice, you whom we beseech, 130
The Angels Praise Mary, 174, 210, 265
You are blessed, 193, 266
Hymn to Saint George (and Mary)
O who is quick for help, 105
Hymns
to Church, 51

to the Christian Sabbath, 51
Hymns, collection
  Does not a man?, 50
Image
  of Arägawi/Zä-Mika'el, 263
  of Fasiledes, 60
  of Gäbrä Mänfäs Qəddus, 60, 105, 263
  of Gabriel, 154, 193, 199, 264
  of George, 234, 264
  of Jesus Christ, 52, 60, 72, 74, 80, 154, 263
  of John the Baptist, 60
  of Kiros, 61, 120
  of Mäzra'tä Krəstos, 61
  of Mary, 72, 74, 79, 106, 154, 204, 263
  of Mary of Qʷəsqʷam, 15, 207
  of Mary's Assumption, 8, 36, 50
  of Mercurius, 101
  of Michael, 61, 74, 149, 154, 164, 234, 263
  of Phanuel, 213
  of Raguel, 109
  of Täklä Haymanot, 62, 104
  of the conception of George, 52
  of the Covenant of Mercy, 61
  of the Eucharist (known in the West as Community of the Faithful, 60
  of the Gate of Light, 105
  of the Icon, 119, 265
  of the Praises of Mary, 105
  of the Saintly Kings of the Zagʷe Dynasty, 58
  of the Savior of the World, 202, 234
  of the suffering of George, 52
  of the Trinity, 18, 61, 62, 117
Image of Mary's Icon, 73
Imposition of the hand of the Anaphora of Our Lord, 77
Imposition of the hand of the Anaphora of the 318 Orthodox Fathers, 77
Introductory Rite to the Miracles of Mary, Amharic commentary, 87
Journey to Heaven, 90
Lamentations of the Virgin, 15, 207
Lectionary for Passion Week, 116
Legend of Susənyos and the Witch Wurzəlya, 201
List of the first forty abbots of Däbrä Libanos, 15
List of the Sufferings of Jesus, 61, 205
Litanies, 123
Liturgical hymn to Jesus Christ, 79
Medical prescription, 138, 172
  against evil eye, 241
  against python and snakebite, 241
  for a person whom the enemy shut up, 242
  for an unspecified illness, 23
  for headache, 242
Miracles
  of *Abunä* Täklä Haymanot, 101, 102
  of Jesus, 102, 261

of Martyr Märqorewos, 102
of Mary, 87, 100, 148, 218, 266, 267
of Mary, Introductory Rite, 218
of Mercurius, 101
of the Archangel Michael, 69
of the Trinity, 17, 80
Missal, 76, 129, 159, 193
Monastic genealogy of the line of *Abunä* Ewosṭatewos, 194
Musical notation, 20, 62, 65, 98, 111, 116, 129, 159, 216, 229, 265, 266
Mystagogia, 10, 92, 111, 150, 175, 199, 204
Nä'a Dawit, 10
Nicene Creed, 220
Notes on orders of the rite of baptism and the Mass, 128
On the Christological controversies of the Gonderite era, 15
On the early life of Däbrä Asbo (Däbrä Libanos), 58
On the meaning of ኢዩ, 15
Ordinary of the Mass, 76, 123, 129, 159
Palace Etiquette at Susənyos's Court, 15
Praises of God, *Wəddase Amlak*, 57
Praises of Mary (see also, Psalter), 65, 123, 168, 174
Prayer
    about Melchisedek and the Paraclete, 178
    about the angel of death, 179
    about which the angels asked the Lord, 178
    after taking Communion, 105
    against abortion of animals, in Amharic, 241
    against demons, 204
    against evil spirits, 13, 176
    against pestilence, 13
    against the enemy, 194
    against the evil eye, 22, 106
    by Abbot Pachomius, 57
    by John Chrysostom, 57
    collection mostly rhyming hymns, 49
    compiled by Athanasius of Alexandria from Coptic hymns, 58
    compiled from the prayers of St. Cyril of Alexandria, 58
    compiled from the words of St. John (Saba), the Spiritual Elder, *Arägawi Mänfäsawi*, 57
    for blessing and the imposition of the hand, 89
    for Gäbrä Mika'el, 3
    for help in learning, 39
    for protection with the power of the Cross, 13
    for salvation from the sea of fire, hell, 207
    for salvation that descended to St. Thomas, 178
    for the de-consecration of the baptismal water, 89
    For the sake of the peaceful holy things, 62, 105
    given to the Apostles and Mary, 178
    God of the luminaries, 92, 105, 175

I take refuge, 92
Layman's prayer, 88
May the names of Christ sanctify us, 178
of Šärawitä mäla'əktihu of the different anaphoras, 77
of incense, 194
of mercy that the angels and the clergy prayed, 177
of the Apostles and Disciples for the forgiveness of sin, 178
of the different anaphoras, 111
of the Disciples for forgiveness of sin, 91
of the Twelve Disciples, 91
of Wäldä Mäsqäl for salvation with the *asmat* found in the *Dərsanä Mika'el* and the Hebrew letters found in Ps 118, 203
reward for praying certain prayers, 35
taken from a homily by St Ephrem the Syrian, 57
Taking Refuge with All Powers, 13
that God gave to Ananiah, Azariah and Michael, 179
that Our Lord told to St. Andrew, 179
that the angels told Enoch, 179
to Christ
for mercy, 178
to de-consecrate blessed baptismal water, 71
to God, 176
for forgiveness, 80
for protection, 220
to heal a wound, 194
to Jesus Christ, 50
for help and protection, 13
For the sake of your, 111
Guard me, 49
to keep Satan away, 178
to Mary, 73, 80, 85
Guard me, 50, 105
I take refuge, 50
to Mary, asking her intercession, 126
to Täklä Haymanot, 80
to the Trinity
I take refuge, 17
Prayer against the Tongue of People, 225
Prayer for the journey to heaven, 237
Prayer of Incense, 193
Prayer of Mary at Bartos, 104
Prayer of Mary at Golgotha, 146, 150, 175, 199, 218, 249
Prayer of the Covenant, 8, 32, 93, 105, 123, 159
Prayer:, 17, 18, 32, 48, 53, 62, 71, 93, 98, 107, 135, 145, 155, 220, 248
Psalms of David (see also, Psalter), 95
Psalter, 1, 5, 10, 21, 26, 29, 31, 36, 39, 54, 66, 70, 79, 82, 85, 97, 113, 119, 125, 132, 138, 140, 152, 156, 160, 164, 167, 187, 190, 197, 210, 213, 216, 220, 226, 228, 238, 241, 245, 247, 253, 256

Psalter with the Psalms of the Virgin, *Mäzmurä Dəngəl*, 5, 181, 250
Psalter, directory for reading, 10
Qəne poem, 80, 107, 229
Record
  Birth, 114
  Copied by, 3, 18, 69, 88, 93, 105, 107, 133, 165, 173, 174, 179, 208
  Copied for, 8, 15, 53, 54, 58, 61, 69, 74, 77, 88, 93, 103, 110, 112, 151, 157, 174, 176, 179, 194, 200, 219, 220, 234, 235, 249, 259, 264, 268
  Death, 22, 114
  Letter, 145
  Letter of Greeting, 35, 107
  List of fourteen contributors, 48
  List of names, 10
  Medical prescription, 112
  name of the intermediary, 226
  note, 32
  Note of age, 93
  Note of condolence, 220
  Note of ownership, 11, 16, 23, 29, 37, 39, 53, 55, 58, 83, 93, 95, 98, 107, 128, 130, 136, 145, 149, 173, 176, 181, 194, 203, 208, 211, 221, 224, 225, 226, 237, 256
  Note of ownership, 3
  Note on land ownership, 82
  Note on the contents of the book, 128
  Note, unintelligible, 6
  Notice of the year in which someone was ordained priest, 114
  of division of land, 136
  of marriage, 136
  of military expedition to Eritrea, 188
  of payment, 124
  of purchase, 30
  of purchase of land, 106, 203
  of purchase of the manuscript, 35, 80, 241, 251
  of settlement of dispute over property, 226
  of the purpose of money, 107
  of transaction, 181
  of transaction of a certain good, 174
  of unidentified incident, 155
  price of the manuscript, 6
  Receipt for money borrowed, 107
  Receipt of loan, 130
  Receipt of money borrowed, 245
  Receipt of the purchase of the manuscript, 150
  Settlement of an unidentifiable dispute, 10
  transaction, 220
  unintelligible note, 23, 27, 63, 130, 181
  vow, 154, 155
  Will, 93, 124, 226
Reward for reading the Gospel regularly, 207
Rogation
  Glorification of the beloved, 266
  of the Archangel Michael, 111
Song of Isaiah, 119

Song of Songs, common version, 2, 5, 10, 26, 29, 31, 36, 39, 54, 66, 70, 82, 85, 97, 132, 135, 140, 152, 156, 160, 164, 167, 181, 187, 197, 210, 213, 216, 220, 229, 238, 241, 245, 247, 250, 253, 256

Song of Songs, Hebraic version, 21, 79, 114, 125, 138, 190, 226

Stamp of ownership, 259

Story of the Sorcerer at the Sea of Tiberias, 10

Story of the Trinity, 90, 117

Supplication, 105, 123

Sword of Divinity, 92, 175

Sword of the Trinity, 17, 91, 117, 177

Symbolic interpretation of parts of a church building and its contents, in Amharic, 71

Synaxary entry of Roch, 13

Table blessing, 53, 71, 111, 181, 261

Table of Contents, 73

What to do when an enemy rises, 242

Wise saying, in Amharic, 144

Wisest of the Wise, 91

Zəmmare, 232

Index of Names and Places in the Codices

NB: Western names are put in the form "lastname, firstname"; Ethiopian names are put in the traditional form.

'Alämayyähu of Morät, *Abba*, 23
'Amäta Śəllase Ağori, 16
'Arkä Śəllus, 16
Abbäbä, 98, 136
Abrəha Kasay, 55
Adära Giyorgis, Fəqrä Śəllase Kəflä Maryam, 181
Addis Ayyänäw, 221
Admaśu, 211
Aläqa Adḥena Bärḥe, 256
Aläqa Fəssəḥa, 95
Aläqa Gäbrä Ṣadəq of Betä Abrəham, 55
Aläqa Wäldä Ḥanna, 16
Amdu of Bašo Däbr, *Qes*, 168
Ankore, *Qes*, 251
Aqba Mika'el, 61
Askalä Ṣəyon, 155
Aśrat, 165
Ayyälä, *Qesä Gäbäz Mämmərə*, 107
Bašära, 16
Balä Ṭäkase, 205
Balambaras Šawəl, 145
Bärtälomewos, 3
Čäkkol Gäbrä Śəllase, 173
Däggu, *Qes Mämmərə*, 117
Däbrä Gännät, 3
Əmmahoy Dässəta Azagä, 226
Əmam, *Abba*, 23

'Ərgätä Qal, 149
Əssetä Mika'el, 80
Ewosṭatewos, 69
Ewosṭatewos, *Abunä*, 102, 197
Fəśśəḥa, *Mämmərə*, 48
Gäbrä Ṣadəq, 112
Gäbrä Śəllase, 114
Gäbrä Ṣəyon, 93
Gäbrä Əgzi'abḥer, 157
Gäbrä Əgzi'bḥer, 53
Gäbrä Iyyäsus, 71, 179, 248
Gäbrä Kidan, 200
Gäbrä Krəstos, 93
Gäbrä Krəstos, *Mämḥərə*, 93
Gäbrä Mädḥən, 219
Gäbrä Mädḥən Abbäbä, 151
Gäbrä Mänfäs Qəddus, 89, 245, 247
Gäbrä Maryam, 93, 225
Gäbrä Mika'el, 208
Gäbrä Iyyäsus Aššäbbər, 11
Gäbrä Iyyäsus Wä[l]dä Śəllase, *Mämmərə*, 18
Gäbrä Mädḥən, *Abba*, 48
Gäbrä Mika'el, 3
Gäbrä Wäld, 18
Gəday, *Mämhər*, 29
Giyorgis, 98
Ḥabtä Maryam, 249
Hadära Abrəha, *Qes*, 55

Haile Sellasie I, 48
Ḥaläqa, 39
Ḥaylä Maryam, 103
Herron, Paul, 3
Iyyo'ab, 93
Iyyob, 77
Iyyosyas, 58
Kəflä Maryam, 220
Kənfe Wäd(d)i, Qes, 251
Kidanä Maryam, 145
Ləssanä Krəstos, 194
Lottu Səbḥat, 93
Märgeta Gäbrä Maryam, 114
Matewos, Bishop/Metropolitan (1881-1926), 98
Mulatu, 230
Qerəlos, *Abba*, 152
Säfonyas, 176
Säyfä Mika'el, 107
Śahlä Ǝgzi', 133
Śahlä Maryam, 174
Śahlä Śəllase, 53
Šašit/Wälättä Śəllase, 224
Täšomä, 226
Täklä Ṣadəq Gäbrä Iyyäsus, 88
Täklä Haymanot, 194
Täklä Haymanot, *Abunä*, 15, 16, 71, 102, 197
Täklä Iyyäsus, *Abba*, 107
Täklä Maryam, 174
Täkläyyäs Dačäw, *Abba*, 107
Täsfa Giyorgis, 251
Taffäsä Azzänä, 107
Takkälä Abbäbä, 136
Täsfa Giyorgis of Wəddo, 15
Täsfaw Bayyuh, 11
Täsfay, *Haläqa*, 55
Tə'əmrtä Həbu'at, 32
Wälättä Śəllase, 103, 237
Wälättä Iyyäsus, 203, 235

Wälättä Maryam 'Omä Gännät, 69
Wälättä Mika'el, 173
Wäldä Ṣadəq, 83, 88, 234, 241
Wäldä Śəllase, 69
Wäldä Ḥəywät, 249
Wäldä Ḥsanna, 208
Wäldä Abib, 74
Wäldä Amanu'el, 241
Wäldä Bərhan, 248
Wäldä Gäbrə'el, 173, 200
Wäldä Giyorgis, 71, 124, 165
Wäldä Iyyäsus, 107, 110
Wäldä Kahən, 93
Wäldä Mädḫən, *Abba*, 124
Wäldä Mäsqäl, 176, 203
Wäldä Maryam, 107, 259, 268
Wäldä Maryam of Gämza Safra, 117
Wäldä Maryam, *Mämmərе*, 53
Wäldä Mika'el, 53
Wäldä Mika'el, *Mämmərе*, 98
Wäldä Täklä Haymanot, 179
Wäldä Täkle, 58
Wäldä Yoḥannəs, 53
Wäldä Zena Marəqos, 264
Wärqu Täsfayä, 80
Wälätta Ǝgzi'bḥer, 83
Wälätta Gäbrə'el, 8
Wälättä Śəllase, 3
Wäldä Ṣadəq Ayyänäw, 11
Wäldä Ḥawaryat, 37
Wäldä Gäbrə'el, 37
Wäldä Giyorgis, 14, 54
Wäldä Maryam, 11, 14, 48
Wäldä Mika'el, 8
Wäldä Ḥanna, 15
WäldäYoḥannəs, 18
Wube, *Abba*, 220

Yəggärämu, 211
Zä'ənb Ḫgru, 267
Ẓäḥay, *Mämmǝre*, 136
Zäwäldä Maryam, 3
Ẓewa Iyyäsus, 208
Zion, *Ṣǝyon*, 181

Index of Miniatures in the Codices

Aaron, 26, 76
Abba Samuel riding a lion, 76
Adam and Eve Eating the Forbidden Fruit, 238
Angel, 85, 210, 261, 262
   Archangel Gabriel, 247, 253
   Archangel Michael, 22, 92, 130, 185
   Archangel Michael and Balaam, 48
   Archangel Michael and the Dedication of the church in Alexandria, 48
   Archangel Michael Enthroned, 92
   Archangel Michael helping Samson to kill the Philistines, 48
   Archangel Michael rescuing the Three Holy Children, 92
   Archangel Michael restores the sight of the blind man, 48
   Archangel Michael with a sword, 259
   Archangel Phanuel, 15
   Kirubel, 112
   Michael with sword, 247
   Raguel, 247
   Raphael with sword, 247
   Surafel, 112
   with staff, 141
   with sword, 26, 106, 120, 128, 147, 148, 149, 150, 170, 201, 203, 218, 232, 235, 237, 247
Angels, 197, 235, 236, 261, 262
   Archangels Michael, Saraphim, Gabriel and Cherubim, 201
Apostles, Twelve, 167
Arägawi holding snake, *Abunä*, 170
Booklet of prayer coming down from heaven, 26, 92
Child being baptized, 197
Church and Angels, 48
Cross, 13, 201, 235, 261, 262
Crosses, 262
Crude drawing, 6, 16, 18, 34, 35, 58, 62, 65, 102, 114, 135, 167, 168, 175, 191, 194, 207, 216, 220
   angel, 58
   Geometric pattern, 62
   man, 58
   Man with prayer stick and animal, 39
   Qes Amdu of Bašo Däbr, 168
   Täklä Haymanot, 194
   two crosses, 97
   two crosses and a man, 97
   two men, 88
David
   Beheading Goliath, 26
   Playing the Harp, 26, 114, 126, 132, 138, 152, 165,

Index of Miniatures in the Codices · 423

167, 188, 191, 197, 216, 229, 232, 238, 245
Drawing of human face, 267
Equestrian Saints, Joab and Abishai on horseback, 70
Ethiopian Dignitary, 147, 152, 235
Ethiopian Dignitary (St. Yared?), 170
Ethiopian saint, 170, 201
Evangelist, writing gospel, 117
Expulsion of Adam and Eve from Eden, 238
Flight to Egypt, 22, 197, 238
Four chief priests, 238
Gäbrä Mänfäs Qəddus, 26, 92, 123, 170, 185, 245, 247
Gabriel, 76
Geometric pattern, 147, 170, 201, 235
George, Saint, 141
   and the Dragon, 8, 22, 72, 76, 102, 106, 110, 112, 114, 117, 120, 123, 125, 130, 132, 138, 140, 145, 149, 150, 170, 172, 175, 185, 203, 207, 210, 213, 216, 226, 229, 232, 264, 267
God, 218
God the Father, 92
Holy Trinity, 128, 149, 152, 161, 165, 167, 172, 207
   surrounded by the Four Living Creatures, 106, 125, 238
Jesus, 175
   Arrest, 114
   Ascension, 92, 95, 135, 138, 145, 150, 188, 229, 234, 253
   Baptism, 110, 114, 130, 132, 197, 238

   Betrayal, 168
   Burial, 165, 188, 232
   carried by Martha and Salome, 198
   carrying the Cross, 126, 135, 138, 141, 145, 159, 165, 167, 188, 210, 229, 237
   Crown of Thorns, 226
   Crucifixion, 8, 26, 73, 123, 126, 135, 138, 145, 152, 165, 167, 170, 172, 185, 188, 216, 220, 226, 229, 232, 234, 238
   debating(?), 237
   enthroned, 267
   Feeding of the Five Thousand, 238
   Flogging, 72, 130, 132, 159, 161
   followed by a line of people, 141
   Foot Washing Ceremony, 238
   heals the paralytic man, 238
   holding a book, 95
   holding orb, 128
   in front of a crowd, 110, 114
   Last Supper, 112, 150, 161, 165, 168, 172, 188, 219, 229, 232, 238
   looking up(?), 92
   raising right hand, 207
   Resurrected Displaying His Wounds, 26, 73, 123
   Resurrected, displays his wounds, 185, 234
   Resurrection, raising Adam and Eve, 95, 102, 106, 112, 126, 135, 138, 141, 145, 150, 165, 172, 188,

207, 210, 213, 226, 229, 238, 253
Savior of the World, 152
Striking of the Head, 72, 95, 120, 128, 138, 149, 161, 168, 172, 216
surrounded by the Four Living Creatures, 48, 76, 203
Taking off the robe of Jesus, 128, 130, 132, 135, 161
Teaching, 120
Temptation by the Devil, 159
Triumphal Entry, 132
with a crowd, 210
with uplifted hands, 66
John, Saint, 109, 172
Joseph, Saint, holding flowers, 152
Lalibäla, Saint, 147
Luke, Saint, 150
Man, 216, 261
Man and a woman, 253
Man being fed by a bird, 72
Man looking ahead and pointing up, 72, 73
Man pointing a dagger to the neck of another, 207
Man riding a horse spears a cow, 207
Man riding horse with spear, 58
Man with a spear, 213
Man with book, 218
Man with crown, 236
Man, seated, 236
Mary, 76, 152, 219, 259
Annunciation, 22, 102, 106, 110, 114, 123, 141, 197, 207, 238
Enthroned, 102, 110, 232
Enthroned with the Trinity, 22
Madonna and Child, 22, 72, 76, 95, 106, 109, 112, 114, 117, 120, 123, 125, 128, 130, 132, 135, 138, 145, 147, 149, 150, 152, 161, 165, 170, 172, 185, 188, 197, 201, 203, 207, 213, 216, 218, 220, 226, 229, 232, 235, 237, 245, 247
Man grasps the cloak of Mary, 185
Man with a stone foot praying for Mary to heal him, 267
Praying in the Temple, 15
raises the painter who fell, 197
Mathew, Saint, 149
Matthew, Saint, 128
Moses, 22, 95, 112, 120, 125, 130, 150, 216
Mounted holy man, 185
Nä'akk^{w}əto Lä'ab, Saint, 147
Nativity, 22, 110, 114, 120, 238
Nine-box panel, 170, 235
Noah and his family, 238
Ornate cross, 13
Peter, Saint, 112
Presentation of Jesus in the Temple, 22
Priest blessing people with his hand cross, 198
Qerəlos, *Abba*, 152
Sacrifice of Isaac, 130, 132, 149, 161
Saint pointing to sky, 234
Saint with a book, 26, 92, 123, 161, 165
Saints, 106

Saints with crosses, 102
Samu'el riding a lion, *Abunä*, 170
Täklä Haymanot, *Abunä*, 15, 170, 185
Talismanic symbol, 236
   Nine-box panel with face, 147
Three men, 135
Three women, 117
Two angels, 197
Two men, 76, 219
Two men before a multitude, 22
Two men with arms outstretched, 13
Two men, probably *Abunä* Täklä Haymanot and *Abunä* Ewosṭatewos, 197
Visitation, 95
Woman holding looking glass, 245
Woman with two children, 236
Yared, Saint, and King Gäbrä Mäsqäl, 213
Zechariah, 95

Index of Scribal Practices in the Codices

Arranged
  for the church calendar, 31
  for the days of the week, 2,
    5, 8, 10, 11, 17, 21, 26,
    29, 31, 36, 39, 54, 57,
    65, 66, 69, 70, 79, 82,
    85, 91, 92, 97, 104, 105,
    109, 114, 117, 119, 123,
    125, 132, 135, 138, 140,
    152, 161, 164, 167, 172,
    174, 177, 181, 187, 190,
    197, 206, 210, 213, 216,
    220, 226, 229, 238, 241,
    245, 247, 251, 253, 256
Binding
  headband and tailband, 1,
    5, 10, 25, 29, 79, 94,
    125, 131, 140, 146, 151,
    157, 167, 170, 171, 202,
    225, 228, 238, 241, 244,
    247, 250
  linen between pastedowns,
    1, 29, 85, 131, 137, 140,
    157, 158, 170, 199, 223,
    228, 238, 241, 244, 247,
    261
  three chain stitches, 89,
    150, 154, 170, 175, 234,
    263
  tooled leather, 1, 5, 9, 25,
    29, 54, 68, 79, 85, 94,
    125, 131, 140, 146, 151,
    157, 167, 170, 171, 180,
    199, 202, 218, 223, 225,
    237, 241, 244, 247, 250,
    261
  untooled leather, 7
Carrying Case
  Double slip, 1, 8, 10, 74,
    125, 146, 172, 204, 220,
    225, 256
  Single slip, 5, 13, 15, 72,
    76, 79, 90, 116, 218,
    236, 245, 247, 263
Colummetric Layout, 232
  a. Psalm 95, 86
  b. Psalm 145, 11, 80, 165,
    188, 211
  c. Psalm 148, 11, 32, 71,
    80, 165, 211, 256
  d. Psalm 150, 6, 11, 29, 32,
    40, 67, 71, 80, 83, 86,
    126, 133, 136, 138, 141,
    165, 168, 211, 214, 221,
    230, 245, 248, 251, 254,
    256
  e. many other places in the
    Psalms, 115, 229
  f. fourth biblical canticle,
    80
  g. ninth biblical canticle,
    242
  h. tenth biblical canticle, 3,
    6, 11, 23, 27, 29, 32, 37,
    67, 72, 80, 83, 86, 114,
    126, 133, 136, 138, 141,
    153, 165, 168, 181, 188,
    191, 198, 211, 214, 217,

221, 226, 230, 239, 242,
  245, 248, 251, 254, 256
Completion of long lines, 3, 6,
  11, 23, 30, 32, 37, 40, 55,
  67, 71, 80, 83, 86, 95, 98,
  115, 126, 133, 136, 139,
  141, 153, 155, 156, 162,
  165, 168, 182, 189, 191,
  198, 211, 214, 217, 221,
  227, 230, 239, 242, 248,
  251, 254, 256
Corrections
  erasure dots, 83
  overlooked lines inserted
    interlinearly, 3, 6, 11,
    18, 23, 27, 30, 32, 35,
    37, 40, 55, 63, 71, 74,
    77, 80, 83, 86, 93, 98,
    103, 112, 115, 121, 126,
    133, 136, 139, 141, 145,
    151, 153, 162, 165, 168,
    173, 176, 182, 188, 191,
    195, 200, 203, 208, 211,
    214, 221, 227, 230, 239,
    242, 248, 249
  overlooked lines inserted
    marginally with symbol,
    23, 32, 35, 40, 63, 71,
    73, 74, 77, 83, 86, 93,
    95, 98, 112, 121, 124,
    133, 136, 141, 145, 173,
    175, 182, 188, 195, 203,
    208, 217, 221, 227, 230,
    245, 246, 264, 268
Inserted lines of text, 40
Midpoint of the Psalms, 32,
  37, 39, 67, 71, 83, 98, 114,
  133, 141, 152, 162, 165,
  181, 211, 214, 221, 239,
  242, 245, 248, 251, 253,
  256
Mirror or mirror niche, 10, 19,
  150
Navigation system

marginal notations for
  readings, 19, 21, 29, 31,
  82, 104, 118, 135, 156,
  197, 210, 220, 245, 263
string for content divisions,
  5, 10, 13, 17, 21, 39, 42,
  54, 65, 66, 68, 70, 76,
  79, 85, 90, 97, 104, 109,
  113, 116, 118, 125, 129,
  135, 140, 160, 164, 172,
  177, 184, 190, 193, 202,
  206, 210, 226, 241, 245,
  250, 263
strings for miniatures, 21,
  26, 72, 76, 90, 95, 109,
  111, 113, 118, 123, 128,
  129, 132, 135, 138, 148,
  150, 160, 164, 167, 172,
  183, 187, 215, 218, 228,
  231, 238
Pen trial, 3, 16, 32, 39, 130,
  145, 234, 264
Quire numbers, 1, 8, 10, 29,
  36, 38, 42, 49, 57, 66, 74,
  79, 82, 85, 90, 113, 125,
  131, 135, 137, 140, 143,
  146, 164, 170, 171, 175,
  177, 183, 190, 193, 199,
  201, 206, 219, 225, 238,
  247, 250, 258
Rejected leaf from another
  manuscript, 6, 23, 89, 220,
  221
Sections
  black and red dotted lines,
    3, 8, 11, 14, 20, 23, 29,
    32, 35, 37, 39, 48, 54,
    58, 63, 67, 71, 73, 74,
    83, 85, 89, 93, 95, 98,
    103, 107, 110, 112, 114,
    132, 136, 138, 155, 165,
    168, 173, 179, 181, 186,
    188, 191, 194, 198, 208,

211, 214, 217, 223, 226,
232, 251, 254, 256, 267
row of full-stop symbols,
16, 63, 107, 121, 124,
149, 155, 156, 161, 173,
181, 188, 203, 208, 254,
256, 259, 264, 267

Index of Works in the Scrolls of Spiritual Healing

Glorification of the Angels, 300
Greeting to Mary, 363
Greeting to Phanuel, 275, 284, 285, 287, 288, 289, 298, 299, 302, 306, 307, 309, 331, 338, 339, 342, 353, 357, 358, 363, 376, 378, 383, 387, 393, 396
Greeting to the pierced side of Jesus, 301, 340, 344, 346, 347, 358, 375
Greeting to Thomas, 347
How Our Lady Mary drove away demons and healed the sick, 369
Hymns to St. George, 289
Image of Jesus, 323
Joseph who came out of a wicked fever, 337
Mystagogia, 322
Net of Solomon, 279, 283, 287, 290, 296, 300, 303, 307, 313, 317, 319, 327, 328, 329, 330, 335, 345, 347, 349, 360, 361, 365, 368, 377, 385, 389, 390, 392, 394, 398
Prayer
  against all kinds of ailments, 274, 331
  against $Aq^w ya\d{s}at$ and charm, 341
  against Barya, 311, 348
  against Barya and Däsk, 298
  against Barya and filthy Legewon, 345, 381
  against Barya and Legewon, 279, 286, 303, 312, 348, 370
  against Barya and the evil eye, 337
  against Barya Təgərtya, and Šotolay, 351
  against Barya, for the days of the week, 320
  against Barya, Legewon, and hemorrhage, 352
  against Barya, Legewon, and Təgrida, 348
  against Barya, Legewon, and the evil eye, 300, 338, 372
  against Barya, Legewon, and the evil eye, and for binding demons, 341
  against Barya, Legewon, hemorrhage, the evil eye and Šotälay, 300
  against Barya, Legewon, the evil eye, Zar, Təgrida, and others, and for binding demons, 338
  against Barya, Legewon, Zar, Šotälay, and the evil eye, 385
  against Barya, Təgərtya, and Belbab, 352
  against Barya, Təgərtya, and Legewon, 353

against Barya, Təgərtya, hemorrhage, Šotälay and Belbab, 370
against Barya, the evil eye, Zar, Qurañña, Mäggañña, Täyayaž, Ṭäbib, Qumäñña and several illnesses, 354
against Buda, 364
against Buda and Carpenter (*Nähabi*), 362
against Buda and Carpenters (*Nähabt*, 311
against Buda, Fälaša, and Qumäñña, 361
against charm, 294, 305, 319, 323, 331, 335, 375, 377, 378, 379, 397
against charm by people, demons, Fälaša, Gudale, Ṭäfinǧ, Buda, Carpenter (*Nähabi*), Dobbi, Dobbit, Zar, Zarit, Muslims, and Christians, 362
against charm, taken from the Eighty-One (Canonical) Books, 293, 318, 353
against charm, the evil eye, Fəgen, Fälaša, the evil eye of Zar, Təgrida, and Mäggañña, 358
against charm, the Jealous, Buda, and Qumäñña, 306
against colic, 284, 289, 291, 310, 352, 358, 363, 370, 372, 378, 380, 390
against colic and headache, 376

against colic, piercing pain, Täyayaž and other demons, 384
against demons, 360, 365
against demons and Šotälay, 368
against demons and for undoing charm, 282
against demons of Zar, Barya, Legewon, Təgrida, Mäggañň, Ṭäbib, and Gudale, 273
against demons which cause stomachache and other illnesses, 378, 382
against demons, Barya, Legewon, the evil eye, Gärgari, Buda, Qumäñña, Fəgen, and others, 351
against evil spirits, 293, 324, 325, 337, 345
against evil spirits, wicked demons, Dədq, noontime demon, Buda, and *Nähabi*, 374
against eye disease and headache, 303, 304
against fever, *gəbṭ* and shivering, 329
against filthy Legewon, 317, 360
against filthy spirits, 288
against Gärgari, the evil eye, 323
against headache, 291, 338
against headache, stomachache, piercing pain, Barya, demons, and others, 379
against hemorrhage, 273, 275, 277, 278, 284, 291, 295, 296, 300, 302, 310,

313, 321, 326, 335, 340, 341, 347, 350, 366, 371, 373, 381, 382, 383, 385, 390, 396, 397
against hemorrhage and Šotälay, 304, 342
against hemorrhage and Šotälay, 273, 274
against hemorrhage and for conception, 275, 380, 389
against hemorrhage and for conception, using the letters of the Hebrew alphabet from Aleph to Heth as given in Ps 119, 341
against hemorrhage and miscarriage, 327, 332
against hemorrhage as Gabriel announced to Mary, 298
against hemorrhage, Šotälay, and menstruation, 342
against hemorrhage, Šotolay, Təgərtya, and Belbab, 352
against hemorrhage, in Gəʻəz and Amharic, 291
against hemorrhage, using the letters of the Hebrew alphabet from Aleph to Heth as given in Ps 119, 343
against illnesses and charm of different demons, including Zar and Quräñña, 350
against illnesses caused by Šotälay, 304
against illnesses caused by (the eye of) Nähab, 370

against illnesses caused by Barya, 349, 361, 378
against illnesses caused by Barya and Legewon, 280, 301, 304, 305, 342, 371
against illnesses caused by Barya and Legewon and for binding demons and Satan, in Gəʻəz and some Amharic., 389
against illnesses caused by Barya and Legewon and for binding demons, that King Alexander uttered before Gog and Magog, 318
against illnesses caused by Barya, and the evil eye, 304
against illnesses caused by Barya, Legewon and Šotolay, 308
against illnesses caused by Barya, Legewon, Šotälay, the evil eye and child killer, 316
against illnesses caused by Barya, Legewon, and the evil eye of Šotälay, 281
against illnesses caused by Barya, Legewon, and Zar, 276, 301
against illnesses caused by Barya, Legewon, Zar, and Mäggäñña other illnesses, and for binding demons, 285
against illnesses caused by Buda and the noontime demon, 366

against illnesses caused by
  Buda, Ṭäbib, Anṭärañña,
  and Fälaša, 353, 371
against illnesses caused by
  charm, 353
against illnesses caused by
  demons Barya,
  Legewon, and the filthy
  demon of the sea, 350
against illnesses caused by
  Qurañña, Täyaž, Zar,
  Təgrida, 364
against illnesses caused by
  Šotälay, 366
against illnesses caused by
  Šotälay and 'Urde, 366
against illnesses caused by
  Šotälay, Galla, and Zar,
  282
against illnesses caused by
  Šotälay, *Qurañña*, Zar,
  Zarit, *Nähabi*, Ṭəfnät,
  and Gudale, 374
against illnesses caused by
  the evil eye of Barya and
  charm, 327
against illnesses caused by
  the evil eye of Barya,
  Zar, Nägärgar, Dədq,
  noontime demon, and
  charm, 327
against illnesses caused by
  the evil eye, Barya, etc.,
  298
against illnesses caused by
  the evil eye, Barya,
  Mäggañña, colic, Däsk,
  and Gudale, 278
against illnesses caused by
  the eye of Šotälay and
  the story of St. Susənyos
  fighting Wərzəlya, 388
against illnesses caused by
  the eye of
  Barya,Täyayaž, Šotälay,
  Mäggañña, Buda, Ṭäbib,
  Qumäñña, and other
  illnesses, 291
against illnesses caused by
  Zar and demons, and for
  drowning demons,
  Legewon, Wəllaǧ, and
  illnesses caused by
  Təgərtya, 315
against illnesses of
  Täyayaž, Q^{w}ərañña,
  Šotälay and hemorrhage,
  307
against illnesseses caused
  by the evil eye of Barya,
  394
against infertility, 312
against Legewon, 279, 288,
  310, 311
against Mäggañña and
  miscarriage, 332
against miscarriage and
  hemorrhage, 317
against *Nähabt*, 375
against *Nähabt*, and
  Artisans, 335
against piercing pain, 275,
  282, 284, 300, 301, 323,
  340, 344, 353, 355, 375,
  390
against piercing pain and
  colic, 343, 375
against piercing pain and
  other illnesses, 313
against piercing pain
  caused by Šotälay and
  the wicked Legewon,
  308
against piercing pain,
  illnesses caused by Zar,

demons of the air, and Legewon, 352
against punching pain, 291, 298
against *Qämäñña* (sic) ... and for binding demons, 305
against rheumatism, 291, 301, 390
against Šätäle, Täyayaž and other demons, 384
against Šätolay, Šätolawit, and hemorrhage, 352
against Šätolay, Šätolawit, Təgərtya, and Belbab, 381
against Šotälay, Šätolayt, and hemorrhage, 371
against Šotälay, 308
against Šotälay, Mäggañña, the eye of Barya, Legewon, Däsk, Gudale, Buda, 308
against Šotälay and hemorrhage, 323
against Šotälay and hemorrhage, 371
against Šotolay, 325
against stomachache, 337, 355, 386
against Täyayaž which brings nightmare, 296
against terror, 323
against terror caused by demon of the day, night, *Sext*, and *None*, Šotälawi, Zar, Qurañña, Barya, and Legewon, 391
against terror that God gave to Adam, 316

against terror that God gave to Noah, 316
against terrorizing demons and the evil eye of Barya, the evil eye of Zar, 394
against the demon Šotolawi, 286
against the demons Šotälay and Qotälay, 271
against the evil eye, 272, 274, 276, 288, 294, 297, 299, 313, 334, 337, 342, 344, 346, 357, 362, 364, 372, 374, 391
against the evil eye and Šätolay and against hemorrhage, Mäggañña, Anṭärañña, Zar, and Təgrida, and against charm, 364
against the evil eye and for binding demons that Alexander uttered before Gog and Magog, 286
against the evil eye and for binding demons, Barya, Legewon, and Mäggañña, invoking the name of the cross, 297
against the evil eye and for binding demons, Satan, Buda, Carpenter, Käyla, Fälaša that Alexander uttered before Gog and Magog, 295
against the evil eye and for drowning the Zar, 299
against the evil eye and Legewon, 296
against the evil eye and miscarriage, 306

against the evil eye and the evil eye of Barya, 393
against the evil eye of Barya, 272, 326, 332, 337, 340, 349
against the evil eye of Barya and charm, 337
against the evil eye of Barya and for drowning demons, 378
against the evil eye of Barya and illnesses caused by Šotolay, 326
against the evil eye of Barya and Legewon, 331, 333
against the evil eye of Barya and others, 314
against the evil eye of Barya Legewon and all filthy spirits, 284
against the evil eye of Barya, demons and Legewon, 330
against the evil eye of Barya, Gärgari, Zar, Mäggañña, all types of stomachache, and the demon Ğuḥa, 394
against the evil eye of Barya, illnesses caused by Šotolay, and Mäggañña, 326
against the evil eye of Barya, Legewon and charm, 333
against the evil eye of Barya, Legewon, and against terror, 333
against the evil eye of Barya, Legewon, Däsk and Gudale, 295
against the evil eye of Barya, Legewon, Zar, Zarit, Təgrida, Mäggäñña, Buda, Fälaša, 297
against the evil eye of Barya, Qurañña, the eye of Buda, Ṭäbib, Dədq and noontime demon, 343
against the evil eye of Buda, artisans and Qumäñña, 314
against the evil eye of demons, 330
against the evil eye of demons, and different ailments, 292
against the evil eye with the *asmat* of the Archanel Michael, 319
against the evil eye, Šätolay, and against hemorrhage, 357
against the evil eye, Šätolay, Mäggañña, Anṭärañña, Marit, Zarit, Gudale, Təgrida, and Šätolawit, 357
against the evil eye, and Šotälay, 314
against the evil eye, and for binding demons, Barya, Legewon, and Šotälay, 322
against the evil eye, Barya and Legewon, 397
against the evil eye, Barya, and Šotolay causing hemorrhage, 355
against the evil eye, Barya, and Legewon, 367

against the evil eye, Barya, Gudale, Däsk, Zar, Šotälay, and Qurañña, 340
against the evil eye, Barya, Legewon, Šätolay, Anṭärañña, Mäggañña, and others, against hemorrhage, 363
against the evil eye, Barya, Legewon, hemorrhage, 304
against the evil eye, Barya, Legewon, Zar, Tägrda ans Šälay, Buda, and Fälaša, 305
against the evil eye, Gärgari, Šotälay, Ğənn, Wəllağ, Täyaž, the eye Zar, the eye of Buda, Fälaša, and the eye of Nas, 365
against the evil eye, Gärgari, Barya, Legewon, and the eye of Barya, 346
against the evil eye, Gärgari, Legewon and the eye of a Muslim, 324
against the evil eye, Gärgari, the evil eye of Barya, Legewon, Buda, Ṭäbib, Mäggañña and others, 317
against the evil eye, illnesses caused by Šotälay, other illnesses, 374
against the evil eye, the evil eye of Šotälay, and the eye of child killer, 316

against the evil eye, the evil eye of Barya, Legewon, 388
against the evil eye, the evil eye of Barya, Legewon, different illnesses, and charm, 357
against the evil eye, the evil eye of Barya, Legewon, Zar and Təgrida, 280
against the evil eye, the evil eye of Barya, Legewon, Zar, and Təgrida, 393
against the evil eye, the evil eye of Barya, Legewon, Zar, Täyayaž, Šotälay and Mäggañń, 315
against the evil eye, the evil eye of Nas, Buda, Wägi, Zar, 398
against the evil eye, the eye of Barya, 303
against the evil eye, Zar and Ṭäbib, 383
against the evil eye, Zar, filthy demons, Gudale, Barya, Legewon, and other demons, 373
against the evil spirit of Gergesenes, 293
against the evil spirit of Luke 4.31-36, 293
against the eye of Šotälay, 318
against the eye of Šotälay and the story of St. Susənyos fighting Wərzəlya, 387
against the eye of Barya, 378
against the eye of Barya and charm, 382

against the eye of Barya
and demons with the
asmat of the *Dərsanä
Mika'el*, 326
against the eye of Barya
and filthy spirits, 369
against the eye of Barya
and for binding demons,
382
against the eye of Barya
and piercing pain, 383
against the eye of Barya,
Legewon, demons, and
the wicked Legewon,
346
against the eye of Barya,
Legewon, eye of Zar,
eye of Täyaž, Šotälay,
Mäggäñña, Buda, Ṭäbib,
Mänšo, and other
illnesses, 387
against the eye of Barya,
Legewon, Qurañña,
Mäggäñña, and filthy
spirits, Dədq and
noontime demon, 368
against the eye of Barya,
the eye of Buda, 376
against the eye that causes
piercing pain, 334
Asmat of Solomon, 277,
298, 321
Asmat of Solomon and the
story of his fight with
the carpenters, *nähabt*,
369
Asmat of Solomon that
Michael gave him, for
drowning demons,
Barya, Legewon (,)
Ǧənn, Däbas, Däsk,
Gudale, Zar, Təgrida,
Mäggäñña, Šotolay,
Buda, and Mänš, 359
Asmat of Solomon, against
the eye of Barya, wicked
people, Šotälay, and
hemorrhage, 349
Asmat of the Archangel
Michael, against Barya,
Təgərtya, and different
illnesses, 362
Asmat of the Qəmant, 294
Asmat prayer that Gabriel
told Mary regarding her
conception of Jesus
Christ, 381
by which Solomon was
saved from evil spirits,
346
for binding Šotälay and
other demons, 392
for binding and driving
away demons, 329
for binding and drowning
demons, 319, 323
for binding Barya and
Legewon, with the
glorification of the
Cross, 392
for binding demons, 272,
276, 279, 290, 292, 301,
303, 311, 314, 337, 342,
359, 367, 375, 380, 385,
387, 388, 396, 397
for binding demons and
against charm, 322
for binding demons and
against headache, 386
for binding demons and
against the eye of Barya,
330
for binding demons and
filthy Legewon, 374

for binding demons and
terrorizing Satan, Barya
and Legewon, Buda,
Anṭərāñña, Qumāñña,
and Təgərtya, 321
for binding demons and the
evil eye, 272
for binding demons and the
evil hand, 280
for binding demons and the
eye of Barya, 344
for binding demons and
Zar, 379
for binding demons,
Šätolay and Šätolawit,
367
for binding demons,
Šotälay and Təgərtya,
368
for binding demons,
[Legewon], Buda, Ṭäbib,
Täyayaž, Dədq, and
noontime demon, 320
for binding demons, against
Šotälay, Mäggäñña, Zar,
and hemorrhage, 344
for binding demons, and
against Qedar,
Carpenters (Nähabt) and
Gärgar, 291
for binding demons, and
for driving Satan, 281
for binding demons, and
for terrorizing satans the
eye of the filthy
Legewon, 283
for binding demons, and
illnesses caused by
Barya, Legewon, Däsk,
Legewon, Mäggäñña,
Zar, Buda, Təgrida,
Šotolay, and Wərzəlya,
287
for binding demons, Barya
and Legewon, 287
for binding demons, Barya,
and Legewon, 292
for binding demons, Barya,
and Legewon, 277
for binding demons, Barya,
Legewon, Däsk and
Gudale, 391
for binding demons, Barya,
the filthy Legewon, and
the evil hand, 299
for binding demons, Buda
and Carpenter, 295
for binding demons,
Legewon, and Barya,
Täyayaž, 391
for binding demons, the
evil eye of Zar, Wəllağ,
the eye of Buda, Ṭäbib,
the eye of jealous
people, the eye of
Muslim and Christian,
the eye of Wärğ, Färäng
and against all their evil
eyes, 340
for binding Satan, 372
for binding Satan and
against charm, 321
for binding Satan and
against the evil eye and
the evil eye of Barya,
386
for binding Satan and
against the evil eye of
Zar, 281
for binding Satan and
demons, 386
for binding Satan and
Legewon, 387

for binding Satan and
  Nägärgar, 311
for binding the evil eye and
  Zar, 379, 391
for casting out evil spirits,
  310
for cleansing sin, 285
for conception, 272, 310,
  344, 366, 382
for conception and against
  Šotälay, 309
for conception and against
  hemorrhage, 344, 368
for conception, to stop
  hemorrhage and against
  Šotälay, 274
for disgracing the arrogant,
  334
for driving away demons,
  356, 366, 369, 373, 384
for driving away evil
  spirits, 306, 308, 325
for drowning and binding
  demons, 355
for drowning Barya and
  Legewon, 396
for drowning Barya,
  Legewon, and Nägärgar,
  342
for drowning demons, 310,
  334, 338, 350, 355
for drowning demons and
  Barya, 338
for drowning demons,
  against Barya, Čänäfär,
  the noontime demon, for
  binding and terrorizing
  demons, and against
  Barya and the noontime
  demon, 282
for drowning demons, and
  against illnesses caused
  by Barya, Qumäñña, the
  eye of Šanqəlla, Däbas,
  Zar, Täzawarit, Šotälay,
  and others, 281
for drowning demons,
  Barya, Legewon Ǧänn,
  Däbas, Däsk, Gudale,
  Zar, Təgrida, Mäggäñña,
  Šotälay, Buda, Qimäñña,
  and others, 336
for drowning demons,
  Barya, Legewon Ǧänn,
  Däbas, Gudale, Zar,
  Təgrida, Mäggäñña,
  Šotälay, and others, 324
for drowning demons,
  Barya, Təgərtya, Däsk,
  Wərzəlya, Legewon,
  Mäggäñña, Gudale, and
  Ṭäfänt, 332
for drowning filthy
  demons, 323
for drowning illness-
  causing demons, 350
for drowning/binding
  demons and against
  Barya and Nähabi, and
  hemorrhage, 316
for protection, 379
for refuge against evil
  spirits, 373
for safety, *adhḥənno*, of the
  owner of the scroll, 376
for the days of the week
  and for drowning
  demons, 381
for the days of the week for
  drowning demons, 324,
  336, 356, 359
illnesses caused by Barya,
  Legewon, Zar and
  Ṭäbib, 383, 384

of *Abunä* Kiros that God may release him from his illness, 326
of Alexander which he utterd on a Friday against illnesses caused by Barya, Legewon, for biding demons, against charm, Mäggañña, Mari, and Marit, 389
of Our Lady Mary which she prayed when they made her drink the bitter water, 361
of St. Susənyos, 368
of St. Susənyos against Barya, Legewon, Däsk, Gudale, 395
of St. Susənyos against hemorrhage, 283
of St. Susənyos against hemorrhage and the story of his fight against Wərzəlya, 367
of St. Susənyos against hemorrhage, Šätälay, the evil eye of Barya, and the story of his fight against Wərzəlya, 277
of St. Susənyos against illnesses caused by Šotälay, and the story of his fight against Wərzəlya, 299
of St. Susənyos against illnesses caused by Barya and Šotälay, and the story of his fight against Wərzəlya, 397
of St. Susənyos against illnesses caused by Barya and Legeon, and the story of his fight against Wərzəlya, 298
of St. Susənyos against illnesses caused by Barya, Legewon, Zar, Ṭäbib, and the story of his fight against Wərzəlya, 384
of St. Susənyos against illnesses caused by evil eye, Šätolay, and others, and against hemorrhage, 357
of St. Susənyos against illnesses caused by Mäggäña, Buda, Carpenter, Šotolay, and the story of his fight against Wərzəlya, 295
of St. Susənyos against infant mortality, 303, 309
of St. Susənyos against infant mortality, prayer against illnesses caused by Barya, Legewon, the evil eye, and for drowning demons, 339
of St. Susənyos against the evil eye, illnesses caused by Buda and the story of his fight against Wərzəlya, 393
of St. Susənyos against the evil eye, Zar, the eye of Buda, Təgrida, Legewon, Muslims and Christians, and the story of his fight against Wərzəlya, 293
of St. Susənyos and the story of his fight against

Wərzəlya, 276, 278, 280, 281, 283, 286, 289, 290, 297, 302, 305, 309, 311, 332, 340, 343, 344, 345, 347, 348, 350, 351, 352, 355, 358, 365, 369, 371, 372, 380, 381, 382, 390
of St. Susənyos for binding demons and against the eye of Barya, filthy Legewon, Mäggäñña, Šotälay, Buda, Carpenter (*Nähabi*), Zar, 362
of St. Susənyos for binding demons, and the story of his fight against Wərzəlya, 396
of St. Susənyos for binding demons, Mäggäñña, Šotälay, Buda, *Qumäñña* and different kinds of illnesses, and the story of his fight against Wərzəlya, 285
of the rampart of the cross, 322
to remove illnesses found from head to feet, against hemorrhage caused by the Zar, Quräñña, Täyayaž, eye of Barya, Legewon, Təgərtya, Mäqawəzi, Mäggäñña, Šotälay and others, and for conception, 349
to subjugate demons, Däsk and Gudale, 385
to subjugate evil spirits, and unbind charm, 310
to subjugate the enemy and Šotälay, 392
to terrorize and bind demons, 347
to terrorize demons, 345, 376
to terrorize the enemy and against charm, 361
to win the love of authorities, 364
Prayer against the eye of Barya, Legewon, the eye of Zar, Šotolay, Täyayaž, the eye of Dədq, noontime demon, and other demons, 289
Rampart of the Cross, 274, 276, 288, 292, 302, 354, 394, 395, 396, 398
Story of St. Susənyos and his martyrdom, 369
Story of St. Susənyos fighting Wərzəlya, 304, 308, 314, 315, 318, 323, 324, 325, 335, 337, 339, 365, 374, 376, 395
Story of the Sorcerer at the Sea of Tiberias, 272, 296, 301, 303, 306, 307, 311, 313, 314, 316, 326, 331, 337, 340, 342, 349, 362, 372, 393
Sword of Divinity, 329, 372
Sword of Trinity, 329

Index of Names in the Scrolls of Spiritual Healing

NB: The two names connected with a forward slash refer to one and the same person, the first being the given name, given by his/her parents on the day the child was born or about that time, and the second the baptismal name, given by the baptizing priest on the day the child was baptized. In such cases the two names have been indexed independently, eg as "x/y" and "y, see x"

'Amätä Iyyäsus, 351
'Amätä Maryam, 348, 363
'Amättä Wäld, 354
'Ayne/ Wälättä Iyyäsus, 329
Abäbay, 332
Abbäbäčč, 335
Abbäbčč/Wälättä Mika'el, 386
Adanäñña, see Wälättä Kidan, 396
Alganäš/Wälättä Gäbrə'el, 373
Amätä Ṣəyon, 349
Amätä Iyyäsus/Dässəta, 395
Amätä Krəstos, 333
Amätä Maryam, see Yaṭenaš, 297
Amätä Maryam/Birarra, 366
Amätä Mika'el, 338
Amätä Ṣadqan, 272
Amätä Gäbrə'el, 277
Amätä Maryam, see Asnaqäy, 285
Amätä Mika'el/Wäynitu Fä(n)taye, 283
Amməḫay, Ləǧ, 289

Askalä Maryam, 311
Asnaqäy/Amätä Maryam, 285
Aster, 295
Bäyyänäčč/Wälättä Sänbät, 322
Bällaṭäč/Wälättä Ḥəwät, 292
Bosäna/Wälättä Iyyäsus, 351
Däbritu, 345
Däbritu Ǝ(n)guday, see Wälättä Kidan, 380, 392
Däbritu/Wälättä Kidan, 339
Dässəta, 395
Dässəta, see Amätä Iyyäsus, 395
Ǝgzi' Ḥaräya, 369, 393
Ǝmmukäy, 327
'Ǝnkʷäy Lul, 396
Faṭima, 367
Fre Maryam, 327
Gäbrä Ṣəllase, 357
Gäbrä Ḥəwät, 364
Gäbrä Ḥəywät, 331
Gäbrä Iyyäsus/Wasehun, 302
Gäbrä Kidan, 375
Gäbrä Kiros, 314
Gäbrä Kiros Gäbre, 344

Gäbrä Maryam, 353, 376
Gäbrä Mika'el Ayyalew, 370
Gäbrä Naryam, see Kaśa, 302
Gäbrä Tənśa'e, 330
Haftä Maryam, 336
Hanna, 290
Haylä Maryam, 330, 331, 379, 385
Haylä Śəllase, 289
Hirutä Śəllase, 346
Kaśa/Gäbrä Naryam, 302
Kiros, 385
Mäśärät/Wälättä Sänbät, 398
Mänän, 335
Mänän, see Wälättä Maryam, 300
Mänbärä Səllase, 336
Mäzgäbä Śəllase, 348
Marsa/Wälättä Maryam, 397
Muluyyä Wälättä Səllase, 395
Qʷadi/Wälättä Iyyäsus, 281
Ṣädalä Maryam, 317
Ṣähaynäši, 332
Śahlä Maryam, see Yayn Waga, 293
Səḫin, 273
Sisay Därräbä, 299
Šiwäqet/Wälättä Mika'el, 302
Təblät, see Wälättä Iyyäsus, 316
Täwabäčč, 380, 392
Ṭäğğətu, 343
Ṭayitu Abägaz, 334
Tayyäčč/Faṭima, 373
Ṭəru, 361
Ṭəruyyä, see Wälättä Hanna, 342
Wälädä Kidan, 313
Wälättä Śəllase, 319
Wälättä Śəllase, 330, 355

Wälättä Ḥəywät, 357, 382, 383
Wälättä Ṣadəq, 397
Wälättä Ḥanna/Ṭəruyyä, 342
Wälättä Ǝgzi', 323
Wälättä Ananya, 311
Wälättä Arägawi, 325
Wälättä Arägawit, 338
Wälättä Arägay, 305
Wälättä Gäbrə'el, 296
Wälättä Gäbrə'el, see Alganäš, 373
Wälättä Gäbr'əl, 350
Wälättä Gäbrel, 299
Wälättä Giyorgis, 298, 330, 374, 395
Wälättä Haymanot, 310
Wälättä Iyyäsus, 296, 340, 360, 370, 395
Wälättä Iyyäsus, see 'Ayne, 329
Wälättä Iyyäsus, see Bosäna, 351
Wälättä Iyyäsus/Təblät, 316
Wälättä Iyyäsus/Yäši, 374
Wälättä Iyyäsus/Yalganäš, 341
Wälättä Kidan, 296, 325, 345, 371, 378
Wälättä Kidan, see Däbritu, 339
Wälättä Kidan/Adanäñña, 396
Wälättä Kidan/Däbritu Ǝ(n)guday, 380, 392
Wälättä Kidan/Wälättä Maryam, 331
Wälättä Kiros, 322
Wälättä Krəstos, 352
Wälättä Libanos, 303

Wälättä Mädḫən, 305, 316, 322, 368
Wälättä Maryam, 307, 324, 336, 347, 354, 365, 396
Wälättä Maryam Fälqa, 299
Wälättä Maryam, see Marsa, 397
Wälättä Maryam, see Wälättä Kidan, 331
Wälättä Maryam, see Yäzabnäš, 322
Wälättä Maryam/Mänän, 300
Wälättä Mika'el, 306, 310, 325, 336, 340
Wälättä Mika'el, see Šiwäqet, 302
Wälättä Mika'el, see Abbäbčč, 386
Wälättä Mika'el, see Wäynitu, 304
Wälättä Rufa'el, 309
Wälättä Səllase, 327
Wälättä Sänbät, 303, 308
Wälättä Sänbät, see Bäyyänäčč, 322
Wälättä Sänbät, see Mäśärät, 398
Wälättä Säsnbät, 341
Wälättä Täklä Haymanot, 336, 359, 387
Wälättä Tənśa'e, 305, 358
Wälättä Tənśa'e, see Yaṭenäš, 378
Wälättä Yoḥannəs, 315, 360, 374
Wälättä Yoḥannəs Ṭəruyyä, 297
Wälättä Ḥəywät, 295
Wälatta Mädḫən, 362
Wälatta Maryam, 363
Wälatta Rufa'el, 364

Wäldä Amlak, 375
Wäldä Gäbrə'el, 325, 331
Wäldä Giyorgis, 346
Wäldä Sänbät, 302
Wände, 336
Wäynitu/Wälättä Mika'el, 304
Wälätä Maryam/Yamrot, 278
Wälättä Śəllase/Wärqnäš, 275
Wälättä Ḥəwät, see Bällätäč, 292
Wälättä Ḥəywät, 287
Wälättä Arägawi Adina, 293
Wälättä Gäbrə'el, 290
Wälättä Iyyäsus, 284
Wälättä Iyyäsus Aškute, 274
Wälättä Iyyäsus, see Qʷadi, 281
Wälättä Maryam, 290
Wälättä Maryam, see Yälfne, 280
Wälättä Mika'el, 293
Wälättä Mika'el, 289
Wälättä Säma't, 286
Wärq Yanṭəf, 276
Wärqnäš, see Wälättä Śəllase, 275
Wasehun, see Gäbrä Iyyäsus, 302
Wätättä Ḥəywät, 280
Wäynitu Fä(n)taye, see Amätä Mika'el, 283
Yäši, see Wälättä Iyyäsus, 374
Yälfəññ, 391
Yäzabnäš/ Wälättä Maryam, 322
Yaṭenäš/Wälättä Tənśa'e, 378
Yaṭenaš/Amätä Maryam, 297
Yälfne/Wälättä Maryam, 280
Yalganäš, see Wälättä Iyyäsus, 341

Yamrot, see Wälätä Maryam, 278

Yayn Waga/Śahlä Maryam, 293

Zälläläw, 351

www.ingramcontent.com/pod-product-compliance
Lightning Source LLC
Chambersburg PA
CBHW052047290426
44111CB00011B/1643